Corel DRAW!®

made Easy

Emil and Sybil Ihrig

Osborne **McGraw-Hill**

Berkeley New York St. Louis San Francisco
Auckland Bogotá Hamburg London Madrid
Mexico City Milan Montreal New Delhi Panama City
Paris São Paulo Singapore Sydney
Tokyo Toronto

Osborne **McGraw-Hill**
2600 Tenth Street
Berkeley, California 94710
U.S.A.

For information on translations and book distributors outside of the U.S.A.,
please write to Osborne **McGraw-Hill** at the above address.

Corel DRAW!® Made Easy

34567890 DOC 99876543210

ISBN 0-07-881627-0

Acquisitions Editor: Liz Fisher
Technical Reviewer: Michael Katz
Copy Editor: Margaret Flynn
Word Processors: Judy Koplan, Carole Latimer
Composition: Bonnie Bozorg
Proofreaders: Julie Anjos, Barbara Conway, Jeff Green
Cover Design: Bay Graphics Design, Inc.
Production Supervisor: Kevin Shafer

DEDICATION

For our parents, with love.

CONTENTS
AT A GLANCE

TABLE OF CONTENTS

ACKNOWLEDGMENTS

The efforts of many individuals contributed to the production of this book. We thank all of them, but would like to recognize three outstanding contributions in particular.

Thanks to Liz Fisher, acquisitions editor at Osborne/McGraw-Hill, who always has an ear for authors' concerns and meets them more than halfway. The twin skills of negotiation and biting speeding bullets are raised to the level of fine arts in her daily routine.

We would like to extend our appreciation to Vivi Nichol, manager of Customer Support at Corel Systems, for her enthusiastic and careful attention to our manuscript. Andrew Knox, also of Corel Systems Customer Support, deserves commendation for his nurturing of the material on the Corel TRACE! batch autotracing utility.

Finally, thanks also go to Shawn Greenberg, our technical support guru in residence at Corel Systems. His dedication to our project from its very inception has been surpassed only by his untiring ability to shed light on the innermost world of Corel DRAW!.

INTRODUCTION

Since its initial release in January 1989, Corel DRAW! has become the most talked-about graphics software package for IBM-compatible PCs. It's easy to understand why the program has received so much favorable attention, including nine major industry awards. Quite simply, no other drawing software offers so many powerful text-handling, autotracing, color separation, and special effects capabilities in a single package.

ABOUT THIS BOOK

Corel DRAW! Made Easy is a step-by-step training guide to Corel DRAW! that leads you from elementary skills to more complex ones. Each chapter contains hands-on exercises that are richly and clearly illustrated so that you can match the results exactly on your computer screen.

This book makes few assumptions about your graphics experience or computer background. If you have never used a mouse or worked with a drawing package, you can begin with the exercises in the early chapters and move forward as you master each skill. On the other hand, if you have experience in desktop publishing, graphic design, or technical illustration, you can concentrate on the chapters that cover more advanced features or features that are new to you. Even the basic chapters contain exercises that stimulate your creativity, however, so it is worth your while to browse through each chapter in order to gain new design ideas.

HOW THIS BOOK IS ORGANIZED

Corel DRAW! Made Easy is designed to let you learn by doing, regardless of whether you are a new, intermediate, or advanced user of Corel DRAW!. You begin to draw right away, and as the book proceeds, you continue to build on the skills you have learned in previous chapters.

The organization of this book is based on the philosophy that knowing how to perform a particular *task* is more important than simply knowing the location of a tool or menu command. The body of the book therefore contains step-by-step exercises that begin with basic drawing skills and progress to advanced skills that combine multiple techniques. The appendixes at the end of the book contain handy reference material that you can turn to when you need to review what you have learned.

The organization of each chapter will help you locate quickly any information that you need to learn. At the beginning of each chapter is a list of major headings, which describe clearly the skills you can expect to learn in that chapter. Each section within a chapter begins with an overview of a particular skill and its importance in the context of other Corel DRAW! functions. In most chapters, every section contains one or more hands-on exercises that allow you to practice the skill being taught.

Chapters 1 through 5 of *Corel DRAW! Made Easy* help you become familiar with the software interface and with basic drawing skills. Chapter 1, "Getting Acquainted with Corel DRAW!," gives you a guided tour of the Corel DRAW! screen and introduces you to the menus, tools, and mouse techniques of the software. Chapter 2, "Drawing and Working with Lines and Curves," introduces you to the Freehand tool and shows you how to create straight lines, polygons, curves, and closed curve objects. Chapter 3, "Drawing and Working with Rectangles and Squares," and Chapter 4,

"Drawing and Working with Circles and Ellipses," introduce the Rectangle and Ellipse tools, respectively. Chapter 5, "Adding Text," shows you how to enter text on the Corel DRAW! page and define the font, point size, alignment, and spacing for text.

Chapters 6 and 7 describe how you can customize the Corel DRAW! screen to enhance your drawing power. Chapter 6, "Using Magnification and View Selection," acquaints you with the Magnification tool and with the five ways you can define a limited or expanded viewing area. In Chapter 7, "Previewing Your Graphics," you will learn how the screen can show you your graphics just as they will look when you print them.

Chapters 8 through 12 show you how to edit objects and text and combine them into more complex images. Chapter 8, "Selecting, Moving, and Arranging Objects," teaches you how to select objects in order to perform further work on them and how to group, combine, move, and change the relative order of objects on the screen. Chapter 9, "Transforming Objects," describes how to stretch, scale, rotate, and skew objects, how to create mirror images in any desired direction, and how to leave a copy of the original object as you transform it. Chapter 10, "Shaping Lines, Curves, Rectangles, and Ellipses," shows you how to use the Shaping tool to turn rectangles into rounded rectangles, circles or ellipses into wedges or arcs, and lines or curves into any shape you desire. Chapter 11, "Shaping and Editing Text," introduces a variety of special effects (such as word pictures) that you can achieve when you edit text with the Shaping tool. Chapter 12, "Cutting, Copying, and Pasting Objects and Pictures," describes how to use the Windows clipboard to transfer objects between Corel DRAW! pictures or between Corel DRAW! and other applications. This chapter also covers Corel DRAW! techniques for duplicating objects and repeating operations and suggests ways to exploit the special-effects potentials of these techniques.

Chapters 13, 14, and 15 cover an especially rich topic: the process of defining outlines and fills for objects within a drawing. In Chapter 13, "Defining the Outline Pen," you will learn how to create calligraphic outlines and define line styles for existing and

new objects. Chapter 14, "Defining Outline Color," lets you practice assigning spot color, process color, or gray shades to any
object's outline or define outlines that contain special PostScript
halftone screen patterns. In Chapter 15, "Defining Fill Color," you
learn how to fill the interior of any object with process or spot
color, shades of gray, or special-effects fountain fills.

Chapters 16 through 19 cover skills and special topics that go
beyond drawing and editing techniques. The ability to use Corel
DRAW! in conjunction with other graphics applications is discussed in Chapter 16, "Importing and Exporting Files." Chapter
17, "Tracing and Working with Bitmapped Graphics," lets you
practice techniques for tracing imported bitmaps manually or
automatically and then editing the resulting object-oriented
graphic. You will also learn how to trace single or multiple bitmaps
rapidly, using the sophisticated new Corel TRACE! batch autotracing utility available with version 1.12. Chapter 18, "Printing
and Processing Your Images," reviews how to set up your printer
and lets you experiment with printing color separations with crop
marks and registration marks, printing to a file, and defining a
variety of printing parameters. In Chapter 19, "Creating and Using
Macros," you will find out how to design custom shortcut commands that can incorporate complex techniques and speed your
work.

Chapter 20, "Combining Corel DRAW! Features and Creating
Special Effects," allows you to integrate all the skills taught in the
earlier part of the book. It contains three lengthy exercises that
review many techniques and help you design a variety of special
effects.

The appendixes at the back of the book provide easy reference
information. To benefit from suggestions for getting the fastest,
most efficient performance from your software, turn to Appendix
A, "Installing Corel DRAW! and Enhancing Performance." Use
Appendixes B and C, "Menu Summaries" and "Keyboard and
Mouse Shortcuts," when you need to look up the function of a
command or the use of a special key combination quickly. For
information on using third-party fonts or clipart, or for help in

using WFNBOSS to convert other manufacturers' fonts to Corel DRAW! format, see Appendix D, "Corel Connectivity: Clip Art and Fonts." Finally, Appendix E, "PostScript Textures," contains a visual mini-catalog of the many fill patterns available for use with PostScript printers.

Note: The exercises in this book were designed with a VGA display adapter and screen driver in mind. If the screen driver that you installed for Windows has a lower or higher resolution in (for example, EGA or 800 X 600), you may need to adjust viewing magnification or rulers for some of the exercises.

CONVENTIONS USED IN THIS BOOK

Corel DRAW! Made Easy uses several conventions designed to help you locate important information quickly. The most important of these are

- Terms important to the operation of Corel DRAW! appear in *italics* the first time they are introduced.

- The first time an icon or tool in the Corel DRAW! toolbox or interface is discussed, it appears as a small graphic in the text (for example, the Freehand tool ℓ). A small icon also appears in the text the first time you are asked to use or refer to a given tool or icon within a chapter.

- You can locate the steps of any exercise quickly by looking for the numbered paragraphs.

- Names of keys appear as small graphics that look similar to the actual keys on your computer's keyboard (for example, CTRL).

- Text or information that you must enter using the keyboard appears in this book in **boldface**.

• Summaries of entire chapters or of sequences of steps are surrounded by a box in order to distinguish them from the rest of the text.

ADDITIONAL HELP FROM OSBORNE/MCGRAW-HILL

Osborne/McGraw-Hill provides top-quality books for computer users at every level of computing experience. To help you build your skills, we suggest that you look for the books in the following Osborne series that best address your needs.

The "Teach Yourself" Series is perfect for people who have never used a computer before or who want to gain confidence in using program basics. These books provide a simple, slow-paced introduction to the fundamental uses of popular software packages and programming languages. The "Mastery Skills Check" format ensures your understanding concepts thoroughly before you progress to new material. Plenty of examples and exercises (with answers at the back of the book) are used throughout the text.

The "Made Easy" Series is also for beginners or users who may need a refresher on the new features of an upgraded product. These in-depth introductions guide users step-by-step from the program basics to intermediate-level usage. Plenty of "hands-on" exercises and examples are used in every chapter.

The "Using" Series presents fast-paced guides that cover beginning concepts quickly and move on to intermediate-level techniques and some advanced topics. These books are written for users already familiar with computers and software who want to get up to speed fast with a certain product.

The "Advanced" Series assumes that the reader is a user who has reached at least an intermediate skill level and is ready to learn more sophisticated techniques and refinements.

"The Complete Reference" Series provides handy desktop references for popular software and programming languages that list every command, feature, and function of the product along with brief but detailed descriptions of how they are used. Books are fully indexed and often include tear-out command cards. "The Complete Reference" series is ideal for both beginners and pros.

"The Pocket Reference" Series is a pocket-sized, shorter version of "The Complete Reference" Series. It provides the essential commands, features, and functions of software and programming languages for users of every level who need a quick reminder.

The "Secrets, Solutions, Shortcuts" Series is written for beginning users who are already somewhat familiar with the software and for experienced users at intermediate and advanced levels. This series provides clever tips, points out shortcuts for using the software to greater advantage, and indicates traps to avoid.

Osborne/McGraw-Hill also publishes many fine books that are not included in the series described here. If you have questions about which Osborne books are right for you, ask the salesperson at your local book or computer store, or call us toll-free at 1-800-262-4729.

OTHER OSBORNE/MCGRAW-HILL BOOKS OF INTEREST TO YOU

We hope that *Corel DRAW! Made Easy* will assist you in mastering this fine product, and will also pique your interest in learning more about other ways to better use your computer.

If you're interested in expanding your skills so you can be even more "computer efficient," be sure to take advantage of Osborne/McGraw-Hill's large selection of top-quality computer books that cover all varieties of popular hardware, software, programming languages, and operating systems. While we cannot list every title here that may relate to Corel Draw!and to your special computing needs, here are just a few books that complement *Corel Draw! Made Easy* .

If you are just beginning WordPerfect 5 and you are unfamiliar with other word processors or even with a computer, see *Teach Yourself WordPerfect 5*, by Mary Campbell, a simple introduction to WordPerfect 5 essentials with plenty of hands-on exercises.

If you are a beginning WordPerfect 5.1 user looking for an in-depth guide that leads you from basics to intermediate-level techniques, see *WordPerfect 5.1 Made Easy*, by Mella Mincberg. If you have WordPerfect 5.0, see *WordPerfect Made Easy, Series 5 Edition*, by Mella Mincberg. Or if you are using WordPerfect 4.2, look for Mincberg's *WordPerfect Made Easy*.

For a quick-paced book that covers WordPerfect 5.0 basics before concentrating on intermediate-level skills and even some advanced topics, see *Using WordPerfect, Series 5 Edition*, by Gail Todd.

WordPerfect 5.1: The Complete Reference, by Karen L. Acerson, is ideal for all users, both beginners who are somewhat familiar with WordPerfect and for pros. This desktop resource lists every WordPerfect 5.1 command, feature, and function along with brief, yet in-depth discussions of how they are used. *WordPerfect: The Complete Reference, Series 5 Edition*, by Karen L. Acerson, covers version 5.0, and Acerson's *WordPerfect: The Complete Reference* covers release 4.2.

Microsoft Word 5 Made Easy, by Paul Hoffman, leads you from basics to intermediate-level techniques. If you have Microsoft Word 4.0, see *Microsoft Word Made Easy, Third Edition*, by Paul Hoffman.

For a quick-paced book that focuses on intermediate-level skills and some advanced topics, see *Using Microsoft Word 5*, by Greg M. Perry.

Using Microsoft Word for Windows, by David Dean, shows you how to take full advantage of all the Windows graphical user interface features including clipboard and dynamic data exchange hot links.

WHY THIS BOOK IS FOR YOU

If you already have purchased or are planning to purchase Corel DRAW! for use in your desktop publishing, graphic design, or technical illustration business, *Corel DRAW! Made Easy* was written for you. It supplements the manufacturer's documentation because it is a step-by-step training guide, providing hands-on exercises to help you learn *and retain* every feature of the software. The ample supply of illustrations accompanying the exercises ensure that you achieve the desired results every time.

Corel DRAW! Made Easy will benefit you no matter whether you are a new, intermediate, or advanced user of Corel DRAW!. If you are new to graphics software, you will find it easy to learn Corel DRAW! because the book begins with basic skills and progresses to more complex ones. The exercises in more advanced chapters build upon skills you have learned in previous chapters. If you already have a background in graphics, desktop publishing, or technical illustration software, but have not used Corel DRAW!, you will find ample instruction about how to use features that are unique to Corel DRAW!. You will also find plenty of attention given to applications that pertain to your field of business.

Regardless of your background, the exercises in *Corel DRAW! Made Easy* are designed to stimulate your imagination while teaching you how to use the software effectively. You will find new ideas for exciting applications as you become familiar with Corel DRAW!'s equally exciting features.

LEARN MORE ABOUT SOFTWARE YOU CAN USE WITH COREL DRAW!

Here is an excellent selection of other Osborne/McGraw-Hill books on software packages you can use with Corel DRAW! that will help you build your skills and maximize the power of the graphics software you have selected.

If you have PageMaker for the PC Version 4.0 and you're looking for a quick-paced book that covers basics before concentrating on intermediate-level skills and even some advanced topics, see *Using PageMaker for the PC, Version 4, Third Edition*, by Martin S. Matthews and Carole Boggs Matthews. If you have PageMaker Version 3.0, see *Using PageMaker for the PC, Version 3, Second Edition*, also by the Matthews.

Ventura: The Complete Reference, by Marilyn Holt and Ricardo Birmele, provides comprehensive coverage of every Ventura command and feature. Whether you need an overview of Ventura's basic procedures or a reference for advanced applications, you'll find it here.

For beginning users of Publish It!, Paul Garrison's book *Publish It! Made Easy* leads you from basics to intermediate-level techniques, step-by-step. This book covers Publish It! version 1.2 and Publish It Lite!.

GETTING ACQUAINTED
WITH COREL DRAW!

Welcome to Corel DRAW!. You have selected one of the most innovative and advanced graphics tools available for the IBM personal computer. Corel DRAW! will sharpen your creative edge by allowing you to edit any shape or character with ease and precision, fit text to a curve, autotrace existing artwork, create custom color separations, explore calligraphic "pens" and fountain fills, and more. You can combine Corel DRAW!'s features to achieve many different special effects, such as mirror images, masks, and 3D simulations. Corel DRAW! makes these and other capabilities work for you at speeds far surpassing those of other graphics programs.

To support your creative and technical endeavors, Corel DRAW! has an almost unlimited number of fonts and clip-art libraries at your disposal. If the more than one hundred fonts provided with Corel DRAW! fail to meet your needs, you can use the WFNBOSS utility (provided with version 1.1 or later) to access thousands of commercial fonts. Your software also supplies 300 clip-art images and you can obtain thousands more from industry vendors. (For more information on fonts and clip art, see Appendix D, "Corel Connectivity: Clip Art and Fonts.")

If you haven't installed Corel DRAW!, turn to Appendix A, "Installing Corel DRAW! and Enhancing Performance," before continuing with this chapter. Even if you have installed the program, browse through the "Enhancing Speed and Performance" section of Appendix A. This appendix contains useful, little-known tips on maximizing the operation speed of Corel DRAW! and will benefit all users, no matter how advanced.

STARTING COREL DRAW!

This section presents a method of starting Corel DRAW! that enhances software operating speed by minimizing the amount of memory used by Windows. See the "Enhancing Speed and Performance" section of Appendix A for suggestions about other ways to start the program.

To start Corel DRAW! for the first time:

1. Change to the Windows directory of your hard drive.

2. Type **win** and press (ENTER). The MS- DOS Executive window appears on the screen, as shown in Figure 1-1.

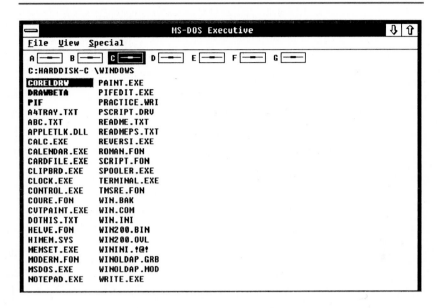

FIGURE 1-1   The MS-DOS Executive window

3. Using your mouse, position the *mouse cursor* (the arrow-shaped cursor) on the word "File." Press the left mouse button to pull down the File menu, shown in Figure 1- 2.

4. Point the mouse cursor at the Run command in the File menu and press (click) the mouse button once to select the command. The dialog box in Figure 1-3 appears. You will find out more about dialog boxes in the section "Working with Dialog Boxes," later in this chapter.

5. If the check box next to "Minimize MS-DOS Executive" is empty, click on it. An "X" should appear in the box. If an "X" is already in the checkbox, you do not need to do anything.

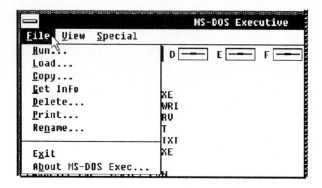

FIGURE 1-2   Pulling down the File menu

6. Click once on the OK command button to save your selection and exit the dialog box. You do not need to enter any text in the rectangular box that is shown at the top of the dialog box in Figure 1-3.

7. Change to the CORELDRW subdirectory of Windows by double-clicking (clicking twice) on the directory name. The

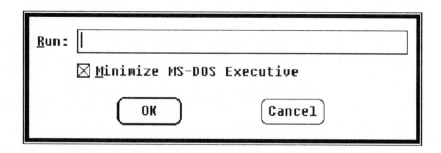

FIGURE 1-3   Minimizing the MS-DOS Executive

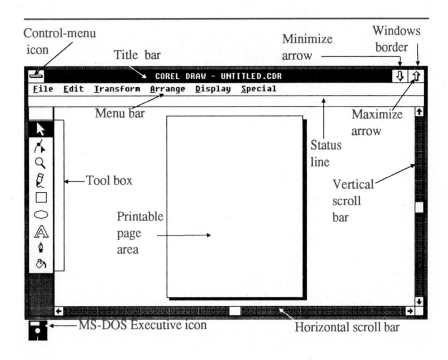

FIGURE 1-4   The Corel DRAW! opening screen

directory name becomes highlighted and an hourglass appears until the directory changes.

8. Double-click on the filename CORELDRW.EXE. After a moment, an information screen about Corel DRAW! is displayed, and then the Corel DRAW! main screen appears, shown in Figure 1-4.

You need to execute the Run command in the Windows File menu only once. Thereafter, it remains in Windows memory, and the MS-DOS Executive automatically runs as an icon in the background each time you load Corel DRAW!.

A QUICK TOUR OF
THE COREL DRAW! SCREEN

You will see references to the various screen components of Corel DRAW! many times throughout the book. Take a moment now to familiarize yourself with these terms and their functions within the program. Figure 1-4 shows the location of each screen component.

Windows Border   The Windows border marks the boundaries of the Corel DRAW! window. You can scale this window to different sizes using your mouse or other drawing device. Refer to your *Microsoft Windows User's Guide* for full details on how to scale the program window.

MS-DOS Executive Icon   If you loaded Corel DRAW! according to the steps in the previous section, the MS-DOS Executive icon appears as a small floppy disk in the lower left corner of your screen. The presence of this icon indicates that you have minimized the MS-DOS Executive, or reduced the amount of memory it is using in the background while you are running Corel DRAW!. When the Windows MS-DOS Executive runs as an icon, it requires only about 10K of memory. You can restore Windows to the foreground at any time while running Corel DRAW!. Just position the mouse over the Windows icon, press the left mouse button once, and select the Maximize option.

Title Bar   The title bar shows the name of the program you are working in and the name of the currently loaded image. All files in Corel DRAW! format have the file extension .CDR directly after the filename. When you first load Corel DRAW!, the screen is blank and so the title bar reads "UNTITLED.CDR."

You can move the Corel DRAW! window around on the screen by pressing and holding down the left mouse button over the title bar, then dragging the mouse in the direction you would like to move your window. When you reach the desired position, release the mouse button.

Minimize Arrow   If you are running other Windows applications at the same time as Corel DRAW!, you will find the minimize arrow ⬇ at the upper right corner of your screen useful. Click on this icon to turn the Corel DRAW! window into a small picture of a man with a moustache. When running as an icon, Corel DRAW! frees up memory that you can use to run another application. To restore Corel DRAW! to the foreground, position the mouse over the icon, click once, and select the Maximize option.

Maximize Arrow   If you want to make the Corel DRAW! window fill the entire screen, click on the maximize arrow ⬆ located next to the minimize arrow. This icon then turns into a two-way arrow. You can return the Corel DRAW! window to its default size by clicking on this icon once more.

Control-Menu Icon   You can use the control-menu icon ⬜ as another easy way to move, minimize, maximize, or otherwise change the size of the Corel DRAW! program window. To use the control-menu icon, simply click on the small bar inside the box, and the control menu will appear. Select the command you want by clicking on it. When you have finished, click anywhere outside the control menu to close it.

   If you select the About command in the control menu, a small message box like the one in Figure 1-5 pops up on the screen, displaying information about the current version of Corel DRAW!. When you are finished reading the message, click on OK to exit and return to the program.

Menu Bar   The menu bar contains six menus that you pull down when you click on one of the menu names. See the "Corel DRAW! Menus" section of this chapter for a brief summary of the command

FIGURE 1-5   The "About Corel DRAW!" message box

options in each menu, or Appendix B for a full description of each command.

Status Line   The status line contains a rich source of information about the image you have on your screen. When you first load Corel DRAW!, this line is blank. When you are drawing or editing images, however, it displays information such as the number, type, and dimensions of objects you select and the distance you travel when moving these objects. The exact nature of the information displayed depends on what you are doing at the time. The status line offers invaluable aid to technical illustration or to any work that requires precision and exactness.

Printable Page Area   You create your images in the printable page area. The exact size of the page depends on the printer or other output device that you installed when you set up Microsoft Windows, as well as on the settings you choose through the Page Setup command in the File menu. When you first load Corel DRAW!, the screen displays the total printable page area. Once you learn about magnification in Chapter 6, you can adjust the area of the page that is visible at any one time.

Scroll Bars   The scroll bars are most useful when you are looking at a magnified view of the page. Use the horizontal scroll bar to move to the left or right of the currently visible area of the page; use the vertical scroll bar to move to an area of the page that is above or below the currently visible area. You will find more information on how to use the scroll bars in Chapter 6.

Toolbox   The toolbox contains tools that carry out the most important and powerful drawing and editing functions in Corel DRAW!. Click on a tool icon to select a tool. The tool icon now appears in reverse video—white images on a black background. Other changes to the screen or to a selected object may also occur, depending on which tool you have selected. For a brief explanation of the function of each tool, see the "Corel DRAW! Tools" section of this chapter.

With a basic understanding of the screen elements, you can get around the Corel DRAW! window easily. The next three sections of this chapter explore three types of interface elements—menus, dialog boxes, and tools—in greater depth.

THE COREL DRAW! MENUS

When you pull down a menu, some commands appear in boldface, while others appear in gray. You can select any command that appears in boldface, but commands in gray are not available to you at the moment. Commands become available for selection depending on the objects you are working with and the actions you perform on them.

This book is a tutorial rather than a reference manual. As such, it organizes information about Corel DRAW! according to the task you want to perform. You'll learn to use program menus by working with particular functions of Corel DRAW!. For quick reference, Appendix B contains a detailed listing of menu commands and their functions. This section briefly describes the major purposes of each menu.

The File Menu   The File menu in Figure 1- 6(a) is common to all Windows applications. Most of the commands in the File menu do not apply to the process of drawing. Instead, they cover program functions that deal with entire files at a time or with running the program as a whole. Examples of such functions are loading, saving, importing, exporting, and printing a file, and quitting Corel DRAW!.

The Edit Menu   The Edit menu in Figure 1- 6(b) is also common to all Windows applications. Use the commands in this menu to copy, cut, and paste objects or images, to undo the last action you performed, and to copy or change attributes of objects and text.

The Transform Menu   The commands in the Transform menu, shown in Figure 1-6(c), allow you to edit the shape of selected objects and text. A more direct way to perform these functions is to use the Select and/or Shape tools, which you'll learn about in Chapters 8 through 11.

The Arrange Menu   The commands in the Arrange menu, shown in Figure 1-6(d), all have to do with the relative placement of objects within an image. Select the commands in this menu to move a selected object or group of objects to the forefront or background of an image, to combine, group, ungroup, or break apart selected objects, and to align objects and text. You will find more details about the Arrange menu commands in Chapter 8.

The Display Menu   The Display menu in Figure 1-6(e) has one very clear function: to help you customize the user interface and make the Corel DRAW! screen work the way you do. Use the

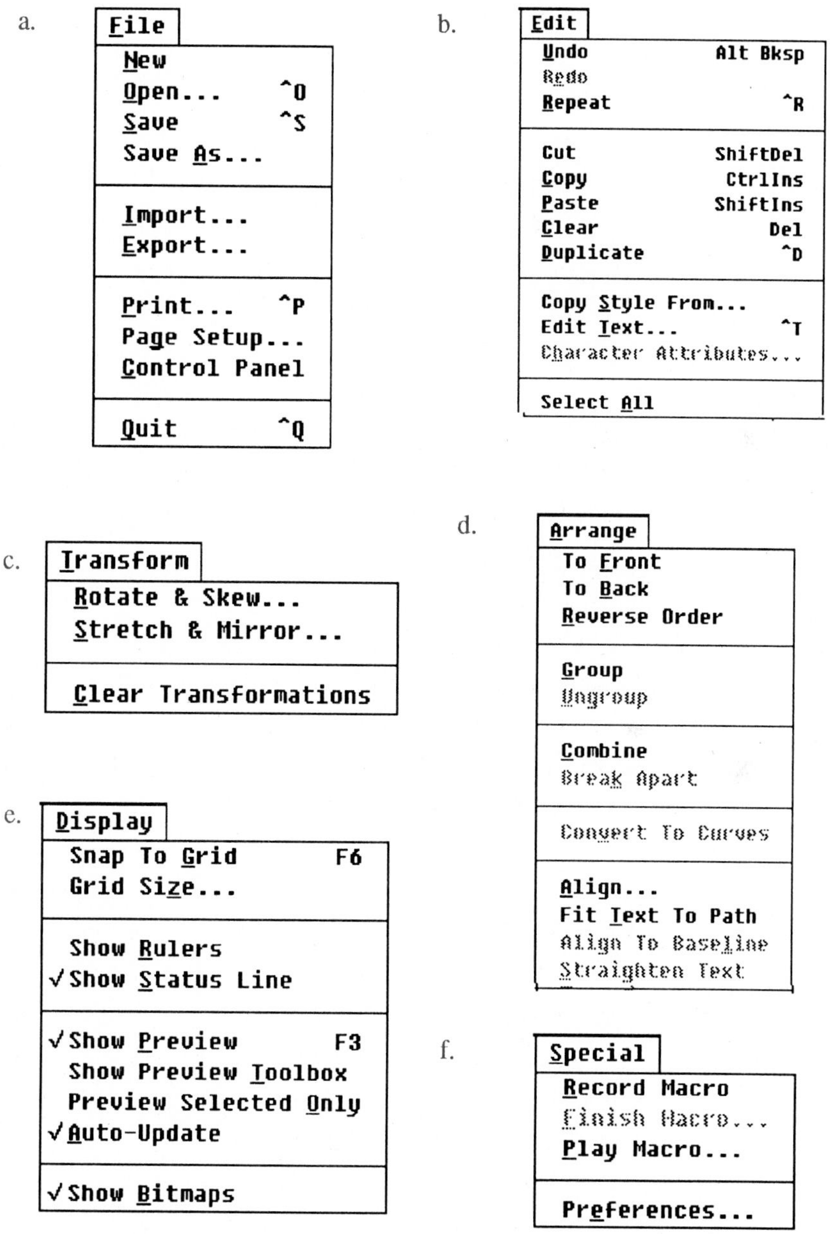

a.
```
┌─────────────┐
│ File        │
├─────────────┴──────┐
│ New                │
│ Open...        ^O  │
│ Save           ^S  │
│ Save As...         │
│                    │
│ Import...          │
│ Export...          │
│                    │
│ Print...       ^P  │
│ Page Setup...      │
│ Control Panel      │
│                    │
│ Quit           ^Q  │
└────────────────────┘
```

b.
```
┌─────────────┐
│ Edit        │
├─────────────┴──────────┐
│ Undo        Alt Bksp   │
│ Redo                   │
│ Repeat            ^R   │
│                        │
│ Cut          ShiftDel  │
│ Copy          CtrlIns  │
│ Paste        ShiftIns  │
│ Clear             Del  │
│ Duplicate         ^D   │
│                        │
│ Copy Style From...     │
│ Edit Text...      ^T   │
│ Character Attributes...│
│                        │
│ Select All             │
└────────────────────────┘
```

c.
```
┌───────────────┐
│ Transform     │
├───────────────┴────────────┐
│ Rotate & Skew...           │
│ Stretch & Mirror...        │
│                            │
│ Clear Transformations      │
└────────────────────────────┘
```

d.
```
┌─────────────┐
│ Arrange     │
├─────────────┴──────────┐
│ To Front               │
│ To Back                │
│ Reverse Order          │
│                        │
│ Group                  │
│ Ungroup                │
│                        │
│ Combine                │
│ Break Apart            │
│                        │
│ Convert To Curves      │
│                        │
│ Align...               │
│ Fit Text To Path       │
│ Align To Baseline      │
│ Straighten Text        │
└────────────────────────┘
```

e.
```
┌─────────────┐
│ Display     │
├─────────────┴──────────┐
│ Snap To Grid       F6  │
│ Grid Size...           │
│                        │
│   Show Rulers          │
│ √ Show Status Line     │
│                        │
│ √ Show Preview     F3  │
│   Show Preview Toolbox │
│   Preview Selected Only│
│ √ Auto-Update          │
│                        │
│ √ Show Bitmaps         │
└────────────────────────┘
```

f.
```
┌─────────────┐
│ Special     │
├─────────────┴──────┐
│ Record Macro       │
│ Finish Macro...    │
│ Play Macro...      │
│                    │
│ Preferences...     │
└────────────────────┘
```

FIGURE 1-6   The Corel DRAW! menus

commands in this menu to display or hide the rulers and the status line, to set up grids for precision drawing, and to choose whether and how to display fully accurate, WYSIWYG (What-You-See-Is-What-You-Get) previews of your images.

The Special Menu   The Special menu in Figure 1-6(f) has two main functions. First, it allows you to control the design and use of *macros,* mini-programs that combine several often-repeated steps in one simple command. Second, it lets you fine-tune many different program parameters using the Preferences command. Discussions about these precision controls, which apply to a wide range of functions, appear in their respective contexts.

WORKING WITH DIALOG BOXES

Some menu commands are automatic: Click on them, and Corel DRAW! performs the action immediately. Other commands are followed by a series of dots, indicating that you must enter additional information before Corel DRAW! can execute the command. You enter this additional information through dialog boxes that pop up on the screen when you click on the command. This section introduces you to the look and feel of typical dialog boxes in Corel DRAW!.

Dialog boxes contain several kinds of controls and other ways for you to enter information. Compare the callouts in Figures 1-7 and 1-8 with the following descriptions to familiarize yourself with operations in a dialog box. Look at Figure 1-7 first.

Circular *option buttons* like those in Figure 1-7 present you with mutually exclusive choices. In a group of option buttons, you can select only one at a time. When you click on an option button to select it, the inner circle becomes black.

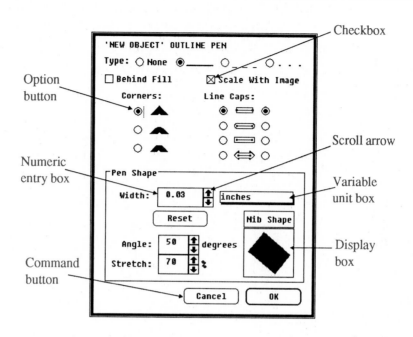

FIGURE 1-7   Representative controls in a dialog box

Square *checkboxes* in a dialog box offer you choices that are not mutually exclusive, so you can select more than one option simultaneously. Checkboxes behave like light switches; you turn them on or off when you click to select or deselect them. When you turn on or enable an option in a checkbox, an "X" fills it. When you turn off or disable the option, the "X" disappears.

The rounded rectangles in a dialog box are *command buttons.* When selected, a command button is highlighted temporarily, and usually Corel DRAW! performs the command instantly. When you click on a command button that has a label followed by dots, you open another dialog box that is nested within it.

A rectangle that contains numeric entries and that is associated with up and down scroll arrows is a *numeric entry box.* You can

change the numeric values in three ways. To increase or decrease
the value by a single increment, click on the up or down arrow
respectively. To increase or decrease the value by a large amount,
press and hold the mouse button over one of the scroll arrows. You
can also click on the value itself, erase the current value, and then
type in new numbers.

Rectangles containing units of measurement represent *variable
unit boxes* that are valid only for the associated option and dialog
box. Click on the variable unit box as many times as necessary to
change to the unit of measurement you prefer.

Some dialog boxes contain *display boxes* that show you just how
your current selection will look after you exit the dialog box. You
do not perform any action on the display box itself; instead, its
contents change as you change your selections in the dialog box.

Figure 1-8 shows an example of a dialog box that contains
different types of controls. Use the *text entry box* available in some

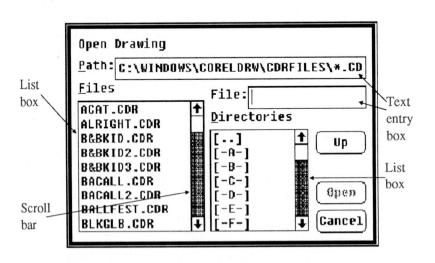

FIGURE 1-8   Additional dialog box controls

dialog boxes to enter strings of text. Depending on the dialog box involved, text strings might represent filenames, path names, or text to appear in an image. To enter new text where none exists, click on the text entry box. To edit an existing text string, click on the string, then use the keyboard to erase or add text. You will become familiar with the specific keys to use as you learn about each type of text entry box.

The *list boxes* within a dialog box list the names of choices available to the user, such as filenames, directory and drive names, or typestyle names. Drive and directory names appear in boldface and in all capital letters within a list box, while filenames do not. You can tell drive names from directory names because the former are surrounded by both brackets and hyphens, [-A-], while the latter are surrounded by brackets only, [CORELDRW]. Click on a name in the list box to select it.

Scroll bars accompany text entry boxes or list boxes when the contents of those boxes exceed the visible area in the dialog box. You can use the scroll bar to access the portions of the list that are outside of the currently visible area. To move up or down one name at a time, click on the up or down arrow of the scroll bar respectively. To move up or down continuously, press and hold the mouse button over the up or down arrow of the scroll bar. Alternatively, you can press (PGUP) or (PGDN) to move up or down the list box in large increments.

Some options in a dialog box appear in gray, indicating that you cannot select them at the moment. On the other hand, a command button within a dialog box may appear in boldface, indicating that you can select it, and also may have a bold outline around it. This command button represents the default selection. You can simply press (ENTER) to activate that selection, exit the dialog box, and return to your graphic.

You will learn more about operating within dialog boxes in the context of each chapter in this book. The following section will acquaint you with the toolbox, the portion of the interface most vital to the operation of Corel DRAW!.

THE COREL DRAW! TOOLBOX

One of the features that makes Corel DRAW! so easy to work with is the economy of the screen. The number of tools in the Corel DRAW! toolbox (Figure 1-9) is deceptively small. Several of the tools have more than one function, and nested sub-menus pop up when you select them. This method of organization reduces screen clutter and keeps related functions together.

The tools in the Corel DRAW! toolbox perform three different kinds of functions. Some allow you to draw objects, others let you edit the objects you have drawn, and a third group permit you to alter the appearance of the screen so that you can work more efficiently. This section describes each tool briefly in the context of its respective function.

FIGURE 1-9   The Corel DRAW! toolbox

Drawing Tools

Corel DRAW! allows you to create or work with nine different types of objects. Because you use the same tools and techniques for some of the objects, however, there are actually only five different *classes* of objects. These classes, and the kinds of objects you can design in each, are

- Lines, curves, and polygons

- Rectangles and squares

- Ellipses and circles

- Text

- Bitmapped (pixel-based) images imported from a scanner or paint program

Figure 1-10 shows an example of each kind of object.

Does nine seem like a small number? Professional artists and graphic designers know that basic geometrical shapes are the building blocks on which more elaborate images are constructed. After you "build" an object using one of the four drawing tools, you can use one or more of the editing tools in the Corel DRAW! toolbox to reshape, rearrange, color, and outline it.

The four drawing tools—the Freehand tool, the Rectangle tool, the Ellipse tool, and the Text tool—are all you need to create eight of the nine object types in Corel DRAW!. You work with the last object type, a bitmapped image, after importing it. (See Chapter 17, "Tracing and Working with Bitmapped Images," for a fuller discussion of this subject.)

The Freehand Tool   The Freehand tool 🖊️ is the most basic drawing tool in the Corel DRAW! toolbox. This single tool allows you to create lines, curves, curve objects, and polygons. Chapter 2, "Drawing and Working with Lines and Curves," guides you through a series of exercises that teach you all the basic Corel DRAW! freehand skills.

To select the Freehand tool, click on the Freehand tool icon once, and then move the mouse cursor into the white space on the page. When you select this tool, the mouse cursor takes the shape of a crosshair ┼, the Freehand tool icon becomes highlighted, and the message "Drawing" appears on the status line.

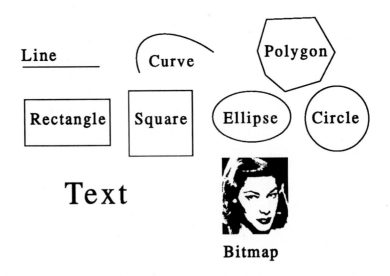

FIGURE 1-10   The nine types of objects

The Rectangle Tool   The Rectangle tool ▢ lets you draw rectangles and squares. You'll create your own rectangles and squares in Chapter 3. To round the corners of a rectangle, however, you need to use the Shaping tool ▱, one of the editing tools in the Corel DRAW! toolbox.

To select the Rectangle tool, click on the Rectangle icon once, and then move the mouse cursor into the white space on the page. The Rectangle icon becomes highlighted and the cursor takes on the shape of a crosshair.

The Ellipse Tool   The Ellipse tool ▱ allows you to design ellipses and perfect circles. You can learn more about using the Ellipse tool in Chapter 4.

To select the Ellipse tool, click on the Ellipse icon once, and then move the mouse cursor into the white space on the page. The Ellipse icon becomes highlighted and the cursor takes on the shape of a crosshair.

The Text Tool   The Text tool ▱ gives you access to more than 100 Corel Systems fonts and (if you use the WFNBOSS utility described in Appendix D) to thousands of other commercial fonts as well. Chapter 5 teaches you how to enter text in Corel DRAW!.

To select the Text tool, click on the Text icon once, and then move the cursor into the white space on the page. The Text icon becomes highlighted, and the mouse cursor changes to an I-beam
I .

If you "scribbled" on the page in trying out any of the drawing tools, clear the screen before proceeding. To do this, click on the File menu name and select the New command. A dialog box appears with the message:

UNTITLED.CDR Has Changed, Save Current Changes?

Select the No command button to exit the message box and clear the screen.

The Editing Tools

Once you have created objects on a page with the drawing tools, you use a different group of tools to move, arrange, reshape, and manipulate the objects. The editing tools include the Select tool, the Shaping tool, the Outline tool, and the Fill tool.

The Select Tool The Select tool is really two tools in one. In the *select mode*, you can select objects in order to move, arrange, group, or combine them. In the *transformation mode*, you can use the Select tool to rotate, skew, stretch, reflect, move, or scale a selected object. This tool does not let you change the basic shape of an object, however. Chapters 8 and 9 introduce you to all the functions of the Select tool.

The Shaping Tool The Shaping tool allows you to edit the shape of an object. Use this tool to smooth or distort any shape, add rounded corners to rectangles, convert a circle into a wedge or arc, modify a curve, or kern individual characters in a text string. Chapters 10 and 11 cover the basics of using this tool.

The Outline Tool The Outline tool , like the Select tool, functions in more than one way. Use the Outline tool and its associated pop-up submenu to choose a standard or custom outline color, or to create a custom outline "pen" for a selected object. Chapters 13 and 14 instruct you in the use of this tool.

The Fill Tool Use the Fill tool and its associated pop-up submenu to select a standard or design a custom fill color for selected objects or text. As you'll learn in Chapter 15, your options include custom colors, PostScript screens, fountain fills, and Post-Script textures.

Tools for Customizing
The Corel DRAW! Screen

The third group of tools help you customize the Corel DRAW! interface so that it works the way you do. Only one of these tools, the Magnification tool, is visible in the Corel DRAW! toolbox. The Magnification tool and its associated pop-up submenu let you control just how much of your picture you will view at one time. Use this tool when you need to work on a smaller area in fine detail, or when you need to zoom in or out of a picture.

Still other screen adjustment tools are available, but you can access them only when you use the preview window (Chapter 7) to view your graphic just as it would appear when you print it.

GETTING ON-LINE HELP
IN COREL DRAW!

Your Corel DRAW! software includes a limited on-line help system that allows you to call up program instructions onscreen whenever you need to refer to them. Currently, this system provides very little data on how to run Corel DRAW!, with the exception of instructions for using the Corel typeface conversion utility WFNBOSS.EXE. The great potential of the help system, however, lies in the relative ease with which you can write your own help files for future reference. You can write files that include custom instructions, handy tips you've learned through experience, and other pertinent information. The following sections will familiarize you with the help system and how it works.

Running CORELHLP.EXE

You activate the Corel DRAW! help system by opening the CORELHLP.EXE file, which is located inside the CORELDRW directory, but outside the program itself. To access help, you must be in the MS-DOS Executive window; therefore, you must either quit Corel DRAW! (not a very convenient solution) or run the MS-DOS Executive as an icon in the background whenever you run Corel DRAW!. This second solution makes accessing the help system as easy as if it were an integral part of the Corel DRAW! software. To run CORELHLP.EXE and the associated data file CORELHLP.CHL,

1. Load Corel DRAW! with the MS-DOS Executive running as an icon in the background, as described in the section of this chapter entitled "Starting Corel DRAW!."

2. Click on the MS-DOS Executive icon in the lower left corner of the screen. The Windows control menu pops up, as shown in Figure 1-11.

FIGURE 1-11   The Windows control menu

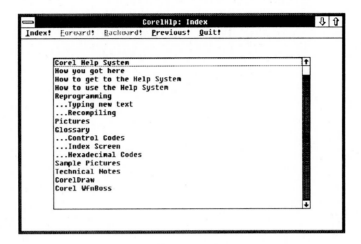

FIGURE 1-12   The index screen of the Corel help system

3. Select the Maximize command. The MS-DOS Executive fills the screen, listing the contents of the CORELDRW directory.

4. Double-click on the filename CORELHLP.EXE. The index screen of the Corel help window appears, as in Figure 1-12.

When you first open the Corel help window, you enter the *index screen*, as shown by the title bar in the figure. The index screen contains an alphabetized listing of all general topics and subtopics in the help data file CORELHLP.CHL. Note that of the five commands in the menu bar, two are gray (Forward! and Backward!). You cannot select them until you choose a specific topic and enter the help screen for that topic.

ACCESSING A HELP TOPIC SCREEN AND MOVING BETWEEN TOPICS   To enter a help topic screen, double-click on the name of the topic you want. If you double-click on the help topic Reprogramming, for example, its help screen displays, as in Figure 1-13. The title bar displays the name of the currently selected help topic, so you always know where you are in the help system. Once you are inside a help screen for a given topic, you can use one of the five commands in the menu bar to move from topic to topic.

- The Index! command returns you to the index screen no matter where you are in the help system.

- The Forward! command is available once you enter a topic screen. Select the Forward! command to move forward to the next topic screen in the index. If you continue clicking on the Forward! command, you will eventually cycle through all of the available screens in all of the available help topics. When you reach the last help topic screen, the Forward! command becomes unavailable once more.

- The Backward! command is available once you enter any help topic screen except the first one in the index. Select Backward! to move to the topic screen before the current topic. If you

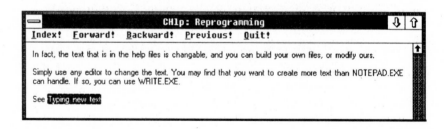

FIGURE 1-13   Accessing another help topic screen

continue clicking on Backward!, you will eventually cycle through all of the available help screens and return to the first topic in the index.

- The Previous! command differs from the Backward! command in that it sends you back to the last screen you viewed before the current screen. For example, if you choose the index screen, then select a topic halfway down the index listing, clicking on Previous! brings you back to the index screen. Clicking on Backward!, on the other hand, would send you to the topic just before the current topic in the index list.

- To leave the help system and return to Corel DRAW!, select the Quit! command. The Corel help window disappears, and the MS-DOS Executive shrinks to an icon once more.

CROSS-REFERENCES BETWEEN HELP TOPIC SCREENS   There is a second way to move between help screen topics. The Reprogramming help topic screen in Figure 1-13 shows the words "Typing new text" in reverse video within a dotted, moving outline. This and other reverse-video text strings in the various help topic screens are *hypertext*. When you click on a hypertext text string, the help system automatically sends you to another help topic screen containing more information about that topic. The hypertext text strings are an excellent means of providing cross-references between topics.

To practice, click on the text string "Typing new text." You immediately go to the associated help topic screen, as shown in Figure 1-14.

VIEWING LONG HELP TOPIC SCREENS   Some of the help topic screens (including some you might create yourself) are longer than the visible screen. When you enter a help topic screen

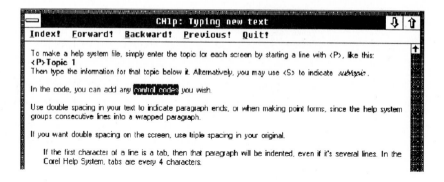

FIGURE 1-14   Using hypertext to move between topics

that extends below the visible window, press (PGDN) to view additional text about that topic.

Running Other Help Data Files (Extension .CHL)

At present, the only help data file available, other than the general CORELHLP.CHL file, is WFNBOSS.CHL (another help file is being included with the Corel Trace batch auto trace utility provided with release 1.2). This help file gives you full information on how to run the WFNBOSS utility, which lets you convert other manufacturers' typefaces into Corel DRAW! format (see Appendix D). To access the help systems for WFNBOSS or other .CHL files, follow these steps:

1. From the CORELDRW directory in the MS-DOS Executive, click once on the filename CORELHLP.EXE to select it and then select the Run command in the File menu. The Run dialog

box appears, with the filename CORELHLP.EXE in the text entry window.

2. Click on the end of the text string in the text entry window, press the spacebar, and type the name of the help file you want to access (for example, type **WFNBOSS.CHL**). This tells CORELHLP.EXE to run the associated help data file.

3. Select the OK command button to exit the dialog box and run the Corel help system with the help file you have chosen.

Creating Your Own Help Data Files

You can create your own help data files in Corel DRAW! using the information in the CORELHLP.CHL data file as a kind of "starter kit." The help data files can contain multiple topics, hypertext cross-references, and even pictures. You can use any Windows text editor, such as NOTEPAD.EXE or WRITE.EXE, to create a help file.

 If you use WRITE.EXE, save the text in Text Only format. Otherwise, Corel DRAW! will not be able to read it.

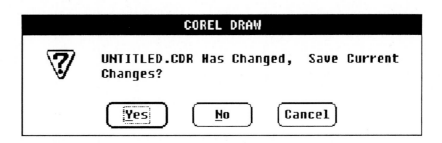

FIGURE 1-15 The Save Changes message box

The subject of how to create help files is a rich one, and it may not be of interest to casual Corel DRAW! users. If you'd like to try writing your own help data files, load the CORELHLP.CHL help data file and follow the instructions under the help topics Reprogramming, Typing New Text, and Recompiling.

When you are finished experimenting with the help system, select Quit to leave the help screen and return to Corel DRAW!.

QUITTING COREL DRAW!

Now that you are familiar with the screen components and help files, exit Corel DRAW! and return to the MS-DOS Executive. You can use the mouse, the keyboard and mouse, or the keyboard alone to quit Corel DRAW!.

To quit by using the mouse, display the File menu by moving the mouse cursor to the File menu name and then click once. Then, select the Quit command by clicking on it once.

To quit by using both mouse and keyboard, display the File menu by clicking on the menu name. Then, with the File menu displayed, type **q**.

To quit by using the keyboard alone, you can either press (CTRL-Q) or press (ALT-F) to display the File menu and then type **q**.

If you have attempted to draw during this session, a screen message like the one in Figure 1-15 appears. Select the No command button to abandon your changes.

If you are like most software users, you will want to begin drawing immediately. This book encourages you to draw. In Chapter 2 you will use the Freehand tool to begin drawing lines and curves.

SUMMARY

Run the Windows MS-DOS Executive as an icon in the background whenever you run Corel DRAW!. This method of working allows you to have ready access to the Windows clipboard, the Corel DRAW! help system, and other Windows applications at all times.

The Corel DRAW! interface features six pull-down menus and a toolbox containing nine tools. Familiarize yourself with the various functions of these menus and tools. Some tools perform drawing functions, others allow you to edit images, and still others help you adjust the look of the screen to fit your working habits.

Knowing how to get around in dialog boxes is a key to working with Corel DRAW! efficiently. Dialog boxes contain several kinds of controls, which allow you to choose among available options, enter text, and preview the results of your selections.

Corel DRAW! also gives you access to a skeletal on-screen help system. You can create your own help files using the Windows Notepad or Write applications.

DRAWING AND
WORKING WITH LINES
AND CURVES

The Freehand tool ⌐ℓ⌐ is the most versatile tool in the Corel DRAW! toolbox. By using this tool in two different ways, you can create both straight and curved lines, and from these simple building blocks you can construct an almost infinite variety of polygons and irregular shapes. Work through the exercises in this chapter to become thoroughly familiar with this most basic Corel DRAW! tool.

DRAWING STRAIGHT LINES

In the language of the Corel DRAW! interface, *line* refers to any straight line, while the term *curve* refers to curved lines, irregular lines, and closed objects you create with such lines. Drawing a straight line requires that you work with the mouse in a different way than when you draw a curved or irregular line. To draw a straight line in Corel DRAW!,

1. Load Corel DRAW! if it isn't running already.

2. Position the mouse cursor over the Freehand tool icon $\boxed{\mathcal{l}}$ and click once. The cursor changes to a crosshair $\boxed{+}$ and the Freehand tool icon appears in reverse video.

3. Position the crosshair cursor at the point where you want a line to begin. This can be anywhere inside the printable page area.

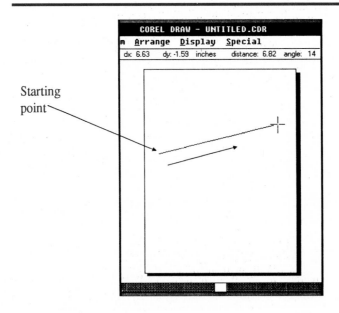

FIGURE 2-1   Extending a straight line

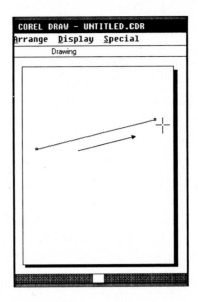

FIGURE 2-2   Nodes on a completed line

4. Click *and immediately release* the mouse button, and then move the crosshair cursor toward the point where you want to end the line. A straight line appears and extends as far as you move the crosshair cursor, as in Figure 2-1. You can move the line in any direction, or make the segment longer or shorter.

5. When you have established the length and direction you want, complete the line by clicking and releasing the mouse button. As Figure 2-2 shows, a small rectangular *node* appears at each end of the line to show that the line is complete and can be selected for further work.

6. Press (DEL) to clear the screen of the line.

 When you begin to draw a line, be sure to release the mouse button as soon as you press it. If you continue to hold down the mouse button while drawing, you create a curve instead of a straight line.

Using the Status Line
To Improve Precision

Chapter 1 introduced you briefly to the status line and its potential for helping you draw with precision and accuracy. In the next exercise, you will draw another straight line, but this time pay attention to the useful information that appears on the status line.

1. With the Freehand tool still selected, begin another line by clicking and releasing the mouse button at a point about halfway down the left side of the page.

2. Move the mouse toward the right side of the page. Don't click a second time yet.

3. Notice that as soon as you clicked once and began to move the mouse, a message appeared on the status line. Look more closely at the status line. It includes the following information about the line you are drawing:

dx   The *dx* code refers to the *x-coordinate* or horizontal location of your line on the page relative to the starting point. The number following this code identifies how far your line is traveling (in other words, its *distance, d*) from that starting point in a horizontal direction. A positive number (one with no minus sign in front of it) indicates that you are extending the line to the right of the starting point, while a negative number indicates that you are extending the line to the left of the starting point.

dy   The *dy* code refers to the *y-coordinate* or vertical location of your line on the page relative to the starting point. The number following this code identifies how far your line is traveling (in other words, its *distance, d*) above or below that starting point. A positive number indicates that you are extending the line below the starting point, while a negative number indicates that you are extending it above the starting point.

inches   The unit of measurement for the current *dx* and *dy* position indicators appears on the status line as well. The Corel DRAW! default is inches, but you can change it to centimeters or picas and points using the Grid Size command in the Display menu. You'll gain experience with the grid later in this chapter.

distance   The number following this text indicates the length of your line relative to the starting point.

angle   The number following this text indicates the angle of the line relative to an imaginary compass, where 0 degrees is at the 3 o'clock position, 90 degrees is at the 12 o'clock position, 180 degrees is at the 9 o'clock position, and -90 degrees is at the 6 o'clock position.

4. Choose an end point for the line and click again to freeze the line in place. Note that the status line indicators disappear as soon as you complete the line, just as they did in Figure 2-2.

5. Press (DEL) to delete the line before going further.

As you may have noticed, information appears on the status line only when you are performing some action on an object. This information makes Corel DRAW! especially powerful for applications requiring great precision, such as technical illustration.

Erasing Unwanted Portions Of a Line as You Draw

In the following exercise, you'll practice erasing part of a line that you have extended but not completed. You can always backtrack and shorten a line in Corel DRAW!, as long as you have not clicked a second time to complete it.

1. With the Freehand tool still selected, select a starting point for another line.

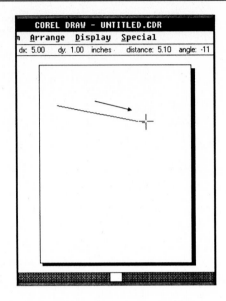

FIGURE 2-3   Extending a line using the status line indicators

2. Move the cursor downward and to the right until the *dx* indicator reads 5.00 inches and the *dy* indicator reads 1.00 inches, as in the example in Figure 2-3.

3. Without clicking the mouse button a second time, backtrack upward until the *dx* indicator reads 4.00 inches. Notice that the line you have drawn behaves flexibly and becomes shorter as you move the mouse backward, as in Figure 2-4.

4. Click a second time to freeze the line at *dx* 4.00 inches.

5. Before going any further, delete the line by pressing (DEL).

Constraining a Straight Line to an Angle

You need not rely on the status line alone when seeking to control the precision of your drawing. You can also use the (CTRL) key

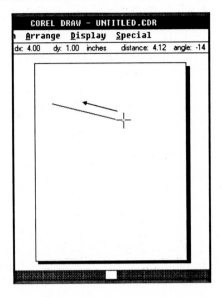

FIGURE 2-4   Backtracking to erase portions of a line

while drawing to *constrain* (force) a line to an angle in increments of 15 degrees. In the following exercise, you'll create a series of seven straight lines this way.

1. With the Freehand tool still selected, press *and hold* (CTRL) and click the mouse button to choose a starting point for the line.

2. Release the mouse button, but continue holding (CTRL) as you extend the line outward and downward from the starting point. Try moving the line to different angles in a clockwise direction; as the angle indicator in the status line shows, the line does not move smoothly, but instead "jumps" in increments of 15 degrees.

3. Now, extend the line straight outward, so that the angle indicator on the status line reads 0 degrees. While still holding down (CTRL), click the mouse button a second time to freeze the line at this angle.

4. Release (CTRL). (Remember always to click the mouse *before* you release (CTRL). If you release (CTRL) first, the line doesn't align to an angle.

5. Draw six more lines in the same way, each sharing a common starting point. Extend the second line at an angle of 15 degrees, the third at an angle of 30 degrees, the fourth at an angle of 45 degrees, the fifth at an angle of 60 degrees, the sixth at an angle of 75 degrees, and the seventh at an angle of 90 degrees. When you are finished, your lines should match the pattern shown in Figure 2-5.

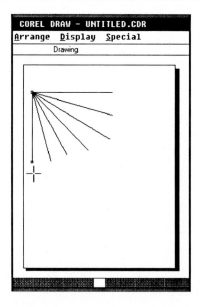

FIGURE 2-5.   Constraining lines to angles in 15-degree increments

Clearing the Screen

Before going any further, clear the screen of the lines you have created so far.

1. Click on the File menu to pull it down.

2. Select the New command.

3. A message box appears with the message:

   UNTITLED.CDR Has Changed, Save Current Changes?

Click on the No command button to exit the message box and clear the screen. The Select tool in the tool box is highlighted by default, just as when you first loaded Corel DRAW!.

Drawing Multi-Segment Lines

With Corel DRAW!, you can easily draw several straight lines in sequence so that each begins where the previous one left off. Use this technique both for drawing open-ended line figures and for constructing polygons. In the present exercise, you will construct a series of peaks and valleys.

1. Select the Freehand tool and then click to choose a line starting point. Extend a line upwards and to the right.

2. When you reach the desired end point for the line, freeze it in place with a *double-click* rather than a single click of the mouse button.

3. Move the mouse downward and to the right, without clicking again. The flexible line follows the crosshair cursor automatically.

4. Double-click again to freeze the second line in place.

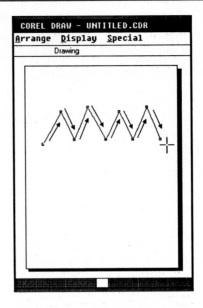

FIGURE 2-6   Drawing multi-segment lines

5. Continue zig-zagging in this way until you have created several peaks and valleys similar to those in Figure 2-6.

6. When you reach the last valley, click once instead of twice to end the multi-segment line.

7. Press (DEL) to clear the screen before proceeding.

 If you make a mistake while drawing, you can erase the last line segment you completed in one of two ways. You either press (ALT-BACKSPACE) or select the Undo command in the Edit menu. Don't press (DEL) when drawing a multi-segment line, or you will erase all of the segments you have drawn so far.

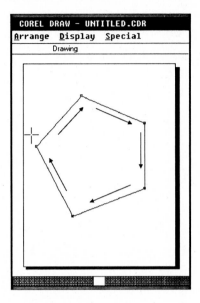

FIGURE 2-7   Drawing a polygon

DRAWING A POLYGON

A *polygon* is a closed two-dimensional figure bounded by straight lines. You create polygons in Corel DRAW! by drawing multi-segment lines and then connecting the end point to the starting point. In the following exercise, you'll create a polygon figure like the one in Figure 2-7.

1. Draw the first line, double-clicking at the line end point so that you can continue drawing without interruption.

2. Draw four additional lines in the same way, following the pattern in Figure 2-7. End the last line segment with a single click at the point where the first line segment began.

Did your last line segment "snap" to the beginning of the first? Or does a small gap remain between them? If you can still see a small gap, don't worry. In the section "Joining Lines and Curves Automatically" later in this chapter, you'll learn how to adjust the level of sensitivity at which one line will join automatically to another. For now, clear the screen and begin the next exercise.

DRAWING CURVES

The Freehand tool has a twofold purpose in Corel DRAW!; you can use it to draw curved or irregular lines as well as straight lines. This section introduces you to the basics of drawing a simple curve, closing the path of a curve to form a closed curve object, and erasing unwanted portions of a curve as you draw.

To draw a simple curve:

1. Select the Freehand tool if it is not still selected.

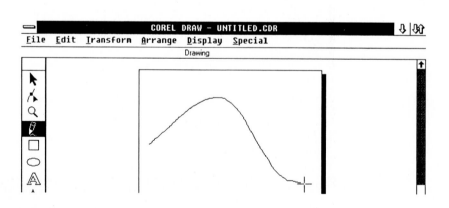

FIGURE 2-8   Drawing a curve

2. Position the crosshair cursor at the point on the page where you want a curve to begin and then press *and hold* the mouse button. The word "Drawing"appears on the status line.

3. Continue to hold the mouse button and *drag* the mouse along the path where you want the curve to continue. Follow the example in Figure 2-8.

4. Upon completing the curve, release the mouse button. The curve disappears momentarily while Corel DRAW! calculates exactly where it should go. Then the curve reappears with many small square nodes, as in Figure 2-9. Note that when you have finished, the word "Curve" appears in the middle of the status

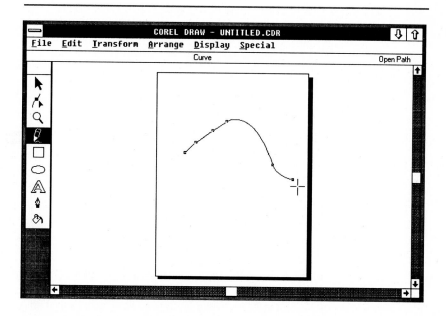

FIGURE 2-9   A completed curve with nodes

line and the message "Open Path" appears at the right side of the status line. "Open Path" indicates that you have drawn a curved line, not a closed figure.

5. Press (DEL) or select the Undo command in the Edit menu to clear the curve you have just drawn.

 To draw a straight line, *click and release* the mouse button. To draw a curve, *press and hold* the mouse button and *drag* the mouse along the desired path.

Erasing Unwanted Portions Of a Curve as You Draw

Should you make a mistake while drawing a curve, you can backtrack and erase what you have drawn, as long as you have not yet released the mouse button. You use (SHIFT) to erase the portion of a curve that you no longer want.

1. Begin another curve by pressing and holding the mouse button over the point at which you want the curve to start.

2. Drag the mouse as desired. Do not release the mouse button yet.

3. While still holding down the mouse button, press and hold (SHIFT) and backtrack over as much of the curve as you wish to erase.

4. After you have erased a portion of the curve, release (SHIFT) and continue to draw by dragging the mouse in the desired direction.

5. Release the mouse button to finalize the curve. Delete the curve by pressing (DEL).

6. Clear the screen by selecting New from the File menu. Do not save your changes.

Drawing Multi-Segment Curves

Just as you drew multi-segment lines, you can also draw multi-segment curves. You can join two successive curves together automatically if the starting point of the second curve is within a few pixels of the end point of the first curve. Refer to Figure 2-10 for this exercise.

1. Select a point for the first curve and begin dragging the mouse.

2. Complete the curve by releasing the mouse button. Do not move the mouse cursor from the point at which your first curve ends.

3. Draw the second curve and complete it. The second curve should "snap" to the first, as in Figure 2-10.

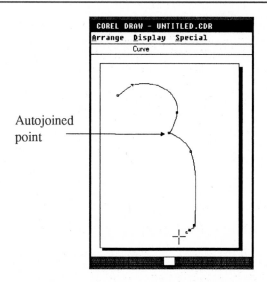

FIGURE 2-10   Drawing two curves that "snap" together

If the two curved lines didn't snap together, you moved the cursor farther than five pixels away before starting the second curve. Don't worry about it at this point. Corel DRAW! has a default value of five pixels distance for automatic joining of lines and curves. In the "Joining Lines and Curves Automatically" section of this chapter, you will learn how to adjust the sensitivity of this AutoJoin feature.

Closing an Open Path

When you drew your first curve, the message "Open Path" appeared at the right side of the status line. This message indicates that your curved line is not a closed object, and therefore that you cannot fill it with a color or pattern (see Chapter 15, "Defining Fill Color"). You can create a closed curve object with the Freehand tool, however. Refer to Figure 2-11 to create an outline of an apple for this exercise. You'll draw the apple and its stem as a single curve.

1. Before beginning the exercise, select New from the File menu to clear the screen. When a message box appears and asks whether you want to save your changes, select No.

2. Select the Freehand tool.

3. Start the curve about midway across the page area. Begin with the stem first.

4. When you reach the bottom of the stem, continue dragging the mouse and tracing the outline of an apple. Your drawing doesn't have to look exactly like the one in Figure 2-11. If you make a mistake, backtrack and erase the portions of the curve that you do not want.

5. When you return to the point at which you began to draw the stem, release the mouse button. After a few seconds, the apple reappears with many square nodes along the path.

Note that the message in the middle of the status line now reads "Curve." At the right side of the status line, the message "Fill:" appears, followed by a representation of a solid black color. This indicates that you now have a closed curve object and that you have filled it with the default color, black. You can't yet see the fill for this object, because you haven't begun to work with the preview window that allows you to see your graphic just as you would print it. You'll become familiar with the preview window in Chapter 7.

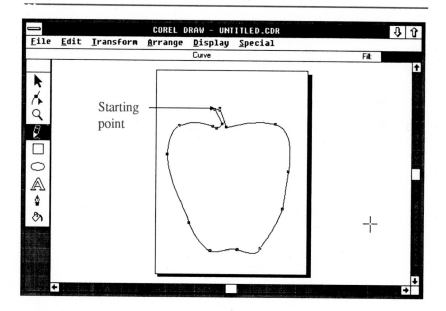

FIGURE 2-11   Drawing a closed curve object

JOINING LINES AND CURVES AUTOMATICALLY

This section shows you how to use rulers and grid spacing to draw with greater precision. This section also introduces you to the AutoJoin feature of Corel DRAW!, which causes lines and curves to "snap" together automatically when their end points are a preset number of pixels apart. You can adjust the sensitivity of the AutoJoin feature using the Preferences command in the Special menu.

Setting the Grid and Displaying Rulers

The invisible grid in Corel DRAW! is a helpful aid when you need to align objects, position them exactly, or draw them to a specific size. You can adjust both the units of measurement and the fineness of the grid spacing.

1. Select the New command from the File menu to clear the screen of the apple you drew in the last exercise.

2. Select the Grid Size command from the Display menu. The dialog box in Figure 2-12 appears. The settings in your software may be different from the ones in the figure.

3. Adjust the grid settings to 8.00 per inch, if necessary. To change the value in the numeric entry box, press and hold the mouse button over the up or down scroll arrow until the number changes to 8.00. Alternatively, you can click on the numeric value itself and type in the new number. To change the unit of measurement in the rectangular units box, just click on it until the word "inch" appears.

4. Click on OK to save this setting and exit the dialog box.

5. Look at the Snap to Grid command in the Display menu. If no check mark appears in front of it, select it to make the grid active. If a check mark already appears in front of it, you don't need to do anything.

6. Select the Show Rulers command from the Display menu. Since you have set the grid size to inches, the rulers will also display in inches, as in Figure 2-13. Notice that the zero point for both the horizontal and vertical rulers begins at the upper-left corner of the page area, as shown by the cursor arrow in the figure. This is a convenient way to mark the rulers so that you can measure everything relative to that corner.

7. Now you are ready to work with the AutoJoin feature. Select the Freehand tool, then move the crosshair cursor to a point 1 inch to the right of the zero point on the horizontal ruler and 2 inches below the zero point on the vertical ruler. Notice that as you move the mouse, dotted "shadow" ruler lines show you the exact location of your cursor.

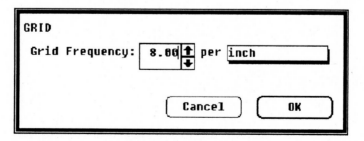

FIGURE 2-12   The Grid dialog box

8. Click once at this point to begin drawing a line. The parameters in the status line appear.

9. Using the rulers and the status line to help you, extend the line 4 inches to the right. The *dx* and distance parameters on the status line should read 4.0 inches, as in Figure 2-14. Click a second time to freeze the line in position.

10. Move the crosshair cursor exactly 1/4 inch to the right of the end point of the line. Use the rulers to help you.

11. Press and hold the mouse button at this point and drag the mouse to form a squiggling curve.

12. Release the mouse button to complete the curve. If you began the curve 1/4 inch or more to the right of the line end point, the

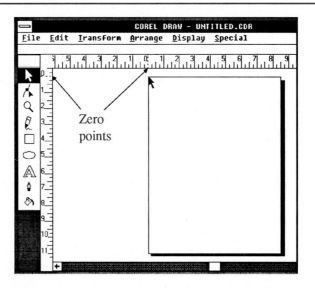

FIGURE 2-13   Displaying the rulers

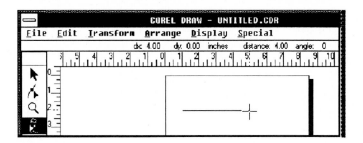

FIGURE 2-14   Extending a line (dx=4.00 inches,
Distance=4.00 inches)

curve remains separate from the line and does not snap to it, as in Figure 2-15. In order to make a curve snap to a line automatically at this distance, you'll need to adjust the AutoJoin threshold value in the Preferences dialog box. (You'll become familiar with this process in the next section.)

13. Select the New command from the File menu to clear the screen before proceeding. Do not save any changes.

Adjusting the AutoJoin Threshold

The AutoJoin feature determines how far apart (in pixels) two lines or curves have to be for them to join together automatically. If the setting in the Preferences dialog box is a very small number, such as 3 or less, lines snap together only if you draw with a very exact hand. Use this lower setting when you want to *prevent* lines from joining accidentally. If your technique is less precise, you can set the AutoJoin threshold value to a number higher than 5 pixels so that lines will snap together even if you don't have a steady hand.

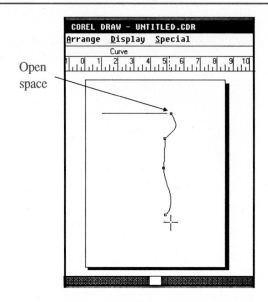

Open space

FIGURE 2-15   Curve failing to snap to a line (AutoJoin value low)

1. Select the Preferences command from the Special menu. The Preferences dialog box in Figure 2-16 appears. The default setting for all of the features in the Lines and Curves section of the dialog box is 5 pixels. You'll use some of the other settings later on, when you learn skills for which these settings are useful. For now, you will concern yourself only with the AutoJoin setting.

2. Set the AutoJoin value to 10 pixels by clicking several times on the up scroll arrow.

3. Select OK to save the new value and return to the drawing.

4. Now you can redraw the line and make the curve snap to it. With the Freehand tool selected, redraw a straight line as you did in steps 7-9 of the previous section.

5. Move the crosshair to a point 1/4 inch to the right of the end point of the line and then press and hold the mouse button to begin drawing a curve. The horizontal ruler on your screen displays only four markings per inch, not eight as you would find on an actual ruler.

6. Drag the mouse and draw the squiggle curve as you did in step 11 of the previous section.

7. Release the mouse button. This time, the curve joins automatically to the line, as shown in Figure 2-17.

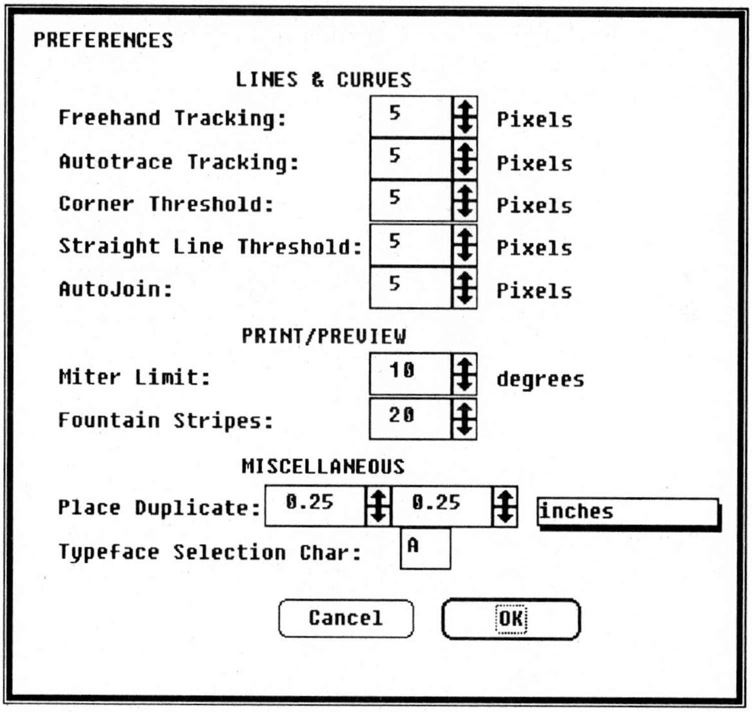

PREFERENCES

LINES & CURVES

Freehand Tracking:	5	Pixels
Autotrace Tracking:	5	Pixels
Corner Threshold:	5	Pixels
Straight Line Threshold:	5	Pixels
AutoJoin:	5	Pixels

PRINT/PREVIEW

Miter Limit:	10	degrees
Fountain Stripes:	20	

MISCELLANEOUS

Place Duplicate: | 0.25 | 0.25 | inches

Typeface Selection Char: | A |

Cancel   OK

FIGURE 2-16   The Preferences dialog box

8. Select New from the File menu to clear the screen before going further.

The AutoJoin feature has other uses in addition to allowing you to connect lines and curves. You can also use it to accomplish the following:

- Join lines to lines or curves to curves.

- Add a curve or line to the end of an existing curve, line, or object that you have selected.

- Create closed curve objects and polygons by starting and ending a curve (or a series of line segments) at the same point.

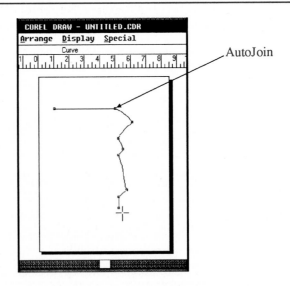

FIGURE 2-17   Curve snapping to a line (AutoJoin value high)

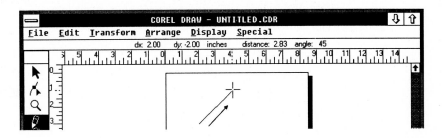

FIGURE 2-18   Drawing a kite: the first line segment

CREATING A DRAWING USING LINES, CURVES, AND POLYGONS

You have learned to create all of the simple objects—line, curve, closed curve, and polygon—that you can make with the Freehand tool. In this exercise, you'll bring together all of the skills you have learned by drawing a kite that consists of lines, curves, and a polygon. Use Figures 2-18 to 2-25 as a guide to help you position the start and end points of the lines and curves.

1. Invoke the rulers (if they do not appear onscreen already) by selecting Show Rulers from the Display menu.

2. Select the Freehand tool.

3. Move to a point 2 inches to the right of the zero point on the horizontal ruler and 3 inches below the zero point on the vertical ruler and then click once to start a line.

4. Extend the line upward and to the right until you reach a point 4 inches to the right of the horizontal zero point and 1 inch below the vertical zero point. Use the status line information to help you and refer to Figure 2-18. Double-click and release the mouse button at this point.

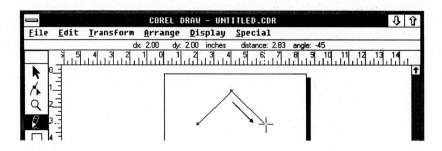

FIGURE 2-19 Drawing a kite: the second line segment

5. Extend the next line segment downward and to the right as shown in Figure 2-19, until you reach a point 6 inches to the right of the horizontal zero point and 3 inches below the vertical zero point. Double-click at this point to add on another line segment.

6. Extend this new line segment horizontally to the left until you reach the starting point. Double-click at this point. The last line segment connects to the first line segment and forms a triangle, as shown in Figure 2-20.

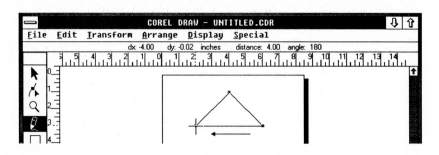

FIGURE 2-20 Drawing a kite: the third line segment

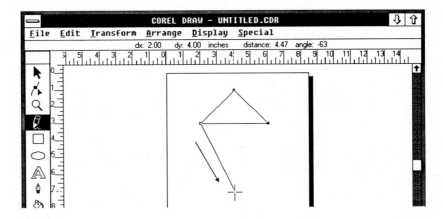

FIGURE 2-21   Drawing a kite: the fourth line segment

7. From this point, extend another line segment downward and to the right until you reach a point 4 inches to the right of the horizontal zero point and 7 inches below the vertical zero point, as shown in Figure 2-21. Double-click at this point to complete this segment.

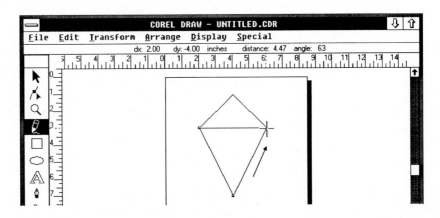

FIGURE 2-22   Completing the basic kite shape

8. Now, extend a final segment upward to the lower-right corner of the original triangle, as in Figure 2-22. Click just once to finish the line and complete the basic kite shape.

9. Next, add a vertical crosspiece to the kite. Since this line must be absolutely vertical, begin by pressing and holding (CTRL) and then clicking once at the top of the kite.

10. Extend this new line to the base of the kite as shown in Figure 2-23 and then click once. You are going to attach a curve to this line.

11. To attach a curve to this point, press and hold the mouse button and then draw a kite tail similar to the one in Figure 2-24. Release the mouse button to complete the curve.

12. Finally, add a string to the kite. Click on the point at which the crosspieces meet and extend a line diagonally downward and to the left until you reach the margin of the printable page area. Use Figure 2-25 as a guide. Click once to complete the line.

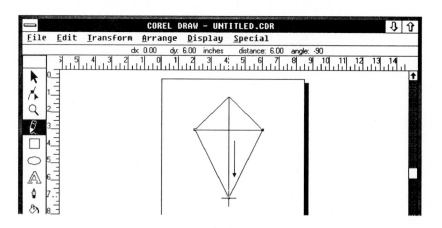

FIGURE 2-23   Drawing the crosspiece

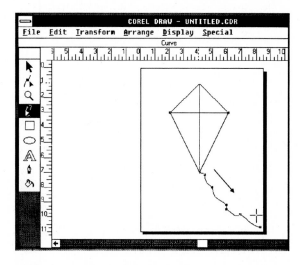

FIGURE 2-24   Drawing the kite "tail" (a curve)

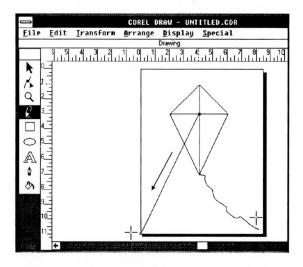

FIGURE 2-25   Adding a string and completing the kite

13. Your kite should now look similar to the one in Figure 2-25. Leave the kite on your screen for the concluding section of this chapter.

SAVING YOUR WORK

As you work on your own drawings, save your work frequently during a session. If you don't save often enough, you could lose an image in the event of unexpected power or hardware failures.

In order to save a new drawing, you must establish a filename for it.

To save the kite you just drew,

1. Select the Save As command from the File menu to display the Save Drawing dialog box in Figure 2-26. If you installed the sample drawings with Corel DRAW!, the directory indicator shows that you are in the \WINDOWS\CORELDRW\ CDRFILES directory of your hard drive. (Path names may vary, depending on how and where you installed the software.) Notice that the limited size of the Path text entry box causes the

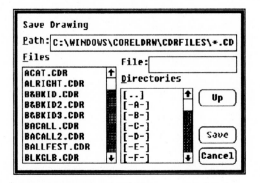

FIGURE 2-26   The Save Drawing dialog box

"R" in the CDR file extension to be hidden from view. To see the end of the text string, click anywhere in the Path text entry box, and then press (END). To return to the beginning of the text line, press (HOME).

2. If the Path text entry box shows some other path, or if you want to save the drawing in a different drive and/or directory, change to the correct drive and directory by double-clicking on the correct entries in the Directories list box. When you double-click, the selected path name will appear in the Path text entry box. If the drive or directory name you want is not visible in the Directories list box, position the mouse cursor over the up or down arrow in the scroll bar, and then press and hold the mouse button until the path name becomes visible. You can then select the drive or directory name.

3. Name the drawing by clicking in the File: text entry box, and then typing the desired name of your file. Use no more than eight characters; Corel DRAW! adds the .CDR extension for you when you select the Save command button. In this case, type **KITE**. The Save command button, which was gray before, now becomes available for selection.

4. Save the file by clicking on the Save command button or pressing (ENTER). Corel DRAW! adds the extension .CDR to the file. You exit the Save File dialog box and return to your drawing. Notice that the title bar now contains the name of your drawing, KITE.CDR.

5. Select New from the File menu to clear the screen before continuing. Since you have just saved a picture, the Save Changes warning box doesn't appear.

The foregoing procedure applies only the first time you save a drawing. To save an existing drawing, either select the Save command from the File menu, or press (CTRL-S).

RETRIEVING A FILE

To open an existing picture, use the following procedure. In this exercise, you'll open the KITE.CDR file you just saved.

1. Select Open from the File menu. The Open Drawing dialog box appears, as in Figure 2-27. Its layout is very similar to the Save As dialog box.

2. If you saved your file in a directory other than the default directory (the CDRFILES subdirectory of CORELDRW), select the drive and/or directory name from the Directories list box. Use the scroll bar if necessary.

3. If you can't see the file KITE.CDR in the Files list box, position the mouse cursor over the down arrow in the scroll bar and then press and hold it until the filename becomes visible.

4. Click once on the filename KITE.CDR. The name appears in reverse video (white lettering on black background) and displays in the File text box.

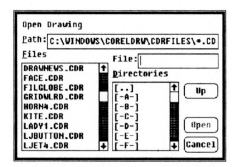

FIGURE 2-27   The Open Drawing dialog box

5. To open the file, select the Open command or press (ENTER). After a moment, the file displays in the window and its name appears in the title bar.

6. Exit Corel DRAW! by pressing (CTRL-Q), or by selecting Quit from the File menu.

 There's a shortcut to opening a file once you are in the Open File dialog box. Instead of clicking once on the filename and then selecting Open, you can simply double-click on the filename.

That's all there is to it. You have created a complete drawing using the Freehand tool, saved it, and loaded it again. Along the way, you have learned how to use the rulers, grid spacing, and status line to help you work.

SUMMARY

The versatile Freehand tool in Corel DRAW! allows you to draw an almost infinite number of shapes using the basic building blocks of lines and curves. In Corel DRAW!, "line" refers to straight lines only, while "curve" refers to both straight and curved lines, irregular lines, and closed objects made with these lines.

The Corel DRAW! interface contains a number of aids to help you attain greater precision when drawing. Among these are the status line, the rulers, and the grid. You can adjust settings for the rulers and the grid through the appropriate dialog boxes.

Another useful aid to freehand drawing is the AutoJoin feature, which you can adjust to cause lines and curves to snap together automatically as you draw them. You adjust the threshold values for AutoJoin through the Preferences command in the Special menu.

chapter **3**

DRAWING AND WORKING WITH RECTANGLES AND SQUARES

Drawing a Rectangle
Drawing a Square
Practicing with the Grid
Creating a Drawing Using Rectangles and Squares

The rectangle is a basic shape that underlies many complex man-made forms. In this chapter, you will begin to use the Rectangle tool to create both rectangular and square shapes. As you work your way through the exercises in this book, you will apply a host of Corel DRAW! special effects, fills, and shaping techniques to rectangles and squares to make them come alive.

DRAWING A RECTANGLE

Using the Rectangle tool in the Corel DRAW! toolbox, you can initiate a rectangle from any of its four corners, as well as from the center outward. Having this degree of freedom and control over the placement of rectangles saves you time and effort when you lay out your illustrations.

Drawing from Any Corner

You can start a rectangle from any of its four corners. The corner that represents the starting point always remains fixed as you draw; the rest of the outline expands or contracts as you move the cursor diagonally. This flexibility in choosing a starting point allows you to place a rectangle more quickly and precisely within a drawing. Perform the following exercise to become familiar with how the Corel DRAW! interface reacts when you use different corners as starting points.

1. Load Corel DRAW! if you are not running it already.

2. Select the Rectangle tool by placing the mouse cursor over the Rectangle icon ▭ and clicking once, and then moving the mouse out of the toolbox and to the right. The mouse cursor turns into a crosshair ┼ , and the Rectangle icon is selected.

3. Position the cursor anywhere on the printable page area, press and hold the left mouse button, and drag the mouse *downward* and to the *right* along a diagonal path, as shown in Figure 3-1. When you draw in this direction, the width and height indicators on the status line display as positive numbers.

4. Experiment with different widths and heights until you achieve the shape you want. You can easily modify the shape of the rectangle by redirecting the movement of the mouse. Notice

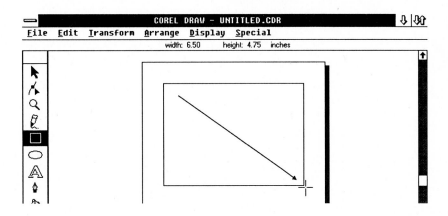

FIGURE 3-1   Drawing a rectangle

that the upper-left corner, which was your starting point, remains fixed.

5. When the rectangle is the shape and size you want, release the mouse button. This action freezes the rectangle in place. Four nodes appear at the corners of the rectangle, and the status line changes to display the messages "Rectangle" and "Fill:" followed by a solid black color, as in Figure 3-2. You will learn more about fills in Chapter 15.

6. Press and hold the mouse button at a new starting point, and then move the cursor along a diagonal path *downward* and to the *left*. This time, the width indicator on the status line displays a negative number, and the height indicator displays a positive number. Release the mouse button when the rectangle has the dimensions you want.

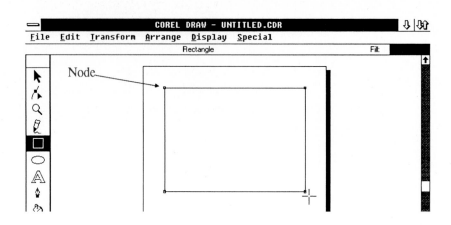

FIGURE 3-2   Completing a rectangle

7. Press and hold the mouse button at a different starting point, and then move the cursor along a diagonal path *upward* and to the *right*. This time, the width indicator displays a positive number and the height indicator displays a negative number. Release the mouse button when the rectangle has the dimensions you want.

8. Move to another new starting point, and then press and hold the mouse button and move the cursor along a diagonal path *upward* and to the *left*. When you use the lower-right corner as your starting point, both of the dimension indicators in the status line display as negative numbers. Release the mouse button when the rectangle has the dimensions you want.

9. To clear the screen before proceeding, select the Clear command from the Edit menu.

 The type of information appearing in the status line reflects the kind of object you are drawing. When you create a line, the status line displays the *x*- and *y*-coordinates, the distance (*d*) traveled, and the angle of the line. When you create a rectangle, the status line displays the width and height.

Keep in mind that while you are drawing, the width and height indicators always show you the direction of the rectangle relative to the starting point.

- A positive width indicator means you are drawing from left to right.

- A negative width indicator means you are drawing from right to left.

- A positive height indicator means you are drawing from top to bottom.

- A negative height indicator means you are drawing from bottom to top.

Drawing from the Center Outward

Corel DRAW! allows you to draw a rectangle from the center outward. Using this technique, you can place rectangular shapes more precisely within a graphic, without having to pay close attention to rulers or grid spacing. The width and height indicators display the exact dimensions of the rectangle as you draw. Draw a rectangle now, using the center as its starting point.

1. With the Rectangle tool selected, press and hold both (SHIFT) and the mouse button at the desired starting point. Keep both (SHIFT) and the mouse button pressed as you move the mouse. As with any rectangle, you can draw in any direction; the width and height indicators in the status line reflect that direction. You can tell that the rectangle in Figure 3-3 is being drawn from the

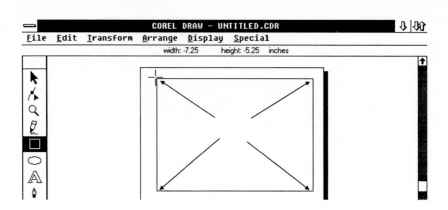

FIGURE 3-3   Drawing a rectangle from the center outward

center to the upper-left corner because both of the indicators display negative numbers.

2. Release both (**SHIFT**) and the mouse button to complete the rectangle.

3. Press (**DEL**) to clear the rectangle from the screen.

DRAWING A SQUARE

In Corel DRAW!, you use the same tool to produce both rectangles and perfect squares. The technique is identical, except that you bring (**CTRL**) into play when creating a square.

Drawing from a Corner

Follow these steps to draw a square. As with a rectangle, you can use any corner as your starting point.

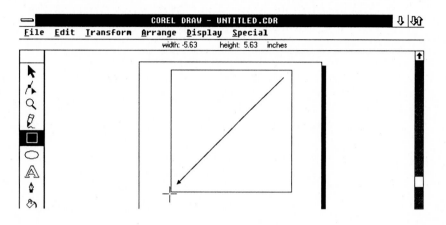

FIGURE 3-4   Drawing a square

1. With the Rectangle tool selected, position the cursor at the point where you want to begin the square.

2. Press and hold both (CTRL) and the mouse button and then draw diagonally in any direction. Note that the status line indicators show that the width and the height of the shape are equal, as in Figure 3-4.

3. To complete the square, release the mouse button first, and then release (CTRL). If you release (CTRL) first, you might draw a rectangle with unequal sides rather than a square.

4. Press (DEL) to clear the square from the screen.

Drawing from the Center Outward

To draw a square in any direction, using the center as a starting point, you must use both (CTRL) and (SHIFT).

1. With the Rectangle tool selected, position the cursor at the point where you want to begin the square.

2. Press and hold (CTRL), (SHIFT), and the mouse button simultaneously, and draw diagonally in any direction.

3. To complete the square, release the mouse button first, and then release (CTRL) and (SHIFT). If you release (CTRL) and (SHIFT) first, you might draw a rectangle with unequal sides, and the center might turn into a corner.

4. Press (DEL) to clear the square from the screen.

PRACTICING WITH THE GRID

If your work includes design-oriented applications such as technical illustration, architectural renderings, or graphic design, you may sometimes find it necessary to align geometrical shapes horizontally or vertically in fixed increments. In this section, you can practice aligning rectangles and squares while drawing; Chapter 8 will introduce you to techniques for aligning shapes *after* you have drawn them.

As you learned in the previous chapter, the grid in Corel DRAW! is invisible. Objects align to it, but you never see a grid on the screen.

One way to align objects while drawing is to take advantage of the Grid Size and Snap To Grid commands in the Display menu. The process of aligning new objects to a grid consists of three steps:

• Adjusting the grid spacing

• Displaying the rulers

- Enabling the Snap To Grid feature.

1. Pull down the Display menu and select the Grid Size command. The Grid dialog box in Figure 3-5 will display.

2. Adjust the Grid Frequency value to 2.00 per inch. To do this, press and hold the mouse button over the upper or lower scroll arrow until the number 2.00 appears. Alternatively, you can click on the current value, backspace, and type **2.00**. If the selected unit of measurement is something other than inches, click on the units box until the word "inch" appears.

3. When you are finished, click on OK to save this setting and exit the dialog box.

4. Display the rulers (if they do not already appear on the screen) by selecting the Show Rulers command in the Display menu. A checkmark will appear next to the command, indicating that the rulers are now active.

5. Pull down the Display menu once more to see if the Snap To Grid feature is currently selected. If a checkmark appears next to the Snap To Grid command, it is already active, and you can

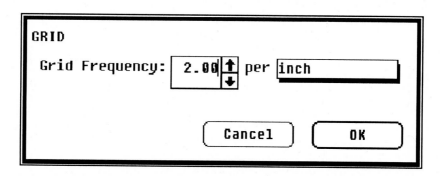

FIGURE 3-5 Adjusting grid frequency to 2.00 per inch

align and place objects automatically at the specified increment. If a checkmark does not appear, select this command to activate the feature.

6. Next, select the Rectangle tool and position the cursor at the 1-inch mark relative to both the horizontal and vertical rulers. Even if you place the cursor inexactly, the corner of the rectangle will align perfectly to the 1-inch marks when you begin to draw.

7. Press and hold the mouse button and draw a rectangle 4 inches wide and 3 inches deep.

8. Draw a second rectangle the same size as the first beginning at a point ½ inch to the right and ½ inch below the first. The shadow rulers align exactly with the ½-inch marks on both rulers. The grid setting prevents you from "missing the mark."

9. Draw a third rectangle from a starting point ½ inch below and ½ inch to the right of the second. Your three rectangles should align like the ones in Figure 3-6.

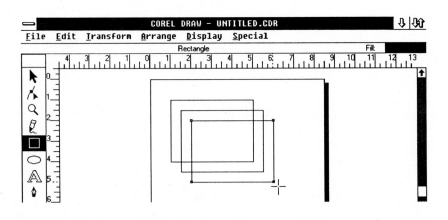

FIGURE 3-6   Drawing rectangles at ½-inch intervals

10. Select New from the File menu to clear all of the rectangles from the screen. When the Save Changes message box appears, select No.

Now that you have practiced drawing all possible types of rectangles, you are ready to build a drawing with rectangular and freehand elements.

CREATING A DRAWING USING RECTANGLES AND SQUARES

In the following exercise, you will integrate all the skills you have learned so far by creating a teacup that includes rectangles, squares, and freehand drawing elements. In the process, you will also learn how to adjust the relative smoothness of curved lines you draw with the Freehand tool. The adjustment involves a feature called Freehand Tracking, which controls how closely Corel DRAW! follows the movements of your mouse cursor when you draw curves.

To prepare for this exercise, select the Grid Size command from the Display menu and adjust Grid Frequency to 8.00 per inch. Refer to the steps in the preceding section if necessary. When you are ready to create the drawing, proceed through the following steps, using the numbers in Figure 3-7 as a guide. If you wish, use the rulers as an aid in laying out your work.

1. Draw a rectangle (1) to represent the body of the teacup. It should be higher than it is wide.

2. Position your cursor at the right side of this rectangle and attach a rectangular handle (2) to the body of the teacup. The handle should touch the edge of the teacup but not overlap it; the grid settings you have chosen will prevent overlapping.

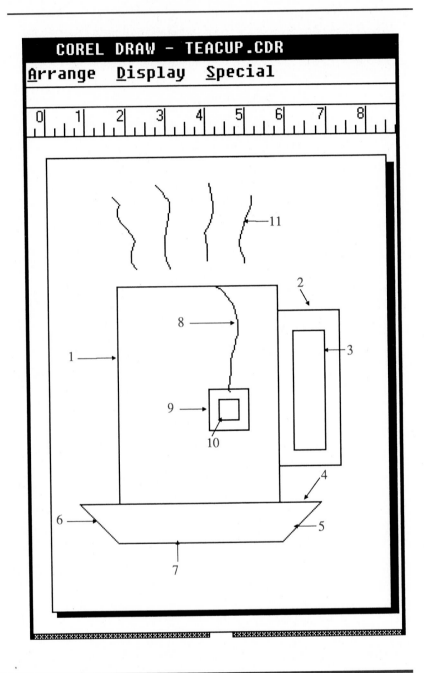

FIGURE 3-7   A teacup using rectangles, squares, and freehand elements

3. Draw a smaller rectangle (3) inside the one you just created (2) to make the opening in the handle.

4. Now select the Freehand tool ⌐ℓ⌐ and add a straight line (4) to the base of the teacup. This represents the top of the saucer. Remember to press and hold (CTRL) while drawing to ensure that the line remains perfectly horizontal; use the information in the status line if you need guidance.

5. Extend a diagonal line (5) and (6) down from each end of the top of the saucer. Check the status line indicators as you draw: The angle for the diagonal line to the left (6) should read -45 degrees, while the angle for the diagonal line to the right (5) should read -135 degrees. Be sure to make both lines the same length. Each line snaps to the saucer base to form a multi-segment line, as you learned in Chapter 2.

6. Now add another straight line (7) to form the bottom of the saucer. Remember to constrain the line using (CTRL). The saucer base snaps to the other line segments to form a single object, a polygon.

7. With the Freehand tool still selected, press and hold the mouse button and draw a curve (8) to represent the string of a tea bag. Does your string appear excessively jagged? If it does, you can adjust the Freehand Tracking setting in the next set of steps.

8. Before adjusting the Freehand Tracking value, erase the tea bag string you have just drawn by selecting Undo from the Edit menu.

9. Select the Preferences command from the Special menu to display the Preferences dialog box, as shown in Figure 3-8. You used this same dialog box in Chapter 2 to adjust the AutoJoin values. The default value in the numeric entry box next to Freehand Tracking: is 5 but you are going to adjust it to a higher number to facilitate smoother curves.

10. Using the scroll arrow, adjust the sensitivity level in the Freehand Tracking option to 10 pixels. This is the highest number possible and causes Corel DRAW! to smooth your curved lines as you draw. Lower numbers, on the other hand, cause the Freehand tool to track every little dip and rise as you move the mouse.

11. Select OK to exit the dialog box and save your setting.

12. Now draw the tea bag string a second time. Your curve should be somewhat smoother now, more like the one in Figure 3-7.

13. Next, attach a tag to the string: Select the Rectangle tool again, position the cursor just below the bottom of the string, press and hold (CTRL) and (SHIFT) simultaneously and draw a square (9) from the center outward.

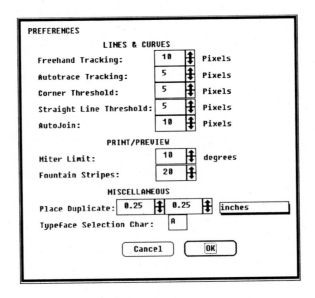

FIGURE 3-8   Adjusting the Freehand Tracking value for smoother curvers

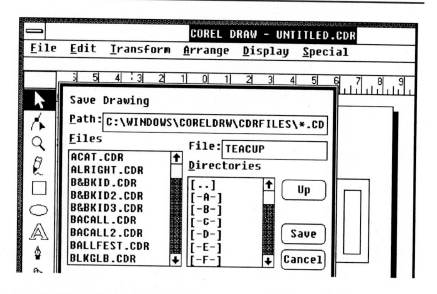

FIGURE 3-9   Saving the drawing as TEACUP.CDR

14. To add a center label to the tag, create a square (10) inside the first square. Select one of the corners as the starting point for this smaller square.

15. To add a finishing touch to your drawing, create some steam (11) by selecting the Freehand tool and drawing some curves. Since you have set Freehand Tracking to a higher number of pixels, you can create more effective "steam" than if you had not adjusted the default setting.

16. Finally, save your drawing. Select the Save As command from the File menu and type the name **TEACUP** as shown in Figure 3-9. When you click on the Save command button, Corel DRAW! adds the extension .CDR automatically.

SUMMARY

Rectangles and squares are important shapes to master if you need to create technical, architectural, or other stylized or design-oriented illustrations. In Corel DRAW!, the Rectangle tool creates both types of shapes.

Add speed and accuracy to the drawing process by constructing rectangles and squares from any corner or from the center outward. Use of these techniques allow you to place shapes more intuitively within a graphic than if you had to rely on the grid and rulers at every step.

Use the grid and display rulers to help you place elements in your drawings when strict precision is required. You can adjust grid spacing to cause elements to align more tightly or loosely according to your needs.

You can also make your freehand curves smoother or rougher by adjusting the Freehand Tracking setting in the Preferences dialog box. A higher value results in smoother curves, while a lower value gives you more jagged curves.

DRAWING AND WORKING WITH ELLIPSES AND CIRCLES

Drawing an Ellipse
Drawing a Circle
Creating a Drawing Using Ellipses and Circles

The ellipse and the circle are basic shapes that underlie more complex forms in nature and in man-made artifacts. The Ellipse tool in Corel DRAW! allows you to create both ellipses and perfect circles. For added convenience in placement, you can choose to initiate ellipses and circles either from any point on the rim or from the center outward.

Follow the exercises in this chapter to begin creating ellipses and circles of many different shapes and sizes using Corel DRAW!. In later chapters, you will expand your skills and apply a rich variety of special effects and shaping techniques to these basic geometrical forms.

DRAWING AN ELLIPSE

All versions of Corel DRAW! allow you to start an ellipse from any point on the rim. You can also draw an ellipse from the center point outward by using the (SHIFT) key. This second method allows you to place ellipses precisely within a graphic.

Using the Rim as a Starting Point

You can initiate an ellipse from any point on its rim. This flexibility in choosing your starting point allows you to position an ellipse easily within a drawing, without sacrificing precision.

When you began creating rectangles in Chapter 3, you saw how the status line width and height indicators displayed positive or negative numbers, depending on the starting point you chose and the direction in which you moved the mouse. The same holds true for ellipses and circles. You cannot use a corner as a starting point, of course, but you can still use the width and height indicators as guides. Keep in mind that a positive width indicator means you are drawing from left to right, while a negative width indicator shows you are drawing from right to left. Similarly, a positive height indicator means you are drawing from top to bottom and a negative height indicator means you are drawing from bottom to top.

Corel DRAW! gives you an additional visual cue when you are drawing ellipses and circles. If your starting point is on the upper half of the rim, Corel DRAW! places the node at the uppermost point of the ellipse; if your starting point is on the lower half of the rim, Corel DRAW! places the node at the bottommost point of the ellipse. Perform the following exercises to become familiar with how the Corel DRAW! interface reacts when you choose different points on the rim as starting points for an ellipse.

1. Load Corel DRAW! if you are not running it already.

2. Select the Ellipse tool ⬭ by positioning the mouse cursor over the Ellipse icon and clicking once. Move the mouse to the right, out of the toolbox. The mouse cursor turns into a crosshair and the Ellipse icon appears highlighted.

3. Position the cursor anywhere on the printable page area, press and hold the mouse button, and drag the mouse downward and to the right along a diagonal path, as shown in Figure 4-1. The indicators on the status line display the width and height of the ellipse as positive numbers.

4. When the ellipse is the shape you want, release the mouse button. This action completes the ellipse and freezes it in place. As in Figure 4-2, a single node appears at the uppermost point of the ellipse, and the status line changes to display the messages "Ellipse" and "Fill:" followed by a solid black rectangle. The "Fill:" message indicates that the ellipse has a default interior color of black.

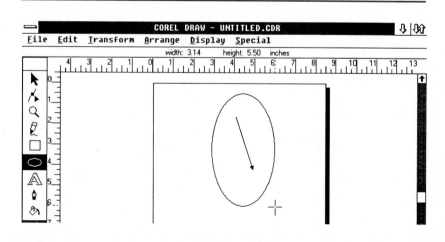

FIGURE 4-1 Drawing an ellipse from top to bottom

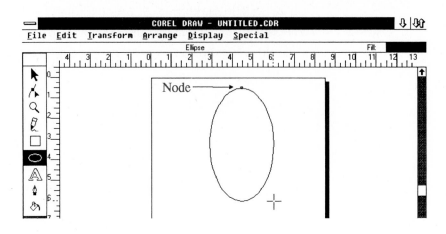

FIGURE 4-2 A completed ellipse showing the node at the top

5. Choose a new starting point and draw an ellipse from bottom to top. Press and hold the mouse button at a desired starting

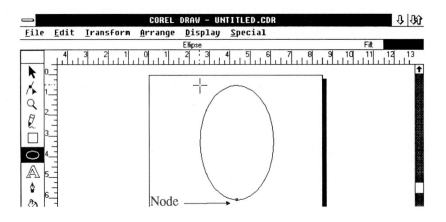

FIGURE 4-3 A completed ellipse drawn from bottom to top (node at bottom)

point anywhere on the bottom half of the rim and then move the cursor *upward* in a diagonal direction. This time the height indicator on the status line displays negative numbers.

6. When the ellipse has the dimensions you want, release the mouse button. Note that the node is now at the bottom of the ellipse, as in Figure 4-3.

7. To clear both ellipses from the screen, select New from the File menu. Do not save any changes.

Drawing from the Center Outward

Corel DRAW! allows you to draw an ellipse from the center outward, just as you did with rectangles in the previous chapter. This feature offers you a more interactive method of working, without sacrificing precision. The width and height indicators continue to display the exact dimensions of the ellipse as you draw. Practice drawing an ellipse using the center as a starting point.

1. With the Ellipse tool selected, press and hold both (SHIFT) and the mouse button at the desired starting point. Keep both (SHIFT) and the mouse button depressed as you move the mouse. As with any ellipse, you can draw in whichever direction you choose; the width and height indicators in the status line reflect that direction, as shown in Figure 4-4.

2. Release the mouse button and then release (SHIFT) to complete the ellipse. Be sure to release the mouse button *before* you release (SHIFT) or the ellipse may "snap" away from the center point you have chosen and your center point will be treated as a rim point.

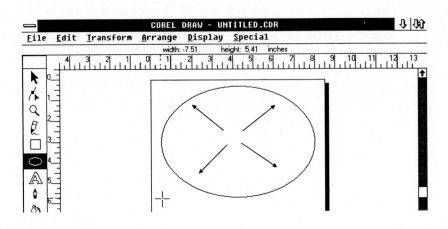

FIGURE 4-4   Drawing an ellipse from the center outward

3. Clear the ellipse from the screen by pressing (DEL).

DRAWING A CIRCLE

In Corel DRAW! you use a single tool to produce both ellipses and perfect circles, just as you used the same tool to produce rectangles and squares. The technique is identical, except that you use (CTRL) to constrain an ellipse to a circle. As with ellipses, you can choose either the rim or the center of the circle as a starting point.

Using the Rim as a Starting Point

Perform the following exercise to create a perfect circle, starting from the circle's rim.

1. With the Ellipse tool selected, position the cursor at a desired starting point.

2. Press and hold both (CTRL) and the mouse button and draw diagonally in any direction. As you can see in Figure 4-5, the status line indicators show that both the width and the height of the shape are equal.

3. To complete the circle, release the mouse button and then (CTRL). Be sure to release the mouse button *before* you release (CTRL) or your circle may turn into an ordinary ellipse of unequal height and width.

4. Clear the circle from the screen by pressing (DEL).

 Because of the way Corel DRAW! works, you are actually creating an imaginary rectangle when you draw an ellipse or circle. That is why the status line indicator for a perfect circle displays width and height instead of diameter. The ellipse or circle fits inside this

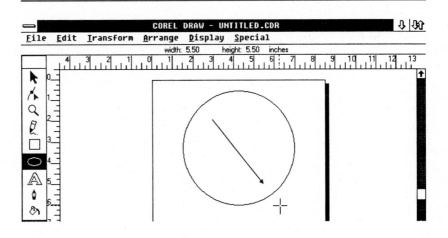

FIGURE 4-5   Drawing a circle using (CTRL)

rectangle, as you will see more clearly when you begin to select objects in Chapter 8.

Drawing from the Center Outward

In the following brief exercise, you will draw a circle using the center as a starting point.

1. With the Ellipse tool selected, position the cursor at the point where you want to begin the circle.

2. Press and hold (CTRL), (SHIFT), and the mouse button simultaneously and draw in any direction.

3. To complete the circle, release the mouse button and then (CTRL) and (SHIFT). If you release the keys before you release the mouse button, you may jeopardize both your circle and its central starting point.

4. Clear the circle from the screen by pressing (DEL).

Now that you have created some circles and ellipses using all of the available techniques, you can integrate these shapes into an original drawing. Continue with the next section to consolidate your skills.

CREATING A DRAWING USING ELLIPSES AND CIRCLES

The following exercise brings together all the skills you have learned so far. You will create a drawing of a house and its environment that will include ellipses, circles, rectangles, squares, and freehand drawing elements. The grid can assist you with some of the geometrical elements of the drawing; other elements you

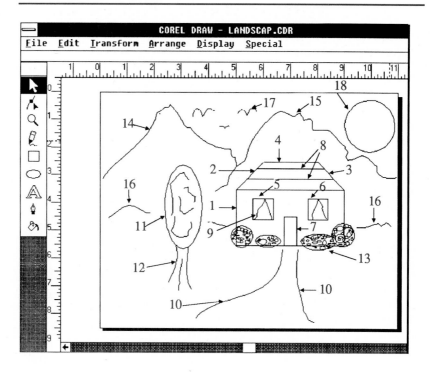

FIGURE 4-6   A drawing using ellipses, circles, rectangles, and freehand elements

can draw freehand. Since this drawing will be wider than it is high, you will also learn how to adjust the page format from portrait (the default vertical format) to landscape (horizontal format). The first few steps get you into the habit of anticipating and preparing for your drawing needs before you actually begin to draw, so that you can draw quickly and without interruption. Use the numbers in Figure 4-6 as a guide in performing this exercise.

1. To prepare for the geometrical portion of the drawing, select the Grid Size command from the Display menu and adjust grid frequency to 4.00 per inch. If you need help, refer to the section of Chapter 3 entitled "Practicing with the Grid."

2. If the rulers are not already visible, display them by selecting the Show Rulers command from the Display menu.

3. Change the page setup so that your page is longer than it is wide. To do this, select the Page Setup command from the File menu. When the Page Setup dialog box in Figure 4-7 appears, select the Landscape option button to set the Orientation option to landscape. Exit by selecting the OK command button.

4. Select the Preferences command from the Special menu and set both the Freehand Tracking and the AutoJoin options to 10 pixels. As you recall from the previous chapter, a high Freehand Tracking setting lets you draw smoother curves and a high AutoJoin setting causes lines and curves to snap together even when their end points are a few pixels apart. Click on the OK command button to exit the dialog box.

5. Select the Rectangle tool 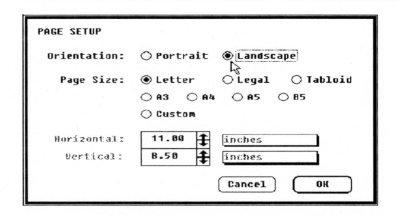 and position the cursor at the 5-inch mark on the horizontal ruler and the 3 ½-inch mark on the vertical ruler. Draw a rectangle that extends from this point

FIGURE 4-7   The Page Setup dialog box

to the 9-inch mark on the horizontal ruler and the 5 ½-inch mark on the vertical ruler. This rectangle will compose the main element of the house (1).

6. Designing the roof of the house requires three steps involving constrained lines and automatic joining of lines to form a polygon. Select the Freehand tool ⬚ and position your cursor at the upper left corner of the "house." Extend a line (2) upward and to the right at a 45-degree angle. Remember to press (CTRL) while drawing to constrain this line to the correct angle automatically. End the line at the 6-inch mark on the horizontal ruler and the 2 ½-inch mark on the vertical ruler.

7. Extend a line (3) upward and to the left at a 135-degree angle. Remember to press (CTRL) while drawing to constrain this line to the control angle automatically. When you reach the 8-inch mark on the horizontal ruler and the 2 ½-inch mark on the vertical ruler, end the line with a double-click so you can continue with another line segment.

8. While continuing to hold (CTRL), extend a horizontal line (4) back to the first diagonal line (2) and single-click to end it. The two line segments should snap together and form a polygon that constitutes the "roof" of the house.

9. You will need smaller grid increments when drawing the next few objects. Select the Grid Size command from the Display menu again and set the grid frequency to 8.00 per inch. Select OK to save this setting and return to your drawing.

10. Create two square windows for the house. To create the first window, select the Rectangle tool and begin a square (5) near the left side of the house, a little below the "roof." Practice drawing a square from the center outward using the (CTRL-SHIFT) key combination. Notice the dimensions of your square just before you complete it, so that you can draw a square of the

same size in the next step.If you do not like the first square you draw, press (DEL) immediately to erase it and try again.

11. Create a second square window (6) near the right side of the house. Make sure this square is the same size as the first and that it begins and ends on the same horizontal plane. The grid settings should help you place it correctly.

12. Make a rectangular door (7) for the house about halfway between the two windows. Use the rulers to help guide your movement. If you make a mistake, press (DEL) or select Undo in the Edit menu to delete the rectangle and try again.

13. To create planes of shingles for the roof, select the Freehand tool, press and hold (CTRL), and draw two perfectly horizontal lines (8) across the roof.

14. Add asymmetrical curtains for the house by drawing some diagonal freehand curves (9) inside the windows. Remember to press and hold the mouse button as you draw to create curves instead of lines.

15. Draw a freehand sidewalk (10) that widens as it approaches the foreground of your picture.

16. Select the Ellipse tool and draw an elongated ellipse (11) to the left of the house. This represents the foliage of a poplar tree.

17. Select the Freehand tool and form the trunk of the poplar by adding some freehand vertical curves (12) beneath it. If you wish, you can add some small lines to the "foliage" of the poplar.

18. Select the Ellipse tool again and draw a series of "bushes" (13) immediately in front of the house. Use ellipses for the outlines of the bushes; create detail in the bushes by inserting a few ellipses and circles inside each one. Insert more ellipses to

create a denser bush. (You can practice this technique on the poplar tree, too.)

19. Select the Freehand tool and create a mountain (14) behind and to the left of the house. Use curved instead of straight lines. Your mountain doesn't have to look exactly like the one in the figure.

20. Before creating the second mountain, select the Preferences command from the Special menu and set Freehand Tracking to 1 pixel. This will make the outline of your subsequent freehand curves more jagged. Select OK to exit the dialog box and save the new setting.

21. Draw the second mountain (15) behind the house. Notice that the outline of this mountain looks rougher than the outline of the first mountain.

22. Continue by using freehand curves to add a little landscaping (16) beneath the mountains and, if desired, a few birds (17).

23. Select the Ellipse tool and create a sun (18) by drawing a circle from the center outward at the upper right corner of the picture.

24. Finally, save your drawing by selecting the Save As command from the File menu. When the Save As dialog box appears, type in the name **LANDSCAP** and select Save. Corel DRAW! adds the .CDR extension automatically.

Congratulations! You have mastered the Ellipse tool and created another masterpiece with Corel DRAW!.

SUMMARY

Ellipses and circles are important shapes to master if you need to create design-oriented, technical, or other stylized illustrations. The Ellipse tool in Corel DRAW! allows you to construct both ellipses and circles, just as the Rectangle tool does double duty for rectangles and squares.

You can draw ellipses and circles from any point on the rim or from the center outward. The latter technique, available when you use the (SHIFT) key, helps you draw more quickly without sacrificing accuracy.

The Corel DRAW! interface offers you a variety of methods to place elements in your drawings quickly and precisely. The interface allows you to draw geometrical shapes from the center outward, adjust grid settings, display ruler settings, and change page format. Also, the Preferences dialog box offers helpful features, including Freehand Tracking and AutoJoin.

Add texture and detail to simple geometrical shapes by placing smaller geometrical shapes inside them. When you become familiar with changing the magnification of your screen (Chapter 6) and with importing and exporting files (Chapter 16), you will see how this technique is used to create original drawings and clipart.

chapter **5**

ADDING TEXT

Corel DRAW!'s advanced text handling features let you turn text into a work of art. You can rotate, skew, reshape, and edit a character or a *text string* (a group of characters) just as you would any other object. You can perform these feats on Corel Systems typefaces and on the extensive library of typefaces available from other manufacturers. The more than 100 Corel Systems fonts provided with your software look similar to standard industry typefaces and will print on any printer with which Corel DRAW! is compatible. If you already have a favorite typeface manufacturer, you can use the WFNBOSS utility discussed in Appendix D to convert popular fonts to the Corel DRAW! format.

In this chapter, you will learn how to insert text into a drawing and select the typeface, typestyle, point size, alignment, and spacing attributes of your text. You will also learn how to enter special foreign language or symbolic characters. After you have completed the exercises in this chapter, you will be ready to tackle more advanced techniques for reshaping your text (Chapter 11) and converting other manufacturers' typefaces to a format that you can use in Corel DRAW! (Appendix D).

ENTERING TEXT: AN OVERVIEW

The Text tool , the last of the four basic drawing tools in Corel DRAW!, is represented by a stylized capital letter A. You use the text tool to insert text into your pictures, just as you use the Ellipse or Rectangle tool to insert geometrical objects. The process of inserting text into a drawing can involve up to eight steps:

1. Select the Text tool.

2. Change the sample character, if desired.

3. Select an insertion point.

4. Enter text in the text window.

5. Choose the point size of your text.

6. Set the alignment for the text.

7. Select a typeface and typestyle.

8. Adjust the spacing between the letters, words, and lines of your text.

The sections that follow treat each of the preceding steps in greater detail. Since most of this chapter consists of exercises, however, the order in which you perform these steps may vary slightly from this list.

SELECTING THE TEXT TOOL

You use the Text tool in Corel DRAW! to enter new text on a page. When you first load Corel DRAW!, the Select tool is highlighted; in order to enter text, you must activate the Text tool. In the following brief exercise, you will adjust the page format, and then activate the Text tool.

1. If the printable page area is in portrait format (vertical instead of horizontal), select Page Setup from the File menu and select Landscape format. If you did the drawing exercise at the end of Chapter 4, the printable page area is already in landscape format. This is because Corel DRAW! always "remembers" the page setup you used the last time you created a new drawing.

2. Select the Text tool ▨ by positioning the mouse cursor over the Text icon and clicking once. The Text tool is highlighted and the mouse cursor turns into an I-beam, as you saw in Chapter 1.

SELECTING AN INSERTION POINT

The *insertion point* is the point on the printable page where you want text to begin. Text aligns itself relative to that point. In Corel DRAW!, you cannot enter text directly on the page; instead, you

Text
cursor

Alignment
buttons

Typeface list
box

Spacing
command
button

Point size
selection

Sample
character
display
window

Typestyle
buttons

Cancel
button

OK button

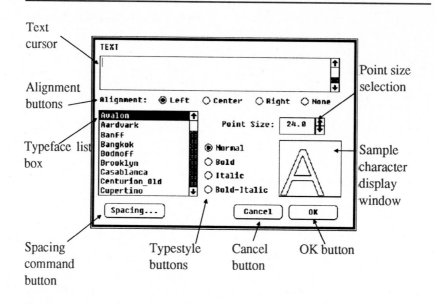

━━━ **FIGURE 5-1**   The Text dialog box

type it in a special dialog box, where you also select its attributes.
To select an insertion point and prepare for the other exercises in
this chapter, follow these steps:

1. Make sure that Snap To Grid is on and set Grid Size to 2 per
   inch. If your screen does not already display rulers, select Show
   Rulers from the Display menu.

2. Position the I-beam cursor at the top center of the page area and
   click once. After a few seconds the Text dialog box displays,
   as shown in Figure 5-1.

GETTING AROUND IN THE TEXT DIALOG BOX

Using the elements of the Text dialog box, you can enter text and
then customize it in five different ways. Take a moment to become

familiar with the layout of this dialog box and the way the keyboard keys function within it.

Elements of the Text Dialog Box

The following are the components of the Text dialog box and their respective functions. Figure 5-1 points out the major components.

Text Cursor   A flashing text cursor appears in the text entry window when you first call up this dialog box. Type your text string, or series of characters, in this window. A text string can include up to 250 characters. You can include an unlimited number of text strings in a single file.

Alignment Buttons   Use the alignment buttons to choose how to align your text relative to the insertion point. The default setting for this text attribute is left alignment.

Typeface List Box   The typeface list box contains the names of all the Corel DRAW! typefaces from which you can choose. If you prefer, you can customize this list and rename the typefaces to their industry equivalents, such as "Times" or "Helvetica." See the "Renaming Corel DRAW! Typefaces" section later in this chapter.

Sample Character Display Window   When you select a typeface, the letter in the sample character display window gives you a true WYSIWYG example of that typeface. In the section, "Changing the Sample Character," you will learn how to change the letter or character that displays in this window.

Typestyle Buttons   Once you choose a typeface, use the typestyle buttons to specify the typestyle in which you want the typeface to appear. In the graphics industry, *typeface* refers to an entire character set that shares the same basic design, regardless of the size (for example, 10 points) or weight (for example, bold or italic). A *typestyle* is narrower in scope. One typestyle includes only a single weight (normal, bold, italic, or bold italic) for a particular typeface. Although there are four possible typestyles, some typefaces are not available in all four styles.

Point Size Selection Box   Use the point size selection box to choose a point size for the text you enter. The default setting for this attribute is 24 points, but you can change this value by adjusting the scroll arrows at the right side of the dialog box (see "Selecting a Point Size" later in this chapter).

Spacing Command Button   The spacing command button gives you access to an additional dialog box where you can specify spacing between characters, words, or lines. See the "Adjusting Text Spacing" section in this chapter for fuller instructions on how to adjust spacing.

OK and Cancel Buttons   You press the OK button to save your attribute settings and display, onscreen, the text you have entered. To exit the Text dialog box without entering any text, press the Cancel button.

Using the Keyboard and Mouse

You can use both the mouse and the keyboard to move between attributes and between attribute settings in the Text dialog box. The only exception is if you have Corel DRAW! version 1.1 or earlier, in which case you can enter the typeface list box only with the help of the mouse.

If you are using a mouse to move around in the Text dialog box, you can select a text attribute in two different ways: by clicking on an option button or by scrolling with a scrollbar or scroll arrow. You work with option buttons to choose alignment and typestyle, and you use scrollbars or scroll arrows to choose the typeface, point size, and spacing attributes.

If you prefer to use the keyboard in the Text dialog box, you can select most text attributes using (TAB), (SHIFT-TAB), and the four arrow keys on your cursor pad. (If you have Corel DRAW! version 1.11 or later, you can select all text attributes this way.) When you first enter the dialog box, the text cursor appears in the text entry window; pressing (TAB) moves you from one attribute to the next, while the (SHIFT-TAB) key combination moves you between attributes in the reverse order. The order in which you can move between attributes depends on which version of Corel DRAW! you have. If you are using version 1.11 or later, you can access the typeface list box using the keyboard alone. If you have an earlier version, you must use the mouse to select a typeface.

Now you are familiar with how to get around in the Text dialog box. In the following sections you will learn how to set text attributes for yourself.

CHANGING THE SAMPLE CHARACTER

The default character that appears in the sample character window is the letter A, as you can see from Figure 5-1. You can change the sample WYSIWYG character, however, so that you can see in advance exactly how a specific letter will appear in the typeface you select. For example, if your text contains a large number of C's, you may want to preview the letter C for each font that you consider.

The next set of exercises uses a text string in which the letter D is important. Change the sample display character to D now, before you begin to type in the text entry window.

1. Select Cancel in the Text dialog box. You exit the dialog box and return to the display without entering any text. Corel DRAW! does not leave a marker at the insertion point when you change your mind about entering text.

2. Select Preferences from the Special menu to display the Preferences dialog box, as shown in Figure 5-2. You can use the Typeface Selection Character option, listed in the Miscellaneous section of the Preferences dialog box, to customize your work with the Text tool.

3. Position the mouse cursor over the box next to "Typeface Selection Char:" and click once. The mouse cursor turns into an I-beam and a flashing text cursor appears in the box.

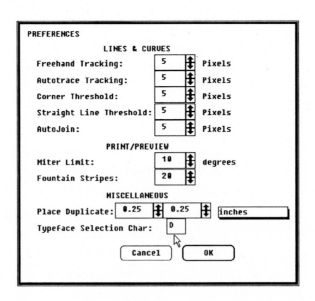

FIGURE 5-2   Changing the sample typeface selection character

4. Change the selected character from a capital A to a capital D by backspacing over the A and then typing **D**.

5. Select OK to save this setting and return to the main Corel DRAW! window.

ENTERING TEXT IN THE TEXT WINDOW

Now you are ready to return to the Text dialog box and enter text. Using the rulers as a guide, select an insertion point at the horizontal 5 ½-inch mark, 1 inch down from the top of the page. The Text dialog box displays again. Because of the changes you made in the Preferences dialog box, a capital D has replaced the capital A in the sample character display window, as in Figure 5-3. When you type the letter D in DRAW! in the following exercise, it will look exactly like the sample character in the specified typeface.

When you first enter the Text dialog box, the Text entry window is automatically selected, as you can see by the text cursor in

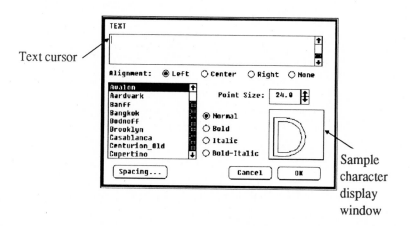

FIGURE 5-3   D as the sample display character

Figures 5-1 and 5-3. (On your monitor, the text cursor is flashing.)
To enter a maximum of 250 text characters, simply begin typing.
For this exercise, enter text in the following way:

1. Type **Corel DRAW!** at the flashing text cursor.

2. Press (**ENTER**) to begin a new line, type **Made**, and press (**ENTER**)
    again.

3. On the third line, type **Easy**.

Your text entry window should now look like this:

Moving Between Lines
And Characters

The way you use your computer keys to move around in the Corel
DRAW! text entry window differs from the way you use them in
a word processor. Whenever you have several lines of text in the
text entry window, you can use the following keyboard commands:

• Press (**ENTER**) to start a new line within the text entry window
  and begin entering text into it. The window will hold as many
  lines of text as you generate, as long as you do not exceed the
  250-character limit.

- Press (↓), the down arrow key, to move the text cursor down one line. (This does not apply if you are already on the last line of text.)

- Press (**PGDN**) to move the text cursor down two lines at a time, as far as the last line of text. The text in the previous two lines may "jump" out of visual range, like this:

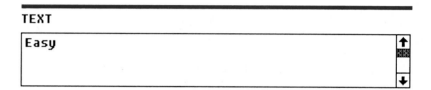

- Press (↑), the up arrow key, to move the text cursor up one line. (This has no effect if you are already on the top line of text.)

- Press (**PGUP**) to move the text cursor up two lines. (This takes effect only if there are at least three lines of text in the text entry window, and the cursor is located on the third line or lower.)

- Press (**HOME**) to move the cursor to the beginning of the current line.

- Press (**END**) to move the cursor to the end of the current line.

- Press (→), the right arrow key, to move the cursor one letter at a time to the right.

- Press (←), the left arrow key, to move the cursor one letter at a time to the left.

- Press (**BACKSPACE**) to delete the character immediately preceding the text cursor.

- Press (DEL) to delete the character immediately following the text cursor.

Mouse Operations in the Text Entry Window

You can also perform some text entry operations using the mouse:

- Use the scroll bar at the right side of the text entry window to locate a line of text that is not currently visible.

- If you want to insert text at a given point, click at that point.

- To select one or more characters in a text string, position the text cursor at the first character you want to select and then drag the mouse across the desired characters. The characters appear highlighted, as shown here:

TEXT

```
Corel DRAW!
Made
Easy
```

- You can delete a text string that you have selected in this way by pressing (DEL).

When you have finished experimenting with the keyboard controls, press (TAB) or (SHIFT-TAB) until you select the numeric value in the point size box and it becomes highlighted.

SELECTING A POINT SIZE

Normally, you will select alignment and typeface settings for a text string before you specify the point size. For this exercise, however, you will want to see results on the full page in a larger size than the default value of 24 points. You can change the default point size in either of two ways, depending on whether you want to use the mouse or the keyboard.

To change the point size from 24 to 40 using the mouse,

1. Position the cursor over the upper scroll arrow next to the Point Size box and depress and hold the mouse button. As you scroll, the numerical value in the Point Size box increases.

2. Release the mouse button when the value in the Point Size box reaches 40.0.

To change the point size from 24 to 40 using the keyboard,

1. Tab out of the text entry window and into the Point Size box by pressing (TAB) or (SHIFT-TAB) until you select the Point Size box. Again, the value in the Point Size box appears highlighted when you select it.

2. Backspace over the current value to delete it and type **40.0**.

ALIGNING TEXT

The next exercise involves deciding how you want to align the text. You have four choices: Left, Center, Right, and None.

Left Alignment

Left is the default alignment setting. When you choose this setting, text will align on the page as though the insertion point were the left margin.

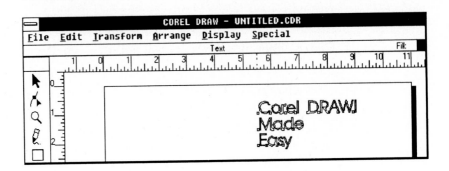

FIGURE 5-4   Left-aligned text

1. Select Left alignment by clicking on the Left button or by tabbing to the Alignment line and using the arrow keys if necessary. The center of the Left option button darkens when you select it.

2. Select OK to exit the Text dialog box. The text that you entered displays on the page in the default typeface, left-aligned at the 5 ½-inch mark, as in Figure 5-4. The text string actually has a default fill of black like other closed objects in Corel DRAW!, but you see it only in outline form. (When you work with the Preview window in Chapter 7, your text will be displayed with its appropriate fill.) The small rectangles at the base of each letter are nodes that help you edit text shape and attributes, as you will learn in Chapter 11.

3. Leave this text on the page and select another insertion point, at the 3-inch vertical mark and the 5 ½-inch horizontal mark, just below the first text string. The Text dialog box displays again.

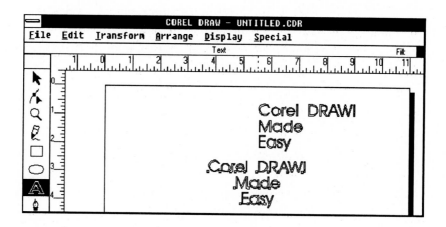

FIGURE 5-5   Center-aligned text added

Center Alignment

When you select Center alignment, text becomes the midpoint of any string you type. Perform these steps to compare center alignment with left alignment:

1. Type **Corel DRAW!** on one line, **Made** on the next, and **Easy** on the third line, as you did in the last section.

2. Using the mouse, change to Center alignment by positioning the mouse cursor over the Center button and clicking once. To select Center alignment using the keyboard, press (TAB) until you reach the Alignment line, and then press (→) or (←) until the Center option button is selected.

3. Select OK to return to the page. The text you entered appears in the default font, center-aligned with respect to the 5 ½-inch mark. Your page should now look like Figure 5-5.

4. Leave this text on the page. Return to the Text dialog box by selecting a third insertion point, this time at the 5-inch vertical mark and the 5 ½-inch horizontal mark, just below the center-aligned text. The Text dialog box displays again.

Right Alignment

When you select Right alignment, the text aligns on the page area as though the insertion point were the right margin. Perform these steps to compare Right alignment with Left and Center alignment:

1. Type **Corel DRAW! Made Easy** on three lines as you did in the previous exercises.

2. Using the mouse, change to Right alignment by positioning the mouse cursor over the Right button and clicking once. To select Right alignment using the keyboard, press (TAB) until you reach the Alignment line, and then press (←) or (→) until the Right option button is highlighted.

3. Select OK to return to the page. The text you entered appears in the default font, right-aligned with respect to the 5 ½-inch mark. Your page should now look like Figure 5-6.

4. Leave this text on the page. Return to the Text dialog box one more time by selecting a fourth insertion point, this time at the 7-inch horizontal and 5 ½-inch vertical mark. The Text dialog box displays once more.

No Alignment

When you select None for alignment, text displays on the page exactly as you enter it. This selection is useful when you want to add unusual spacing at the beginning of a line in a text string.

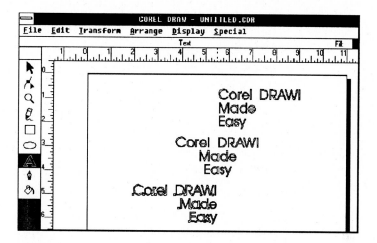

FIGURE 5-6   Right-aligned text added

Perform these steps to compare text with no alignment to text with Left, Center, and Right alignment:

1. Type **Corel DRAW!** on the first line of the text entry window and press (**ENTER**).

2. On the second line, indent two spaces, type **Made**, and press (**ENTER**) again.

3. On the third line, indent four spaces and type **Easy**.

4. Using the mouse, change the alignment to None by positioning the mouse cursor over the None button and clicking once. To change alignment to None using the keyboard, press (**TAB**) until you reach the Alignment line, and then press (→) or (←) until the None option button is highlighted.

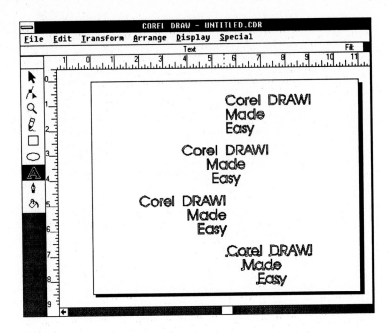

FIGURE 5-7   Unaligned text added

5. Select OK to return to the page. The text that you entered appears in the default font, with the spacing exactly as you typed it. Your page should now look like Figure 5-7.

6. Clear the page of text by selecting New from the File menu. Do not save the changes.

SELECTING A TYPEFACE AND TYPESTYLE

So far, you have used only the Avalon typeface, which is the default typeface in Corel DRAW! because it appears first in the typeface list box. In this section, you will have the opportunity to

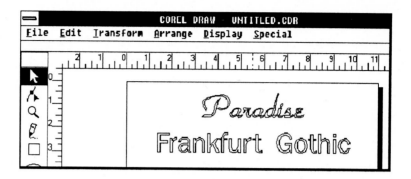

FIGURE 5-8   Comparing the "tone" of typefaces

experiment with some of the different typefaces and typestyles supplied with your software.

Selecting a Typeface

Many books and trade magazines offer guidelines for selecting appropriate typefaces. A thorough discussion of the subject is beyond the scope of this book; however, when choosing the typeface you will use in a Corel DRAW! graphic, you should consider the tone and purpose of your work, as well as your intended audience. Look at the two fonts in Figure 5-8, for example. You probably would not choose an elaborate, flowery font such as Paradise for a graphic that you would present to a meeting of civil engineers; a typeface such as Frankfurt Gothic might prove a better choice.

Practice selecting typefaces in the following exercise.

1. To prepare for this exercise, select Preferences from the Special menu and change the sample typeface character back to the capital letter A. Select OK to save the new setting.

2. Select the Text tool and then select an insertion point that is at the 1 ½-inch mark on the horizontal ruler and the 1-inch mark on the vertical ruler. The Text dialog box appears, with the sample letter A for the default Avalon typeface in the sample character window.

3. Type the word **Paradise** in the text entry window.

4. Select the Paradise typeface from the typeface list box. You can select a typeface in one of three ways:

   Click directly on the typeface name if it is visible in the list box. When you do this, the typeface name becomes highlighted and a faint dotted outline surrounds it. If the typeface you want is not visible, use one of the following techniques.

   Scroll up or down the list one line at a time: Position the mouse cursor over the up or down scroll arrow at the top or bottom of the scroll bar in the typeface list box. Click repeatedly until the name of the typeface you want comes into view. Select that typeface name by clicking on it.

   Scroll continuously up or down the list: Position the mouse cursor over the up or down scroll arrow and then depress and

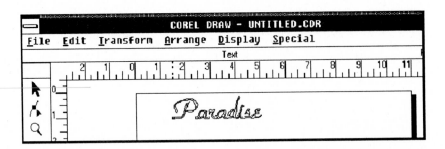

FIGURE 5-9   A text string using the Paradise typeface

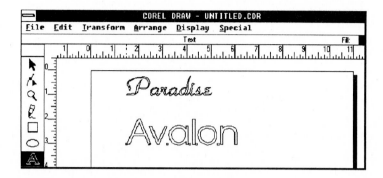

FIGURE 5-10   Text strings using Paradise and Avalon

hold the mouse button until the desired typeface comes into view. Click on the typeface name to select it.

5. Set the point size to 100 points, using either the mouse or keyboard technique described earlier in this chapter.

6. Set Alignment to Left.

7. Select OK to return to the page, where you will see the Paradise text string with the selected attributes, as shown in Figure 5-9. Nodes appear between each letter.

8. Select another insertion point at the 1 ½-inch mark on the horizontal ruler and the 3-inch mark on the vertical ruler.

9. When the Text dialog box appears, type **Avalon** in the text entry window.

10. Select the Avalon typeface in the typestyle list box.

11. Select OK to return to the page, where you will see the Avalon text string beneath the Paradise text string, as in Figure 5-10.

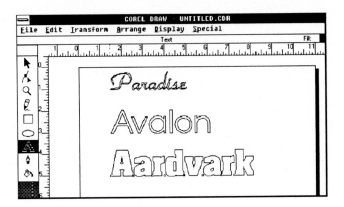

FIGURE 5-11   Comparing Paradise, Avalon, and Aardvark
typefaces

12. Select a third insertion point at the 1 ½-inch mark on the
    horizontal ruler and the 5-inch mark on the vertical ruler.

13. When the Text dialog box displays, type the word **Aardvark**
    into the text entry window.

14. Select the Aardvark typeface from the list box.

15. Select OK to exit the Text dialog box. Your page now looks
    like Figure 5-11.

16. Select a fourth insertion point at the 1 ½-inch mark on the
    horizontal ruler and the 7-inch mark on the vertical ruler.

17. When the Text dialog box displays, type the word **Dixieland**
    in the text entry window.

18. Select the Dixieland typeface from the list box and notice that
    a nonalphabetic symbol, rather than a letter, appears in the
    sample character window. This typeface, like the Geographic

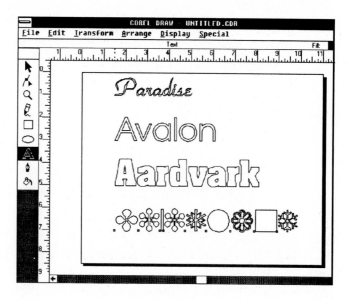

FIGURE 5-12   Adding a text string from a nonalphabetic
(symbol) typeface

Symbols, Greek/Math Symbols, and Musical Symbols typefaces, consists of symbols rather than letters. You see only
letters when you type, however, because Microsoft Windows
cannot display these characters in the text entry box. See
Appendix D for a complete list of all Corel DRAW! typefaces
and the character sets for each.

19. Select OK to see the text on the page. Your page now resembles
    Figure 5-12. You will notice that even though you have entered
    all of the text strings at the same point size, some appear larger
    than others. Each typeface has its own characteristic width and
    height.

20. Clear the screen by selecting New from the File menu. Do not
    save any changes.

Practice trying out different typefaces. When you are ready for the next section, clear the screen by selecting New from the File menu. You are ready to learn how to select one of the four available typestyles for a given typeface.

Selecting a Typestyle

While you were experimenting with typefaces in the foregoing exercise, you may have noticed that the appearance of the typestyle option buttons to the right of the typeface list box kept changing. This is because some typefaces have only one or two typestyles available, while others have three or four. When a typestyle is not available for a specific typeface, it displays in gray and you cannot select it.

Perform the following exercise to practice selecting available typestyles for the Corel DRAW! typefaces.

1. Select the Text tool and then choose an insertion point that is at the 1 ½-inch mark on the horizontal ruler and the 1 ½-inch mark on the vertical ruler. The Text dialog box displays.

2. Change the point size to 75.0 points.

3. Type **Frankfurt Gothic** in the text entry window.

4. Select Frankfurt Gothic from the typeface list box.

5. Select the Italic typestyle. A dark dot fills the center of the option button beside Italic and the letter in the sample character window changes its appearance.

6. Select OK to display the resulting text on the page, as in Figure 5-13. Leave this text on the page for now.

7. Select another insertion point at the 1 ½-inch horizontal and 3-inch vertical ruler marks to display the Text dialog box once more. The Frankfurt Gothic typeface is still selected; Corel

DRAW! remembers the last typeface you selected during the current session.

8. Type **Frankfurt Gothic** in the text entry window again.

9. Select Bold from the typestyle list and watch the character in the sample character window change to reflect this choice.

10. Select OK to display the resulting text on the page, as in Figure 5-14.

11. Select a third insertion point at the 1 ½-inch horizontal and the 4 ½-inch vertical ruler marks.

12. When the Text dialog box displays, type **Frankfurt Gothic** in the text entry window.

13. Select Bold Italic from the typestyle list. A dotted outline surrounds the typestyle name, the center of the associated option button darkens, and the character in the sample character window changes to reflect the new choice.

14. Select OK to display the resulting text on the page. Your screen should resemble Figure 5-15.

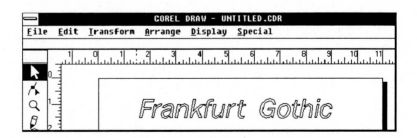

FIGURE 5-13   Text string in Frankfurt Gothic italic

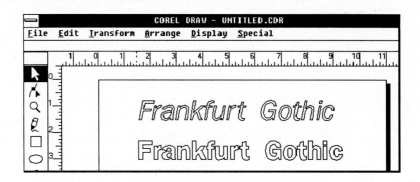

FIGURE 5-14   Comparing italic and bold typestyles

15. Select New from the File menu to clear the screen before continuing with another exercise.

FIGURE 5-15   Comparing italic, bold, and bold italic typestyles

Take a few moments to practice selecting typestyles for other typefaces. When you have finished, continue with the next section to learn how to adjust spacing when you enter a new text string.

ADJUSTING TEXT SPACING

The Spacing command button in the lower-left corner of the Text dialog box may be easy to overlook, but it can give you enormous control over text. When you select this button, the Spacing dialog box appears, which allows you to control the spacing between characters, words, and lines of text. Spacing is the last attribute you should adjust when entering text. As soon as you select OK to save your changes, you exit immediately to the page, and the text you have entered displays. If you adjust spacing attributes before you have finished changing other attributes, your text will display before you are ready.

 In this chapter, you are working with attributes only as you enter text. However, Corel DRAW! also allows you to adjust text spacing *interactively*. This means that even after text displays on the page, you can change the spacing of one character, several characters, or an entire text string without going back to the Text dialog box. You will learn more about how to edit spacing attributes for existing text in Chapter 11.

Setting Up the Exercise

In the following exercise, you will have the opportunity to review what you have learned thus far about setting all of the attributes in the Text dialog box. If you have forgotten how to perform any of these functions, go back to the relevant section and review it.

1. Select the Text tool if it is not selected already.

2. Select an insertion point near the top of the page, aligned to the 5 ½-inch horizontal and 1-inch vertical marks on the rulers.

3. When the Text dialog box displays, enter four lines of text in the text entry window. Type your name on the first line, your address on the second, your city, state, and zip code on the third, and your telephone number on the fourth.

4. Change the point size in the Point Size box to 50.0.

5. Select Center alignment.

6. Select Gatineau as the typeface and Normal as the typestyle. The Text dialog box should now look like Figure 5-16, except that the actual text you have entered into the text entry window will differ. You will also see only the last three lines you have

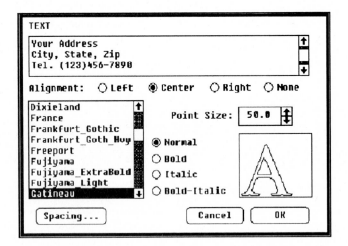

FIGURE 5-16   Settings: Gatineau normal, Center Alignment, 50 points

entered, since the text entry window can display only three lines at a time.

7. Select the Spacing command button by clicking on it once. The Text Spacing dialog box in Figure 5-17 appears. If you had not entered text into the text entry window, Corel DRAW! would display an error message and not permit you to enter the Text Spacing dialog box.

Getting Around in the Text Spacing Dialog Box

The Text Spacing dialog box features three options for adjusting inter-word, inter-character, and inter-line spacing. You will not change them at this point in the exercise, but take a moment to become familiar with your options.

Inter-Word   The Inter-Word option controls spacing between each word of the text that you enter. The default value is 1.00 em. An *em* is a unit of measurement that is equal to the width of the capital letter M for the current point size of the selected typeface and typestyle. This measurement is relative, because the width of

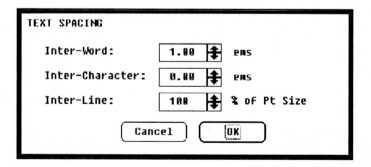

FIGURE 5-17   The Text Spacing dialog box

a capital M varies, not only between different typefaces, but also between different styles and sizes of the same typeface. You can adjust the value of inter-word spacing in increments of .10 of an em automatically using the scroll arrow, or in increments of .01 of an em if you type the value manually.

Inter-Character   The Inter-Character option controls spacing between each character within each word of the text. The default value is 0.00 ems. In other words, Corel DRAW! inserts no space at all between characters unless you change that value. You can adjust the value of inter-character spacing in increments of .10 of an em automatically using the scroll arrow, or in increments of .01 of an em if you type the value manually.

Inter-Line   When your text contains more than one line, the Inter-Line option controls the amount of space between each line. In the printing industry, this type of spacing is also known as *leading*. The default value is 100% of the point size, which means that if your text size is 10 points, the total amount of space between two lines is exactly 10 points and no more. You can adjust inter-line spacing in increments of 1%.

You can adjust the values in the Text Spacing dialog box in two ways: by scrolling with the mouse or by using a combination of mouse and keyboard.

To adjust values using the mouse only,

1. Position the mouse cursor over the up or down scroll arrow. If you want to increase the value, position it over the up arrow; if you want to decrease the value, position it over the down arrow.

2. Press and hold the mouse button until the value you want displays in the adjoining box and then release the mouse button.

To adjust values using both mouse and keyboard,

FIGURE 5-18   Address text string with default spacing attributes

1. Position the mouse cursor over the numeric value in the box adjoining the scroll bar and click once. A flashing cursor appears there.

2. Press (DEL) or (BACKSPACE) over the current value to delete it and type in the value you want. To go to the next setting, press (TAB).

Leave the spacing options at their default settings for the current text string and select OK. You exit the Text Spacing dialog box, and the text that you typed in the text entry window now appears on the page. Your text string has the default settings of 1.00 em spacing between words, no spacing between characters, and no extra leading between lines, as shown in Figure 5-18.

Adjusting and Comparing Text Spacing

Now that you are acquainted with the way the Text Spacing dialog box works, you will create another text string, identical to the first except that its spacing values differ. You can then visually compare the results of your spacing adjustments.

1. Select an insertion point at the 5 ½-inch mark on the horizontal ruler and the 4-inch mark on the vertical ruler, just beneath the last line of text on the page.

2. When the Text dialog box displays, type your name, street address, city, state, and zip, and telephone number on four separate lines. Leave all of the other attribute settings just as they are.

3. Select the Spacing command button to display the Text Spacing dialog box.

4. This time, adjust the spacing in the Inter-Word Option box to 2.00 ems, Inter-Character to 0.50 ems, and Inter-Line to 130%. This means that the space between words will equal the width of two capital M's, the space between characters will equal the width of half a capital M, and the space between lines will equal 1.3 times the height of the typeface itself.

5. Select OK to save these settings and exit to the page. The second text string now displays beneath the first. Your page resembles Figure 5-19, except that the text in the figure does not display the text nodes.

6. Select New from the File menu to clear the screen. Do not save any changes.

ENTERING SPECIAL CHARACTERS

Corel DRAW! supports five different proprietary character sets beyond the standard alphabet and characters that appear on your computer keyboard. You enter special characters in the text entry

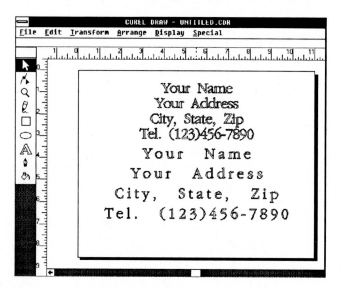

FIGURE 5-19   Comparing default and custom spacing
attributes

window of the text dialog box, and can adjust alignment, point
size, and spacing for these special characters, just as you can for
alphabetic characters.

- The Corel character set includes alphabetic and keyboard characters, foreign language characters, currency symbols, and
copyright and other popular commercial symbols. This character set applies to most of the typefaces you will use in Corel
DRAW!.

- The character set in the Dixieland typeface includes decorative
and directional symbols and callouts.

- The character set in the Greek/Math typeface includes a variety of scientific and mathematical symbols.

- The character set in the Musical typeface contains common musical notes and notations.

- The character set in the Geographic typeface includes geographical, military, and industrial symbols.

A complete listing of the contents of each character set appears in Appendix D and on the Character Reference Chart provided with your software.

No matter which of the five character sets you are using, characters above ASCII 128 are not accessible by pressing a single key on your keyboard. To type one of these special characters, depress and hold (ALT) and then type the appropriate number on your numeric keypad. Be sure to include the "0" that precedes each number. For example, to type the character ü in the Corel character set, type **0129**.

The Corel character set differs in some respects from the standard Windows character set, which is common to all Windows applications. For instance, the four symbol typefaces provided with Corel DRAW! have nothing in common with the Windows character set. As a result, the text you enter in the Text dialog box may not always match what displays on the screen. Always refer to your Corel DRAW! Character Reference Chart or to Appendix D of this book when you are entering special characters.

RENAMING COREL DRAW! TYPEFACES

Corel DRAW!'s proprietary typefaces closely resemble standard industry typefaces from well-known manufacturers. In fact, Corel

Systems has named the typefaces to remind you of their existing counterparts. If you already use some of these counterparts with other programs, or if you find it easier to remember common industry names than Corel's proprietary ones, you can rename the typefaces. Then each time you call up the Text dialog box, the standard industry names will appear in the typeface list box. Refer to Appendix D for full instructions on how to rename typefaces.

SUMMARY

The Text tool allows you to enter text on the Corel DRAW! page. You enter text by first selecting an insertion point and then entering text and adjusting settings in the pop-up Text dialog box.

The Text dialog box contains settings for five different text attributes: alignment, typeface, typestyle, point size, and spacing. You can adjust these settings using either the keyboard or the mouse.

You can enter up to 250 characters in the text entry window each time you select an insertion point. The group of characters you type is called a text string. Selecting Left, Center, Right, or no alignment (None) in the Text dialog box will cause the text you type to align in a certain way on the page.

Select a point size, typeface, and typestyle to match the tone and purpose of your text, using the WYSIWYG sample character window as a guide. Change sample characters using the Preferences dialog box to preview specific letters of your text.

Adjust spacing between characters, words, and lines of text using the pop-up dialog box that you access by clicking on the Spacing command button of the Text dialog box. Corel DRAW! measures inter-word and inter-character spacing in ems (the width of a capital letter M in the currently selected typeface), and inter-line spacing in terms of a percentage of the selected point size.

Use Corel DRAW! typefaces as display headers in electronic publications such as newletters and annual reports, or create brief, eye-catching graphic documents in Corel DRAW! instead of in a word processor.

chapter **6**

USING MAGNIFICATION AND VIEW SELECTION

About the Magnification Tool
Zooming In on a Selected Area
Zooming Out
Viewing a Graphic at Actual Size
Fitting a Graphic Within the Window
Showing an Entire Page
Panning Outside the Current Viewing Area

U ntil now, you have done all your work in Corel DRAW! using the full-screen view. This is the default view when you load Corel DRAW! or open a file, but it has obvious limitations if you need to edit images or do fine detail work. The Magnification tool, however, can customize the viewing area of your screen any way you wish. As you become familiar with this tool, you will experience greater drawing convenience and ease in editing.

ABOUT THE MAGNIFICATION TOOL

The Magnification tool ⌖ , the third tool in the Corel DRAW! toolbox, resembles a small magnifying glass. Unlike the Freehand, Rectangle, Ellipse, and Text tools, the Magnification tool is not a drawing tool. It could be called a view adjustment tool, because it allows you to zoom in or out of the viewing area in a variety of different ways. Because the Magnification tool gives you complete control over the content of the viewing area, it helps enhance every object you draw and increases the usefulness of every tool in the Corel DRAW! toolbox.

Selecting the Magnification Tool

The Magnification tool is five tools in one. When you select this tool, the pop-up menu shown in Figure 6-1 appears, giving you five options for adjusting your viewing area.

Zoom-In   The Zoom-In tool ⌖ allows you to zoom in on any area of a drawing that you select.

Zoom-Out   The Zoom-Out tool ⌖ either zooms out of your current image by a factor of two or, if your screen currently shows a zoom-in view, returns you to the previous view.

1:1   Selecting the 1:1 icon allows you to see an actual-size area of your drawing.

ALL   Selecting the ALL icon fits all of the currently displayed graphic into your viewing window.

Show Page   The Show Page icon ⬜ returns you to the default full-page view of your graphic.

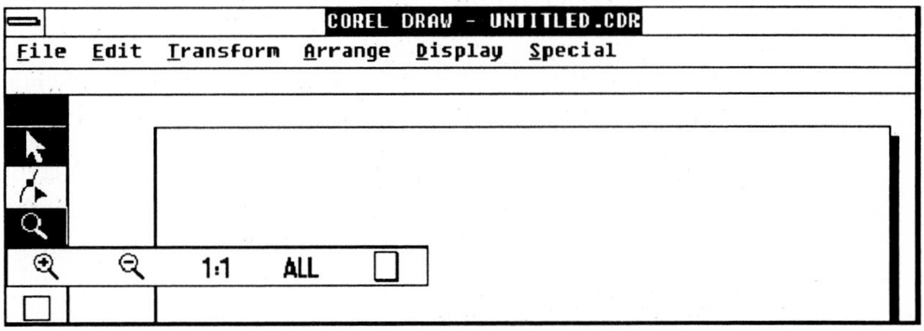

FIGURE 6-1   The five viewing options for the Magnification tool

To select one of these five options, you must first have an image on your screen. Open the sample file CATS.CDR that was provided with your software and perform these steps:

1. Select the Magnification tool by positioning the mouse cursor over the Magnification tool icon and clicking once. The menu containing the five viewing options pops up below and to the right of the Magnification tool.

2. Select an icon from the pop-up menu using either the mouse or your keyboard. To select an icon using the mouse, simply click on it or drag the mouse cursor until you highlight the tool and then click. To select an icon using the keyboard, press (→) until you highlight the desired tool and then press (ENTER).

All of the five Magnification tools except the Zoom-In tool perform their functions automatically. The following sections discuss each Magnification tool and present hands-on exercises that allow you to practice using these tools.

ZOOMING IN ON A SELECTED AREA

The Zoom-In tool icon [🔍] looks like the main Magnification tool icon, except that it is smaller and contains a plus sign. The Zoom-In tool is the most versatile of the five Magnification tools, because it lets you define precisely how much of your picture you want to view at once. It is therefore invaluable for drawing fine details or editing small areas of a picture.

Selecting the Zoom-In Tool and Defining the Viewing Area

Unlike the other Magnification tools in the pop-up menu, the Zoom-In Tool does not perform its function automatically. You have to define the zoom-in area in a series of four general steps. Try this yourself now on the CATS3.CDR file:

1. Select the Zoom-In tool by first activating the Magnification tool and then selecting the Zoom-In tool icon from the pop-up menu. The cursor changes to an image of a magnifying glass containing a plus sign (+).

2. Position the cursor at any corner of the area you want to magnify; usually it is most convenient to start at the upper-left corner.

3. Press and hold the mouse button at that corner and then drag the mouse diagonally towards the opposite corner of the area on which you want to zoom in. A dotted rectangle (the *marquee*) will follow your cursor and "lasso" the zoom-in area, as in the example in Figure 6-2.

4. When you have surrounded all of the objects on which you want to zoom in, release the mouse button. The screen redraws as in

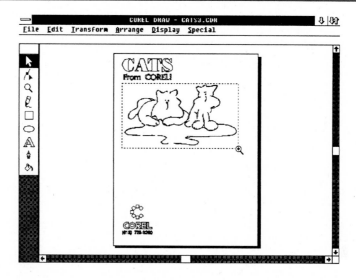

FIGURE 6-2   Lassoing an area with the marquee

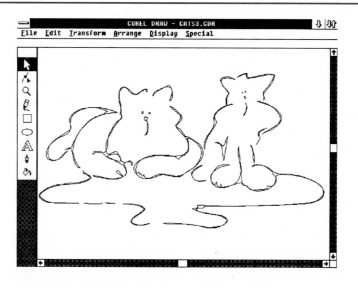

FIGURE 6-3   A close-up view of the lassoed area

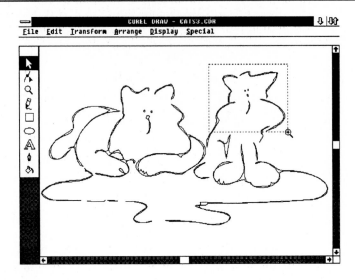

FIGURE 6-4   Zooming in a second time

Figure 6-3, and the viewing window now contains a close-up view of only the objects you lassoed.

You can zoom in on successively smaller areas of the screen using the Zoom-In tool. You must re-select the Zoom-In tool each time you wish to magnify further, however, for as soon as you have redrawn the screen, Corel DRAW! automatically returns to the Select tool. Simply select the Zoom-In tool again and lasso another area, as in Figure 6-4. The number of times you can zoom in depends on the type of monitor and display adapter you use. Try zooming in on progressively smaller areas; eventually, you reach a point where you are unable to zoom in any further. When this occurs, you have reached the maximum magnification possible for your monitor and display adapter. At that point, 1 pixel on the screen represents approximately $\frac{1}{1000}$ of an inch. You must use another magnification tool first before you can use the Zoom-In tool again.

 You can change the dotted rectangle of the marquee into a solid rectangle, if you prefer. Using the Windows Notepad, edit your WIN.INI file by scrolling to the [CDrawConfig] section of the file, which contains configuration information for Corel DRAW!. Change the line that says "DrawDotted=1" to "DrawDotted=0." Thereafter, when you lasso any area of the screen, the marquee will appear as a solid rather than as a dotted rectangle.

Zooming In and Editing TEACUP.CDR

The following exercise lets you practice using the Zoom-In tool on the teacup illustration you created in Chapter 3, "Drawing and Working with Rectangles and Squares." You will edit this illustration by entering text inside a tiny area of the drawing, a function you couldn't perform without using the Magnification tool. This exercise also allows you to practice the text entry skills you learned in Chapter 5.

1. Select Show Rulers from the Display menu if the rulers do not already appear on the screen.

2. Make sure that a checkmark appears in front of the Snap To Grid command in the Display menu. If a checkmark does not appear, select this command.

3. Select Grid Size from the Display menu and set grid spacing to 16 per inch.

4. Select Open from the File menu, select the file TEACUP.CDR, and click on the Open button.

5. Select the Magnification tool, and then select the Zoom-In tool from the pop-up menu. The cursor changes into a replica of the Zoom-In tool as soon as you move into the drawing window.

6. Zoom in on the tag for the teabag: Position the cursor at the top left corner of the tag, press the mouse button, and drag the mouse diagonally downward until you have surrounded the tea tag, as in Figure 6-5.

7. Release the mouse button. The screen redraws and displays only the tea tag and its immediate environment, as in Figure 6-6. Notice that in magnified view, the scale of the ruler changes from ½ inch to ¹⁄₁₆ inch.

8. Select the Text tool. The mouse cursor turns into an I-beam.

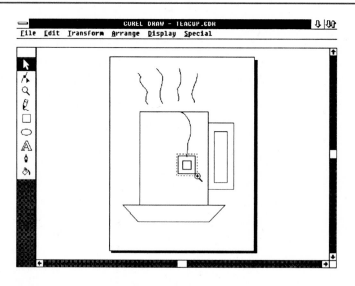

FIGURE 6-5   Lassoing the tea tag

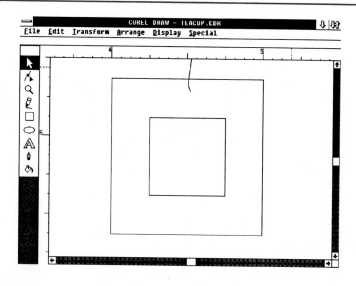

FIGURE 6-6   A close-up view of the tea tag

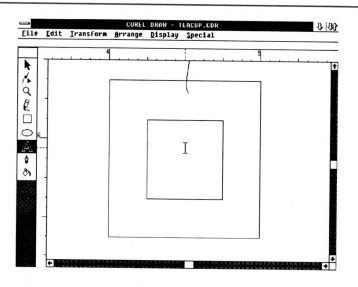

FIGURE 6-7   Selecting a text insertion point

9. Position the I-beam cursor near the top center of the inner tea tag square and align it with a horizontal ruler marker, as in Figure 6-7.

10. Click once to select this point as the insertion point.

11. When the Text dialog box displays, type **JASMINE TEA** in all capital letters on two separate lines in the text entry window. Then select the following text attributes: Center alignment, Fujiyama Normal, 10.0 points. The Text dialog box should look like Figure 6-8.

12. Select the Spacing button within the Text dialog box and change the values to Inter-Word: 1.00 ems, Inter-Character: .30

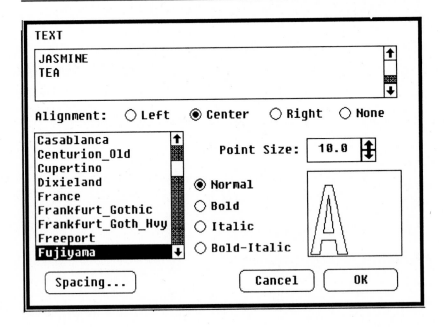

FIGURE 6-8   Text attributes for JASMINE TEA

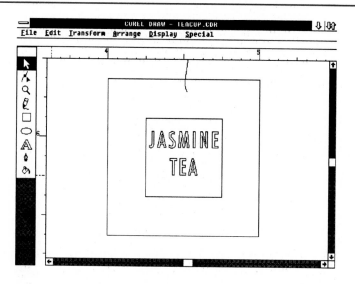

FIGURE 6-9   Entering text in a close-up view

ems, Inter-Line: 125% of point size.

13. Select OK to return to the magnified display window. The text you typed now appears within the tea tag label, as in Figure 6-9.

14. Finally, select the Save As command from the File menu. When the Save As dialog box appears, type **TEACUP2** in the File text entry box, and then select Save.

ZOOMING OUT

The Zoom-Out tool ⌐Q⌐ looks exactly like the main Magnification tool, except that it contains a minus (-) sign. As soon as you select this tool, it defines the zoom-out area for you automatically in one of two ways:

- If you are currently in a 1:1, ALL, or Show Page viewing magnification, selecting the Zoom-Out tool causes your current viewing area to zoom out by a factor of two.

- If you are currently in a Zoom-In viewing magnification, selecting the Zoom-Out tool causes you to return to the previously selected view. You can therefore use the Zoom-Out tool to back out of successive zoom-ins.

The maximum zoom-out you can achieve is a full view of the page at 50% of the original size.

To use the Zoom-Out tool, select the Magnification tool, drag the mouse, and click when you have highlighted the Zoom-Out tool icon. The cursor does not change shape when you select this tool, but the screen redraws according to the preceding rules.

In the following simple exercise, you will practice using both the Zoom-In and Zoom-Out tools while editing the LAND-SCAP.CDR file that you created in Chapter 4. Remember the few extra circles and ellipses you drew inside the bushes of that picture? Now that you can see the bushes up close, you can add even more detail. Turn Snap To Grid off before you begin.

1. Select Open from the File menu and open the file called LANDSCAP.CDR that you created in Chapter 4. The image first appears in full-page view.

2. Select the Magnification tool and then click on the Zoom-Out tool icon to select the Zoom-Out tool. You can still see the full page, but it now appears at half size, as in Figure 6-10.

3. Select the Zoom-Out tool again. This time, you zoom out only a little further. You cannot zoom out further than this.

4. Select the Zoom-In tool and then lasso the house and bushes. The screen redraws to include just these objects.

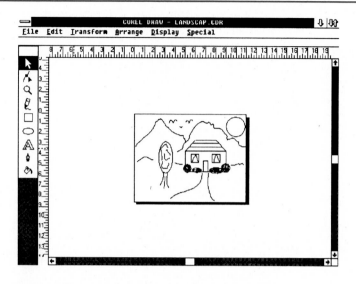

FIGURE 6-10   Zooming out to a 50% page view

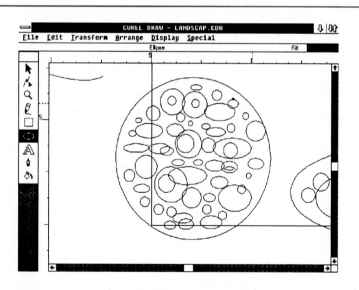

FIGURE 6-11   Adding detail to a magnified view

5. Select the Zoom-In tool again and magnify the bushes only.

6. Select the Zoom-In tool once more and lasso a single bush.

7. Select the Ellipse tool ⬭ and add detail to the bush by inserting small ellipses and circles, as shown in Figure 6-11.

8. Now, select the Zoom-Out tool. The screen displays the view you magnified in step 5 but the bush you worked on has more detail.

9. Select the Zoom-Out tool again. This time, the screen displays the view you selected in step 4.

10. Select the Zoom-Out tool a third time. This time, the screen displays the full page at 50% of its size, as in step 2. The bush you edited probably looks denser than the others because of the detail you have added.

11. Select the Save As command from the File menu. When the Save As dialog box appears, type **LANDSCA2** in the File text entry box, and then select Save.

12. Select New from the File menu to clear the screen.

You have seen how the Zoom-In and Zoom-Out tools work well together when you are interested in editing a picture in minute detail. In the next section, you will learn how to achieve the kind of view that is useful when you want to print your image.

VIEWING A GRAPHIC AT ACTUAL SIZE

When you want to see approximately how large your image will look when printed, use the 1:1 tool in the Magnification pop-up menu. At a 1:1 viewing magnification, 1 inch on your screen

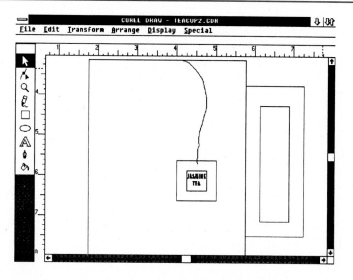

FIGURE 6-12   Viewing an image at actual size

corresponds to about 1 inch on the printed page. The amount of the page you see at this magnification may vary, depending on the way Microsoft Windows works with your monitor.

To achieve a 1:1 viewing magnification, select the Magnification tool and then drag the mouse and click when you have highlighted the 1:1 icon. You can practice using this tool on the TEACUP2.CDR image that you edited earlier in this chapter.

1. Open the file TEACUP2.CDR using the Open command from the File menu. Unless you have a full-page, 19-inch, or 24- inch monitor, the full-page view of the image is too small to allow you to read the text you entered earlier in this chapter.

2. Select the 1:1 tool. The screen redraws to display an area of your image similar to Figure 6-12. The actual area may vary because of the variety of monitors and display adapters available. At this viewing magnification, your text still appears small but it is legible.

3. Select the Zoom-In tool and lasso the tea tag with the marquee. The screen redraws to display only this portion of the image.

4. Select the Zoom-Out tool. Since you were in a 1:1 view previously, you zoom out by a factor of two.

5. Clear the screen by selecting New from the File menu.

The next section shows you how to fit an entire image within the viewing window. This is a different type of magnification than the 1:1 ratio.

FITTING A GRAPHIC WITHIN THE WINDOW

When the pictures you draw extend all the way to the edge of the page, they already fit within the viewing window. The ALL tool is not of much use to you in such cases. When some blank space exists, however, you can use the ALL tool to view everything you have drawn, but no more. This can be especially useful for small designs, such as logos.

To select the ALL tool, select the Magnification tool, move the mouse along the pop-up menu, and click when you have high-lighted the ALL tool. The screen redraws to fill the entire viewing area with the graphic image. Practice using this tool on one of the sample Corel DRAW! files in the following exercise.

1. Open the file ACAT.CDR. Note that there is a large amount of blank or "white" space at the top of the page, as in Figure 6-13.

2. Select the ALL view by selecting the Magnification tool, moving the mouse, and clicking when you have highlighted the icon ALL. Now you see only the cat itself and the logo beneath it, as shown in Figure 6-14.

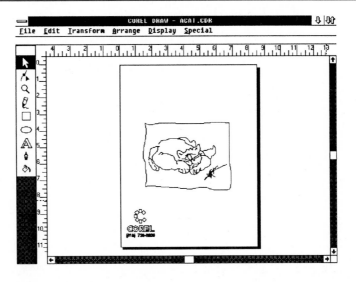

FIGURE 6-13   Image with unused blank space at top

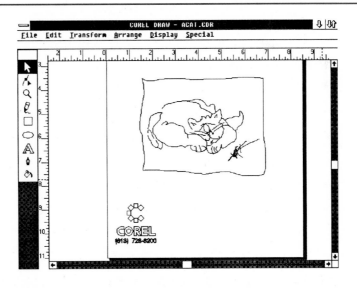

FIGURE 6-14   Fitting the image within the viewing area

SHOWING AN ENTIRE PAGE

The full-page view is the default view when you load Corel DRAW! or open a picture. It is easy to return to this view from any other view you have selected. Simply select the Magnification tool, drag the mouse along the pop-up menu, and click when you have highlighted the Show Page icon □ .

You have mastered all of the view selection tools but there is still another method, called panning, that you can use to control your viewing area.

PANNING OUTSIDE THE CURRENT VIEWING AREA

Regardless of which view you are in, you can always move beyond your current viewing area to see what lies beyond it. This operation is called *panning.* The horizontal and vertical scroll bars at the bottom and right sides of your screen are the tools you use to pan a picture. The callouts in Figure 6-15 point out the three different parts of the scroll bars you can use for panning.

- To pan in very small increments, click on a scroll bar arrow. The size of the increment varies, depending on your monitor and display adapter combination. If you click on the right horizontal scroll arrow, the image in the viewing window appears to move to the left. If you click on the left horizontal arrow, the image appears to move to the right. This is an excellent method to use when you need to edit an image in fine detail.

- To pan in large increments, click on either side of the blank box, or *thumb,* located in the middle of the horizontal and vertical scroll bars. Once again, the image appears to move in the opposite direction from your panning direction. This method has

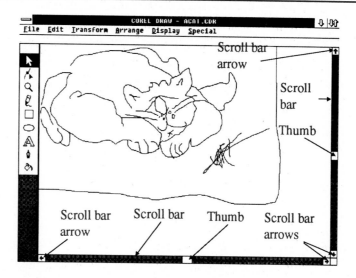

FIGURE 6-15   The parts of the scroll bar

only limited usefulness for editing, because the movement of the screen is rather jumpy and unpredictable.

- To control the exact distance that you pan, position the cursor over the thumb and drag it across the scroll bar in the direction that you want to pan. Release the mouse button when you reach the desired area.

Now that you are familiar with all of the magnification tools and with the scroll bars, you have complete control over the portion of your picture that you display at any one time. In the next chapter, you will put this new skill to work to help you select, arrange, and move objects and text.

SUMMARY

The Magnification tool is actually five tools in one. When you select the Magnification tool, a menu pops up, allowing you to customize your viewing area in five different ways. You can zoom in to any area of a picture, zoom out to a previous or reduced view, see a portion of an image at actual size, fill the viewing area with a graphic, or see the entire page.

Use the Zoom-In tool to edit small portions of an image or to add fine detail that, though too small to see in full view, is important to the total look of the picture. Use this tool again to gain precise control over the shaping of curves and the placement of their nodes in both objects and text. Technical drawings and realistic illustrations benefit greatly from the use of this tool.

Use the Zoom-Out tool to gain perspective on work you have done in other views.

Use the 1:1 view to see how large portions of your image look at actual size.

Use the ALL view when you need the perspective of seeing how your image looks in its entirety, without distracting white space.

Use the scroll bars, the scroll arrows, and the scroll bar thumbs to pan a picture in discrete increments. Use the scroll bar arrows to pan when detail is an issue, such as in technical or realistic illustrations.

PREVIEWING YOUR GRAPHICS

Displaying the Preview Window
Sizing the Preview Window
Working with the Preview Toolbox
Improving Preview Operation Speed

When you first open a file in Corel DRAW!, only a skeleton view of the image appears on the screen. You can see the basic shapes of objects and text, but not the custom outlines or fill colors with which you flesh them out. (You will begin working with outlines and fills in Chapters 13, 14, and 15.) This "bare bones" view is designed for speedy editing, but it doesn't give you as much visual information or accuracy as you would see in an actual printout of the image. For example, if an image contains several layers of objects, the editing view doesn't make it easy to tell which objects are in the foreground and which are in the background. The advantage of this stripped-down view is that it allows you to edit an image rapidly and conveniently. The disadvantage is that when you are moving, shaping, or editing objects, or working with colors, you need to see a true WYSIWYG display of your pictures to work efficiently.

Fortunately, WYSIWYG graphic displays are always available in Corel DRAW!. Just invoke the preview window and a second, more accurate view of your image appears next to the editing window. This preview image redraws automatically every time you make a change to a selected object in the editing window. You can edit an image and then check the results immediately. Frequent redrawing of the preview image can lower the performance speed of your software, so use this feature sparingly.

Like the Magnification tool discussed in the previous chapter, the preview window helps you customize the user interface of Corel DRAW! in many different ways. You can decide just how much of the screen you want the preview window to occupy, where you want to place the preview window on the screen, and even how much of your image you want shown in the preview window at any given moment. Follow the exercises in this chapter to make the preview window suit the way you work.

DISPLAYING THE PREVIEW WINDOW

In this exercise, you will open one of the sample images that came with your software. Because this image contains several colors and multiple layers of objects, it can show you the benefits of working with the preview window. Prepare for the exercise by setting up the Corel DRAW! window as follows:

1. Select the Display menu. If a checkmark appears in front of the Snap To Grid command, click on it to turn this feature off.

2. Select the Display menu again and turn off the Show Rulers command by clicking on it.

Displaying and Concealing The Preview Window

You can choose to display or conceal the preview window at any time while editing an image. Practice turning the preview window on and off now, using the MATH.CDR sample file.

1. Select Open from the File menu and open the file MATH.CDR. The image appears on the screen in skeletal form, as in Figure 7-1. Notice that the multiple layering of objects makes it

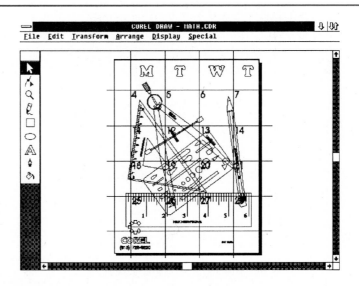

FIGURE 7-1   Skeletal image for speedy editing

difficult for you to tell objects apart or to guess which objects are in the foreground.

2. Pull down the Display menu and select the Show Preview command, or press the (F3) function key as a shortcut. The skeletal, or editing, view of the image now takes up only the left half of the screen, while a second view apppears on the right, as shown in Figure 7-2. If you have a color display adapter and monitor, this second image appears in pastel colors.

What a difference! The preview window shows you the outlines, fill colors, and layering of each object in the picture—all informa-

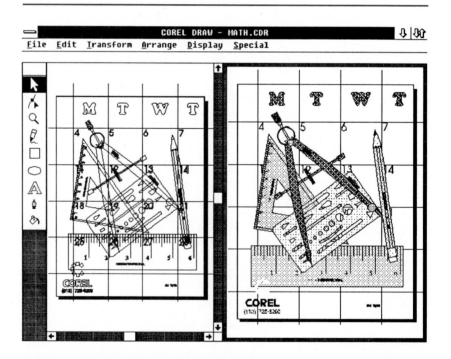

FIGURE 7-2   Comparing the editing and preview windows

tion that the default editing window does not provide. Also, you can see which objects lie closer to the foreground of the picture and which ones lie behind other objects. In the preview window, the template clearly falls between the compass and the triangle, but you couldn't be sure of that just from looking at the editing window.

To turn the preview window off, select the Show Preview command from the Display menu once more or just press (F3) again. The preview window disappears and you are left with the editing window only.

Limitations of the Preview Window

Since the preview window lets you see the results of editing a picture immediately, you may prefer to leave it turned on most of the time. The preview window does have two important limitations, however, and these make it advisable to turn it off under certain circumstances.

POSTSCRIPT EFFECTS The first limitation of the preview window applies if you plan to output your images to a PostScript laser printer or imagesetter. Corel DRAW! includes many advanced features that make use of PostScript graphics capabilities, but not all of them are visible onscreen. To see how such features really look, you must print the files that contain them. Corel DRAW! cannot display the following PostScript features with true WYSIWYG accuracy in the preview window:

- Custom PostScript textures

- PostScript halftone screens

- Dotted and dashed lines

- Grayscale tones

You will learn about these features when you create custom outlines and fills for objects and text in Chapters 13 through 15.

DISPLAYING FOUNTAIN FILLS IN COLOR   Another limitation of the preview window involves the ability to display fountain fills in color. You will learn more about fountain fills in Chapter 15. For now, however, it is sufficient to know that a fountain fill involves a gradual transition between two colors or two shades of a color in the interior of an object. The generic VGA and EGA screen drivers supplied with Microsoft Windows 2.1 or earlier contain a "bug" that causes problems when Corel DRAW! users attempt to preview fountain fills in color. Because of this problem, the default setting for Corel DRAW! allows you to preview fountain fills in black and white only. If you are running Windows version 2.11 or later, however, *and* if you installed it with one of the generic screen drivers, you can change this setting so that fountain fills display in color in the preview window. You may also try changing the setting if you installed any version of Windows using a custom screen driver supplied with your display adapter, but the results depend on your driver.

To change the setting, simply edit the [CDrawConfig] portion of your WIN.INI file and change the line "PreviewFountScreen=1" to "PreviewFountScreen=2." See your Microsoft Windows manual if you need help editing your WIN.INI file.

SCREEN REDRAW TIME   A third limitation of the preview window applies to all Corel DRAW! users and involves screen redraw time, the time needed for all details of the WYSIWYG image to redisplay in the preview window. Select the Show Preview command to turn on the preview window for MATH.CDR again and note that the screen redraws the preview image more slowly than the skeletal format. The preview contains much more visual information and is therefore more memory intensive. Also, the screen redraw occurs every time you make changes to the picture in the editing window. Fortunately, you can overcome this limitation in several different ways; see the "Improving Preview Operation Speed" section near the end of this chapter. The following sections show you how to change the size and shape of the preview window to suit your needs.

SIZING THE PREVIEW WINDOW

Since the shapes and sizes of pictures vary, you sometimes need to adjust the preview window to match the format of a picture. You can place the preview window beneath or beside the editing window and make it broad or long. The more closely you make the preview window fit the size and shape of your picture, the more control you have over the editing process.

Sizing with the Two-Way Arrows

To move or change the size of the preview window, you need only click on one of the window's boundaries and drag it to the desired position. Look again at the preview window and notice the narrow gray frame, or boundary, that surrounds it. When you move the mouse cursor to any part of the preview window boundary, a white two-way arrow appears, indicating which boundary you have approached and the direction in which you can drag the preview window from this point. With the file MATH.CDR open and the preview window displayed, move the mouse cursor as follows:

1. Move the cursor to any point along the upper boundary of the preview window. A vertical two-way white arrow appears, like this:

This arrow indicates that from this point, you can move the preview window upward or downward.

2. Move the mouse to the upper-left corner of the preview window. Now, the two-way arrow points diagonally, indicating that you can drag the preview window diagonally from the corner:

3. Finally, move the cursor to any point along the left side of the preview window. The two-way arrow becomes horizontal, which tells you that you can drag the preview window back and forth in a horizontal direction:

In the following exercises, you can experiment with changing the size or shape of the preview window.

Displaying the Preview Window In Top-to-Bottom Format

The first time you display the preview window, it appears automatically at the right side of the normal editing window, as it did in Figure 7-2. Sometimes a side-by-side format is inconvenient to work with. If you are editing a graphic that is wider than it is long, for example, you could see the graphic better if you positioned the preview window *below* the editing window.

1. Open the file BALLFEST.CDR and then select the Show Preview command from the Display menu. The two windows appear side by side, as in Figure 7-3. This picture has a vertical

format, but you are going to zoom in on a section that has a horizontal orientation.

2. Select the Magnification tool $\boxed{\mathbb{Q}}$ and then select the Zoom-In tool and lasso the balloon and the words "Balloon Fest" at the top of the editing window, as shown in Figure 7-4. Release the mouse button when you have surrounded the entire section. Both the editing window and the preview window redraw to show the magnified area (Figure 7-5). You can see some of the graphic below the specified zoom-in area as well, because Corel DRAW! adjusts the zoom to the proportions, or *aspect ratio*,

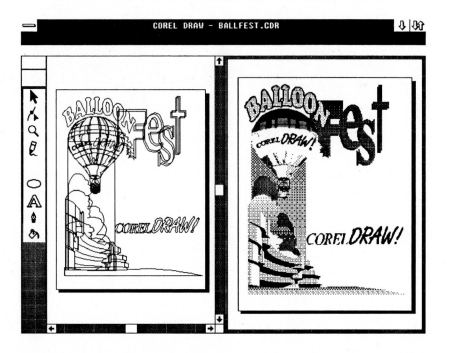

FIGURE 7-3   Previewing BALLFEST.CDR

of the page. To obtain a better view, you must change the arrangement of the preview and editing windows.

3. Position the mouse cursor along the upper boundary of the preview window. The two-way vertical arrow appears, as shown in Figure 7-5.

4. Press and hold the mouse button and drag the upper preview boundary downward until it is below the midpoint of the screen, as in Figure 7-6.

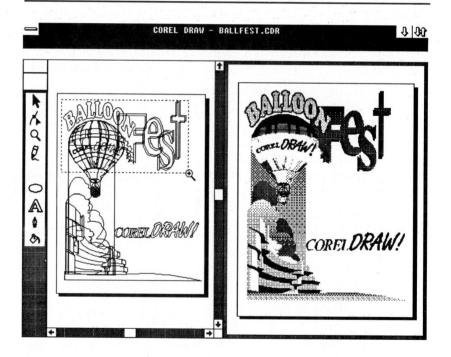

FIGURE 7-4   Magnifying the upper portion of the picture in the editing window

5. Release the mouse button. Corel DRAW! adjusts the windows so that the preview window appears below the editing window, as in Figure 7-7. Now you can see exactly the area you zoomed in on and no more, because you have tailored the aspect ratio of the editing and preview windows to the dimensions of the zoom-in area.

6. Leave the two windows in this top-to-bottom format for now.

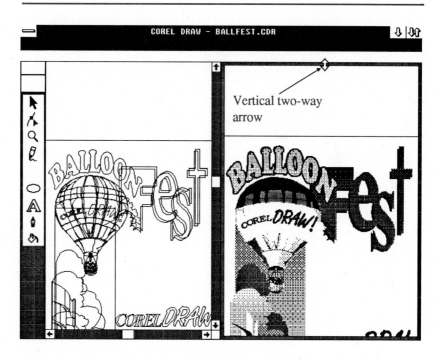

FIGURE 7-5   Screen redraw showing magnified view in both windows

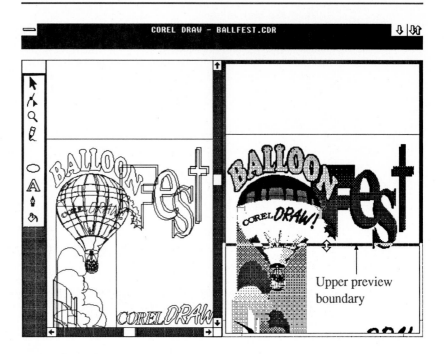

FIGURE 7-6   Dragging the upper preview boundary downward

  You can also place the preview window below the editing window by dragging the diagonal boundary instead of the vertical boundary. To do so, drag the diagonal boundary first downward and then to the left. The result is the same.

Changing the Size of the Preview Window (Top-to-Bottom Format)

You can alter the relative size of the preview and editing windows once you have them in a top-to-bottom format. If you wanted to see large, clear results of an edit involving color or outline, you

FIGURE 7-7   Preview window in top-to-bottom format

could make the preview window larger than the editing window. Practice altering the size of the preview window in the next exercise.

1. With the BALLFEST.CDR image still in top-to-bottom format on the screen, move the mouse cursor to the top boundary of the preview window until the vertical two-way arrow appears.

2. Drag this boundary upward until it covers approximately 75% of the screen and release the mouse button. The two windows redraw, with the preview window taking up most of the display area, as in Figure 7-8.

3. Take this sizing a step further. Drag the upper boundary of the preview window until you reach the top of the screen, and then release the mouse button. The preview window now fills the entire display area, crowding out the editing window entirely.

4. Drag the upper boundary back to a point more than halfway down the screen. The preview and editing windows return to a top-to-bottom format.

5. Select New from the File menu to clear the screen before proceeding.

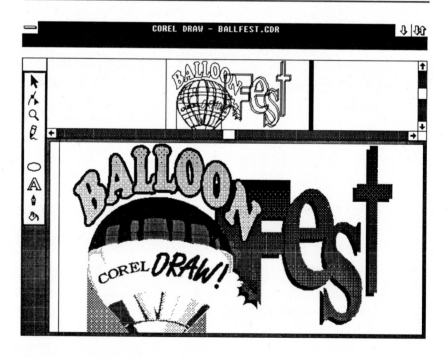

FIGURE 7-8   Increasing the size of the preview window (top-to-bottom format)

caution Never attempt to edit a graphic directly through the preview window. Corel DRAW! doesn't allow you to edit anything but the skeletal image in the editing window. You cannot edit the preview image. When you have finished checking the results of your edits using a full-screen preview window, return the display to either a top-to-bottom or side-by-side format to continue editing.

Displaying the Preview Window in Side-by-Side Format

Corel DRAW! "remembers" the most recent format you chose for the preview window during the current session. This format appears automatically until you either change it or exit the program. In this section, you will change back to the side- by-side placement of the editing and preview windows.

1. Open the file BALLFEST.CDR again and display the preview window once more. The editing and preview windows appear automatically in top-to-bottom format, as in Figure 7-9, because that was the last format you chose. Since you are displaying the entire graphic, however, the top-to-bottom arrangement makes the image in both windows too small to work with comfortably.

2. Move the mouse cursor to any point along the left boundary of the preview window; a two-way horizontal arrow appears.

3. Press and hold the mouse button and drag the left preview boundary toward the right until you have passed the halfway point of the screen, as shown in Figure 7-10.

4. Release the mouse button. Corel DRAW! redraws the screen so that both the preview and editing windows are side-by-side in vertical format, just as they were in Figure 7-3 earlier in the chapter. Since the vertical format fits the proportions of the

graphic, the images in both windows seem larger than they did before.

5. Leave this image on the screen for now.

 Another way to change from a top-to-bottom to a side-by-side format is to drag the diagonal boundary of the preview window instead of the horizontal one. To do this, drag the diagonal boundary first to the right and then upward. Similarly, to change from a

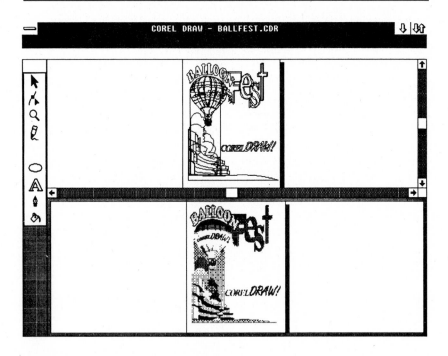

FIGURE 7-9   Full view of BALLFEST.CDR in top-to-bottom preview format

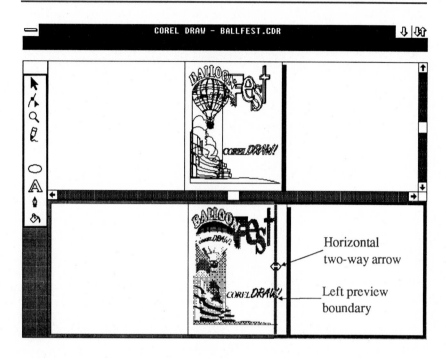

FIGURE 7-10   Dragging the left preview window boundary to the right

side-by-side to a top-to-bottom format, drag the diagonal boundary first downward and then to the left.

Changing the Size of the Preview Window (Side-by-Side Format)

You can alter the relative size of the preview and editing windows once you have them in a side-by-side format. Make the preview window larger than the editing window if you want to view results more clearly; make the editing window larger if you want to concentrate on manipulating the image.

1. With the BALLFEST.CDR image still on the screen, move the mouse cursor to the left boundary of the preview window so that the horizontal two-way arrow appears.

2. Drag this boundary to the left until it covers approximately 75% of the screen, and then release the mouse button. The two windows redraw, with the preview window taking up most of the display area, as in Figure 7-11.

3. Now drag the boundary of the preview window about 75% of the way to the right and then release the mouse button. This time, the editing window takes up most of the display area.

FIGURE 7-11   Increasing the size of the preview window in side-by-side format

4. Take this sizing a step further by dragging the left boundary of the preview window all the way to the left edge of the screen and then releasing the mouse button. The preview window fills the entire display area, crowding out the editing window entirely. Remember to use this full-screen preview only to *view* a picture; never try to edit on the preview window directly.

5. Select New from the File menu to clear the screen before proceeding.

Changing the format of the preview window manually is convenient, especially since it takes only a second to alter the relative size of the editing and preview windows. By dragging the appropriate two-way arrow, you can change both the format and the sizing of the preview window. If you prefer to switch preview window format (not size) automatically, however, you can activate the preview toolbox.

WORKING WITH THE PREVIEW TOOLBOX

The preview window has its own toolbox, which you can turn on or off using the Show Preview Toolbox command in the Display menu. Unlike the regular toolbox for the editing window, the preview toolbox contains no drawing tools. The sole function of its tools is to customize the format or content of the preview window relative to the editing window. Using this toolbox, you can choose between top-to-bottom and side-to-side preview format and magnify custom areas of the preview window.

 When the preview toolbox is turned on, the preview window does not update itself automatically to match changes made in the editing window.

Displaying the Preview Toolbox and
Adjusting the Preview Window Format

Perform the following brief exercise to display the preview toolbox
and adjust the format of the preview window automatically.

1. Open the file MATH.CDR and press (F3) to show the preview
   window. Since the last change you made to the preview window
   was to stretch it across the entire screen, the preview window
   fills the screen as soon as you display it.

2. Select the Show Preview Toolbox command from the Display
   menu. At the right side of the preview window, three icons
   appear, as in Figure 7-12. The top icon, the Magnification tool,

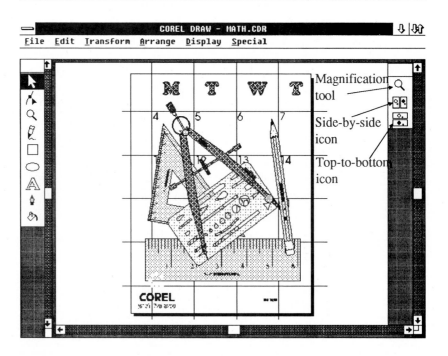

FIGURE 7-12   Displaying the preview window toolbox

works exactly like the Magnification tool for the editing window. The second icon allows you to arrange the editing and preview windows in a side-by-side format. The third icon allows you to arrange the editing and preview windows in a top-to-bottom format.

3. Click anywhere on the second icon in the preview toolbox to return the preview window to a side-by-side display. Note that the preview and editing windows occupy equal areas of the screen. You can adjust the relative size of the two windows by manually dragging the left boundary of the preview window, just as you did earlier.

4. Change to a top-to-bottom arrangement of the two windows by clicking anywhere on the third icon in the preview toolbox.

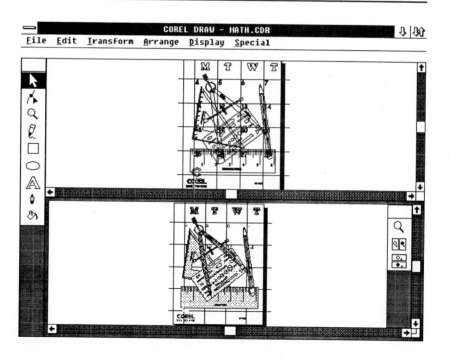

FIGURE 7-13   Returning to a top-to-bottom format

Your screen should now look like Figure 7-13. Again, the preview and editing windows occupy equal areas of the screen.

5. To conceal the preview toolbox, click on the Show Preview Toolbox command from the Display menu once more. Leave the MATH.CDR image on the screen for the next exercise.

Working with Magnification In the Preview Window

The Magnification tool in the preview toolbox contains the same five icons (Zoom-In, Zoom-Out, 1:1, ALL, and Show Page) as its counterpart in the editing window. Both Magnification tools work the same way—but they work independently. The Magnification tool in the preview toolbox controls only the content of the preview window, so you can look at different sections of the same image in each window. Perform the following brief exercise for a quick example of the potential of this feature.

1. With the MATH.CDR file on the screen, drag the left boundary of the preview window to the right and adjust the windows to a side-by-side format.

2. In the editing window, select the Magnification tool and then select the Zoom-In tool and lasso the compass only. Both windows redraw automatically, as in Figure 7-14.

3. Select Show Preview Toolbox from the Display menu. Notice that as soon as you activate the preview toolbox, scroll bars appear along the bottom and right boundaries of the preview window. You can now adjust the preview window magnification using the same techniques you learned in Chapter 6.

4. In the editing window, select the Magnification tool and the Zoom-In tool again. Zoom in on the square of the calendar that contains the number "6." As Figure 7-15 shows, the editing

window redraws to show the new magnification, but the preview window does not redraw. Whenever the preview toolbox is turned on, the preview window no longer changes magnification automatically; you must change it yourself using the preview Magnification tool.

5. Select the Text tool 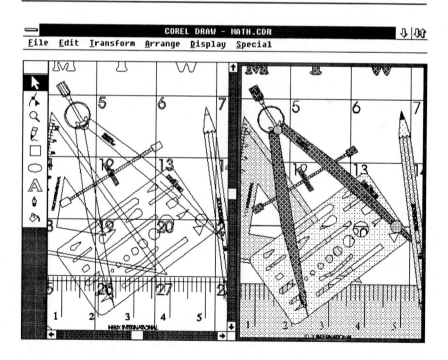 in the editing window toolbox and then select an insertion point in the middle of the calendar box.

6. When the Text dialog box appears, type a capital **X** in the text entry window. Set the text attributes to left aligned, Avalon Normal, 75 points.

FIGURE 7-14   Automatic magnification of both windows (preview toolbox off)

7. Select OK to confirm these settings. The letter X now appears in both the editing and preview windows, as in Figure 7-16, but in the preview window you see it in perspective, among all the surrounding objects, and with a default fill color of black.

8. To practice varying the magnification in the preview window, click on the Magnification tool in the preview toolbox and again on the Zoom-In icon. Lasso the "X" in the preview window; the screen redraws to show approximately the same area that appears in the editing window. The other icons in the Magnification tool pop-up menu of the preview toolbox work just like their counterparts in the editing window, too.

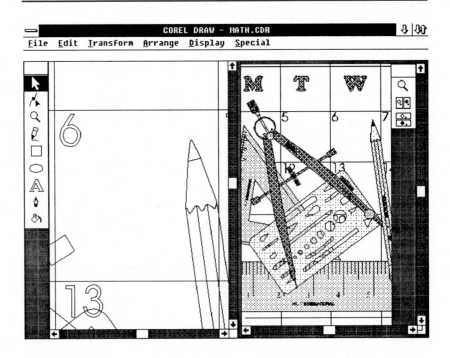

FIGURE 7-15   Showing different magnification in each window (preview toolbox on)

9. Turn the preview toolbox off by selecting the Show Preview toolbox command from the display window once more.

10. Select New to clear the screen. Do not save the changes you made to the picture in this exercise.

You have mastered all of the basic techniques for customizing the preview window to best view your images. The next section of this chapter contains tips on advanced techniques for reducing the amount of memory and time that is needed to redraw the preview window.

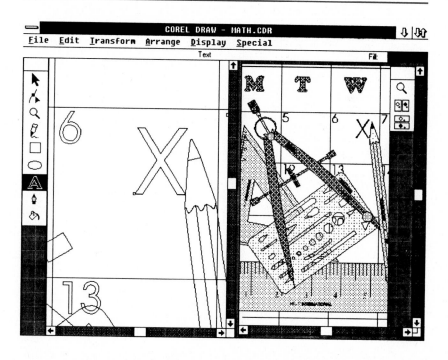

FIGURE 7-16   Previewing edits with different magnification in each window

IMPROVING PREVIEW OPERATION SPEED

If you allow Corel DRAW! to redraw the preview window whenever you edit a picture, you can spend a lot of potential drawing time waiting, especially if you are working on a complex image. Fortunately, you can slash redraw time while still retaining all the most important editing benefits of the preview window. Just use any of these four techniques:

- Interrupt the screen redraw before it has finished.

- Turn off the Auto-Update feature so the preview will no longer redraw automatically every time you make a change.

- Turn off the display of bitmaps in the editing window.

- Use the Preview Selected Only command so the screen will display only those objects on which you are currently working.

The following sections describe each of these techniques and offer suggestions for their use.

Interrupting the Screen Redraw

You can interrupt the redraw of the preview window at any time before it is finished. Simply begin another operation using the mouse button. Corel DRAW! senses the signals from the mouse and stops redrawing the preview as soon as the object it is currently redrawing is complete. This means that if the object that is currently being redrawn is a complex one, your interruption of the process may take effect only after a few seconds.

Turning Off the
Auto-Update Feature

One of the most effective ways to speed up Corel DRAW! operation while retaining the preview window is to turn off the Auto-Update feature, controlled by the Auto-Update command in the Display menu. This feature is turned on by default, so that the preview window redraws with every change you make to the editing window. To turn this feature off, click on the Auto-Update command in the Display menu and the checkmark in front of the command should disappear. This prevents the preview window from redrawing unless you click on any point in the window. Practice this technique by performing the following brief exercise:

1. Open the MATH.CDR file. When the image appears, click on the Auto-Update command in the Display menu to turn off this feature.

2. Embellish the editing window any way you like. For example, select the Freehand tool and draw an "X" on one of the calendar windows with the Freehand tool or add geometric shapes. The preview window does not redraw at any time.

3. When you have finished doodling in the editing window, click anywhere on the preview window. In a few seconds, you see the results of your actions. If your "doodles" do not appear in the preview window and you have drawn a line or curve, click on the Outline tool $\boxed{\text{\textcolor{black}{◊}}}$ and again on the word "HAIR" in the first row of the pop-up menu. This ensures that the outlines of your lines and curves are visible. Then draw the same doodles over again. You will learn more about the Outline tool in Chapter 13.

4. Select New from the File menu to clear the screen.

You can see why toggling the Auto-Update command on and off is a favorite work habit of seasoned Corel DRAW! users. If you use this method most of the time, you will always have the preview handy, while avoiding its potential drawbacks.

Concealing Bitmaps in The Editing Window

Bitmapped images take a long time to redraw, even in the editing window, as you will learn when you work with bitmapped images and autotracing in Chapter 17. A useful technique is to turn off the Show Bitmaps command in the Display menu. This command, which you can turn on and off like the Auto-Update command, is normally turned on and has a checkmark in front of it. When you select it to turn it off, bitmapped images display in the editing window as an empty rectangle, but continue to appear in the preview window. Turn Show Bitmaps and Auto-Update off when you are finished cropping and editing bitmaps; this will allow you to work at maximum speed and still check the results of your edits.

Previewing Selected Objects Only

When your main concern is to view the specific object or objects you are editing, you can select the Preview Selected Only command in the Display menu. Invoking this command causes Corel DRAW! to redraw only the object(s) you have selected. This is a particularly useful technique when you are trying to figure out which objects are in the foreground and which are in the background. Chapter 8, "Selecting, Moving, and Arranging Objects," introduces the Select tool and gives you ample opportunity to practice displaying selected objects in the preview window.

SUMMARY

The preview window in Corel DRAW! has several useful functions. It allows you to see immediate results of editing, to identify superimposed objects, and to check color and outline selections. The area in which you make changes to objects, called the editing window, shows the objects in a skeletal form only.

You can alter the relative position of the preview and editing windows in several ways to suit the format of your graphic and the level of magnification you are using. When you work with images or magnified views of images that are in a vertical format, position the editing and preview windows side-by-side. Position the editing and preview windows in top-to-bottom format when you work with images or magnified portions of images that are in a horizontal format. To reposition the preview window automatically, use the appropriate icon in the preview toolbox. To customize the size of the preview window in any format, drag the window boundary in the desired direction.

The preview window has its own toolbox, which consists of controls for changing the magnification and format of the preview window. You can turn the preview toolbox on or off. When you turn it on, the preview window no longer updates itself automatically to match changes you make to the editing window. A very useful feature of the preview toolbox is that it enables you to work with different magnifications in each window.

When the preview toolbox is turned off, the Auto-Update command determines whether the preview window is updated automatically as you edit the picture. Turn Auto-Update off to reduce preview window redraw time and preserve a high program operating speed. To redraw the contents of the preview window and see your changes with Auto-Update off, click anywhere on the preview window. When Auto-Update is on, you can reduce screen redraw time by interrupting the redraw process or by selecting the Preview Selected Only command. This command causes only the currently selected objects to appear in the preview window.

chapter **8**

SELECTING, MOVING, AND ARRANGING OBJECTS

Selecting and Deselecting Objects
Moving Objects
Arranging Objects

I n order to change the appearance or position of any object or text string, you must first *select* it. Once you have selected an object, you can move and rearrange it, stretch, scale, rotate or skew it, give it a custom outline, or fill it with a color or pattern. Learning how to select an object is therefore an important prerequisite to mastering most of the skills in Corel DRAW!.

You use the Select tool 🖰 , the first tool in the Corel DRAW! toolbox, to select objects and text. When you first load Corel DRAW!, the Select tool is automatically active and remains active until you choose a different tool. If you are already working with one of the other tools, you can activate the Select tool by clicking on the Select tool icon in the toolbox, but pressing the spacebar once is more efficient. This is a time-saving shortcut that allows you to switch back and forth between tools quickly. To reactivate the tool you were working with before you selected the Select tool, press the spacebar again. Use this shortcut often when you want to draw objects, immediately move, rearrange, or transform them, and then continue drawing.

The Select tool performs more than one function; it has both a select mode and a transformation mode. The select mode includes all those functions—selecting, moving, and arranging—that do not require you to change the size or structure of the object. The transformation mode allows you to stretch, scale, rotate, skew, or create mirror images of objects. This chapter covers the functions of the select mode; Chapter 9 will acquaint you with the use of the Select tool in the transformation mode.

SELECTING AND DESELECTING OBJECTS

You can select objects only when the Select tool is active. This tool is always active when you first open a picture, when you begin a new picture, and immediately after you save your work. To activate the Select tool when you're using the Shaping tool or one of the drawing tools, you either press the spacebar or click on the Select tool icon once.

Once the Select tool is active, you can select objects by clicking on their outlines, using (SHIFT) with the mouse, or lassoing the objects. The technique you choose depends on the number of objects you are selecting, the placement of the objects within the graphic, and whether it's more convenient to select objects with the mouse or with the keyboard shortcuts.

The Corel DRAW! screen gives you three visual cues to let you know that an object is selected. First, a *highlighting box* consisting of eight small rectangles, called *boundary markers,* surrounds the object. These markers allow you to stretch and scale the object, as you'll learn in Chapter 9. Second, one or more tiny hollow nodes appear on the outline of the object or group of objects. The number of nodes displayed depends on the type and number of objects selected. The nodes are the means by which you can change an object's shape, as you'll learn in Chapters 10 and 11. Finally, the status line tells you the type of object you have selected (rectangle, ellipse, curve, and so on) or the number of objects you have selected if you have selected more than one. Figure 8-3 will identify each of these aids.

Selecting and Deselecting Single Objects

Any time you activate the Select tool while working on a graphic, it automatically selects the last object you created. If you want to select a different object, simply click once anywhere on the object's *outline*. Clicking on the inside of a rectangle or ellipse, or on an open space inside a letter, has no effect. Also, you must click on a point unique to that object; it cannot share that point with the outline of any other object. Only when an object is the same type and size as another object on top of it does it have no unique selection point available. For information on how to select superimposed objects without unique selection points, see the "Cycling Through Objects" section of this chapter.

To *deselect* an object or text string so that the tools or menu commands you use no longer affect it, click in any open area on the page. Alternatively, you can select a different object and thereby automatically deselect the previously selected object.

 When you click twice on an object instead of once, arrows surround the object in place of the boundary markers. These arrows indicate that you have enabled the stretch, scale, rotate, and skew functions of the Select tool. This can happen to you accidentally, since the Select tool covers transformation mode as well as select

mode functions. If you enable the transformation mode accidentally at any time, just click on the object's outlines again to toggle
back to the select mode.

In the following exercise, you will practice selecting and deselecting single objects in the LANDSCA2.CDR file that you
edited in Chapter 6. You will use the spacebar to select objects that
you have just drawn and the mouse to select other objects.

1. Make sure that the Show Status Line command in the Display
   menu is turned on and the Snap To Grid command is turned off.

2. Open the LANDSCA2.CDR file. Note that when the picture
   displays on the screen, the Select tool is already active.

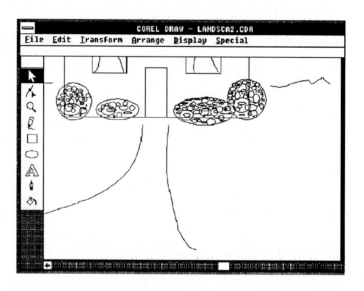

FIGURE 8-1   Magnifying the lower-right quarter of the file
LANDSCA2.CDR

3. Select the Magnification tool 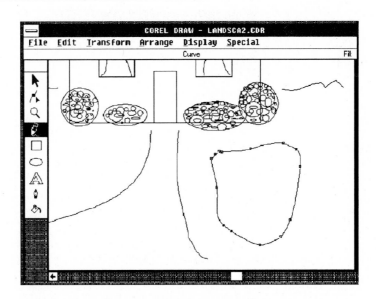 and then select the Zoom-In tool from the pop-up menu and lasso the lower-right quarter of the picture. The screen redraws an area of the image similar to Figure 8-1.

4. Select the Freehand tool and drag the mouse button to draw a large pond in the lower-right corner of the picture. Be sure to connect the starting point to the finish point, so that the curve representing the pond becomes a closed path that you can fill later. Notice that as soon as you finish drawing this object, nodes appear all along the path of the curve, as in Figure 8-2.

5. As soon as the pond appears, press the spacebar to activate the Select tool . Since the pond is the last object you drew, Corel DRAW! automatically selects it. A highlighting box

FIGURE 8-2   Adding a pond to the drawing

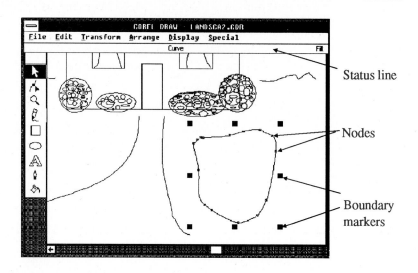

Status line

Nodes

Boundary
markers

FIGURE 8-3   Selecting the last object drawn using the
spacebar

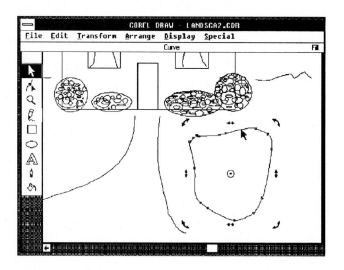

FIGURE 8-4   Enabling the transformation mode of the Select
tool

surrounds the pond and the status line indicates "Curve" as in Figure 8-3.

6. Click on the outlines of the curve object again. As Figure 8-4 shows, black two-way arrows replace the boundary markers of the highlighting box. Your second click has enabled the rotate and skew functions of the Select tool. Click on the object's outlines again to toggle back to the select mode.

7. Now, zoom out of your magnified view using the Zoom-Out tool in the Magnification tool pop-up menu. Practice selecting objects that you drew in previous sessions. For example, click on one of the curves that form the branches of the poplar tree. Each time you select a new object, the previously selected object becomes deselected; the highlighting box disappears from the previously selected object and surrounds the new one instead. The name of the currently selected object type always appears in the status line. If you select any objects within other objects (the detail inside one of the bushes, for example), you may notice that the highlighting box is sometimes much larger than the object itself. If several objects of the same type are crowded closely together, it may be difficult to tell which one you have selected. Use the Zoom-In tool to magnify a small portion of a crowded area before you attempt to select single objects.

8. When you have practiced enough to feel comfortable with selecting objects, select Save As from the File menu and type in the name **LANDSCA3.CDR** to save the file.

9. Select New from the File menu to clear the screen.

Selecting and Deselecting
Multiple Objects

It's often more convenient to perform an operation on several objects simultaneously than to perform the same operation on a series of single objects individually. Assume, for example, that you want to move the tree in the LANDSCA3.CDR file to another location within the picture. Since the tree consists of several separate objects, moving each component object individually would be tedious and might even lead to inaccurate placement.

Corel DRAW! gives you three alternative solutions to this type of problem. The first solution, simply *selecting* the objects, is appropriate when you want to keep multiple objects together only temporarily, without merging them into a single entity. For example, you might want to fill a certain number of objects in a picture with the same color or pattern or move them all by the same distance. You can select multiple objects by using the mouse and (SHIFT) key, by drawing a marquee around them, or by using the Select All command in the Edit menu. Your choice of technique depends on both the number of objects you want to select and their location within the graphic.

If the multiple objects are components of a larger whole and should remain together at all times, you might choose to *group* them, as you will learn to do later in this chapter. Corel DRAW! will still remember that grouped objects have separate identities. If the multiple objects belong together and contain many curves, you can choose to *combine* them into a single object. Combining objects, unlike grouping them, reduces the amount of memory they require and also allows you to reshape the entire resulting object.

You will learn more about the uses of grouping and combining multiple objects in the "Arranging Objects" portion of this chapter. The following group of sections lets you practice common methods of selecting multiple objects.

SELECTING AND DESELECTING MULTIPLE OBJECTS WITH THE (SHIFT) KEY

When you want to select a few objects at a time, you can conveniently select them one after another using the mouse and (SHIFT) together. The (SHIFT) key method is especially useful when the objects you want to select are not next to one another within the graphic. Practice selecting multiple objects using this method:

1. Select the first object by clicking on its outline.

2. Depress and hold (SHIFT) and select the next object.

3. Continue selecting objects in this way, holding down (SHIFT) continuously.

4. When you have selected all desired objects, release (SHIFT).

To deselect one or more of the objects you have selected in this way, hold down (SHIFT) and click again on that object's outline. This action affects only that object; other objects in the group remain selected. To deselect all of the selected objects simultaneously, click on any free space.

Each time you select another object using (SHIFT), the highlighting box expands to surround all the objects you have selected so far. Objects that you did not select also may fall within the boundaries of the highlighting box, making it difficult for you to see just which objects you have selected. The following exercise shows how you can use the status line information and the preview window as aids in selecting multiple objects with (SHIFT).

1. Open the TEACUP2.CDR file that you edited in Chapter 6.

2. Use the Maximize arrow to enlarge the size of the working area. Magnify the area that extends from the upper-left corner of the picture to the bottom of the tag on the teabag.

3. Click on the leftmost wisp of "steam" above the teacup to select it. A highlighting box surrounds the object, and the status line indicates that you have selected a curve.

4. Depress and hold (SHIFT) and click anywhere on the outlines of the text "JASMINE TEA." The message in the status line changes to "2 objects selected," but the highlighting box shown in Figure 8-5 seems to surround many more objects. It is difficult to tell whether you have selected the text string or one of the rectangles on the tea tag surrounding it. To find out, you need help from the preview window.

5. Press (F3) to display the preview window. Do not be concerned at this point that all of the objects in your drawing seem to blend into a solid black mass. You will learn how to edit the outlines and colors of individual objects in Chapters 13, 14, and 15.

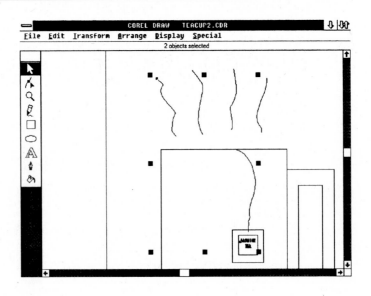

FIGURE 8-5   Selecting non-adjacent objects using (SHIFT)

6. Select Preview Selected Only from the Display menu. This command, first introduced in Chapter 7, causes only the currently selected objects to appear in the preview window. The text string is too small to read clearly but, as Figure 8-6 shows, you can now be certain that you selected the correct objects. Or did you?

 If you cannot see the "steam" when it is selected, click on the Outline tool and again on the word "HAIR" in the first row of the pop-up menu. This action ensures that selected lines and curves have a visible outline.

7. If you accidentally selected one of the tea-tag rectangles instead of the text string, deselect the incorrect object by holding (SHIFT) while clicking again on that object. When the highlighting box

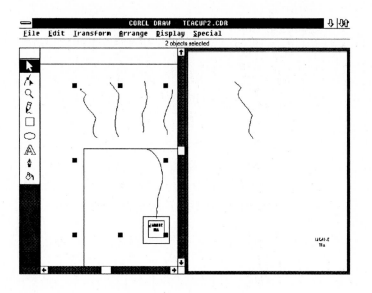

FIGURE 8-6   Using Preview Selected Only to confirm object selection

no longer surrounds that object, continue to hold down (SHIFT)
and select the text string instead.

8. Still holding down (SHIFT), select the rightmost wisp of "steam"
and add it to the group of selected objects. The status line now
displays the message "3 objects selected," and the preview
window displays all three objects. Again, if you can't see the
steam when it is selected, click on the Outline tool and again
on the word "HAIR" in the pop-up menu.

9. Click on the Preview Selected Only command in the Display
menu again to turn off this feature, and then select New from
the File menu to clear the screen.

SELECTING AND DESELECTING OBJECTS WITH THE MARQUEE

If you need to select a large number of objects at
once, using the mouse and (SHIFT) can be tedious. A quick shortcut
is to draw a marquee around all of the desired objects with the
Select tool. Perform the following exercise to practice using a
marquee:

1. Position the mouse cursor just above and to the left of the first
object you want to select. (You can begin from any corner of
the group of objects, but the upper-left corner is usually most
convenient.)

2. Depress the mouse button and drag the mouse diagonally in the
direction of the other objects you want to select. A dotted
rectangle (the marquee) follows the cursor. Make sure that
every object you want to select falls completely within this
rectangle, or Corel DRAW! will not select it.

3. When you have enclosed the last object you want to select
within the marquee, release the mouse button. The highlighting
box appears, encompassing all of the objects within the selected
area.

If you want to exclude some of the objects that fall within the selected area, you can deselect them using (SHIFT). Lasso the entire group of objects first, depress and hold (SHIFT), and click on a particular object's outline to deselect that object. You can also use the status line and preview window as "quality control" aids to guide you in selecting exactly the objects you want.

Perform the following exercise to gain skill at selecting objects quickly with the marquee. Use magnification, status line information, and the preview window to make the selection process more efficient. Use (SHIFT) to fine-tune your selection and add or subtract objects to the group you selected with the marquee.

1. Open the file LANDSCA3.CDR. Note that the poplar tree you drew in an earlier lesson contains several objects: the ellipse that forms the main body of the foliage, a few curves that form the branches, and curves that make up the trunk. Since all of these objects are adjacent to one another, the tree is a perfect example of the types of multiple objects you can select easily with the marquee.

2. Select the Magnification tool and then select the Zoom-In tool from the pop-up menu. Zoom in to display the left half of the picture. As soon as you have magnified this area, the Select tool becomes highlighted again.

3. Press (F3) to turn on the preview window. Do not be concerned that many of the objects seem to be solid black; you can practice giving them different outline and fill colors after you work with Chapters 13, 14, and 15.

4. Select Preview Selected Only. The preview window now appears blank.

5. Position the mouse cursor above and to the left of the poplar tree. Drag the mouse downward and to the right until the marquee surrounds all of the component objects of the tree

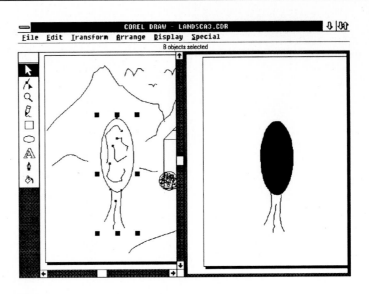

FIGURE 8-7   Selecting all component objects of the tree

completely and release the mouse button. The highlighting box appears and the status line indicates the number of objects you have selected, as in Figure 8-7. However, the preview window displays the foliage of the tree as a solid elliptical mass, without the detail of the curves you have entered inside it. You cannot distinguish between objects because the foliage curves and the ellipse have the same fill color.

6. Depress and hold (SHIFT) and then click once anywhere on the outline of the ellipse that makes up the main body of the foliage. Corel DRAW! deselects it and the status line shows there is one less selected object. You can now see the internal details in the preview window, as shown in Figure 8-8. As in the previous exercise, if you cannot see the foliage curves when they are

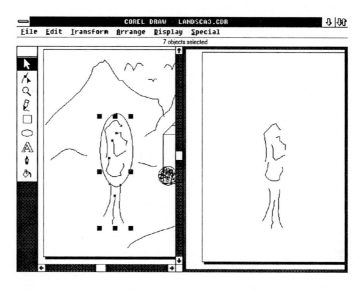

FIGURE 8-8   Deselecting one object in a group of selected objects

selected, click on the Outline tool and again on the word "HAIR" in the pop-up menu.

7. Click on any white space to deselect all of the objects, and then select New from the File menu to clear the screen.

SELECTING AND DESELECTING ALL OBJECTS IN A GRAPHIC   If you want to perform an operation on all the objects in the graphic, you can select them by drawing a marquee. A quicker way to select all objects is simply to invoke the Select All command in the Edit menu. Using this command, you can be sure that you haven't left out any objects.

You now know several methods for selecting single and multiple objects. Most of the time, selecting objects is a straightforward process in Corel DRAW!. But what if your graphic contains many small objects or you want to select an object that may have several other layers of objects on top of it? The next section makes that process easy for you.

Cycling Through Objects

The object selection techniques you have learned so far in this chapter are adequate for most applications. However, when working with complex drawings containing many objects or superimposed objects, you may find it more convenient to cycle through the objects using (TAB). The following exercise summarizes this technique:

1. Select an object near or on top of the object you want to select.

2. Press (TAB). Corel DRAW! deselects the first object and selects the next object in the drawing. The "next" object is the one that was drawn just prior to the currently selected object. Each time you press (TAB), Corel DRAW! cycles backward to another object. If you press (TAB) often enough, you eventually select the first object again, and the cycle begins once more.

The following sections show you two different situations in which you might choose to cycle through objects in a drawing. The first section provides an example of objects that have other objects superimposed on them. The second section demonstrates how to locate and select small objects in a complex drawing.

CYCLING THROUGH SUPERIMPOSED OBJECTS   You may recall that in order to select an object in Corel DRAW!, you must click on a unique point on its outline, a point not shared by any other object. This limitation does not apply to most superimposed objects, because you can always see separate outlines in the preview window. The only exception is when two or more objects are the same size and shape and overlay one another exactly.

Why might you choose to create two identical overlapping objects? You could achieve interesting design effects by varying the color and thickness of their respective outlines and fills, as shown in the example in Figure 8-9. The preview window shows that what appears to be a single rectangle in the editing window is actually two separate rectangles, each with its own outline color, outline thickness, and fill color. In Chapters 13, 14, and 15, you will learn more about outlines and fill colors. For now, you need only know that to select the object in the background, you can select one object and then press (**TAB**), checking the preview window for confirmation.

SELECTING SMALL OBJECTS IN A COMPLEX DRAW-ING   There is another, more common use for (**TAB**) when selecting objects in Corel DRAW!. Clipart, technical illustrations, and other complex drawings often contain many small objects close

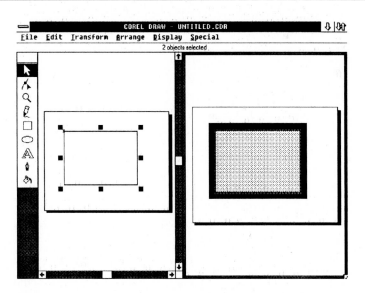

FIGURE 8-9   An example of objects exactly superimposed

together. Even in magnified view, trying to select one or more of these with the mouse can be difficult at best. To ease the process, you can select one object, and then press (**TAB**) repeatedly until the fine little detail you are looking for is selected. Corel DRAW! cycles backward through the objects, selecting them in the reverse order to which you drew them. To cycle forward through the objects in a drawing, press (**SHIFT-TAB**). Perform the following brief exercise to gain a clearer understanding of how the (**TAB**) key method of selection works.

1. Open the file MATH.CDR, turn on the preview window by pressing (**F3**), and select Preview Selected Only from the Display menu.

2. Choose the Select All command from the Edit menu. The status line shows you that there are 173 separate objects that have not been grouped or combined.

3. Click on any white space to deselect all the objects, and then select the template as shown in Figure 8-10.

4. Press (**TAB**) several times. Corel DRAW! cycles through the objects layered below the template, displaying a different fine ruler marker, ruler number, or other detail each time that you press (**TAB**).

5. Press (**SHIFT-TAB**) several times. Now Corel DRAW! selects objects in the opposite order, eventually selecting objects layered above the template.

6. If you have the patience to cycle through all 173 objects, keep pressing (**TAB**) or (**SHIFT-TAB**) until Corel DRAW! selects the template again.

7. Select New from the File menu to clear the screen before proceeding.

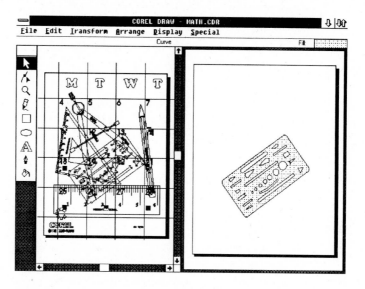

FIGURE 8-10   Cycling through multiple objects in a complex drawing

Now you are familiar with all of the available techniques for selecting any number of objects. In the next portion of this chapter, you will begin moving selected objects to other areas within the illustration.

MOVING OBJECTS

Once you have selected an object, you can move it by positioning the cursor over any point on its *outline* (not on the highlighting box) and then dragging the mouse to the desired location. The status line provides you with precise, real-time information about the distance you are travelling, the *x*- and *y*-coordinates, and the angle of movement. You can achieve precision worthy of the most demanding technical illustrations if you choose to work with the status line and grid.

Factors such as the number of objects you want to move, whether you want to constrain movement to a 90-degree angle, and whether you want to make a copy of the object determine your choice of technique. The following sections provide examples and exercises that show how to move objects in specific situations.

Moving a Single Object

The appearance of an object undergoes several changes during the process of moving it. Try the following simple exercise to become familiar with those changes.

1. Select the Ellipse tool ⬭ and draw an ellipse in the upper area of the page.

2. Activate the Select tool and select the ellipse. (Recall that you can simply press the spacebar to select the last object you have drawn.) The highlighting box surrounds the ellipse.

3. Move the mouse to any point on the outline of the ellipse, press and hold the mouse button, and begin dragging the mouse downward and to the right. The screen does not change imme-diately, because Corel DRAW! has a built-in, 3-pixel safety zone; you must drag the mouse at least 3 pixels away from the starting point before the object begins to "move." As soon as you pass the 3-pixel safety zone, the cursor changes to a four-way arrow, and a dotted replica of the highlighting box follows the cursor, as shown in Figure 8-11. This dotted box represents the object while you are moving it; as you can see in the figure, the object itself seems to remain in its original position.

4. When you have dragged the dotted box to the lower edge of the page, release the mouse button. The ellipse disappears from its original position and reappears in the new location.

5. Select New from the File menu to clear the screen before proceeding.

These are the basic steps involved in moving an object, but Corel DRAW! offers you additional refinements as well. The next three sections provide details on moving multiple objects, constraining an object to move at a 90-degree angle, and retaining a copy of an object while moving it.

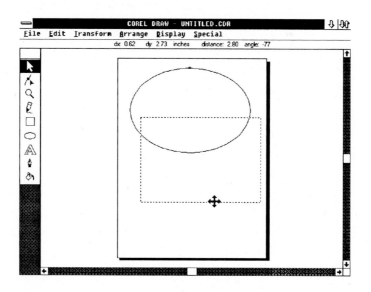

FIGURE 8-11   Dragging the dotted move box to move an object

Moving Multiple Objects

The technique for moving multiple, selected objects differs very little from the way you move single objects. When more than one object is selected, you simply press and hold the mouse button on the outline of *any one* of the objects within the selected group. The entire group moves together as you drag the mouse. Complete the following exercise to practice moving multiple objects in the LANDSCA3.CDR file.

1. Open the file LANDSCA3.CDR. The Select tool is automatically activated when you open a new picture.

2. Draw a marquee and lasso the entire poplar tree in the front foreground of the picture to select it. The status line displays the number of selected objects. If you are not sure whether you have selected all of the objects that make up the tree, get confirmation by turning on the preview window and selecting Preview Selected Only from the Display menu.

3. Position the cursor over any of the outlines in the tree, and then drag the mouse until the dotted move box reaches the extreme right of the picture, as shown in Figure 8-12.

4. Release the mouse button. The tree disappears from its original location and reappears in the new location. The tree is now in the middle of the pond, so you will move the pond next.

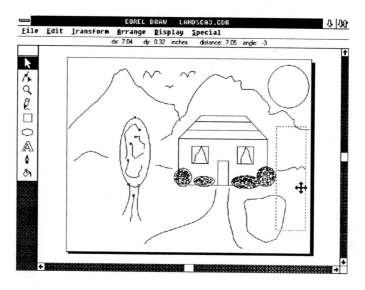

FIGURE 8-12   Moving multiple objects to a new location

5. Select the pond and move it to the left side of the picture where the poplar tree formerly stood.

6. Select the Zoom-In tool from the Magnification tool pop-up menu and magnify the area around the leftmost bush in front of the house. Your viewing area should look similar to Figure 8-13.

7. Activate the Select tool again and select (lasso) the entire bush, including the detail you drew inside it, and then move the bush a little to the left of the house.

8. Zoom out to full-page view. Your picture should now resemble Figure 8-14.

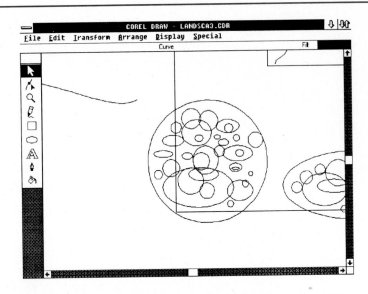

FIGURE 8-13   Magnifying the area around the leftmost bush

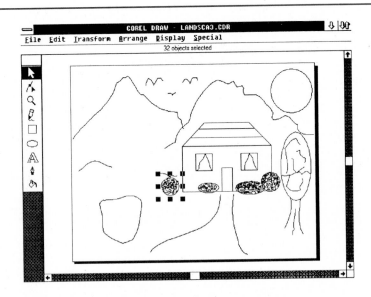

FIGURE 8-14   LANDSCA3.CDR after moving the
multiple-object bush

9. Save this altered picture as LANDSCA4.CDR and leave it on the screen.

Constraining Movement
To a 90-Degree Angle

The techniques you have learned so far in this chapter apply to moving objects in any direction. But what if the nature of your drawing requires that you move objects straight up or down or directly to the right or left? You could, of course, use the coordinates information in the status line to reposition the object precisely. But Corel DRAW! also offers you a more intuitive method of moving objects at an exact 90-degree angle using (CTRL). This is a convenient method for obtaining precision without slowing your drawing pace. Perform the following exercise to practice constraining the movement of objects vertically or horizontally.

1. With the LANDSCA4.CDR file still displayed, select one of the birds at the top of the picture.

2. Press and hold (CTRL) and then drag the bird to the right. Even if you don't have a steady hand, the bird remains at exactly the same horizontal level of the picture. The information on the status line verifies the steadiness of your movement: both the *dy* indicator and the angle indicator remain at zero, as in the following illustration:

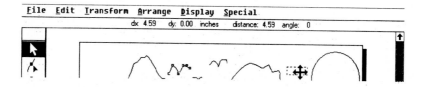

Release the mouse button first and then release (CTRL) to reposition the bird at the new location. If you release (CTRL) first, the selected object is no longer constrained and can move up or down relative to the starting point.

3. Press and hold (CTRL) and the mouse button a second time. This time, drag the bird to the left of its current location. Again, the bird remains at the same horizontal level and the *dy* indicator remains at zero. This time the angle indicator displays 180 degrees:

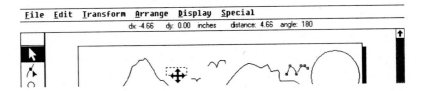

Release the mouse button and (CTRL) when you reach a satisfactory location.

4. Press and hold (CTRL) and the mouse button again and drag the bird directly downward. This time, the *dx* indicator remains at zero, and the angle indicator displays -90 degrees:

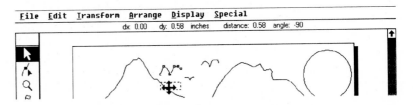

Release the mouse button and then (CTRL) to reposition the bird at the new vertical location. If you accidentally release (CTRL) first, the select object is not constrained, and you can move it both horizontally and vertically relative to the original location.

5. Continue to depress both (CTRL) and the mouse button and drag the bird directly upward. The *dx* indicator remains at zero, but the angle indicator reads 90 degrees:

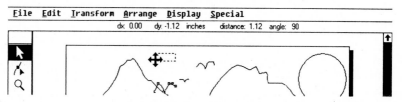

6. Continue practicing this technique with other objects in the picture. When you are finished, select New from the File menu but do not save any changes.

Copying an Object While Moving It

You may recall that while you are moving an object, it seems to remain in place and you appear to be moving only a dotted rectangular substitute. Corel DRAW! lets you take this feature a step further; you can make an identical copy of the object as you move it. The copy remains at the initial location while you move the original to a new location. This handy technique has interesting design possibilities, as you can discover for yourself by performing the next exercise.

1. Select the Grid Size command in the Display menu and set the grid to 2.0 per inch. Activate the Snap To Grid and Show Rulers commands in the Display menu. Since you just finished working on a picture in Landscape (horizontal) mode, the blank page area is also in this mode. (If you worked on something else in the meantime, change to Landscape mode now, using the Page Setup command in the File menu.)

2. Select the Text tool and then select an insertion point at the 1-inch mark on both the horizontal and vertical rulers. When the Text dialog box appears, type the word **Arrow** in upper and lower case in the text entry box. Set the text attributes to Bangkok normal, left aligned, 100 points. Select OK to exit the

dialog box. The word "Arrow" displays in the upper-left corner of the page.

3. Press the spacebar to activate the Select tool and select the text string. Press and hold the mouse button over the outline of any letter and begin to drag downward and to the right. Since you have set grid spacing in large units, the dotted move box travels and snaps in visibly discrete increments.

4. Continue holding down the mouse button. When the upper-left corner of the dotted move box snaps to a point half an inch below and to the right of the starting point (about midway down and across the letter "A"), press the ⊙ key on the numeric keypad. At the right of the status line, the message "Leave Original"appears, as in Figure 8-15. The ⊙ key in Corel DRAW! is also called the Leave Original key.

5. Release the mouse button. An exact copy of the object appears at the starting point and the original appears at the new location.

6. Make four more copies of the text string in the same way, using the ⊙ key and moving the text object in ½-inch increments downward and to the right. You should now have a total of six identical text strings.

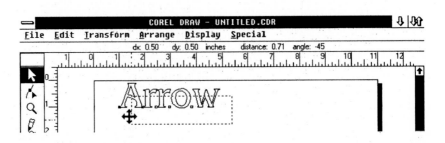

FIGURE 8-15   Copying an object while moving it

7. Change the direction in which you move the text object. Make five additional copies as you move the text object downward and to the left in ½-inch increments. When you are finished, 11 identical text strings form an arrowhead shape.

8. Activate the preview window. If the Preview Selected Only command is active, click on the command again to deselect this feature and then drag the preview window to the left until it fills the entire screen, as in Figure 8-16. This gives you a better view of how your design really looks.

9. Select Save As from the File menu and save this picture under the name ARROW1.CDR. Before leaving this exercise, return the preview window to a side-by-side display format.

Using the preceding exercise as an example, you can probably think up additional design ideas for copying single or multiple

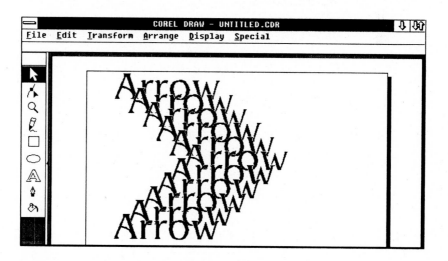

FIGURE 8-16 A preview of the arrow design

objects as you move them. Go on to the final portion of this chapter to discover ways of changing the relative order of objects within a drawing.

ARRANGING OBJECTS

In Corel DRAW!, you can change the order of superimposed objects, group and combine separate objects, and align objects relative to one another. All of these techniques are ways of arranging objects on the page. The Arrange menu contains all of the commands you will use in this chapter, plus a few others (such as Fit Text To Path) that are discussed in Chapter 20, "Combining Corel DRAW! Features and Creating Special Effects." The next four sections demonstrate the most common methods of arranging selected objects.

Changing the Order of Superimposed Objects

When you draw a series of objects, Corel DRAW! always places the object you drew *last* on top of all of the other objects. If you could look at the ARROW1.CDR file in 3D, for example, you would see that the first text string you created is beneath all of the others you subsequently copied.

You can change the order of objects at any time by applying one of the first three commands in the Arrange menu—To Front, To Back, and Reverse Order—to a selected object or group of objects. The To Front and To Back commands rearrange the selected objects *relative to* the other objects on the page, but they do not rearrange objects within a selected group. The Reverse Order command, on the other hand, rearranges the objects *within* a selected group, but it does not alter the relationship between the selected objects and the other objects in the picture. Practice

working with these commands now, using the sample file
DRAWNEWS.CDR that came with your software.

1. Select the Open command from the File menu and open the file
    DRAWNEWS.CDR. This image represents a stylized newslet-
    ter masthead.

2. Press (F3) to activate the preview window and display the object
    in color.

3. Select the Zoom-In tool in the Magnification tool pop-up menu
    and magnify just the masthead portion of the image. The
    preview window also redisplays automatically, but the aspect
    ratio in both windows is inappropriate for the magnification you
    have chosen.

FIGURE 8-17   The masthead and preview window in
horizontal format

4. Drag the preview window down below the halfway point on the screen to display it underneath the editing window. Now both windows should display a close-up of the masthead in horizontal format, as in Figure 8-17.

5. In the editing window, select the four letters "D-R-a-W" and the two stylized rectangles behind them. You can use the marquee or the (SHIFT) key method to select them, but make sure that the status line reads "6 objects selected."

6. Pull down the Arrange menu and select the To Back command. The entire group of selected objects disappears behind the rectangle that forms the background of the masthead, as shown in Figure 8-18. When you apply this command to a group of objects, however, the relative order of the objects *within* the group does not change.

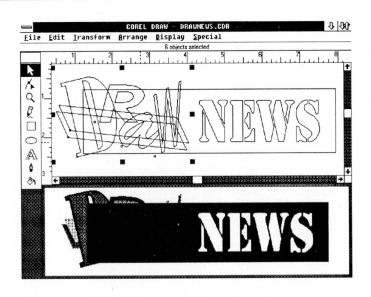

FIGURE 8-18   Using the To Back command on selected objects

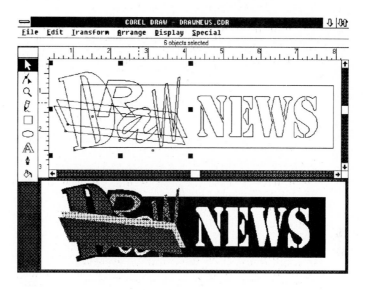

FIGURE 8-19   Using the Reverse Order command on selected objects

7. With the same group of objects still selected, select the To Front command in the Arrange menu. Now the objects reappear in their original order, in front of the masthead rectangle.

8. Leave these objects selected and select the Reverse Order command from the Arrange menu. This command reverses the relative order of the objects within the selected group. As the preview window redraws, you can see the letters appear one by one in reverse order. The stylized rectangles appear last of all, as in Figure 8-19. The yellow rectangle and the black rectangle that formed the "shadow" now make it impossible to read the letters!

9. Select the Reverse Order command once more to return the objects to their original order on the screen. Leave this drawing on the screen for the next exercise.

Grouping and Ungrouping Objects

Selecting multiple objects with the marquee or (SHIFT) key is fine
if you want to apply certain commands or operations to them on a
one-time basis only. However, most drawings contain subsets of
objects that belong together, such as the elements of a logo on a
business card. If you want the same set of objects to form a single
entity at all times, consider *grouping* them instead of merely
selecting them.

To group multiple objects, you first select them and then apply
the Group command in the Arrange menu. Thereafter, the group
responds to any operation collectively. You can move, align, color,
and outline them together, without individually selecting each
component of the group. However, Corel DRAW! still "knows"
that the component objects have separate identities. As a result,
you cannot apply the Reverse Order command to a group or
reshape the group using the Shaping tool. You can also create
groups within groups, and then use the Ungroup command to break
them down into their component objects again.

Continue working with the DRAWNEWS.CDR file to become
familiar with the basics of grouping and ungrouping objects.

1. Drag the preview window to the right and rearrange the preview
    and editing windows into a side-by-side format. The entire
    upper half of the page should be visible now.

2. Select all of the separate letters in the word "Draw" plus the two
    stylized background rectangles using the (SHIFT) key technique.
    To check that you have selected the correct objects, click on the
    Preview Selected Only command in the Display menu to get
    confirmation. When you are finished, the status line should
    display the message "6 objects selected." Deselect the Preview
    Selected Only command so that you can see everything in the
    preview window.

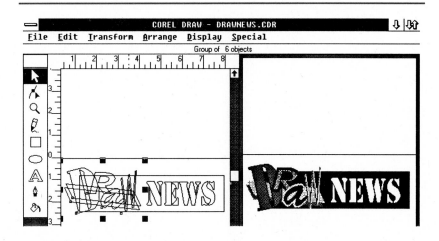

FIGURE 8-20   Grouping multiple objects

3. Select the Group command in the Arrange menu. The status line message changes immediately from "6 objects selected" to "Group of 6 objects," as shown in Figure 8-20.

4. Press and hold the mouse button at any point along the outline of any of the letters and drag the mouse to the bottom of the screen. The entire group moves together and relocates when you release the mouse button.

5. Select the rectangle that forms the background for the word "NEWS" and move it down the page, too. What happened to the word "NEWS" in Figure 8-21? Since it has a white fill color and no outline, you cannot see it when you take away the blue background.

6. Move the rectangle back up to its original location and apply the Group command to this rectangle and the single curve object that constitutes the word "NEWS." When you try to move either object now, both move together. As a group, they cannot be separated from one another unintentionally.

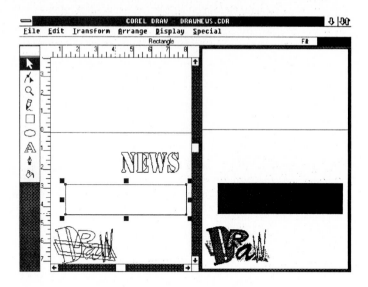

FIGURE 8-21   Moving the background object away from a
hollow foreground object

7. Move the group consisting of the word "Draw" and the background rectangles over the group consisting of the word "NEWS" and the masthead rectangle. Select both groups and apply the Group command again. You now have a group within a group; when you select and move any component, the entire masthead moves together.

8. Select the group consisting of all the objects in the masthead and then select the Ungroup command from the Arrange menu. You now have only the two separate subgroups of objects that you formed in steps 3, 4, and 7. Select each group in turn and ungroup it until you can select individual objects again.

9. Select New from the File menu to clear the screen before proceeding. Do not save any changes to this picture.

Practice grouping and ungrouping objects on your own, perhaps using some of the image files you created in previous chapter exercises. Before and after grouping objects and text strings, look at the menus to see how grouping affects which commands you can and cannot select.

Combining Objects and Breaking Objects Apart

The Arrange menu contains two sets of commands that seem almost identical in content, but are actually two different operations: Group/Ungroup and Combine/Break Apart. Combining objects differs from grouping them in several complex respects that are beyond the scope of the current chapter; you will gain more experience with the Combine command in Chapters 15 and 20. In general, however, you use Combine in the following situations:

- When you want multiple objects to *become* a single object that you can reshape with the Shaping tool

- When the objects contain many nodes and curves and you want to reduce the total amount of memory they consume

- When you want to create special effects such as transparent masks, behind which you can place other objects.

In these situations, simply grouping objects would not yield the desired results.

Later chapters contain several examples of creative uses for the Combine command. There is one interesting use of Combine, however, that you can practice in this chapter. Recall that when you first activated the preview window in Chapter 7, you couldn't distinguish the component objects of the TEACUP2.CDR file because they all contained a default fill of black. If you combine objects with other objects contained within them, however, the net result is a reverse video effect that makes alternating objects transparent and creates contrast. For a clearer understanding of how this works, try the following exercise.

1. Open the TEACUP2.CDR file, activate the preview window, and zoom in on the area immediately surrounding the "handle" of the cup, as shown in Figure 8-22. The preview window displays a solid black mass because you haven't yet applied different fill colors or outlines to separate objects.

2. Select both the larger rectangle that forms the outline of the handle and the inner rectangle. Use either the marquee or the (SHIFT) key method.

3. Select the Combine command from the Arrange menu. The inside of the inner rectangle becomes transparent, as shown in

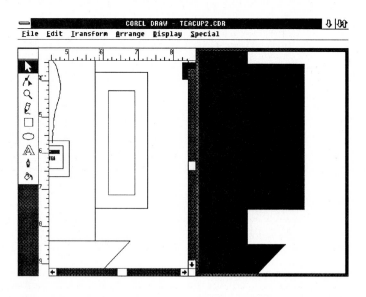

FIGURE 8-22   Magnifying the handle of the teacup

Figure 8-23. This "special effect" comes about because the Combine command causes all overlapping areas in a graphic to appear transparent. Notice that the status line now refers to the combined object as a single curve object.

4. Zoom out to full-page view. Because of the hollow areas you created when you selected the Combine command, you can now distinguish the handle from the rest of the cup.

5. Save this file under the new name TEACUP3.CDR.

6. Select the newly combined handle if it is not still selected, and then select the Break Apart command from the Arrange menu. All objects revert to their previous state and become black again.

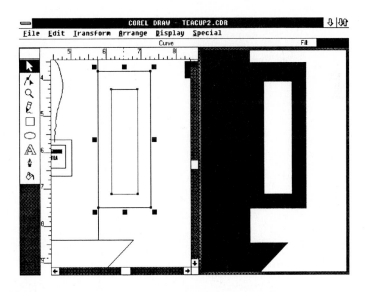

FIGURE 8-23   Using the Combine command to create a hollow inner region

7. Clear the screen using the New command in the File menu. Do not save any changes.

Aligning Objects

Earlier in this chapter, you saw how you can move objects precisely using the (CTRL) key as a substitute for the grid. The Align command in the Arrange menu offers you another quick and easy method for aligning selected objects without having to spend all of your drawing time measuring. To align objects, you simply select the objects, click on the Align command, and then adjust the horizontal and vertical alignment settings in the Align dialog box.

You could try to memorize the abstract effects of all 15 possible settings, but experiencing those settings for yourself might be more meaningful. In the following exercise, you will create the surface of a billiard table complete with six pockets, combine all the elements of the table into one object, and then add a billiard ball and apply various alignment settings to the ball and the table.

1. Start with the page in Landscape orientation. Select the Rectangle tool and draw a rectangle 9 inches wide and 4 inches deep. This rectangle represents the surface of the billiard table.

2. Magnify the area of the page that contains the rectangle, select the Freehand tool, and draw six billiard "pockets," as shown in Figure 8-24. You can draw the pockets either as curved or multi-segment lines as you wish.

 If you want to draw the billiard pockets as curves, set Freehand tracking in the Preference dialog box to 10 pixels and then magnify each area as you draw a pocket in it. The smaller the area in which you are drawing, the smoother your curves become. Zoom out when you have finished drawing the fine details.

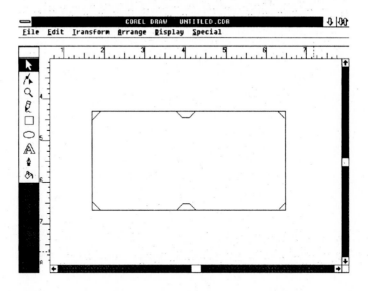

FIGURE 8-24   A billiard "table" with six "pockets"

3. Activate the Select tool and draw a marquee around the billiard table to select both the table and the pockets and then apply the Combine command in the Arrange menu. This combines the pockets and the table surface into a single object to prevent accidental realignment of the pockets later on in this exercise.

4. Select the Ellipse tool, press and hold (CTRL), and draw a perfectly circular "ball" in the center of the table.

5. Select both the table and the ball, and then select the Align command in the Arrange menu. The Align dialog box in Figure 8-25 appears. The dialog box contains two rows of option buttons; the settings in the top row pertain to the relative *horizontal* alignment of the selected objects, while the settings in the bottom row pertain to their relative *vertical* alignment. You can set horizontal and vertical alignment independently of

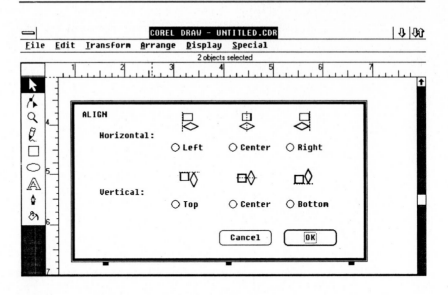

FIGURE 8-25   The Align dialog box

each other or mix them, for a total of 15 possible settings. When multiple objects are selected and you choose the Horizontal Left, Horizontal Right, Vertical Top, or Vertical Bottom alignment option, Corel DRAW! repositions all but one of the objects. The object whose highlighting box extends furthest in the direction of alignment remains in place. When you select Horizontal Center or Vertical Center alignment, however, Corel DRAW! repositions all of the selected objects, unless one of them is already in the desired location.

6. Select Horizontal Left and then click on the OK command button. The billiard ball reappears in position (1) in Figure 8-26, aligned to the left edge of the table.

7. Select the Align command repeatedly and choose each of the numbered settings in the following list, one at a time. As you

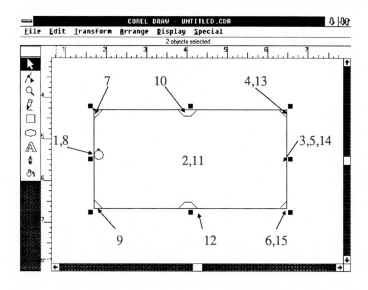

FIGURE 8-26   Results of Align dialog box settings

select each setting, check the location of the billiard ball against the corresponding callout numbers in Figure 8-26. Six of the following settings will cause your ball to "go" into one of the billiard table pockets.

(1)   Horizontal Left
(2)   Horizontal Center
(3)   Horizontal Right
(4)   Vertical Top
(5)   Vertical Center
(6)   Vertical Bottom
(7)   Horizontal Left—Vertical Top
(8)   Horizontal Left—Vertical Center
(9)   Horizontal Left—Vertical Bottom
(10)   Horizontal Center—Vertical Top

(11) Horizontal Center—Vertical Center
(12) Horizontal Center—Vertical Bottom
(13) Horizontal Right—Vertical Top
(14) Horizontal Right—Vertical Center
(15) Horizontal Right—Vertical Bottom

Experiment on your own, perhaps with other objects in drawings you have already created. Other objects may align in a slightly different way, depending on the order in which you select alignment settings.

By now, you have had an opportunity to practice all of the functions of the Select tool that do not require you to change the size or structure of selected objects. In the next chapter, you will explore the transformation mode of the Select tool and learn to stretch, scale, rotate, skew, and mirror a selected object or group of objects.

SUMMARY

The Select tool performs many different functions. You can use it to select an object, to move or rearrange its location, and to size, scale, rotate, or skew it. When you use the Select tool to select, move, and arrange objects, you do not change the size or outward appearance of the objects.

When you select objects, the status line provides information about the number of objects selected and how they are grouped. To select a single object, click anywhere on its outline. To select multiple objects, you can use the mouse and (SHIFT) key or surround the objects with a marquee. Use the Select All command in the Edit menu to select all of the objects in a drawing. When working with graphics that contain many small objects, you can cycle through and find objects by pressing (TAB) repeatedly. To deselect objects, click on any free space, or select another object instead.

To move selected objects, press and hold the mouse over any point on the objects' outline and then drag the object to the desired location. A dotted replica of the highlighting box represents the object as you move it. You can constrain objects to move straight up, down, or sideways using (CTRL), or you can make copies of the object as you move it using the Leave Original key (+) on the numeric keypad.

Many of the commands in the Arrange menu allow you to change the relative position of selected objects within a graphic. To change the order of superimposed objects, use the To Front, To Back, or Reverse Order commands. To align selected objects, change the settings in the Align dialog box, which you access with the Align command. When you want to treat multiple objects as a single entity, use the Group/Ungroup commands. When working with multiple objects that contain many lines and curves, use the Combine/Break Apart commands to conserve memory and create special effects.

chapter **9**

TRANSFORMING OBJECTS

Stretching and Mirroring an Object
Scaling an Object
Rotating an Object
Skewing an Object
Repeating a Transformation

In Chapter 8, you learned how to use the Select tool to select, move, and arrange objects. In this chapter, you will use the Select tool to _transform_ the size or shape of selected objects.

When you transform an object with the Select tool, you do not alter its fundamental shape; a rectangle continues to have four corners and an ellipse remains an oval. (This is not the case when you _reshape_ an object using the Shaping tool, which you will learn about in Chapters 10 and 11.) The five basic transformation techniques you will learn in this chapter enable you to stretch, scale, mirror, rotate, and skew an object in any direction. You will also learn how to retain a copy of the original object, repeat transformations automatically, and return an object to its original format even if you have transformed it several times.

The exercises in this chapter introduce not only the basic skills that make up the art of transformation, but also the alternative ways you can practice them. Corel DRAW! lets you customize the way you work when transforming objects. If you like to work interactively, you can carry out these functions using the mouse and keyboard alone. For a little extra guidance, you can look to the status line and rulers. And, if you have to render a technical illustration that requires absolute precision, you can specify transformations using the commands and dialog boxes in the Transform menu.

Throughout most of this chapter, you will practice each skill using a sample text string that you create in the following section. However, the stretch, scale, rotate, and skew functions of Corel DRAW! work exactly the same way with multiple selected objects as with single ones. In later exercises, you can practice combining transformation operations with other skills you have learned in previous chapters.

STRETCHING AND MIRRORING AN OBJECT

As you discovered in Chapter 8, a rectangular highlighting box, made up of eight black boundary markers, surrounds an object when you select it. These boundary markers, shown in Figure 9-1, have special functions in Corel DRAW!; you use them to stretch and scale objects. When you *stretch* an object, you change its *aspect ratio* (the proportion of its width to its height), because you lengthen or shorten it in one direction only. When you *scale* an object, you change the object's length and width at the same time, so the aspect ratio remains the same. To stretch an object, you must drag one of the four *middle* boundary markers, as shown in Figure

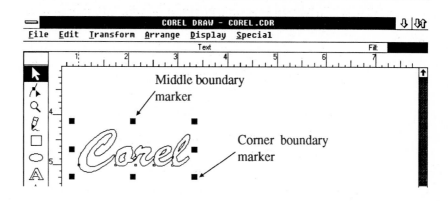

FIGURE 9-1   A selected text object showing boundary markers

9-1. To scale an object, you drag one of the four boundary markers in the *corners* of the highlighting box.

This section covers all of the available techniques for stretching objects. You have the additional option of creating a mirror image or making a copy of the original object as you stretch it. The exercises in this section introduce you to both the interactive and menu-assisted methods for stretching, mirroring, and copying objects.

Stretching an Object Interactively

If you prefer to work interactively, bypassing menu commands and dialog boxes, you can stretch a selected object using the mouse and keyboard alone. You do not sacrifice precision when you work this way, for the status line assists you in setting precise values as you stretch an object. Practice stretching a text string interactively in the following sections.

STRETCHING AN OBJECT HORIZONTALLY You can stretch an object in either a horizontal or vertical direction. In the following exercise, you will create a text string and stretch it toward the right.

1. Make sure your page is in portrait format before you begin. If it is not, choose the Page Setup command from the File menu and select the portrait and letter option buttons.

2. Select the Magnification tool and choose 1:1 from the pop-up menu. Turn on the Show Rulers command and make sure that the Snap to Grid command is inactive.

3. Select the Text tool and select an insertion point at the 1-inch mark on the horizontal ruler and the 5-inch mark on the vertical ruler.

4. When the Text dialog box appears, type the word **Corel** in the text entry box. Set text attributes to Banff, 75 points, Left alignment, and then select OK. The text appears on your screen.

5. Select the Save As command from the File menu and type in the filename **COREL.CDR**.

6. Press the spacebar to activate the Select tool . A highlighting box surrounds the text string immediately, since it was the last object you drew. Your screen should resemble Figure 9-1.

7. Position the cursor directly over the center right boundary marker of the highlighting box. The mouse cursor changes to a white cross like the one in Figure 9-2.

8. Depress and hold the mouse and drag the boundary marker to the right. The original object seems to stay in the same place, but a dotted rectangular box follows the cursor, which turns into a two-way horizontal arrow as shown in Figure 9-3. As you drag, the status line displays the message: "x scale:" followed

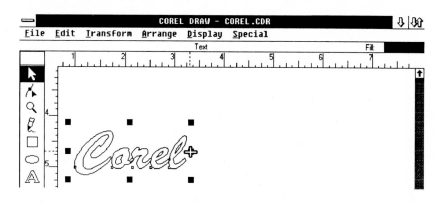

FIGURE 9-2   Preparing to stretch a selected object horizontally

by a numeric value and a percent sign. This value tells you by how much you are stretching the selected object in increments of $\frac{1}{10}$ of a percentage point.

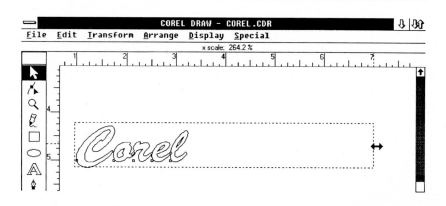

FIGURE 9-3   Stretching an object horizontally to the right

9. After you have stretched the object to the desired size, release the mouse button. Corel redraws a horizontally stretched version of the original object, like the one in Figure 9-4.

10. Select the Undo command from the Edit menu to return the text string to its original size. The original text string remains selected for the next exercise.

To stretch a selected object to the left instead of to the right, drag the middle boundary marker at the *left* side of the highlighting box. Practice stretching the text string from the left side if you wish, but select Undo after you are finished so that the original text string remains on the screen.

STRETCHING AN OBJECT VERTICALLY   You can also stretch an object in a vertical direction. The mouse cursor and status line information change to reflect the direction of your stretch.

1. Select the "Corel" text string if it is not selected already.

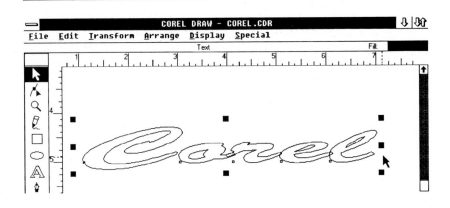

FIGURE 9-4   A text object stretched horizontally

2. Position the mouse cursor directly over the middle top boundary marker of the highlighting box. The mouse cursor changes to a white cross.

3. Depress and hold the mouse and drag the boundary marker upward. The original object seems to stay in the same place, but a dotted rectangular box follows the cursor, which turns into a two-way vertical arrow, as shown in Figure 9-5. As you drag, the status line displays the message: "y scale:" followed by a numeric value and a percent sign. This value tells you by precisely how much you are stretching the selected object in increments of $\frac{1}{10}$ of a percentage point.

4. After you have stretched the object to the desired size, release the mouse button. Corel redraws a vertically stretched version of the original object.

5. Select the Undo command from the Edit menu to return the text string to its original size.

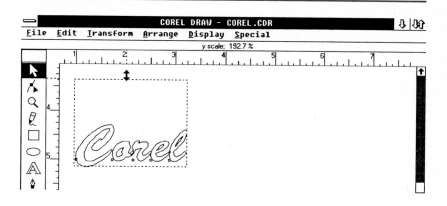

FIGURE 9-5   Stretching an object vertically and upward

If you wish, practice stretching the text string downward in a vertical direction. When you are finished, undo your changes to the original object and then proceed with the next exercise.

STRETCHING AN OBJECT IN INCREMENTS OF 100%

In previous chapters, you saw how to use (CTRL) to constrain your drawing or moving operations to fixed increments or angles. The same holds true when you are stretching a selected object. To stretch an object in fixed increments of 100%, press and hold (CTRL) as you drag the boundary marker in the desired direction. The status line keeps track of the increments in which you are stretching the object. As always, remember to release the mouse button *before* you release (CTRL), or the object may not stretch in exact increments. In the following exercise, you will triple the width of the original object using (CTRL).

1. Select the text string if it is not selected already.

2. Press and hold (CTRL) and then drag the middle right boundary marker to the right. Notice that the dotted rectangular outline does not follow the two-way arrow cursor continuously; instead, it "snaps" outward only when you have doubled the width of the object.

3. When the status line displays the message, "x scale: 300%" as shown in Figure 9-6, release the mouse button first and then (CTRL). The text string redisplays at triple its original width.

4. Select the Undo command from the Edit menu to revert to the original unstretched object.

If you wish, practice stretching the text string vertically as well as horizontally in fixed increments of 100%. Undo your changes after each practice stretch. When you are finished, proceed to the next exercise.

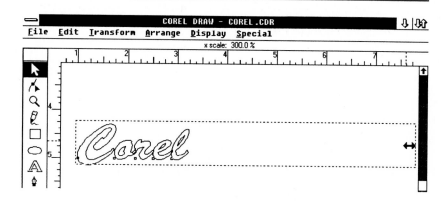

FIGURE 9-6   A horizontal stretch constrained to 300%
original size

RETAINING A COPY OF THE ORIGINAL OBJECT   A
useful design technique is to make a copy of the original object as
you stretch it, so that both the original and the stretched objects
appear on the screen. To retain a copy of the original object, just
press the (•) key once as soon as you begin the stretching, when
the outline box appears.

You can also retain a copy of the original object when using
(CTRL). Try this technique now:

1. Select the text string "Corel" if it is not already selected.
   Position the mouse cursor over the bottom middle boundary
   marker and begin to drag this marker downward.

2. As soon as the dotted outline box appears, press the (•) key on
   your numeric keypad once. The message "Leave Original"
   appears at the right side of the status line.

3. Press and hold (CTRL) and continue to drag the bottom middle boundary marker downward until the status line reads "y scale: 200%."

4. Release the mouse button and then (CTRL). The screen displays both the original and stretched object, as in Figure 9-7.

5. Undo your changes to the original text string before continuing.

If the stretched object does not appear in the correct proportion, you either failed to press and hold (CTRL) or you released (CTRL) before releasing the mouse button. Keep practicing until you feel comfortable with the technique, but remember to undo your changes. In the next exercise, you will create mirror images of both the original and stretched text string.

CREATING A HORIZONTAL OR VERTICAL MIRROR IMAGE OF AN OBJECT Using the middle boundary markers on the highlighting box, you can create a horizontal or vertical

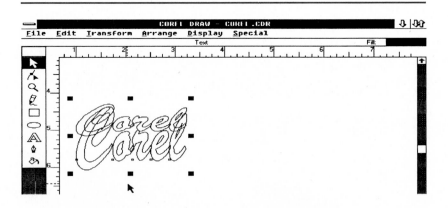

FIGURE 9-7   Retaining a copy of the original object while stretching

mirror image of an object. You have several choices of technique, depending on your needs. If, for example, you choose to retain a copy of the original object, you need to use the ⊙ key. If you choose to make the size of the mirror image an exact multiple of the original, you need to use (CTRL). You can just as easily decide not to copy the original object, or make the mirrored object a custom size. In every case, however, you will drag the *opposite* center boundary marker until it "flips" in the direction in which you want the mirror image to appear.

The following exercise assumes that you want to create a perfect horizontal mirror image of an object, like the one in Figure 9-9. In this figure, the original object is retained but neither the original nor the mirrored object is stretched. At the end of the exercise are suggestions for obtaining other results.

1. Select the text string "Corel" if it isn't selected already.

2. Position the mouse cursor over the left middle boundary marker and begin to drag this marker to the right.

3. As soon as the dotted outline box appears, press the ⊙ key on your numeric keypad once. The message "Leave Original" appears at the right side of the status line.

4. Press and hold (CTRL) and continue to drag the marker to the right. The (CTRL) key ensures that the size of the mirrored object will be an exact multiple of the original, in this case the identical size (100%).

5. When the dotted outline box "snaps" beside the original object and the status line reads "x scale: 100%," as in Figure 9-8, release the mouse button and then (CTRL). Corel DRAW! redraws the screen showing both the original and the mirrored object, as in Figure 9-9. The mirrored object is selected. If your text strings look different, select Undo and try the exercise again.

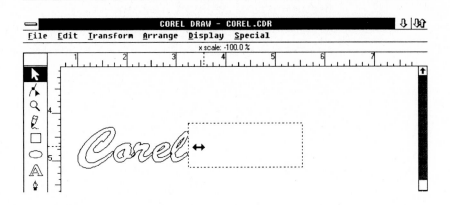

FIGURE 9-8 Creating a perfect horizontal mirror image of an object

6. Select Undo from the Edit menu to return the text string to its original unmirrored state.

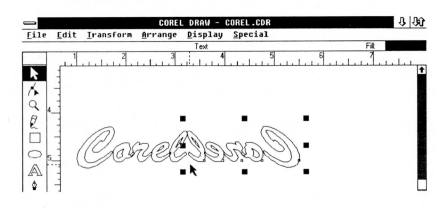

FIGURE 9-9 Retaining a copy of the original object while mirroring it

You can vary this exercise to achieve different results. For example, to create a vertical mirror image that appears beneath the object, drag the upper middle boundary marker downward. To make the mirror image double or triple the size of the original, keep stretching the mirror object using (CTRL). To make the mirror image a custom size, just drag the boundary marker *without* using (CTRL). If you want to create a mirror image only, without retaining the original object, do not use the (•) key.

If you want to create a mirror image appearing at a diagonal to the original object, you first need to be familiar with how to scale an object. See the section "Scaling an Object" later in this chapter for instructions.

Stretching and Mirroring an Object Using the Stretch & Mirror Command

If you find the use of the keyboard controls inconvenient, you can perform all of the possible stretch operations using the Stretch & Mirror command in the Transform menu. The dialog box that pops up when you select this command allows you to choose the direction of the stretch, specify the exact amount of stretching, retain a copy of the original object, and create horizontal or vertical mirror images.

STRETCHING AN OBJECT USING THE STRETCH & MIRROR COMMAND   Take another look at the COREL.CDR file that you created in the first part of this chapter. Then try the following exercise to become familiar with the Stretch & Mirror command.

1. Select the "Corel" text string and then click on the Stretch & Mirror command from the Transform menu. The dialog box shown in Figure 9-10 appears. The controls at the left side of the dialog box allow you to specify the direction and amount

of stretch in increments of 1/2%. The controls at the right allow you to mirror the object horizontally or vertically. The Leave Original checkbox controls whether you make a copy of the original object as you stretch or mirror it.

2. Set the numeric value next to Stretch Vertically to 175%, using either the scroll arrow or the keyboard, and then select OK. The text string has increased in height. Notice, however, that when you stretch an object using the Stretch & Mirror dialog box instead of the mouse, the stretched object occupies the same position as the original. If you want it to appear in another location, click on the object's outline and drag it to the desired location.

3. Select the Clear Transformations command from the Transform menu to return the object to its original size.

4. Select the Stretch & Mirror command again, set the Stretch Horizontally value to 175%, and then select OK. This time, the

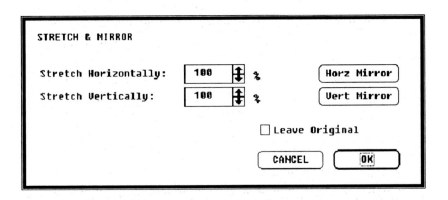

FIGURE 9-10   The Stretch & Mirror dialog box

text string increases in width. Notice that when you stretch an object using the Stretch & Mirror command and dialog box instead of the mouse, the stretched object occupies the same position as the original.

5. Clear the current transformation by selecting the Clear Transformations command in the Transform menu. Then select Stretch & Mirror again. This time, you will constrain the stretch of the image to an exact multiple of the original, as you did using (CTRL) and the mouse button.

6. Set the Stretch Vertically value to 300% and then click on the Leave Original checkbox to retain a copy of the original object.

7. Select OK to exit the dialog box. Corel DRAW! redisplays the original object against a vertically stretched image three times the size of the original. Notice that when you use the Stretch & Mirror dialog box for these operations, the stretched object is superimposed on the original and both objects share a common center point. If you want the stretched object to appear below or to the side of the original, you must drag its outline to the desired location.

8. To erase the transformed copy of the object so that only the unaltered original remains, select the Undo command from the Edit menu.

If you desire to erase the copy of the original object after a transformation, use the Undo command rather than the Clear Transformations command. If you use the Clear Transformations command, the object on the top layer is not erased, but instead becomes an exact copy of the original. The transformation is cleared, but not the object itself. As a result, what looks like one object on the screen is actually two objects.

MIRRORING AN OBJECT USING THE STRETCH & MIRROR COMMAND   The following exercise shows you how to create a vertical or horizontal mirror image using the Stretch & Mirror command instead of the mouse and keyboard. Once you create a mirror image, you can choose whether or not to retain a copy of the original object. You should continue working in a 1:1 viewing magnification for this exercise.

1. With the text string in the COREL.CDR file selected, select the Stretch & Mirror command.

2. Click on the Vert Mirror command button in the Stretch & Mirror dialog box. Notice that the value next to Stretch Vertically becomes a negative number automatically. Leave this value at -100%.

3. If a checkmark appears in the Leave Original checkbox, click on the checkbox again to remove it. Then select OK to exit the dialog box. A vertical mirror image of the object replaces the original, as shown in Figure 9-11.

4. Select Clear Transformations to return the object to its original state.

5. Select the Stretch & Mirror command again, but this time click on the Horz Mirror command button. Notice that the Stretch Horizontally value becomes a negative number automatically.

6. Select OK to exit the dialog box. A horizontal mirror image of the original text appears.

7. Select Clear Transformations to return the image to its original state.

You can customize the settings in the dialog box to achieve different results. If you want to merge a copy of the original object

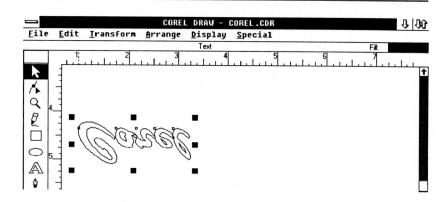

FIGURE 9-11   A vertical mirror image of the original object

with the mirrored version, for example, just click on the Leave Original checkbox. If you want to make the mirror image larger or smaller than the original, set the Stretch Horizontally value accordingly. Remember that this value must always be a negative number if it is to result in a mirror image.

Keep in mind, too, that when you use the Stretch & Mirror dialog box instead of the mouse to create a mirror image, the mirror image occupies the same position as the original. If you want the mirrored object to appear below or to the side of the original, you must drag its outline to the desired location.

SCALING AN OBJECT

As you have just seen, stretching an object involves changing its size in one direction (horizontal or vertical) only. When you *scale* an object, you change its size horizontally and vertically at the same time, thereby maintaining the same proportions and aspect ratio. You can scale an object interactively using the keyboard and mouse, or you can scale an object using the Stretch & Mirror dialog box instead.

Scaling an Object Interactively

If you prefer to work more spontaneously, without menus and dialog boxes, you can scale an object using the mouse and keyboard controls. Recall that when you stretch an object, you drag it by one of the *middle* boundary markers. Scaling an object is similar, except that you drag one of the *corner* boundary markers instead.

To practice scaling objects interactively, try this exercise:

1. Open the COREL.CDR file if it is not open already and select the "Corel" text string.

2. Position the mouse cursor directly over one of the corner boundary markers. You can scale from any corner but, for the sake of this exercise, use the lower-right corner marker. The cursor changes to a white cross, just as when you prepared to stretch an object.

3. Drag the lower right boundary marker diagonally downward. As you drag, the cursor changes to a four-way arrow, similar to the move arrow except that it is rotated diagonally, as in Figure 9-12. The original object appears to stay in the same place, but a dotted outline box follows the scaling cursor. The scaling cursor increases or decreases in size, depending on the direction in which you drag the marker. Figure 9-12 shows an object increasing in scale from the lower-right corner marker. Note that the status line displays the message "scale:" followed by a percentage value. This value tells you precisely how much larger or smaller you are making the object.

4. When the dotted outline box is the size you want the text string to be, release the mouse button. The selected object reappears in a scaled version.

5. Select Clear Transformations in the Transform menu or Undo in the Edit menu to return the object to its original size.

SCALING AN OBJECT IN INCREMENTS OF 100%   To scale an object in increments of 100% of its size, all you need to do is press and hold (CTRL) while scaling the object. Just as when you stretched objects using (CTRL), the dotted outline box does not move smoothly but instead "snaps" at each 100% increment. Likewise, the message in the status line changes only when you reach the next 100% increment. Remember to release the mouse button *before* you release (CTRL), or the increments will not be exact.

Keep in mind, too, that an object scaled to 200% of its original size takes up four times the area of the original object, not twice as much, because you are increasing both the height and width of the object by a factor of two.

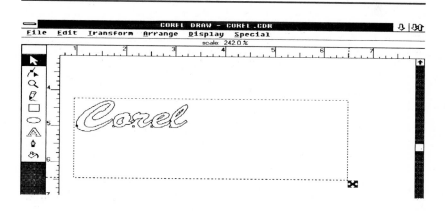

FIGURE 9-12   Dragging the scaling cursor to scale an object

RETAINING A COPY OF THE ORIGINAL OBJECT WHILE SCALING IT   To retain a copy of the object in its original location as you scale it, just press and release the (•) key on the numeric keypad as soon as you begin to scale the object. The status line displays the message, "Leave Original," just as when you leave a copy while stretching an object.

CREATING A DIAGONAL MIRROR IMAGE OF AN OBJECT   Using the corner boundary markers on the highlighting box, you can create a mirror image that appears at a *diagonal* to the original object. You have several choices of technique, depending on your needs. If you choose to retain a copy of the original object, you need to use the (•) key. If you choose to make the size of the mirror image an exact multiple of the original, you need to use (CTRL). You can just as easily decide not to copy the original object or to make the mirrored object a custom size. In every case, however, you drag the *opposite* corner boundary marker until it "flips" in the direction in which you want the mirror image to appear.

The following exercise assumes that you are going to create a perfect diagonal mirror image of an object like the one in Figure 9-13. In this figure, the original object remains, but neither the original nor the mirrored object is scaled beyond the original size. At the end of the exercise you will find suggestions for obtaining other results.

1. Select the text string "Corel," if it is not selected already.

2. Position the cursor over the boundary marker in the upper-left corner of the highlighting box and begin to drag the marker downward and to the right.

3. As soon as the dotted outline box appears, press the (•) key on your numeric keypad once to leave a copy of the original object.

The message "Leave Original" appears at the right side of the status line, as shown in Figure 9-13.

4. Press and hold (CTRL) and continue dragging the boundary marker until the dotted outline box "snaps" at a diagonal to the original object and the status line reads "scale: 100%." (The (CTRL) key ensures that the size of the mirrored object will be an exact multiple of the original, in this case 100%.)

5. Release the mouse button and then (CTRL). Corel DRAW! redraws the screen showing both the original and the mirrored object, as in Figure 9-14. The mirrored object is selected. If your text strings do not match this figure, try the exercise again.

6. Select Undo from the Edit menu to return the object to its original unmirrored state.

You can vary this exercise to achieve different results. For example, to place the mirror image at the upper-right corner of the original object, drag from the lower-left corner marker upward. To make the mirror image double or triple the size of the original, keep

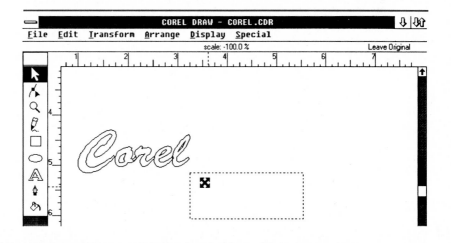

FIGURE 9-13   Creating a diagonal mirror image of an object while scaling

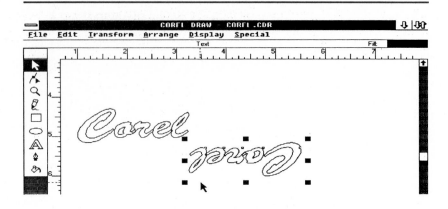

FIGURE 9-14   An original object with a diagonal mirror image

stretching the mirror object using (CTRL). To make the mirror image a custom size, just drag the opposite boundary marker without using (CTRL). If you want to create a mirror image only, without retaining the original object, do not use the (•) key.

Scaling an Object Using the Stretch & Mirror Command

If you find the use of keyboard controls inconvenient, you can perform all of the scaling operations precisely, using the Stretch & Mirror command in the Transform menu. You can specify the amount of scaling desired, retain a copy of the original object, and create mirror images that overlay the original. Work through the following exercise to become familiar with using the Stretch & Mirror command to scale an object.

1. With the COREL.CDR file open and in a 1:1 viewing magnification, select the "Corel" text string, and then select the Stretch & Mirror command from the Transform menu.

2. To scale an object, you need to set both the Stretch Horizontally and the Stretch Vertically values to the same number. Set both of these values to 150%, using either the scroll arrow or the keyboard.

3. Make certain that a checkmark does not appear in the Leave Original checkbox, and then select OK. The text string has increased in both height and width. Notice, however, that a scaled object created with the Stretch & Mirror command appears in the same location as the original and has the same center point. If you want the scaled object to appear elsewhere, move it to the desired location.

4. Select the Clear Transformations command from the Transform menu to return the object to its original size.

RETAINING A COPY OF THE ORIGINAL OBJECT USING THE STRETCH & MIRROR COMMAND

It is easy to make a copy of the original object from the Stretch & Mirror dialog box. Simply place a checkmark in the Leave Original checkbox before you exit the dialog box.

1. Select the text string "Corel" and then select the Stretch & Mirror command. This time, you will constrain the stretch of the image to an exact multiple of the original, as you did using (CTRL) and the mouse. You will also leave a copy of the original object in its original location.

2. Set the Stretch Vertically and Stretch Horizontally values to 200% and then click on the Leave Original checkbox to retain a copy of the original object.

3. Select OK to exit the dialog box. Corel DRAW! redisplays the original object along with a scaled text string four times the size of the original. Notice that when you copy and scale an object using the Stretch & Mirror dialog box, the scaled object is superimposed on the original and the two objects share a common center point. If you want the stretched object to appear elsewhere, you must move it by dragging its outline.

4. To erase the transformed copy of the object so that only the unaltered original remains, select the Undo command from the Edit menu. If you have moved the copy of the original, select it and press (DEL) to clear it.

ROTATING AN OBJECT

When you click on an object once using the Select tool, you can move, arrange, stretch, or scale it. In addition, the Select tool can *rotate* and *skew* an object. Rotating involves turning an object in a clockwise or counterclockwise direction, at an angle that you define. When you skew an object, on the other hand, you slant it toward the right, left, top, or bottom in order to create distortion or three-dimensional effects.

As with stretching and scaling, you can rotate an object interactively, using the mouse and keyboard, or you can use the Rotate & Skew command in the Transform Menu. If you feel more comfortable working with dialog boxes than with the mouse and keyboard, you can select the Rotate & Skew command after clicking on an object only once. To rotate an object interactively, however, you must either click on a selected object a second time, or double-click on an object that you have not yet selected.

Rotating an Object Interactively

Practice entering the interactive rotate/skew mode now, using the text string in the COREL.CDR file.

1. With the COREL.CDR file open and displayed at a 1:1 viewing magnification, click once on the outline of the text string. The normal highlighting box with its eight black boundary markers appears.

2. Click on the outline of the text string a second time. Corel DRAW! replaces the eight boundary markers with eight two-way arrows, as shown in Figure 9-15. You can drag any one of the corner arrows to rotate the object but, for the sake of this exercise, you will work with the upper-right corner arrow.

3. Position the mouse cursor over the two-way arrow in the upper-right corner of the rotate/skew highlighting box. When the cursor becomes a cross, press and hold the mouse button

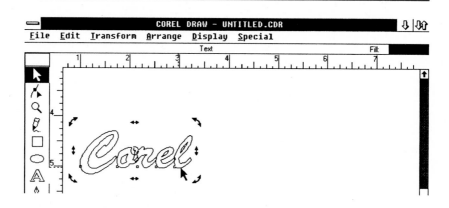

FIGURE 9-15   A selected object in rotate/skew mode

and drag the mouse in a counterclockwise direction. As soon as you begin to drag, the mouse cursor changes to an arc with arrows at either end. A dotted outline box representing the text string begins to rotate in a counterclockwise direction, as in Figure 9-16. Notice that the status line displays the angle of rotation as a positive number.

4. Continue to drag the corner highlighting arrow in a counter-clockwise direction until you have rotated the object more than 180 degrees. At that point, the status line begins to display a negative number for the angle of rotation, and the number begins to decrease from -180 downward. Use the number on the status line to inform yourself how far you have rotated a selected object.

5. Continue rotating the text object until the number becomes positive again. Release the mouse button when the status line indicates an angle of 17 degrees. Corel DRAW! redisplays the object at the selected angle of rotation, as shown in Figure 9-17.

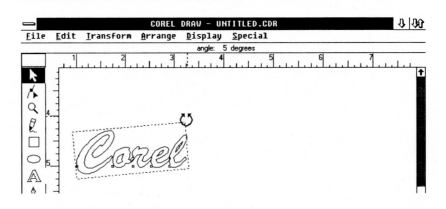

FIGURE 9-16   Rotating an object in a counterclockwise direction

6. Select the Clear Transformations command from the Transform menu to return the object to its original angle.

7. Drag the highlighting arrow in the upper-right corner again, but in a clockwise direction. The angle indicator on the status line displays a negative number until you rotate the text string more than 180 degrees. At that point, the number becomes positive and begins to decrease from 180 degrees downward.

8. Release the mouse button to redisplay the object at the new angle of rotation.

9. Select the Clear Transformations command from the Transform menu to return the object to its original angle.

note You may sometimes rotate an object several times in succession. The angle of rotation displayed in the status line, however, is an absolute value and refers to the amount of the *current* rotation, not to the cumulative angle.

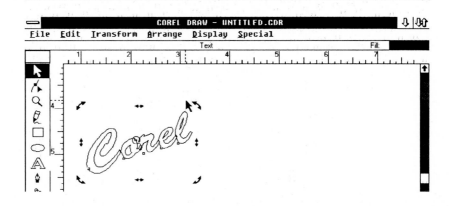

FIGURE 9-17   A selected object after rotation

Continue with the next section to find out how you can constrain rotation of an object to increments of 15-degree angles.

ROTATING AN OBJECT IN INCREMENTS OF 15 DE-GREES   As in almost every drawing or editing function of Corel DRAW!, you can use (CTRL) to constrain movement in the rotation of objects. Simply press and hold (CTRL) while dragging a corner arrow of the rotate/skew highlighting box, and the object rotates and "snaps" to successive 15-degree angles. The status line keeps track of the angle of rotation. As always, remember to release the mouse button before you release (CTRL), or you will not constrain the angle of rotation. You will use the constrain feature in the following exercise.

1. Double-click on the text string if it is not selected already or click once on its outline if it is selected. The two-way arrows appear to show that you are in the rotate/skew mode.

2. Position the cursor over the upper-right corner highlighting arrow until the cursor turns into a cross. Press and hold the (CTRL) key and drag the highlighting arrow in the desired direction. Notice that the dotted rectangular box does not follow the rotation cursor continuously; instead, it "snaps" each time you reach an angle that is a multiple of 15 degrees.

3. When you reach the desired angle, release the mouse button first, and then release (CTRL). The object redisplays at the new angle of rotation.

4. Select Clear Transformations from the Transform menu to return the object to its original angle.

RETAINING A COPY OF AN ORIGINAL OBJECT   I f you like to experiment with design, you may find it useful to make

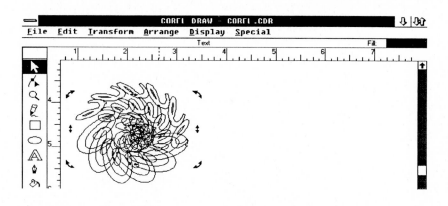

FIGURE 9-18   A text pinwheel created by rotating and
retaining a copy of a text string repeatedly

a copy of the original object as you rotate it. Figure 9-18 illustrates one design effect you can achieve easily. This text pinwheel, suitable for desktop publishing applications, was created by rotating a text string in increments of 30 degrees and copying the original each time.

You can also retain a copy of the original object using (CTRL), but this operation requires a bit more coordination. Try this technique now:

1. With the COREL.CDR file open and in a 1:1 viewing magnification, click on the text string "Corel" if it is already selected, or double-click if it is not selected. The rotate/skew highlighting arrows appear.

2. Position the mouse cursor over the upper-right highlighting arrow marker and begin to drag this marker upward. As soon as the dotted outline box appears, press the (+) key on your numeric keypad once to leave a copy of the original.

3. Press and hold (CTRL) and continue dragging the arrow marker upward until the status line reads "angle: 30 degrees."

4. Release the mouse button and then the (CTRL) key. The screen displays both the original and the rotated object, as shown in Figure 9-19.

5. Continue copying and rotating the text strings four more times at the same angle to create the design shown in Figure 9-18. Then undo your changes to the original text string before going further.

CHANGING THE CENTER OF AN OBJECT'S ROTATION

Look at an object on your screen when it is in rotate/skew mode. In the center of the object is a small dot surrounded by a circle. This graphic aid appears every time you activate the rotate/skew mode and represents the center of rotation of an object. The object turns on this axis as you rotate it. The center of rotation does not have to be the center of the object, however. If you want

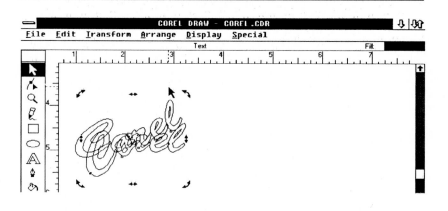

FIGURE 9-19   Retaining a copy of the original object while rotating

the object to rotate on a different axis, you can alter the center of rotation freely by dragging the center of rotation symbol to the desired location using the mouse. In the following exercise, you will create a simple text design that involves changing the center of a text string's rotation.

1. Select the text string if it is not selected already and move it to the center of the display. Click on its outlines again to access the rotate/skew mode.

2. When the rotate/skew highlighting box appears, position the mouse cursor over the center of rotation symbol until it becomes a cross. Drag the rotation symbol to the upper-right corner of the rotate/skew highlighting box, as shown in Figure 9-20. Then release the mouse button.

3. Position the mouse cursor over any one of the corner highlighting arrows and begin dragging the arrow in a clockwise direction. As soon as the dotted outline box appears, press the ⊙ key

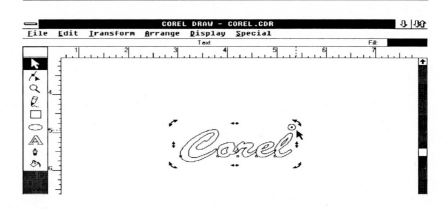

FIGURE 9-20   Relocating an object's center of rotation to a corner of the highlighting box

on your numeric keypad once to leave a copy of the original. Notice that because you have changed the center of rotation, the text string turns on its end rather than relative to its center point.

4. Press and hold (CTRL) and continue dragging the marker until the status line shows that you have rotated the text string by -90 degrees.

5. Release the mouse button first, and then (CTRL). Both the original object and the rotated object display at 90-degree angles to one another.

6. Repeat this process two more times, until you have a text design similar to the one in Figure 9-21. To make all the text strings behave as though they were one object, click on the Select All

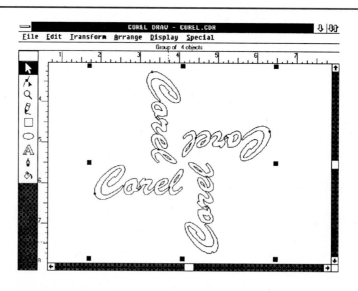

FIGURE 9-21   A text design created by rotating and copying an object with an altered center of rotation

command in the Edit menu, group the text strings, and then reposition the group to the center of the display.

7. Save this figure as 4CORNERS.CDR.

8. Clear the screen by selecting New from the File menu.

Your new center of rotation does not have to be a highlighting arrow; you can relocate the center anywhere within the highlighting box. But a corner or boundary of the selected object often proves to be a convenient "handle" when you are performing rotations.

Rotating an Object Using the Rotate & Skew Command

If you find the use of the keyboard controls inconvenient, you can perform all of the preceding rotation operations with precision using the Rotate & Skew command in the Transform menu. You can select this command regardless of whether the normal highlighting box or the rotate/skew highlighting box is visible around a selected object. Perform the following brief exercise to familiarize yourself with the workings of the Rotate & Skew dialog box.

1. Open the COREL.CDR file and set the viewing magnification to 1:1. Click once on the text string to select it.

2. Select the Rotate & Skew command from the Transform menu. The Rotate & Skew dialog box appears as in Figure 9-22.

3. Enter a number in the numeric entry box next to "Rotation Angle:". You can enter a number either by scrolling in increments of 5 degrees or by clicking on the numeric entry box and typing in a number in increments of 1 degree. Note that as soon as you enter a number in this box, the Skew Horizontally and

Skew Vertically entry boxes become unavailable for selection. You cannot skew and rotate an object at the same time.

4. If desired, click on the Leave Original checkbox to make a copy of the original object as you rotate it.

5. Select OK to exit the dialog box and see the results of your settings. When you are finished, select Undo to return the original object to its former angle. Leave this image on the screen for the next exercise.

That's all there is to rotating an object at the angle and axis of your choice. You can leave a copy of the original object while rotating it, just as when you copy an object that you are stretching or scaling. In the next section, you will practice skewing an object to achieve interesting distortion effects.

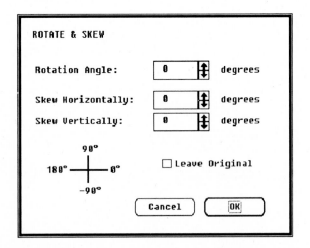

FIGURE 9-22   The Rotate & Skew dialog box

SKEWING AN OBJECT

When you *skew* an object, you slant and distort it at a horizontal or vertical angle, thus warping its appearance. This technique can be useful for creating three-dimensional or surrealistic effects. As with the other techniques you have learned in this chapter, you can skew an object either interactively or using the controls in the Rotate & Skew dialog box.

Skewing an Object Interactively

When you wanted to rotate objects in the preceding exercises, you dragged one corner highlighting arrow when the object was in rotate/skew mode. To skew an object, you drag one of the middle highlighting arrows along the sides of the rotate/skew highlighting box. You can skew an object horizontally or vertically, at angles of up to 75 degrees in either direction. Practice skewing the text string in the COREL.CDR file in the following exercise.

1. With the COREL.CDR file open and in a 1:1 viewing magnification, select the "Corel" text string. Then click a second time anywhere on its outline to enter the rotate/skew mode.

2. To begin skewing the object horizontally, position the mouse cursor directly over the upper middle highlighting arrow and drag it to the right. The mouse cursor changes to two half arrows pointing in opposite directions, and a dotted outline box slants to the right, the direction you are moving your mouse, as shown in Figure 9-23. The status line keeps track of the current angle of horizontal skew.

3. When you reach the desired skewing angle, release the mouse button. Corel DRAW! redisplays the object as you have skewed it, as shown in Figure 9-24.

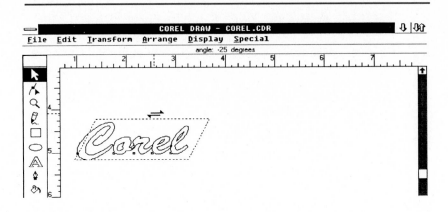

FIGURE 9-23 Skewing an object to the right

4. Select Clear Transformations from the Transform menu to return the object to its original unskewed state.

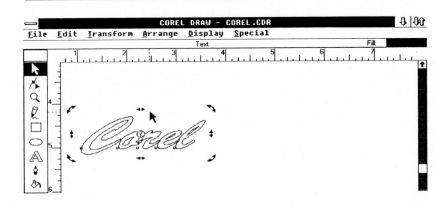

FIGURE 9-24 An object skewed horizontally to the right

5. Practice different angles of horizontal skewing. You can skew an object up to 75 degrees to the right or left. If you drag one of the middle highlighting arrows along the left or right *side* of the highlighting box, you can skew the object in a vertical direction.

6. When you feel comfortable with basic skewing operations, select Clear Transformations from the Transform menu. Leave the text string on the screen for the next exercise.

SKEWING AN OBJECT IN INCREMENTS OF 15 DE-GREES

Once again, you can use (CTRL) to introduce an extra measure of precision to the interactive transformation of objects. When skewing an object, pressing and holding (CTRL) forces the object to skew in increments of 15 degrees. Try using this constraint feature now.

1. Select the text string "Corel" and enter the rotate/skew mode.

2. Position the mouse cursor over the upper middle highlighting arrow, press and hold (CTRL), and begin dragging the mouse to the right or left as desired. The mouse cursor changes to the skew cursor, and the dotted outline box "snaps" in the desired direction in increments of 15 degrees.

3. When you reach the desired angle, release the mouse button first, and then release (CTRL). If you release (CTRL) first, you might not constrain the skewing operation to a 15-degree increment.

4. Select Clear Transformations from the Transform menu to return the skewed object to its original state. Leave the text string on the screen.

**RETAINING A COPY OF THE ORIGINAL OBJECT WHILE
SKEWING** For an interesting design effect, you can skew an
object and then make a copy of the original. As you will see in the
following exercise, you can then position the skewed object behind
the original to make it seem like a shadow.

1. Select the "Corel" text string and enter rotate/skew mode.

2. Position the mouse cursor over the upper-middle highlighting
    arrow and begin dragging the arrow to the right. As soon as the
    dotted outline box appears, press the (+) key on your numeric
    keypad to leave a copy of the original.

3. Press and hold (CTRL) and continue dragging the marker until
    the status line shows a -60-degree skewing angle.

4. Release the mouse button first and then release (CTRL). The
    skewed object, which is selected automatically, appears on top
    of the copy of the original, as in Figure 9-25.

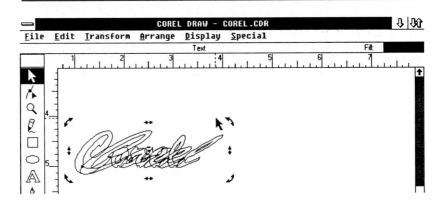

FIGURE 9-25   Retaining a copy of an object while skewing

5. Select the To Back command from the Arrange menu to position the skewed object behind the unskewed original.

6. You can manipulate the skewed object like any other object. Click once on its outline to toggle back to the select mode, and then scale it to a smaller size by dragging the upper-right corner boundary marker of the highlighting box.

7. Adjust the viewing magnification to ALL and activate the preview window to obtain a WYSIWYG display of the original object and its skewed "shadow." Your preview should look roughly similar to Figure 9-26. When you learn about filling objects in Chapter 15, you can refine the appearance of skewed background images to create a clearer "shadow" than this one.

8. To remove the transformed copy of the object so that only the unaltered original remains, select the Undo command from the Edit menu.

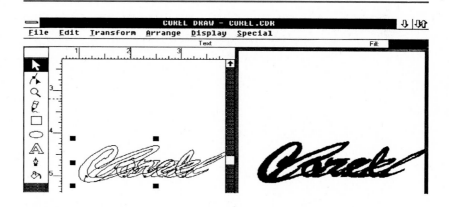

FIGURE 9-26   A "shadow" created by skewing and resizing an object

Skewing an Object Using the Rotate & Skew Command

If you find the use of keyboard controls inconvenient, you can perform all of the possible skewing operations using the Rotate & Skew command in the Transform menu. You can select this command regardless of whether the normal highlighting box or the rotate/skew highlighting box is visible around a selected object. Perform the following brief exercise to familiarize yourself with using the Rotate & Skew command to skew an object.

1. Open the COREL.CDR file and set the viewing magnification to 1:1. Click once on the text string to select it.

2. Select the Rotate & Skew command from the Transform menu. The Rotate & Skew dialog box appears.

3. First, skew the text object horizontally. Enter a number in the numeric entry box next to "Skew Horizontally:." You can enter a number either by scrolling in increments of 5 degrees or by clicking on the numeric entry box and typing in a number in increments of 1 degree. Only values between -75 and 75 degrees are valid. You will recall that a positive number results in skewing to the left, while a negative number results in skewing to the right.

4. If desired, click on the Leave Original checkbox to make a copy of the original object as you rotate it.

5. Select OK to exit the dialog box and see the results of your settings. When you are finished, select Undo to return the original object to its former angle (and erase the copy, if you have made one).

6. Select the Rotate & Skew command from the Transform menu once more. This time, enter a number in the numeric entry box

next to "Skew Vertically:." You can adjust this value in the same way that you adjusted the "Skew Horizontally:" value in step 3.

7. Select OK to exit the dialog box and see the results of your settings. When you are finished, select Clear Transformations from the Transform menu to return the original object to its former angle.

In the final section of this chapter, you will have the opportunity to combine additional transformation techniques and apply your most recently performed operation to other objects in a drawing.

REPEATING A TRANSFORMATION

Corel DRAW! stores the most recently performed transformation in memory until you quit the current session. You can save design and drawing time by automatically repeating your most recent stretch, scale, rotate, or skew operation on a different object or set of objects. Just remember that the second object, the one on which you wish to repeat the transformation, must exist on the screen *before* you perform the transformation the first time. If you perform a transformation and then create another object and try to repeat that transformation on it, nothing happens. Perform the following brief exercise to see how this feature can work for you.

1. With the COREL.CDR file open and in a 1:1 viewing magnification, select the Ellipse tool ⬭ and draw a long, narrow ellipse next to the "Corel" text string.

2. Press the spacebar to activate the Select tool. Select the "Corel" text string and then scale the text string to 200% using the lower right corner boundary marker and (CTRL). Leave a copy of the original using the ⊙ key, as described earlier in this chapter.

3. Press the spacebar to activate the Select tool and then select the ellipse that you drew next to the text string.

4. Select the Repeat command from the Edit menu or press the shortcut keyboard combination (CTRL-R). Corel DRAW! scales the ellipse to 200%, leaving a copy of the original, as shown in Figure 9-27. If the objects extend beyond your viewing window, adjust viewing magnification to ALL.

5. Select New from the File menu to clear the screen. Do not save any changes to your work.

You have seen how stretching, scaling, rotating, and skewing objects can lead to creative ideas for advanced designs. Continue

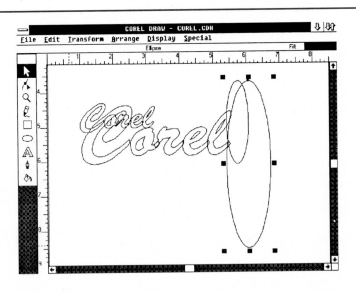

FIGURE 9-27   Repeating a transformation on a different object

practicing some of the techniques you have learned and see what original ideas you can come up with on your own. Chapter 20, "Combining Corel DRAW! Features to Create Special Effects," will expand on these and other techniques and provide additional stimulation for your imagination.

SUMMARY

You can use the Select tool not only to move and rearrange selected objects, but also to edit their appearance, or transform them. Transformative operations you can perform with the Select tool include stretching, scaling, rotating, skewing, and creating mirror images of objects. You can perform each of these five functions interactively using the mouse and keyboard, or you can use the Stretch & Mirror command in the Transform menu.

You can stretch or scale an object when you have clicked on it once to select it. To stretch an object in one direction, you drag one of the middle boundary markers that surround a selected object. Other options include stretching an object in exact multiples of the original size, making a copy of the original object as you stretch it, and creating a horizontal or vertical mirror image.

To scale an object, you drag one of the four corner boundary markers that surround a selected object. When you scale an object, you increase its width and height at the same time. Other options include scaling an object in exact multiples of its original dimensions, making a copy of the original unscaled object, and creating a diagonal mirror image.

When you click on a selected object's outline a second time, you enter the rotate/skew mode of the Select tool. Instead of eight rectangular boundary markers, eight two-way arrows appear around the highlighting box of the object. In this mode you can rotate or skew the object. Again, you can choose between the interactive method (using the mouse and keyboard) and the menu command and dialog box method.

To rotate an object, you drag it by one of the four corner arrows that make up the rotate/skew highlighting box. You can rotate a selected object in any direction up to 360 degrees.

When you rotate more than 180 degrees in a counterclockwise direction at one time, the status line displays the angle degree as a negative number. Other options include constraining rotation to increments of 15-degree angles, retaining a copy of the original object, and changing the center or axis of an object's rotation.

Skewing an object involves slanting it at a horizontal or vertical angle. You can skew an object horizontally or vertically in Corel DRAW! by up to 75 degrees in either direction. To skew a selected object, drag one of the four middle two-way arrows that make up the object's highlighting box in rotate/skew mode. Other options you can choose are constraining skewing to increments of 15-degree angles and retaining a copy of the original object.

To return a transformed object to its original state at any time, select the Clear Transformations command from the Transform menu. To repeat the most recently performed transformation on an object, select that object, and then select the Repeat command in the Edit menu or press (CTRL-R).

chapter **10**

SHAPING LINES, CURVES, RECTANGLES, AND ELLIPSES

About the Shaping Tool
Selecting Objects with the Shaping Tool
Shaping Lines and Curves
Shaping Rectangles and Squares
Shaping Ellipses and Circles

The power to reshape any object to the limits of the imagination is at the very heart of Corel DRAW! Using the Shaping tool, you can change any type of object into an image that can showcase your creativity.

The Shaping tool ⟨⟨🖈⟩⟩ , the second tool in the Corel DRAW! toolbox, allows you to change the underlying shape of an object. Although the Select tool, in transformation mode, allows you to resize, rotate, or skew an object, it leaves the fundamental shape of the object intact. When you edit an object with the Shaping tool, however, it becomes something quite different from what you originally drew.

You can apply the Shaping tool to all object types: lines and curves, rectangles and squares, ellipses and circles, text, and pixel-based (bitmapped) graphics. Shaping functions for text and bitmapped graphics, however, are part of a broader range of editing functions that apply specifically to those object types. You will find information specifically about shaping text in Chapter 11, "Shaping and Editing Text," and about shaping curves to fit traced bitmaps in Chapter 17, "Tracing and Working with Bitmapped Images." This chapter covers techniques for shaping lines, curves, rectangles, and ellipses.

ABOUT THE SHAPING TOOL

The Shaping tool performs several different functions, depending on the kind of object to which you apply it. You take advantage of the most powerful capabilities of the Shaping tool when you use it to edit curves, but it has specific effects on other kinds of object types as well.

When you are working with lines and curves, the Shaping tool is at its most versatile. You can manipulate single curve points (nodes) interactively, move single or multiple curve segments, control the angle of movement, and add or delete curve points in order to exercise greater control over the degree of curvature. You can break apart or join segments of a curve and change one type of node into another. You can even convert curves to straight lines and back again.

When you apply the Shaping tool to rectangles and squares, you can round the corners of a rectangle and turn rotated, stretched, or skewed rectangles into near-ellipses and circles. When you apply the Shaping tool to ellipses and circles, you can create pie-shaped wedges or arcs. If these shaping options for rectangles and ellipses seem limited, you will be pleased to learn that you can convert any object in Corel DRAW! to curves—and then proceed to apply the most advanced shaping techniques to it.

SELECTING OBJECTS WITH THE SHAPING TOOL

You must select an object with the Shaping tool before you can edit it. Corel DRAW! allows you to select only one object with the Shaping tool at a time. Although the Shaping tool affects each type of object in a different way, the basic steps involved in editing are similar with all object types. To select an object for editing,

1. Activate the Shaping tool ⬚ by clicking on it. The cursor turns into a thick arrowhead ⬚ as soon as you move it away from the toolbox and toward the page area.

2. If the object you want to work with is already selected, its nodes enlarge in size automatically as soon as you select the Shaping tool, and the highlighting box around the object disappears. The number of nodes may vary, depending on the object type and (in the case of curves) the way your hand moved when you drew it. If the object you want to work with is not selected, click on any point of the object's outline with the arrowhead cursor. Enlarged nodes appear on the object, while the status line shows the object type and information about the nodes on the object. If the selected object has multiple nodes, the first node appears larger than the others, as in the example in Figure 10-1. The first node is the one furthest to the left on lines and curves, the one at the top left corner in rectangles, and at the top- or bottommost point on ellipses.

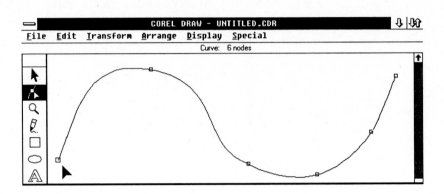

FIGURE 10-1   Selecting an object with the Shaping tool

3. Refer to the chapter that covers your object type for more help on how to edit the shape of that object.

If multiple objects were selected prior to activating the Shaping tool, Corel DRAW! automatically deselects all of them, and you must select a single object to edit with the Shaping tool. If you try to apply the Shaping tool to grouped objects, the outlines of the objects become dotted and your mouse actions have no effect. The only time you can edit more than one object simultaneously is when you *combine* the objects prior to selecting the Shaping tool. You will see examples of editing combined objects in the "Shaping Lines and Curves" section of this chapter.

To deselect an object that you are editing with the Shaping tool, either click on the outline of a different object, or select another drawing tool from the Corel DRAW! toolbox.

The following sections show you how to use the Shaping tool to edit specific types of objects. These sections follow the order of the drawing tools in the Corel DRAW! toolbox: lines and curves, rectangles, and ellipses.

SHAPING LINES AND CURVES

The Shaping tool is at its most powerful when you use it to edit a curve. Ways in which you can reshape a curve include moving, adding, or deleting nodes, changing node shape, breaking nodes apart or joining them together, and manipulating the control points that define the shape of a curve segment.

You may recall that every object in Corel DRAW! has nodes, which appear when you first draw an object and become enlarged when you select it with the Shaping tool. Nodes on a curve (shown in Figure 10-1) are the points through which a curve passes, and each node is associated with the curve segment that immediately precedes it. The *control points* that appear when you select a single node with the Shaping tool (see Figure 10-5) determine the curvature of the node and of the curve segments on either side of it. You can use the Shaping tool to manipulate both nodes and curves.

Your options for shaping straight lines with the Shaping tool are mucn more limited than for curves; lines have no angles of curvature and, therefore, no control points that you can manipulate. When you edit a line segment with the Shaping tool, you can only move the nodes or stretch or diminish the length of the line segment. In the course of creating and editing a complex curve object, however, you often need to fuse curve and line segments, change curves into lines, or turn lines into curves. The Shaping tool allows you to do all of these things, and so a discussion of shaping both kinds of freehand objects belongs together.

Selecting a Line or Curve for Shaping

You must select a line or curve with the Shaping tool before you can begin to manipulate its nodes. The status line provides you with information about the number of nodes in the object.

In the following exercise, you will draw a straight line and a freehand curve and then select each object in turn. Turn off the Snap To Grid and Show Rulers options before you begin this exercise.

1. Activate the Magnification tool 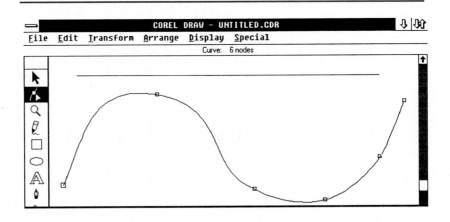 and set your viewing magnification to 1:1. Then, select the Freehand tool and draw a straight horizontal line across the top half of the screen, as shown in Figure 10-2.

2. Below the line, draw a Freehand curve in a horizontal "S" shape. Small nodes appear on the curve.

3. Select the Shaping tool. The cursor turns into an arrowhead, and the S-curve is automatically selected, because it was the last object you drew. The nodes of the S-curve increase in size, and the status line displays the number of the nodes in the curve, as shown in Figure 10-2. The number of nodes in your curve may differ from the number in the figure. Notice that the node furthest to the left appears larger in size than the others, because it is the first node of the curve.

FIGURE 10-2   Displaying the number of nodes in a curve

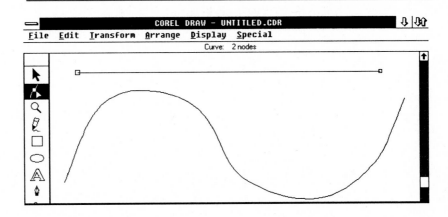

FIGURE 10-3   Displaying the number of nodes in a line

4. To deselect the S-curve and select the line, simply click on any point of the line with the Shaping tool. Only two nodes appear on the line, one at each end. Again, the node furthest to the left is larger. The status line displays the message, "Curve: 2 nodes," as shown in Figure 10-3. (As far as the Shaping tool is concerned, every line has the potential of becoming a curve.)

5. Clear the screen before continuing by selecting New from the File menu. Do not save your work.

Your next step in shaping a selected line or curve is to select one or more of its nodes. Continue with the next section to explore the choices open to you.

Selecting Nodes of a Line or Curve

Although you can shape only one curve or line at a time, you can select and shape either single or multiple nodes. The shaping options available to you depend on whether you select one node or several. You can reshape a single curve node interactively in one of two ways: by dragging the node itself or by dragging the control points that appear when you select the node. Moving a node stretches and resizes the associated curve segment(s), but does not allow you to change the angle of curvature. Dragging the control points, on the other hand, allows you to change both the angle of curvature at the node and the shape of the associated curve segment(s). When you select multiple nodes, you can move only the nodes, not their control points; as a result, you reshape all of the selected segments in the same way.

 No control points are available for any straight line segment.

In general, you should select single nodes when you need to fine-tune a curve, and multiple nodes when you need to move or reshape several segments in the same way without changing their angle of curvature.

The exercises in the following sections guide you through the available techniques for selecting nodes in preparation for moving or editing them. Along the way, you will become familiar with the different types of nodes that Corel DRAW! generates and how they indicate the shape of a particular curve. Nodes of a straight line segment are always cusp nodes and contain no control points. They become important only when you begin adding or deleting nodes or changing a line into a curve. You will concentrate on working with curves in the next few sections.

SELECTING AND DESELECTING SINGLE NODES AND IDENTIFYING NODE TYPE   When you click on a single curve node, the status line provides information about the type of node you have selected. There are three node types: cusp, smooth, and symmetrical. Each type of node indicates what will happen when you drag the control points to reshape a curve. In the following exercise, you will practice selecting and deselecting single nodes in the sample file FACE.CDR that came with your software.

1. Open the sample file FACE.CDR and magnify only the area that contains the objects representing the left eye, eyebrow, and eyelashes, as shown in Figure 10-4.

2. With the Shaping tool selected, click anywhere on the outline of the curve object that represents the eyelashes (see Figure 10-4). The status line indicates that this curve object contains 12 nodes.

3. Click on the node furthest to the left on the selected curve object. The node becomes a black filled square, and two control points—tiny black rectangles connected to the node by dotted

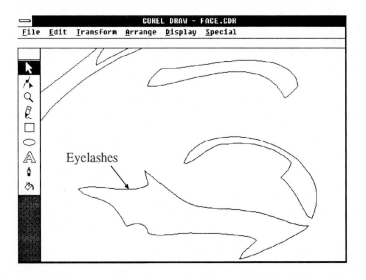

FIGURE 10-4   Magnifying the eye area of FACE.CDR

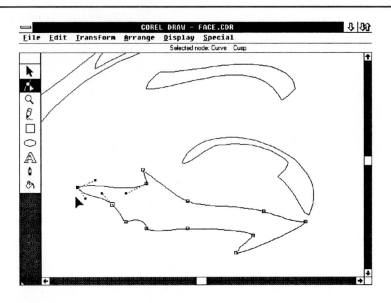

FIGURE 10-5   Selecting a single node and displaying control points

lines—pop out, as shown in Figure 10-5. (You will also see a control point extending from each of the nodes on either side of the selected node.) The messages "Selected node: Curve" and "Cusp" appear on the status line. "Cusp" refers to the node type, which you will learn about shortly.

4. Click on each node in turn to select it and deselect the previous node. Each time you select a node, control points pop out, and the status line tells you what type of node you have selected. Notice that some of the nodes are cusp nodes, while others are smooth.

5. Leave this magnified view of FACE.CDR on the screen for the next exercise.

Corel DRAW! generates three different kinds of nodes when you draw lines and curves: cusp nodes, smooth nodes, and symmetrical nodes. These names describe both the curvature at the node and, in the case of curve objects, the way you can shape the node. Straight lines contain only cusp nodes, while curves can contain all three node types.

Cusp Nodes   Cusp nodes occur at the end point of a line or curve or at a sharp change of direction in a curve. When you edit the control points of a cusp node, you can alter the curvature of the segment that precedes the node without affecting the segment that follows it.

Smooth Nodes   Smooth nodes occur at smooth changes in direction of a curve. When you edit a smooth node, you alter the shape and direction of both the segment preceding and the segment following the node. The curvature of the two segments do not change in identical degrees, however.

Symmetrical Nodes   Symmetrical nodes occur where the segments, preceding and following the node, curve in identical ways. (Symmetrical nodes occur less frequently than other node types in freehand drawing, but you can change any node type to symmetrical using the Node Edit menu, which you will learn about shortly.) When you edit a symmetrical node, you alter the shape and direction of the curve segments before and after the node in identical ways.

You can always change the node type by using the pop-up Node Edit menu, as you will see shortly. But you can also control whether the majority of nodes you generate during the freehand drawing process are smooth or cusped. To generate mostly cusped nodes (and create more jagged curves), select the Preferences command in the Special menu and set the Corner Threshold option in the Preferences dialog box to 3 pixels or lower. To generate mostly smooth nodes and create smoother curves, set the Corner Threshold option to 8 pixels or higher.

You will become familiar with techniques for moving control points in a moment. First, finish the next section to learn how to select more than one node at a time.

SELECTING AND DESELECTING MULTIPLE NODES   You select multiple nodes with the Shaping tool in the same way that you select multiple objects with the Select tool, using either (SHIFT) or the marquee technique. When multiple nodes are selected, you are unable to move control points to shape your object. You can only move the nodes and reshape their associated curve segments in a more limited way. Review the selection techniques in the following brief exercise.

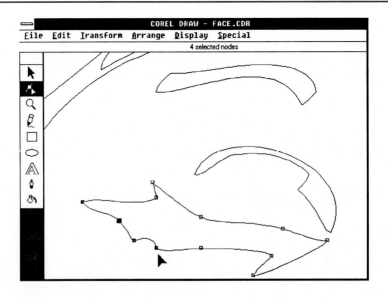

FIGURE 10-6   Curve with multiple nodes selected

1. Select the node that the cursor is pointing to in Figure 10-6. While pressing and holding (SHIFT), select three additional nodes to the left of the first node. As in Figure 10-6, the nodes turn dark but display no control points, and the status line changes to show the total number of nodes you have selected.

2. Deselect the node furthest to the right of the selected group by pressing and holding (SHIFT) and then clicking on the node with the Shaping tool. The other nodes remain selected.

3. Deselect all of the selected nodes by clicking on any white space. The curve object itself remains selected for further work with the Shaping tool, however.

4. Select the six nodes at the left side of the eyelashes by drawing a marquee around them, as shown in Figure 10-7. The selected nodes turn dark after you release the mouse button, and the status line tells you how many nodes you have selected.

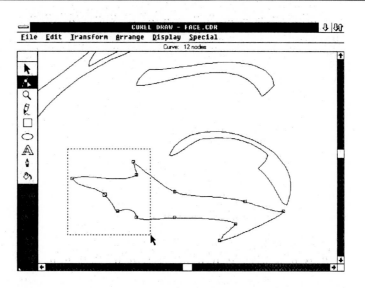

FIGURE 10-7   Selecting multiple nodes with the marquee

5. Deselect one node at a time using (SHIFT) and the mouse button, or deselect all of the nodes by clicking on any other node or on any white space.

6. When you have finished, clear the screen by selecting New from the File menu. Do not save the changes you have made.

Now that you are familiar with how to select nodes, you are ready to begin editing a curve object. You can edit a curve by moving nodes and control points interactively or by selecting options in a pop-up Node Edit menu. The next portion of the chapter discusses the first of these methods.

Moving Nodes and Control Points

You can reshape a curve interactively in one of two ways: by moving one or more nodes or by manipulating the control points of a single node. You can move any number of nodes, but in order to work with control points, you can select only one node at a time.

You move nodes when your aim is to stretch, shrink, or move the curve segments on either side of a node. The angle of curvature at selected nodes doesn't change as you move them, because the control points move along with the nodes. The end result of moving nodes is a limited reshaping of the selected area of the curve object.

In general, your best strategy when reshaping curves is to move the nodes first. If just repositioning the nodes does not yield satisfactory results, you can fine-tune the shape of a curve by manipulating the control points of one or more nodes. When you drag control points to reshape a curve, you affect both the angle of curvature at the node and the shape of the curve segment on one or both sides of the node. The effects of this kind of reshaping are much more dramatic. The way you move control points is determined by the type of node you select.

Try the exercises in each of the following sections to practice moving single or multiple nodes, manipulating control points, and constraining node movement to 90-degree increments.

MOVING A SINGLE NODE   To move a single node, you simply select the curve and then select and drag the node in the desired direction. In the following exercise, you will draw a wave-form curve, select a node, and move the node to reshape the curve.

1. To prepare for the exercise, make sure that the Snap To Grid and Show Rulers options are turned off. Check to see that all of the settings in the Lines & Curves section of the Preferences dialog box are at 5 pixels. (This will result in curves with a fairly even distribution of cusp and smooth nodes.) Set viewing magnification to a 1:1 ratio.

2. Select the Freehand tool and draw a wave-form curve similar to the one in Figure 10-8. Don't be concerned if your curve is shaped a little differently.

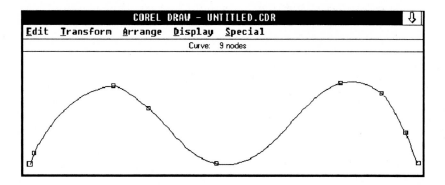

FIGURE 10-8   Drawing a wave-form curve

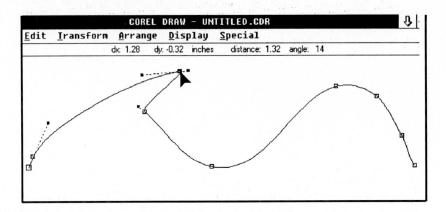

FIGURE 10-9   Moving a single selected node

3. Select the Shaping tool and then select a node near the crest of one of the curves. Elongate this curve by dragging the node (not the control points) upward and to the right, as shown in Figure 10-9. As you begin to move the node, the status line provides information about *dx*- and *dy*-coordinates, the distance you have traveled, and the angle of movement relative to the starting point. Release the mouse button when you are satisfied with the stretch of your curve.

4. Select Undo from the Edit menu to return the curve to its original shape. Leave this curve on the screen for now. You can use it to move multiple nodes in the next exercise.

MOVING MULTIPLE NODES   There are many cases in which you might choose to move multiple nodes instead of a single node at a time. You might move multiple adjacent nodes, for example, if you need to reposition an entire section of a curve at one time. Or you might select nonadjacent nodes and move them all in the same direction for special design effects. Whatever the case, all you need do is select the nodes and drag them.

1. Using the mouse button and (**SHIFT**), select one node near the beginning of your wave-form curve and one near the end. Again, do not be concerned if the nodes in your curve are in different positions from the nodes in the figure. The process of freehand drawing is so complex that two people rarely produce the same results.

2. Drag one of the nodes downward and to the right. Even though the two selected nodes are separated by several others, they move at the same angle and over the same distance, as shown in Figure 10-10.

3. Release the mouse button when you are finished. Select Undo from the Edit menu to return the curve object to its former shape.

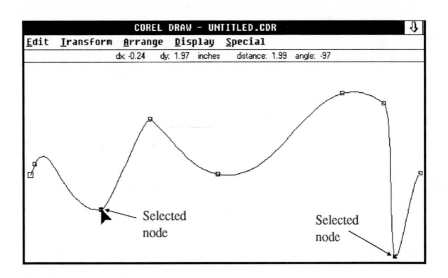

FIGURE 10-10   Moving multiple selected nodes

If you prefer to draft even the most "creative-looking" freehand curves with precision, you may wish to exercise greater control over the angle at which you move nodes. The next section will show you how to move nodes with precision.

CONSTRAINING NODE MOVEMENT TO 90-DEGREE ANGLES You have the option of moving nodes and their associated curve segments in increments of 90 degrees relative to your starting point. You use the now-familiar (CTRL) key to achieve this kind of precise movement.

1. Select the same two nodes you worked with in the preceding section, press and hold (CTRL), and drag one of the nodes to the left. At first the two nodes do not seem to move at all; then, they "snap" at a 90-degree angle from their starting point. The status line on your screen reflects this precise angle of movement, as in Figure 10-11.

2. Release the mouse button when you reach the desired angle. Select New from the File menu to clear the curve from the screen. Do not save your changes.

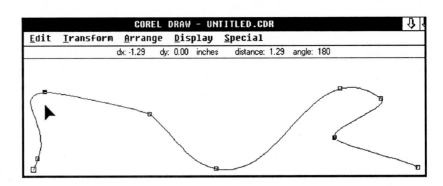

FIGURE 10-11   Moving multiple nodes by increments of 90-degree angles

What if you have moved one or more nodes every which way but you are still not satisfied with the shape of the curve segments on either side of the node? In the next section you will fine-tune your curves by manipulating the control points of a node.

MOVING CONTROL POINTS   By moving one or both control points of a node, you can control the shape of a curve segment more exactly than if you move just the node itself. The effect of moving control points varies, depending on the type of node—cusp, smooth, and symmetrical. Figure 10-12 (a through d) illustrates this difference.

The control points of cusp nodes are not in a straight-line relationship to one another. This means that you can move one control point and change the shape of one curve segment at a time, without affecting the other associated segment. The control points of smooth nodes, on the other hand, *are* in a straight line relative to one another. If you move one control point of a smooth node, you affect the curvature of both line segments at once, though not to the same degree. Finally, the control points of a symmetrical node are at an equal distance from the node. When you move one control point of a symmetrical node, the curvature of both associated curve segments changes in exactly the same way. Your wave-form curve may not have a symmetrical node, because symmetrical nodes rarely occur naturally in freehand drawing due to the steadiness of hand required. You can practice moving the control points of smooth and cusp nodes, however, by following the steps in the next exercise.

1. Select the Freehand tool and draw a curve similar in shape to the one in Figure 10-12a. Don't be concerned if your curve has a slightly different shape. You should draw part of the curve with a steady hand and part using more jagged movements. This will result in an even distribution of node types.

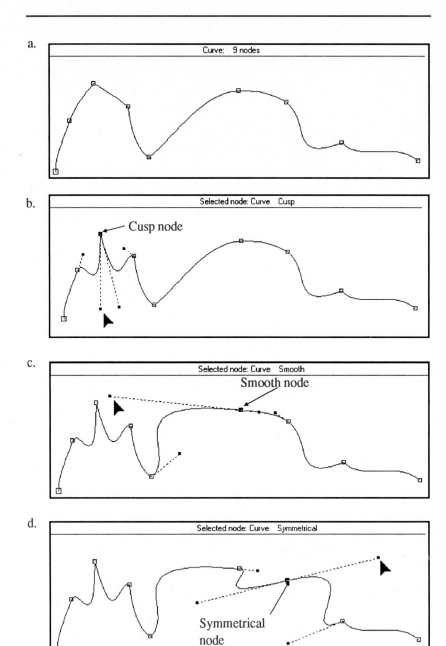

FIGURE 10-12   Moving controls points of a cusp, smooth, and symmetrical node

2. Select individual nodes on your wave-form curve until you find a cusp node. You will know what type of node you have selected by referring to the status line. Do not use one of the end nodes, however; end nodes have only one control point, because only one curve segment is associated with them. If you can't find a cusp node, redraw the curve to be more jagged, and then try again. For your reference, Figure 10-12a shows the wave-form curve with no nodes selected and no control points moved.

3. Drag one of the cusp node's control points outward as far as you can without extending it beyond the viewing window. The further you drag the control point outward from the node, the more angular the curvature of the associated segment becomes. Note also that the curve segment associated with the other control point does not change.

4. Drag the other control point in any direction you choose. The angle of the second curve segment associated with the node changes, independently of the first one. If you have extended both control points independently, you will see a sharp change in curve direction at the node, as in Figure 10-12b.

5. When you have played with this technique to your satisfaction, find and select a smooth node. Note that the two control points of this node lie along a straight line.

6. Drag one of the control points of the smooth node outward, and notice that the curvature of *both* of the segments associated with the node changes. As shown in the example in Figure 10-12c, however, the two segments do not change in exactly the same way. (The curvature of your curve segments may differ from those in the example, depending on how you drew the curve.)

7. If your wave-form curve contains a symmetrical node, select it and move the control points. If you do not have a symmetrical

node, observe the curvature changes in Figure 10-12d when the control points of a symmetrical node are moved. The curvature of these segments changes by an identical angle.

8. When you have played with control points to your satisfaction, activate the Select tool ▶ and press (DEL) to delete the waveform curve from the screen.

Now you have a working knowledge of all the possible interactive techniques for moving and editing curves. It may sometimes happen, however, that even these techniques are not enough to shape your curve just as you want it. What if you are working with a cusp node and just can't make it smooth enough? Or what if you need an additional node at a certain point to enable you to fit a curve to an exact shape? To accomplish these and other node-editing tasks, you can call up the Node Edit menu. How to edit curves using this menu is the subject of the remaining sections on shaping lines and curves.

Editing Nodes

Selecting a curve object and moving nodes and control points are interactive operations that you can perform without invoking a special command or menu. There are times, however, when you need to *edit* the nodes themselves: to change their shape, or to add nodes, delete nodes, join nodes together, or break them apart. Editing nodes requires that you use a special Node Edit menu that pops up when you double-click on a node or on the curve segment that immediately precedes it.

Working with the Node Edit Menu

To call up the Node Edit menu, you double-click on the node you wish to edit. Alternatively, you can double-click on the curve or line segment that immediately precedes the node. As the example in Figure 10-13 shows, double-clicking on a node or curve segment causes that segment to thicken temporarily. The Node Edit menu appears exactly at the selected node. If multiple nodes are selected, their associated curve segments thicken.

The commands in the Node Edit menu allow you to add or delete selected nodes, join two nodes or break them apart, convert lines to curves and curves to lines, or change the node type. Not all commands are available to you for every node, however. Some commands appear in gray and are unavailable, depending on the number and type of node(s) you have selected. See the section pertaining to the relevant Node Edit command for more information about why particular commands are not available at certain

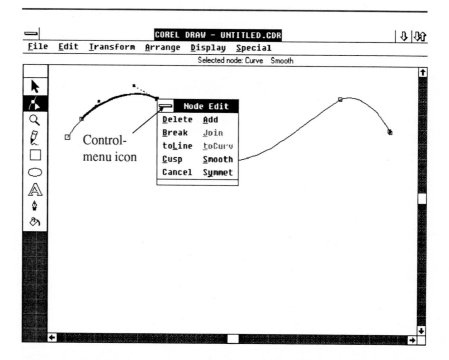

FIGURE 10-13   Invoking the Node Edit menu

times. To select commands that are available, click once on the command name.

 Disregard the underlined letters in the command names of the Node Edit menu. Although Windows conventions might suggest that you can select a command by pressing (ALT) and the underlined letter, it is not possible to do so.

If the Node Edit menu conceals an area of a curve that you want to view, just click on the control-menu icon at the upper left corner of the Node Edit menu. When the control menu (which looks just like the control menu in the Corel DRAW! window) appears, select the Move command and drag the entire menu out of the way by dragging the menu title. Figure 10-14 shows the Node Edit menu being moved to the right of its original pop-up location. A shortcut to invoking the control menu of the Node Edit menu is to press

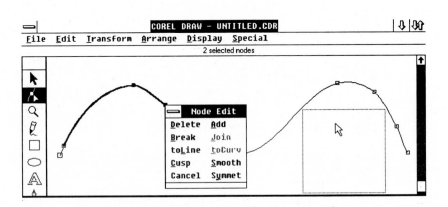

FIGURE 10-14   Moving the Node Edit menu away from the selected node(s)

(ALT-F7). You can close the control menu by pressing (ALT-F4) or selecting the Close command.

As soon as you select a command from the Node Edit menu, the menu disappears, and Corel DRAW! immediately applies the command to the selected node(s). If you accidentally invoke the Node Edit menu at any time, select Cancel to remove it from the display.

Try the exercises in each of the following sections to become familiar with using the commands in the Node Edit menu.

ADDING SINGLE OR MULTIPLE NODES If you have moved nodes and manipulated control points to the best of your ability but still cannot achieve the exact shape you want, consider adding one or more nodes where the curvature seems most inadequate. You can add a single node or multiple nodes, depending on how many nodes are selected.

 If the node you have selected is the first node of a line or curve, you cannot add a node to it. In Corel DRAW!, a first node can never have a node or segment preceding it.

The following exercise furnishes the necessary steps to add a single node between two existing nodes. Set the viewing magnification to 1:1. Make sure that the Snap To Grid and Show Rulers commands are turned off for this and all of the other exercises in the "Editing Nodes" portion of this chapter.

1. Select the Freehand tool and draw a wave-form curve similar to the one shown in Figure 10-15a. Activate the Shaping tool to select the curve for editing. Your curve may contain a different number of nodes from the one in Figure 10-15a.

2. Double-click with the Shaping tool on either the node or the curve segment immediately in front of the point at which you

a.

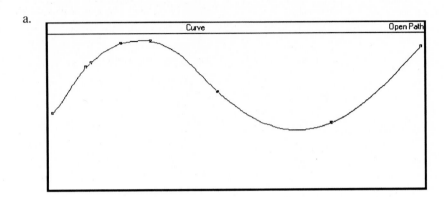

b.

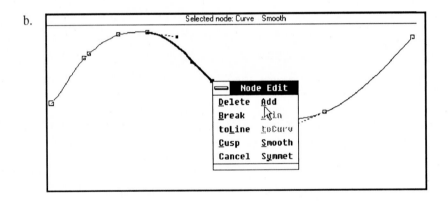

c.

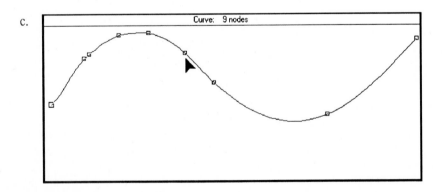

FIGURE 10-15   Adding a single node

want to add a node. The Node Edit menu appears, with its upper left corner at the selected node, as shown in Figure 10-15b.

3. Select the Add command from the Node Edit menu. A new node appears on the curve or line segment preceding the selected node, as shown in Figure 10-15c. If you first deselect all of the selected nodes by clicking on any white space, you can move this added node or manipulate its control points just like any other node.

4. Select New from the File menu to clear the screen. Do not save your work.

If you add a node to a straight line segment instead of to a curve, then move the new node, you effectively add a new line segment.

Perform the following brief exercise to add several nodes to a curve at one time. The technique is the same as when you add a single node, except that multiple nodes must be selected.

1. Make sure that magnification is set to 1:1, and then draw another wave-form curve similar to the one you did for the previous exercise. Activate the Shaping tool to select the curve. Your rendition of the curve may include more or fewer nodes than the one in Figure 10-16a.

2. Select two or more nodes using either (SHIFT) or the marquee method. You will add nodes in front of each of these selected nodes. All of the squares that mark the selected nodes blacken.

3. Using the Shaping tool, double-click on any of the selected nodes or segments. The Node Edit menu appears at the node on which you double-clicked, as in Figure 10-16b.

4. Click on the Add command of the Node Edit menu. A new node appears in front of each of the selected nodes, as shown in

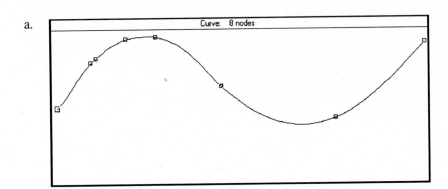

a.

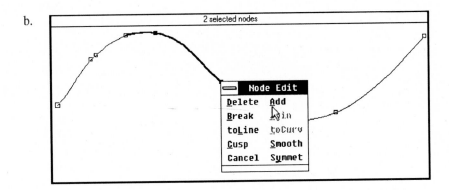

b.

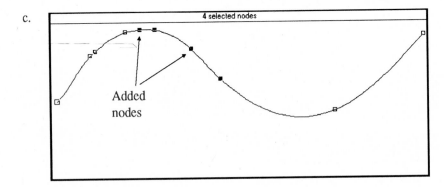

c.

FIGURE 10-16   Adding multiple nodes

Figure 10-16c. If you deselect all of the currently selected nodes, and then select the added nodes, you can move any or all of them. If you select the new nodes individually, you can manipulate their control points to suit your drawing needs.

5. Select New from the File menu to clear the screen. Do not save your work.

The counterpart to adding nodes is deleting them. Continue with the next section to practice deleting one or more nodes from a curve.

DELETING SINGLE OR MULTIPLE NODES When you draw freehand curves, it is often difficult to control mouse movement completely. Changing the Freehand Tracking, Corner Threshold, and AutoJoin settings in the Preferences dialog box may help, but erratic movements while you execute a curve still can produce occasional extraneous nodes. You can smooth out an uneven curve quickly and easily by deleting single or multiple extraneous nodes.

caution Always use the Delete command in the Node Edit menu with caution. Deleting a node at random, without checking to see if other nodes are nearby, can radically alter the shape of a curve in ways that are not always predictable.

Perform the following exercise to delete a single node from a curve.

1. Set viewing magnification to 1:1 and draw a curve similar to the one in Figure 10-17a. Select the curve with the Shaping tool. Your curve may contain a different number of nodes from the one in this figure.

a.

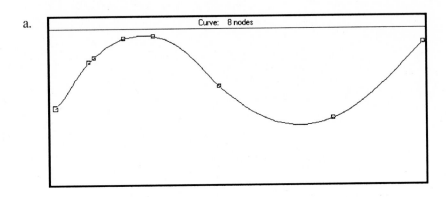

b.

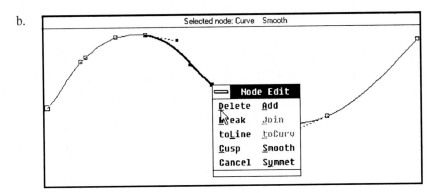

c.

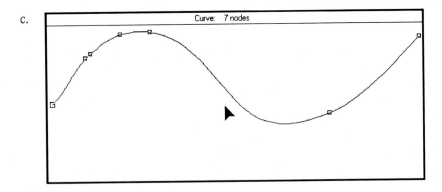

FIGURE 10-17   Deleting a single node

2. Using the Shaping tool, double-click on either the node or segment that you want to delete. The Node Edit menu appears, as in Figure 10-17b.

3. Select the Delete command from the Node Edit menu. Corel DRAW! deletes the node that you selected and redraws the curve without it, as in Figure 10-17c. The shape of your redrawn curve could be quite different from your original one; just how different it is depends on the location of the node you selected for deletion.

4. Select New from the File menu to clear the screen. Do not save your work.

Keep in mind that if you delete one of the end nodes of a curve, you delete the associated curve segment as well. If you try to delete either node of a straight line, you delete the entire line in the process.

 As a shortcut to deleting a node, you can first select a node and then press (DEL) instead of invoking the pop-up menu.

You can delete multiple nodes as well as single nodes from a curve, as long as all of the nodes you want to delete are selected. To delete multiple nodes,

1. Set viewing magnification to 1:1 and draw a curve similar to the one shown in Figure 10-18a. Activate the Shaping tool to select the curve. Your rendition of the curve may include more or fewer nodes than the one in the figure.

2. Select the nodes you want to delete, using either (SHIFT) or the marquee method; Figure 10-18b shows four nodes selected. The squares marking all of the selected nodes blacken. Keep in

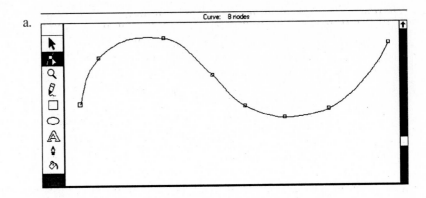

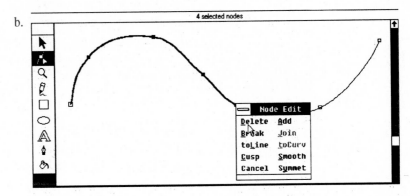

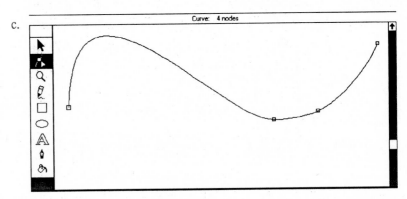

FIGURE 10-18   Deleting multiple nodes

mind that if you try to delete an end node, you will delete the associated curve segment along with it.

3. Double-click with the Shaping tool on one of the nodes or curve segments in the selected group. The Node Edit menu pops up, as in Figure 10-18b.

4. Select the Delete command in the Node Edit menu. Corel DRAW! immediately deletes the selected nodes from the screen and redraws the curve without them, as in Figure 10-18c. The shape of the curve can change subtly or dramatically between node positions; the extent of the change depends on the original positions of the selected nodes.

5. Select New from the File menu to clear the screen. Do not save your work.

You have learned to add and delete nodes when you need to reshape a curve more than the existing nodes allow. Sometimes, though, you may want your curve to flatten to the extent that you need to replace a curve segment with a straight line segment. You accomplish this by converting one or more curve segments to straight lines.

CONVERTING SINGLE OR MULTIPLE CURVE SEGMENTS TO STRAIGHT LINE SEGMENTS   Corel DRAW!

allows you to convert curve segments to line segments. Before you convert a curve to a line, you need to be able to identify whether a selected segment is a curve or a straight line. Some important guidelines to follow are

- A curve segment has two control points; a straight line segment has none.

- When you select the segment or its node, the status line indicates whether the segment is a line or curve.

a.

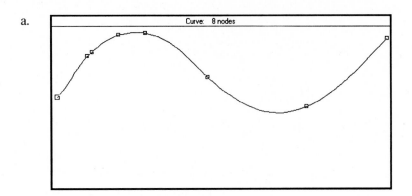

b.

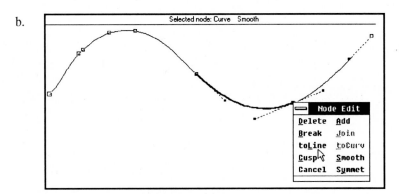

c.

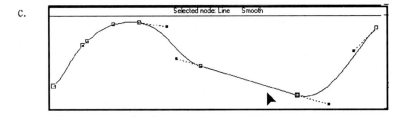

FIGURE 10-19   Converting a curve segment to a straight line segment

- The shape of the *selected* node identifies the type of segment that precedes it. A black fill in the selected node signifies a curve segment, while a hollow selected node signifies a straight line segment.

Perform the following exercise to gain experience in converting a single curve segment into a straight line segment.

1. Set viewing magnification to 1:1, then select the Freehand tool and draw a wave-form curve, as shown in Figure 10-19a.

2. Select the curve object with the Shaping tool. Your curve may contain a different number of nodes from the one in the figure.

3. Using the Shaping tool, double-click on a segment or node of a curve that you want to convert to a straight line. The Node Edit menu pops up, as in Figure 10-19b.

4. Now, select the toLine command in the Node Edit menu. The two control points related to the selected curve disappear and the curve segment becomes a straight line segment, as shown in Figure 10-19c. You can reposition, stretch, or shorten this line segment by using the Shaping tool to drag the nodes at either end.

5. Select New from the File menu to clear the screen. Do not save your work.

If you want a curve object in your drawing to be more angular, you can change its appearance by selecting multiple nodes or curve segments and converting them to straight lines. To convert multiple curve segments to straight line segments,

1. Draw a wave-form curve similar to the one shown in Figure 10-20a and then select the curve with the Shaping tool. Your rendition of the curve may contain more or fewer nodes than the one in the figure.

2. Select the curve segments or nodes you want to convert to straight lines, using either (SHIFT) or the marquee technique.

3. Using the Shaping tool, double-click on any one of the selected nodes or curve segments. The Node Edit menu appears, as shown in Figure 10-20b.

4. Select the toLine command in the Node Edit menu. The selected curve segments convert to straight lines and all associated control points are eliminated (straight lines do not include control points). The object becomes much more angular, as in Figure 10-20c. You can now reposition, stretch, or shrink any or all one of the line segments by dragging the node(s).

5. Select New from the File menu to clear the screen. Do not save your work.

If your object consists of angular line segments but you want to give it much smoother contours, you can convert line segments to curves. The next section shows you how.

CONVERTING SINGLE OR MULTIPLE STRAIGHT LINE SEGMENTS TO CURVE SEGMENTS   With Corel DRAW!

you can convert straight line segments to curve segments through the Node Edit menu. Before you convert a line segment to a curve segment, you need to identify whether a selected segment is a straight line or a curve. If you are uncertain about identifying segments, review the guidelines in the last section before you proceed.

Try the following exercise to practice converting a single line segment into a curve segment.

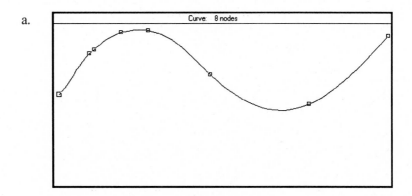

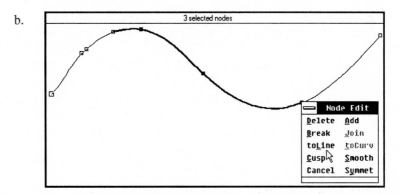

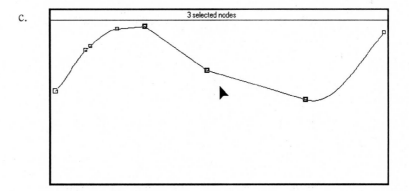

FIGURE 10-20   Converting multiple curve segments to lines

a.

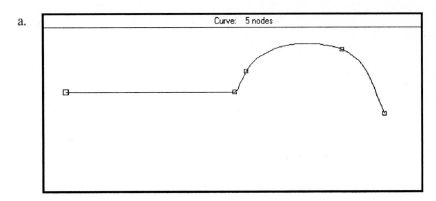

b.

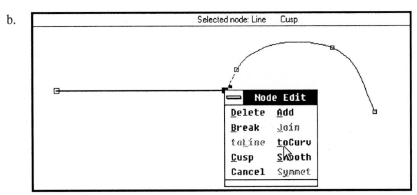

c.

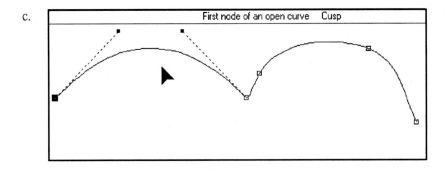

FIGURE 10-21   Converting a line segment to a curve segment

1. Set magnification to 1:1, and then select the Freehand tool. Draw a straight line, double-click, and drag the mouse to continue with a wave-form curve, as shown in Figure 10-21a.

2. Activate the Shaping tool to select the curve object. Your drawing may show a different number of nodes from the one in the figure.

3. Using the Shaping tool, double-click on the straight line segment of the object or on the *second* node of the straight line. The Node Edit menu pops up, as in Figure 10-21b. (If you select the first node of the line segment, you will not be able to convert it to a curve.)

4. Now, select the toCurv command in the Node Edit menu. Corel DRAW! turns the selected straight line segment into a curve, causing two control points to appear on the line segment. You can now manipulate the control points of this node, just as in Figure 10-21c.

5. Select New from the File menu to clear the screen.

You can turn several straight line segments into curve segments at the same time, as long as they are part of the same object. Try the following exercise to convert multiple straight line segments to curves.

1. Select the Freehand tool and draw a multi-segment "sawtooth" shape like the one in Figure 10-22a. Remember to double-click as you complete each line segment in order to attach the next one to it.

2. Activate the Shaping tool to select the multi-segment line for editing.

a.

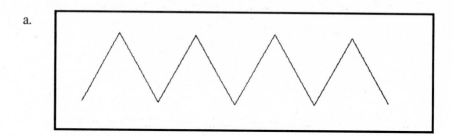

b.

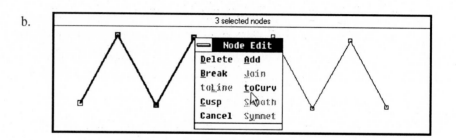

c.

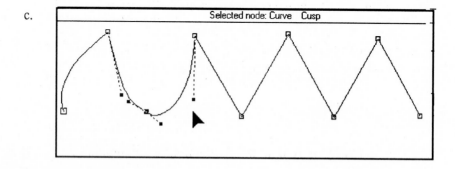

FIGURE 10-22   Converting multiple line segments to curves

3. Select the line segments or nodes you want to convert to curves, using either (SHIFT) or the marquee technique.

4. Double-click with the Shaping tool on one of the selected straight line segments or on the node that follows it. The Node Edit menu appears, as in Figure 10-22b.

5. Select the toCurv command in the Node Edit menu. The selected straight line segments convert to curve lines. On the surface, the segments do not appear to have changed. However, if you deselect all nodes and then select any one of the converted nodes, two control points appear. You can reshape the peaks and valleys like any other curve, as in Figure 10-22c.

6. Experiment with the nodes and control points of the converted segments to prove to yourself that you really are working with curves now. When you are finished, select New from the File menu to clear the screen before continuing.

You have experimented with adding and deleting nodes, and with changing lines to curves and curves to lines. Another group of commands in the Node Edit menu allows you to change the type of single or multiple nodes. These commands are Cusp, Smooth, and Symmetrical and are the subject of the next several sections.

CUSPING SINGLE OR MULTIPLE NODES   When you work with a cusp node, you can move either of its control points independently of the other. This makes it possible to control the curvature of one of the two curve segments that meet at the node, without affecting the other segment. Cusp nodes are especially desirable when you want to render an abrupt change in direction at a node.

The following exercises show you how to turn a single smooth or symmetrical node into a cusped node.

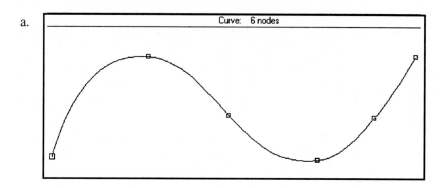

a.

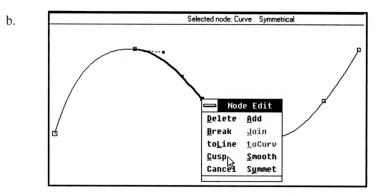

b.

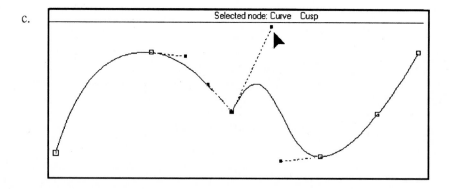

c.

FIGURE 10-23   Cusping a single node

1. Set magnification to 1:1, then activate the Freehand tool and draw a wave-form curve similar to the one shown in Figure 10-23a.

2. Activate the Shaping tool to select the curve automatically. It is not important if your node count does not match the one in the figure. Find a smooth or symmetrical node that you want to cusp.

3. Using the Shaping tool, double-click on the node you want to cusp. Select any node except an end node; Corel DRAW! designs all end nodes as cusp nodes.

4. When the Node Edit menu appears as in Figure 10-23b, select the Cusp command. The appearance of the curve will not change. However, if you manipulate the control points of this node as shown in Figure 10-23c, you will find that you can move one control point without affecting the curve segment on the other side of the node.

5. Clear the screen by selecting New from the File menu. Do not save your work.

When you want a curve object to have a relatively jagged appearance but you do not want to turn your curves into straight lines, the next best solution is to change multiple smooth or symmetrical nodes into cusp nodes. You can then shape the cusped nodes to create a more angular appearance for the affected portions of the object.

1. Draw a wave-form curve similar to the one in Figure 10-24a.

2. Activate the Shaping tool to select the curve automatically, and then find the nodes that are smooth or symmetrical.

a.
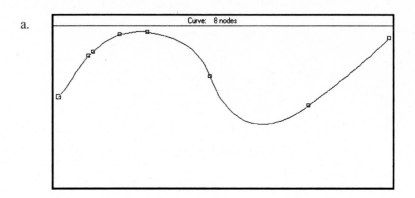

b.
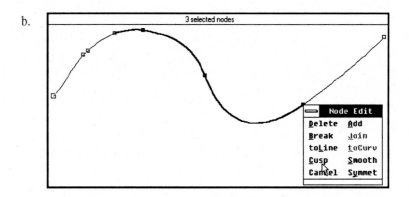

c.
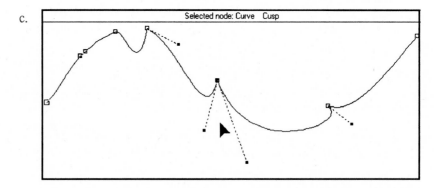

FIGURE 10-24   Cusping multiple nodes

3. Select the smooth and symmetrical nodes, using either (SHIFT) or the marquee technique. All of the selected nodes blacken.

4. Double-click with the Shaping tool on any of the nodes or segments of the curves you selected for cusping. The Node Edit menu appears, as shown in Figure 10-24b.

5. Select the Cusp command in the Node Edit menu. The curves selected for cusping will not change in appearance. However, if you select each cusped node separately and manipulate its control points (Figure 10-24c), you can move one control point without affecting the curve segment on the other side of the node.

6. Select New from the File menu to clear the screen. Do not save your work.

In the next section, you will become familiar with changing cusped or symmetrical nodes into smooth nodes.

SMOOTHING SINGLE OR MULTIPLE NODES   In the previous section, you saw that cusp nodes are desirable when you want to create a rougher, more jagged appearance for an object. When you want to make an object's curves smoother, you need to seek out the cusped nodes and turn them into smooth ones.

A smooth node can be defined as a node whose control points always lie along a straight line. A special case exists when a smooth node is located between a straight line and a curve segment, as in Figure 10-25a. In such a case, only the side of the node that leans toward the curve segment contains a control point, and you can only move that control point along an imaginary line that follows the extension of the straight line. This restriction maintains the smoothness at the node.

In the next exercise, you will convert a single cusp node that lies at the juncture between a straight line and curve segment into a smooth node.

a.

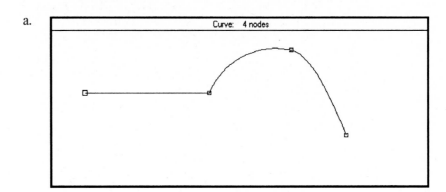

b.

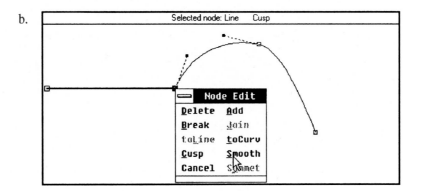

c.

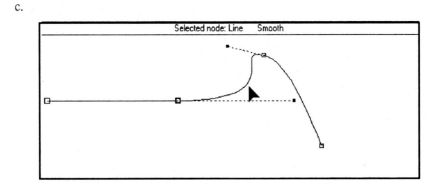

FIGURE 10-25   Smoothing a single cusped node

1. Set viewing magnification to 1:1. Then select the Freehand tool and draw a straight line connected to a curve segment, as shown in Figure 10-25a. Remember to double-click at the end of the line segment to attach it to the curve segment automatically.

2. Activate the Shaping tool. Your curve object may not include the same number of nodes as the one in this figure, but that is not important for the purpose of this exercise.

3. Using the Shaping tool, double-click on the cusp or symmetrical node that you want changed to a smooth node. When the Node Edit menu appears (Figure 10-25b), select the Smooth command. The curve passing through the selected node is smoothed, like the one in Figure 10-25c, and will remain smooth when you move either the node itself or its control points. The straight line segment does not change, of course.

4. Select New from the File menu to clear the screen.

To smooth multiple nodes, you simply select multiple nodes and then repeat the steps for smoothing a single node.

1. Set magnification to 1:1, then select the Freehand tool and draw a wave-form curve with several peaks and troughs, like the one in Figure 10- 26a. Attempt to draw each curve with sharp peaks in order to see final smoothing results.

2. Activate the Shaping tool and select two or three cusp nodes at the peaks of the curve object, using either (SHIFT) or the marquee.

3. Using the Shaping tool, double-click on any of the selected nodes. The Node Edit menu pops up, as in Figure 10-26b.

a.

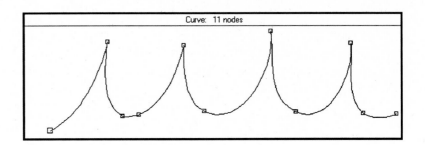

b.

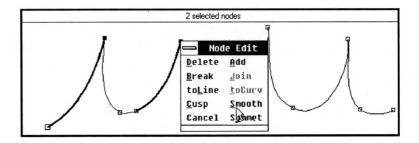

c.

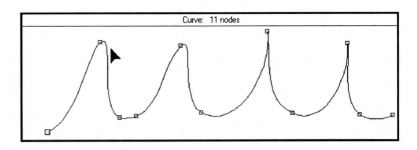

FIGURE 10-26   Smoothing multiple cusped nodes

4. Select the Smooth command. The selected curves convert to smooth curves and pass through the nodes smoothly, similar to the curves in Figure 10-26c.

5. Deselect all of the nodes by clicking on any white space. Then select each node that you smoothed and work with its control points to see how the control points of a smoothed node behave.

6. Clear the screen by selecting New from the File menu.

Go on to the next section to learn how you can turn smooth or cusp nodes into symmetrical nodes and how this affects the drawing process.

MAKING SINGLE OR MULTIPLE NODES SYMMETRICAL   Symmetrical nodes share the same characteristics as smooth nodes, except that the control points on a symmetrical node are equidistant from the node. This means that the curvature is the same on both sides of the symmetrical node. As with the smooth nodes, when you move one of the control points, the other control point moves. In effect, symmetry causes the two control points to move as one.

Another important point to remember is that you cannot make a node symmetrical if it connects to a straight line segment. The node must lie between two curve segments in order to qualify for a symmetrical edit.

Perform the following brief exercise to convert a single cusped node to a symmetrical node.

1. Set viewing magnification to 1:1, then select the Freehand tool and draw a curve similar to the one in Figure 10-27a.

2. Activate the Shaping tool to select the curve. Your curve may contain a different number of nodes from this figure, but that is not important for the purposes of this exercise.

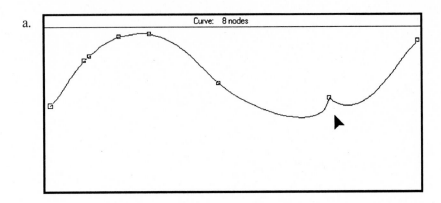

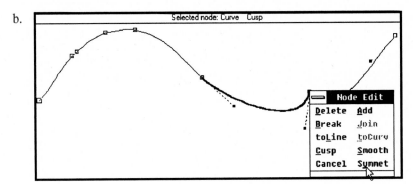

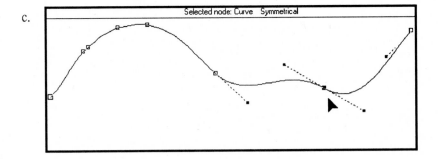

FIGURE 10-27   Making a cusp node symmetrical

3. Find a cusp node that you want to make symmetrical and then double-click on it. The Node Edit menu appears, as shown in Figure 10-27b.

4. Click on the Symmet command. The selected node is now converted to a symmetrical node and Corel DRAW! redraws the curve so that it passes through the node symmetrically, as in Figure 10-27c.

5. Move the control points of this node until you have a satisfactory understanding of how symmetrical nodes work. Then select New from the File menu to clear the screen.

Making multiple nodes symmetrical is just as easy as making single nodes symmetrical. The only difference is that you select more than one node at a time, using either (SHIFT) or the marquee method.

1. Set viewing magnification to 1:1, then select the Freehand tool and draw a curve, as shown in Figure 10-28a.

2. Activate the Shaping tool to select the curve. Your rendition of the curve may have a different number of nodes.

3. Find and select several cusped and smooth nodes that you want to make symmetrical.

4. Use the Shaping tool to double-click on one of the nodes or related curve segments. The Node Edit menu appears, as in Figure 10-28b.

5. Select the Symmet command in the Node Edit menu. As in Figure 10-28c, Corel DRAW! converts all of the selected nodes to symmetrical nodes, and the curve changes to pass through the nodes symmetrically. If you want to see how the converted symmetrical nodes behave, deselect all of them, then select

a.

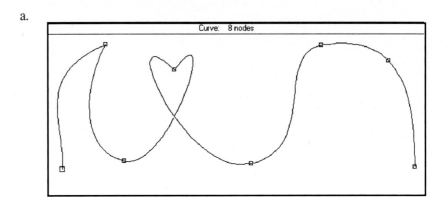

b.

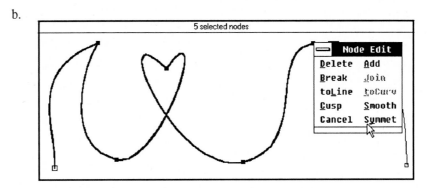

c.

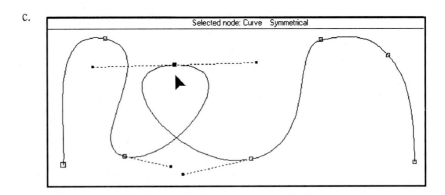

FIGURE 10-28   Making multiple nodes symmetrical

them one at a time and move their control points. When you move the control points of these nodes, you affect both associated line segments in the same way.

6. Select New from the File menu to clear the screen.

In the next sections, you will find out how to master the art of breaking nodes apart and joining them together—and why you might choose to do so.

BREAKING CURVES AT SINGLE OR AT MULTIPLE NODES

Breaking a node involves splitting a curve at a selected node, so that two nodes appear where before there was one. Although you can move the separate sections of a broken node as though they were separate curves, Corel DRAW! does not regard them as separate. These split segments actually constitute different *subpaths* of the same curve. A good example of an image created with node-breaking techniques is the sample file ACAT.CDR that came with your software. If you ungroup the cat and its background mat and then select the cat with the Shaping tool, you see a very large number of nodes. The status line displays the message, "196 nodes on 27 subpaths." Breaking a node into separate subpaths gives the impression of spontaneous freehand drawing, yet it allows you to keep separate "drawing strokes" together as one object. Breaking curves at the nodes is also a useful "trick" when you need to delete a portion of a curve and leave the rest of the curve intact.

Keep in mind that you cannot break a curve at an end node, because there is no segment on the other side of the end point with which to form a separate subpath.

When you break a node, it becomes two unconnected end nodes. You are then free to move either end node and the entire subpath to which it is connected. The two subpaths remain part of the same object, however, as you can see when you select either subpath with the Select tool. In the following exercise, you will draw another curve, break it at a single node, and then observe how Corel DRAW! handles the two resulting subpaths.

1. Select the Freehand tool and draw a wave-form curve similar to the one in Figure 10-29a.

2. Activate the Shaping tool to select the curve and then select a node in the trough of the curve.

3. Double-click on the selected node to cause the Node Edit menu to pop up, as in Figure 10-29b.

4. Select Break from the Node Edit menu. The single node splits into two nodes. Since they are close together, however, the change is not visible until you begin to move the new end nodes.

5. Move the left end point away from the subpath to the right as shown in Figure 10-29c, and then deselect both nodes. The object itself remains selected for editing, and the status line informs you that the curve now has two subpaths.

6. Press the spacebar to activate the Select tool. Notice that the Select tool treats these two subpaths as a single object, even though they look like separate curves. There may be times when you want to make subpaths into truly separate objects, so that you can manipulate and edit them independently. As the next step shows, Corel DRAW! provides a means for you to turn the subpaths into independent curves.

7. To separate the two subpaths into two truly distinct objects, leave the Select tool active and then select the Break Apart command from the Arrange menu. This command is available only when multiple subpaths of a single curve object are selected.

8. Select New from the File menu to clear the screen.

a.

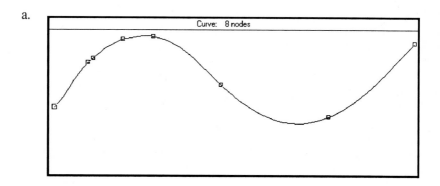

b.

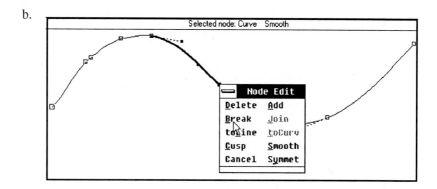

c.

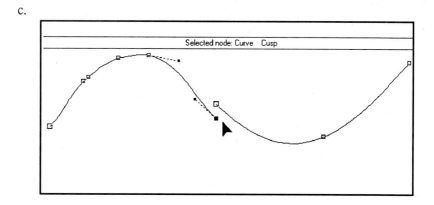

FIGURE 10-29   Breaking a curve at a single node

In this brief exercise, you have seen some applications for breaking a curve at a node. For example, you can create two separate objects from a single object, or create separate subpaths that move together as a single object.

caution   If you break a closed curve object at a node, you will not be able to fill the object with a color or pattern.

When you break a curve at multiple nodes, the result is multiple subpaths, which still remain part of the same object. The file ACAT.CDR contains a good example of a curve object that has been broken apart at multiple nodes. To break your own curve at multiple nodes, perform the following exercise.

1. Set magnification to 1:1, then select the Freehand tool and draw a wave-form curve like the one in Figure 10-30a.

2. Activate the Shaping tool to select the curve and then select three or four nodes using (SHIFT). Do not select one of the end nodes; as previously mentioned, you cannot break an end node into separate subpaths.

3. Double-click on any of the selected nodes to call up the Node Edit menu, as shown in Figure 10-30b.

4. Select Break from the Node Edit menu. The status line displays the message, "*xx* selected nodes on *x* subpaths," indicating how many subpaths you have created and how many nodes the entire curve object contains.

5. Move the end points of the subpaths away from each other until the subpaths look like separate curves, as in Figure 10-30c.

6. Press the spacebar to activate the Select tool. All of the subpaths are selected automatically as a single object.

a.

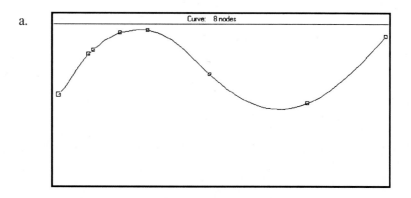

b.

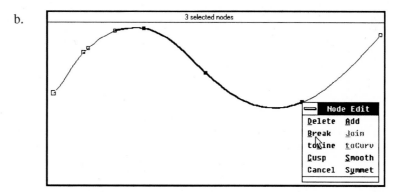

c.

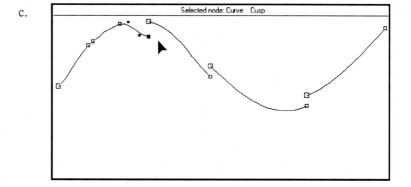

FIGURE 10-30   Breaking a curve at multiple nodes

7. Select Break Apart from the Arrange menu. Now each subpath constitutes a separate object.

8. Select New from the File menu to clear the screen before going on to the next exercise.

The reverse of breaking curves apart is joining them together. In the next section, you will learn when you can and cannot join nodes together, and some reasons why you might want to do so.

JOINING NODES   By now, you have probably noticed that the Join command is rarely available for selection when you invoke the pop-up Node Edit menu. You can join nodes only under very specific conditions.

- You can join only two nodes at a time, so only two nodes can be selected.

- The two nodes must be either end nodes of the same object or end nodes of separate subpaths of the same object.

- You cannot join an end node of an open curve to a closed object such as an ellipse or a rectangle.

When might you want to join two nodes, then? The two chief occasions are when you want to close an open path, or when you want to make a single continuous curve from two separate paths.

Joining Nodes to Close an Open Path   An open path, as you will recall from your previous freehand drawing experience in Corel DRAW!, is a curve object whose end points do not meet and which therefore cannot be filled with a color or pattern. To prevent open paths, you can set the AutoJoin option in the Preferences dialog box to a higher number and make it easier for end nodes to snap together as you draw. There are still times, however, when you might choose to join end points after drawing an open curve. In such cases, you use the Join command in the pop-up Node Edit menu. The following exercise presents a situation in which you could use the Join command to make the drawing process easier.

1. Set magnification to 1:1. Select the Freehand tool and draw a more or less oval curve, but do not finish the curve at a point close to where you started it. See Figure 10-31a for an example.

2. Activate the Shaping tool to select this curve object, and then select both of the end nodes using the marquee or (SHIFT) key technique.

3. Double-click on either of the selected end nodes to call up the Node Edit menu, as shown in Figure 10-31b.

4. Select the Join command in the Node Edit menu. Corel DRAW! redraws the curve as a closed path, like the one in Figure 10-31c. You can then fill this path with a color or pattern, as you will learn in Chapter 15.

5. Select New from the File menu to clear the screen before going further.

It is easy to close an open path with the Shaping tool. Joining nodes from separate curves, however, is a bit trickier. Read on to learn how to combine the curves so that you can join the nodes.

Joining Nodes on Separate Subpaths to Form a Continuous Curve (Combined Objects)   You can also join two end nodes if they are on two subpaths of the same curve. The two subpaths then become a single, continuous curve segment. A special case exists when you have two separate curve objects (not two subpaths of the same curve) and want to make them into a single continuous curve. Knowing that you cannot join nodes from two separate objects,

a.

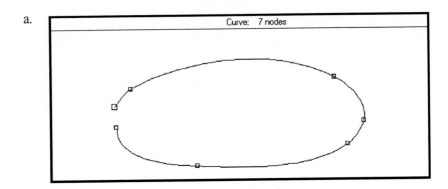

b.

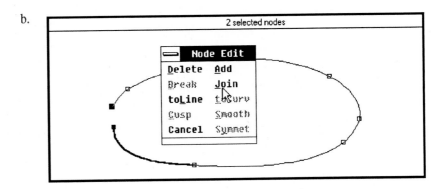

c.

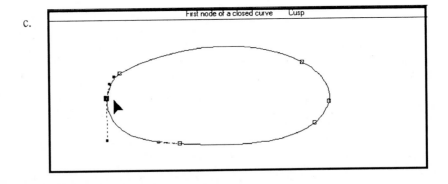

FIGURE 10-31 Joining nodes to close an open path

what do you do? Your best option is to combine the curves using the Select tool and the Combine command in the Arrange menu. Even though the curves continue to look like separate objects, from the standpoint of the software they become two subpaths of a single curve. You can then join their end nodes to unite the subpaths.

In the following exercise, you will practice joining separate subpaths of the same curve by reconstructing portions of the ACAT.CDR sample file that came with your software.

 If you have version 1.11 or later of Corel DRAW!, your ACAT.CDR image differs from the one shown in Figure 10-32a through 10-32c in several ways. For example, the cat and the mat behind are not grouped. More important, the ACAT.CDR image supplied with version 1.11 or later contains no subpaths; all of the curves in the image are separate. To simulate the following exercise, you can break a curve of the cat's hind quarters at the node using the Break command in the Node Edit menu. You can also use the Combine command to combine some of the separate curves into one curve object, thereby creating subpaths that you can then join again.

1. Open the sample file ACAT.CDR. Select a 1:1 viewing magnification. Most of the image fits into this viewing window, as you can see in Figure 10-32a.

2. The Select tool is already active, so click on any point of the outline of the cat. The cat and the mat it is lying on have been grouped, so the Select tool selects both images.

3. Select the Ungroup command from the Arrange menu and then deselect all of the objects in the group by clicking on any white space.

4. Activate the Shaping tool and click on any point of the cat's outline. A multitude of nodes appear and the status line displays

a.

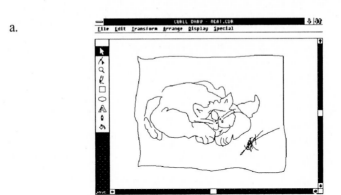

b.

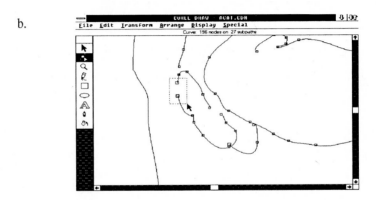

c.

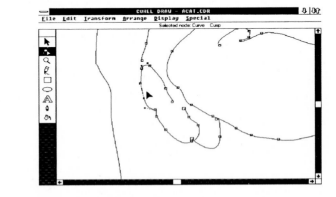

FIGURE 10-32   Joining nodes to form a continuous curve

the message, "196 nodes on 27 subpaths." As you can see, this object was created by breaking curves at many different nodes.

5. Select the Magnification tool and zoom in on the area that represents the cat's hind quarters, as shown in Figure 10-32b. The enlarged figure includes two clearly visible end nodes of different subpaths; you are going to join these end nodes and thereby reduce the number of nodes and subpaths by one.

6. With the Shaping tool, select both of the end nodes marked in Figure 10-32b, and then double-click on either one to call up the Node Edit menu.

7. Select the Join command in this menu. The two end nodes fuse to form a single curve segment, as shown in Figure 10-32c.

8. Zoom out to a 1:1 viewing magnification again, leaving the Shaping tool selected. The status line now displays the message, "195 nodes on 26 subpaths." By joining the end nodes, you have reduced both the number of nodes and the number of subpaths by one. If you want to get a clearer look at what you have done, activate the Select tool and deselect the cat.

9. Select New from the File menu, but do not save the changes you have made.

Going through this process is a good way to familiarize yourself with all the steps involved in both joining and breaking nodes apart. Perhaps you have some new ideas for using the Join command for some of your own original drawings.

EDIT CANCELLATION   If you invoke the Node Edit menu by accident or change your mind about editing a node once the Node Edit menu has appeared, simply select the Cancel command. The Node Edit menu disappears from the screen but the selected node or nodes remain selected for further work.

This concludes your exploration of the techniques for shaping lines and curves. In the remaining sections of this chapter, you will have a hands-on opportunity to explore techniques for shaping rectangular and elliptical objects.

SHAPING RECTANGLES AND SQUARES

The Shaping tool has a specific function when you apply it to rectangles and squares in Corel DRAW!. It rounds the corners of a rectangle, thus creating a shape separate from a rectangle or square. The status line keeps track of the radius of the rounded corner as you drag. You can control the degree of rounding either interactively or by using the grid to ensure exactness.

For interesting distortions, you can stretch, rotate, or skew the rectangle or square before rounding its corners.

Rounding the Corners of a Rectangle or Square Interactively

Complete the following exercise to practice rounding rectangles and squares using the Shaping tool. You will begin by rounding corners interactively; later, you will use the grid to perform the same work.

1. For the beginning of this exercise, make sure that the Snap To Grid and Show Rulers commands are inactive and that you are working in a 1:1 viewing magnification. Then select the Rectangle tool and draw a rectangle of unequal length and width.

2. Activate the Shaping tool and select a node at one of the corners of the rectangle. As shown in Figure 10-33a, the status line indicates that the corner radius of this rectangle is 0.00 inches.

The corner radius helps you measure the degree to which you have rounded the corners of a rectangle or square with the Shaping tool.

3. Position the Shaping cursor at this node and begin to drag the mouse away from the corner slowly. As shown in Figure 10-33b, each corner node separates into two separate nodes, with each node moving farther away from the original corner as you drag. The status line also informs you just how much of a corner radius you are creating. The further you drag the nodes from the corners, the rounder the corners become and the more the corner radius increases.

4. Continue dragging the mouse until you reach the logical limit of rounding: when the nodes from adjacent corners meet at the sides of the rectangle. At this point, your rounded rectangle has become almost an ellipse, similar to the rectangle shown in Figure 10-33c.

5. Begin dragging the selected node from the middle of the line back to the former corner. As you do so, the corner radius diminishes. You can return the rectangle to its original shape by dragging the nodes all the way back to the corner.

6. Delete the rectangle from the screen, then draw a square and repeat steps 2 through 5. Notice that when you begin with a square and then round the corners to the logical limit, the square becomes a nearly perfect circle rather than an ellipse, as in Figure 10-34.

7. Select New to clear the screen of the square.

Although the status line information helps you round corners precisely, you can gain even greater precision using the grid and rulers. The next exercise steps you through the process of rounding corners of a rectangle or square with the help of these aids.

a.

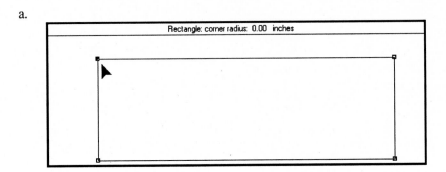

b.

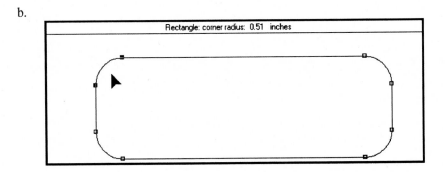

c.

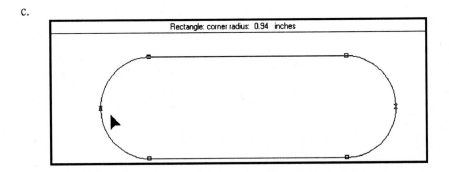

FIGURE 10-33 Rounding the corners of a rectangle

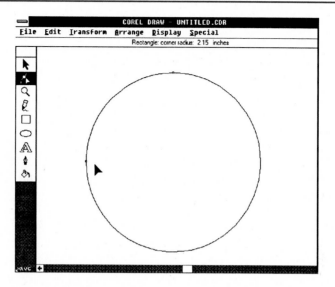

FIGURE 10-34   Rounding the corners of a square

1. Activate the Snap To Grid command, set the grid spacing to 4 per inch, and then display the rulers.

2. Draw a rectangle 2 inches wide by 1.25 inches deep. Activate the Shaping tool and select one of the corner nodes of the rectangle.

3. Drag this corner node away from the corner to round the rectangle. This time, the corner radius changes in increments of 0.25 inches because of the grid setting.

4. Draw a square and round its corners. The radius of the square also changes in increments of 0.25 inches.

5. When you have finished experimenting with the rectangle and the square, select New from the File menu to clear the screen.

In the next section, you will see what can happen when you stretch, rotate, or skew a rectangle or square before attempting to round its corners.

Shaping Stretched, Rotated, or Skewed Rectangles and Squares

When you transform a rectangle or square by stretching, rotating, or skewing it with the Select tool and then round its corners, the value of the corner radius may be distorted. The corner radius indicator on the status line is followed by the word "distorted" in parentheses. As Figure 10-35 shows, the final shape of such a rounded rectangle may also be distorted; in extreme cases it can resemble a skewed flying saucer or rotated ellipse. Figure 10-36 shows a skewed square whose corners have been rounded.

Practice this technique on your own and then go on to the final section on shaping rectangles. In this next section, you will find out how to turn a rectangle into a curve so that you can shape it in an infinite number of ways.

Converting a Rectangle to a Curve Object

If the shaping options for rectangles or squares seem limited to you, don't worry. You can convert any rectangle or square into a curve object and, from that point onward, you can turn a formerly four-cornered object into anything at all. The technique is simple, as you will see in the following brief exercise.

1. Set magnification to 1:1 and turn the ruler off in preparation for this exercise.

2. Select the Rectangle tool if it is not selected already and then draw a rectangle of any size or shape.

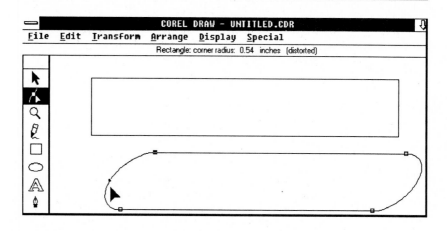

FIGURE 10-35   Rounding the corners of a skewed rectangle

3. Activate the Select tool to select the rectangle and select the Convert To Curves command from the Arrange menu. The status line message changes from "Rectangle" to "Curve." Note

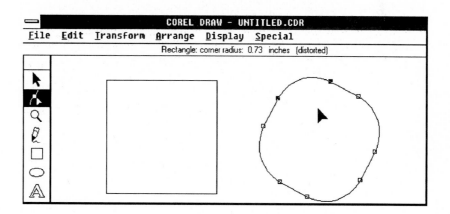

FIGURE 10-36   Rounding the corners of a rotated square

that the new four-cornered "curve" still has the same number of nodes as when it was a rectangle.

4. Activate the Shaping tool and then select and drag one of the nodes in any direction. As the example in Figure 10-37 shows, dragging the node no longer forces the associated line/curve segment to move parallel to the other line segments.

5. Continue warping the shape of this rectangle-turned-curve in a variety of ways. For example, you could add nodes, convert line segments to curves, create symmetrical nodes, or even turn the former rectangle into a candy cane or other hybrid object.

6. Select New from the File menu to clear the screen before going further.

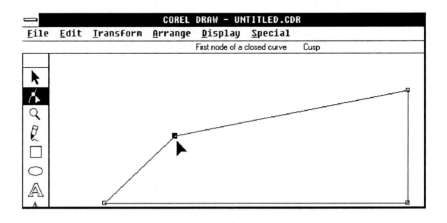

FIGURE 10-37   Editing a rectangle that has been converted to curves

Now that you have mastered the art of shaping rectangles and squares, you are ready to apply the Shaping tool to Ellipses and Circles for some quite different effects.

SHAPING ELLIPSES AND CIRCLES

When you shape ellipses or circles with the Shaping tool, you can create either an open arc or a pie wedge. You can even shift back and forth between these two shapes as you draw, depending on whether the tip of the shaping cursor lies inside or outside the ellipse or circle. You also have the option of constraining the angle of an arc or pie wedge to 15-degree increments.

Creating an Open Arc

To turn an ellipse or circle into an arc, you position the tip of the shaping cursor just *outside of* the rim at the node and then drag the node in the desired direction. Make certain that the tip of the cursor remains outside the rim of the ellipse as you drag, or you will create a wedge instead of an arc. The status line provides information about the angle of the arc as you draw. Practice creating arcs from both ellipses and circles in the following exercise.

1. Turn off the Snap To Grid command if it is active and set the viewing magnification to 1:1.

2. Select the Ellipse tool and draw a perfect circle.

3. Activate the Shaping tool to select the circle automatically.

4. Position the tip of the Shaping tool exactly at the node but just outside the rim of the circle, and then drag the node downward slowly in a clockwise direction. As Figure 10-38 shows, the single node separates into two nodes, with the second node following your cursor as you drag. If the circle seems to be

turning into a pie wedge instead of an arc, the tip of your mouse cursor is inside the rim of the circle. Move it outside of the rim and try again.

 Note that the status line provides information about the angle position of the first and second nodes and about the total angle of the arc. This information is based on a 360-degree wheel, with 0 degrees at 3 o'clock, 90 degrees at 12 o'clock, 180 degrees at 9 o'clock, and 270 degrees at 6 o'clock.

5. Continue to drag the shaping cursor, but now press and hold the (CTRL) key as well. The angle of the arc snaps in increments of 15 degrees. Release the mouse button when your arc has the angle you want.

6. Select the Ellipse tool and draw a perfect circle. Then repeat steps 4 and 5, completing this arc at a 105-degree angle. If you use an ellipse instead of a circle, the "total angle" information

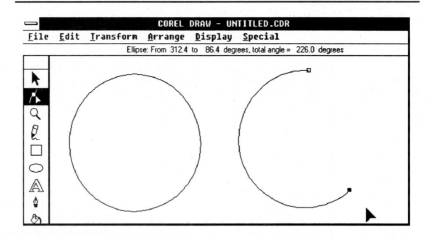

FIGURE 10-38   Creating an arc from a circle

on the status line is followed by the message "distorted" in parentheses. This message occurs because Corel DRAW! bases its calculation of an arc on a perfect circle rather than on an ellipse with different height and width. The angle assignments for arcs created from an ellipse are therefore approximate.

7. Press the spacebar to activate the Select tool and select the newly created arc. Notice that the highlighting box, like the one in Figure 10-39, is much larger than the arc itself; in fact, it seems to surround the now invisible but complete original ellipse. The purpose of this large highlighting box is to make it easy for you to align an arc or wedge concentrically, using the Align command in the Arrange menu. The disadvantage of this large highlighting box is that when you are selecting objects with the marquee, you must make certain that your marquee surrounds the entire highlighting box.

8. Select New from the File menu to clear the screen before going further.

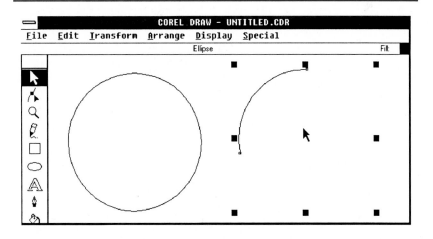

FIGURE 10-39   Selecting an arc for alignment purposes

Creating a wedge shape from an ellipse is just as easy as creating an arc, as you will see in the next section.

Creating a Pie Wedge

The only difference between creating an arc and creating a pie wedge is that in the latter case, you position the tip of the shaping cursor *inside* the ellipse or circle as you drag. Perform the following exercise to see the difference for yourself.

1. Set magnification to 1:1, and then select the Ellipse tool and draw a circle. Activate the Shaping tool to select it for editing.

2. Position the tip of the shaping cursor inside the circle exactly at the node, and then begin dragging the node downward in a clockwise direction. The two nodes separate as before, but this time the circle turns into a shape like a pie missing a piece, suitable for pie charts and wedges, as shown in Figure 10-40.

3. Press and hold (CTRL) and continue dragging the mouse. The angle of the wedge shape now moves in fixed increments of 15 degrees. Release the mouse button when you have obtained the desired angle.

4. Just as you did with the arc, press the spacebar to activate the Select tool and select the wedge. Notice the oversized highlighting box once more. Make sure to surround this highlighting box completely whenever you attempt to select a wedge with a narrow total angle.

5. Select New from the File menu to clear the screen.

That's all there is to creating arcs and wedges from ellipses and circles. If these shaping techniques are not flexible enough for you, you can always convert the arc or wedge to a curve object, as you will see in the next section.

Converting Ellipses and Circles to Curves

If the shaping options for ellipses and circles seem limited to you, don't worry. You can convert any ellipse, circle, arc, or wedge into a curve object and, from that point onward, you can add and delete nodes, drag nodes and control points, or change node types. In the following exercise, you will create a wedge from a circle, convert the wedge to curves, and then reshape the new curve object into the body of a baby carriage.

1. Select the Ellipse tool and draw an ellipse that is wider than it is high, starting from the upper left area of the rim and moving downward as you drag.

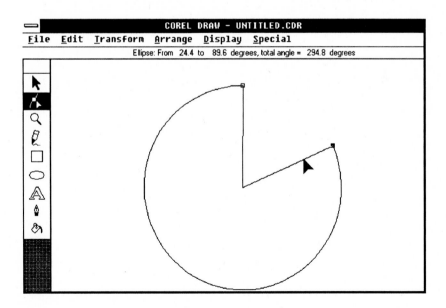

FIGURE 10-40   Creating a pie wedge from a circle

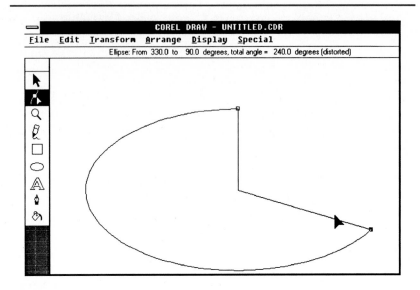

FIGURE 10-41   A wedge created from an ellipse, with a total angle of 240 degrees

2. Activate the Shaping tool and position the arrowhead cursor over the node of the circle. Drag the node downward, keeping the tip of the shaping cursor inside the rim, and create a wedge with a total angle of 240 degrees, as shown in Figure 10-41.

3. Press the spacebar to activate the Select tool and select the wedge, and then select the Convert To Curves command from the Arrange menu. Notice that because of the shape of the wedge, the new curve object has five nodes, whereas the circle had only one node.

4. Reactivate the Shaping tool and drag the node furthest to the right upward and outward, as shown in Figure 10-42. Since the

segment next to this one is a straight line, the selected node has only one control point. Moving this node upward and outward has the effect of stretching the straight line.

5. The curvature of the segment associated with the node you just moved is not adequate to round out the bottom of the "carriage." To remedy this, double-click on the curve segment and select Add from the pop-up Node Edit menu. A new node appears between the selected node and the one below and to the left of it, as shown in Figure 10-43. It's a symmetrical node because of the existing curvature and because the object originated as an ellipse.

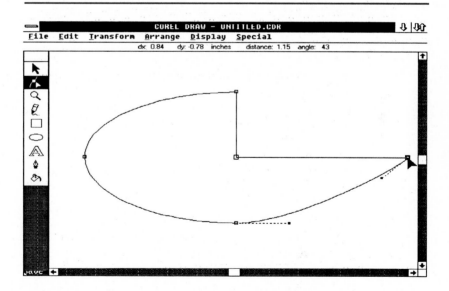

FIGURE 10-42   Dragging a node to form the top of a carriage

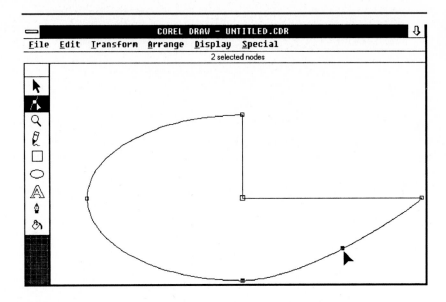

FIGURE 10-43   Adding a node to obtain better curve control

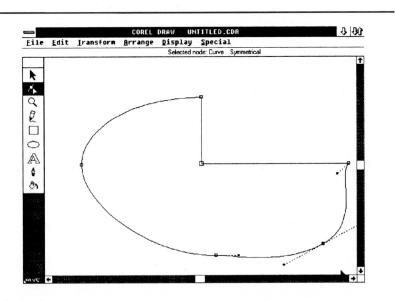

FIGURE 10-44   Rounding out the bottom of the carriage

6. Select and drag this newly added symmetrical node downward and to the right, until it forms a nicely rounded bottom to the "carriage" body, as shown in Figure 10-44.

Perhaps the example in the preceding exercise will stimulate your imagination to create any number of complex objects from the basic objects available to you through the drawing tools. The Shaping tool makes it all possible!

SUMMARY

An ability to reshape objects is one of the most critical skills in Corel DRAW! You reshape objects with the Shaping tool, which performs different functions depending on the type of object to which you apply it. To select any object with the Shaping tool, first select the Shaping tool and then click once anywhere on the outline of the object. To show that you are in shaping mode, the nodes of the selected object become enlarged. You can select and shape only one object at a time with the Shaping tool. If you need to shape more than one object simultaneously, you must first combine the objects using the Select tool and the Combine command in the Arrange menu, and then apply the Shaping tool to the combined object.

When you use the Shaping tool with lines and curves, you have complete control over the shape, angle, and direction of curvature. You achieve this control in one of three ways: by moving nodes, by moving the control points of nodes, or by editing the nodes using a pop-up Node Edit menu. Nodes, represented by tiny square boxes, are the points through which a curve passes and are associated with the curve or line segments on either side of a node. Control points, available when you select one node at a time, allow you to reshape one or both curve segments of a node manually, depending on the type of node you select. The Node Edit menu, which pops up when you double-click on a node or on the preceding line or curve segment, allows you to add and delete nodes, break curves apart and join them together, and change node type.

When you use the Shaping tool with rectangles and squares, you can round the corners of these objects. Rounding the corners of rotated, skewed, or stretched rectangles and squares produces distorted semi-elliptical shapes. You can also convert any square or rectangle to a curve object, and then reshape that object more freely than if it remained a rectangle or square.

When you use the Shaping tool with ellipses and circles, you can create open arcs or wedge shapes. To create an arc, you drag the node of the ellipse or circle with the tip of the Shaping tool cursor *outside* the rim of the ellipse or circle while dragging. To create a wedge shape, you place the tip of the Shaping tool cursor *inside* the rim of the ellipse or circle while dragging. You can also convert circles and ellipses to curve objects and then reshape that object even more freely.

chapter **11**

SHAPING AND EDITING TEXT

Text can be an important design element, whether you specialize in original art, graphic or industrial design, technical illustration, or desktop publishing. Every choice you make concerning typeface, typestyle, spacing, alignment, point size, and placement can affect how your intended audience receives your work. You should have the option of editing text attributes at any time, not only when you first enter text on a page.

With Corel DRAW!, you do have that option. Using the Select tool and the Shaping tool, you can edit existing text in ways that enhance both its typographic and pictorial value. You already edited text as a graphic element in Chapters 8 and 9, by using the Select tool to rotate, stretch, scale, skew, and reflect text strings. In this chapter, you will concentrate on editing the *typographical* text attributes (such as typeface and point size) of individual characters, groups of characters, and complete text strings. You will also learn to customize your text picture even further by converting a text string to a set of curves and then reshaping each curve. The Select and Shaping tools share these editing functions between them.

EDITING ATTRIBUTES FOR AN ENTIRE TEXT STRING

Remember the Text dialog box you used to select attributes when you first entered a text string? You can also use this dialog box to change attributes for text that already exists: Simply click on the text string with the Select tool and then select Edit Text from the Edit menu. This menu option is available only when you have selected a text string with the Select tool and the changes you make apply to every character in the text string. To change attributes for selected characters within a text string, you need to use the Shaping tool as described in the section entitled "Selecting and Editing Characters with the Shaping Tool."

In the following exercise, you will create a short text string that you will use in many different exercises throughout this chapter. Then, you will select the text string and change some of its attributes using the Edit Text command from the Edit menu. Set your viewing magnification to 1:1 and turn the Show Rulers and Snap To Grid commands off for this portion of the chapter.

1. Select the Text tool ◮ and then select an insertion point midway down the left edge of your viewing window. When the Text dialog box appears, type the following text string on three separate lines:

   Doing
   what comes
   naturally

2. Use the default text attributes in the dialog box: Avalon Normal, 24.0 points, and Left Alignment. Adjust your dialog box if it shows other settings.

3. Select OK to exit the dialog box and display the text on the page.

4. Press the spacebar to activate the Select tool ◤ and select the text string. A highlighting box surrounds the text string.

5. Select Edit Text from the Edit menu. The Text dialog box shown in Figure 11-1 appears. This dialog box is the same one you use when you enter a new text string.

6. Change the text attributes to Cupertino Italic, 65.0 points, and Center Alignment and then select OK. Because you have changed the alignment, some of the text may not appear within viewing range. If this is the case, drag its outlines until it fits within the viewing window, as shown in Figure 11-2.

7. Deselect the text string and save your work as the file named DOINWHAT.CDR. Leave the text on the screen for the next exercise.

You can change attributes for a text string as often as desired. However, as long as you use the Select tool to select text, any attribute changes you make will affect the entire text string. If your work requires highly stylized text designs, where attributes must

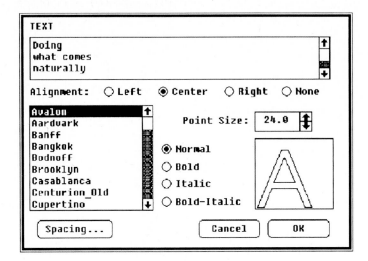

FIGURE 11-1   Editing attributes in the Text dialog box

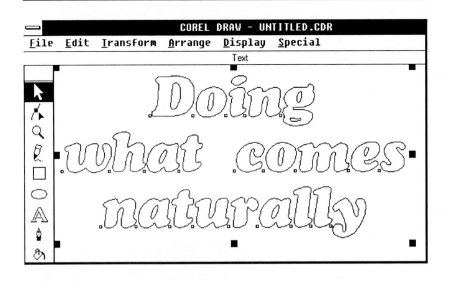

FIGURE 11-2   Changing typeface, typestyle, alignment, and
point size

be decided on a character-by-character basis, you need to use the Shaping tool.

SELECTING AND EDITING CHARACTERS WITH THE SHAPING TOOL

When the Shaping tool is active, you can select any number of characters within a text string and edit their typographical attributes. Depending on how you prefer to work, you can edit attributes either interactively or with the Character Attributes command in the Edit menu. Some of these attributes, specifically typeface, typestyle, and point size, overlap with the attributes in the Text dialog box. Others, including horizontal and vertical shift and character angle, are adjustable only through the Character Attributes dialog box. And you can move letters and adjust spacing and kerning interactively, without using menu commands or dialog boxes. If all these adjustments fail to give your text the desired look, you can gain more editing control by converting text to curves and then manipulating its nodes and control points.

Before you can edit text attributes on a character-by-character basis, you must first use the Shaping tool to select the text string in which the characters are located. This is similar to selecting a curve object as a prerequisite to selecting one or more of its nodes. After you select a text string, you can select a specific character, multiple adjacent or non-adjacent characters, or all characters in the text string. Practice selecting different combinations of characters in the following exercise.

1. Open the DOINWHAT.CDR text file that you created in the last exercise, if it is not open already. If the Select tool is active, make sure that the text string is not selected; it should not be surrounded by a highlighting box.

2. Activate the Shaping tool  and click once on the outline of any character in the text string. A square node appears at the base of each letter in the text string, and vertical and horizontal arrow symbols appear at the lower left and lower right corners of the text string, respectively:

You will become acquainted with the meaning of these symbols in a moment. For now, it is enough to recognize that this change in the text string's appearance indicates that you have selected it for editing with the Shaping tool. The status line shows that you have not yet selected specific characters.

3. Select a single character in the text string, the letter "n" in "naturally." Do this by clicking *once* on the node of this character. The status line now contains the message "1 character(s) selected," and the node at the bottom left of the letter turns black, like this:

4. Deselect the letter "n" by clicking anywhere outside the text string. Notice that the string itself remains selected, however.

5. Select the initial letter of each word. Click once on the node for the "D" in "Doing." Then press and hold the (SHIFT) key and

click on the node for the initial letter of each of the other words. Check the status line to keep track of the number of characters you select.

6. To deselect these characters, either click on any white space, or press and hold (SHIFT) and click on each selected character node one by one.

7. Select the entire word "Doing" by lassoing its nodes with a marquee:

Your marquee does not have to surround the letter characters completely, as long as it surrounds the nodes. All the nodes of this word become highlighted after you release the mouse button.

8. Deselect these characters, and then draw a marquee that surrounds all of the text string. All of the characters are now selected for editing.

9. Deselect all of the characters by clicking on any white space. Leave the text on the screen, with the text string selected for editing with the Shaping tool, but with no individual characters selected.

You may be wondering, "Why should I bother to select all the characters with the Shaping tool, when I could activate the Select tool and change attributes for the entire text string?" You can control *some* attributes that way, but the Character Attributes dialog box, which you can access only when the Shaping tool is active, offers you even more options for altering the appearance of text. Read on to find out how those additional attributes can enhance the design of text in Corel DRAW!.

WORKING WITH THE CHARACTER ATTRIBUTES DIALOG BOX

When you use the Character Attributes dialog box, you can control other characteristics of selected characters besides typeface, typestyle, and point size. You can tilt characters at any angle, shift them up, down, or sideways, or make them into small subscripts and superscripts. Practically the only thing you can't do is change the text message itself. In this section, you will learn how to access this dialog box and work with each of the controls in it. As you work through the exercises, you will learn about useful applications for each type of attribute. By the end of the section, you will have altered the design of the DOINWHAT.CDR text string substantially.

Accessing the Character Attributes Dialog Box

You can access the Character Attributes dialog box either by double-clicking on a selected character node, or by selecting a menu command. Any attributes that you alter in this dialog box apply only to the characters you have selected. Make sure, then, that you have selected all of the characters you want to edit before accessing the Character Attributes dialog box.

1. With the Shaping tool active, select the node in front of the letter "n" in "naturally."

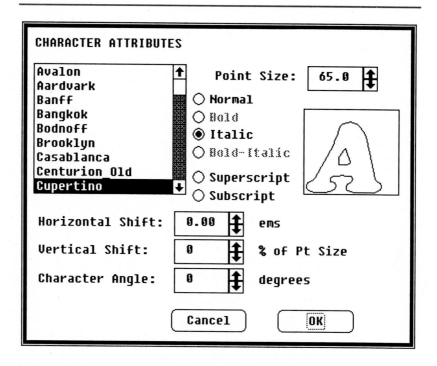

FIGURE 11-3   The Character Attributes dialog box

2. Access the Character Attributes dialog box in the way that is most convenient for your working habits. If you prefer to use menu commands, select the Character Attributes option from the Edit menu. If you like using the mouse best, double-click on any of the selected nodes. The Character Attributes dialog box shown in Figure 11-3 appears.

Take a moment to become familiar with the options available to you in this dialog box and with the significance of each attribute.

Getting Around in the Character Attributes Dialog Box

The options in the Character Attributes box in Figure 11-3 allow you to control eight different types of text attributes: typeface, typestyle, point size, horizontal shift, vertical shift, character angle, superscript, and subscript. You are familiar with the first three attributes, but the concepts behind horizontal and vertical shifts, character angle, superscript, and subscript may be new to you. If so, browse through this section to find out more about these attributes.

Horizontal Shift   The Horizontal Shift option controls the distance, in ems, by which selected characters shift to the right or left of their original location. You may recall from Chapter 5 that one em equals the width of the capital letter M in the current typeface. This unit is therefore variable, depending on the typeface of the selected characters.

Vertical Shift   The Vertical Shift option controls the distance by which selected characters shift above or below their starting location (baseline). Corel DRAW! expresses this distance as a percentage of the point size of the selected characters. This distance is therefore variable, too.

Character Angle   The Character Angle option allows you to tilt the selected characters in any direction and at any angle. You can turn characters upside down, sideways, or anywhere in between.

Superscript and Subscript   The Superscript and Subscript options let you place selected characters above or below the rest of the text respectively. Superscript text bottom-aligns with the imaginary line at the top of surrounding text (example: the "2" in

$E=mc^2$). Subscript text top-aligns with the baseline of surrounding text, for example the "2" in H_2O. The term baseline refers to the imaginary straight line to which text is normally anchored and with which it aligns.

 The values that display in the Character Attributes dialog box depend on how you invoked the dialog box. If you access this dialog box by double-clicking on a character, you will see the settings assigned to that character, even if you have selected other characters at the same time. If you call up the dialog box by selecting the Character Attributes command, the values displayed correspond to the first character in the selected group.

You can move between options in the Character Attributes dialog box either by using the mouse, or by pressing the (TAB) or (SHIFT-TAB) and cursor keys. The only controls you cannot select with the keyboard are the Superscript and Subscript option buttons.

In the next five sections, you will have the opportunity to redesign text imaginatively, using all of the options in the Character Attributes dialog box.

Editing Typeface and Typestyle

In the following exercise, you will assign a different typeface and/or typestyle to each letter in the word "naturally." You selected the first letter of the word before entering the dialog box, so you will alter the letter "n" first of all.

1. Select the Aardvark typeface in the typeface list box and then select OK. Your text string redisplays on the screen, but now the letter "n" looks quite different from the surrounding letters.

2. Double-click on the character node of the "n" once more. When the dialog box appears this time, it shows the current typeface

of the *selected* character or characters. (See the note in the previous section.) Select Cancel to exit the dialog box.

3. Select each of the other letters in the word "naturally" in turn. Assign typefaces and typestyles to them in the following order: Paradise Normal, Frankfurt Gothic Bold Italic, Cupertino Normal, RenfrewNormal, Switzerland Italic, Unicorn Normal, USA Black Italic, Banff Normal. When you are finished, the word "naturally"displays an interesting patchwork of fonts:

4. Save the changes you have made by pressing (CTRL-S), and leave your work on the screen for the next exercise. Note that whenever you save the picture you are working on, Corel DRAW! activates the Select tool automatically.

Go on to the next section to apply different point sizes to the letters whose typefaces and typestyles you have already altered.

Editing Point Size

When you changed typefaces for each letter in the word "naturally," you left the point sizes unaltered, yet the letters do not appear to be the same size. You have probably guessed by now that different typefaces have different heights and widths and that point size is only one way to measure text size. In the following exercise, you will make the letters in this word closer to one another in actual size.

1. Activate the Shaping tool again and then double-click on the character node of the first letter "a" in "naturally." When the Character Attributes dialog box appears, change the point size for this letter to 140.0 and then select OK. Even though you have more than doubled its point size, this letter only now approximates the height of its neighbors.

2. In the same way, select the first letter "l" and change its point size to 75.0.

3. Finally, select the letter "y" and change its point size to 90.0. Now, all of the letters seem more uniform in height and size:

4. Save your work by pressing (**CTRL-S**), and leave the text string on the screen.

To edit the word "naturally" so that it conveys a sense of a more natural state, you can shift some of the characters up or down relative to the baseline and move others sideways. In the next exercise, you will practice moving individual characters.

Editing Horizontal and Vertical Shift

When you shift selected characters horizontally, you move them to the right or left of their starting position, causing them to overlap with other characters on the same line. You can use this technique to convey a sense of being rushed or crowded, or simply to adjust spacing between letters precisely. When you shift characters vertically, they fall above or below the baseline, which can create a feeling of spontaneity or excitement (see the DRAWNEWS.CDR sample file for a good example of this kind of treatment).

In the next exercise, you will shift some of the characters in the word "naturally" to enhance the sense of spontaneity and a natural look in the text.

1. Activate the Shaping tool and then double-click on the character node for the letter "n" in the word "naturally" to enter the Character Attributes dialog box. Set Horizontal Shift to -0.50 ems and then select OK. Because you set the value to a negative number, the letter shifts to the left of its original position.

2. Select the character node for the next letter "a" and set Vertical Shift to 20% of point size. When you select OK, the position of the letter shifts above the baseline.

3. Select the following letters in turn and change the shift settings for each as follows. Change "r" to Vertical Shift -25%, the second "l" to Vertical Shift 10%, and the "y" to Horizontal Shift .40 ems and Vertical Shift 25%. Notice that a negative value for Vertical Shift causes the selected character, "r," to reposition itself below the baseline. The resulting text should now look like this:

4. Save your changes and leave this text on the screen.

So far, you have edited attributes for one letter at a time. In the next section, you will select a group of characters and practice positioning them as superscripts and subscripts.

Creating Superscripts and Subscripts

Perform the following exercise to simulate a superscript and subscript.

1. Reactivate the Shaping tool and then select the character nodes of all of the letters in the word "comes" except the letter "c." Double-click on the node in front of "o" to access the Character Attributes dialog box.

2. Click on the Superscript option button and then select OK. The selected letters have become small and appear as a superscript to the letter "c," like this:

3. Select the Undo command in the Edit menu to return the selected characters to their original position.

4. Select the same characters again and return to the Character Attributes dialog box by double-clicking on the "o" node. This time, click on the Subscript option button. When you select OK, the letters display as a subscript to the letter "c."

5. Select the Undo command in the Edit menu to return the selected characters to their original position.

In the next section, you will complete the last exercise pertinent to the Character Attributes dialog box. You will practice tilting the characters in the word "naturally" to different angles.

Editing Character Angle

You can tilt selected characters at any angle using the Character Angle setting in the Character Attributes dialog box. Values between 0 and 180 degrees indicate that you are tilting the characters above an imaginary horizon, in a counterclockwise direction. Values between 0 and -180 degrees indicate that you are tilting the characters below an imaginary horizon, in a clockwise direction. At a 180-degree angle, the characters are upside down. Practice adjusting character angle in the following exercise.

1. With the Shaping tool active, select the character nodes of the first letter "n," the letter "u," and the last letter "y" in the word "naturally." Double-click on one of these nodes to access the Character Attributes dialog box. Set Character Angle to -15 degrees and then select OK. The selected characters now appear tilted toward the right.

2. Deselect these three letters and select the letter "t," the second letter "a," and the second "l." Double-click on one of their nodes to access the Character Attributes dialog box. Set Character Angle for these letters to 15 degrees and then select OK. These characters appear tilted toward the left. The word "naturally" now seems to fly off in all directions:

3. Save your changes and then select New from the File menu to clear the screen.

This concludes the tutorial on the use of the settings in the Character Attributes dialog box. No doubt you have come up with a few creative ideas of your own while practicing the exercises in the preceding sections. When you are ready to proceed, continue through the next portion of this chapter, where you will learn some convenient ways to kern text and adjust spacing interactively.

KERNING TEXT INTERACTIVELY

Kerning, simply defined, is the art of adjusting the space between individual pairs of letters for greater readability. There are many possible letter pair combinations in the 26 letters of the English alphabet, but most typeface manufacturers provide automatic kerning for only a few hundred commonly used pairs. Occasionally you will see too much or too little space between adjacent letters. You can kern these letter pairs by moving one of the letters subtly to the right or left.

Using kerning as a design element can enhance the power of your message. For instance, you will draw more attention to your text when you kern letters to create special effects, such as expanded letter spacing in selected words of a magazine or newspaper headline.

The exercises in this section offer more extreme examples of kerning than you are likely to find in most text, but they will help you become familiar with the concept of kerning. Follow the steps in each exercise to learn how to kern single or multiple characters. Integrated within the exercises is information on using constraint and alignment techniques to kern more easily and precisely.

Kerning Single Characters

The following exercise lets you practice adjusting spacing between any two text characters. As you work through the steps, you will learn how to ensure that characters align properly with the surrounding text after you move them. Before starting the exercise, adjust viewing magnification to a 1:1 ratio. Turn on the Snap To Grid, Show Rulers, and Show Status Line commands, and set the Grid Frequency to 8 per inch. Retain these settings for both exercises on kerning.

1. Select the Text tool and then select a text insertion point at the 1-inch mark on the horizontal ruler and the 4 ½-inch mark on the vertical ruler.

2. After the Text dialog box appears, type the word **Kerning** in upper- and lowercase letters. Leave a space after the "K" and another after the "e." Press (ENTER) to begin a new line and type the word **Text** on this line. Leave one space after the letter "T," one space after the "e," and two spaces after the letter "x."

3. Set the alignment to None, the point size to 80.0, and the typeface to Bodnoff.

4. After the text string appears on the screen as in Figure 11-4, select the Shaping tool. Since the text string was the last object you created, the Shaping tool selects it automatically. A node appears next to each character in the text string; vertical and horizontal spacing control handles appear at each end of the last line of the text string.

5. You will need to bring the letter "e" in "Kerning" much closer to the "K" and the letters "rning" closer to the "e." To adjust the spacing between "K" and "e" so that the text will appear more uniform, click on the node in front of the letter "e." When the cursor turns into a + sign, drag the letter 0.75 inches to the left,

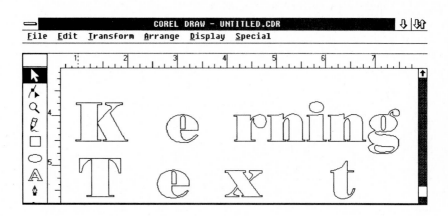

FIGURE 11-4   Text in need of kerning

as shown in Figure 11-5. A dotted outline of the letter follows the cursor as you drag. When you release the mouse button, the letter itself appears in this location.

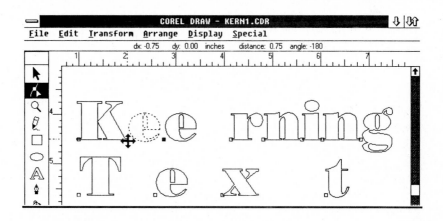

FIGURE 11-5   Kerning a single letter

6. If the "e" is not aligned with the rest of the text, snap this letter back to its original position by selecting the Straighten Text command in the Arrange menu, and then repeat step 5. This command erases any previous kerning information, so use it only when you want to return text to its original location. Alternatively, you can select the Align To Baseline command, also in the Arrange menu. When you accidentally position a character above or below the baseline, this command forces the character to align with the baseline again. Unlike the Straighten Text command, the Align To Baseline command does not erase any previous kerning information.

7. Save your kerned text as KERN1.CDR and leave it on the screen for the next exercise.

 If you require a high degree of precision in the placement of kerned text, zoom in on the character(s) you want to move. Alternatively, you can press and hold (CTRL) while moving the characters, thereby constraining the text to align with the nearest baseline. Be sure to release the mouse button before you release (CTRL) to make certain of proper alignment.

Kerning Multiple Characters

In this section, you will learn how to move and kern multiple characters within a text string simultaneously. In practice, your most common use for this feature will be to move the remaining characters of a word closer to another letter that you have already kerned. However, you can select and reposition any group of characters, including non-adjacent characters, to another location in the same way.

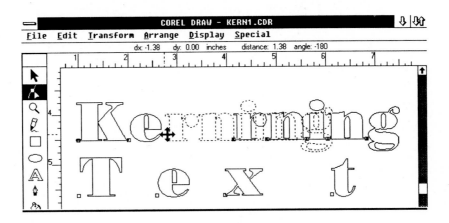

FIGURE 11-6   Kerning multiple adjacent letters

1. With the KERN1.CDR file displayed in a 1:1 viewing magnification, select the Shaping tool and draw a marquee around the letters "rning."

2. Click on the node for the letter "r" and then drag the mouse 1.38 inches to the left. Refer to the status line for assistance. All the letters in the selected group follow, as shown in Figure 11-6. If the selected characters do not line up with the adjoining text when you release the mouse button, review step 6 in the previous exercise. You may want to use the Align To Baseline and Straighten Text commands. Deselect the letters "rning" when you have them in the desired location.

3. Use (**SHIFT**) to select the "e" and the second "t" in "Text," as shown in Figure 11- 7a. Click on the node in front of the letter "e" and drag it 0.60 inches to the left. Both selected letters

a.
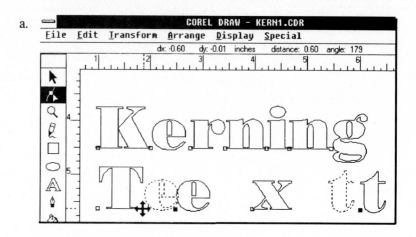

b.
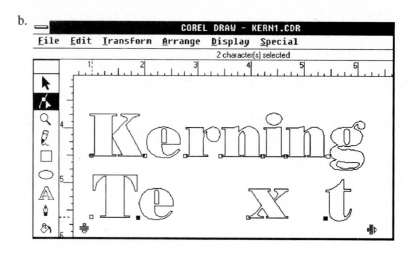

FIGURE 11-7   Kerning multiple non-adjacent letters

should move together across the screen without disturbing the "x." After you release the mouse button the letters "e" and "t" will appear, as shown in Figure 11-7b.

4. As you can see, the letters "x" and "t" still are not close enough to the "e." Experiment by moving these two letters on your screen until the text string appears normal.

5. Save your changes to the file by pressing (CTRL-S). Then select New from the File menu to clear the screen.

Kerning is not the only text attribute that you can adjust interactively with the Shaping tool. In the next section, you will learn how to adjust spacing between characters, words, and lines for an entire selected text string.

ADJUSTING SPACING INTERACTIVELY

There are two ways to edit inter-character, inter-word, and inter-line spacing of existing text in Corel DRAW!. The first way, as you will recall, is to select the text string with the Select tool and then invoke the Text dialog box using either (CTRL-T) or the Edit Text command in the Edit menu. Using this method, you can click on the Spacing command button in the Text dialog box and set spacing in the sub-dialog box provided. You enjoy the advantage of precision but experience the disadvantage of going through a series of additional steps.

If you prefer to work more spontaneously, Corel DRAW! offers you an interactive method of spacing as well. This method involves selecting the text string with the Shaping tool and then dragging one of the two stylized arrows that appear at the text string's lower boundary. Keep in mind, however, that you adjust spacing for *all* of the characters in the text string when you use this technique. To adjust spacing between individual characters, see the "Kerning Characters Interactively" section of this chapter.

To alter inter-character spacing interactively, you drag the horizontal arrow at the lower right boundary of the text string. To alter inter-word spacing, you drag the same arrow while holding down

FIGURE 11-8   Displaying the spacing adjustments arrows

(CTRL). And to alter inter-line spacing, you drag the vertical arrow at the lower left boundary of the text string.

FIGURE 11-9   Adjusting inter-character spacing

The next three sections provide a short tutorial on altering each of the three types of spacing interactively.

Adjusting Inter-Character Spacing

In the following exercise, you will create a text string and adjust the inter-character spacing, observing the changes in the Corel DRAW! interface as you work.

1. Set viewing magnification to 1:1, then activate the Text tool and select an insertion point near the upper left corner of your viewing window.

2. When the Text dialog box appears, type **Running out of** on the first line of the text entry window and **space?** on the second. Set text attributes to Fujiyama Normal, Left Alignment, and 75.0 points, and then select OK. The text displays in your viewing window. If the text string is not completely visible on the display, select the text string and move it to the location shown in Figure 11-8.

3. Activate the Shaping tool. Each character node increases in size, and stylized vertical and horizontal arrows appear at the lower left and right boundaries of the text object, just as in Figure 11-8.

4. Position the Shaping cursor directly over the horizontal arrow at the lower right boundary of the text object, until the cursor turns into a white cross. Then, drag this arrow to the right. Notice that, just as in the example in Figure 11-9, the characters do not seem to move immediately; instead, you see a dotted outline following the two-way arrow cursor. As you drag, the status line displays the message "Inter-Character," followed by information about the horizontal distance by which you are increasing the size of the text boundary.

FIGURE 11-10   Increasing inter-character spacing

5. When the right boundary of the text string (represented by the dotted outline) reaches the desired point, release the mouse button. The text repositions itself to align with that boundary, and the space between each character increases proportionally, as shown in Figure 11-10.

6. If you would like to know the exact inter-character spacing measurement you have obtained, select the text string with the Select tool and access the Text and Spacing dialog boxes. This is a good way to check for precision.

7. Select the Undo command from the Edit menu to return the text to its former position. Then *decrease* the space between characters by dragging the horizontal arrow to the left instead of to the right. If you decrease the space drastically, letters may even overlap each other, like this:

8. Select Undo once more to return the characters to their original positions. Leave this text on the screen for now.

This method is useful when you want to fit text into a defined space within a drawing, without changing the point size or other attributes. Go on to the next section to practice changing inter-word spacing independently of the spacing between characters.

Adjusting Inter-Word Spacing

Suppose that you don't need to change the spacing between letters but your design calls for increased or decreased spacing between words. To adjust inter-word spacing interactively, you drag the same horizontal arrow that you used for inter-character spacing. The difference is that you also hold down (CTRL) at the same time. Try the following exercise, using the text string you created in the previous section.

1. With the Shaping tool active and the text string selected, position the cursor over the horizontal arrow until the cursor turns into a white cross. Then press and hold (CTRL) and drag the two-way arrow cursor to the right. The status line displays the message "Inter-Word," followed by the horizontal distance by which you are stretching the text boundary.

2. When the outline that you are dragging has the desired width, release the mouse button first, and then (CTRL). (If you release

FIGURE 11-11   Increasing inter-word spacing

(CTRL) first, you will adjust the inter-character rather than the inter-word spacing.) The text redisplays with increased space between each word, as shown in Figure 11-11.

3. Select the Undo command in the Edit menu to return the text to its original inter-word spacing.

4. Try decreasing the amount of inter-word spacing by dragging the horizontal arrow to the left instead of the right. When you are finished experimenting, select the Undo command once more. Leave this text on the screen for the next exercise.

You can change the spacing between lines of a text string, as well as between words or characters. The next section gives you hands-on practice in editing inter-line spacing.

Adjusting Inter-Line Spacing

To edit inter-line spacing with the Shaping tool, you drag the vertical arrow located at the lower left of the text boundary. Try increasing and decreasing the space between lines now, using the same text string you have been working with for the past two sections.

1. With the Shaping tool active and the text string selected, position the mouse cursor directly over the vertical arrow that appears at the lower left text boundary and drag this arrow downward. The cursor turns into a two-way vertical arrow. Simultaneously, the status line displays the message "Inter-Line," followed by the vertical distance measurement, which tells you how much you have increased the size of the text boundary.

2. When you have increased the boundary by the desired size, release the mouse button. The text repositions itself to fit the new boundary; as in Figure 11-12, only the spacing between lines changes, not the length or size of the text itself.

3. To see the precise amount of inter-line spacing that you have added, activate the Select tool and select the Edit Text command in the Edit menu. Then, click on the Spacing command button to see the Spacing dialog box. When you are finished, select Undo from the Edit menu to return the text string to its former inter-line spacing.

4. Reduce the inter-line spacing of the text string by dragging the vertical arrow upward instead of downward. When you are finished, select Undo to return the text to its former spacing.

5. Select New from the File menu to clear the screen before beginning the next section.

 If your text string contains only one line, dragging the vertical arrow has no effect.

By now, you have explored all of the possible text attributes that you can change using the Select and Shaping tools. If you need to give your text an even more customized look, however, you have the option of converting text to a curve object and then editing its nodes. This is the topic of the next and final section of this chapter.

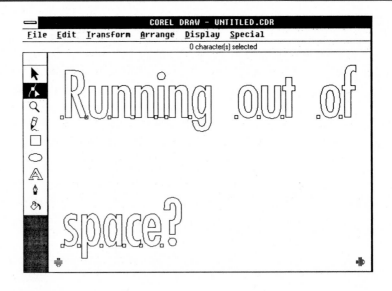

FIGURE 11-12   Increasing inter-line spacing

RESHAPING CHARACTERS

Graphic designers and desktop publishers often have need of stylized text characters that give their messages extra flair, but which just don't exist in standard typefaces. Corel DRAW! can help you create such "text pictures" easily. All you have to do is select text attributes that approximate the effect you want to achieve, and then convert the text string to curves. You can then reshape the text using the Select and Shaping tools.

The following exercise contains a simple step-by-step example of how to create stylized text pictures. Carry out the steps and give your own imagination a boost!

1. To prepare for this exercise, turn off the Show Rulers command and set the viewing magnification to 1:1. Set the Typeface Selection Char: option in the Preferences dialog box to a capital "S." You will need to see how this letter looks in the Text dialog box so that you can select an appropriate typeface more easily.

2. Activate the Text tool and select an insertion point about midway down the left edge of your viewing area. The Text dialog box appears.

3. Type the word **Snake** in upper- and lowercase letters in the text entry box. Test each of the typefaces in the typeface list box against the sample display character. The capital "S" of the Gatineau typeface bears a fairly strong resemblance to a snake, so set text attributes to Gatineau Bold Italic, 150.0 points, and Left Alignment. Select OK to exit the Text dialog box and display your text on the page, as shown in Figure 11-13.

4. Activate the Shaping tool and double-click on the node for the letter "S" to invoke the Character Attributes dialog box.

5. Your aim is to increase the size of the letter "S" and make it a *drop cap*—a first capital letter that falls below the baseline of the remaining text. To achieve this aim, set the point size for the letter "S" to 250.0 and set Vertical Shift to -25% of point size. Select OK to make these changes take effect. Your text should now look like Figure 11-14.

6. Activate the Select tool to select the entire text string, and then click on the Convert To Curves option in the Arrange menu. The text redisplays with many little nodes, indicating that it has become a curve object. If you activate the Shaping tool again, the status line displays the message, "Curve: 66 nodes on 8 subpaths." This message indicates that Corel DRAW! now considers this text string to be one object with eight combined segments.

7. Activate the Select tool again and select the Break Apart command in the Arrange menu. Each letter is now a separate object.

FIGURE 11-13   "Snake" text: Gatineau Bold Italic, 150.0 points

FIGURE 11-14   Increasing the size of the letter "S"

8. Deselect all of the letters and then click on the letter "S" with the Select tool. Stretch the letter vertically by dragging the middle boundary markers on the upper and lower sides of the

FIGURE 11-15   "S" converted to curves and reshaped with the Shaping tool

highlighting box. Your goal is to elongate the letter, thereby enhancing a "snake-like" appearance.

9. Now, activate the Shaping tool and manipulate the nodes of the "S" so that you achieve the general look of Figure 11-15. Make some areas of the "snake" narrower and others broader. You will want to reshape and move the snake's head, too. Make the "tail" of the snake narrower, as well.

10. You can try to match the results in Figure 11-15 exactly or develop your own creative enhancements utilizing all of the skills you have learned at this point in the book. When you are satisfied with the appearance of the snake, save the image under the filename SNAKE.CDR.

11. Select New from the File menu to clear the screen.

As you can see, the possibilities for creating custom characters for text are virtually endless. If you find yourself fired-up with new ideas for your own projects, experiment until you design a word picture that best enhances your message.

SUMMARY

Text in Corel DRAW! can express your message in terms of both its typography (text-specific attributes) and its pictorial value. You can edit text attributes any time after you first enter your text, using features available to you through the Select and Shaping tools.

When you want to edit text attributes for all of the characters in a text string, use the Text dialog box. This dialog box becomes available to you through the Edit Text command in the Edit menu when you click on a text string with the Select tool. Typeface, typestyle, point size, alignment, and spacing are the attributes you can adjust using this method.

To edit attributes for one or several selected characters only, you need to select characters with the Shaping tool rather than the Select tool. You select one character by clicking on its associated node; you select multiple characters using (SHIFT) or the marquee. The Shaping tool allows you to edit many text attributes using the Character Attributes dialog box, and other attributes (kerning and spacing) interactively using the mouse alone. You can also adjust some of these text attributes with the options in the Text dialog box. Others, however—specifically character angle, horizontal and vertical shift, and subscript or superscript—are available for selected characters only. These last attributes allow you to customize characters beyond the parameters of a normal typeface.

Using the Shaping tool with selected characters, you can also kern text interactively, without having to use menus or dialog boxes. To adjust kerning, you simply move one or more selected characters along the baseline, using (CTRL) to keep the characters properly aligned.

You also have the ability to adjust inter-character, inter-word, and inter-line spacing using the Shaping tool. These spacing adjustments apply to *all* of the characters in the selected text string; you cannot select specific characters for these operations. To adjust spacing, you drag either the horizontal or vertical arrow along the lower edge of the text boundary.

To give text a truly customized or pictorial look, convert a text string to curves, and then reshape the letter or letters, using both Select and Shaping tool techniques. Once you convert a text string to curves, you can stretch, scale, rotate, and skew the text objects, or manipulate their nodes and control points.

chapter 12

CUTTING, COPYING, AND PASTING OBJECTS AND PICTURES

So far, you have learned how to select, move, rearrange, transform, and reshape objects within a single graphic. An equally important part of the editing process involves the *transfer* of image information within a graphic, between pictures, or between Corel DRAW! and other Windows applications. The editing functions that allow you to transfer image data include copying, cutting, and pasting objects and pictures, deleting or duplicating objects, and copying object attributes. You access these operations using the Cut, Copy, Paste, Clear, Duplicate, and Copy Style From commands in the Edit menu.

These editing functions have many uses that will save you time and design effort. You don't have to start from scratch each time you need to duplicate an object or its style attribute. You can simply transfer image information, using the editing commands. You perform some of the transfer operations within a single picture; others allow you to transfer information between Corel DRAW! files, and even between Corel DRAW! and other Windows applications.

Starting with Version 1.1, Corel DRAW! allows you to transfer objects to and from the Windows clipboard. This means that you can copy or cut objects between different image files in Corel DRAW!, or from Corel DRAW! to a file in another Windows application. Conversely, you can copy or cut objects from files in other Windows applications and paste them to the page of your choice in Corel DRAW!.

This chapter covers the use of the Windows clipboard, both within Corel DRAW! and between Corel DRAW! and other Windows applications. It also introduces you to some additional object and style copying functions in Corel DRAW! that complement the use of the Windows clipboard. You'll find out how to duplicate objects within a drawing and how to copy attributes from one object to another. You'll also review the difference between cutting objects from a file and deleting them permanently.

ABOUT THE WINDOWS CLIPBOARD

If you haven't used Windows applications before, you may be wondering how the clipboard works. Think of the Windows clipboard as a temporary storage bin that can contain only one item at a time. When you select an object and then click on the Copy or

Cut command in the Edit menu, you send a copy of the object to the clipboard. When you use the Paste command, you retrieve a copy of that object from the clipboard to place it in your drawing at the desired location. The copy you sent to the clipboard remains there until you overwrite it by copying or cutting another object, or until you exit Windows and end a session.

Windows creates its own file format, called a *metafile,* out of the information that you send to the clipboard. This standard metafile format allows you to share information between different applications that run under Windows. A metafile can be larger or smaller than the object you send to the clipboard, depending on the complexity of the information you are trying to transfer. Versions of Windows previous to 3.0 accept only 64K of data at a time into the clipboard. However, as you will see later in the chapter, this limitation does not always apply when you are simply transferring information between different Corel DRAW! files. As a rule of thumb, the more complex an object is in terms of its attributes, the more memory it requires when you send it to the clipboard.

Theoretically, all Windows applications should be able to trade information through the clipboard. In practice, however, some types of information in objects or files transfer better than others. When you have completed the basic exercises on copying, cutting, and pasting objects within Corel DRAW!, turn to the section entitled "Copying, Cutting, and Pasting Objects Between Applications." There you will find tips for trouble-free transfer operations through the clipboard.

SELECTING OBJECTS TO COPY, CUT, DUPLICATE, OR CLEAR

In order to duplicate or delete one or more objects, or copy or cut them to the clipboard, you must first select the objects with the Select tool. The Edit menu commands and their keyboard shortcuts are unavailable to you unless one or more objects are already selected.

You can select a single object, multiple objects, or all objects in a graphic for any of the Edit menu operations discussed in this chapter. To select a single object for one of the transfer operations, just click on its outline once. To select multiple objects for a transfer operation, use (SHIFT) or the marquee method you first learned in Chapter 8. (You might also want to group the objects after you select them in order to avoid separating them from each other accidentally.) To select all of the objects in a graphic, click on the Select All command in the Edit menu.

Once you have selected one or more objects, you are ready to apply the commands in the Edit menu.

COPYING AND PASTING OBJECTS

The Copy and Paste commands in the Edit menu enable you to copy Corel DRAW! objects and paste them to the same file, to another file in Corel DRAW!, or to another Windows application. When you *copy* an object to the clipboard, the original object remains in position on the page. When you *paste* the object, Windows makes another copy from the copy in the clipboard. The copy in the clipboard remains there until you overwrite it by copying or cutting another object or group of objects, or until you exit Windows.

To practice copying objects to the clipboard and pasting them to the same or different pictures, you will use a file that you created in Chapter 8, as well as two sample files provided with your software.

Copying and Pasting
Objects Within a Picture

When you copy an object to the clipboard and then paste it to the same picture, the copy overlays the original object exactly. The copy is selected as soon as it appears on the page, however, so you can move it safely without displacing the original object.

A more convenient way to copy an object within the same picture is to use the Duplicate command. When you invoke this command, Corel DRAW! automatically offsets the copy of the object from the original by a fixed distance that you specify. As a result, you can see both the original and the copy at the same time. See the "Duplicating Objects" section of this chapter for more details.

1. Open the ARROW1.CDR file and group all of the text strings in the picture, using the Select All command in the Edit menu and then the Group command in the Arrange menu.

2. To copy the grouped objects to the clipboard, either select the Copy command from the Edit menu as shown in Figure 12-1, or press (CTRL-INS). The cursor turns into an hourglass until Corel DRAW! finishes copying the selected object to the clipboard. If the error message shown in Figure 12-2 appears, click on the OK command button to return to the picture. In most cases, Corel DRAW! will actually have copied the selected objects to the clipboard in spite of the 64K limit. Check the Paste command in the Edit menu; if it is now available for selection, the objects have been successfully copied. If this command is not available, Corel DRAW! could not copy the selected objects.

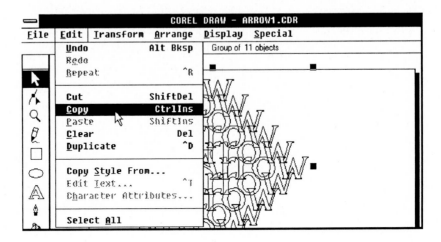

FIGURE 12-1   Selecting the Copy command

3. Select Paste from the Edit menu or press (**SHIFT-INS**). The screen redraws, with the pasted object selected. You will not notice anything different because the pasted object appears exactly on top of the original.

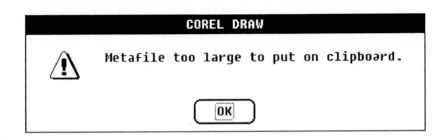

FIGURE 12-2   The Windows clipboard error message

4. To move the pasted object away from the original, press and hold the mouse button directly over any outline of the selected object and drag it as desired. You can now scale, rotate, stretch, skew, or otherwise edit the pasted object.

5. Select New from the File menu to clear the screen before continuing. Do not save any changes to the ARROW1.CDR document.

Text is the most complex kind of object that Corel DRAW! copies to the clipboard. If you try to copy a text string that contains attributes such as custom calligraphic outlines (Chapter 13), PostScript halftone screens (Chapter 14), or PostScript or fountain fills (Chapter 15), you are likely to see the "Metafile too large" error message, just as you did in the previous exercise. The clipboard may accept an object in spite of the error message, however, as long as you remain in Corel DRAW! and do not go to another software application. Check the Edit menu to see whether the Paste command becomes available. If the Paste command is still gray, the object has not been copied. You may have to break it down into smaller components (such as a few characters) and then try to copy each component separately.

In the previous exercise, you copied a group of objects to the same picture. In the next section, you will copy an object to a different picture and use it as a design enhancement there.

Copying and Pasting Objects Between Different Corel DRAW! Pictures

In the following exercise, you will copy a group of objects from ACAT.CDR and paste them to the DRAWNEWS.CDR file.

1. Open the ACAT.CDR file and select the cat. If you have Corel DRAW! Version 1.10 or earlier, the status line informs you that

this is a group of five objects. If you have Version 1.11 or later, the cat is not grouped with any other object.

2. If the cat in your version of Corel DRAW! is grouped with other objects, select the Ungroup command from the Arrange menu and then use (SHIFT) to deselect the artist's signature and the cat's blanket. When the status line informs you that three objects are selected, click on the Group command in the Arrange menu to keep these three objects together. If the cat in your image consists of several different curve objects, select them all by using the marquee, and then use the Group command to keep them together as one entity.

3. Position the cursor at any of the four corner boundary markers of the group. Then, drag the cursor and scale down the cat to approximately 50% of its original size.

4. Press (CTRL-INS) to copy the selected group of objects to the clipboard. The cursor temporarily turns into an hourglass until Corel DRAW! finishes copying the selected objects to the clipboard. Click on the OK button if the "Metafile too large" error message appears; Corel DRAW! will copy the selected objects to the clipboard anyway.

5. Select Open from the File menu. Select No when the message box asks you if you want to save changes. Now, open the sample file DRAWNEWS.CDR. Magnify just the masthead and adjust the viewing window so that the masthead appears near the top of the screen, as in Figure 12-3.

6. In preparation for pasting the cat, you are going to reduce the scale of the elements on this masthead, so the cat will fit alongside the text in the masthead. In order to reduce the scale of the elements, draw a marquee around the entire masthead, and then deselect the background rectangle by using (SHIFT) and a single click of the mouse button. Group the remaining objects.

7. Scale down the selected objects to 60% of original size, starting from the upper right corner boundary marker. Then move the scaled-down objects upward until they are centered on the background rectangle, leaving an empty space at the right side of the rectangle.

8. Zoom out to full-page view and then press (**SHIFT-INS**) to paste the copy of the cat from the clipboard onto this picture. Notice that it appears on the same area of the page that it occupied in the ACAT.CDR file after you scaled it down.

9. Move the cat to the right side of the background rectangle and then magnify the masthead again. Your screen should now resemble Figure 12-4.

10. Select the Save As command from the File menu. When the Save As dialog box appears, type **NEWSCAT** and select Save.

11. Select New from the File menu to clear the screen.

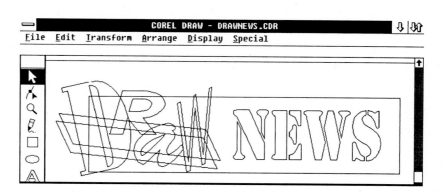

FIGURE 12-3   The masthead of DRAWNEWS.CDR

FIGURE 12-4   Copying and pasting an object to an existing image

As you can see from the preceding exercise, you don't have to start from scratch to design an attractive picture. You can copy and paste existing objects and images to an illustration in progress, saving yourself work without sacrificing quality or originality. In the next group of sections, you will experiment with the Cut and Paste menu commands and see how their operation differs from that of Copy and Paste.

CUTTING AND PASTING OBJECTS

When you select an object and then invoke the Cut command in the Edit menu, the object disappears and goes to the clipboard. When you then select the Paste command, Windows places a copy of the cut object on the page. The original object that you cut remains in the clipboard until you overwrite it by cutting or copying another object, or until you end a Windows session.

To begin practicing cutting and pasting objects, you will use the DRAWNEWS.CDR sample file that came with your software.

Cutting and Pasting Objects
Within a Picture

There are two ways to remove an unwanted object from a picture in Corel DRAW!. You can either cut it to the clipboard using the Cut command, or delete it from the program memory entirely by using the Clear command. Use the Cut command unless you are absolutely certain that you will never need the object again. If you delete an object using the Clear command, Corel DRAW! doesn't store a copy anywhere; unless you immediately select the Undo command, you won't be able to recover the object.

Corel DRAW! always pastes a cut or copied object as the top layer of the picture. Therefore, when you cut and paste objects within an image that contains several layers of objects, remember to restore the original object arrangement using the commands in the Arrange menu. The DRAWNEWS.CDR sample file that came with your software provides a good example of how to maintain object order after performing a cut and paste operation.

1. Open the DRAWNEWS.CDR file that was provided with your software and then turn on the preview window.

2. Select the Magnification tool and then the Zoom-In tool, and zoom in on just the masthead at the top of the page. Activate Show Preview and adjust the preview window to a top-to-bottom format.

3. Select the background rectangle and the two skewed rectangles behind the letters of the word "Draw" and group them.

4. Press (**SHIFT-DEL**) or select the Cut command from the Edit menu to cut the grouped objects from the page. As you can see in Figure 12-5, the characters in the word "News" are still part of the drawing. Their fill color is white, however, so you can't see these characters in the preview window when the colored background rectangle is missing.

5. Select Paste from the Edit menu, or press (SHIFT-INS). The skewed and background rectangles now appear on top of all of the other objects and obscure the letters, as demonstrated in Figure 12-6.

6. With the pasted objects still selected, select the To Back command from the Arrange menu. Corel DRAW! restores the original order of the objects.

7. Select New to clear the screen before continuing. Do not save any changes to the picture.

In the next section, you will cut and paste objects between different pictures in Corel DRAW!.

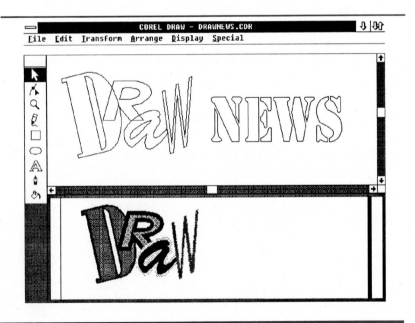

FIGURE 12-5   Cutting objects from the masthead

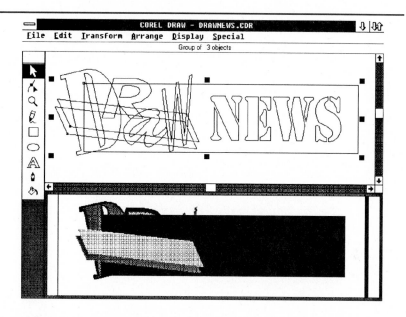

FIGURE 12-6   Pasted objects overlaying all other objects in a picture

Cutting and Pasting Objects Between Different Corel DRAW! Pictures

Earlier in this chapter, you redesigned the masthead in the DRAWNEWS.CDR file by copying and pasting a scaled-down object from another image file. In the following exercise, you will redesign the same masthead a different way: by cutting a balloon from the BALLFEST.CDR file to the clipboard and pasting it to the DRAWNEWS.CDR file.

1. Open the sample file BALLFEST.CDR that came with your software and turn on the preview window. Adjust the preview window to a side-by-side format and then click on the Preview

Selected Only command in the Display menu. The use of this command will assist you in selecting the objects you wish to cut from the picture.

2. Click once on the balloon. The status line informs you that a "Group of 1 object(s)" is selected. The balloon is the only object appearing in the preview window, as you can see in Figure 12-7.

3. Select Cut from the Edit menu or press (**SHIFT-DEL**). If the error message in Figure 12-2 appears, click on OK. Look at the Paste option in the Edit menu when the cursor returns to normal; you will see that the clipboard has accepted the objects anyway.

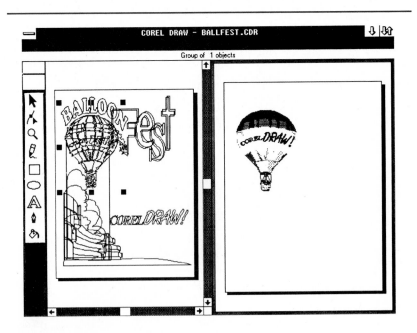

FIGURE 12-7   Isolating the balloon for a cut and paste operation

4. Select Open from the File menu. When a message box pops up to ask you if you want to save changes, select No. Then, open the DRAWNEWS.CDR file.

5. Turn on the preview window and adjust it to a top-to-bottom format. Magnify only the masthead of the picture.

6. In preparation for pasting the cut object to this picture, you are going to edit the masthead. Select all of the objects in the masthead *except* the background rectangle, and group them. Scale the grouped objects to a smaller size, so that they fit into an area of the background rectangle similar to what you see in Figure 12-8. Move the grouped objects after you scale them in order to center them vertically on the background rectangle.

7. Select Paste from the Edit menu or press (**SHIFT-INS**). After a few seconds, the objects that make up the balloon appear on the page, on top of the existing objects.

8. Turn off the preview window so that you can see the whole balloon. Scale the balloon to a smaller size, and then move it onto the right side of the background rectangle. The passenger basket of the balloon should extend beyond the bottom edge of the background rectangle.

9. Redisplay the preview window. Your screen should resemble Figure 12-8.

10. Select Save As from the File menu. When the Save As dialog box appears, type **NEWSLET** in the File text box, and then click on the Save command button.

11. Select New from the File menu to clear the screen before continuing.

The balloon transferred to the clipboard in spite of its complexity because you remained in Corel DRAW! If you see a "Metafile

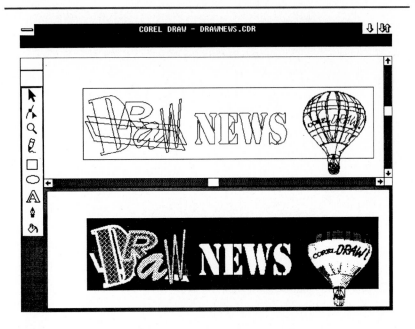

FIGURE 12-8   Redesigning the masthead using a pasted object

too large" error message when trying to cut or copy an image in order to transfer it to another Windows application, however, you will not be able to paste it. Go on to the next section to explore the possibilities for copying and pasting objects between Corel DRAW! and other Windows applications.

COPYING, CUTTING, AND PASTING OBJECTS BETWEEN APPLICATIONS

The number of software packages running under Microsoft Windows is increasing almost daily. These programs include such diverse applications as word processors, desktop publishing and presentation software, database managers and forms generators, and, of course, paint and illustration software. If your other favorite Windows applications also support the Windows clipboard, you should be able to transfer data back and forth between them and Corel DRAW!.

Features and techniques differ with every application, however; as a result, not all visual information transfers equally well between programs. There are too many Windows applications to catalog what happens to each file type as it transfers to or from Corel DRAW! through the clipboard. However, the following sections should give you an idea of how the clipboard handles graphic information that you transfer between Corel DRAW! and some of the most popular software.

Clipboard Memory Limits

Microsoft Windows, not Corel DRAW!, determines just how much information you can transfer to the clipboard at one time. The limit for Microsoft Windows 2.11 and earlier is 64K. This number refers to the size of the Windows metafile (WMF) that is created when you send information to the clipboard; 64K is *not* the file size that you see in a DOS directory. Since you cannot predict exactly how large a metafile a certain object or group of objects will generate, it's not easy to define how many or which kinds of objects you can transfer easily. If the objects you want to place on the clipboard exceed the 64K metafile limit, however, the error message box shown in Figure 12-2 appears. As previously mentioned, the clipboard accepts these objects if you paste them to another file within Corel DRAW!, but if you leave Corel DRAW! and then try to paste the objects to another application, the clipboard will appear to be empty.

In general, you'll have the best chance of success when copying, cutting, and pasting Corel DRAW! objects that don't take advantage of too many advanced features at one time. Text, custom calligraphic outlines, PostScript fills, and fountain fills, for example, are more difficult to transfer to the clipboard than an apparently complex geometrical image that contains none of these features.

Windows version 3.0, which may be available by the time you read this, should allow you to transfer a metafile larger than 64K to the clipboard.

Transferring Objects from Corel DRAW! to Other Applications

When you copy or cut a Corel DRAW! object to the clipboard, you are transferring not only the shape of an object, but also its attributes. Attributes include outline, outline fill, object fill, and text characteristics. Some attributes do not transfer well in their original form, owing in some cases to the diversity of Windows applications and in others to the complexity of Corel DRAW! features.

Most problems with transferring Corel DRAW! objects into the clipboard have to do with the extremely low 64K metafile memory limit. The following tips should help you avoid clipboard memory or Windows metafile compatibility problems.

Avoid using fountain fills and PostScript fills (both discussed in Chapter 15). These types of fills are extremely memory intensive from the standpoint of the Windows clipboard, and they often go through unpredictable changes when transferred to another program. For example, the following incompatibilities have been observed when objects containing fountain and PostScript fills are transferred to Micrographx Designer:

- Fountain fills imported into Micrographx Designer tend to fill the entire highlighting box area that would surround the object if it were still in Corel DRAW!.

- Objects containing fills of any kind tend to import into Micrographx Designer as two separate objects—an object consisting of only the outline and an object consisting of only the fill.

In addition, the clipboard does not know how to interpret PostScript fill patterns (Chapter 15). This kind of object information therefore does not transfer to any other programs.

Text sent from Corel DRAW! files to the clipboard can be sensitive also. The observations about special fills apply to text as well as to other object types. In general, the greater the number of letters and/or attributes in a text string, the more likely that some information will not transfer properly. The specific program to which you want to send the text may influence the transfer of information, too. For example, text imported into Micrographx Designer from Corel DRAW! transfers as curve objects rather than as editable text.

Other differences between what you send to the clipboard from Corel DRAW! and what you receive in another application are program-specific. For example, ellipses become four connected line segments (quadrant curves) when imported into Micrographx Designer from Corel DRAW!. Bitmapped objects sent from Corel DRAW! do not reach Micrographx Designer, either. Grouped objects transferred to the clipboard from Corel DRAW! are received by Arts & Letters as a single "Picture"that you cannot break down into component objects.

Transferring Objects from Other Applications to Corel DRAW!

When you transfer objects from your other favorite Windows applications to Corel DRAW!, you may not always receive exactly what you sent to the clipboard. Sometimes this limitation depends on what the Windows clipboard can interpret; at other times, the apparent discrepancy is specific to the interaction between the other program and Corel DRAW!.

The clipboard, for example, has difficulty transferring special text kerning or text rotation information, pattern or flood fills, pixel-by-pixel manipulations, and combined pen colors from other Windows applications to Corel DRAW!. As upgraded versions of

Windows become available, ask your Microsoft Windows dealer if these limitations still apply.

Text that you import into Corel DRAW! from another Windows application comes in with the default text attributes. If you know the typeface, typestyle, alignment, and other attributes you want, set these first, before importing the text. You can import a maximum of 250 text characters at a time. Since there is no setting for justified alignment in Corel DRAW!, text that is justified in another application won't maintain its alignment when you bring it into Corel DRAW!.

Some features that do not transfer well into Corel DRAW! are specific to a particular program. Bitmaps, for example, don't transfer well from either Arts & Letters or Micrographx Designer. Text sent from other graphics applications (as opposed to a word processor) often arrives in Corel DRAW! as curves. Fills and fountain fills from other programs may transfer into Corel DRAW! as solids, or as an outline and separate fill object. Circles and ellipses from Arts & Letters come into Corel DRAW! as connected line segments, while curves from Micrographx Designer become straight line segments. As Corel DRAW!, Microsoft Windows, and other Windows applications are constantly being upgraded, however, you can expect compatibility to improve over time.

This concludes the information on using the Windows clipboard in Corel DRAW! to transfer information within a file, between files, and between Windows applications. In the remaining sections of the chapter, you will learn about special commands in the Corel DRAW! Edit menu that make it easy for you to copy objects or their attributes within a Corel DRAW! file.

DUPLICATING OBJECTS

As you saw earlier in the chapter, you can use the Copy and Paste commands in the Edit menu to make a copy of an object within a picture. This process can be somewhat time-consuming if you use it frequently, because you need two separate menu commands or keyboard combinations to perform one action. A more convenient way of achieving the same end is to use the Duplicate command in the Edit menu or its keyboard shortcut, (CTRL-D).

The Duplicate command causes a copy of the selected object or objects to appear at a specified *offset* from the original. In other words, the duplicate copy does not appear directly on top of the original, but at a horizontal and vertical distance from it, which you specify. This makes it easier to move the duplicate to a new location.

You can also use the Duplicate command alone or with the Combine command in the Arrange menu to achieve unusual logo or graphic designs, or special effects. In the next exercise, you will create and duplicate three different series of rectangles, each with a different specified offset. Then you will combine them to create the design shown in Figure 12-12.

1. Starting with a blank page, change the page format to Landscape using the Page Setup command from the File menu.

2. Select the Preferences command from the Special menu. Check the Place Duplicate: setting near the bottom of the Preferences dialog box. Both of the values in the numeric entry and units boxes should show the default setting of 0.25 inches, as follows:

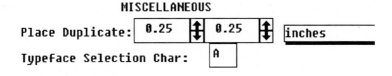

If the values are correct, select OK and exit the dialog box. If you see a different setting, change it to 0.25 inches.

3. Select the Rectangle tool and draw a rectangle about halfway down the left edge of the page. The rectangle should be wider than it is long.

4. Press **(CTRL-D)** or select the Duplicate command from the Edit menu. An exact copy of the rectangle appears 0.25 inches to the right and above the original. Press **(CTRL-D)** repeatedly until you have created 14 copies of the rectangle, as in Figure 12-9.

5. Change the Place Duplicate: setting in the Preferences dialog box to 0.05 inches in both numeric entry boxes.

6. With the Rectangle tool still selected, draw another rectangle to the right of the first series. Then, press **(CTRL-D)** 20 times in succession. This time, the duplicates appear at much shorter intervals, as shown in Figure 12-10, giving a smooth appearance to the transitions between the series of duplicated objects.

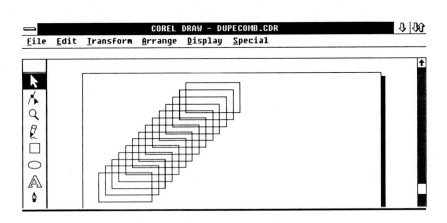

FIGURE 12-9   Creating and duplicating the first set of rectangles

7. Refer to the Place Duplicate: setting in the Preferences dialog box one more time and change both values to - 0.10 inches. The negative numbers indicate that the duplicates will appear below and to the left of the original object.

8. Draw a third rectangle between the first and second series of rectangles and then press (CTRL-D) 20 times in succession. This time, the duplicates appear to the left of and below the original object, as shown in Figure 12-11.

9. Turn on the preview window in side-by-side format and then activate the Select tool. Beginning with the first series of objects you created, select each series and apply the Combine command in the Arrange menu. You will recall from Chapter 8 that the use of the Combine command causes alternating objects in a group to become transparent.

10. When you have combined all three series of objects, adjust the

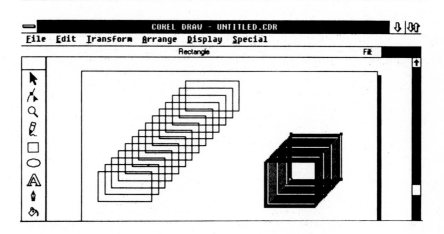

FIGURE 12-10   A second set of duplicate rectangles with smaller offset values

preview window so that it fills the entire screen. As you can see from Figure 12-12, the various offset settings lead to different special effects when you combine each group of rectangles.

11. Save this file as DUPECOMB.CDR and then select New to clear the screen.

The preceding exercise shows you only one potential use for the Duplicate command. You can probably think of many others that will spark your creativity and enhance your design abilities, especially since you can apply this command to multiple or grouped objects as well as single objects. In the next section, you will see an example of another interesting Corel DRAW! copying technique—one that transfers attributes rather than the objects themselves.

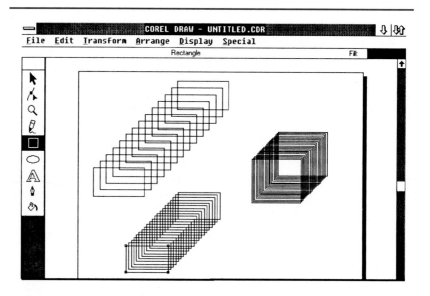

FIGURE 12-11   Creating and duplicating a third set of rectangles

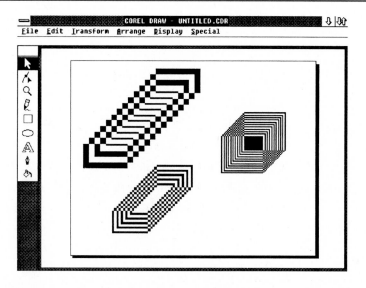

FIGURE 12-12   Special effects created with the Duplicate and
Combine commands

COPYING THE STYLE
OF AN OBJECT

Suppose that you have spent a lot of time designing an object,
giving it a custom calligraphic outline, special fills, or a unique
combination of text attributes. You would like to give the same set
of attributes to another object, but you don't want to waste time
setting up all those attributes from scratch. Corel DRAW! allows
you to save time and enhance the design of your image by using
the Copy Style From command in the Edit menu. You will practice
using this command in the following exercise.

1. Select the Page Setup command in the File menu and change
   the page format to Portrait.

2. Adjust magnification to 1:1, then activate the Text tool and select an insertion point near the top left of the page. When the Text dialog box appears, type **Corel** in the text entry window. Set text attributes to Aardvark bold, 100.0 points, and None alignment. Click on the Spacing command button, change inter-character spacing to 0.30 ems, and then select OK.

3. Select a second insertion point a little below the first one. This time, type **DRAW!** in the text entry window and set attributes to Avalon Italic, 50.0 points, and Left Alignment. Click on the Spacing command button, readjust inter-character spacing to 0.00 ems, and then select OK. When this text string appears, change the viewing magnification to ALL. Your screen should look similar to the one in Figure 12-13.

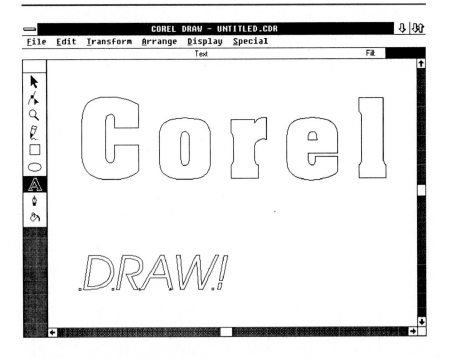

FIGURE 12-13   Preparing to copy text attributes from one text string to another

4. Activate the Select tool to select the second text string automatically and then click on the Copy Style From command in the Edit menu. The Copy Style dialog box shown in Figure 12-14 appears. This dialog box contains four options—Outline Pen, Outline Color, Fill, and Text Attributes—each with its own checkbox. You can choose to copy any or all of these attributes to the selected object. Since you haven't worked with the Outline or Fill tools yet, just click on the Text Attributes checkbox to place a checkmark in it. Notice that a message at the bottom of the dialog box instructs you to select the object from which you want to copy the attributes.

5. Click on the OK command button to exit to the page. The cursor turns into a thick arrow containing the word "From?" This reminds you to click on the object from which you want to copy attributes.

6. Select the "Corel" text string by clicking anywhere on its outlines. The "DRAW!" text string immediately changes to

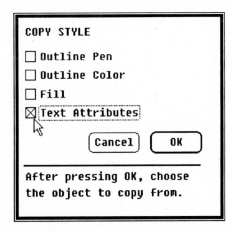

FIGURE 12-14   The Copy Style dialog box

reflect the same attributes as the "Corel" text string, as shown in Figure 12-15.

7. Select New from the File menu to clear the screen. Do not save these changes.

You will have opportunities to use this dialog box again in Chapters 13 through 15. In the final section of this chapter, you will review techniques for deleting objects in Corel DRAW!.

DELETING OBJECTS

As mentioned previously, you can delete objects from a Corel DRAW! file in one of two ways: by cutting them to the clipboard ((SHIFT-DEL)) or by selecting the Clear command from the Edit

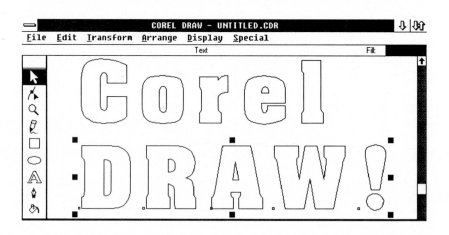

FIGURE 12-15   Selected object with attributes copied from adjoining object

menu (keyboard shortcut: (DEL)). It is generally advisable to cut objects to the clipboard if you might want to paste them back to the same or to a different image later. Use the Clear command or its keyboard shortcut only if you are certain that you will not need the deleted objects later, because Corel DRAW! doesn't save a cleared object anywhere in memory.

To delete a single object, select the object, and then apply the Clear command. You can also choose to delete multiple objects or all objects in the picture, using any of the selection techniques you learned in earlier chapters.

You have experimented in this chapter with the available techniques for copying, cutting, and pasting objects and attributes within or between Corel DRAW! files, and between Corel DRAW! and other applications. In the next three chapters, you will learn about outline width, outline fill, and object fill—important attributes that you can assign to any new or existing object.

SUMMARY

Using the Windows clipboard, you can cut, copy, or paste one or more objects within a single Corel DRAW! file, between different Corel DRAW! files, or between Corel DRAW! and other Windows applications. In any cut or copy and paste operation, the clipboard stores the object(s) temporarily in memory, until you either overwrite the object(s) or end a Windows session. You must select the desired object(s) before you can cut or copy and paste them.

When you copy or cut and paste objects within the same picture, the pasted objects always appear in front of all other objects. Remember to rearrange objects when you are finished copying and pasting, if necessary. Copying or cutting and pasting operations allow you to enhance images while cutting down on design and editing time.

Copying and pasting objects is a convenient way to shorten image editing and design time; you don't have to create new objects from scratch. However, special restrictions apply when you use the clipboard to transfer information between Corel DRAW! and other Windows applications. The clipboard creates a metafile, a special format file, from the information that you cut or copy. The size of this file can differ a great deal from the actual file size of the cut objects if you were to see their value in DOS terms. The clipboard in Windows versions 2.12 and earlier can accept only 64K in a metafile; if you try to transfer larger files, an error message may appear. As long as you remain within Corel DRAW!, even complex objects may transfer successfully through the clipboard, in spite of error messages. If you go outside of Corel DRAW!, however, objects larger than 64K won't transfer.

Because of these memory limits and also because of discrepancies between the features of various programs, not all visual information in objects transfers equally well between applications. In general, avoid using long text strings, fountain fills, PostScript fills, or outline fills, and your information should arrive at its destination safely.

Corel DRAW! contains additional commands in the Edit menu that help you edit and enhance objects within Corel DRAW!. The Duplicate command allows you to create copies of selected objects at specified offsets to the original. Use the Duplicate command with the Combine command to create special effects, logos, and designs. You can also choose to copy attributes (outline, outline fill, object fill, and text attributes) from one object to another, using the Copy Style From command. This command saves you additional editing time, since you do not have to recreate settings from each object.

13

DEFINING THE
OUTLINE PEN

Preparing to Define Outline Pen Attributes
Customizing the Outline Pen
Selecting a Preset Outline Pen Width
Outline Pen Hints

In Corel DRAW!, all objects have outline pen, outline color, and object fill attributes. In addition, text has its own set of attributes, as you learned in Chapter 11. All of the objects you created and edited until now had standard black fills and fixed-width black outlines. In this chapter, however, you will start to modify outline attributes, using the Corel DRAW! Outline tool ◊ .

The Outline tool is actually two tools in one. In order to create an outline for any object, you need to define the *outline pen* and the *outline color* in two separate steps. Think of the Outline tool as a calligraphic pen having an almost infinite number of replaceable nibs. The outline pen, which you will explore in this chapter, represents the shape of the nib and emulates the possible ways you can slant your hand while drawing. And the outline color, which you will learn about in Chapter 14, represents the ink and textures that flow from the pen.

When defining an outline pen for any object, you can vary the width, line type, corner shape, line end styles, and nib shape of the pen. You can also control the placement of the outline relative to the object's fill color. Only Corel DRAW! allows you so great a degree of control over the shape and appearance of your drawings. With your first try, you can create ornate calligraphic effects and simulate a hand-sketched look electronically.

PREPARING TO DEFINE OUTLINE PEN ATTRIBUTES

The method you use to define outline pen attributes depends on whether you are creating new objects with the current default settings, editing attributes for existing objects, or altering default outline settings. The following checklist summarizes the order of steps involved.

- To create an object with the current default outline pen attributes, you select the appropriate drawing tool and draw the object. You can then select the Outline tool to view the current default outline attributes (optional).

- To edit outline pen attributes for an existing object (including grouped or combined objects), you activate the Select tool, select the object, and then click on the Outline tool.

- To begin setting new outline pen default attributes, you click on the Outline tool and then on the desired icon.

Once you have selected the Outline tool, you can choose between defining a custom outline pen or selecting a preset outline width. In the remaining sections of this chapter, you will practice customizing outline pen attributes and selecting preset outline pen widths for both planned and existing objects.

 Always work with the preview window turned on when you define outline pen attributes. The editing window doesn't show you how the outline pen really looks, but the WYSIWYG preview window lets you see the results of your settings instantly.

CUSTOMIZING THE OUTLINE PEN

You have complete control over the attributes of the outline pen in Corel DRAW!, thanks to a dialog box that appears when you click on the outline pen icon in the Outline tool pop-up menu. By altering the settings in this dialog box, you can vary the outline's placement and width, change the shape of corners and line end styles, design custom nibs, and create an array of calligraphic effects.

The way you access this dialog box varies, depending on whether you are creating objects with default attributes, editing attributes for existing objects, or altering default attributes. In the following exercises, you will create an object with default outline pen attributes and become familiar with the settings in the Outline Pen dialog box. Then, you will edit outline pen attributes for existing objects in the sample files that came packaged with your software. Finally, you will set up new default outline pen attributes that will apply to objects you draw later.

If you simply want to specify outline width, without creating a custom outline pen, turn to the section "Selecting a Preset Outline Pen Width." There, you will find out how to alter the width of the outline pen quickly, without accessing a dialog box.

Creating Objects with Default
Outline Pen Attributes

When you create a new object, Corel DRAW! applies the current default settings to it automatically. You can leave those settings as they are or edit them. When you edit outline pen settings for a newly created object, however, your changes apply only to that object. Other objects that you create continue to have the default outline pen attributes until you set new defaults.

In the exercise that follows, you will create a text string, select the Outline tool pop-up menu and access the Outline Pen dialog box, and observe the default outline pen attributes that come standard with Corel DRAW!.

1. Make sure that the Show Rulers and Snap To Grid commands are turned off, select the Magnification tool [Q] and set magnification to 1:1.

2. Activate the Text tool [A] and select an insertion point near the upper-left edge of the page. When the Text dialog box appears, type **outline pen** in the text entry box. Set text attributes to Gatineau Normal, 90.0 points, and Left Alignment. Set inter-character spacing to 0.10 ems, and then select OK.

3. When the text string appears, turn on the preview window and adjust the editing and preview windows to a top-to-bottom format. Magnify the text string by using the Zoom-In tool [Q] in the Magnification tool pop-up menu. You do not have to activate the Select tool to select the text string; the presence of the nodes indicates that as a newly drawn object, it's already selected.

4. The interior of the text string in the preview window is black. For the purposes of this exercise, you want to remove the fill color to cleary view your outline. To do this, click on the Fill

tool icon 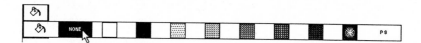 at the bottom of the Corel DRAW! toolbox and then select None from the pop-up menu that appears:

The text string in the preview window redisplays with just the outline. The center is hollow, as shown in Figure 13-1. (If your text seems to have vanished completely in the preview window, you will find a solution in the next step.)

5. Click on the Outline tool 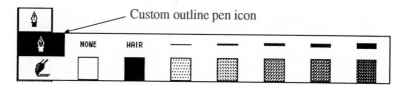. A pop-up menu appears, with the first icon in the top row highlighted:

Custom outline pen icon

The Outline tool pop-up menu contains two rows of options. The top row consists of controls for the outline pen, which you will use throughout this chapter. The second row of the pop-up menu, which you will work with in Chapter 14, contains controls for the outline fill color. (If the text string has disappeared from your preview window, click on the solid black icon in the second row of this pop-up menu to make it reappear.)

6. Ignore all but the first control in the top row of the pop-up menu. The seven controls after the first one allow you to specify quickly fixed outline widths (but no other attributes) for the outline pen. You will practice working with these seven controls in the "Selecting a Preset Outline Pen Width" section of this chapter. For now, click on the first icon in the top row, the *custom outline pen* icon. It looks just like the Outline tool icon, but it has the more specialized function of allowing you to specify all the possible attributes of the outline pen. The Outline

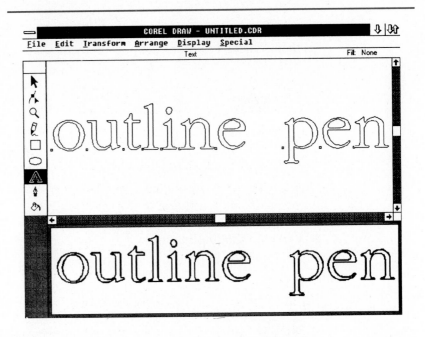

FIGURE 13-1   Outline text with fill removed

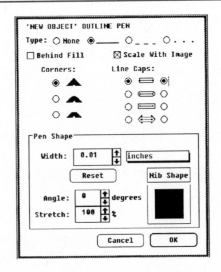

FIGURE 13-2   The Outline Pen dialog box

Pen dialog box displays, as in Figure 13-2. Leave this dialog box on the screen for now.

The Outline Pen dialog box contains controls for eight outline pen attributes. The default settings on your screen should match the settings in Figure 13-2, unless you or another user has altered them since installing the software. If your dialog box shows different settings, adjust them to match the ones in the figure. Then, take a moment to become familiar with the attributes and how they function.

Line Type   At the top of the dialog box is the word "Type:" followed by four option buttons. These options allow you to choose between four line types for the outline pen: none, solid lines, dashed lines, and dotted lines. The default line type is none. If you select None, Corel DRAW! will not draw an outline for the selected object, regardless of your settings for other outline pen attributes. You can use the dashed or dotted outline types only if you have a PostScript printer and they will not display on your screen. The preview window displays dotted and dashed outlines as normal solid lines.

Behind Fill   The Behind Fill checkbox lets you specify whether the outline of an object should appear in front of or behind the object's fill. The default setting is in front of the fill (empty checkbox), but if you create objects with thick outlines, you will want to activate Behind Fill. This is especially advisable with text, where thick outlines appearing in front of the fill can obliterate empty spaces and cause text to appear smudged, like this:

When you place an outline behind the fill, only half of it is visible. The outline therefore appears to be only half as thick as specified.

Scale With Image   When the Scale With Image checkbox contains an "x," the width and angle of the outline change proportionally as you resize, rotate, or skew the object. Corel DRAW! automatically updates the width and angle settings in the Outline Pen dialog box when Scale With Object is active. When the Scale With Object setting is *not* active, the width and angle of an object's outline do not change, no matter how you stretch, scale, rotate, or skew the object. This can lead to some interesting but unintended changes in appearance when you define a calligraphic pen nib for the object, as you will see in the "Scaling an Outline with the Image" section of this chapter

Corners   The Corners options pertain to objects that tend to have sharp corners: lines, open and closed curve objects, rectangles, and some angular typefaces. The three option buttons in this area of the dialog box allow you to choose just how Corel DRAW! shapes those corners. The first (default) option shows a sharp or *miter* corner, where the outer edges of two joining line or curve segments extend until they meet. By altering the Miter Limit setting in the Preferences dialog box, you can control the angle below which Corel DRAW! flattens or bevels the edge of a sharp curve. When you choose the second option button, Corel DRAW! *rounds* the corners where two lines or curve segments meet. When you choose the third or *bevel* corner option button, corners of joining curve or line segments are flattened. The results of the Corners settings are usually subtle, unless you magnify an object or combine Corners settings with Pen Shape attributes for calligraphic effects.

Line Caps   The Line Caps options apply to lines and open curves, but not to closed path objects such as rectangles, closed curves, or ellipses. These settings determine the end styles of lines and curves. The first or default option is a *butt* line end style, where the line ends exactly at the end point. The second option gives you *rounded* line end points. When you choose the third or *square* line end type, the line extends beyond the end point for a distance equal to half of the line thickness. The fourth line end style from which you can choose gives an *arrowhead* shape to the end points of lines and curves. When you select any of the first three line end styles, that style applies to both end points of the line or curve. When you choose an arrowhead line end style for either end point, you can select a different end style for the remaining end point. If you have selected dashed lines as your line type for an object, each dash takes on the shape of the line end style you choose. The exception to this rule is the arrowhead line end style, which applies only to the end points of dashed or dotted lines.

Width, Angle, and Stretch   The remaining three outline pen attributes—width, angle, and stretch—all help you define a custom pen shape, analogous to the *nib* or point of a calligraphic fountain pen. With default values of 0.01-inch width, a 0 degree angle, and 100% stretch, the pen shape is square, resulting in a plain outline. On their own, these settings will not create calligraphic effects. When you alter them in combination, however, they allow you to outline objects with varying thick and thin strokes at the angle of your choice. The Corners settings work with the Pen Shape settings to define the appearance of calligraphic strokes, as you will learn in the "Creating a Custom Nib for Calligraphic Effects" section of this chapter.

Now that you are familiar with the functions of the attributes in the Outline Pen dialog box, exit the dialog box by selecting Cancel. Clear the screen by selecting New from the File menu before going further. After you complete the following section, you will experiment with each setting in the Outline Pen dialog box.

Editing Outline Pen Attributes of Existing Objects

To define outline pen attributes for an existing (not newly created) object, you must select the object before you access the Outline tool pop-up menu. If you try to access the Outline Pen dialog box without having selected an object, Corel DRAW! assumes that you want to set new defaults for the outline pen, and changes you make in the Outline Pen dialog box will not affect existing objects.

When you define outline pen attributes for an existing object that is selected, you are in effect *editing* its current outline style. The changes you make apply to that object only and have no effect on the default settings for objects you create later.

 If you use the Shift key method to select multiple objects in order to change their outline pen attributes, the Outline Pen dialog box displays the settings for the last object that you selected in the group. If you use another method to select the objects, the dialog box displays the settings for the last object that you draw. Any changes you make will apply to all of the selected objects, however, so be very careful about changing outline pen attributes for more than one object at a time.

Each of the following sections concentrates on the effects of editing a specific attribute or related set of attributes in the Outline Pen dialog box. You will work with sample files that best demonstrate how changes to an attribute can alter the overall design and mood of a picture.

ADJUSTING LINE TYPE   The line type you assign to an object's outline pen helps define the balance and weight of that object within a picture. In the following exercise, you will alter the line type for several elements in the sample picture called BALL-FEST.CDR and observe how your changes affect the overall balance of the picture.

1. Open the file BALLFEST.CDR and turn on the preview window in side-to-side format. Note that the balloon seems to dominate the picture, even though it is not the largest object on the page.

2. Activate the Preview Selected Only command in the Display menu, and then magnify just the area containing the word "Fest."

3. Select the word "Fest" by clicking on the outline of any letter. The status line informs you that this is a group of five objects. As the word redraws in the preview window, notice that the apparent shadow behind each letter is the result of overlaying light objects on black ones. Your screen should now display an area similar to Figure 13-3.

FIGURE 13-3   Light and airy text with no outline

4. Select the Outline tool and access the Outline Pen dialog box. Because the outline pen for this group of objects has None selected for line type, no outline at all appears around the objects and none of the other settings in the dialog box have any visible effect. This setting makes the word appear lighter and airier in spite of its large size, especially since the shadow letters appear below and to the left of each colored letter. The upper edges of the letters do not have sharp boundaries separating them from the "sky."

5. Change the outline type from None to a solid line. In order to emphasize the difference between these two Type settings, increase the Width setting to 0.14 inch.

6. Select OK to exit the dialog box. "Fest" redisplays with a thick outline, as shown in Figure 13-4.

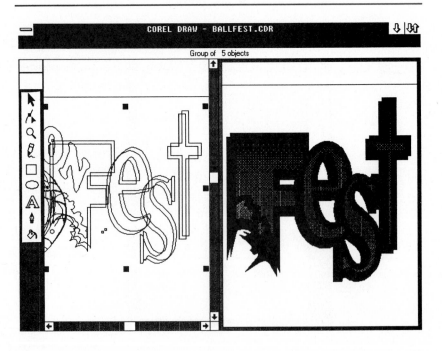

FIGURE 13-4 Text made heavier with a thick outline

7. Adjust the horizontal and vertical scroll bars of the editing window until you can see the full balloon, and then select the balloon. Access the Outline Pen dialog box. The "Group of one objects" that makes up the balloon has a solid outline type and an outline width of 0.00 inch.

8. Change the Type setting to None. Notice that as soon as you select None, all of the other outline pen options go gray and you cannot select them. Exit the dialog box. The balloon redisplays in the preview window with no external outlines and no thin lines to mark the creases in its pleats, as shown in Figure 13-5. In addition, the word DRAW! on the balloon has disappeared. As you will recall, setting outline Type to None causes lines and open curve objects to become invisible. The entire balloon appears lighter because of your changes.

9. Return the picture to a full-page viewing magnification and

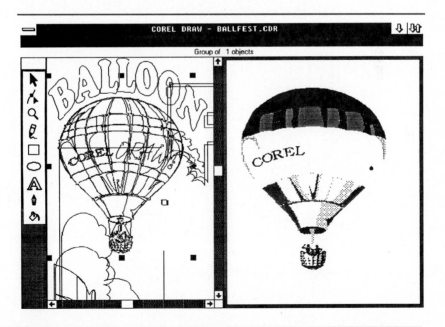

FIGURE 13-5   Balloon with outlines removed

deactivate the Preview Selected Only command in the Display menu. The entire picture redisplays, as shown in Figure 13-6. The end result of the changes you have made is a visual imbalance in the picture. The increased heaviness of the word "Fest," combined with the lighter look of the balloon, causes the text to seem more important in the overall image than the balloon.

10. Clear this picture from the screen by selecting New from the File menu. Do not save the changes you have made.

By altering the outline type for objects in a finished picture, you have gained a deeper appreciation of this attribute's value as a design element. The next section explores the design possibilities of placing outlines of objects behind or in front of their fills.

FIGURE 13-6   Outline affects weight and balance of a picture

ADJUSTING PLACEMENT OF OUTLINE AND FILL The Behind Fill setting in the Outline Pen dialog box determines whether the outline of a selected object is placed behind or in front of the object's fill. This attribute is most important when you are working with text. Thick outlines appearing in front of the fill can clog up the open spaces in letters, making the letters appear unclear. In the following exercise, you will adjust outline placement for the letters in the DRAWNEWS.CDR file.

1. Open the sample file DRAWNEWS.CDR. Turn on the preview window and adjust it to a top-to-bottom format. Activate the Preview Selected Only command.

2. Magnify the masthead of the file. The creator of this file converted all of the letters in "Draw" to curve objects, so you can select each letter separately. Select the letter "R." As shown in Figure 13-7, it appears with a thick outline that is a different color than the fill.

FIGURE 13-7   The letter "R" with a thick outline in front of fill

3. Select the Outline tool and then the Custom Outline Pen icon to access the Outline Pen dialog box and see the current attribute settings for this letter. The outline has a width of 0.11 inch, and the Behind Fill option is not active.

4. Click on the Behind Fill checkbox to activate it and then select OK to exit the dialog box. The letter reappears with what seems to be a thinner outline, as shown in Figure 13-8. Actually, the outline is just as thick as before, but half of it is hidden behind the fill.

5. Select the Undo command in the Edit menu to return this letter to its former settings.

6. Select each of the other letters in "Draw" in turn, and toggle their Behind Fill settings on or off. The "a," with an outline

FIGURE 13-8   The letter "R" with outline behind fill (Behind Fill active)

width of 0.14 inch (thicker than the outline of the "R"), becomes clogged when you deactivate its Behind Fill setting. The thin outline of the "W," on the other hand, becomes more visible when you turn Behind Fill off. Deselect any letter that remains selected before continuing with Step 7.

7. Now, select all four of the letters using the (SHIFT) key in the order D-R-a-W, and then access the Outline Pen dialog box. The dialog box displays settings for the object that was selected last in the group, in this case the letter "W." Even if you made no changes to the settings of the object that was selected last, Corel DRAW! applies these settings to *all* of the selected objects as soon as you select OK.

8. Make sure that the Behind Fill checkbox contains an "x" (activated). Then increase the Width setting to 0.20 inch, a fairly thick outline. Select OK to exit the dialog box. All four letters now have a uniform outline width placed behind their respective fills, as shown in Figure 13-9.

9. Clear the image from the screen by selecting New from the File menu, but do not save any changes.

You have seen how the Behind Fill option affects the appearance of objects and can be especially useful with text. In the next section, you will observe how the Scale With Image setting impacts the appearance of resized or transformed objects.

SETTING SHARP (MITER), ROUNDED, OR BEVELED OUTLINE CORNERS   The effect of changing corner attributes of the outline pen is so subtle that it is almost unnoticeable—unless the selected object has a thick outline as well as sharp corners. A thick outline enables you to see the shape of the object change as you cycle through the Corners options. Perform the following

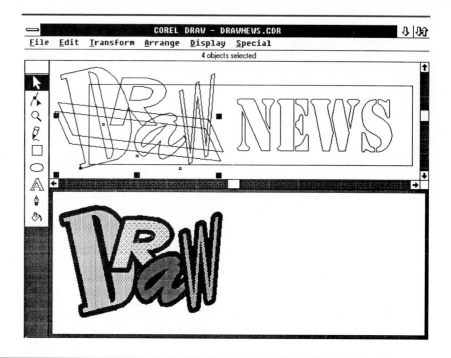

FIGURE 13-9   Activating Behind Fill for a selected group of objects

exercise to practice altering Corners settings for a letter in the DRAWNEWS.CDR file.

1. Open the DRAWNEWS.CDR file and turn on the preview window, with the Preview Selected Only command activated. Adjust the preview and editing windows to a side-to-side format.

2. Magnify just the area of the masthead that contains the letter "D," and then select the "D." Your screen should resemble Figure 13-10.

3. Select the Outline tool and the Custom Outline Pen icon to access the Outline Pen dialog box. This letter, which was

converted to curves, has an outline only 0.06 inch wide. Select the sharp (miter) corners option button and then select OK. Not much of a change is visible at this outline width.

4. Select Undo to return the "D" to rounded corners, and then access the Outline Pen dialog box again. This time, increase the width of the outline to 0.14 inch and select OK to exit the dialog box. The outjutting corners in Figure 13-11a appear even more rounded than before because the thicker outline makes their shape more obvious.

5. Access the Outline Pen dialog box once more and select the sharp (miter) corners option button. When you exit the dialog

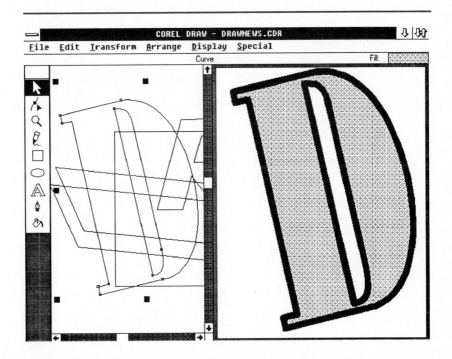

FIGURE 13-10   The letter "D" with a thin outline and rounded corner setting

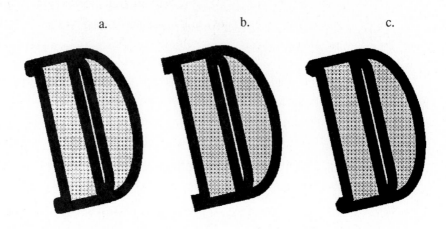

a.   b.   c.

FIGURE 13-11   The letter "D" with (a) rounded, (b) sharp
(miter), and (c) beveled corner settings

box, the outjutting corners of the "D" are obviously squared off,
as shown in Figure 13-11b.

6. Access the Outline Pen dialog box a final time, and select the
beveled corners option button. When you exit the dialog box
now, the beveled edges are clearly visible, as shown in Figure
13-11c.

7. Select New from the File menu to clear the screen. Do not save
your changes.

In creating your own drawings, you will find the effects of the
Corners options most dramatic when you assign thick outlines to
objects that contain at least some cusp nodes. In the next section,
you will explore when and how changes to the line end styles can
alter an object's appearance.

SELECTING LINE END STYLES Line end options apply only to straight lines and open-ended curves and curve objects, never to closed curve objects, rectangles, text, or squares. It is difficult to see the difference between line end types unless you create very thick lines, which you haven't learned how to do yet. Figure 13-12 contains six thick example lines. The first four lines (a, b, c, and d) exhibit butt, rounded, square, and arrowhead line caps, respectively. The last two lines (e and f) should remind you that when you select an arrowhead line cap for one end of the line, you may choose a different style of line cap for the other end. If you use the line with rounded line caps (b) as a reference, you can see the difference between the butt (a) and square (c) line caps: the choice of square line caps causes the line to extend further than its nominal length.

If an image contains many open-ended curves, selecting rounded line end styles can soften the image, even if the lines are thin. Conversely, you can select butt or square line end styles to

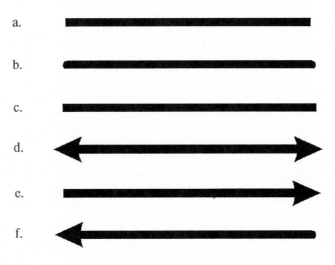

FIGURE 13-12 The four line cap styles

give an object a more rough-hewn, sharp appearance. Arrowhead line end styles are well suited to callouts for technical illustration.

In the next section, you will begin working with the pen shapes—Width, Angle, and Stretch—that make calligraphic effects possible in Corel DRAW!.

DESIGNING A CUSTOM PEN SHAPE FOR CALLI-GRAPHIC EFFECTS   The Width, Angle, and Stretch settings in the Outline Pen dialog box are in a separate enclosed area subtitled "Pen Shape." The Pen Shape options—Width, Angle, and Stretch—allow you to create variable calligraphic "nibs" that can be highly effective with freehand drawings and text. If you adjust all three of these settings in various combinations, you can approximate a freehand style of drawing.

In the following exercise, you will experiment with the Pen Shape settings using the ACAT.CDR file and achieve both hand-sketched and comic-strip style looks. The first six steps require you to set up the exercise so that you have a convenient image with which to work.

1. Open the sample file ACAT.CDR. Turn on the preview window and make sure that it is in side-by-side format. Turn off Preview Selected Only.

2. Delete the Corel Systems emblem at the bottom of the page and then select the cat. As the status line informs you, this is a group of five objects. (If you have version 1.11 or later, the cat is made up of 28 curve objects and is separate from the mat that surrounds it. Select the mat, the emblem, and the signature and delete them, and then proceed to step 4.)

3. Apply the Ungroup command in the Arrange menu and deselect all objects. Select just the mat surrounding the cat and delete it. Then select the cat again.

4. Adjust viewing magnification to ALL. With the cat selected, click on the Break Apart command in the Arrange menu to break the subpaths of the cat into separate curves. Deselect all of the curves, and then select and delete all of the curves except for the ones visible in Figure 13-13. (If you have version 1.11 or later, magnify just the cat's head. Do not delete any curves. Then continue with step 5.)

5. When you have deleted all of the unnecessary curves, group the remaining ones, and then adjust magnification to ALL again. Your screen should now display an image similar to the one in Figure 13-13. (If you have version 1.11 or later, select all of the curves that make up the cat and group them, using the Group command in the Arrange menu.)

6. Save this image under a new file name by selecting Save As in the File menu. When the Save As dialog box appears, type **CATSPAWS** and then click on the Save command button.

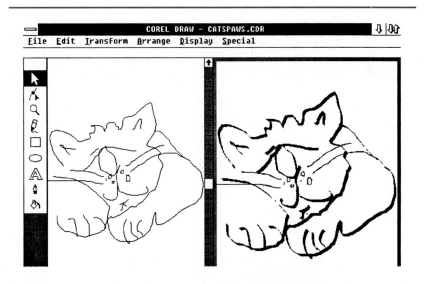

FIGURE 13-13   Outline Width 0.04 inch, Angle 42 degrees, Stretch 14%

7. You are ready to begin experimenting with pen shape attributes. Select the grouped image. Notice that the WYSIWYG outlines in the preview window have a more hand-sketched look than their counterparts in the editing window, with varying thick and thin lines. (This does not apply if you have version 1.11 or later.)

8. Activate the Outline tool and access the Outline Pen dialog box. The current Pen Shape settings for this object are Width 0.04 inch, Angle 42 degrees, and Stretch 14%. This translates into a moderately thin outline and a relatively narrow nib, with the "pen" held at a 42-degree angle. (If you have version 1.11 or later, change the settings so that they match these.)

9. Decrease the width to 0.02 inch and select OK to exit the dialog box. Now the outline is finer than before but the variations in line thickness have not changed.

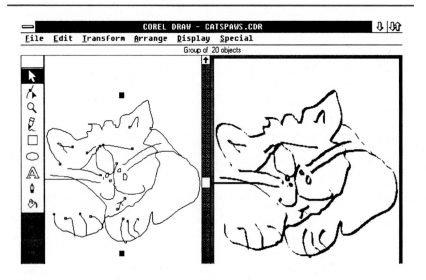

FIGURE 13-14   Outline Width 0.02 inch, Angle 42 degrees, Stretch 2%

10. To vary line thickness, experiment with the stretch of the nib, expressed as a percentage of the nib width. Keep decreasing the Stretch value all the way to 2%, and then select OK. The cat's whiskers, right ear, and left front leg show more pronounced variations in thickness than before, as shown in Figure 13-14. As the value in the Stretch numeric entry box decreases, you effectively flatten the nib in one direction; the black symbol representing a pen nib in the Nib Shape window flattens horizontally. The resulting nib is broad in one dimension and extremely narrow in the other, which makes more extreme calligraphic effects possible. If you were to increase the Stretch value all the way to 100%, the curves of the image would have the same thickness everywhere, and no calligraphic effects could result.

11. Access the Outline Pen dialog box once more. This time, adjust the Angle of the nib from 42 to 0 degrees. You will recall that the Angle setting is analogous to the way you hold a calligraphic pen in your hand; at a 0-degree setting, the Nib Shape window alters to show you a perfectly vertical nib.

12. Select OK to exit the dialog box. Now the areas that display the thickest and thinnest lines have shifted by 42 degrees. Adjusting the Angle value is therefore a convenient way to control where thick and thin lines appear on any selected object.

13. Access the Outline Pen dialog box again and click on the Reset button. This resets the Angle and Stretch settings (though not Width) to the default values of 0 degrees and 100%, respectively—a square nib with no variations in thickness. Now set Width to 0.06 inch, and then select OK. The cat is redrawn with a consistently thick outline, much like a cartoon character, as shown in Figure 13-15.

14. Experiment with angle and stretch settings at this outline width, too. For example, to obtain greater variation in line thickness,

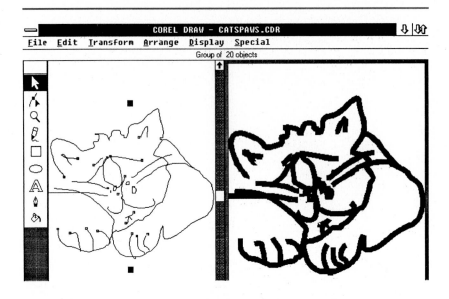

FIGURE 13-15   Outline Width 0.06 inch, Angle 0 degrees, Stretch 100%

set Stretch at a reduced value, such as 4%. To change the placement of the thinner segments of the curve, try different angle settings.

15. When you have finished experimenting, set Width to 0.02 inch, Angle to 42 degrees, and Stretch to 14%. Leave this image on the screen for now.

The possibilities for creating custom calligraphic nibs should spark your imagination. An interesting use for an image sketched faintly at 0.01-inch width might be as a background illustration in a newsletter, where the text overprints the image without obscuring it totally. You have probably seen applications like this involving outlines of scanned-in photographs. Chapter 17 will give you more information on how to outline bitmapped and scanned images.

Avoid using 0.00-inch widths, unless your draft printer is also the printer you will be using for your final output. As an outline Width setting, 0.00 inch represents the thinnest line your printer is capable of printing. For PostScript printers, this is 1 pixel or 1/300 of an inch, but for a Linotronic or other high-resolution imagesetter, 0.00 inches could represent something even thinner. Because of the variations among printers, this setting does not truly represent a fixed width, and the preview window does not display a WYSIWYG representation of it.

Angle settings are especially useful to help you fine-tune the exact location of thick and thin lines within a drawing. With precise, degree-by-degree control available, you can make sure that thinner areas of a selected curve are positioned exactly where you want them.

The Stretch settings represent the relative squareness or roundness of the nib, with 100% representing a square nib and 1% representing a long and narrow nib. As the stretch percentage value decreases, the variation in line thickness of a drawn object increases.

In the next section, you will refine your understanding of how objects drawn with custom nibs behave when you stretch, scale, rotate, or skew them.

SCALING AN OUTLINE WITH THE IMAGE   You will remember that when the Scale With Image option is active, the pen shape (width, angle, and stretch) changes automatically as you stretch, scale, rotate, or skew the object. When you activate this setting for objects that are drawn with a custom calligraphic "nib," the objects maintain a uniform appearance, no matter how you transform them. The following exercise shows you examples of how an object with a calligraphic outline pen behaves when Scale With Image is turned on and off.

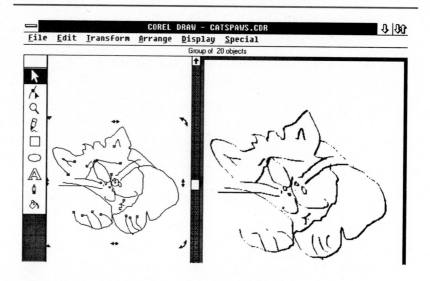

FIGURE 13-16 CATSPAWS.CDR skewed by 15 degrees, Scale With Image active

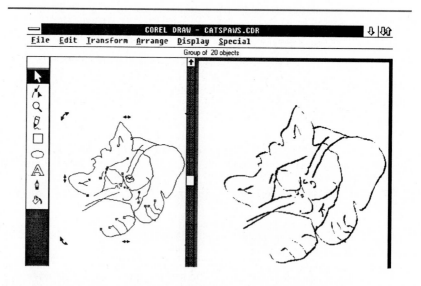

FIGURE 13-17 CATSPAWS.CDR rotated by 30 degrees, Scale With Image inactive

1. Select the Outline tool and access the Outline Pen dialog box. Activate the Scale With Image setting by clicking on the checkbox next to it, and then select OK. This setting ensures that even when you rotate, skew, or resize the image, the thick and thin lines will remain in their proper places without shifting.

2. Make sure the cat is still selected, and then click on its outline a second time with the Select tool to enter rotate/skew mode. Skew the cat at a 15-degree angle in a counterclockwise direction, as shown in Figure 13-16. Even though the cat is distorted, the relative variations in line thickness do not change.

3. Select Undo in the Edit menu to return the cat to its former shape.

4. Access the Outline Pen dialog box once more, and click on the Scale With Image checkbox to deactivate this selection. Select OK to exit the dialog box with the new setting.

5. Rotate the cat at a 30-degree angle in a counterclockwise direction, as shown in Figure 13-17. Since Scale With Image is turned off, the positions of the thick and thin portions of the lines in the image shift by the exact angle of rotation. The same effect would occur if you had skewed the image by a specified number of degrees. In other words, the cat now appears as if you had drawn it from scratch at this new angle, holding your hand (and your calligraphic pen) in the same position as before the cat was rotated.

6. Select Undo in the Edit menu to return the cat to its former shape.

7. Select the Outline tool and then the Custom Outline Pen icon to enter the Outline Pen dialog box once more. Reactivate the Scale With Image option, and then select OK to exit the dialog box.

8. Save your changes by pressing (CTRL-S), and then select New from the File menu to clear the screen.

If you enjoy experimenting, you may not want to have Scale With Image activated most of the time; it may be more interesting for you to allow calligraphy to shift every which way as you transform an image. But if you prefer to "nail down" the appearance of an object as soon as you have it to your liking, Scale With Image is an ideal outline pen attribute for this purpose.

The next few sections show you how to change the default outline pen attributes. Objects that you create after altering the attributes will exhibit the new attributes automatically.

Defining a Custom Outline Pen
For New Objects (Setting Defaults)

So far in this chapter, you have learned to create objects with the outline pen settings that are standard with your software, and to adjust current outline pen settings for existing objects. Different artists have different styles, however, and you may prefer to create most of your objects with outline pen styles that differ from the standard settings. If so, perform the exercise in this section to learn how to customize outline pen defaults. Objects that you create after changing the default attributes will then conform to the appearance that characterizes your working style.

Creating objects with new outline pen defaults is a three-stage process. First, you access the 'New Object Outline' Pen dialog box. Then you change the outline pen attributes. Finally, you create new objects, which automatically adhere to the new default attributes. The dialog box that you use to edit default settings is identical to the Outline Pen dialog box, except for its title and the way you access it.

1. Start with a blank page. (If you are in an existing drawing and want to change default settings, make sure that no object is selected.) Then select the Outline tool and click on the Custom Outline Pen icon. Since no object is selected, the message box in Figure 13-18 appears. This message is somewhat misleading, because the settings you are about to alter will not apply to newly created objects but, rather, to objects that you haven't created at all yet.

2. Select OK to access the 'New Object' Outline Pen dialog box. The contents of this dialog box are identical to the contents of the normal Outline Pen dialog box. Only the title is different, to remind you that you are changing default attributes for the outline pen.

3. Imagine that you are a cartoonist who prefers to work with broader strokes and a more pronounced calligraphic "nib" than the standard outline pen settings offer you. Accordingly, change Width to 0.10 inch, Angle to 40 degrees, and Stretch to 8%. Set Line Caps to a rounded style, and then select OK.

4. Turn on the preview window, select the Freehand tool 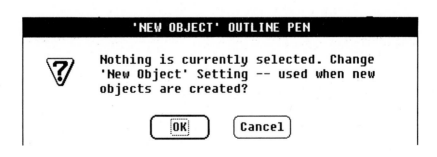, and draw a few scribbles or an image of your choice. The

'NEW OBJECT' OUTLINE PEN

Nothing is currently selected. Change 'New Object' Setting -- used when new objects are created?

OK   Cancel

FIGURE 13-18   'New Objects' Outline Pen message

resulting lines are much thicker and more calligraphically varied than the new lines you used to draw with the standard default settings.

5. When you have finished experimenting, select New to clear the screen.

It's that easy to alter default settings for the outline pen. As with almost every other Corel DRAW! feature, customization is the key word. Corel DRAW! encourages you to create images according to your unique working habits and style.

On the other hand, if you are involved in technical illustration or your normal Corel DRAW! tasks are relatively uncomplicated, you may seldom require calligraphy or other special options in the Outline Pen and 'New Object' Outline Pen dialog boxes. The next section shows you how to change outline pen width quickly and interactively, without the use of a dialog box.

SELECTING A PRESET OUTLINE PEN WIDTH

If Width is the outline pen attribute you change most frequently, Corel DRAW! offers a shortcut that saves you time and keeps you out of the Outline Pen dialog box. The first row of the pop-up menu that appears when you select the Outline tool, as shown in Figure 13-19, contains seven preset outline widths from which you can choose.

You can choose one of these options for a currently selected object, or you can set a fixed line width as a new default. When you choose a preset outline width for a selected object, you apply that width to the selected object only. When you click on one of these options without having first selected an object, however, Corel DRAW! assumes that you want to set the option as a new default width and the message box shown in Figure 13-18 pops up. Select OK to set the selected line width as a new default for objects that you draw in the future. If you meant to select an existing object first, click on the Cancel command button instead.

The first option next to the Custom Outline Pen icon (see Figure 13-19) is NONE; click on this option when you want a selected object to have no outline at all. When an object has an outline style of NONE, an outline will appear in the editing window, but not in the preview window.

The next option, HAIR, represents 1/4 point. The preview window, however, does not display a true WYSIWYG representation of an outline this thin. The outlines in the editing and preview windows appear to be the same width when you choose this option.

As Figure 13-19 shows, the remaining five options in the pop-up menu represent fixed outline widths from 1/2 point to 8 points. Think of these options as "package deals," with each selection including an Angle of 0 degrees and a stretch value of 100% in the Outline Pen dialog box.

If you have altered any of the other default outline pen settings using the 'New Object' Outline Pen dialog box, they are still effective when you select a preset outline pen width. For example, if you previously had selected the Behind Fill or Scale With Image options as defaults, your outlines will exhibit these attributes even when you select a preset outline width. Since the Angle, and

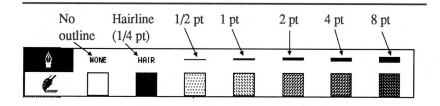

FIGURE 13-19   Preset outline widths available in Outling tool pop-up menu

Stretch settings are standardized for preset widths, however, you cannot achieve calligraphic effects.

You have mastered all of the basic skills involved in customizing the Corel DRAW! outline pen. Browse through the next and final section for a few hints on when to use certain settings for best results.

OUTLINE PEN HINTS

The range of choices available to you makes the outline pen one of the richer areas of Corel DRAW!. The following sections contain selected hints for making the most of your choices and coordinating your settings with the type of work you are doing.

Defining an Outline Pen for Text

Do you want text in your drawings to appear normally? Or are you aiming for exaggerated or stylized effects? For a clean-cut look, it's best to create text with a line type of None, using either the Outline Pen dialog box or the Outline tool pop-up menu. When text has a visible outline, some characters appear to be drawn thicker, with the result that spaces within letters (such as in a small "a" or "e") are partially or wholly filled in. This is especially the case when you create text in small point sizes.

If your design calls for outlined text, a good way to maintain readability in smaller point sizes is to activate the Behind Fill option in the Outline Pen dialog box. As mentioned earlier, Behind Fill causes the outline to appear half as thick as it really is, because the other half of the outline is hidden behind the object's fill.

In some cases, you may really prefer a slightly "smudgy" graphic look of text with thick outlines. Let the purpose and design of your illustration be your guide in choosing how to outline text.

Varying Your Calligraphic Style

Unless you have a prior background in calligraphy, the wealth of width, angle, stretch, and corners settings available to you in the Outline Pen dialog box can be confusing. The following hints should help put you on the right track if you know the effect you would like to achieve.

Desktop publishers can create faint background illustrations from original artwork or scanned photos and then overprint them with text. The result is a visible but not distracting piece of artwork that enhances the mood of an article or feature. Recommended settings for this kind of graphics effect are Width, 0.03 inch or less; Stretch, 14% or less; and a variable angle according to your tastes. Keep in mind that if you reduce the outline Width below 0.02 inch (or 1.2 fractional points), you will not be able to see an accurate representation of the calligraphy on your screen. The outline will still print according to your specifications, however.

Illustrators, cartoonists, and other artists seeking a traditional hand-sketched look should set Pen Shape options to achieve the desired variation in line thickness. For finer lines, outline pen width should be fairly thin, below 0.05 inch, and for blunter strokes, above 0.06 inch. Stretch should be set to 1 to 2% for the maximum variation in line thickness, and closer to 100% for minimal variation. The fine-tuning possible with angle settings permits illustrators to place thicker or thinner lines at exact locations. Miter corner settings promote a more angular look, while rounded corner settings create a smoother appearance.

For those who are interested in extremely broad calligraphic strokes, consider setting Stretch above 100%, removing the fill of an object, and then varying the Angle settings in the Outline Pen dialog box. The example text that follows has a three-dimensional look because it was created at a Width of 0.06 inch, at an Angle of 75 degrees, and with a Stretch of 225%:

outline pen

Copying Outline Styles

In Chapter 12, you transferred text attributes from one text string to another using the Copy Style From command in the Edit menu. You can do the same with outline pen attributes, as you will see by performing the following brief exercise.

1. Open the DRAWNEWS.CDR sample file. Turn on the preview window, magnify just the letters in the word "Draw," and adjust the preview and editing windows to a top-to-bottom format.

2. Select the "a" in "Draw" and then select the Copy Style From command in the Edit menu. The Copy Style dialog box appears.

3. Click on the Outline Pen checkbox to place a checkmark in it, and then select OK. The cursor changes to an arrow containing the word "From?," which indicates that you should now select the object with the outline pen attributes you want to copy to the letter "a."

4. Select the letter "D." The letter "a" now redraws with a thinner outline placed behind the fill color, just like the outline of the letter "D." The hollow space in the "a" no longer appears smudged.

You can imagine how useful the Copy Style From command can be if you need to copy outline pen styles to, or from, even larger blocks of text or groups of objects.

SUMMARY

The Outline tool in the Corel DRAW! toolbox allows you to define a preset or custom outline for any object. The top row of the pop-up menu that appears when you select the Outline tool contains choices for defining the outline pen shape. The bottom row contains choices for defining the colors and textures that flow from the pen.

Whenever you create a new object, it automatically has the current outline pen defaults. To change the defaults, you select the Outline tool and click on the Custom Outline Pen icon (the first icon in the pop-up menu) without first selecting an object. This action accesses the 'New Object' Outline Pen dialog box, where you set the new defaults.

To edit the outline pen attributes of an existing object, you select the object, and then click on the Outline tool and the Custom Outline Pen icon in the pop-up menu. You can customize the outline pen by altering the settings of up to eight different options: Type, Behind Fill, Scale With Image, Corners, Line Caps, Width, Angle, and Stretch. The Width, Angle, and Stretch settings are especially useful for defining variable "nibs" of a calligraphic pen. By altering these settings, you can exercise great control over the variation in line thickness and the placement of thick and thin strokes on a selected object.

If you rarely need to alter most of the settings in the Outline Pen dialog box, you have the "shortcut" option of selecting a preset outline width from the Outline tool pop-up menu. These preset widths range from no outline at all to an outline 8 points thick.

Once you have defined an outline pen for any object, you can copy that object's outline pen style to other single or multiple objects using the Copy Style From command in the Edit menu.

chapter 14

DEFINING OUTLINE COLOR

Preparing to Define an Object's Outline Color
Outlining with Spot Color
Outlining with PostScript Halftone Screen Patterns
Outlining with Process Color
Outlining with Black, White, or Preset Shades of Gray
Copying Outline Color and Pen Styles

To define an object's outline completely in Corel DRAW!, you must define both the outline pen shape and the outline color attributes. You learned how to select attributes for the outline pen in Chapter 13; in this chapter, you will begin to define outline color. As you may recall, the outline pen allows you to draw with the characteristic style of a calligraphic pen, using "nibs" of various sizes. The outline color represents the colors and textures that flow from the pen.

Corel DRAW! offers you a choice between two different color systems—*spot color* and *process color*—for assigning color to an object's outline. In the spot color system, each color is assigned a unique name or number. The Pantone Color Matching System, which is the standard of the printing industry, has licensed its spot color specifications for use in Corel DRAW!. Spot color works best for images that contain only a few colors, such as headings in newsletters or single-color objects within black-and-white graphics. The process color system, on the other hand, specifies colors in terms of a mix of cyan, magenta, yellow, and black. Process color is more appropriate to use when you plan traditional four-color printing of images that contain a large number of colors. You will find more information concerning color systems and color separation principles in Chapter 18, "Printing and Processing Your Images."

Your options for assigning outline colors do not end with spot and process colors, however. Unlike a hand-held pen, the Corel DRAW! pen not only dispenses "ink" in all colors of the rainbow, it can lay down an assortment of halftone screens for PostScript printing. Appendix E contains examples of these screens for your reference.

The exercises in this chapter will give you practice in specifying spot color, process color, gray shades, and halftone screen patterns for your object outlines. The preview window faithfully reproduces your settings, except in the case of halftone screens. Since you cannot preview an outline consisting of a halftone screen, you must print out your work in order to view it. See Chapter 18 for assistance with printing.

PREPARING TO DEFINE AN OBJECT'S OUTLINE COLOR

Your first step in defining outline color attributes is to determine whether you want to define the attributes for existing objects or for objects not yet rendered. When defining outline color attributes for an existing object, you are in effect editing its current or default attributes. The changes you make apply to that object only, not to additional objects you may create later. When you define outline color attributes for a new object, on the other hand, you are changing default attributes. The next object or series of objects you draw will incorporate automatically the newly defined outline color attributes.

Always work with the preview window turned on when you alter outline color attributes. The editing window does not show you how the selected outline color looks, but for most attributes, the WYSIWYG preview window lets you see the results of your changes instantly.

Preparing to Define an Existing Object's Outline Color Attributes

An existing object can be either a newly created object or one that you have drawn previously. To begin the process of defining outline color attributes for an existing object, proceed as follows:

1. Activate the Select tool ⬚ and select an object whose outline color attributes you wish to edit.

2. Click on the Outline tool ⬚ . When the Outline tool pop-up menu appears, select the Custom Outline Color icon ⬚ , the first icon in the second row, which looks like a paintbrush. The Outline Color dialog box appears, as shown in Figure 14-1. You will practice working with this dialog box later in this chapter; for now, click on Cancel.

   Alternatively, if you have just drawn an object, it is selected automatically, as you will recall from Chapter 8. To invoke the Outline Color dialog box, follow step 1 above without activating the Select tool.

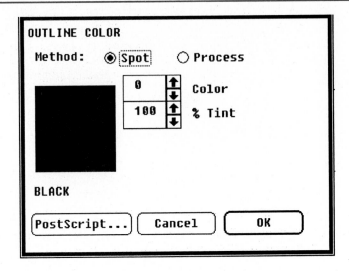

FIGURE 14-1   The Outline Color dialog box with default settings

The next section explains the process of defining outline color attributes for objects that you haven't created yet.

Preparing to Set New Outline Color Defaults

When you click on an option in the Outline tool pop-up menu without first having selected an object, Corel DRAW! assumes that you want to change the standard or default attributes for objects that you draw in the future. Here's how to begin the process:

1. Click on the Outline tool and then proceed to select the Outline Color tool. The message box shown in Figure 14-2 appears, asking you whether you want to change the default settings.

2. Click on OK. The 'New Object' Outline Color dialog box appears. The contents of this dialog box are the same as those

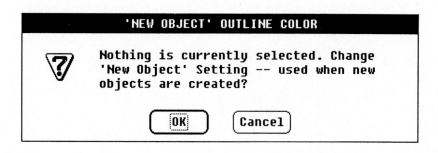

FIGURE 14-2   The 'New Object' Outline Color message box

of the Outline Color dialog box; only the title is different. For now, click on Cancel.

The next set of sections introduces you to the concept of spot color and lets you practice assigning a spot color to an existing or planned object. You gain access to the spot color display as soon as you invoke the Outline Color or 'New Object' Outline Color dialog box.

OUTLINING WITH SPOT COLOR

You should base your choice of a color system (spot or process color) in Corel DRAW! on the type of printer you have and the ultimate destination of your work. You can use either color system if your printer is not a PostScript printer. If you have a PostScript printer, however, let the number of colors in your picture guide you. If an image contains more than half a dozen colors, you would probably find spot color too expensive and time-consuming to produce, and should opt for process color instead. If an image contains fewer than six colors and you require close color match-

ing, you should use the spot color system to assign a unique
Pantone color name to each color. Spot color is also the system to
use with a PostScript printer, since it gives you access to special
PostScript halftone screen patterns.

You define spot colors in Corel DRAW! using the Outline Color
dialog box that you access when you click on the Custom Outline
Color icon in the Outline tool pop-up menu. This dialog box
contains settings for both spot color and process color systems, but
the options visible in the dialog box vary depending on which
system you choose. PostScript halftone screens, for example, are
an option with the spot color system only.

The colors you select using the spot color system are from the
Pantone Matching System that is the standard for the printing
industry. Since the colors that appear in the dialog box preview
color window are only approximations, you should use the Pantone
Color Reference Manual to evaluate your choice of colors prior to
printing. In addition, you can specify a percentage of the tint of
any spot colors you select. The effect of settings below 100% is to
render a lighter shade of the selected color on your monitor or color
printout.

 If you work with a PostScript printer, you can create color separations for spot color and CMYK (process color) objects when you
print your images.

In the following set of exercises, you will learn how to specify
spot colors for the outlines of your Corel DRAW! objects. If you
are working with a color monitor, you will see your drawings come
alive in living color. If you are working with a black and white
monitor, an exercise is included to show you how to set up your
outlines in shades of gray. The exercises in these sections assume
that you understand how to invoke the correct dialog box for either
a planned object or an existing object. If you need to review this
process, refer to the section of this chapter entitled "Preparing to
Define an Object's Outline Color" before continuing.

Assigning Spot Color Outlines
To Existing Objects

To assign spot color to an object's outline, you adjust the settings in the Outline Color dialog box. You access this dialog box by clicking on the Custom Outline Color icon in the Outline tool pop-up menu. This same dialog box allows you to assign process color to an outline, too, but the content of the dialog box changes depending on which option you choose. In the following exercise, you will assign spot colors and shades of gray to the outline of an existing object.

1. Load the CATSPAWS.CDR file that you created in Chapter 13 and magnify the cat. If you didn't create this file, use the ACAT.CDR file and magnify just the head and front paws of the cat.

2. Activate the preview window in a side-by-side format. Make sure that Preview Selected Only is *not* active.

3. To begin editing the cat's existing outline color attributes, select the cat, and then click on the Outline tool and the Custom Outline Color icon. The Outline Color dialog box appears. If you have not altered the default selections, the dialog box still looks like Figure 14-1. If the Process option button rather than the Spot option button is selected, the contents of your dialog box will differ from this figure. Click on the Spot option button if it is not already highlighted.

4. Using the scroll arrow for the Color numeric entry box, scroll to color number 4. As shown in Figure 14-3, the selected color appears in a color preview window at the left side of the dialog box. The Tint numeric entry box shows a value of 100% (the default value). The Pantone identification name or number for this color, in this case "PANTONE Rhodamine Red CV," displays at the bottom of the window. If you have the Pantone

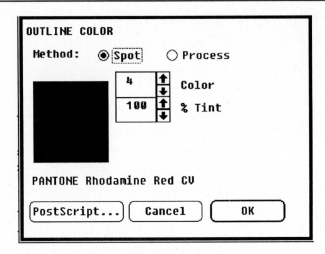

FIGURE 14-3   Setting a new spot color for a selected object

Color Reference Manual or know a color's number, you can type it into the numeric entry box instead of scrolling to it.

5. Click OK in the dialog box. Notice that the outlines of the cat have changed from black to Rhodamine Red. If you are not working with a color monitor, step 7 is especially for you.

6. Invoke the Outline Color dialog box again. This time, set the Color value to 0 (Black) and the Tint value to 51%. Notice that as soon as the Tint value decreases below 100%, the color name beneath the color preview window appears in gray instead of black. The color preview window in the dialog box now displays a 51% gray shade.

7. Click OK in the dialog box. If you have a VGA or Super VGA display card, you will see an actual representation of a 51% gray shade in the cat's outline, as shown in Figure 14-4. If you have

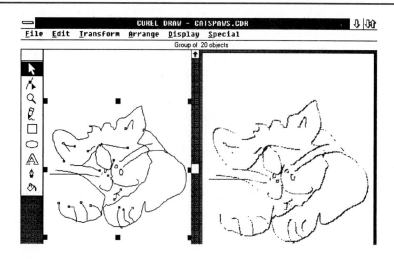

FIGURE 14-4   An outline at 51% gray shade

an EGA display card, however, the outline appears not to have changed from pure black.

8. Access the Outline Color dialog box once more and set the Color value to 4, but leave the Tint value at 51%. You have just selected a lighter tint of PANTONE Rhodamine Red. Whenever the numeric value of the Tint setting is below 100%, the color name in the color preview window is rendered in gray rather than black.

9. Select OK to exit the dialog box with the new outline color setting. If you have a VGA color monitor, you will see an actual representation of the tint. If you have an EGA monitor, the outline color appears the same as if it were a 100% tint.

10. Clear the screen by selecting New from the File menu. Do not save changes to your work.

If you have an EGA display card and monitor, the outline color functions of Corel DRAW! give you less than WYSIWYG displays in two respects. First, you cannot see an actual representation of less than 100% tints in the preview window. In addition, if you select a tint of any color of less than 51%, the outline in the preview window disappears completely. The object is still there, however, and you can print it normally. Should any selected object in a drawing not be visible, therefore, check its Outline Color settings. It could simply be that you have assigned a tint of 50% or less to that object.

In the next exercise, you will practice assigning new spot color outline default values. These values apply automatically to objects that you create after assigning the new defaults

Setting New Spot Color Outline Defaults

When you access the Outline Color dialog box with no objects selected, Corel DRAW! assumes that you intend to change the default outline color values. If this is not the case, select Cancel and select an object before trying again. In the following exercise, you will change defaults for both the outline pen and outline spot color attributes, and then create new objects that exhibit those defaults automatically.

1. Begin with an empty page. Set the display magnification to 1:1.

2. Without creating or selecting any objects, click on the Outline tool and on the Custom Outline Pen icon in the first row of the pop-up menu. The message box that you saw in Figure 14-2 appears, asking whether you want to change default outline pen values. Click on OK to clear the message box from the screen and access the 'New Object' Outline Pen dialog box.

3. When the 'New Object' Outline Pen dialog box appears, set the outline pen attributes as follows: Type solid line, Corners sharp (miter), Line Caps butt, Width 0.15 inch, Angle −45 degrees, Stretch 10%. Do not activate Behind Fill or Scale With Image. Select OK to save these settings and exit the dialog box.

4. Still without selecting an object, click on the Outline tool and on the Custom Outline Color icon in the pop-up menu. As before, the "Nothing is currently selected" message box pops up, but this time it has the title 'New Object' Outline Color. Click on OK to signal that you wish to change the default outline color values. The 'New Object' Outline Color dialog box appears. This is identical to the Outline Color dialog box, except that the title and the purpose of each are different.

5. Set up the new object outline color attributes as follows: Spot Method, Color value 7 (PANTONE Process Blue CV), Tint value 100%. Select OK to save these settings and exit the dialog box.

6. Activate the display rulers, turn on the preview window, and then click on the Text tool ⬚ . Select an insertion point at the 2 5/8-inch horizontal mark and the 7-inch vertical mark.

7. When the Text dialog box appears, type a capital **A** in the text entry window. Select the following text attributes: None Alignment, Banff Normal, 300.0 points. Select OK to exit the dialog box and display the text. If you followed all the steps up to this point, the text should have a default fill of black. Your screen should look like Figure 14-5, except that the color of the outline is blue. Remember that *all* of the new outline pen and color attributes you have selected apply to the new object automatically.

8. Clear the screen by selecting New from the File menu. Do not save your work.

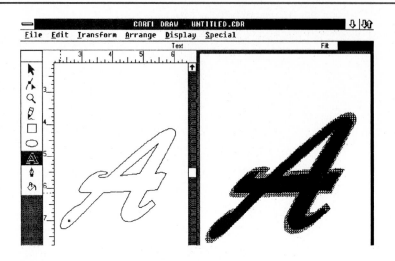

FIGURE 14-5   Letter created with new default Pantone spot color outline

If you create the same kinds of images regularly in your line of work, you probably have strong individual preferences for what you would like default outlines to look like. If you wish, start a new drawing on your own, setting up the outline pen and outline color default attributes that will apply to the basic elements in your drawing. You can edit settings for objects that should have different outline fills, by selecting them after you draw them and accessing the appropriate dialog boxes. If you are not satisfied with the results of your outline pen or outline color attribute settings, you can make any adjustments during the drawing process.

If you have or occasionally use a PostScript printer, go on to the next section to learn how to assign a PostScript halftone screen as an outline color. This option is available only when you choose the spot color method, and it takes effect only if you have a PostScript printer.

OUTLINING WITH POSTSCRIPT HALFTONE SCREEN PATTERNS

If you work with a PostScript printer, you can elect to fill an outline with a *halftone screen pattern* of the currently selected spot color. This option is available only when you have selected spot color as your outlining color method. The preview window displays Post-Script halftone screen patterns as solid colors only; to see the patterns, you must print the images that have PostScript patterns.

The concept of a halftone screen is probably familiar to you already: it is a method of representing continuous tone or color by patterns of dots. Black-and-white and color photographs in newspapers and magazines are examples of halftone images that you see every day.

You define a PostScript halftone screen by clicking on the PostScript command button at the lower-left corner of the Outline Color or 'New Object' Outline Color dialog box. Corel DRAW! offers 11 different types of halftone screen patterns. You can vary the frequency (number of occurrences per inch) and angle of any screen to achieve dramatic differences in outline appearance, even within a single pattern. To see how a PostScript halftone really looks, however, you must print it; the preview window cannot display these screens. Appendix E provides examples of PostScript halftone screens at various frequency and angle settings.

Defining a PostScript halftone screen outline requires the following steps:

1. Select the spot color (and tint, if desired) in which you want to print a screen pattern.

2. Click on the PostScript command button at the lower-left corner of the Outline Color or 'New Object' Outline Color dialog box.

3. Specify a halftone screen pattern from among the 11 patterns available.

4. Select the frequency or number of occurrences of the pattern per inch.

5. Determine the angle at which the pattern should print. Since you cannot view the results of your selections in the preview window, this section does not feature any exercises. Following, however, are brief instructions for selecting a halftone screen pattern, frequency, and angle and some guidelines you should keep in mind when working with these patterns. You can refer to Chapter 18 for instructions on printing with PostScript printers, or to Appendix E to see sample outline fills using halftone screens.

Accessing the PostScript Halftone Screen Dialog Box

To begin defining a halftone screen outline, make sure you have selected the spot color and tint in which you want to print your outline. Then click on the PostScript command button at the lower-left corner of the Outline Color or 'New Object' Outline Color dialog box. The PostScript Halftone Screen dialog box shown in Figure 14-6 appears. This dialog box contains settings for pattern Type, Frequency, and Angle attributes.

Selecting the Halftone Screen Type

The Type option in the PostScript Halftone Screen dialog box features 11 halftone patterns that are available for your outline color work. Your choices are Default, Dot, Line, Diamond, Dot2, Grid, Lines, MicroWaves, OutCircleBlk, OutCircleWhi, and Star. To select a halftone pattern type, scroll through the list until you see the name of the desired pattern, and then click on the name to highlight it. Sample printouts of each of the 11 halftone screens are shown in Appendix E.

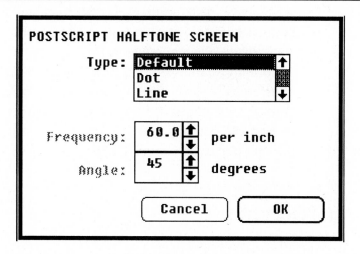

FIGURE 14-6   The PostScript Halftone Screen dialog box with default settings

Selecting the Halftone Screen Frequency

The Frequency option in the PostScript Halftone Screen dialog box allows you to determine how many times per inch the pattern should occur within the outline. The available range is from 10 to 1000 per inch, and the default setting is 60. The number you should select depends upon the resolution of your ultimate output device; refer to Chapter 18 for more details on frequency settings for PostScript halftone screens.

Setting the Halftone Screen Angle

The third and last option in the PostScript Halftone Screen dialog box allows you to specify the angle of the screen pattern when you print it. Keep in mind that the halftone screen angle remains constant, no matter how you transform an object. If you stretch, scale, rotate, or skew an object after assigning it a halftone screen outline, you could alter its appearance significantly. If you do not want this to happen, remember to change the screen angle after performing a transform operation, to match the offset of the transformed object. You will achieve the best results by setting your screen angle at 0, 45, 90, and 180 degrees. In the next group of sections, you will begin defining process color (CMYK) outlines for objects in Corel DRAW!.

OUTLINING WITH PROCESS COLOR

Process color is the term used for specifying color in percentages of cyan, magenta, yellow, and black (CMYK). This is the four-color standard for the printing industry. You can specify greater than 64 million colors by using various CMYK percentages. In general, you should specify process color instead of spot color when your drawing includes more than a half dozen colors and you plan to reproduce it through the four-color printing process.

Corel DRAW! supports color separation for process as well as spot color if you send your work to a PostScript printer. When you specify color in CMYK terms, your printer generates only four sheets (one each for cyan, magenta, yellow, and black percentages) for every image page, no matter how many colors the image contains. When you specify in spot color terms, on the other hand, the printer generates a separate page for every single color used in the drawing. You will learn more about printing spot and process colors in Chapter 18.

To specify process colors for an existing object, you select or create the object, click on the Outline tool, and click again on the Custom Outline Color icon in the pop-up menu. When the Outline Color dialog box appears, you select the Process option button and set the color mix using the CMYK numeric entry boxes. To specify default process colors for planned objects that you haven't drawn yet, you access the Outline Color dialog box without having selected an object.

In the following exercise, you will specify both the outline pen and outline process color for a text string in the sample file ORG4.CDR.

1. Deactivate the Show Rulers command, and then open the sample file ORG4.CDR. Magnify just the area containing the text string "Org Chart." Turn on the preview window and adjust preview and editing windows to a top-to-bottom format. Your screen should now appear similar to Figure 14-7.

2. Select the text string "Org Chart." Notice that it has a fill of white, no apparent outline, and the contrast between this text and the light green rectangle behind it is very poor. You are

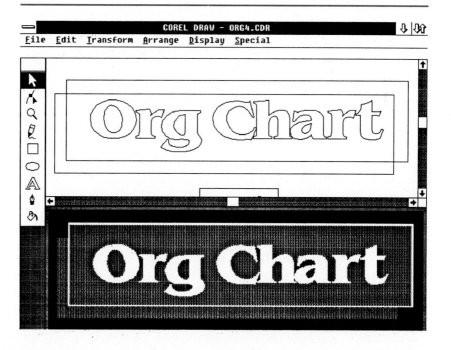

FIGURE 14-7   Magnified text string with no outline

going to improve this contrast by adding an outline of the appropriate color and thickness to the text.

3. Select the Outline tool and the Custom Outline Pen icon to invoke the Outline Pen dialog box. The current settings for the text string are shown as in Figure 14-8. The text has no outline, so even though the Nib Shape window displays a yellow nib, the color has no effect.

4. Change the Type setting to solid and increase the outline pen Width to 18.0 fractional points. Select rounded instead of sharp corners, and activate the Behind Fill option by clicking on the checkbox in front of it.

5. Select OK to save your settings. Your changes have resulted in a fairly thick text outline, and by the calligraphic Pen Shape and

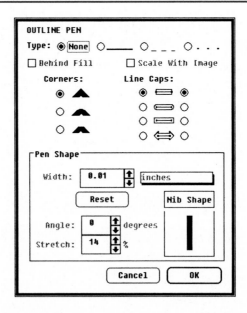

FIGURE 14-8   Current outline pen settings for the "Org Chart" text string

the location of the outline behind the fill color give an "artistic" look. The rounded corners setting adds a more polished look to the outlines of corners of angular letters, such as the "t" in "Chart." The yellow color of the outline still does not provide enough contrast to the background rectangle, however, so you will change it now.

6. With the text string still selected, click on the Outline tool once more. This time, select the Custom Outline Color icon [icon] in the second row of the pop-up menu to invoke the Outline Color dialog box. Notice that the current outline color was assigned using the spot color method.

7. Click on the Process option button to switch color selection methods. The options in the dialog box change instantly to percentages of cyan, magenta, yellow, and black. Using the scroll bar or your mouse and keyboard, set the following color mix: Cyan 100%, Magenta 55%, Yellow 0%, and Black 45%. The color preview window in the Outline Color box displays a real-time approximation of changes to the color as you scroll to or type in each specified value. When you have specified all of the values, the color window displays a deep royal blue.

8. Select OK to exit the dialog box. If you have a color monitor, the text string's outline displays as a deep royal blue, providing a high contrast to the light rectangle behind. This contrast is shown in Figure 14-9.

9. Select the Save As command in the File menu and save this altered file as ORG4-1.CDR. If you are continuing with the next exercise, leave this image on the screen. If not, select the New command to clear the screen.

You could continue altering outline colors throughout the ORG.CDR file to improve contrast or for other design purposes. When specifying process colors, you can include as many colors

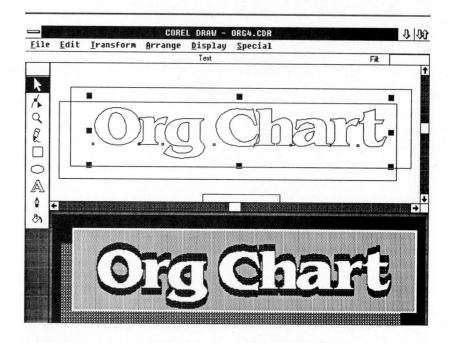

FIGURE 14-9   Magnified text string with thick outline
contrasting with background

in the picture as you like. When you finally print the image, the results will still be separated into no more than four sheets.

In the next section of this chapter, you will learn a shortcut to specifying outline color that will be useful if you usually print to a black-and-white printer.

OUTLINING WITH BLACK, WHITE, OR PRESET SHADES OF GRAY

When you worked with the outline pen in Chapter 13, the first row of the Outline tool pop-up menu contained seven preset outline widths that you could select simply by clicking on the desired icon. The arrangement of the second row of the Outline tool pop-up

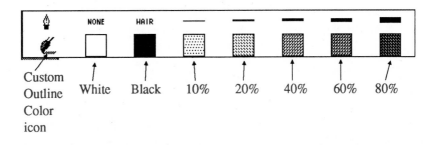

FIGURE 14-10   Preset black, white, and gray shades in the
Outline tool pop-up menu

menu is similar. Following the Custom Outline Color icon is a
series of seven symbols that let you select a preset outline color
quickly, without having to set attributes in a dialog box. As Figure
14-10 shows, the seven preset outline color options are white,
black, and 10%, 20%, 40%, 60%, and 80% gray.

To select one of these preset outline colors for an existing object,
you select the object, access the Outline tool pop-up menu, and
then click on the appropriate icon. To select one of these options
as the default outline color, you click on the desired icon in the
Outline tool pop-up menu without first selecting an object.

In the following exercise, you will select several of the preset
outline color options and apply them to the text outline in the
ORG4-1.CDR file you edited in the previous exercise.

1. Open the ORG4-1.CDR file if you did not leave it on the screen
    after the last exercise. Magnify the area containing the "Org
    Chart" text as before. Once again, turn on the preview window
    and place it beneath the editing window.

2. Select the "Org Chart" text, and then select the Outline tool.
    When the pop-up menu appears, click on the black square in

the second row of the menu. The outline of the text string changes from dark blue to solid black.

3. Select the Outline tool again, and this time click on the 40% gray symbol (the third symbol in from the right in the second row). Now the text outline shows a much lighter color, as in Figure 14-11.

4. Experiment with different preset outline color settings. When you have finished, select the New command from the File menu to clear the screen. Do not save your changes.

Remember that you are not limited to these preset shades of gray if you use a black-and-white printer. You can use either the spot color or the process color system to define custom shades of gray.

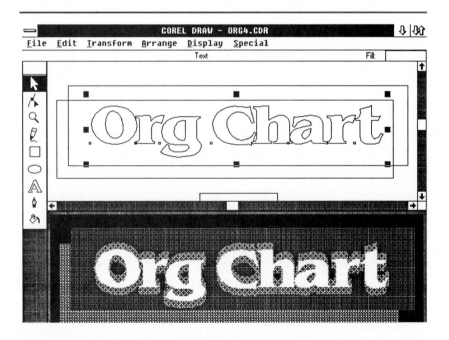

FIGURE 14-11   Magnified text string with preset outline of 40% gray

To define custom shades of gray using the spot color method, access the Outline Color dialog box and set shades of gray by setting the Color to 0 and the % tint in increments of 1%. To define custom shades of gray using the process color method, define a percentage for Black only, leaving cyan, magenta, and yellow all at 0%.

You can use the preset shades of gray in the Outline tool pop-up menu in combination with the PostScript halftone screens.

COPYING OUTLINE COLOR AND PEN STYLES

In previous chapters, you have learned how to use the Copy Style From command in the Edit menu to copy text or outline pen attributes from one object to another. You use the same command to copy outline color attributes between objects, too, as you will see in the following exercise.

1. Open the ORG4-1.CDR file once again. Magnify the "Org Chart" text and set up the preview window in top-to-bottom format as before.

2. Select the upper of the two background rectangles located behind the text string. This object currently has a thin white outline.

3. Select the Copy Style From command in the Edit menu. When the Copy Style dialog box appears, click on both the Outline Pen and the Outline Color checkboxes, and then select OK. The cursor turns into an arrow containing the words "Copy From?" to indicate that the next object you select will copy its outline attributes to the selected object.

4. Select the "Org Chart" text string. The background rectangle redisplays to show the same outline thickness and color as the text string, as shown in Figure 14-12.

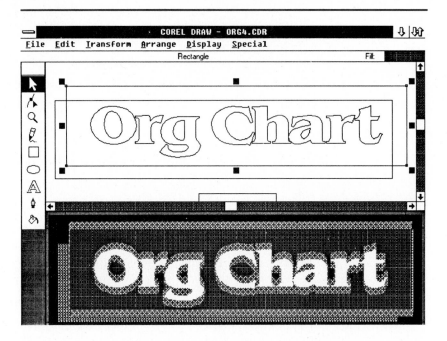

FIGURE 14-12   Rectangle with outline color and pen styles
copied from text string

5. Save your changes by pressing (**CTRL-S**). Then clear the screen
    by selecting the New command.

For more practice with the Outline color tool, you could go back
to the LANDSCA4.CDR or other landscape drawing that you
created and edited in Chapters 4 through 8. The default outlines
and fills of all of the objects in those files are black, but you can
begin to differentiate objects by varying their outlines. You can
give custom outlines to interior objects or copy outline styles to
multiple objects at a time.

SUMMARY

When defining the outline for an object in Corel DRAW!, you can specify not only the outline pen, but also the outline color, using the options in the second row of the Outline tool pop-up menu. You can define a custom spot or process color, assign a PostScript halftone screen pattern, or select one of seven preset shades ranging from white to black. When you assign outline colors for selected objects, you are editing the existing settings for those objects. When you define outline colors without first selecting any objects, you are creating new default colors that apply automatically to objects you create later.

To define a custom outline color, you set the attributes in the Outline Color dialog box. You access this dialog box by clicking on the Custom Outline Color icon in the Outline tool pop-up menu. You can choose from two color systems—spot color and process color—when specifying the color of an outline. Use spot color when an image has fewer than six colors and you need a perfect color match. Use process color when an image contains a larger number of colors and you have a limited production budget. The contents of the Outline Color dialog box change, depending on which color system you select.

When you assign spot color to an outline, you use the Pantone Matching System, the industry standard licensed for use by Corel DRAW!. You express each color in terms of a Tint value between 1% and 100%. Using the spot color system also gives you the added advantage of being able to assign one of 11 Corel DRAW! PostScript halftone screen patterns to the outline. You can use these patterns in conjunction with any spot color and vary their frequency and angle within the outline.

When you assign a process color to an outline, you specify colors in terms of a color mix, expressed as percentages of cyan, magenta, yellow, and black (CMYK). PostScript halftone screen patterns are not available with the process color system.

Corel DRAW! supports color separation for PostScript printers for both spot color and process color. When you request color separation for spot color outlines, your printer generates one page for every color in the picture. When you request color separation for process color, your printer generates only four pages, one each for cyan, magenta, yellow, and black.

If you print only to a black-and-white printer, you can specify exact gray shades through the Outline Color dialog box. Alternatively, you can select one of seven preset colors (black, white, and five gray shades) from the Outline tool pop-up menu.

Just as with the outline pen, you can copy outline color styles from one object to another. Use the Copy Style From command in the Edit menu for this purpose.

chapter 15

DEFINING FILL COLOR

In Chapters 13 and 14, you learned how to enhance your drawings by defining outline pen and outline color attributes for objects. The outline color attributes make up the "ink" that flows from a pen, while the outline pen is like the calligraphic pen or marker from which the ink flows.

This chapter introduces you to the Corel DRAW! Fill tool. The Fill tool, as its icon suggests, functions like a paint bucket with a limitless supply of paint, capable of filling the interior of any leakproof object. A leakproof object is any object that is a closed path; all Corel DRAW! objects are leakproof, except straight lines and open curves. If you have drawn a curve object in which the two end nodes do not join, the object remains an open path, and you cannot fill it. When you select such an object, the words "Open Path" appear at the right side of the status line. (You can close an open path by joining its end nodes, as you will recall from Chapter 10.)

The Fill tool is similar to the Outline Color tool in that it can dispense spot color, process color, and PostScript halftone screen patterns. It can also dispense other types of fills that the Outline Color tool does not provide: fountain fills in any combination of colors, and 42 different gray-scale PostScript fill textures. You will learn more about these types of fills in the "Defining Custom Fountain Fills" and "Defining PostScript Fill Textures" sections of this chapter.

The exercises in this chapter give you practice in specifying spot or process color, gray shades, PostScript halftone screen patterns, fountain fills, and PostScript fill textures for objects. The preview window faithfully reproduces your settings, unless you have chosen a PostScript halftone screen or fill texture. Since you cannot preview these types of fills, you must print out your work in order to view it. See Chapter 18 for assistance with printing, and Appendix E for examples of PostScript halftone screens and fill textures.

PREPARING TO DEFINE FILL COLOR

Before you define fill attributes for the interior of an object, you must determine whether you want to define the attributes for existing objects or for objects not yet rendered. When defining fill attributes for an existing object, you are editing its current fill. The color or name of the fill will appear in the status line when you select the object. The changes you make apply to that object only, not to additional objects you may create later. When you set new default fill attributes, on the other hand, you are specifying how objects you create in the future will be filled automatically. In this respect, the Fill tool works like the Outline tool.

Always work with the preview window turned on when you alter fill attributes for new or existing objects. Except for PostScript textures and halftone screen patterns, the WYSIWYG preview lets you see the results of your changes instantly.

Preparing to Define Fill Color For Existing Objects

An existing object can be either a newly created object or an object that you have drawn previously. In general, it's a good idea to define fill color for one object at a time. If you define fill colors for multiple objects that you have selected using the (SHIFT) key technique, the fill colors of all of the objects change to match the fill of the last object you selected. If you select multiple objects using the marquee, the fill colors of all the objects change to match the fill of the most recently drawn object in the group.

To begin the process of defining fill attributes for an existing object, select the object and the Fill tool in the following way:

1. Activate the Select tool and click on an object that has fill attributes you would like to edit. The current fill color of the object displays on the status line. Alternatively, if you have just drawn an object, it is automatically selected and available for further work, and you do not have to activate the Select tool.

2. Click on the Fill tool in the Corel DRAW! toolbox . The Fill tool pop-up menu appears and looks like this:

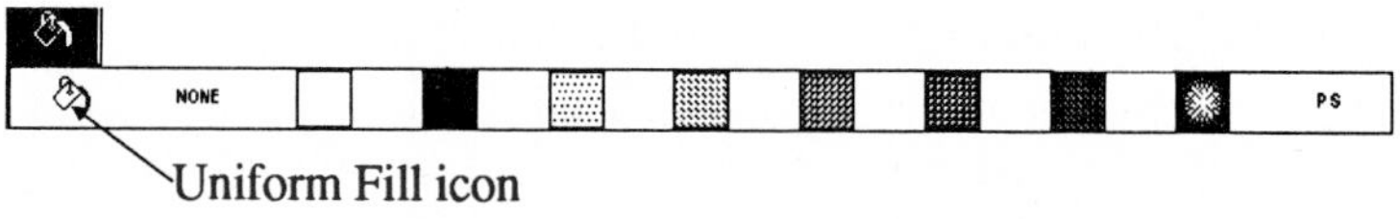
NONE
PS
Uniform Fill icon

The first icon in the Fill tool pop-up menu is the Uniform Fill icon. Although this icon looks just like the Fill tool icon, it has the specialized function of helping you define custom spot and process color fills and PostScript halftone screen patterns. The NONE icon causes an object to have a transparent fill. The seven icons following NONE let you specify preset fill colors of white, black, and shades of gray automatically. The last two icons in the pop-up menu let you access dialog boxes to customize specific types of fills, known as fountain fills and PostScript textures.

3. Click on the icon that accesses the desired dialog box or specifies the desired preset fill shade, as described in the previous step. To remove the pop-up menu from the screen without making any selections, click anywhere outside the menu or press (ESC).

The major sections in this chapter offer you extensive practice in working with each dialog box and selecting fill attributes for each of the major types of fills. Whether you are setting fill attributes for selected objects or altering default attributes for objects you haven't drawn yet, the main steps involved are similar. The next section explains the minor differences in steps that change default fill attributes.

Preparing to Define New
Default Fill Attributes

When you click on an option in the Fill tool pop- up menu without first having selected an object, Corel DRAW! assumes that you want to change the default attributes for objects that you will draw in the future. To begin defining new default attributes:

1. Click on the Fill tool without first creating a new object or selecting an existing one.

2. Click on the icon that accesses the desired dialog box or specifies the desired fill of black, white, or shade of gray. No matter which icon you select, the message box shown in Figure 15-1 appears, asking you whether you want to change the default settings. Only the title of the message box will differ, depending on which pop-up menu icon you select.

3. If you meant to select an existing object and edit its fill, click on Cancel; otherwise, click on OK. If you clicked on the first, next to last, or last icon in the pop-up menu (the Uniform Fill, Fountain Fill, or PostScript Textures icon), a dialog box appears. If you clicked any other icon, the next object or series of objects you draw will have the specified fill color automatically. To remove the pop-up menu from the screen without making a selection, click anywhere outside the menu.

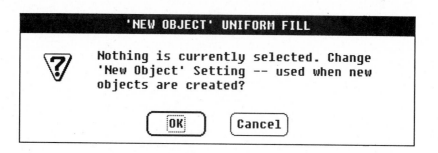

FIGURE 15-1   A sample 'New Object' message box for setting default fill attributes

The major sections in this chapter describe how to set fill attributes in the respective dialog boxes. The first dialog box you will encounter is the Uniform Fill dialog box. This dialog box allows you to specify a fill color as a spot color, PostScript halftone screen pattern, or process color.

DEFINING UNIFORM SPOT COLOR FILLS

To fill an object with spot color, process color, or a PostScript halftone screen pattern, you use the settings in the Uniform Fill dialog box. This dialog box appears when you click on the Uniform Fill icon, the first icon in the Fill tool pop-up menu. Its name, Uniform Fill, distinguishes it conceptually from Fountain and PostScript Texture fills, which involve multiple hues or patterns rather than a single color. Except for the title, the Uniform Fill dialog box is identical in appearance and function to the Outline Fill dialog box you worked with in Chapter 14.

You will recall from Chapter 14 that spot color is the preferred color system when an image contains six or fewer colors or if you want to experiment with PostScript halftone screen patterns. If you do not have a PostScript printer at your disposal and your work does not require spot color or four-color printing, you can use either the spot or process color system to specify fill colors.

 If you have a black-and-white display adapter and monitor, you can still specify spot color fills, but your screen will not display them in color. Refer to the Pantone Color Reference Manual to see the color you have selected.

As mentioned at the beginning of the chapter, an object must be a closed path in order for you to fill it. However, a closed path does not assure a solid object. If you combine two or more objects as you learned to do in Chapter 8, "holes" result where the combined objects overlap. You can then create interesting design effects by surrounding the "holes" with outline and fill colors. Perform the following exercise to create a logo with transparent text, outline it, and assign a uniform fill spot color to it. You will edit this logo throughout the chapter as you learn new ways to use the Fill tool pop-up menu. If you are working with a color monitor, you will see the example drawings come alive in living color! If you are working with a black-and-white monitor, you will see the specified colors as shades of gray.

1. To prepare the screen, set magnification at 1:1. Activate the Snap To Grid command and set Grid Frequency to 1 per pica. If the units box displays a unit of measurement other than picas, click on it until the word "pica" displays. Activate the Show Rulers command; because of the grid settings, the rulers display in picas rather than in inches.

2. Before beginning to draw, set the default outline pen and outline fill attributes back to the original Corel DRAW! defaults. To do this, click on the Custom Outline Pen icon in the Outline tool pop-up menu. Select OK when the 'New Object' Outline Pen message box appears to ask you whether you want to set a new default value. Adjust settings in the Outline Pen dialog box as follows: line Type none, Corners sharp, width 0.01 inches, Angle 0 degrees, Stretch 100%. No checkboxes should be filled. Select OK to make these settings the default outline pen attributes.

3. To specify the default outline color as black, click on the Outline tool again and then select the black icon in the second row of the Outline tool pop-up menu. Select OK when the 'New Object' Outline Color message box asks you whether you want to set a new default.

4. Select the Ellipse tool ⬭, and position the cursor at the 24-pica mark on the horizontal ruler and the 33-pica mark on the vertical ruler. Draw a perfect circle from the center outward, starting from this point. Make the circle 28 picas in diameter, using the information on the status line to help you.

5. Activate the Text tool Ⓐ. Select an insertion point near the top of the circle, at the 25-pica mark on the horizontal ruler and the 23-pica mark on the vertical ruler. You do not have to position the cursor exactly, because you can align the text and circle later. When the Text dialog box appears, type **The World of Corel DRAW!** in the text entry window, one word per line, and select the following text attributes: Aardvark Bold, 50.0 points, Center alignment. Click on the Spacing command button, set inter-character spacing to 0.20 em and inter-line spacing

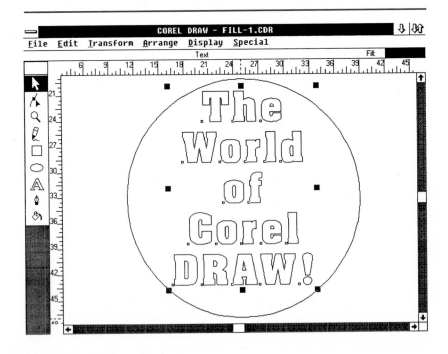

FIGURE 15-2   Centering a text string within a circle

to 115%, and then select OK. The text appears centered vertically and horizontally within the circle, as shown in Figure
15-2. If the text is not centered perfectly within the circle, select
both the text and the circle and align them using the Align
command in the Arrange menu.

6. Click on the Show Rulers command in the Display menu again
   to deactivate the rulers. Turn on the preview window and adjust
   it to a top-to-bottom format. You cannot clearly distinguish the
   text from the circle yet, because they have the same outline and
   fill colors.

7. Select the Preferences command in the Special menu. When the
   Preferences dialog box appears, adjust both of the numeric
   settings beside the Place Duplicate option to −2,0 picas and
   points. Make sure that you place a comma rather than a period
   after the 2. Duplicate objects that you create with this setting
   are offset from the original by the specified amount (in this case,
   2 picas below and to the left of the original). Select OK to exit
   the dialog box.

8. Activate the Select tool, select the circle, and then click on the
   Duplicate command in the Edit menu. A duplicate of the circle
   appears below and to the left of the original and is selected
   immediately.

9. Change the fill of this duplicate circle to None by clicking on
   the Fill tool and then on the NONE option in the pop-up menu.

10. Select the original circle and the text string again using the
    (SHIFT) key, and click on the Combine command in the Arrange
    menu. The message in the status line changes from "2 objects
    selected" to "Curve." The "Fill:" message at the right side of the
    status line displays a default fill of black, but the text now
    appears white, as shown in the full-screen preview window
    illustration in Figure 15-3. In combining the two objects, you

have converted both the circle and the text string to curves. The area behind the text has become not white but transparent.

11. Select the Save As command in the File menu. When the Save As dialog box appears, type the name **FILL-1** in the File text box, and then select Save.

12. With the curve object still selected, click on the Fill tool and again on the Uniform Fill icon. The Uniform Fill dialog box appears. Click on the Spot option button if it is not selected already, and then define the fill color as Color 1, Pantone Yellow CV, and Tint 55%. Your settings should match those in Figure 15-4.

FIGURE 15-3   Combining two objects to form a curve object with transparent "holes"

13. Select OK to exit the dialog box. Now you can see some contrast between the black outline and the fill colors, even if you do not have a color monitor. The text has the same outline style as the circular shape, because Corel DRAW! treats the text curves as "holes" or edges within the single combined object. The outline is very thin, however, so you will thicken it in the next step.

14. With the curve object still selected, click on the Outline tool. Access the Outline Pen dialog box by clicking on the Custom Outline Pen icon. Change the Width setting for the outline pen to 5.0 fractional points. Place a checkmark in the Behind Fill option and then select OK to apply these settings to the object. Now you see a heavier outline around both the outer rim of the circle and the text, as shown in Figure 15-5. Because you activated the Behind Fill option, the "ink" of the outline doesn't completely clog up the transparent spaces in the text.

15. You are ready to give the finishing touches to the curve object. Click on the Outline tool once more, and select the Custom

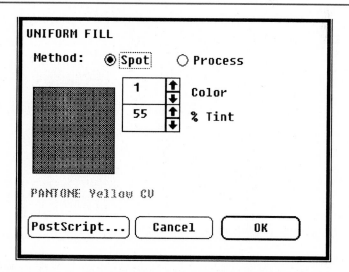

FIGURE 15-4   Settings for a spot color uniform fill

Outline Color icon to access the Outline Color dialog box. Select the Spot option button if it is not selected already, and set outline color to Pantone 293 CV, Tint 52%. Select OK to exit the dialog box.

16. Click on the Preview Selected Only command in the Display menu, and then select the duplicate circle. Click on the Fill tool and the Uniform Fill icon to access the Uniform Fill dialog box. Scroll to or type in Color 281, Pantone 281 CV (a dark purplish blue), Tint 100%. Select OK to save this setting and exit the dialog box.

17. Deactivate the Preview Selected Only command. The image redisplays to show the background circle creating a dramatic "shadow" effect against the curve object. The alignment is not

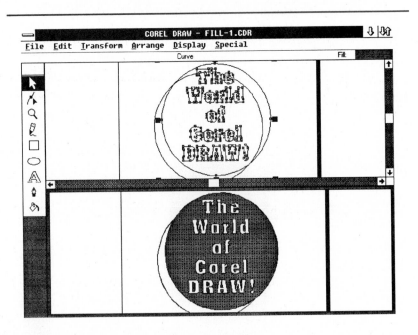

FIGURE 15-5   Outline appearing behind fill for clearer text appearance

quite right yet, however; white space is visible behind the upper portion of the word "The." To remedy this situation, deactivate the Snap To Grid command and adjust the position of the curve object slightly so that the background circle fills the word "The" completely. Now all of the transparent spaces behind the letters in the curve object have an apparent fill behind them.

18. To see this apparent fill more closely, adjust the size of the preview window so that it fills the entire screen. Your screen should look similar to Figure 15-6.

19. Group the curve object and the circle behind it, and then press (CTRL-S) to save the changes you have made to this graphic. Leave the graphic on the screen to use in the next exercise.

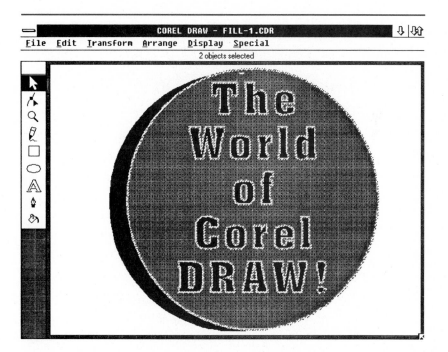

FIGURE 15-6   Apparent fill of transparent areas using a background object

If you have an EGA display card and monitor, the colors you select in the Uniform Fill dialog box will not be quite as WYSIWYG as if you had a VGA or Super VGA display. Tints of less than 100% display as though they were the fully saturated color, for example. In addition, if you select a tint of any color that is less than 51%, the color seems to disappear in the preview window completely. If you are filling an object whose outline has a fill of None, you will not be able to preview the object at all. The object is still there, however, and you can print it normally.

The kind of object you have just created makes an excellent specimen for outline and fill experiments of all kinds. You will continue to use this graphic throughout the chapter. In the next section, you will add an interesting design effect by specifying a PostScript halftone screen pattern for the background circle in FILL-1.CDR.

DEFINING POSTSCRIPT HALFTONE SCREEN FILL PATTERNS

When you choose the spot color rather than the process color system in the Uniform Fill dialog box, another set of fill specifications becomes available. If you work with a PostScript printer, you can fill an object with a halftone screen pattern of the currently selected spot color. You will recall from your work with outline color in Chapter 14 that the Corel DRAW! preview window displays PostScript halftone screen patterns as a solid color; to see how they actually look, you have to print them.

You define a PostScript halftone screen pattern by clicking on the PostScript command button at the lower-left corner of the Uniform Fill or 'New Object' Uniform Fill dialog box. Corel DRAW! offers 11 different screen options. You can vary the frequency (number of occurrences per inch) and angle of any screen pattern to achieve dramatic differences in the appearance of a spot color fill. Appendix E provides examples of PostScript halftone screens with various attribute settings.

In the following exercise, you will assign a PostScript halftone screen pattern of a specified angle and frequency to the background circle in the FILL-1.CDR image and save the altered image under a new name. If you have a PostScript printer, you can print this image out once you have mastered the printing techniques covered in Chapter 18.

1. With the magnified view of the image in FILL-1.CDR still on the screen, return the preview window to a top-to-bottom format and activate the Preview Selected Only command in the Display menu.

2. Select the image and ungroup its component objects by clicking on the Ungroup command in the Arrange menu. Deselect both objects and then click on the outline of the curve object that you combined earlier.

3. With the curve object selected, click on the Fill tool and the Uniform Fill icon in the Fill tool pop-up menu. When the Uniform Fill dialog box appears, click on the PostScript command button at the lower-left corner of the dialog box. The PostScript Halftone Screen dialog box appears.

4. Select the MicroWaves screen type by scrolling through the Type list box until MicroWaves is highlighted.

5. Adjust screen frequency in the Frequency numeric entry box to 20.0 per inch. This is a very low frequency (the minimum is 10, the maximum 1000) and will display a dramatic pattern on a 300 dpi PostScript printer.

6. Using the scroll arrow, adjust the number in the Angle numeric entry box to 45 degrees. This will cause the screen pattern to tilt at a 45-degree angle.

7. If your settings match the ones in Figure 15-7, select OK to exit the PostScript Halftone Screen dialog box. Click on OK again to exit the Uniform Fill dialog box and return to the screen image. You will not notice anything different, because the preview window cannot display PostScript patterns.

8. Select the Save As command in the File menu and type **FILL-2** in the File text box of the Save As dialog box. Select Save to save the file under this new name. After you complete Chapter 18, you can print this file to see the results of your settings.

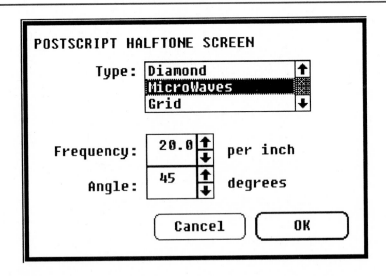

FIGURE 15-7   Defining a custom PostScript halftone screen pattern

9. Select New to clear the screen.

When you assign PostScript halftone screen pattern fills to objects, base your choice of frequency on the resolution of the PostScript printer you will use. On any PostScript printer, low frequencies result in more dramatic pattern effects, while high frequencies result in the pattern being hardly visible. The resolution of the printer, not any absolute number, determines what constitutes a low or a high frequency. To achieve the same visual effect on different printers, you should vary the frequency assigned to a screen. For example, you should assign lower screen frequencies when the printer resolution is 300 dpi, and higher frequencies for Linotronic or other image-setting equipment at a resolution of 600 or 1270 dpi. Table 15-1 provides information on the number of visible gray levels for each printer resolution at a given screen frequency.

You can specify a PostScript halftone screen pattern as a default fill in the same way that you would specify a normal spot color. In the next section, you will change the fill and outline colors of both of the objects in the original FILL-1.CDR file, using the process color system instead of spot color.

Selected Frequency	Number of Gray Levels		
	300dpi	600dpi	1200dpi
30 per inch	101	401	1600
60 per inch	26	101	401
100 per inch	10	37	145
120 per inch	7	26	101

TABLE 15-1   Printer Resolution and Number of Gray Levels Visible for PostScript Halftone Screen Patterns

DEFINING UNIFORM PROCESS COLOR FILLS

As you will recall from Chapter 14, process color is the term used for expressing colors as percentages of cyan, magenta, yellow, and black (CMYK). Process color is the industry standard for four-color printing. In general, you should specify process color instead of spot color when your drawing includes more than six colors or when you plan to reproduce it through the four-color printing process.

Corel DRAW! supports color separation for process as well as spot color if you send your work to a PostScript printer. When you specify color in CMYK terms, your printer generates only four sheets (one each for cyan, magenta, yellow, and black percentages) for every image page, no matter how many colors the image contains. When you specify color in spot color terms, on the other hand, the printer generates a separate page for each color used in the drawing. Spot color is more exact for purposes of color, matching than process color but also more expensive to produce.

To specify process colors for an existing object, you create or select the object, click on the Fill tool, and then click again on the Uniform Fill icon in the pop-up menu. When the Uniform Fill dialog box appears, you select the Process option button and set the color mix using the CMYK numeric entry boxes. To specify default process colors for objects that you plan to draw in the future, you access the Uniform Fill dialog box without first having selected an object.

In the next exercise, you will specify fill and outline color for the original FILL-1.CDR file using the process color system instead of spot color.

Assigning Process Color Uniform
Fills to Existing Objects

If you plan to generate color separations for an image in preparation for printing, remember to specify outlines and fills for all objects in terms of the same color system. In the following exercise, you will change fill color specifications for FILL-1.CDR from spot to process color.

1. Open the original FILL-1.CDR file that you created in the first exercise of this chapter. The curve object and background circle are currently grouped; to make them accessible as separate objects, select them and apply the Ungroup command from the Arrange menu.

2. Magnify the image using the ALL icon in the Magnification tool pop-up menu, and then turn on the preview window. Deselect both objects and select the background circle.

3. With the background circle selected, click on the Fill tool and then the Uniform Fill icon. The Uniform Fill dialog box appears, displaying the object's current spot color fill.

4. Click on the Process option button. The contents of the dialog box change immediately, as shown in Figure 15-8. Now, instead of two settings for specifying each color, you have four: Cyan, Magenta, Yellow, and Black. The PostScript command button has gone gray, too, indicating that this option is not available with process color.

5. Adjust the color values to Cyan 55%, Magenta 55%, and Black 75%. Leave Yellow at the default value, 0%. The color preview

window displays a royal blue. Select OK to redisplay the background circle with the new fill color.

6. Select the combined curve object and access the Uniform Fill dialog box again. Select the Process Method option button, set fill color values to Magenta 30% and Yellow 10% (leaving Cyan and Black at 0%), and then select OK.

7. Whenever you are preparing an image for four-color printing, make sure that *both* outline and fill colors are specified using the process color system. In the present illustration, the outline color for the curve object is still specified with spot color. To switch color systems for the outline of the curve object, select the Outline tool and the Custom Outline Color icon to access the Outline Color dialog box. Click on the Process Method option button and set outline fill color values to Cyan 35%, Magenta 30%, and Black 10% (leaving Yellow at 0%). Click on OK to exit the dialog box and redisplay the curve object. If

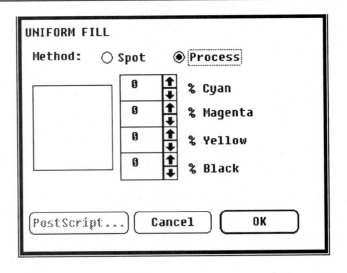

FIGURE 15-8   The Uniform Fill dialog box with process color method selected

you adjust the size of the preview window so that it fills the screen, the image should appear similar to Figure 15-9.

8. Deactivate the Preview Selected Only command and select the Save As command in the File menu. When the Save As dialog box appears, type **FILL-3** in the File text box and then click on Save.

9. Select the New command in the File menu to clear the screen.

Go on to the next section to review how to specify new process color default settings. New objects that you create thereafter will contain those settings automatically.

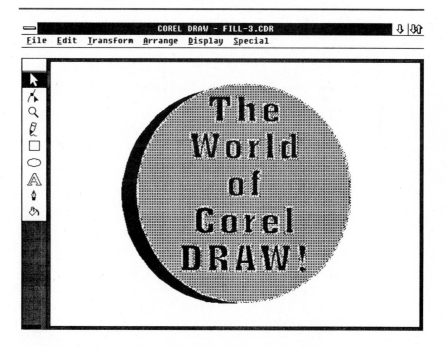

FIGURE 15-9   Curve objects with process color fill of 35% cyan, 30% magenta, 0% yellow, 10% black

Setting New Process Color
Uniform Fill Defaults

The Fill tool works much like the Outline tool when you are defining new default attributes. There is very little difference between editing process color uniform fills for existing objects and setting new process color uniform fill defaults. You simply access the Uniform Fill dialog box without selecting any objects first. Objects that you draw after specifying new defaults will appear with the new fill attributes automatically.

Specifying process color uniform fills is easy; you will begin working with color separation for process color in Chapter 18. Many Corel DRAW! applications require only black and white graphics, however. In the next section, you will learn a shortcut to specifying fill color that will be useful if you usually print to a black-and-white printer.

FILLING OBJECTS WITH WHITE,
BLACK, OR PRESET SHADES OF GRAY

When you specified outline fill colors in Chapter 14, the second row of the Outline tool pop-up menu contained seven preset colors (white, black, and five shades of gray) that you could select quickly by clicking on the desired icon. The arrangement in the Fill tool pop-up menu is similar. Following the Uniform Fill tool is a series of eight icons that allow you to select a preset outline color without having to set attributes in a dialog box. These eight options represent preset uniform fills in the following order: NONE (transparent), white, black, and 10%, 20%, 40%, 60%, and 80% gray.

To select one of these preset uniform fill colors for an existing object, you simply select the object, access the Fill tool pop-up menu, and then click on the appropriate icon. If you had previously assigned a PostScript halftone screen fill to the selected object, the pattern remains the same but now has the new shade that is assigned to it.

To select one of the preset options as the default uniform fill, you click on the desired icon in the Fill tool pop-up menu, without first selecting an object. Again, if the previous default fill involved a PostScript halftone screen pattern, that pattern remains active but in the new default gray shade.

In the following exercise, you will assign black, white, or preset gray shade fills to the objects in the FILL-2.CDR file.

1. Open the FILL-2.CDR file. As you will recall, this is the file in which you assigned a PostScript halftone screen pattern to the background circle.

2. Adjust viewing magnification to ALL, turn on the preview window, activate the Preview Selected Only command, and then select the curve object.

3. With the curve object selected, click on the Fill tool. When the Fill tool pop-up menu appears, select the 80% gray icon (the third one from the right). After a moment, the curve object redisplays with a dark gray shade fill.

4. Select the Outline tool and click on the 10% gray icon, the fifth icon in the second row of the Outline tool pop-up menu. The curve object redisplays with a faint gray outline around the outside and the letters.

5. Turn off Preview Selected Only. Since the background circle has a fill that contrasts poorly with the 10% gray outline, you cannot see the letters very well.

6. Select the background circle and click on the Fill tool and then the black icon. The background circle now contrasts strongly with the 10% gray outline of the letters. If you adjust the size

of the preview window so that it fills the screen, the image should appear similiar to Figure 15-10.

7. To save this altered image, select the Save As command in the File menu. When the Save As dialog box appears, type **FILL-4** in the File text window and select Save.

8. Clear the screen by selecting New from the File menu.

Although the preview window cannot show it to you, the background circle still contains a custom PostScript halftone screen fill in the MicroWaves pattern. When you reach Chapter 18, you can print out this file to see the effect of combining this pattern with the gray shades.

In the next section, you will begin working with one of the most

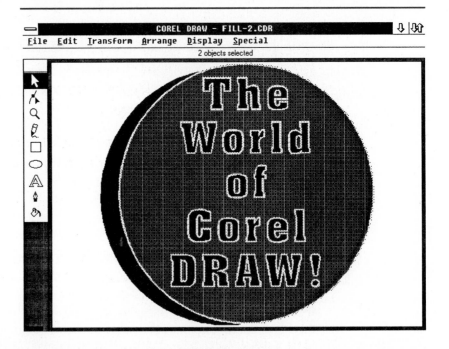

FIGURE 15-10   Preset fills: curve object 80% gray, outline 10% gray, background curve black

creative types of fills in Corel DRAW!: fountain fills, which involve a smooth transition of two different colors through the interior of an object.

DEFINING CUSTOM FOUNTAIN FILLS

When you specify fill colors using the Uniform Fill and 'New Object' Uniform Fill dialog boxes, you are limited to one color per object. When you select the Fountain Fill icon ▨ in the Fill tool pop-up menu, however, you can define a fill that blends two different colors or shades of color. If you are familiar with state-of-the-art paint programs or business presentation slides, you have probably seen *fountain fills,* which are smooth transitions of two different colors or tints. Corel DRAW! makes the color drama of fountain fills available to you through the Fountain Fill dialog box.

By adjusting settings in the Fountain Fill dialog box, you can fill any object with two different colors or tints in such a way that the colors blend evenly from one extreme to the other. Corel DRAW! allows you to create two different types of fountain fills: *linear* and *radial.* Think of the difference between these two fills as similar to the difference between drawing a circle or rectangle from the outer rim or from the center outward. In a linear fountain fill, the color transition occurs in one direction only, determined by the angle that you specify. In a radial fountain fill, the blend of start and end colors proceeds concentrically, from the center of the object outward or from the outer rim inward. Whichever type of fountain fill you select, you can specify colors using either the spot color or process color system. If you choose spot color, you can also define PostScript halftone screen patterns to add an extra visual "punch" to your fountain fills.

Because of an incompatibility problem with Microsoft Windows versions 2.1 and earlier, the default setting for Corel DRAW! allows you to preview fountain fills in black-and-white only. If you have a later version of Windows, refer to the next section, "Displaying Fountain Fills in the Preview Window," to learn how you can view fountain fills in color. Then continue with the exercises in the following sections to practice defining linear and radial fountain fills using spot color, PostScript halftone screen patterns, and process color.

Displaying Fountain Fills In the Preview Window

Early users of Corel DRAW! experienced problems when displaying fountain fills in color in the preview window. These problems stemmed from incompatibilities with Microsoft Windows versions 2.1 and earlier, and do not occur when running Corel DRAW! under later versions of Windows. To avoid potential problems with users who have Windows 2.1 or earlier, however, the manufacturer ships Corel DRAW! with default settings that allow you to preview fountain fills in black-and-white only. You can change this setting, and enable the preview window to display fountain fills in color, by editing a single line of your WIN.INI file.

To change the fountain fill preview setting, just follow these steps:

1. With the MS-DOS Executive running, change to the Windows directory.

2. Double-click on the filename WIN.INI to open this file under the Notepad text editor.

3. Scroll through the WIN.INI file until you reach the [CDraw-Config] section, as shown in Figure 15-11. The settings in your file may differ from the ones in the figure, but the number after "PreviewFountScreen=" is 1 unless you have changed this setting already.

4. Backspace over the "1" and type in **2**. The line should now read, "PreviewFountScreen=2."

5. Select the Save command to save the changes to the WIN.INI file, and then select the Exit command to exit the Windows Notepad.

6. Exit Windows and restart it to activate changes to WIN.INI.

Fountain fills that you specify from now on will display in the preview window in the colors you assign to them.

In the next section, you will begin defining your own fountain fills. You will begin with linear fountain fills, which involve a smooth transition of color in one direction.

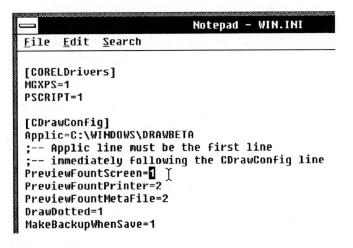

FIGURE 15-11   Editing the PreviewFountScreen setting in WIN.INI

Defining Linear Fountain Fills

When you specify a linear fountain fill, the start color begins at one edge of the object and the end color appears at the opposite side. In between is a smooth blending occurring along an imaginary line that extends from one edge to the other. The direction of the color blend depends on the angle of the fill, over which you have complete control.

You can use either spot color or process color to define a linear fountain fill. When you use spot color, you have the additional option of selecting a PostScript halftone screen pattern.

To control both the speed and the fineness of the display that defines the fountain fill in the preview window, adjust the Fountain Stripes setting in the Preferences dialog box. A low setting (2 is the lower limit) causes the fountain fill to display rapidly with a small number of circles. A high value (100 is the upper limit) causes the filled object to redraw very slowly in the preview window, but it also results in a very finely graded transition of color. For all output devices *except* PostScript printers, the Fountain Stripes setting also determines the resolution at which the fountain fill will print. You will have the opportunity to practice adjusting this setting and viewing the results on the screen in the "Fill Tool Hints" section of the chapter.

As with the outline pen and outline fill, you can define a linear fountain fill for existing objects or set defaults for objects that you have not yet created. To define a linear fountain fill for an existing object, you first select the object and then access the Fountain Fill dialog box by clicking on the Fountain Fill icon in the Fill tool pop-up menu. To define a linear fountain fill as the default fill for the next object you create, you click on the Fountain Fill icon without first selecting an object. The exercises in the next few sections use existing objects as examples. Once you enter the 'New Object' Fountain Fill dialog box, however, the techniques for specifying the fill are the same as when you work with an existing object.

DEFINING LINEAR FOUNTAIN FILLS WITH SPOT COLOR   Theoretically, you can select any two colors as the start and end colors when you specify a linear fountain fill using the spot color system. In practice, however, it's best to select two tints of the *same* color if you intend to send color separations of the resulting image to a commercial reproduction facility. The reason for this has to do with the way spot color is physically reproduced, which makes it difficult to blend two discrete colors evenly.

In the following exercise, you will define a spot color linear fountain fill for the objects in the FILL-1.CDR file, which you created earlier in the chapter.

1. Open the original FILL-1.CDR file you set up in the first exercise of this chapter, not one of the edited versions. Then, turn on the preview window. If you have a color monitor, your screen displays a curve object containing a Pantone Yellow CV spot color at 55% Tint and a blue Pantone 293 CV outline at a 52% Tint. A darker blue (Pantone 281 CV) fills a circle behind the object. (To check the current fill colors for an existing object at any time, just ungroup and select the object, click on the Fill tool, and click on the Uniform Fill icon to display the Uniform Fill dialog box.)

2. Adjust the viewing area to an ALL viewing magnification and then turn on the preview window, adjusting it to a top-to-bottom format.

3. Select the grouped objects. Apply the Ungroup command in the Arrange menu to ungroup them and then deselect both objects and reselect the curve object alone.

4. Click on the Fill tool and then on the Fountain Fill icon in the Fill tool pop-up menu. The Fountain Fill dialog box displays, as shown in Figure 15-12. The upper portion of the screen contains controls for the type of fountain fill (linear or radial)

and the angle that determines the direction of the fill. A degree indicator displays on the upper-right side of the dialog box to guide you in specifying the angle in Corel DRAW! terms. In the lower portion of the dialog box are controls for specifying the start and end colors of the fill according to either the spot or process color system. The default settings are Type of Fountain Linear, Angle 90 degrees, Color Method Spot, start color (From) 0% black, end color (To) 100% black. These settings would result in a fill that is white at the bottom, blending gradually into solid black at the top.

5. Leave the Linear and Spot option buttons selected. Change the start color (From) to color 1, Pantone Yellow CV, at a 100% Tint. Change the end color (To) to color 1 also, but at a 0% Tint, which will look virtually white. Remember that when you define color using the spot color method, both the start and end colors should be different tints of the same color.

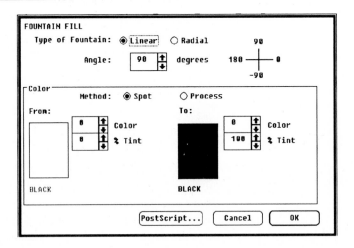

FIGURE 15-12   The Fountain Fill dialog box with linear and
spot color selected

6. Select OK to exit the dialog box with the new settings. The curve object now shows a darker yellow fill at the bottom, with a gradual transition to white at the top. If you adjust the size of the preview window so that it fills the screen, and if you have a black-and- white monitor, the transition in tones is similar to the one shown in Figure 15-13.

7. Access the Fountain Fill dialog box again. This time, change the Angle setting to 45 degrees and then select OK to exit the dialog box. Now, the curve object redisplays with a fountain fill that is lighter at the upper right than at the lower left. If you adjust the size of the preview window so that it fills the screen, the image should appear similar to Figure 15-14.

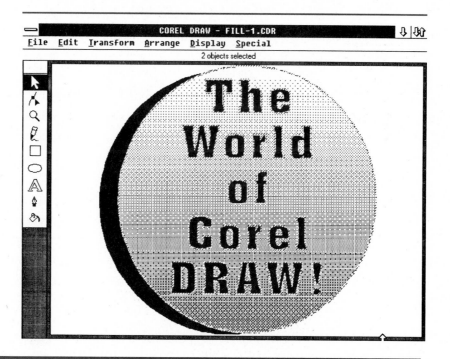

FIGURE 15-13 Spot color linear Fountain Fill at 90-degree angle

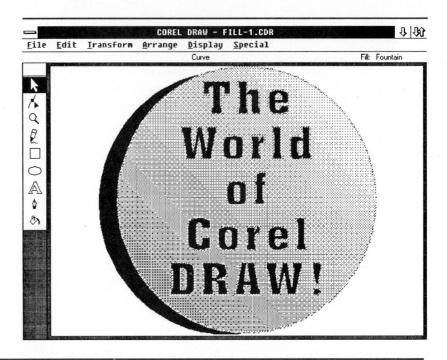

FIGURE 15-14   The same fountain fill at a 45-degree angle

8. For an interesting enhancement, create a fountain fill for the background circle that runs in the opposite direction from the fill for the curve object. To do this, select the background circle and then click on the Fill tool and the Fountain Fill icon. When the Fountain Fill dialog box appears, set the start color to Pantone 281 at a 100% Tint and the end color to 281 at a 30% Tint. Change the Angle setting to −135 degrees, the exact opposite of the 45 degree setting you chose for the fill of the curve object. As the degree indicator in the dialog box shows, this will result in a fill running in the exact opposite direction than the fill for the foreground object.

9. Select OK to exit the dialog box. When the objects are redrawn, you can see that the area behind the letters is a richer color at the upper right than at the lower left. This arrangement adds some visual tension to the mock logo. If you adjust the size of

the preview window so that it fills the screen, the image should
appear similar to Figure 15-15.

10. Group the two objects and then select the Save As command
    from the File menu. When the Save As dialog box appears, type
    the filename **FILL-5** in the File text box, and then click on the
    Save command button to save the altered picture under this new
    name.

11. Clear the screen by selecting the New command from the File
    menu.

 If you plan to use a commercial process to reproduce images that
contain spot color fountain fills, make the start and end colors two

FIGURE 15-15 Background linear fountain fill at a reverse
angle from foreground

tints of the same color. If you do not plan to reproduce your images by a commercial process, however, this restriction does not apply.

When you select the spot color method of assigning start and end colors, you can create a fountain fill from black to white by specifying colors as 0% or 100% black. Spot color is especially useful for black-and-white linear fountain fills if you are interested in assigning a PostScript halftone screen pattern to the object at the same time. In the next section, you will review the process of specifying a PostScript halftone screen pattern with a linear fountain fill.

COMBINING SPOT COLOR LINEAR FOUNTAIN FILLS WITH POSTSCRIPT HALFTONE SCREENS   You will recall from your work with outline fill colors in Chapter 14 that the preview window cannot show you how a selected PostScript halftone screen pattern will look when printed. You must actually print the object with such a fill on a PostScript device in order to see the results. The same is true of PostScript halftone screens when you combine them with fountain fills, which is possible when you use the spot color system to specify start and end colors.

You cannot see the results of your work immediately when you select a PostScript halftone screen pattern with a linear fountain fill. Nevertheless, here are some tips that should help you achieve a better design on the first try:

• Set the angle of the PostScript halftone screen either at the same angle as the linear fountain fill or at an angle that complements it in a design sense. (You do not want the eye to travel in many directions at once.) Sometimes, you can determine the best angle only by experimentation; varying the angle of the halftone screen from the angle of the fountain fill can produce unexpected results.

- If you want the halftone screen to be visible when you print it, use a low frequency setting in the PostScript Halftone Screen dialog box. This is most important if the Fountain Stripes setting in the Preferences dialog box, which controls the fineness of the fountain fill itself, is high.

In the next section, you will practice defining a linear fountain fill, using the process color system instead of spot color.

DEFINING LINEAR FOUNTAIN FILLS WITH PROCESS COLOR
When you assign colors for a linear fountain fill using the process color instead of the spot color system, you can specify two discrete start and end colors, rather than just two different tints of the same color. As you will recall from the exercises in the earlier sections of this chapter, you specify the colors as percentages of cyan, magenta, yellow, and black.

In the following exercise, you will edit the FILL-3.CDR file you saved earlier in the chapter, using the same process colors as before but this time creating a fountain fill from them.

1. Open the FILL-3.CDR file. This file contains a curve image with a uniform process fill color specified as 30% magenta and 10% yellow.

2. Adjust the viewing magnification to ALL, and then turn on the preview window and adjust it to a top-to-bottom format.

3. Select the curve object. Click on the Fill tool and the Fountain Fill icon in the pop-up menu to access the Fountain Fill dialog box.

4. Click on the Process option button to set the controls for percentages of the four process colors. The Angle setting defaults to 90 degrees, which indicates that the start color begins

at the bottom and the end color appears at the top of the object. Specify the start color (From) as 50% magenta and 30% black, and the end color (To) as 10% magenta. Your settings in the Fountain Fill dialog box should match the ones in Figure 15-16.

5. Select OK to exit the dialog box. The curve object redisplays with a graded fill in the specified colors at a 90-degree angle.

6. Select the background circle. To create a fountain fill behind the letters that will complement the fill of the curve object, access the Fountain Fill dialog box and click on the Process option button. Set the Angle to 0 degrees (a fill from left to right). Specify the start color (From) as 55% cyan, 55% magenta, and 75% black, and the end color (To) to 70% cyan and 40% magenta. Select OK to exit the dialog box. If you adjust the size of the preview window so that it fills the screen, the

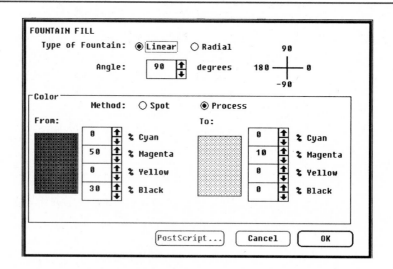

FIGURE 15-16   The Fountain Fill dialog box with linear and process color selected

image should appear similar to Figure 15-17. The somewhat richer hues behind the letters complement the pastels of the curve object. Even if you have a black-and-white monitor, you can see the difference in tones.

7. Select the Save As command in the File menu. When the Save As dialog box appears, type **FILL-6** in the File text box, and then select the Save command button.

8. Select New from the File menu to clear the screen.

To create black-and-white fountain fills using the process color system, define the start and end colors as 0% or 100% black. Leave the percentages for all other process colors at 0.

FIGURE 15-17   Linear foreground fountain fill with
complementary background fountain fill

Go on to the next set of sections to experiment with fountain fills that radiate from the center outward or from the rim inward.

Defining Radial Fountain Fills

When you specify a radial fountain fill, the start color appears all around the outer area of the object and the end color appears at its center, or vice versa. The blending of colors or tints occurs in concentric circles. Because color density in radial fountain fills changes gradually in a circular pattern, a 3-D look is easy to achieve.

You cannot specify an angle when you select a radial fountain fill, but you can control the location of the fill's apparent center. For more information about how to change the center of a radial fountain fill, see Chapter 20, "Combining Corel DRAW! Features and Creating Special Effects."

You can use either spot color or process color to define a radial fountain fill. When you use spot color, you have the additional option of selecting a PostScript halftone screen pattern. The tips contained in the section "Combining Spot Color Linear Fountain Fills with PostScript Halftone Screens" apply to radial fountain fills, too.

You can control both the speed and the fineness of the display that defines the fountain fill in the preview window by adjusting the Fountain Stripes setting in the Preferences dialog box. A low setting (2 is the lower limit) causes the fountain fill to display rapidly with a small number of circles. A high setting (100 is the upper limit) causes the filled object to redraw very slowly in the preview window. It also results in a very finely graded transition of color, however. For all output devices *except* PostScript printers, the Fountain Stripes setting also determines the resolution at which the fountain fill will print. You will have the opportunity to practice adjusting this setting and see the results on the screen in the "Fill Tool Hints" section at the end of the chapter.

As with the linear fountain fill, you can define a radial fountain fill for existing objects or set defaults for objects that you haven't yet created. To define a radial fountain fill for an existing object, you first select the object and then access the Fountain Fill dialog box by clicking on the Fountain Fill icon in the Fill tool pop-up menu. To define a radial fountain fill as the default fill for the next object you create, you click on the Fountain Fill icon without first selecting an object. The exercises in the next few sections use existing objects as examples.

DEFINING RADIAL FOUNTAIN FILLS WITH SPOT COLOR   Theoretically, you can select any two colors as the start and end colors when you specify a radial fountain fill using the spot color system. In practice, however, it is best to select two tints of the *same* color if you intend to send color separations of the resulting image to a commercial reproduction facility. The reason for this has to do with the way spot color is physically reproduced, which makes it difficult to blend two discrete colors evenly.

In the following exercise, you will define a black-and-white spot color radial fountain fill for the objects in the FILL-4.CDR file that you created earlier in the chapter.

1. Open the FILL-4.CDR file. As you will recall from a previous section, the curve object in this file contains a preset uniform fill of 80% black. (Remember, you can find out the current fill specifications by accessing the Uniform Fill dialog box.)

2. Adjust viewing magnification to ALL, and then turn on the preview window and adjust it to a top-to-bottom format. Select the curve object and access the Fountain Fill dialog box by clicking on the Fill tool and the Fountain Fill icon in the pop-up menu.

3. Click on the Radial option button and make sure that the Spot option button is highlighted. Notice that the Angle numeric

entry box is not accessible when the Radial option is selected. Specify the start color (From) as a 100% Tint of Color 0 (black) and the end color (To) as a 20% Tint of Color 0. Then, select OK to exit the dialog box. The curve object redisplays with a brighter area (the 20% black of the color range) in its center. If you adjust the preview window until it fills the screen, your screen will resemble Figure 15-18. The apparent play of light you achieve with this kind of fill creates a 3-D effect, making the surface of the "globe" appear to curve outward.

4. Select the Save As command in the File menu. When the Save As dialog box appears, type the name **FILL-7** in the File text box and then select Save.

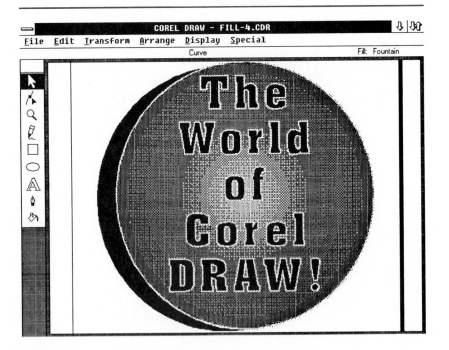

FIGURE 15-18   Spot color radial fountain fill with lighter shade at center

5. Select New from the File menu to clear the screen before going further.

As long as you choose the spot color method of specifying color, you can select a PostScript halftone screen pattern with a radial fountain fill. The added 3-D effect possible with radial fountain fills can lead to quite dramatic results when you add a halftone screen.

In the next section, you will specify a radial fountain fill using the process color method.

DEFINING RADIAL FOUNTAIN FILLS WITH PROCESS COLOR   When you assign colors for a radial fountain fill using the process color system instead of spot color, you can specify two discrete start and end colors, rather than just two different tints of the same color. As you will recall from the exercises in the earlier sections of this chapter, you specify the colors as percentages of cyan, magenta, yellow, and black.

In the following exercise, you will edit the FILL-3.CDR file you saved earlier in the chapter, using the same process colors as before but this time creating a radial fountain fill from them.

1. Open the FILL-3.CDR file. The curve object in this file contains a process color uniform fill specified as 30% magenta and 10% yellow.

2. Set viewing magnification to ALL. Turn on the preview window and adjust it to a top-to-bottom format.

3. Select the curve object, and then click on the Fill tool and the Fountain Fill icon to access the Fountain Fill dialog box. Make sure that the Radial and Process options are selected. Specify the start color (From) as 15% cyan, 75% magenta, and 10% yellow, and the end color (To) as 5% cyan and 10% magenta, and then select OK to exit the dialog box. The curve object now

displays a very light center, with the richer color at its outer rim. The apparent play of light brought about by the radial fill makes the curve object seem like a 3-D globe. To make the light seem to fall along the outer rim of the globe, you need only reverse the color combination, which you will do in the next step.

4. With the curve object still selected, access the Fountain Fill dialog box once more. This time, specify the start color (From) as 5% cyan and 10% magenta, and the end color (To) as 15% cyan, 75% magenta, and 10% yellow. Leave the other settings as before, and then select OK to exit the dialog box. The curve object now displays with the richer color at the center and the

FIGURE 15-19   Process color radial fountain fill with lighter color at rim

lighter color near the outer rim, as shown in Figure 15-19. This color arrangement results in a rounded appearance, but with a different play of light than before.

5. Select the background circle and access the Fountain Fill dialog box. Select the Radial and Process option buttons, and set the start color (From) to 55% cyan, 55% magenta, and 75% black, and the end color (To) at 50% cyan, 15% magenta, and 25% black. If you adjust the size of the preview window so that it fills the screen, the image looks similar to Figure 15-19. Compare your screen with the relative contrast of the tones in Figure 15-19. The background circle has a fill that is lighter at the center, while the foreground object has a fill that is lighter at the rim.

6. Select the Save As command in the File menu. Type the name **FILL-8** in the File text box of the Save As dialog box, and then select Save.

7. Select New from the File menu to clear the screen.

You can change the center of a radial fountain fill to create an off-center highlight for the object. Two methods for accomplishing this effect are available; both are included among the special effects techniques discussed in Chapter 20.

The Fill tool pop-up menu contains one more icon that you have not explored yet, but which unlocks the door to a very rich "palette" of patterns and graphic designs. This icon is the subject of the remainder of this chapter.

DEFINING POSTSCRIPT
FILL TEXTURES

The last icon in the Fill tool pop-up menu is the PostScript Textures icon $\boxed{\text{PS}}$. If you print to a PostScript printer, you can select this icon to fill selected objects with a choice of 42 different textures. This number is deceptive; although only 42 basic patterns exist, you can alter the parameters for each texture to achieve wide variations in appearance. Take a quick glance at the examples in Appendix E to see just how different four versions of a single texture can look.

When you assign a PostScript fill texture to an object, the preview window displays the object with a small gray "PS" pattern on a white background. The Fill designation in the status line, however, indicates the name of the particular texture assigned. Unfortunately, you cannot view these textures until you print them. Chapter 18 contains more information about printing these textures, and Appendix E contains samples of each of the 42 textures with different parameter settings.

Because you cannot adequately preview an object filled with a PostScript texture, this section contains no practical exercise. It does summarize the steps involved in defining a PostScript fill texture, however: accessing the PostScript Texture dialog box, selecting a texture, and adjusting parameters.

1. To begin the process of defining a PostScript fill texture, you select the object you'd like to fill, and then click on the Fill tool and the PostScript Textures icon $\boxed{\text{PS}}$ at the extreme right of the Fill tool pop-up menu. The PostScript Texture dialog box shown in Figure 15-20 appears.

2. To select a texture, scroll down the list of texture names in the Name list box. The currently highlighted name is the selected texture. See Appendix E for help in choosing a specific texture.

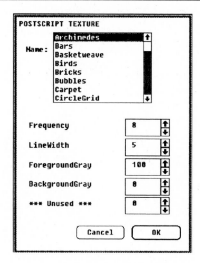

FIGURE 15-20   The PostScript Texture dialog box

3. Adjust each of the parameters in turn. The parameters vary, depending on the texture; Appendix E contains notes on some of the more commonly used parameter names. You will often see references to Frequency, Foreground and Background Gray, Maximum or Minimum Size or Distance, and Random Seed (a built-in mathematical "chance" formula).

4. When you have adjusted parameters to your satisfaction, select OK to exit the dialog box and return to your drawing.

5. Print the filled object to see whether you need to adjust parameters further. Since the mathematical algorithms used to calculate the textures are very complex, some textures contain "chance" elements and may not print in a predictable way.

Working with PostScript fill textures is an adventure because of the *aleatory,* or chance, characteristics built into the mathematical formulas for the textures. Think of these textures as a way to bring more creative design elements into your drawing, even if your own powers of draftsmanship are limited.

FILL TOOL HINTS

The hints contained in this section by no means exhaust the many uses to which you can put the Fill tool. Rather, they represent tips to help you gain speed in your work or to introduce creative effects.

Copying Fill Styles

In previous chapters, you have learned how to use the Copy Style From command in the Edit menu to copy text, outline pen, or outline fill attributes from one object to another. You can use that same command and its associated dialog box to copy fill styles between objects, too. The following summarizes how to use this feature to best advantage:

1. Select the object or group of objects to which you would like to copy the fill attributes of another object.

2. Select the Copy Style From command in the Edit menu. When the Copy Style dialog box appears, activate the Fill Styles checkbox by clicking on it. If you want to copy text, outline pen, or outline fill attributes at the same time, activate those checkboxes, too.

3. Select OK to exit the dialog box. The cursor turns into an arrow containing the message "Copy From?," indicating that you should select the object from which you want to copy the fill style.

4. Select the object whose style you want to copy to the selected object. The selected object redisplays with the new fill style.

The entire continuum of fill styles is available to you when you use this command. You can copy spot or process color uniform fills, PostScript halftone screen textures, preset shades of gray, or even PostScript textures. Use this command and dialog box as a handy shortcut to defining fill attributes for one or more objects.

Adjusting the Fountain Stripes Setting To Enhance Preview And Printing

You will recall that the Preferences dialog box (accessible when you select the Preferences command in the Special menu) contains many useful settings to customize the way Corel DRAW! works. One of these settings, Fountain Stripes, applies to the use of linear and radial fountain fills.

Corel DRAW! displays a fountain fill in the preview window by creating a series of concentric circles that begin at the highlighting box for the object and work their way inward. You have probably noticed this process each time the preview window redraws an object containing a fountain fill. The Fountain Stripes setting in the Preferences dialog box lets you determine how many circles Corel DRAW! creates to represent a fountain fill. The number ranges from 2 to 100, with 2 representing two circles with coarse outlines, and 100 representing a high number of finely drawn circles. As you can imagine, the preview window redraws more quickly when Fountain Stripes is set to a low number, and extremely slowly when the Fountain Stripes setting is high. Furthermore, if you print to a device other than a PostScript printer, the number of circles you select in the Fountain Stripes setting represents what will actually print. You can achieve some interesting effects by varying this setting, as you will see in the following exercise.

1. Open the FILL-7.CDR file you edited in an earlier section of this chapter. The curve object in this file contains a gray-shade radial fountain fill specified with spot color.

2. Set the viewing magnification to ALL and turn on the preview window, adjusting the preview and editing windows to a top-to-bottom format.

3. Select the Preferences command in the Special menu to display the Preferences dialog box. Unless you have altered the settings since you first installed Corel DRAW!, the numeric entry box next to the Fountain Stripes option contains the number 20.

4. Use the scroll bar to adjust this number downward to 2, the lowest setting possible. Select OK to exit the dialog box.

FIGURE 15-21   Radial fountain fill with Fountain Stripes set at 2 (coarse)

5. Click on the preview window to cause the image to redraw. Notice how much more quickly the screen redraws now. Only two coarse concentric circles mark the fountain fill, however; as the full preview screen shows in Figure 15-21, the color transition is abrupt rather than smooth. Depending on your design, such a setting could work to your advantage.

6. Select the Preferences command in the Special menu once more. Adjust the Fountain Stripes setting in the Preferences dialog box upward to 100, the highest setting possible. Select OK to exit the dialog box.

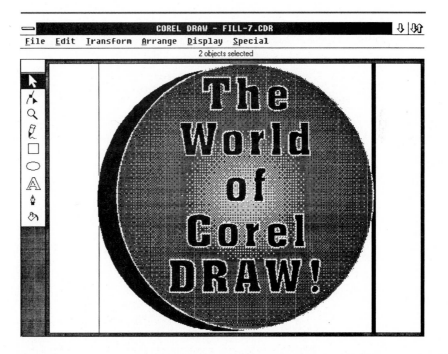

FIGURE 15-22   Radial fountain fill with Fountain Stripes set at 100 (fine)

7. Click on the preview window once more to cause the image to redraw. This time, the redraw takes much longer, because of the high number of fine stripes used to recreate the fountain fill. The resulting blend of color is extremely smooth, as the full screen preview in Figure 15-22 shows.

8. Select New to clear the screen. Do not save any changes.

If you do not have a PostScript printer, you can select a high setting for Fountain Stripes to maximize the printer output quality. If you do have a PostScript printer, you can set Fountain Stripes to a low number to speed up the redraw time in the preview window.

SUMMARY

You can fill the interior of any object in Corel DRAW! with a solid color, gray shade, fountain fill, PostScript halftone screen, or PostScript fill texture. To fill an existing object, you click on the Fill tool and select the desired icon in the Fill tool pop-up menu. To alter the default fill attributes, you select the desired icon in the Fill tool pop-up menu without first selecting any objects.

The first icon in the Fill tool pop-up menu is the Uniform Fill icon, which accesses the Uniform Fill dialog box. Using this dialog box, you can specify a single fill color for an object according to either the spot color or process color method. If you specify a uniform fill in spot color terms, the start color and end color should be tints of the same color. If you specify a uniform fill in process color terms, the start and end colors can be different.

If you select the spot color method for defining a uniform fill color, you can also define a PostScript halftone screen pattern as a fill for the selected object. This fill can be in any spot color, but you must print it in order to see how it looks, because the preview window cannot display PostScript halftone screens.

If you normally print to a black-and-white printer, you can quickly select a fill of white, black, or five preset shades of gray. Simply click on the appropriate icon in the Fill tool pop-up menu. Selecting a preset gray shade allows you to bypass the more time-consuming settings in the Uniform Fill dialog box.

Corel DRAW! also lets you specify linear and radial fountain fills for new or existing objects. A fountain fill is a smooth transition of two colors or tints in the interior of an object.

When you first install Corel DRAW!, fountain fills display as gray shades, but you can display fountain fills in color by editing the PreviewFountScreen line of your WIN.INI file. When you specify a linear fountain fill, the transition from one color to the other occurs in one direction only, at an angle that you specify. When you specify a radial fountain fill, the transition of color occurs concentrically, from the center of the object to its outer edge or from its outer edge inward. You can specify fountain fill colors using either the spot color or process color method. When you specify color using the spot color method, you can also assign a custom PostScript halftone screen pattern to the object's fill. You can achieve interesting design effects by varying the Fountain Stripes setting in the Preferences dialog box. This setting controls the number of concentric circles used to represent a fountain fill in the preview window.

The last option in the Fill tool pop-up menu lets you define a custom PostScript screen texture as an object's fill. There are 42 textures available. You define each texture according to different parameters, so you can achieve many different looks for each texture. Like the PostScript halftone screen patterns, the PostScript fill textures cannot be displayed on your screen; you must print them in order to see the results of your settings.

chapter 16

IMPORTING AND EXPORTING FILES

Bitmapped Versus Object-Oriented Graphics
Importing Graphics: An Overview
Importing Bitmapped Graphics
Importing Object-Oriented Graphics
Exporting Graphics: An Overview
Exporting to Bitmapped Graphics Formats
Exporting to Object-Oriented Graphics Formats

A s more graphics applications for IBM-compatible computers become available, the need to transfer files between different applications becomes more acute. *Connectivity*, or the ability of a software program to import and export data to and from different file formats, is rapidly becoming a requirement for graphics applications. Whether your work involves desktop publishing, technical illustration, original art, or graphic design, it is essential to be able to export your Corel DRAW! graphics to other programs, to import clipart, and to polish your work from other programs.

Corel DRAW! offers you two different methods of connectivity. In Chapter 12, you learned how to use the Windows clipboard to transfer files between Corel DRAW! and other applications that run under Microsoft Windows. The Windows clipboard is not your only option for transferring files, however. Corel DRAW! has its own independent import and export utilities specifically for transferring data between different graphics formats. These utilities allow you to import graphics from and export them to a variety of drawing, painting, desktop publishing, and word processing applications, even though some of these programs may not run under Windows. The use of the Import and Export commands in Corel DRAW! is the subject of this chapter.

Corel DRAW! imports from and exports to both bitmapped and object-oriented applications. If you are unfamiliar with the basic differences between the two graphics formats, the next section will acquaint you with the advantages and disadvantages of each.

BITMAPPED VERSUS OBJECT-ORIENTED GRAPHICS

Corel DRAW! users come from a variety of backgrounds. Some have many years of experience with electronic drawing and design; others are experts at word processing and desktop publishing, but have little experience with graphics applications. Still others have worked with many different paint (bitmap) programs, but Corel DRAW! represents their first drawing (object-oriented) application. Whatever your background, it is important to have a clear understanding of the differences between bitmapped and object-oriented graphics. You then have a firm basis for choosing how and when to import and export graphic files.

There are many different graphics file formats, but only two kinds of graphics: *bitmapped*, also known as *pixel-based*, and *vector-based*, also known as *object-oriented*. The differences between these two kinds of graphics involve the kinds of software applications that produce them, the way the computer stores them in memory, and the ease with which you can edit them.

Paint programs and scanners produce bitmapped images by establishing a grid of *pixels*, the smallest visual unit that the computer can address, on the screen. These applications create images by altering the colors or attributes of each individual pixel. This way of storing images makes inefficient use of memory, however. The size of an image—the number of pixels it occupies—is fixed once it is created, and is dependent on the resolution of the display adapter on the computer where the image first took shape. As a result, finished bitmapped images are difficult to edit when you transfer them from one application to another. If you increase the size of a finished bitmapped image, you can see unsightly white spaces and jagged edges. If you greatly decrease the size of a finished bitmapped image, parts of the image may "smudge" because of the compression involved. Distortion can also occur if you transfer bitmapped graphics to another computer that has a different display resolution.

Object-oriented graphics, on the other hand, have none of these limitations. They are produced by drawing applications such as Corel DRAW! and are stored in the computer's memory as a series of numbers (not pixels) describing how to redraw the image on the screen. Since this method of storing information has nothing to do with the resolution of a given display adapter, line art is considered to be *device-independent*. No matter what computer you used to create an object-oriented graphic, you can stretch, scale, and resize it flexibly without distortion. Object-oriented graphics also tend to create smaller files than bitmapped graphics because the computer does not have to "memorize" the attributes of individual pixels.

How can you use each type of graphic in Corel DRAW!? As you will learn in greater detail in Chapter 17, you can import bitmapped images in order to trace them and turn them into object-oriented graphics. Alternatively, you can simply import them and incorporate them into an existing picture. Your options for editing an imported bitmapped image do not end with the editing capabilities available in Corel DRAW!, however. When you need your finished work to issue from a paint application, or if you prefer to polish your artwork in pixel format, you can export Corel DRAW! graphics back to your favorite paint program.

If you work with other object-oriented drawing and design programs, you can import line art in order to enhance it with advanced features that only Corel DRAW! offers. You can introduce clipart and edit it flexibly. When you are finished editing, you can export Corel DRAW! artwork back to your favorite object-oriented application or to the desktop publishing application of your choice. If you have version 1.10 or later, you can even export your Corel DRAW! graphics to a format that film recorders and slide scanners will be able to use to create professional-looking presentation materials.

Corel DRAW! supports an ever-growing number of file formats that include both pixel-based and object-oriented graphics. Table 16-1 lists all of the file formats you can import into Corel DRAW!, while Table 16-2 lists the file format to which you can export Corel DRAW! graphics. Both tables categorize each file format by format type, graphics type—bitmapped (pixel) or object-oriented (line)—file extension, and the release version of Corel DRAW! in which the particular import or export option first became available. A forthcoming release of Corel DRAW! will include import options for both HPGL plotter and Macintosh PICT formats, as well as an Export option for the HPGL format. Contact Corel Systems regarding the availability of these export filters.

The first half of this chapter addresses the process of importing graphics files into Corel DRAW! and special notes on importing specific file formats. The second half of the chapter covers the process of exporting graphics to other programs, as well as notes pertinent to exporting each type of file format.

File Format	Graphics Type	Extension	Release
Corel DRAW!	line/object	.CDR	1.0
PC Paintbrush	pixel	.PCX, .PCC	1.0
TIFF (Scanners)	pixel	.TIF	1.0
Lotus PIC (graphs)	line/object	.PIC	1.0
Adobe Illustrator	line/object	.AI, .EPS	1.0
IBM PIF (GDF)	line/object	.PIF	1.02
Graphics Metafile	line/object	.CGM	1.1
AutoCAD DXF	line/object	.DXF	1.11
GEM	line/object	.GEM	1.11
Macintosh PICT	pixel	.PICT	1.2
HPGL Plotter	line/object	.HPG	1.2

TABLE 16-1   Corel DRAW! Import File Formats

File Format	Graphic Type	Extension	Release
PostScript	line/object	.EPS	1.0
Windows Metafile	line/object	.WMF	1.0
PCX	pixel	.PCX	1.0
TIFF	pixel	.TIF	1.0
IBM PIF (GDF)	line/object	.GDF	1.02
Graphics Metafile	line/object	.CGM	1.1
SCODL (video)	line/object	.SCD	1.1
VideoShow	line/object	.PIC	1.11
WordPerfect Graphic	line/object	.WPG	1.11
AutoCAD DXF (outlines)	line/object	.DXF	1.11
GEM applications	line/object	.GEM	1.11
Macintosh PICT	pixel	.PICT	1.2
HPGL Plotter	line/object	.HPG	1.2

TABLE 16-2   Corel DRAW! Export File Formats

IMPORTING GRAPHICS: AN OVERVIEW

The process of importing graphics into Corel DRAW! from other file formats always involves these four steps:

1. Select the Import command from the File menu.

2. Select one of the file formats listed in the Import dialog box.

3. Decide whether you want to trace the imported graphic (this applies to bitmapped image files only).

4. Specify the filename and directory location of the graphic you want to import, using the secondary dialog box that appears after you choose a file format.

Once you import the file, you have several editing options, depending on what kind of application it comes from. If the imported graphic originated in a paint program, you can trace it automatically or manually and turn it into a distortion-free object-oriented image. You will find more information on the Corel DRAW! bitmap tracing features in Chapter 17. If you use a great deal of imported clipart, you will be interested in the listing of clipart manufacturers provided in Appendix D.

Selecting the Import Command and Invoking the Import Dialog Box

When you select the Import command from the File menu, the Import dialog box shown in Figure 16-1 appears. The list box at the top of the dialog box contains the filenames and extensions of formats available for import. Below the list box, the For Tracing checkbox lets you specify whether or not you wish to trace a bitmapped graphic. The following sections explain how to work with each of these controls.

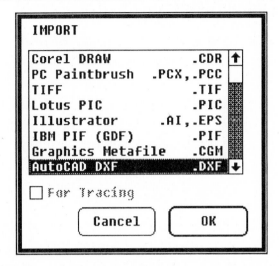

FIGURE 16-1   The Import dialog box

Selecting a File Format

To select and highlight the format for the file you wish to import, click on the file format name. If the name of the file format is not visible, scroll through the list box until you can see it, and then click on it. Versions of Corel DRAW! earlier than 1.11 have a smaller number of file format options; if your dialog box contains fewer options than are shown in Figure 16-1, check your software version against Table 16-1. This table indicates which formats are available for your version.

If you want to import a file that is in an object-oriented format, the For Tracing option is gray and cannot be selected. If the file is a bitmapped graphic, however, the For Tracing option becomes available. The next section provides information about what happens to your graphic when you activate or deactivate this option.

The For Tracing Option
(Bitmapped Graphics)

You can import two different pixel-based file formats: .TIF files generated by scanners and software, and .PCX files generated by scanners or popular paint programs such as the ZSoft PC Paintbrush and Publisher's Paintbrush family of applications. Corel DRAW! handles the display, printing, and memory allocation of an imported bitmap in two different ways, depending on whether or not you activate the For Tracing option.

MEMORY ALLOCATION   Corel DRAW! allocates more program memory for an imported bitmap if the For Tracing option is active. This results in a higher-resolution screen version of the bitmap in the editing window, so that you can more easily trace the bitmap to produce a curve object. The disadvantage is that program operation can slow down noticeably, particularly if the bitmapped graphic file is large or if you have an 80286-based computer.

If you leave the For Tracing option deactivated when you import a bitmap, the bitmap requires less memory, and program operation speed benefits as a result.

DISPLAYING THE BITMAP   When For Tracing is enabled, the pixel-based bitmap appears only in the editing window, not in the preview window. The preview window displays only the object-oriented curves that result after you trace the bitmap. The bitmap that displays in the editing window, however, has a higher resolution.

When you import a bitmapped graphic without enabling the For Tracing option, it is visible in both the preview and editing windows, but the screen version of the bitmap appears rather coarse.

This is because Corel DRAW! allocates less memory for the bitmap in the interest of maintaining program speed.

PRINTING THE BITMAP When you import a bitmapped graphic with the For Tracing option active, you can print only the object-oriented curves that result from the tracing process, not the pixels in the original bitmap. When you import a bitmapped graphic without selecting the For Tracing option, the screen version of the bitmap may appear coarse, but you can print the bitmap at its full original resolution.

With these considerations in mind, you should activate the For Tracing option only if you are sure that you will trace the imported bitmap manually, automatically, or using the Corel Trace utility provided with release 1.2. If you plan to incorporate the bitmap "as is" into your picture, or even if you are not sure you want to trace it, leave the For Tracing checkbox blank. You can always choose to trace the bitmap later, with your only disadvantage being that Autotrace curves will be somewhat more jagged. You can edit Autotrace curves easily with the Shaping tool, however, or simply trace the curves manually instead. Chapter 17 describes the Autotracing process in greater detail.

Specifying the Filename And Destination Directory

After you select a file format and any other applicable options, click on the OK command button. The secondary file selection dialog box appears for you to specify the location and filename of the image you want to import. The header of the secondary dialog box varies, reflecting the file format you have chosen; the header of the dialog box in Figure 16-2, for example, reads "Import AutoCAD DXF."

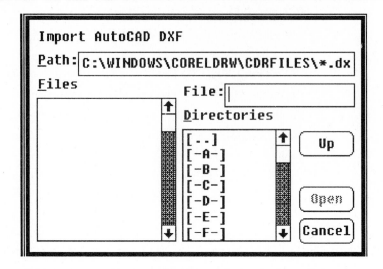

FIGURE 16-2   The secondary Import dialog box

To specify the drive and directory where the import file is located, double-click on the appropriate drive or directory designation in the Directories list box at the right side of the Files list box. Use the scroll bars if the desired drive or directory name is not visible. The name of the highlighted drive and directory appears in the Path text box. To select the filename of the image you want to import, double-click on the filename in the Files list box at the left side of the dialog box. The filename will appear in the File text box. Click on the Open command button to begin the transfer of the image to the Corel DRAW! page.

What happens to the image during the import process depends on the specific file format you have chosen. The following sections offer notes on importing each file format for which a Corel DRAW! filter exists.

IMPORTING BITMAPPED GRAPHICS

All versions of Corel DRAW! since its first release are able to import bitmapped graphics in either .PCX or .TIF format. The most common source of .PCX files is the ZSoft family of paint applications, although some other paint programs also allow you to save files in this format. TIFF files (extension .TIF) are generated by gray-scale scanners and by paint and draw programs that allow you to save bitmapped images with gray-scale information.

Bitmapped images appear inside a rectangle in the editing window after you import them. You cannot break bitmapped images down into their component parts, because Corel DRAW! treats the entire bitmapped image as a single object. You can crop a bitmap after importing it, however, so that only a specified section is visible. You can also select, move, rearrange, stretch, scale, outline, and fill a bitmap as though it were any other type of object.

In some respects, imported bitmaps behave differently from other objects when you edit them. If you rotate or skew a bitmap, you can no longer see the original image in the editing window; it becomes a gray rectangle with a white triangle in the corner to indicate its orientation. A rotated or skewed bitmap will not print unless you output it to a PostScript printer.

The following sections describe the limitations on importing bitmaps as they apply to a specific file format.

Importing Files in PC Paintbrush (.PCX) Format

If the file you choose to import is in .PCX or .PCC format, Corel DRAW! translates it as black-and-white only, interpreting all colored pixels as black. Some recent versions of .PCX formats allow you to save a bitmap with gray-scale information, but Corel

DRAW! does not support this kind of information for the .PCX file format.

Importing Scanner-Generated or Gray-Scale Bitmaps (TIFF)

Scanners and some paint programs save bitmapped images in the .TIF file format. This is the only format for which Corel DRAW! saves gray-scale information, so if your paint application allows it, you should save gray-scale paint images in this format if you intend to import them into Corel DRAW!.

Several different versions of TIFF formats are available. Corel DRAW! supports most of these. Extra time is needed to decompress and import a compressed TIFF file, however. Although Corel DRAW! cannot display gray-scale bitmap information on your monitor screen, it saves this information. If you use a PostScript output device, the gray-scale information will be reproduced faithfully when you print the image.

The following group of sections provides tips on importing and working with graphics files in each of the object-oriented formats that Corel DRAW! supports.

IMPORTING OBJECT-ORIENTED GRAPHICS

The original release of Corel DRAW! supported the import of three object-oriented graphics file formats: .CDR (the native Corel DRAW! format), Lotus .PIC graphs, and .ART files created by Adobe Illustrator or clipart manufacturers. Since then, the ranks of supported object-oriented file formats have swelled to include .GDF, .CGM, .GEM, and .DXF files. Table 16-1 lists each type of object-oriented file format and the release version that first supported it.

Specific notes on importing and working with each file format are provided in the following sections. Keep in mind, however, that software applications are being upgraded continually, however, and that the process of change may alter the way certain file formats interact with Corel DRAW!.

Importing Corel DRAW! Files and Clipart

As you will recall from Chapter 12, you can copy or cut and paste objects or images between different Corel DRAW! files using the Windows clipboard. The Windows clipboard memory limit of 64K renders this solution less than satisfactory, especially if you attempt to transfer images that contain many nodes or complicated attributes. A better solution in such cases is to import the .CDR file into the current graphic, using the Import command.

You can also use the Import command to import clipart in .CDR format. Corel Systems and ArtRight Software Corporation are among the clipart manufacturers who provide files in this format.

A file that you import in .CDR format appears as a group of objects. You can select the group, apply the Ungroup command in the Arrange menu, and then edit the objects normally.

Importing Lotus .PIC files

You can import graphic images in Lotus 1-2-3 format into Corel DRAW! and modify them. When you import a Lotus .PIC file, Corel DRAW! groups the entire file. To manipulate individual objects within the imported graphic, select the graphic, apply the Ungroup command, and then edit objects normally.

Importing Adobe Illustrator Files

A wide variety of clipart files is available in either Adobe Illustrator (.AI) or Adobe Illustrator's own Encapsulated PostScript (.EPS) format, which is different from the .EPS format used by other PostScript applications. If you have a version of Corel DRAW! prior to version 1.02, you will see the extension .ART listed in the Import dialog box; later versions display the file extensions .AI and .EPS. If the extension of the file you want to import does not match the one generated automatically by Corel DRAW!, just backspace over the incorrect extension and type the desired extension instead. Corel DRAW! will recognize the correct files.

caution Keep in mind that the Corel DRAW! .EPS Export filter allows you to save files in a format that most desktop publishing applications can use. However, you cannot edit these files in other graphics applications that use the .EPS format. In addition, the Corel DRAW! .EPS Import filter supports only the Adobe Illustrator version of .EPS. Therefore, if you export a Corel DRAW! file in .EPS format without having saved it as a .CDR file first, you will not be able to re-import it to make changes. Always save your work in Corel DRAW! before exporting it if you think you might need to edit it later.

Corel DRAW! imports an Adobe Illustrator-compatible image file as a group of objects. To edit individual objects in the imported file, select the group, apply the Ungroup command, and then select the desired object(s).

Importing IBM Mainframe Graphics Files (.PIF, .GDF)

Files in the Base .PIF format are most familiar to graphics users in the mainframe IBM environment. The .PIF import and export filters have been available since version 1.02 release of Corel DRAW!.

Not all information in a .PIF file transfers smoothly into Corel DRAW!. For example:

- You may sometimes need to scale and/or center the image on the page before you can edit it.

- Objects that are white in the .PIF file will not show up on the white Corel DRAW! page unless you place a page-sized colored rectangle in the background as contrast.

- Base .PIF specifications for "Set Background Mix," "Set Foreground Mix," "Call Segment," "Set Character Set," "Set Paper Color," and "Set Pattern Symbol" do not transfer into the Corel DRAW! format.

- Base .PIF "Line Types" specifications do not match Corel DRAW! outline pen line types on a one-to-one basis. .PIF line types 0 and 7 become solid; 1, 4, 2, 5, 3, and 6 become one of the dashed or dotted line styles available in Corel DRAW!; and line type 8 becomes a line type of None. The dashed lines, like normal dashed lines in Corel DRAW!, print only on PostScript printers and display as solid lines on the screen.

- Text strings from Base .PIF files come into Corel DRAW! as text in the font that appears at the top of the typeface list in the Text dialog box.

As with most other line-art files, a graphic imported from a .PIF application arrives in Corel DRAW! as multiple grouped objects. To edit individual objects in the graphic, select the group, apply the Ungroup command in the Arrange menu, and then select the object you wish to manipulate.

Importing Graphics Metafiles (.CGM)

Corel DRAW! release 1.10 was the earliest version of the software to include an import filter for the object-oriented .CGM format, which appears in the Import dialog box as the Graphics Metafile option. Unlike the other file formats discussed so far, the .CGM format has many variants because it is used by a wide variety of popular software applications, including Harvard Graphics, Lotus Freelance Plus, Zenographics Mirage, Arts & Letters, Micrographx Designer, ISSCO Displa, and some CAD applications. A number of clipart libraries that make use of the .CGM format exist as well.

Since these programs all have different features, the limitations on transferring .CGM file information into Corel DRAW! vary from application to application, but two general limitations apply to all programs. The first limitation involves the size of the imported file relative to the Corel DRAW! page. As with Base .PIF files, if the imported .CGM file is larger than the page, adjust viewing magnification to ALL and then select and scale the grouped image. You may then apply the Ungroup command to the image to break it into its component objects. The second general limitation with .CGM imports involves bitmapped graphics, which are supported in many applications that use .CGM file formats but which do not transfer into Corel DRAW!.

The following sections describe application-specific limitations on importing .CGM files into Corel DRAW!

HARVARD GRAPHICS   Harvard Graphics treats colors and fills differently than Corel DRAW!, and you should keep some of these differences in mind when importing a .CGM file. Specific-

ally, a filled shape saved in Harvard Graphics transfers into Corel
DRAW! as two separate objects: an outline and a fill. You will
need to group these two objects in order to edit them as a single
entity. In addition, colored objects created in Harvard Graphics
come into Corel DRAW! darker than in their original form. This
problem is due to features of the Harvard Graphics environment
and has no remedy at the present time. Circles, straight lines, and
curves retain their original object identity when imported, but
rectangles, ellipses, and arrows transfer into Corel DRAW! as
curve objects. Text transfers into Corel DRAW! as text in the
Toronto typeface, but *only* if you do not save the file in Harvard
Graphics with a native Harvard Graphics typeface. If you opt to
use a Harvard Graphics typeface, the text turns into curves when
you import it into Corel DRAW!.

Corel DRAW! uses the Windows character set for most of its
native typefaces, but the extended character set for Harvard Graphics differs somewhat from the Windows set. If you use foreign-
language or other special characters above ASCII 128 in Harvard
Graphics, some may not transfer as expected.

MICROGRAPHX DESIGNER   As you will recall from Chapter 12, you can transfer objects from Micrographx Designer images
into Corel DRAW! through the Windows clipboard, as long as they
do not exceed the 64K Windows metafile limit. If you want to
transfer complex objects or entire images into Corel DRAW!,
however, you can use the Import command and dialog box instead,
and import the file in .CGM format.

Most file information from the .CGM format transfers into Corel
DRAW! as expected. Exceptions do exist, however. For example,
circles and ellipses come into Corel DRAW! as curve objects, and
both fountain fills and *hatching* fills (a series of lines of varying
density) transfer as solid color fills. Although Micrographx De-

signer uses bitmapped graphics, these do not import into Corel DRAW!.

LOTUS FREELANCE PLUS   Some text-related information in Lotus Freelance Plus .CGM files may not transfer quite as expected. As with Harvard Graphics, for example, Freelance Plus uses a character set that differs slightly from the Windows character set. If text strings created in Freelance Plus contain characters above ASCII 128, you may notice some character substitutions. In addition, text transfers into Corel DRAW! in the Toronto typeface.

Colors and fills created in Freelance Plus do not always come into Corel DRAW! as originally specified. For example, hatching fills transfer as solid color fills. More importantly, colors specified in the Freelance Plus .CGM file may not transfer accurately unless the printer installed for Freelance supports color printing. If a black-and-white printer was installed with Freelance Plus, colors may transfer into Corel DRAW! as gray shades.

As with Micrographx Designer, bitmapped graphics do not transfer into the Corel DRAW! file format.

ARTS & LETTERS   Most of the file information that does not transfer well into the Corel DRAW! format has to do with object types. Circles, ellipses, and text come into Corel DRAW! as curve objects and can only be edited as such. Rectangles transfer over as connected straight line segments. And, as with other .CGM file formats, bitmapped objects saved in Arts & Letters do not transfer into Corel DRAW! at all. In addition, filled objects come into Corel DRAW! as two separate objects: an outline and a fill. This is the same situation you encounter with filled objects created in Harvard Graphics.

Importing AutoCAD Data
Exchange File (.DXF) Files

Beginning with release 1.11, you can import AutoCAD files into Corel DRAW! in .DXF format. This step represents an important advance, since the .DXF format retains more AutoCAD information than any alternative format. Nonetheless, not all information resident in the AutoCAD .DXF file transfers into the Corel DRAW! format. The following sections give some examples.

3-D INFORMATION   In order to retain as much 3-D information from an AutoCAD file as possible, you should take special steps to prepare the file carefully before importing it. A recommended procedure is to save the AutoCAD 3-D file in .DXB format, then begin a new drawing and transfer the .DXB file to it, and finally save the file in .DXF format using the DXFOUT utility. You should also save the 3-D image in the specific view that you want to transfer into Corel DRAW!.

Because of the complexity of information stored in a 3-D AutoCAD image, the imported file may be much larger than will fit on the Corel DRAW! page. If this happens, adjust the viewing magnification to ALL, then select the imported .DXF graphic and scale it downward.

Some precision is lost in the transfer of information, however. For example, Corel DRAW! does not support 3-D extrusion of circles, arcs, text, or polylines with dashed patterns.

COLORS   When you save a 3-D file in AutoCAD according to the procedure just mentioned, color information is lost. You must respecify colors once the file has arrived in Corel DRAW!. In other cases, however, colors should match the 256-color scheme that AutoCAD uses for the IBM Professional Graphics Controller.

LINES, OUTLINES. AND FILLS   Since Corel DRAW! does not support variable widths on a single line, variable-width lines in AutoCAD are imported as single-width lines. The width of the line in Corel DRAW! is equal to the *minimum* width that the variable-width line had in AutoCAD.

Dashed lines in the .DXF file transfer into Corel DRAW! as the first dashed line pattern in the Outline Pen dialog box. You can choose another line type later.

Objects that are specified as invisible in AutoCAD come into Corel DRAW! with no outline and no fill. You can see these objects in the editing window but not in the preview window.

A point in AutoCAD transfers into Corel DRAW! as an ellipse of the smallest possible size. An extruded point (a point seeming to extend outward in 3-D format) comes into Corel DRAW! as a line segment with two nodes.

TEXT   Text generated in AutoCAD may appear stretched in Corel DRAW!, since Corel DRAW! attempts to keep the physical length of text the same. Some differences in text length may still occur, however.

If the point size or degree that text is skewed in the original AutoCAD file exceeds the limits allowed by Corel DRAW!, the text transfers over within the Corel DRAW! limits and may not match the original.

Non-standard characters imported into Corel DRAW! appear as a question mark (?), and some special characters are ignored. Corel DRAW! will provide some limited matching of AutoCAD fonts.

Importing GEM Applications Files (.GEM)

As of release 1.11, Corel DRAW! supports the import of images created in the object-oriented .GEM format. This includes artwork from GEM Draw and GEM Artline. You will notice a few differences between the original file and its imported version in Corel DRAW! as follows:

- Corel DRAW! does not support the custom fill patterns (grids, ball bearings, and so on) offered in GEM applications. Objects containing these fills in the .GEM format transfer into Corel DRAW! with a tinted spot color fill of the same color as the original pattern fill.

- Corel DRAW! allows only ten levels of object grouping, but GEM applications allow more. If you import a file that has more than ten levels of object groups, some of the objects transfer over as ungrouped. The best solution is to regroup objects after importing the file.

- In GEM applications, you can mix line cap styles in the same line. For example, a line can be rounded at one end and flat on the other. In Corel DRAW!, however, you can mix line cap styles only if one end of the line or curve is an arrow. When you import a GEM file that contains lines with mixed line cap styles, therefore, Corel DRAW! assigns the line cap style of the starting point to both ends of the line or curve.

- Text created in GEM Artline transfers into Corel DRAW! as curve objects. Text created in other GEM applications transfers as text. The Dutch, Swiss, and System typefaces under GEM come into Corel DRAW! as Toronto, Swiss, and Avalon, respectively. Text alignment and spacing settings are not maintained, but you can edit these features after importing the file. Text with underlines in GEM Draw, however, transfers into Corel DRAW! without outlines.

A forthcoming Corel DRAW! release (version 1.2) will include import options for Macintosh PICT graphics and HPGL plotter files. Contact Corel Systems regarding the date on which this version becomes available.

The Corel DRAW! import filters offer you a rich world of possibilities. But the uses to which you can put Corel DRAW!'s advanced graphics features are even richer when you consider the software applications to which you can export your images. The remainder of this chapter covers the process and pitfalls of exporting Corel DRAW! files to other applications.

EXPORTING GRAPHICS: AN OVERVIEW

Connectivity is a two-way street. The ability to import any number of different file formats would be of limited use if you could not export your work to other applications as well. Corel DRAW! has an even greater number of export filters than import filters. After perfecting a masterpiece in Corel DRAW!, you can send it to your favorite paint program, object-oriented drawing software, desktop publishing application, or film recording device.

In some cases, you may have a choice of more than one export format. Popular desktop publishing applications such as Xerox Ventura Publisher and Aldus PageMaker, for example, accept .EPS, .CGM, .PCX, and .TIF graphics files. When several file formats are available, how do you determine which is the best for your needs? The notes on each type of export file format attempt to cover this issue, as well as to describe any features of the original Corel DRAW! artwork that transfer differently than expected.

The process of exporting a Corel DRAW! file to another application always involves these five steps:

1. Open the Corel DRAW! image file you want to transfer and save it before beginning the export procedure. If you want to export only certain objects rather than the entire file, select those objects.

2. Select the Export command from the File menu.

3. Select a file format from the choices in the Export dialog box.

4. Choose whether to export the entire file or selected objects only.

5. Specify the filename and directory location of the graphic you want to export, using the secondary Export file selection dialog box that appears.

Depending on the export file format you choose, other choices in the Export dialog box may also become available to you. Each of these will be detailed in the following sections.

Opening and Saving the File and Selecting the Objects to Export

If you are planning to export an existing file, open it before you select the Export command. If the page is empty when you begin the export procedure, an error message occurs.

If you are preparing to export a new file or one you have imported and edited, always save the file as a .CDR image before exporting it. This is extremely important if there is any chance that you might need to edit the image again later. In several cases, potential problems or inconveniences may occur when you try to re-import an exported file that you never saved in Corel DRAW! format:

- *.EPS*   The Corel DRAW! .EPS import filter supports only Adobe Illustrator files. The .EPS export filter, on the other hand, supports the standard .EPS format used by desktop publishing applications such as Aldus PageMaker and Xerox Ventura Publisher. If you export a Corel DRAW! file to .EPS without saving it first, you will not be able to import it again later.

- *.PCX and .TIF*   If you export a Corel DRAW! image to a pixel-based format without saving it first, and then re-import it, the imported image will be pixel-based as well. You would have to retrace and edit it extensively before you could make changes.

If you want to export only a part of the Corel DRAW! file rather than the entire image, select the desired objects before beginning the export procedure. An option in the Export dialog box will allow you to specify the export of selected objects only.

Selecting the Export Command and Invoking the Export Dialog Box

When you select the Export command from the File menu, the Export dialog box shown in Figure 16-3 appears. If you have a version of Corel DRAW! prior to release 1.10, the Export dialog box on your screen may show fewer options than shown in the figure.

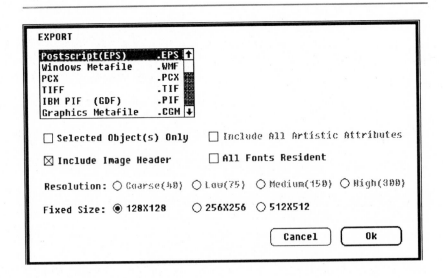

FIGURE 16-3   The Export dialog box

At the upper-left corner of the dialog box, the file format list box contains the names and extensions of the file formats to which you can export the current file. Immediately below the file format list box are four checkboxes. These allow you to export selected objects within the file, include outline and fill attribute information, include an image header (.EPS), or use the fonts resident in the printer instead of the native Corel DRAW! fonts (extension .WFN). Not all of these checkboxes are available for selection with every file format. Below the four checkboxes are two rows of option buttons. The Resolution option buttons let you specify screen resolution when you export to a bitmapped format, while the Fixed Size option buttons let you determine the size of an image header for .EPS file exports. Again, the availability of these options depend on the file format you select. The following sections explain how to work with each of the controls in the Export dialog box.

Selecting a File Format

To select and highlight the file format to which you will export the Corel DRAW! image, click on the file format name. If the name of the file format is not visible, scroll through the list box until you can see it, and then click on it. Versions of Corel DRAW! earlier than 1.11 have a smaller number of file format options; if your dialog box contains fewer options than the one in the figure, check your software version against Table 16-2.

The Selected Objects Only Option

This option is available for any export file format that you choose. However, if you activate this option without first selecting one or more objects in the current image, the message box in Figure 16-4 appears after you specify a filename for the exported file.

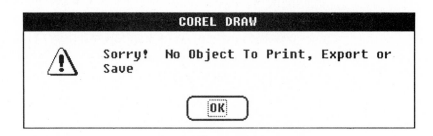

FIGURE 16-4   Error message when no objects are selected for
exporting

The Include All Artistic Attributes Option
(Versions 1.02 and Later)

The purpose of this option is to export not only the objects in the
Corel DRAW! image, but also their text, outline, outline fill, and
fill attributes. This option is available only for object-oriented
export file formats that Corel DRAW! introduced in versions 1.02
and later: IBM .PIF, .CGM, SCODL, VideoShow, WordPerfect
.CGM, .DXF, and .GEM. For these formats, the Include All
Artistic Attributes option is automatically activated. Due to inher-
ent differences in the features of various software applications,
however, not every format translates these attributes accurately.
The "Exporting to Object-Oriented Graphics Formats" section of
this chapter provides information about attributes that may not
transfer well for a specific export file format.

Including an Image Header (.EPS)

An image header is a visual representation of a PostScript graphic
on screen. The Include Image Header option is available (and

automatically activated) only when you select the .EPS export file format for PostScript images. While not truly WYSIWYG, the image header helps you position or crop the .EPS image in desktop publishing applications such as Aldus PageMaker and Xerox Ventura Publisher. If you choose to deactivate the Include Image Header option, you will not have a visual representation of an .EPS image in your desktop publishing application.

Deactivate the Include Image Header option only if you plan to use the exported .EPS image in an application that cannot display an EPS image header. Versions of Xerox Ventura Publisher earlier than 2.0, for example, do not support the display of EPS image headers.

The All Fonts Resident Option (.EPS)

When you activate this option, which is also available only when you choose to export to the .EPS format, you tell Corel DRAW! to assume that all fonts used in your graphic are resident in the output device. Text strings in the exported graphic will be printed using the printer-resident fonts rather than the original Corel DRAW! fonts.

In versions of Corel DRAW! prior to release 1.1, the main use for this option was to create a PostScript output file for printing by a laser service bureau. Most laser service bureaus have access to all of the Adobe PostScript fonts and can substitute them for the Corel DRAW! fonts automatically. With the advent of the WFNBOSS utility that converts major manufacturers' fonts into usable Corel DRAW! fonts, the All Fonts Resident option has even wider applications. If you use the WFNBOSS utility (described in Appendix D), you can activate the All Fonts Resident option whenever you want to use the original manufacturers' fonts in printing.

Specifying a Resolution
(Bitmapped Graphics)

The option buttons following "Resolution:" in the Export dialog box become available for selection only when you have chosen a pixel-based export file format (.PCX, .TIF). You can choose from Coarse (40 dpi), Low (75 dpi), Medium (150 dpi), or High (300 dpi) resolutions. High resolution is the option to choose if you want to give the exported image the best possible appearance.

Because of the way a computer stores pixel-based graphics, however, an image that is large in Corel DRAW! can occupy an enormous amount of memory (up to 1 MB for a full-page image) when you export it at a high resolution. Rather than export the graphic at a lower resolution, consider using the Select tool to scale the Corel DRAW! image down to the size it should be in the final application. For example, if you plan to export the graphic to a desktop publishing program and know the desired image size on the page, scale it down to that size before exporting it from Corel DRAW!. This precautionary action will also prevent you from having to resize the bitmap later, thereby causing its appearance to deteriorate.

Specifying a Fixed Size
Image Header (.EPS)

Although an Encapsulated PostScript (EPS) file is object-oriented, the image header that represents it is a pixel-based approximation. The Fixed Size option buttons in the Export dialog box let you specify, in pixels, the size of the visible image header in the exported file. Like the Include Image Header and All Fonts Resident options, these options become available only when you have chosen .EPS as the export format.

The image header size you select does *not* affect the size of the actual PostScript graphic. If conserving memory and disk space is a concern, you should select the 128-by-128-pixel option for the smallest image header. If accurate representation is more important to you than memory conservation, however, select the 512-by-512-pixel option to obtain an image header that is true to the proportions of the actual graphic. The size of the resulting .EPS files may exceed 64K if you select the 512-by-512 option.

SPECIFYING THE FILENAME AND THE DESTINATION DIRECTORY   After you select a file format and any other applicable options, click on the OK command button. The secondary file selection dialog box appears for you to specify the destination drive and filename of the exported image. The header of the secondary Export dialog box varies, reflecting the file format you have chosen; the header of the dialog box in Figure 16-5, for example, reads "Export GEM."

To specify the destination drive and directory for the exported image, click on the appropriate drive or directory designation in the Directories list box. Use the scroll bars if the desired name is not visible. The name of the highlighted drive and directory appears in the Path text box. To name the exported image file, click on the File text box. When the flashing cursor appears, type the desired filename; Corel DRAW! adds the extension for the specified file format automatically. Click on the Save command button to begin the transfer of the image to the designated file format.

What happens to the image during the export process depends on the specific file format you have chosen. The following sections offer notes on exporting images to each available file format. Equally important, they explore the practical uses of exporting to various file formats.

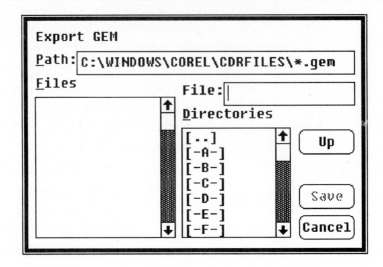

FIGURE 16-5   The secondary Export dialog box

EXPORTING TO BITMAPPED GRAPHICS FORMATS

When you have a choice of several different export file formats, your primary concerns should be the end use to which you will put the exported graphic, the Corel DRAW! features that can or cannot be retained, and the convenience of working with the image in the export file format. The advantages of the bitmap formats supported by Corel DRAW!—.PCX and .TIF—are that they command wide support throughout the software industry and that the paint programs in which you edit them are usually easier to learn and use than most object-oriented drawing and design applications. The disadvantages are that they do not display well on monitors that support resolutions different from the resolutions in which the bitmaps were created, and that they are inconvenient to resize. If you design a bitmap on Corel DRAW! and then export it, however, your image will not suffer from this limitation.

If you have a version of Corel DRAW! previous to 1.1, the bitmap file formats are still good choices for export to desktop publishing programs if you do not use a PostScript printer and cannot take advantage of the .EPS file format. Starting with release 1.1, however, one of the object-oriented formats such as .CGM is a better choice for desktop publishing applications. Unlike the bitmapped formats, the object-oriented formats are easy to resize without distortion and preserve more attribute information. If you have one of the more recent versions of Corel DRAW!, you should select a bitmapped file format only when one of the following conditions applies:

- Your application accepts only bitmapped graphics

- You plan to alter the Corel DRAW! graphic, using techniques available only in the pixel-by-pixel editing environment of a paint program

The following sections provide details on the limitations of exporting to each of the supported bitmapped file formats.

Exporting to .PCX Format

The .PCX format supported by Corel DRAW! describes a graphic as a collection of black-and-white dots. Since this format supports no color information, the files created when you export a Corel DRAW! image can be relatively small—*unless* the original image fills at least half of an 8 1/2-by-11-inch page. The Corel DRAW! .PCX export filter does not support the transfer of gray-scale information.

Exporting to .TIF Format

Although an image that you *import* from a TIFF file can transfer gray-scale information, the export of a Corel DRAW! image to the TIFF format cannot. Therefore, the information exported to a pixel-based file format is roughly the same, whether you choose .PCX or .TIF.

The next group of sections explores the advantages and disadvantages of exporting Corel DRAW! objects and images to each of the available object-oriented file formats.

EXPORTING TO OBJECT-ORIENTED GRAPHICS FORMATS

The original release of Corel DRAW! supported export to two object-oriented file formats only: Encapsulated PostScript (.EPS) and Windows Metafile (.WMF). Since then, export filters for .CGM, VideoShow, AutoCAD .DXF, .GEM, WordPerfect Graphics (.WPG), mainframe .PIF, and film recorder formats have become available as well. As mentioned earlier in this chapter, object-oriented formats transfer color, outline, fill, and attribute information more accurately than is the case with bitmapped formats. In addition, object-oriented formats are *device-independent*, which means that their images look the same despite resizing or changes in the display resolution.

Your main concerns when choosing an object-oriented export format are the final use to which you plan to put the image and the kinds of information you cannot afford to lose during the export process. The following sections provide information on the uses and limitations of each type of export file format.

Exporting to Encapsulated PostScript (.EPS) Format

The .EPS file format is the export format of choice when your Corel DRAW! image contains features that are available for Post-Script output devices only. Such features include PostScript half-tone screen patterns and textures, dashed and dotted lines, and rotated or skewed bitmapped images. If you export a Corel DRAW! graphic containing both line art and bitmaps to the .EPS format, both types of graphics will transfer properly. The Graphics Metafile (.CGM) format, on the other hand, cannot accept bitmaps.

The main limitations of exporting to .EPS file format concern complex curves, the bitmapped image header, and the fact that it is a one-way export from Corel DRAW!.

- *Complex graphics*   If the graphic that you want to export to .EPS format contains approximately 200 or more nodes per curve object, you may have trouble printing it in your desktop publishing or other PostScript application. The same difficulty may occur if your image is laden with PostScript textures, halftone screen patterns, combined objects, and fancy text strings.

- *Image header*   As explained previously, the image header in an .EPS graphic is an approximate bitmap representation made available for the purposes of positioning and cropping the graphic. It is not always convenient to work with this header, because it's not truly WYSIWYG.

- *One-way export*   The Adobe-standard .EPS import format supported by Corel DRAW! works with Adobe Illustrator files only. If you export a Corel DRAW! graphic to the *standard* .EPS format and then decide you need to make changes, you will not be able to re-import the graphic to Corel DRAW!. The importance of saving your graphic in .CDR format in Corel DRAW! before exporting it cannot be overstated.

All in all, the .EPS file format offers you the best opportunity to transfer Corel DRAW! image information if you use a PostScript printer or imagesetter and a relevant application. Other object-oriented formats work nearly as well for other applications, as you will see in the ensuing sections.

Exporting to IBM .PIF Format

When you choose to export a Corel DRAW! graphic to the IBM mainframe .PIF graphics format first made available with Corel DRAW! release 1.02, two additional options in the Export dialog box become available. The first option, Selected Objects Only, allows you to transfer just a portion of your graphic rather than the whole file. The second, Include All Artistic Attributes, allows you to choose whether to transfer outline and fill attributes such as calligraphic outlines, special line caps, and fountain fills. The export filter translates these attributes into polygons and fills them accordingly. Some radial fills may not transfer exactly as they appear in Corel DRAW! and PostScript fills do not transfer at all. If you choose not to include all artistic attributes when exporting a graphic, the .PIF export filter translates custom outlines to default .PIF line thicknesses and omits fountain.

Color information transfers to the mainframe format regardless of whether you activate the Include All Artistic Attributes option. Corel DRAW! colors transfer over as the closest match to one of the 16 colors available in the .PIF graphic format.

Exporting to Computer Graphics Metafile (.CGM) Format

The .CGM, or Computer Graphics Metafile format, first became an export option with version 1.10 of Corel DRAW!. In reality, .CGM represents not a single format, but rather a group of closely related object-oriented file formats. The application determines which file format will be used. Since there are so many versions available, each with its own characteristics, graphics information does not always translate in exactly the same way. The Corel DRAW! .CGM export filter cannot "know" automatically the software application to which you are planning to export a graphic.

In general, however, most color, line thickness, and fill attributes transfer well, even if you do not export a graphic with the Include All Artistic Attributes option selected. Calligraphic outlines transfer to .CGM format only if the Include All Artistic Attributes option is active. If you transfer an object containing a custom calligraphic outline and do not activate this option, the object's outline in the .CGM file will have the same width as the thickest part of the callligraphic outline in the original Corel DRAW! image.

The .CGM option is an excellent choice for exporting files to desktop publishing applications. The WYSIWYG representation of a .CGM file is much easier to work with than an .EPS header and takes the guesswork out of cropping and positioning graphics within a document. If you do not work with a PostScript printer, or if your Corel DRAW! graphics do not contain PostScript-only attributes, you might prefer the .CGM option to the .EPS format.

Exporting to Windows Metafile (.WMF) Format

The .WMF format, like the .PCX, .TIF, and .EPS formats, was one of the earliest export options in Corel DRAW!. This object-oriented format makes a Corel DRAW! graphic available to a wide variety of Microsoft Windows applications. This export format does not transfer PostScript-only features, so it is best suited for graphics that do not contain such features. In addition, if the artwork in your graphic has many outline and fill attributes, many curves and nodes, or complex text, the exported .WMF file might exceed the 64K limit imposed by Microsoft Windows. In this case, try using the .CGM export filter instead.

Exporting to Film Recorders (SCODL)

SCODL, which stands for Scan Conversion Object Description Language, is an image description language that many popular film recorders use to create object-oriented slides at high resolution. Some ink-jet and thermal printers also make use of this language and its associated .SCD file format. The SCODL export option first became available with Corel DRAW! release 1.1. When you select the SCODL option in the Export dialog box, the additional options Include All Artistic Attributes and Selected Objects Only become available for selection.

In general, you should activate the Include All Artistic Attributes option if you want the Corel DRAW! graphic to transfer over exactly as it appears. If you do not activate this option, your export file will automatically contain sharp (miter) corners and will not support calligraphic outlines. Even if you do activate Include All Artistic Attributes, PostScript halftone screen patterns and textures translate as a shade of light gray.

After you specify the filename and destination directory of the exported graphic in the file selection dialog box, a third dialog box displays, as shown in Figure 16-6. Use this dialog box to set the background color of the slide to black, white, or none (Null Color).

If you are new to the world of film recorders and slide generation equipment, you may be interested in the following tips that will help you create a SCODL (.SCD) export file that will not produce visual surprises.

FIGURE 16-6   The SCODL Background Color dialog box

ASPECT RATIO CONSIDERATIONS   The graphic that you plan to export to SCODL format should have the same width-to-height aspect ratio as the film that will be used to create your slide. In most cases this will be the aspect ratio of 35 mm film, which is 0.67. On an 8 1/2-by-11-inch page, this translates into 7.33- inch width by 11-inch height (or 11-inch width by 7.33-inch height in landscape format). The easiest way to ensure that a graphic will conform to the aspect ratio required for slidemaking is to define a custom page size using the Page Setup command in the File menu. Alternatively, you can activate the Show Rulers command in the Display menu to help you fit the graphic within the appropriate dimensions.

FOUNTAIN FILL TIPS   The SCODL format does not support fountain fills as Corel DRAW! understands them. Recall that when you watched a fountain fill redisplay in Chapter 15, the fill began as a rectangle equal to the space occupied by the highlighting box that surrounded the object. The fill outside the object boundary disappears as the redraw of the object proceeds. SCODL does not recognize the last step in this process. As a result, linear fountain fills export to SCODL correctly *only* for rectangles. Radial fountain fills do not, however, export correctly for perfect circles.

If the graphic from which you want to create a slide contains fountain fills for other types of objects, there is a way to work around the problem. You can overcome this limitation by creating a *mask* that includes a background rectangle with a fountain fill. If you performed the "World of Corel DRAW!" series of exercises in Chapter 15, you are already familiar with the principles of a mask. In summary,

1. Create the object to which you want to assign a fountain fill.

2. Create a rectangle that is larger than the object you created in step one. Place it on top of the previous object so that it covers the object completely.

3. Use the Combine command in the Arrange menu to combine both objects into one object. This creates a transparent "hole" with the shape of the first object.

4. Assign the same color fill to the combined object that you assigned to the background color of the drawing. Assign an outline of NONE to the object.

5. Create another and slightly smaller rectangle, and place it on top of the combined object so that the transparent "hole" is completely covered. Assign any desired fountain fill to this rectangle.

6. Use the To Back command in the Arrange menu to place the filled rectangle behind the combined object. The result is that the fountain fill shows through the transparent hole.

7. Apply the Group command in the Arrange menu to group the two objects and treat them as a unit.

This may seem like a complicated solution, but SCODL understands it perfectly and delivers a flawless fill in your slide if you follow the directions carefully.

Exporting to VideoShow Format (.PIC)

Beginning with Corel DRAW! version 1.11, you can export your drawings to VideoShow format to create on-screen presentations or professional slides for portfolios, business presentations, or other applications. Just use the VideoShow option in the Export dialog box to convert your drawings to the .PIC format supported by General Parametrics Corporation's VideoShow and Slidemaker slide production equipment, and by Photometric equipment and Printmaker software.

 The .PIC format supporting by slidemaking equipment is not the same as the .PIC *import* filter used for importing Lotus graph images.

When you select the VideoShow option in the Export dialog box, two additional options become available: Include All Artistic Attributes and Selected Objects Only. In general, you should leave the Include All Artistic Attributes option activated if you wish to preserve as many Corel DRAW! attributes as possible. If you do not activate this option, you may lose calligraphic outlines, rounded, butt, and arrowhead line caps, beveled and rounded outline corners, and dashed outlines. However, a .PIC file created with the Include All Artistic Attributes option active may be up to twice as large as a file created with this option inactive. Since the VideoShow format has a nominal size limit of 100K, you may want to consider the amount of memory you have available.

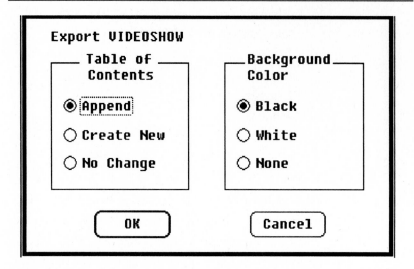

FIGURE 16-7   The VideoShow Table of Contents and
Background Color dialog box

After you specify the desired slide file name in the file selection
dialog box, a third dialog box appears, as shown in Figure 16-7.
The three Table of Contents option buttons let you determine how
VideoShow updates its catalog of pictures. If you select Append,
you add the new drawing to an existing table. If you select Create
New, the drawing you are about to export opens a new table of
contents. And if you select No Change, you are telling VideoShow
that you are updating an existing file and do not wish to change
the order in which it appears in the current catalog.

The second group of option buttons under Background Color
let you specify a background color of white, black, or none for the
drawing. If you select None (invisible), you can overlay objects in
different files. Note that you may have difficulty displaying a file
with an invisible background if it is the first file in the catalog.

The next two sections on exporting to VideoShow format provide guidelines for preparing your drawing before export and

information about Corel DRAW! features that do not transfer exactly as expected.

File Preparation Guidelines

If you plan to use PhotoMetric equipment or PrintMaker software for multiple slide pictures, the first picture listed in the VideoShow Table of Contents should have a background color of either white or black. A picture having a different background color setting will not display. If you will be using VideoShow equipment instead, you may experience difficulties displaying a picture that has a background of NONE, unless you advance through the full cycle of files again.

The cautions about aspect ratio that apply to the preparation of pictures for SCODL export apply to VideoShow export as well. The aspect ratio of your picture should match the aspect ratio of the film used in the slidemaking equipment, or 0.67 for 35 mm film. To achieve the correct aspect ratio for your drawing, you can define a custom page size using the Page Setup command in the File menu. Alternatively, you can use the Select All command and the Select tool to stretch and scale the picture, or use the rulers as a guide when creating the artwork in Corel DRAW!.

Even when you prepare your drawing according to these guidelines, some information may not transfer, owing to the differences in software features. The next section summarizes these limitations.

VIDEOSHOW FORMAT LIMITATIONS   The main differences between what you create in Corel DRAW! and what transfers to the VideoShow format have to do with Corel DRAW! fills, outline widths, and bitmaps. The VideoShow format does not support any PostScript halftone screen patterns or textures, and translates these into a gray shade during the export process. Fountain fills display correctly only if the object containing the fill is a rectangle, because VideoShow applies the fill to the entire high-lighting box that surrounds the object. You can get around this limitation by creating a mask for fountain-filled objects, as described in the "Exporting to Film Recorders (SCODL)" section. If your drawing contains bitmapped objects, these do not appear in the VideoShow picture.

Above all, make certain that the version of the VideoShow operating system is 3.11 or later. Otherwise, the information that transfers from your drawing to the export file may differ from the preceding descriptions.

Exporting Graphics to WordPerfect (.WPG)

As of release 1.11, Corel DRAW! allows you to export images to WordPerfect using the .WPG format. A good use of this feature is to create clipart libraries for use in WordPerfect 5.0 or 5.1.

After you select the .WPG format in the Export dialog box and specify the filename and directory in the file selection dialog box, a third dialog box containing color options displays on your screen, as shown here:

You have a choice of 16 or 256 colors. Select the option button that best matches your display adapter's capabilities, the output device you will be using, and the colors in your drawing, and then select OK.

The following kinds of information do not transfer into the WordPerfect environment:

- PostScript halftone screens and textures

- Radial or linear fountain fills

- Text as text (WordPerfect converts it to curves)

- Corel DRAW! line type settings of None

- Bitmaps

In addition, you cannot rotate a drawing once it is in .WPG format, or it will not print properly from within WordPerfect.

Exporting to AutoCAD (.DXF) Format

Beginning with release 1.11 of Corel DRAW!, you can export as well as import files using the AutoCAD .DXF format. The .DXF files tend to be memory-intensive, however, so it may happen that a complex drawing that occupies only 20-30K in Corel DRAW! can take up half a megabyte or more in the AutoCAD format. Make certain that your hard drive contains enough free space to accommodate potentially large files.

A few Corel DRAW! features either export to .DXF format differently than expected, or do not transfer at all. For example, text preserves its appearance but turns into curves in AutoCAD format. Calligraphic outlines preserve their visual appearance as well, but the .DXF filter interprets them as polygons rather than as lines. Colors match fairly closely, as the .DXF format uses a 256-color scheme.

More important, the present .DXF filter supports the transfer of *outlines only*. This means that no fills at all are exported to the AutoCAD format. If you require fills for certain objects, you must add them using the CAD application.

Exporting to GEM Applications (.GEM)

Corel DRAW! versions 1.11 and later allow you to import and export graphics using the .GEM graphics format. There is an important difference between the import and export filters, however. You can import .GEM files from both GEM Draw and GEM Artline, but you can export only to GEM Artline and Xerox Ventura Publisher. The present GEM export filter does not support export to GEM Draw. As always, save your drawing in Corel DRAW! format before exporting it if you think you might need to edit it later.

As with all object-oriented formats, you can choose whether or not to activate the Include All Artistic Attributes option. It is preferable to activate this option if you want as much visual information as possible to translate correctly. Even with this option selected, however, there are a few limitations in what kinds of features you can transfer. For example, GEM applications support only 16 colors, so colors may not match exactly. In Xerox Ventura Publisher, colored images display as black-and-white unless you have a VGA or compatible display adapter. Another limitation concerns the number of nodes in an exported file. GEM applications can handle a maximum of 128 nodes, so you should limit the size or complexity of your drawings accordingly. If your drawing contains more than 128 nodes, it may transfer, but the GEM application may segment curves into multiple sub-paths (see Chapter 10) and the object will appear differently.

A forthcoming Corel DRAW! release will include an export option for HPGL plotter format. When exporting to this format, you can specify scale factors, curve resolution, pen velocity, plotter pen color, and whether to add a form feed when printing. Since plotters reproduce only outlines, any fill colors in the original Corel DRAW! objects will be stripped when you export them to HPGL format. Contact Corel Systems regarding the availability of the version that contains the HPGL export option.

SUMMARY

The ability to import and export files between different graphics formats is essential for anyone who uses more than one software application. Corel DRAW! now supports the import of nine different graphics formats and allows you to export pictures created in Corel DRAW! to 11 formats. The range of applications Corel DRAW! can now support includes desktop publishing, other drawing software, popular paint programs, and slide generation processes.

You can import pictures from both bitmapped (paint) applications and object-oriented applications. If you import graphics from paint programs, you can trace them and turn them into object-oriented pictures using the AutoTrace feature or the Corel Trace utility provided with Corel DRAW! version 1.12. Alternatively, you can use a bitmapped image as part of your drawing without tracing it.

You also have a variety of object-oriented formats from which to choose. These formats include the .DXF format used by many CAD applications, Lotus .PIC, the .GEM format used by GEM Artline and GEM Draw, Adobe Illustrator .AI and proprietary .EPS files, and the .CGM file format used by many other graphics programs. The available import possibilities make countless clipart libraries as well as original graphics available to you for editing in Corel DRAW!.

In choosing a file format to which you will export a Corel DRAW! graphic, you should be guided by the needs of your application and the complexity of the Corel DRAW! features that you want to transfer. If you need to retain special PostScript fills, fountain fills, and outlines without alteration, you should select the .EPS format if it is supported by your application. If retaining everything but PostScript fills and features is sufficient, you might prefer using the .CGM format instead. The VideoShow and SCODL export formats are specialized formats that allow you to transfer your images to a format that makes slide generation possible.

If you edit an image imported from another application, or if you create an original image in Corel DRAW!, always be certain to save your work in Corel DRAW! format before exporting it. In some cases, you cannot re-import your image once you export it, because not all import and export filters match exactly. If you re-import a bitmapped image without having saved a Corel DRAW! version of it previously, you need to recreate many features before you can continue editing, thereby making unnecessary work for yourself.

Each image format has its own set of limitations regarding the visual information it can transfer correctly. Inform yourself about the limitations that apply to importing from or exporting to the applications you use most frequently.

chapter **17**

TRACING AND WORKING WITH BITMAPPED IMAGES

Creating a Bitmapped Image for Tracing or Editing
Importing a Bitmapped Image
Autotracing an Imported Bitmap
Tracing a Bitmapped Image Manually
Editing Lines and Curves of a Traced Bitmap
Coloring a Bitmap
Moving, Stretching, Scaling, Rotating, and Skewing Bitmaps
Tracing Bitmaps with the Corel TRACE! Utility

In Chapter 16, you learned about the two types of graphics that you can import into Corel DRAW!: bitmapped images and object-oriented art. When you import an object-oriented image, you can edit it just as you would any picture created in Corel

DRAW!. Bitmapped images, however, contain no objects for you to select; they consist entirely of a fixed number of tiny dots, called pixels. If you enlarge or reduce the size of the bitmap without converting it to a Corel DRAW! object, distortion or unsightly compression of the pixels results. The solution is to *trace* the bitmap in Corel DRAW! and turn it into a curve object. You can then change the shape of its outline and the color of its fill, edit it normally, and print it, all without distortion. Corel DRAW! offers you three different methods for tracing an imported bitmap. The newest and most sophisticated of these is the Corel TRACE! batch autotracing utility, available with version 1.2. You will be amazed at the speed and accuracy with which this product, similar to Adobe Streamline, can turn even the most complex bitmap into a finished curve object ready for editing. Turn to the section "Tracing Bitmaps with the Corel TRACE! Utility" to learn more about how to use this exciting feature.

If you have a version of Corel DRAW! earlier than 1.2, you can choose between manual tracing and the semiautomatic Autotrace feature. These methods are less rapid than the newer Corel TRACE! and require more work on the part of the user, but they still offer you a high degree of control over the curves that result from your tracing.

You also may choose to import a bitmap into an existing picture *without* tracing it. This chapter guides you through the entire process of importing a bitmap, tracing it if desired, and editing both traced and untraced bitmaps. You will review most of the skills you learned in previous chapters, for in working with bitmapped images, you make use of six of the nine tools in the Corel DRAW! toolbox.

CREATING A BITMAPPED IMAGE FOR TRACING OR EDITING

Corel DRAW! treats a bitmapped image as a unique object type, separate from other object types such as rectangles, ellipses, curves, and text. Unlike all of the other object types, bitmaps must be created outside of Corel DRAW!.

There are several ways to secure a bitmapped image for importing into Corel DRAW!. The easiest method is to import a finished clipart image having one of the supported file extensions, .PCX or .TIF (see Chapter 16). The next easiest method is to scan an existing image from a print source, such as a newspaper or magazine. Alternatively, you can sketch a drawing by hand, and then scan the image in .PCX or .TIF format. If you are experienced with paint software, you can create your own original pixel-based images.

Once the bitmapped image is available, you are ready to import it into Corel DRAW!. You will practice importing bitmapped images in the next section.

IMPORTING A BITMAPPED IMAGE

You may recall from Chapter 16 that Corel DRAW! accepts only two bitmapped file formats for import: .PCX and .TIF. The .PCX format is native to the ZSoft PC Paintbrush and Publisher's Paintbrush family of paint software, while the .TIF format is the one that most scanners support. If the bitmap you want to import is in another format, you can convert it to .PCX or .TIF using an image conversion program such as Inset Graphics' Hijaak or Symsoft's HotShot Graphics.

To import a bitmap, you use the Import command in the File menu and select the appropriate bitmap file format in the Import dialog box. You also have a choice of whether or not to activate the For Tracing option when importing the image. As explained in Chapter 16, this option determines how Corel DRAW! displays the bitmap, whether or not you can print it, and how much program memory Corel DRAW! allocates for bitmap editing operations.

The next two sections let you practice importing a bitmapped image, first with the For Tracing option selected, and then with this option inactive. The visual comparison should help you better understand how Corel DRAW! handles each type of bitmap.

Importing a Bitmap for Tracing

The standard Corel DRAW! package includes 300 sample clip-art images from 12 different manufacturers, together with a sampler catalog. You can either install these images on your hard disk drive as instructed in Appendix A, or import them from a floppy disk drive as you need them. In the following exercise, you will import one of the sample clip-art images, PEOPLE.PCX, from Metro Image Base. You will select the For Tracing option in order to autotrace this image later.

1. Starting with a blank screen, pull down the Display menu and make sure that a checkmark appears in front of the Show Bitmaps command. If no checkmark appears, click on the command. This enables you to see the bitmap in the editing window after you import it.

2. Select the Page Setup command from the File menu and make certain that the page is set for Portrait format and that the size

is 8 1/2-by-11-inches. Click on the OK command button to save this setting.

3. Select the Import command from the File menu. The Import dialog box appears.

4. Click on the PC Paintbrush .PCX, .PCC format option. The For Tracing option now becomes available for selection.

5. Activate the For Tracing option by clicking on the checkbox next to it. An "x" appears in the box, as shown in Figure 17-1.

6. Select OK to access the secondary Import dialog box. Specify the drive and directory that contains the PEOPLE.PCX image from Metro Image Base, which is shown on page 64 of the Corel DRAW! clip-art sampler catalog. (If you have not installed or used the clip-art samples, see Appendixes A and D.) Figure 17-2 shows the file being loaded from the METRO directory of drive A.

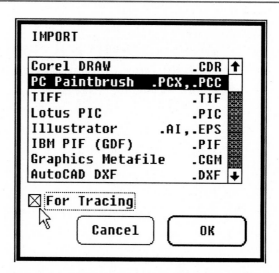

FIGURE 17-1   The Import dialog box

7. To open the PEOPLE.PCX file, double-click on the filename in the Files list box, or highlight the filename and click on the Open command button. After a few seconds, the image appears, centered on the screen and surrounded by a rectangular frame, as shown in Figure 17-3. The status line displays the messages "Bitmap" and "For Tracing."

8. Press (F3) to turn on the preview window. The bitmapped image does not display here. When you import a bitmap using the For Tracing option, Corel DRAW! assumes that you want only the curves that result from your tracing to appear in the preview window. A bitmap imported in this way will neither print nor display in the preview window.

9. Select the Save As command from the File menu. When the Save As dialog box appears, type **AUTTRACE** in the File text box, and then click on the Save command button.

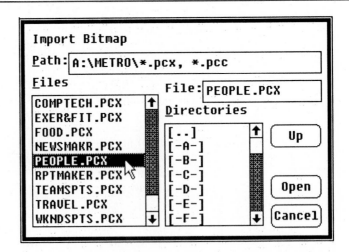

FIGURE 17-2   The secondary Import dialog box

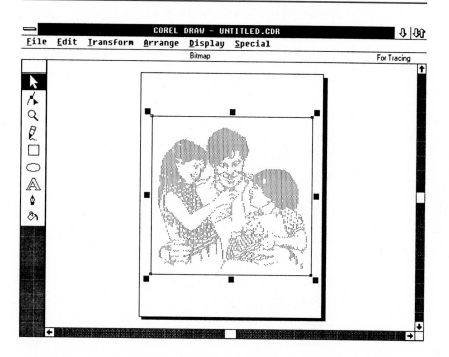

FIGURE 17-3   A bitmapped image (PEOPLE.PCX) imported for tracing

10. You will return to this image later in the chapter to autotrace it. For now, clear the screen by selecting New from the File menu.

When you first import a bitmap, it is selected automatically. At any other time, you must click on the rectangular frame surounding the bitmap in order to select it. Clicking on any of the subjects within the bitmap has no effect and it does not select the entire bitmap object.

Corel DRAW! translates bitmaps in .PCX format into black-and-white pixels only, regardless of the colors of the original image. The on-screen resolution of the image you have just imported is higher than if you had imported it without the For Tracing option selected. That's because Corel DRAW! allocates more program memory for a bitmap that you import for tracing, so that you can trace its curves more accurately. The disadvantage of this approach is that program operation can slow down noticeably, particularly if the bitmapped graphic file is large or if you have an 80286-based computer. Once you have finished tracing and editing a bitmap, however, you can reduce the amount of screen redrew time by deactivating the Show Bitmaps command in the Display menu. Thereafter, the bitmap itself is represented by the surrounding frame only, but the objects you have traced still continue to display in both the editing and preview windows.

note   When you import a bitmap for tracing, it does not appear in the preview window. Only the curves that result from your tracing operations display there. By the same token, a bitmap that you import for tracing does not print; you can print only the object-oriented curves that result from the tracing process.

In the next section, you will import the same bitmap again, but without activating the For Tracing option. You can then compare the visual differences in the way Corel DRAW! handles each type of imported bitmap.

Importing a Bitmap with the For Tracing Option Disabled

When you import a bitmap without activating the For Tracing option, it appears at a lower screen resolution than when you import it for tracing. You can also print the pixel-based image at its full resolution and display it in the preview window, which you cannot do with a bitmap imported for tracing.

If you want to incorporate a printable bitmapped image into an existing picture, you must import the bitmap without activating the For Tracing option. This also holds true if you are unsure whether you will trace the bitmap later. Even without tracing the bitmap, you can still crop it, change its position within the picture, and fill it with a single color. You also will save memory, and you always have the option of tracing the bitmap at a later time.

In the next exercise, you will import the same bitmap that you imported in the previous section. This time, however, you will not activate the For Tracing option, and you will save the image under a different filename.

1. Select the Import command from the File menu. The Import dialog box appears.

2. Select the .PCX format option. The For Tracing option becomes available for selection.

3. Deactivate the For Tracing option by clicking on the checkbox next to it. The "x" disappears from the box.

4. Select OK to access the secondary Import dialog box. Specify the drive and directory that contains the PEOPLE.PCX image from Metro Image Base, shown on page 64 of the Corel DRAW! clip-art sampler catalog. (If you have not installed or used the clip-art samples, see Appendixes A and D.)

5. To open the PEOPLE.PCX file, double-click on the filename in the Files list box, or highlight the filename and click on the Open command button. After a few seconds, the image appears, centered on the screen and surrounded by a rectangular frame. The message "Fill: None" appears on the status line instead of "For Tracing."

6. Press (F3) to turn on the preview window. The bitmapped image displays here as shown in Figure 17-4, because you deselected

the For Tracing option when you imported it. Depending on the resolution of your display adapter, the bitmap in the editing window may look somewhat coarser than the one you imported for tracing in the previous exercise. This is due to the lower amount of memory that Corel DRAW! reserves for a bitmap not intended for tracing. However, this lower on-screen resolution affects only the *display* of the bitmap. The bitmap will print at its ful original resolution.

7. Select the Save As command from the File menu. When the Save As dialog box appears, type **MANTRACE** (short for

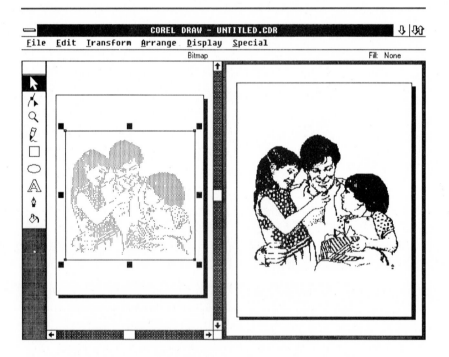

FIGURE 17-4   A bitmap imported with the For Tracing option deactivated

manual trace) in the Filename text box, and then click on the Save command button.

8. Clear the screen by selecting New from the File menu.

In a later section of this chapter, you will return to this bitmap and trace portions of it manually. First, however, you will reopen the AUTTRACE.CDR file and use the Autotrace feature to create curve objects from a bitmap.

AUTOTRACING AN IMPORTED BITMAP

As mentioned earlier in the chapter, Corel DRAW! lets you turn an imported bitmapped image into a resolution-independent curve object by tracing the image. You can trace a single bitmapped image either semiautomatically, using the Autotrace feature, or manually. (If you have version 1.2 or later, you can use the fully automatic Corel TRACE! batch autotracing utility described later in this chapter.) Manual tracing is an excellent choice if you desire total control over the appearance and placement of the outline curves. If you find it cumbersome to use the mouse for tracing long paths manually, however, use the Autotrace feature instead. You have less control over the results, but you will spend less time manipulating the mouse.

The Autotrace feature becomes available to you when the bitmap object is selected. Autotrace is semiautomatic in the sense that the software draws the actual curves for you, but you must define a number of parameters before tracing begins. You control the shape of the outline pen, the color of the outline fill, the interior fill of the object, and the smoothness of the curves.

In the following exercise, you will use Autotrace to trace portions of the AUTTRACE.CDR image that you imported earlier from the PEOPLE.PCX file. Later in the chapter, you will edit some of the curves that you have traced.

1. Open the AUTTRACE.CDR file that you saved earlier in the chapter.

2. Select the bitmap object as soon as it appears, and then adjust magnification to ALL.

3. All bitmap objects are imported with a preset outline color of black and a preset fill of None. You can adjust the Outline pen settings as desired. With the object still selected, click on the Outline tool 🖊 and then on the HAIR icon in the first row of the pop-up menu. This will result in hairline curves of a very fine width.

4. Now you will crop the bitmap just enough to tighten the frame, so that no empty space extends beyond any of the objects in the image. With the bitmap still selected, activate the Shaping tool 🖱 and position it over the middle boundary marker along the bottom edge of the rectangular frame. When the cursor turns into a white cross, press and hold the mouse button and drag the bottom edge of the boundary marker upward. As you drag, the status line displays the percentage by which your cropping is diminishing the height of the bitmap frame. Release the mouse button when the status line displays the message, "Bitmap: Crop bottom: 5%."

5. Crop the left side of the bitmap frame by 5%, the top by 6%, and the right side by 2%. When you have finished, the bitmap extends all the way to the edge of its frame, and the status line displays all four cropping percentages, as shown in Figure 17-5.

6. Select the Preferences command from the Display menu and adjust the settings for the Lines and Curves options as follows: Autotrace Tracking, 10 pixels; Corner Threshold, 8 pixels;

Straight Line Threshold, 3 pixels; and AutoJoin, 10 pixels. These settings will result in smoother curves, smooth (rather than cusp) nodes, curves rather than straight line segments, and curve segments that snap together when they are as far as 10 pixels apart. Click on OK to make these settings take effect.

7. Turn on the preview window. Select the Magnification tool  and then the Zoom-In tool ⊕ when the pop-up menu appears. Magnify only the smaller child on the right side of the screen. Your editing window should look similar to Figure 17-6.

FIGURE 17-5   AUTTRACE.CDR showing a cropped bitmap

8. Now you are ready to begin Autotracing. Make sure that the bitmap is still selected, and then select the Freehand tool ℓ . Notice that the cursor looks different than usual; instead of being a perfectly symmetrical crosshair, it has a wand-like extension on the right: ⊢ . This is the Autotrace cursor. It appears only when you activate the Freehand tool with a bitmap object selected. The word "AutoTrace" appears on the status line, indicating that you are now in Autotrace mode.

9. Position the wand of the Autotrace cursor to the left of the child's earlobe, and then click once. After a waiting period, a closed curve object appears, completely enclosing the contours

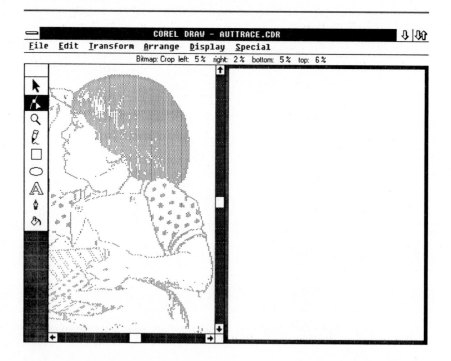

FIGURE 17-6   Magnified view of a child in the bitmap

of the little girl's face, as shown in Figure 17-7. If you do not achieve the same result, select Undo from the Edit menu and try again. If you see an error message like the one in Figure 17-8, try to position the cursor up against a group of dark pixels, or magnify the view further and aim the wand of the Autotrace cursor at an area that could become an outline of a closed path. Autotrace looks for a pattern of pixels as a basis for tracing an outline.

10. Position the Autotrace cursor along the child's hairline, but a little above the point where the child's hairline meets the father's shoulder, and click. Some seconds later, a complex curve containing many nodes appears, as shown in Figure 17-9.

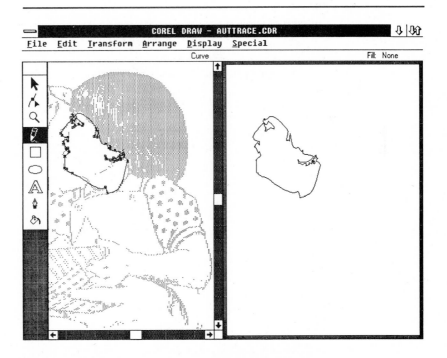

FIGURE 17-7   Autotracing a closed region of the child's face

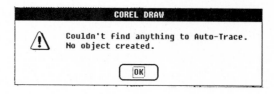

FIGURE 17-8   Error message: "Couldn't find anything to autotrace"

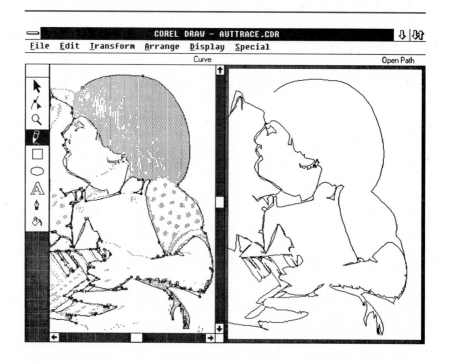

FIGURE 17-9   A complex curve resulting from Autotracing

This curve outlines most of the child's hair, her dress, her hand, and even the package she is opening. You may even see outlines extending to portions of the father. Don't worry about these now; you will practice editing out unwanted curves in a later section of the chapter.

If your screen shows that a different curve was traced, select Undo and try again. Keep in mind that Autotrace does not give you the same high degree of control available with manual tracing.

11. Select the Zoom-In tool from the Magnification tool pop-up menu and zoom in on the child's hair. Then position the intersection point of the Autotrace cursor inside one of the

FIGURE 17-10   Creating highlights in child's hair with the Autotrace cursor

closed regions that represent the highlights of the hair, and click. A closed curve object appears quickly.

12. Create a few more highlighting curves in the same way, until your screen more or less resembles Figure 17-10.

13. Save your changes to the image by pressing (CTRL-S).

14. Select New from the File menu to clear the screen.

 If you have trouble selecting a region that results in the curve you need, try pointing at the desired region using the *wand* of the Autotrace cursor instead of the center point of the crosshair. You will find that you can aim the wand more accurately when you are working in a magnified view.

As you have seen in the previous exercise, the results of the Autotrace feature depend on your choice of the area to outline and on how exactly you can position the Autotrace cursor. Even if you use Autotrace in tracing the same area twice, Corel DRAW! may change the number and positions of the nodes each time. The path that an Autotrace curve takes can sometimes seem to be quite unpredictable, especially if the subjects within the bitmap have overlapping or connected pixels. With practice, you will gain skill in positioning the Autotrace cursor for the best possible results.

TRACING A BITMAPPED IMAGE MANUALLY

You don't have to be a superb draftsman to trace a bitmap with precision in Corel DRAW!. By magnifying the areas you trace and adjusting the Lines and Curves settings in the Preferences dialog box, you can trace swiftly and still achieve accurate results. To trace a bitmap manually, you deselect the bitmap just before you

To summarize, your preparation for tracing an image with the Autotrace feature should always include the following steps in sequence:

1. Import the bitmap with the For Tracing option enabled.

2. Select the bitmap object and adjust outline and fill defaults as you learned to do in Chapters 13 through 15.

3. Crop the imported bitmap as desired, using the Shaping tool.

4. Activate the preview window.

5. Adjust the Lines and Curves settings in the Preferences dialog box—Autotrace Tracking, Corner Threshold, Straight Line Threshold, and AutoJoin—so that the Autotrace curves will be as smooth or as jagged as your image requires. Autotrace Tracking controls how closely the Autotrace curves follow the movement of your mouse; the Corner Threshold sensitivity value determines whether most of your curve nodes are cusps or smooth; the Straight Line Threshold value tells Corel DRAW! whether to turn a segment into a curve or a straight line; and the AutoJoin value determines how close together two end nodes of separate segments must be in order to join together. Table 17-1 summarizes how the Lines and Curves settings affect the tracing of a bitmap.

6. Zoom in on the area to be traced.

7. With the bitmap object selected, activate the Freehand tool, which turns into the Autotrace cursor. You can access the Autotrace mode only when the bitmap object is selected.

8. Position the center of the Autotrace cursor crosshair on an exterior or interior area of the selected bitmap, and click once. The Autotrace feature does the rest.

9. After tracing as many areas of the bitmap as desired, reshape the contours of the resulting curves by editing their nodes and control points.

An alternative to Autotrace is to trace an imported bitmap manually. In the next section, you will learn how easy it is to control the precise shape and direction of manually traced curves.

Option	Determines	Settings	
		Low no. (1-3)	High no. (7-10)
Freehand Tracking	how closely Corel follows your freehand drawing	many nodes	few nodes
Autotrace Tracking	how closely Autotrace cursor follows bitmap edges	rough curve	smooth curve
Corner Threshold	whether a node is a cusp or smooth type	cusp nodes	smooth nodes
Straight Line Threshold	whether segment should be curve or straight line	more curves	more lines
AutoJoin	how close together two line or curve segments must be in order to join	less joining	more joining

TABLE 17-1   Guidelines for Setting Lines and Curves Options in the Preferences Dialog Box

activate the Freehand tool. This action prevents the Freehand tool from becoming the Autotrace cursor.

Manual tracing is faster and easier than using Autotrace if the imported bitmap contains multiple subjects with no clear separations between the pixels that compose these subjects. Most commercial clip-art fits this description. Using the manual method avoids the problem of Autotrace curves that extend beyond the subject with which you are working. As a result, you usually need to do less editing after your initial manual tracing than when you use Autotrace.

Just as when you use the Autotrace feature, you can define the shape of the outline pen, the outline color, the interior fill of the object, and the smoothness of the curves before you begin tracing. In the following exercise, you will trace portions of the MANTRACE.CDR image you imported earlier from the PEO-PLE.PCX file.

1. Open the MANTRACE.CDR file.

2. When the bitmap object appears, click on it with the Select tool, and adjust magnification to ALL.

3. Adjust the outline pen attributes of the bitmap. With the object still selected, click on the Outline tool and then on the HAIR icon in the first row of the pop-up menu. This will produce hairline curves of a very fine width.

4. Click on the Fill tool and again on the NONE icon to change the object fill color to none. This prevents any closed paths that you trace from filling with an opaque color and obscuring other traced areas that lie beneath. You can edit the fill colors of individual objects later.

5. Crop the bitmap so that only the child on the right is fully visible. With the bitmap still selected, select the Shaping tool

and position it directly over the boundary marker at the upper-left *corner* of the bitmap object. When the cursor turns into a white cross, depress and hold the mouse button and drag this corner downward and to the right. Release the mouse button when the status line reads, "Bitmap: Crop left: 30% top 30%", as in Figure 17-11.

6. The left side of the bitmap "frame" needs additional cropping. Position the Shaping tool directly over the *middle* boundary marker on the left side of the bitmap. When the cursor turns into a white cross, press and hold the mouse button and drag this marker to the right. Release the mouse button when the status line reads, "Bitmap: Crop left: 59%."

FIGURE 17-11   Cropping a bitmap in preparation for manual tracing

7. Position the Shaping tool directly over the *middle* boundary marker along the bottom edge of the bitmap. When the cursor turns into a white cross, press and hold the mouse button and drag the marker upward. Release the mouse button when the status line shows that you have cropped the bottom of the image 37%. Then magnify your view to ALL, as shown in Figure 17-12.

8. Select the Preferences command from the Display menu and adjust the settings for the Lines and Curves options as follows: Freehand Tracking, 1 pixel; Corner Threshold, 10 pixels; Straight Line Threshold, 1 pixel; and AutoJoin, ten pixels. These settings will result in curves that closely follow the movements of your mouse. You will generate smooth (rather

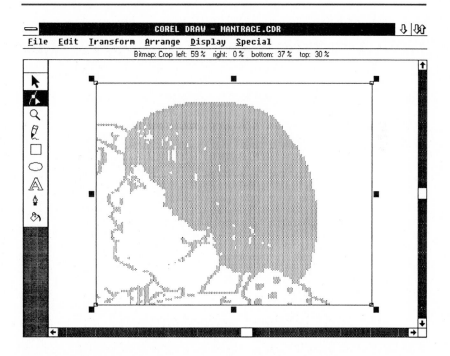

FIGURE 17-12   Enlarged view of child's head in preparation for manual tracing

than cusp) nodes, curves rather than straight line segments, and curve segments that snap together when they are as far as 10 pixels apart. These settings promote ease of editing should you need to smooth out the traced curves later. Click on OK to save these settings.

9. Deselect the bitmap object, and then activate the Freehand tool. (If you see the Autotrace cursor instead of the regular Freehand cursor, you haven't deselected the bitmap.) Position the Freehand tool anywhere along the hairline of the little girl, then depress and hold the mouse and trace all the way around the hairline. End the curve at the starting point. Should you make any errors, you can erase portions of the curve by pressing the

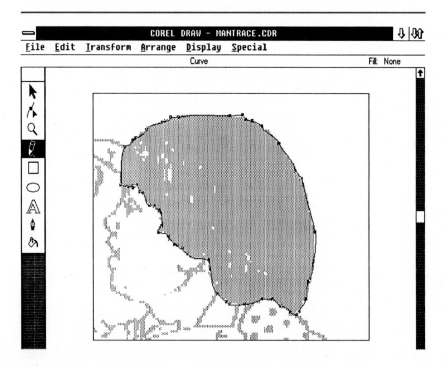

FIGURE 17-13   A manually traced closed curve

(SHIFT) key as you drag the mouse backward. If you end the curve within 10 pixels of the starting point, the two end nodes snap together and form a closed path, as shown in Figure 17-13. If the end nodes are further apart than 10 pixels, the curve remains an open path. To close the path, activate the Shaping tool and draw a marquee around the two end nodes, double-click on one of them to invoke the Node Edit menu, and select Join.

10. Trace the outline of the girl's face as an open path. Follow the line of the neck down to the collar and up again to the point where it meets the hairline.

11. Magnify just the area around the eye and trace two closed paths: one around the outer eye and eyelash structures, and the other around the highlighted area of the eyelid. Don't worry about being exact; you can always reshape your curves later.

12. Use the Zoom-Out tool to return to the previous magnification showing the child's head and neck. Then, activate the Select tool and select the entire bitmap object. Remember that unless the bitmap is selected, you cannot enter Autotrace mode.

13. To enter the Autotrace mode, activate the Freehand tool again with the bitmaps selected. Position the Autotrace cursor inside one of the highlighted areas of the hair and click to trace a curve around this tiny area automatically.

14. Using Autotrace, trace a few more highlights of the girl's hair. When you have finished, your screen should look roughly similar to Figure 17-14. Save the image at this point by pressing (CTRL-S).

15. Turn on the preview window. Since you did not activate the For Tracing option when importing this bitmap, the bitmap appears in the preview window. As a result, you cannot see the traced curves clearly.

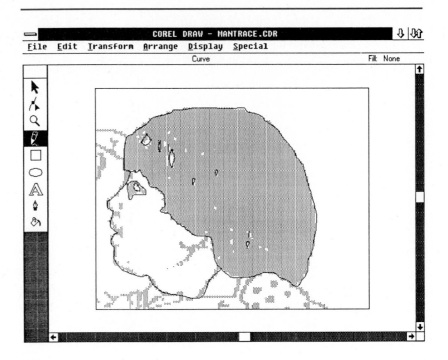

FIGURE 17-14   Combining Autotracing with manual tracing
to create highlights

16. Activate the Preview Selected Only command in the Display
menu, and then select all of the traced curves, including the
highlights of the child's hair. Now you can see the traced objects
clearly in the preview window, as in Figure 17-15.

17. Save the changes you have made by pressing (CTRL-S), and then
select New from the File menu to clear the screen.

As you have just seen, it is possible and sometimes even
preferable to combine both the manual and Autotrace methods
when tracing complex bitmap images. Manual tracing is best
for obtaining exact control over the placement of curves in

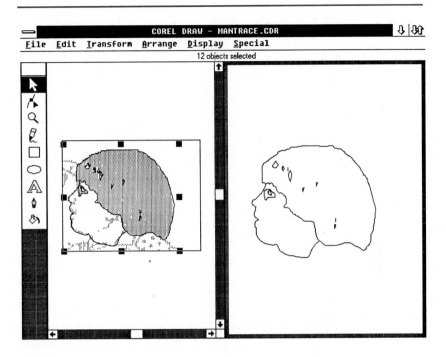

FIGURE 17-15   Preview showing all traced objects in bitmap

bitmaps that contain several subjects close together, as is the case with most clip-art. The Autotrace method is useful for tracing small closed regions like the highlights of the girl's hair in the previous exercises. The Autotrace method is also more convenient to use when the bitmap image has a single, clearly-defined subject with sharp contours.

Whether you use the Autotrace feature, manual tracing, or a combination of both methods, you can always edit the curve objects you create. Of the two files you have worked with in this chapter, the Autotrace bitmap in AUTTRACE.CDR requires the most extensive cleanup. In the next section, you will return to and edit some of the Autotrace curves in this file.

To summarize, your preparation for tracing a bitmap manually should always include the following steps in sequence:

1. Select the bitmap object and adjust outline and fill attributes as discussed in Chapters 13 through 15.

2. Crop the bitmap with the Shaping tool as desired.

3. Adjust four of the Lines and Curves settings in the Preferences dialog box—Freehand Tracking, Corner Threshold, Straight Line Threshold, and AutoJoin—so that the Autotrace curves will be as smooth or as jagged as your image requires. Use table 17-1 as a guide.

4. Zoom in on the area to be traced.

5. Deselect the bitmap object, and then select the Freehand tool. (If you leave the bitmap selected when you activate the Freehand tool, you will enter Autotrace mode.) Position the Freehand tool at the point where you want to begin tracing an outline.

6. Press and hold the mouse button and drag the mouse along the desired path, just as when you draw a normal curve.

7. After you have traced as many areas of the bitmap as desired, reshape the contours of the resulting curves by editing their nodes and control points (see Chapter 10). Manual tracing usually requires less curve editing than the Autotrace method.

EDITING LINES AND CURVES
OF A TRACED BITMAP

You already learned how to edit nodes and control points in Chapter 10, and to alter outline and fill attributes in Chapters 13, 14, and 15. After you use Autotrace to trace a bitmap object, you can use the Shaping tool to remove unwanted curves and smooth or roughen the contours of other curves that didn't turn out just as you expected. When you trace a bitmap manually, you can alter the contours of curves and fill some of the closed objects you have created. The exercises in the following two sections let you refresh these skills.

Removing Unwanted Curve Segments
From an Autotrace Curve

In the following exercise, you will reopen the AUTTRACE.CDR file and remove an unwanted curve segment that appeared during the Autotrace process. Your task is to separate the unwanted curve segment and delete it from the rest of the curve.

1. Open the AUTTRACE.CDR file and adjust viewing magnification to ALL. As in Figure 17-16, a large curve segment extends to the left of the outline of the child.

2. Activate the Shaping tool and click anywhere on the curve segment that includes part of the father. The arrangement of the nodes shows that this is part of a much larger curve that includes most of the outline of the child's body.

3. Activate the Zoom-In tool in the Magnification tool pop-up menu and zoom in on the area where the line extends outward from the child's face, toward the father. This should cover an area approximate to the one shown in Figure 17-17.

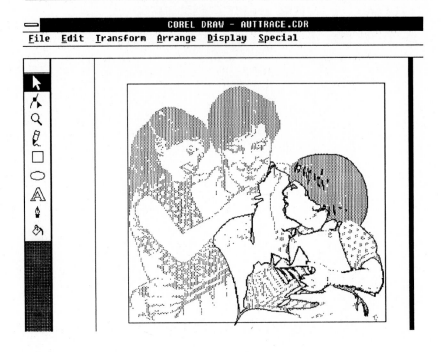

FIGURE 17-16   Full view of Autotraced bitmap showing unwanted curve segments

4. With the Shaping tool still selected, double-click on the node that comes closest to the point where the curve begins to move away from the child's forehead. When the Node Edit menu appears, select the Break command. As you will recall from Chapter 10, this causes the single selected node to break into two end nodes. Corel DRAW! now regards the curve segments on either sides of these nodes as two separate subpaths of the same curve.

5. Move the two end nodes of the newly created subpaths away from each other, as shown in Figure 17-18.

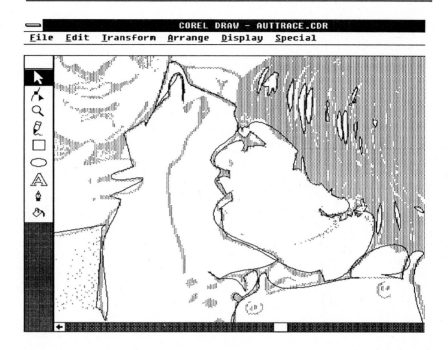

FIGURE 17-17   Zoom-in of child's head showing unwanted curve segments

6. Zoom out to the previous view, and then zoom in to the area near the bottom of the image, where the curve extends outward from the child's gift box to the other subjects in the bitmap.

7. Double-click on the node identified by the Shaping tool cursor (left of screen's center) in Figure 17-19. If no node is present at that location, double-click on the node closest to and above the one in the figure.

8. Select Break from the Node Edit menu, and repeat step 5 to completely isolate the unwanted curve segment from the child on the right.

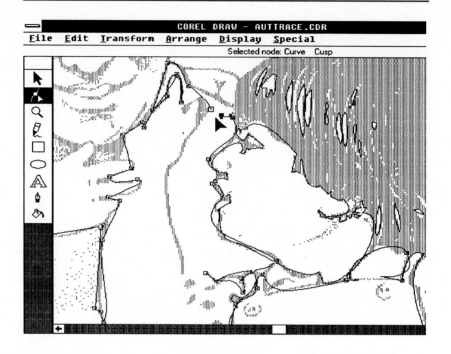

FIGURE 17-18   Nodes broken and moved apart to show separate subpaths

9. With the curve object still selected, change to a magnification of ALL.

10. Activate the Select tool, then click on the Break Apart command in the Arrange menu. This causes Corel DRAW! to handle the disconnected subpaths as separate curves.

11. Deselect both of the curves, and then select just the curve that extends away from the child and toward the other subjects.

12. Press (DEL) or select the Clear command in the Edit menu to delete this curve. As shown in Figure 17-20, Corel DRAW! removes the unwanted curve segment from the screen.

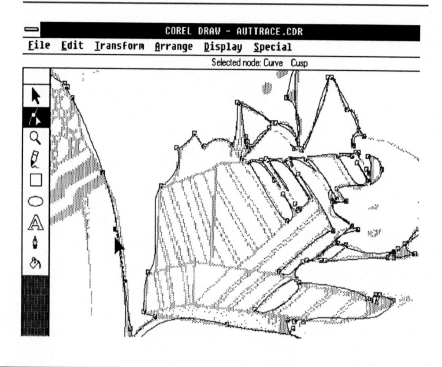

FIGURE 17-19 Locating node to break in order to isolate
curve subpath

13. Go on and remove other curve segments if desired. When you
    are finished, save your changes by pressing (CTRL-S), and then
    select the New command from the File menu to clear the screen.

You may find the curve editing process easier in the
MANTRACE.CDR file, where you traced the bitmap manually
with greater precision. In the next exercise, you will edit the nodes
of the curve objects you generated with manual tracing.

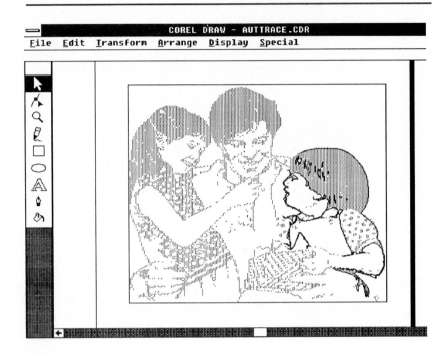

FIGURE 17-20   Full view of Autotraced bitmap with unwanted curves eliminated

Editing Contours of a Manually Traced Curve

Even though it is easy to manually trace a curve with precision, you always have the option of altering the shape of the curve later. In the following exercise, you will enhance manually traced features of the child's face in the MANTRACE.CDR file.

1. Open the MANTRACE.CDR file and magnify the viewing window to ALL. Select the open curve path that constitutes the outline of the child's face, as shown in Figure 17-21. You are going to reshape this curve so that the upper and lower lips stand

out more prominently and the chin shows a more decisive contour.

2. Activate the Shaping tool and select the node that marks a change in direction at the child's chin. This may be either a cusp node or a smooth node, depending on the way you held your hand while tracing. Double-click on this node to invoke the Node Edit menu, and then select Symmetrical.

3. Pull the control points of this node outward to give the child a more pronounced chin. Recall that since it is a symmetrical node, you can reshape the curve around it evenly on both sides.

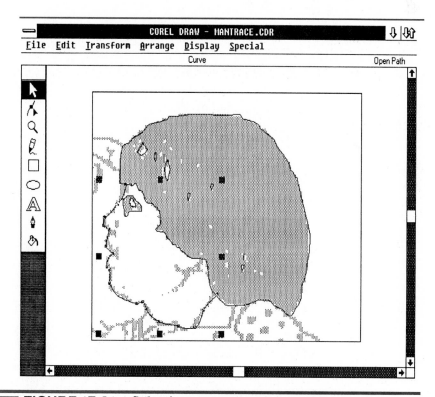

FIGURE 17-21 Selecting an open path in preparation for curve editing

4. Select a node that marks the curve of the lower lip. If manipulating the node does not cause the lip to stand out more prominently without loss of smoothness, add a node just below it and move the resulting control points as required.

5. Increase the prominence of the upper lip in the same way, adding a node above the lip if necessary. Then deselect the Show Bitmaps command in the Display menu. Your screen should now resemble Figure 17-22.

6. Perhaps you would like to edit other curves and nodes on the child's face. When you have finished, press (CTRL-S) to save your changes, and then select New from the File menu to clear the screen.

As you have seen in the preceding exercise, it doesn't matter whether your drafting skills are strong or weak. Using the Magnification and Shaping tools, you can edit your traced curves to take on any shape you choose.

In the next group of sections, you will explore some options for colorizing an entire untraced bitmap and selected closed curves of a traced bitmap.

COLORING A BITMAP

When you trace a bitmap manually or automatically, it is advisable to set the fill color to None, just as you did earlier in this chapter. That way, you won't obscure your view of objects within other objects when you view the traced bitmap in the preview window. The time to edit fill colors is after you have traced all of the areas that make up your curve object and reshaped the resulting curves to your satisfaction. You can fill a closed path traced from a bitmap with as many colors or patterns as there are closed curve objects.

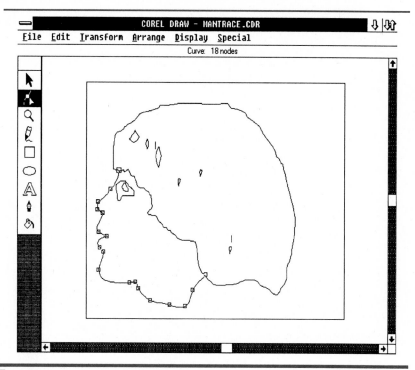

FIGURE 17-22   Traced curve object showing edited facial contours

You can also unify traced objects with the Combine command and fill them with a single color for special color distribution effects.

When you color an untraced bitmap, on the other hand, you can select only one fill color, unless you assign a fountain fill to the bitmap. The color covers the entire rectangle that encloses the bitmap, not just the pixels, as you will see for yourself in the next section.

Coloring an Untraced Bitmap

As you will recall from the early sections of this chapter, a bitmap that you import without the For Tracing option selected appears in the preview window as a collection of black pixels. When you assign a fill color to an untraced bitmap, the color fills the entire rectangle that surrounds the bitmap, as you will observe in the following exercise.

1. Starting with a blank screen, select the Show Bitmaps command. Then select the Import command and import the PEO-PLE.PCX file again, but without the For Tracing option active.

2. When the bitmap appears on the screen, turn on the preview window. Notice that the bitmap is selected automatically as soon as you import it.

3. Select the Fill tool, and then the 20% gray icon in the pop-up menu (the fourth icon after NONE). The preview window shows that you have applied the color to the entire background rectangle that surrounds the bitmap, as shown in Figure 17-23.

4. If you like, experiment with spot and process color fills and fountain fills. Remember that if you select a PostScript halftone screen or fill texture, it will not display in the preview window. You will have to print the bitmap on a PostScript output device to see the results.

5. When you finish experimenting, select New from the File menu to clear the screen. Do not save the changes you have made.

 The current windows driver for the HP Paintjet contains a "bug" that will not allow you to print a filled bitmap properly.

The technique of filling an entire bitmap can produce attractive results for desktop publishing applications, where you might choose to display a scanned photo with a custom color or screen. If you have traced a bitmap and produced filled curve objects, you can design even more varied fills, as you will see in the next exercise.

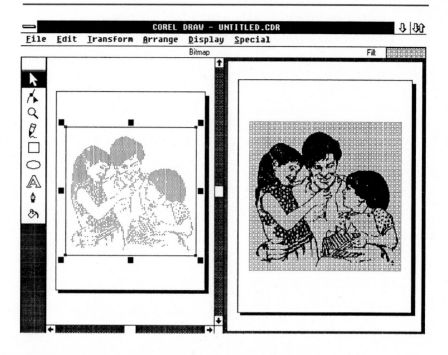

FIGURE 17-23   Coloring an untraced bitmap

Coloring a Traced Graphic

You have several options when deciding how to color closed curve objects created by tracing a bitmap. You can select each object and fill it separately, or combine all objects and assign a single color to create alternating colored and transparent regions. You will practice both of these techniques in the next two sections.

Filling Each Closed Path and Rearranging Fills   Traced bitmaps often contains closed regions within other closed regions. If you assign different colors to different regions, make certain that you don't cover an interior region's color with an outer region's color. You may need to rearrange objects using the commands in the Arrange menu. Working with the preview window on is good insurance against achieving undesired fill results. In the following exercise, you will assign two different fill colors to closed objects in the MANTRACE.CDR file you created earlier in the chapter.

1. Open the MANTRACE.CDR file. Change viewing magnification to ALL and turn on the preview window. Deactivate the Preview Selected Only command in the Display menu if it is currently activated. The original bitmap, which you will not need for this exercise, still appears in the preview window and interferes with your view of the curves.

2. Select the original bitmap and press (DEL) to clear it from the screen.

3. Select the closed region that constitutes the child's hair, and then click on the Fill tool. Click on the black rectangular icon in the pop-up menu to assign a fill color of black to the hair.

4. Draw a marquee or use the (SHIFT) key technique to select all of the closed regions that represent the highlights of the child's hair.

5. Click on the Fill tool and on the 20% gray icon in the pop-up menu to assign this fill color to all of the highlights. If you extend the preview window so that it covers the entire screen, the contrasting shades in the child's hair now resemble Figure 17-24.

6. Select Save As from the File menu. When the Save As dialog box appears, type **HAIRFIL1** in the File text box, and then click on the Save command button.

7. Select the New command in the File menu to clear the screen.

You can also fill traced objects with any spot or process color, or (if you work with a PostScript printer) with any PostScript halftone screen or texture. In the next section, you will experiment with a different method of filling interior and exterior traced regions.

Combining Curves and Creating Transparent Inner Regions A visually interesting way to fill interior and exterior objects in a traced bitmap is to combine all of the closed objects, and then assign a single fill color or texture to them. As you have seen in previous chapters, the use of the Combine command causes interior objects to become transparent. Apply this technique in the next exercise to recreate the highlights in the child's hair.

1. Open the MANTRACE.CDR file once more. Adjust viewing magnification to ALL and turn on the preview window.

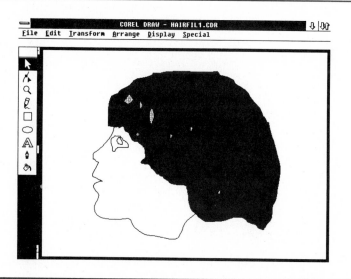

FIGURE 17-24   Filling background and foreground objects with different colors

2. Select the original bitmap and delete it so that only the traced objects appear in the preview window.

3. Draw a marquee around the curve that represents the hair and all of the closed regions that represent the highlights. To avoid including the outline of the child's face, use the (SHIFT) key selection method or the Preview Selected Only command.

4. Select the Combine command in the Arrange menu to unify all of these objects. Since they all have a default fill of None, a change does not occur immediately in the preview window.

5. Click on the Fill tool and then on the 80% gray icon in the pop-up menu (the third icon from the right), and then extend the preview so that it covers the entire screen. The preview window now displays the exterior object (the mass of hair) with the 80% gray fill and the interior regions (the highlights) as transparent "holes," as shown in Figure 17-25.

6. Select Save As from the File menu. When the Save As dialog box appears, type **HAIRFIL2** in the File text box, and then click on the Save command button.

7. Select the New command to clear the screen.

So far, you have learned how to edit and color traced curves, and how to color and crop untraced bitmaps. A few other editing operations function differently with untraced bitmaps than with other objects; you will explore these in the next and final section.

MOVING, STRETCHING, SCALING, ROTATING, AND SKEWING BITMAPS

You have already practiced cropping an imported bitmapped image, and you know that the Shaping tool allows you to perform this function. In the "Editing Lines and Curves of a Traced Bitmap" section, you also used the Select tool briefly to scale the image to a larger size. In the following exercise, you will review how all the functions of the Select tool interact with an imported bitmap image.

1. Starting with a blank page, select the Import command from the File menu. Do not activate the For Tracing option. Import the PEOPLE.PCX image once again.

2. When the bitmap appears, turn on the preview window. The bitmap displays in both windows, because you didn't import it specifically for tracing. Adjust magnification to ALL to see the

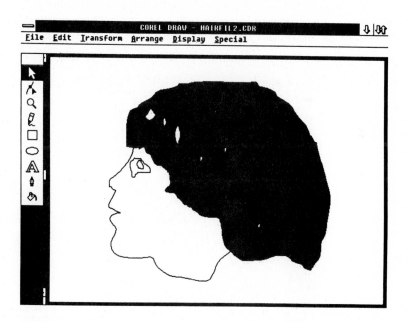

FIGURE 17-25   Combining traced objects to create transparent highlights

complete image extended to as large a size as possible on the screen.

3. The bitmap arrived on the Corel DRAW! screen already selected. Position the cursor over the boundary marker in the upper-left corner of the highlighting box. Drag the mouse downward and to the right to scale the bitmap proportionally to a smaller size. When the status line shows a value of approximately 70%, release the mouse button. The bitmap reappears in perfect proportion but at a smaller size, as shown in Figure 17-26.

4. With the bitmap still selected, position the cursor at any point along the rectangle that surrounds the bitmap. To move the

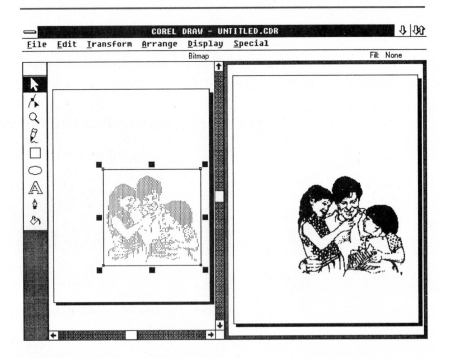

FIGURE 17-26   Scaling an untraced bitmap

bitmap, drag it from this point and place it at the left edge of the page.

5. To stretch the bitmap rather than scale it, position the cursor at the middle right boundary marker and drag this marker almost to the right edge of the page. The bitmap reappears looking distorted as though you were viewing it through an extreme wide-angle camera lens, as shown in Figure 17-27.

6. Click on the rectangle a second time to enter rotate/skew mode. Then, position the mouse cursor over the boundary marker at the upper-right corner of the bitmap rectangle. Drag this marker upward and to the left (counterclockwise), and then release. As shown in Figure 17-28, the bitmap itself is no longer visible in either the preview window or the editing window. In its place is a shaded rectangle with a white triangle at one corner. This triangle shows the orientation of the rotated bitmap relative to

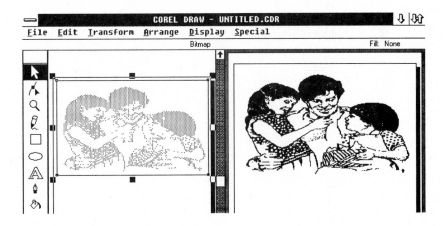

FIGURE 17-27   Stretching an untraced bitmap horizontally

its lower-left corner. Although you cannot view a rotated bitmap, it will still print normally if you have a PostScript printer. If you use another type of printer, only the gray rectangle will print.

7. Select Undo from the Edit menu to return the bitmap to its normal orientation. It is still in rotate/skew mode, however.

8. Position the mouse cursor at the top-middle boundary marker. Drag this marker to the right to skew the bitmap horizontally, then release. Just as when you rotated the bitmap, it now appears as a shaded rectangle with a triangle marking the orientation of the lower-left corner.

9. Select New to clear the screen. Do not save any changes.

This brief experimentation has probably given you some ideas

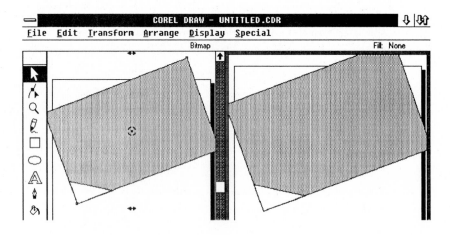

FIGURE 17-28   Rotating an untraced bitmap

for using bitmaps in your own applications. Distorted stretched, rotated, or skewed bitmaps can be highly effective on a visual level when you use them sparingly and for the purpose of communicating your message.

TRACING BITMAPS WITH THE COREL TRACE! UTILITY

Beginning with release 1.2 of Corel DRAW!, a third method of tracing bitmapped images is available to you—one that is more rapid, sophisticated, and efficient than either the manual or Autotrace method. The Corel TRACE! batch tracing utility, similar to Adobe Streamline, allows you to trace one or more bitmaps automatically at high speeds and save them in either Adobe .EPS or .AI format. You can choose from two default methods of tracing, or customize tracing parameters to suit your needs. Corel TRACE! is provided with sample files with which you can practice editing tracing parameters. When you are finished tracing files, you can edit the resulting vector-based images in any drawing program that can read the Adobe .EPS or .AI file format.

Corel TRACE!, like Corel DRAW!, requires only 640K of main memory. Like Corel DRAW!, Corel TRACE! cannot take advantage of a math coprocessor if you have one.

The following sections provide instructions for preparing to use Corel TRACE! for selecting and tracing bitmaps, and for customizing and editing tracing parameters. Some of the figures may look different from your screen because they were created using a pre-release version of Corel TRACE!.

PREPARING TO USE COREL TRACE!   If you have version 1.2 or later, Corel TRACE! is installed in the same directory

where you installed Corel DRAW!. Before you begin using Corel
TRACE! for the first time, check the amount of memory available
in the root directory of your hard drive C:. When you trace bitmaps
using Corel TRACE!, temporary files are generated in the root
directory of your hard drive unless you specify a different directory
in your AUTOEXEC.BAT file. If you trace large bitmaps or more
than one bitmap during a session, you are almost certain to require
several megabytes of hard drive space for these temporary files. A
good recommendation is to have at least 4 Mb of space free.

If the root directory of your hard drive does not have enough
space available, you can either remove unnecessary files or specify
a different directory where Corel TRACE! can place the large
temporary files it generates. For example, if Corel DRAW! and
Corel TRACE! are installed in drive C: and you wish to locate
temporary files in the TEMP directory of drive D:, edit you
AUTOEXEC.BAT file and add the following line to it:

set temp=d:\temp

This statement tells Windows always to place temporary files in
the specified directory. Be sure to reboot you computer after you
edit the AUTOEXEC.BAT file in order to make your changes take
effect, and be sure that the directory exists on the specified hard
drive.

 Never select the Windows directory as the directory in which to
store the temporary files that Windows applications generate.
Errors could result that might cause your system to crash unex-
pectedly.

Loading Corel TRACE!

Do not run any other Windows applications in the background
while you are running Corel TRACE!. Corel TRACE! requires a
large amount of memory to work efficiently. If you run other

applications concurrently, Corel TRACE! may not run or may function very slowly.

To load Corel TRACE!, follow these steps:

1. Run Windows to start the MS-DOS Executive. If you are not in the drive and directory where Windows is installed, change to that directory first.

2. Double-click on the name of the directory where Corel DRAW! is located.

3. Double-click on the filename CORELTRC.EXE. The opening screen shown in Figure 17-29 appears for a few seconds, and then is replaced by the program window depicted in Figure 17-32.

The opening screen of Corel TRACE! is almost bare. It contains only three items in the menu bar: a File menu, a Tracing Options

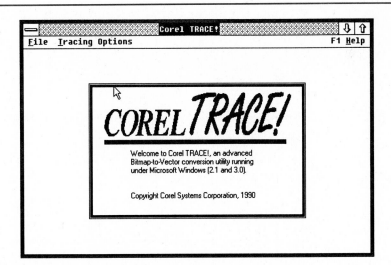

FIGURE 17-29   The Corel TRACE! main screen

menu, and the F1 Help indicator. To obtain help information on running Corel TRACE!, you click on the F1 Help indicator or press the (F1) function key at any time after the small information box disappears from the screen. To begin the process of specifying and tracing files once the program wiindow displays, you click on the File menu and again on the Open option.

Getting Help in Corel TRACE!

You can access Corel TRACE! help screens in one of two ways. If you are running Corel TRACE!, you can press (F1) or click on the F1 Help indicator in the menu bar at any time. If you are not running Corel TRACE! but wish to access the help screens directly from the MS-DOS Executive, follow these steps:

1. From the MS-DOS Executive, go to the directory where Corel DRAW! and Corel TRACE! are located.

2. Click once on CORELHLP.EXE and then select the Run command from the Windows File menu. The Run dialog box

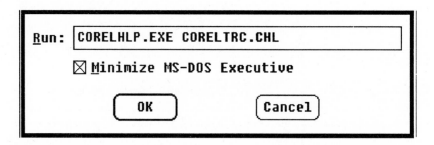

FIGURE 17-30   Running the Corel TRACE! help system from the MS-DOS Executive

appears, with the CORELHLP.EXE filename already in the text box.

3. Place your cursor at the end of the filename in the text box, and click once. Press the spacebar and type **CORELTRC.CHL**.

4. Make certain that an "x" appears in the Minimize MS-DOS Executive checkbox, as shown in Figure 17-30, and then select OK. The Index screen of the Corel TRACE! Help System window appears as in Figure 17-31.

The help system for Corel TRACE! works exactly like the main Corel DRAW! help system you learned about in Chapter 1. To see

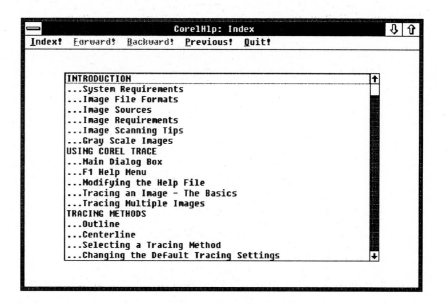

FIGURE 17-31   The Index screen of the Corel TRACE! Help System window

the help information for any topic, double-click on the line that contains the topic name in the Index screen. To move to the next screen, select the Forward! command in the menu bar. To go back to the previous *topic*, select the Previous! command in the menu bar. A single topic can contain more than one screen. To go back to the previous *screen* (which may or may not belong to the same topic), select the Backward! command in the menu bar. You can return to the general Index screen at any time by selecting the Index! command in the menu bar. To exit the Corel TRACE! help system and return to what you were doing previously, select Quit!.

Continue with the next section to learn how to work in the Corel TRACE! program window.

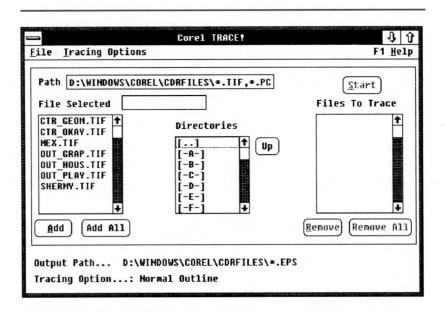

FIGURE 17-32   The Corel TRACE! applications window

Getting Around in the Select Files To Trace Dialog Box

In order to trace one or more bitmaps, you must work with the options in the Corel TRACE! program window shown in Figure 17-32. This is the main operating screen of the Corel TRACE! utility.

You can edit several of the options in this dialog box prior to tracing a file. Take a moment to become acquainted with the components of this screen.

Path, Directories   The Path text box indicates the source directory and file extension of the bitmaps to be traced. Valid input file extensions are .PCX and .TIF. When you first install Corel DRAW!, the default source path is the directory where either Corel DRAW! or its sample files are located. You can change the source drive and directory by double-clicking on the appropriate options in the Directories list box. This list box is located in the center of the Corel TRACE! program window.

File Selected, Files List Box   The list box just below the File Selected text box displays the names of all of the files in the specified directory that match the selected file format. To make a filename appear in the File Selected text box, click once on the desired filename in the Files list box. To select a file for tracing, double-click on the filename, or click on the Add command button, which you will learn about in a moment.

Files To Trace   With Corel TRACE!, you can *batch trace*, or trace multiple files at once. The Files To Trace list box contains the names of the files, in the specified directory, that you have chosen to trace. To make a filename appear here, select it from the Files list box in one of two ways: double-click on the filename, or click on the filename once and then click on the Add command button. To remove a file from the Files To Trace list box, click on the filename in the list box once, and then click on the Remove command button.

Add, Add All, Remove, Remove All These command buttons work in conjunction with the list boxes above them. To add a file from the Files list box to the Files To Trace list box, click on its name once to highlight it, and then click on the Add command button. To transfer all of the filenames in the Files list box to the Files To Trace list box, simply click on the Add All command button. To remove a single file from the Files To Trace list box, click once on the desired filename, and then click on the Remove command button. To remove all of the filenames from the Files To Trace list box, simply click on the Remove All command button.

Output Path The Output Path statement at the bottom of the dialog box specifies the directory where Corel TRACE! sends the files after tracing them. The default is the directory where you installed Corel TRACE!. You can change the output path by clicking on the Output Options! command in the menu bar and making adjustments to the options in the dialog box that appears.

Tracing Options The Tracing Option statement at the bottom of the dialog box tells Corel TRACE! exactly how to trace the files. There are two default methods, Normal Outline and Normal Centerline. You can also define up to eight custom tracing methods by selecting one of the blank dotted line (. . .) options and then selecting the Editing Option command in the Tracing Options menu. Most of the time, the two default methods will be adequate for your needs. To learn more about using the default methods and customizing the tracing methods, see the "Customizing Your Tracing Options" section later in this chapter.

Start Command Button   When you have specified all of the tracing parameters using the other options in the dialog box, click on the Start command button to begin the tracing process.

Now that you are familiar with the contents of the Select Files To Trace dialog box, you are ready to practice tracing bitmapped graphics files. Continue with the next section to obtain hands-on practice.

Tracing a Bitmap with the Corel TRACE! Utility

Tracing one or more bitmaps involves several steps:

1. Specify the source directory of the files you want to trace, using the Directories list box if necessary.

2. Select one or more files to trace. To do so, either double-click on their names in the Files list box, or click on a filename and then on the Add command button.

3. Edit the Output Options—On name conflict messages and output path using the Output Options! command in the File menu.

4. Edit the tracing method options, if desired, by selecting a command from the Tracing Options menu.

5. Click on the Start command button to begin tracing the selected file(s).

In the following exercise, you will tell Corel TRACE! to batch trace (trace one after another) two bitmap files. The sample TIFF files used in the exercise were installed automatically if you installed the sample files with Corel DRAW!. If you wish, you can substitute any two bitmapped graphics files of your own.

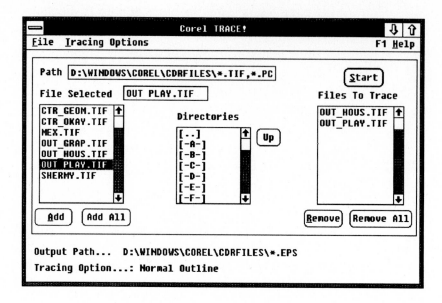

FIGURE 17-33   Selecting two files to trace from the source directory

1. If you did not install the sample files with Corel DRAW!, change to a drive and directory where .PCX or .TIF files are located. If you did install the sample files with your software, make certain that the .TIF files shown in Figure 17-33 appear in the File Selected dialog box. Use the Directories list box to change the path if necessary.

2. Double-click on the OUT_HOUS.TIF and OUT_PLAY.TIF filenames in the Files list box at the left side of the dialog box. Both filenames now appear in the Files To Trace list box, as shown in Figure 17- 33.

3. Check the Output Path statement at the bottom of the dialog box. If you want Corel TRACE! to send the traced files to a different directory than the one specified, click on the Output Options command in the File menu. The Output Options dialog box appears, as shown in Figure 17-34.

4. Check the option settings in the On name conflict area of the Output Options dialog box. These settings determine what happens if you attempt to retrace a bitmap for which an output file of the same name already exists. If you select Always replace, Corel TRACE! overwrites the existing file automatically. If you select Always prompt, Corel TRACE! warns you about the conflict and lets you rename the output file before proceeding.

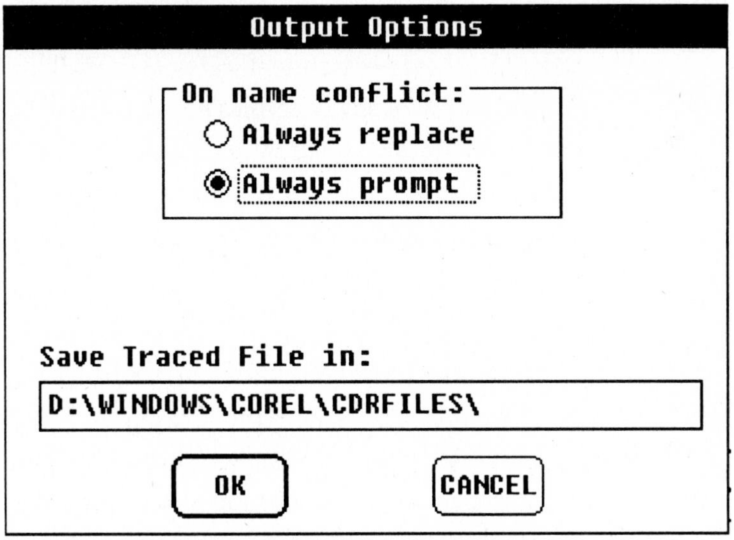

```
┌─────────────────────────────────────────────┐
│              Output Options                  │
│                                              │
│      ┌─On name conflict:──────────┐          │
│      │  ○ Always replace          │          │
│      │  ⦿ Always prompt           │          │
│      └────────────────────────────┘          │
│                                              │
│                                              │
│    Save Traced File in:                      │
│    ┌───────────────────────────────────┐     │
│    │ D:\WINDOWS\COREL\CDRFILES\         │     │
│    └───────────────────────────────────┘     │
│         ┌────────┐      ┌────────┐           │
│         │   OK   │      │ CANCEL │           │
│         └────────┘      └────────┘           │
└─────────────────────────────────────────────┘
```

FIGURE 17-34   The Output Options dialog box

5. Check the Save Traced File in setting. This determines the destination directory of the traced .EPS file. To change the current drive and/or directory, backspace over the current drive and/or directory names and type the desired names in their place.

6. Select the OK command button to save your Output Options settings and return to the Corel TRACE! application window.

7. As a last step before you click on the Start command button, check the Tracing Option statement at the bottom of the dialog box. The default tracing option is Normal_Outline. If the option that appears in your dialog box is Normal_Centerline or something else, pull down the Tracing Options menu and click on the Normal Outline command, as shown in Figure 17-35. This tells Corel TRACE! to trace a line around each of the black or white regions of the bitmap image and then fill each area with black or white to match the original bitmap. The Outline method is best for tracing bitmaps with thick lines, many fills, and a hand-sketched look. The Centerline method, on the other hand, is best for architectural or technical illustrations that have lines of fairly uniform thickness and no fill colors. See the next section of this chapter for more details on the differences between the Outline and Centerline methods of tracing.

8. Click on the Start command button to begin tracing the two sample files. After a few seconds, a small window containing the first of the two bitmaps pops up at the right side of the screen. You can actually watch as Corel TRACE! traces each fine detail of the bitmap. When the tracing is complete, the window containing the first bitmap disappears automatically and is replaced by a pop-up window that contains the second bitmap. Once more, you watch as the bitmap is traced. The window containing the traced image of the second bitmap remains on

the screen after the tracing is complete, as shown in Figure 17-36.

9. To make the window that contains the second traced file disappear, click on the control-menu icon in the upper-left corner of the window and select Close. If you quit Corel TRACE! without closing the window of the last file you traced, the window closes automatically.

10. Select the Exit! command from the menu bar to exit Corel TRACE! and return to the MS-DOS Executive. Now you can load Corel DRAW!, import one or both of the traced files, and edit them just as you would any other object-oriented image. Remember that when you import an Adobe .AI or .EPS file, the

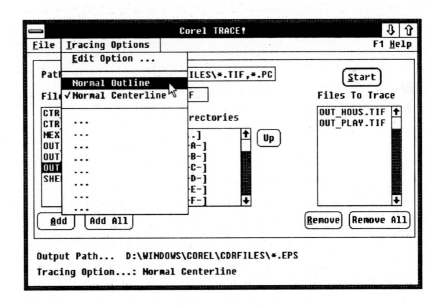

FIGURE 17-35   Selecting the Normal Outline tracing method

image takes some time to load onto the screen fully.

The preceding exercise gave you a brief taste of what Corel TRACE! can do. In the next section, you will learn more about how you can customize the options that determine the smoothness, fineness, and clarity of the curves during the tracing process.

Customizing Your Tracing Options

The Tracing Options menu in the Corel TRACE! application window contains two preset tracing algorithms, Outline and Centerline. If you wish, you can modify the options associated with these two algorithms to define up to eight custom tracing methods. When you modify tracing options, you can save your settings as a new option in the Tracing Options menu, using one of the eight

FIGURE 17-36   A real-time representation of the traced bitmap

blank entries shown in Figure 17-35. In the following sections, you will find out more about the two preset methods, Normal_Outline and Normal_Centerline, and when you will want to choose each method to obtain the best results.

THE NORMAL OUTLINE TRACING METHOD   When you select Normal_Outline as the tracing method, Corel TRACE! seeks out the *outlines* of black or white areas and traces around them. Every curve becomes a closed object that is then filled with black or white to match the original bitmap as closely as possible. (Corel TRACE! does not support gray scale, halftone, or color information in a .PCX or .TIF bitmap.) This method is most appropriate when the images that you trace contain many filled objects or have lines of variable thicknesses.

THE NORMAL CENTERLINE TRACING METHOD   When you select Normal_Centerline as the tracing method, Corel TRACE! seeks out the *center* point of lines in a bitmap and traces down the middle of those lines. No attempt is made to close paths or fill them. The resulting accuracy and attention to fine detail makes this tracing method the best choice for scanned images of technical or architectural drawings. Normal_Centerline is also appropriate for tracing drawings in which line thicknesses are fairly uniform.

DEFINING A CUSTOM TRACING METHOD   What if the image you want to trace contains both filled areas and line art? In Corel TRACE!, you can adjust a variety of tracing options by selecting the Edit Option command in the Tracing Options menu. Follow these steps to access this command and define a custom tracing option.

1. Load Corel TRACE! from the MS-DOS Executive window.

2. Without selecting any files, pull down the Tracing Options menu and click on one of the blank (. . .) menu options. The Tracing Options dialog box shown in Figure 17-37 appears. Using this dialog box, you can edit any of eight tracing parameters, then save them under a unique name that will appear as an option in the Tracing Options menu. You can define up to eight additional tracing options using this dialog box.

3. Position the cursor in the Option Name text box at the lower-left corner of the dialog box and type the name of the new tracing option you are about to define.

4. Edit the tracing options as desired, referring to the descriptions that appear further on in this section.

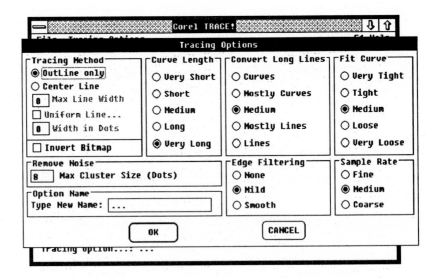

FIGURE 17-37   The Tracing Options dialog box

5. When you are finished editing, select the OK command button to save the tracing option under a new name that will now appear in the Tracing Options menu, as shown in Figure 17-38. The name of the new tracing option and the settings that define it also appear in the WIN.INI file.

Information about tracing methods that you define is saved in the WIN.INI file. Keep a backup copy of your WIN.INI file so that you can restore your custom tracing options in the event that you reinstall Windows or lose your original WIN.INI file due to some other cause.

Each of the eight parameters in the Tracing Options dialog box has a special function in the tracing process.

Tracing Method, Line Width   This tracing parameter is important only if you want to trace an image based on the Centerline

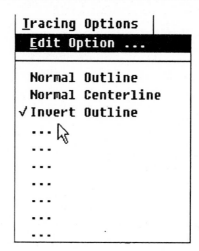

FIGURE 17-38   The Tracing Options menu

rather than the Outline method. If you click on the Center Line checkbox, an "x" appears in the checkbox and the Line Width option becomes available. The number in the Line Width option defines the maximum width, in pixels, that you want Corel TRACE! to treat as a line. If areas in the bitmap contain higher numbers of pixels grouped together, Corel TRACE! treats them as closed objects rather than as lines. The valid range for Line Width is from 2 to 99 pixels or dots. If you select 0 or 1, the setting defaults to a value of 6.

Invert Bitmap   When the Invert Bitmap checkbox contains an "x," this option is active. Corel TRACE! will convert black areas of the bitmap to white and white areas to black.

Curve Length   This parameter determines the maximum length of each curve segment within the traced image. If you select Very Short or Short, each segment may be short, but the number of nodes in each segment remains high. As a result, the curves will fit the outline of the bitmap very closely. If you select Long or Very Long, on the other hand, the traced image will have smoother curves, but they will follow the bitmap more loosely. Select the desired option based on the characteristics of your input file and the way you want the resulting object-oriented picture to look.

Convert Long Lines   Your setting for this option determines whether Corel TRACE! treats a particular curve segment as a straight line or as a curve. If you select the Curves option, for example, Corel TRACE! will convert all traced segments to curves. If you select Lines, Corel TRACE! will convert all traced segments to straight lines. The other settings permit a mixture of curve and straight line segments in the traced drawing. If you frequently trace technical illustrations or other drawings that are made up of mostly straight lines, consider creating a custom tracing option that converts all segments to straight lines.

Fit Curve   This parameter affects how closely Corel TRACE! follows the outline of the bitmap when tracing it. A Very Tight setting results in a curve that follows the bitmap closely, while a Very Loose setting results in a looser curve. You should always set this option to the *opposite* of the setting chosen for the Sample Rate option. For example, if you select Very Loose for Match Bitmap, choose Fine for Sample Rate.

Sample Rate   The Sample Rate option determines how closely Corel TRACE! matches its curve segments to the original bitmap. A setting of Fine results in a close match with many nodes, while a setting of Coarse results in a less exact match with fewer nodes per curve segment. Set this option in conjunction with the Match Bitmap option, as described under "Match Bitmap" earlier in the chapter.

Edge Filtering   Sometimes a bitmap image contains rather jag-ged outlines. You can select the Smooth option from the Edge Filtering selections to tell Corel TRACE! to smooth those outlines when tracing. Selecting the Mild option causes Corel TRACE! to smooth the outlines to a less extreme degree.

Remove Noise   Many scanned images contain unwanted flecks that are not truly part of the images themselves. The Remove Noise option lets you tell Corel TRACE! when to consider clumps of pixels as unwanted flecks and when to treat them as part of the picture. The number to which you set this option determines the minimum pixel cluster size that Corel TRACE! will consider to be a part of the picture. All pixel clusters smaller than or equal to the specified number will be ignored during the file conversion and tracing process. You can set this option to any number between 2 and 999. When you are tracing a poorly scanned image, set the number slightly higher; when you are tracing a "clean" file, keep the number low. You'll rarely need to set this option above 10.

Option Name   As mentioned previously, you can define and name up to eight tracing options beyond the two standard options provided with Corel TRACE!. To save a modified tracing option under a new name, you must be sure to type a name in this text box *before* you exit the Tracing Options dialog box. Otherwise, the new settings will be valid only during the current session of Corel TRACE!. Then select OK to cause this new option to appear in the Tracing Options menu.

If you trace and import many bitmaps, you probably tend to trace the same kinds of files over and over again. Defining custom Tracing Options to fit the kinds of files you trace most often can be a powerful time-saving tool.

EDITING AN EXISTING TRACING OPTION Once you have defined a tracing option, you can alter its parameters permanently using the Edit Options command in the Tracing Options menu. This command always applies to the *currently selected* tracing option. You must therefore select the option you wish to edit *before* you click on the Edit Option command.

To edit an existing tracing option,

1. With the Corel TRACE! application window open, click on the Tracing Options menu and on the name of the option you wish to edit. The name of this option appears in the Tracing Option statement at the lower-left corner of the Corel TRACE! application window, showing that it is the currently selected tracing option.

2. Now, select the Edit Option command from the Tracing Options menu. The Tracing Options dialog box for the currently selected tracing option appears.

3. Edit the tracing options as desired, then select OK to save the new settings permanently.

Editing parameters for existing tracing options, like defining new tracing options, helps you save time when you import traced graphics into Corel DRAW! and edit them. For example, if you know in advance that you need to invert colors of a particular bitmap or that you require a larger or smaller number of nodes in the traced graphic, you can change tracing parameters to give you the desired results automatically.

SUMMARY

Corel DRAW! treats a bitmapped graphic that you import as a separate type of object, just as a text string and an ellipse represent object types. You can import a bitmap either for tracing, or in order to include it in an existing picture.

If you intend to trace a bitmap either manually or with the Autotrace feature, import it with the For Tracing option activated. A bitmap imported for tracing appears with a higher screen resolution than other bitmaps, is visible in the editing window only, and does not print. Bitmaps not imported for tracing appear in both the preview and editing windows, and you can print them in their native pixel-based format.

The Autotrace method of tracing offers convenience, but it is not always easy to predict or control the path that the Autotraced curves will follow. The best subjects to automatically trace are therefore paint program or clip-art images that contain only a single subject. Before beginning to trace a bitmap using Autotrace, you should select it, alter outline and fill attributes, crop the bitmap, adjust Lines and Curves settings in the Preferences dialog box, and magnify the area you want to trace. In order to enter Autotrace mode, the bitmap must be selected before you activate the Freehand tool.

The manual method of tracing is best suited to complex bitmap images that contain several subjects with overlapping pixels. In order to trace a bitmap manually instead of through Autotrace, you must deselect the bitmap before you activate the Freehand tool. By magnifying areas that you want to trace, you can obtain precise curves swiftly and easily.

After you trace a bitmap, you can edit the resulting lines and curves, using the shaping techniques you learned in

Chapter 10. You often need to edit out unwanted curve segments of an Autotrace bitmap. You can also edit the outline and fill attributes of manually or automatically traced bitmaps.

If you choose to incorporate a bitmap into your picture without tracing it, you can assign a single fill color to it, crop it, move it, stretch or scale it, and rotate or skew it. Stretching a bitmap causes distortion. Rotated and skewed bitmaps display in both the preview and editing windows as shaded opaque rectangles with a triangle at one corner to show the orientation of the bitmap. You can print them normally, however, if you use a PostScript printer.

The Corel TRACE! utility available with Corel DRAW! version 1.2 is an advanced autotracing utility that allows you to trace single or multiple bitmaps rapidly and with accuracy of detail. You can choose from a preset Outline or Centerline method of tracing, or define up to eight additional tracing methods through the Tracing Options dialog box. You can also specify the source directory, destination directory, input file format, and output file format for the original bitmap and traced files.

chapter 18

PRINTING AND PROCESSING YOUR IMAGES

Output Devices Supported by Corel DRAW!
Preparing to Print
Working with the Print Options Dialog Box
Hardware-Specific Printing Tips
Hints for Printing Complex Artwork on PostScript Printers

No matter how sophisticated an image may look on your computer monitor, you can judge its true quality only after it has traveled from your hard drive to the outside world. The means by which graphics travel from your computer to your intended audience is a question of output, and until recently, output meant printer and paper. In today's world, however, paper is only one possible means by which your artwork can reach the outside world. As you learned in Chapter 16, film negatives, videotape, and 35 mm slides are equally valid output media. Corel DRAW! offers you your choice of all these media and their associated output devices.

If print media remain your preferred end products, you can output your images using the Print command in the File menu. Corel DRAW! allows you to print selected objects within an image, scale your image to any desired size, print oversize images on multiple tiled pages, or print to a file that you can send to a service bureau. If you work with a PostScript printer, even more advanced printing functions are available to you. You can prepare color separations for process color images, add crop marks and registration marks, print in film negative format, and add file information to your printouts. With a PostScript printing device, you can also reproduce the dotted and dashed outlines, custom halftone screens, and PostScript textures you learned to create in Chapters 14 and 15.

If you want your image produced as slides or used in presentations, refer to Chapter 16. You will use the Export command, not the Print command, to generate your output.

The first part of this chapter describes the output devices and media that Corel DRAW! supports. The middle portion of the chapter guides you step-by-step through the process of printing, using the Print Options dialog box. The concluding sections of the chapter contain tips to help you achieve satisfactory printing results, based on the type of printer you use.

OUTPUT DEVICES SUPPORTED BY COREL DRAW!

In considering how your images will travel from your computer to your audience, you are actually concerning yourself with both equipment and the product of that equipment, or with both *output device* and *output medium*. The output device you work with determines what media you can produce, or what the end product of your work will be. For example, all printers produce paper output. PostScript printers and imagesetters, however, also allow you to prepare your images as color separations or in film negative format, so that you can eliminate costly steps in the commercial printing process. Corel DRAW! supports some printing devices better than others. As you may recall from Chapter 1, Microsoft Windows provides drivers for many different printers and plotters, but not all of them work equally well with Corel DRAW!. The following list shows the printing devices that Corel DRAW! supports best, in the order in which you are likely to reproduce the fullest range of Corel DRAW! features.

- PostScript Plus black-and-white printers, color printers, and imagesetters (Linotronic)

- HP LaserJet with Adobe-licensed PostScript controller boards

- Older PostScript printers compatible with the original Apple LaserWriter

- HP LaserJet printers and 100% compatibles

- HP DeskJet

- HP PaintJet

The PostScript Plus printers, older PostScript printers, printers with genuine Adobe-licensed PostScript controller boards, and printers with PostScript emulation boards are the only ones in this list that let you generate output using PostScript printing options.

You can print your Corel DRAW! images with other printers, too, but the results may vary depending on the complexity of your images and the characteristics of a given manufacturer's device. With some of the following printers, your output may match your expectations exactly. With others, you may experience problems that are hard to predict because of the variety of standards in the industry.

- HP LaserJet clones that are not 100% compatible

- HP LaserJet printers, compatibles, and clones with PostScript-compatible controller boards *not* licensed by Adobe

- Genuine HP Plotters

- HP Plotter clones and other plotters

- Dot-matrix printers

The "Hardware-Specific Printing Tips" section of this chapter contains information about designing your images to obtain the best output results for the printer that you use. It also describes the kinds of limitations you are most likely to encounter with a specific type of printer and provides suggestions on how to solve them. The "Hints for Printing Complex Artwork on PostScript Printers" section provides tips specific to working with PostScript printers.

In the next section, you will learn about general steps you can take before you print to ensure trouble-free output.

PREPARING TO PRINT

Before you select the Print command, you should make certain that your printer is correctly installed to run under Microsoft Windows. You should also adjust several other default settings in Microsoft Windows in order to customize printing for the special needs of Corel DRAW!. Two of these other settings, called *Printer Timeouts,* determine how long Windows waits before sending you messages about potential printer problems. The settings you need to review are all in the Windows Control Panel, which is available in Corel DRAW! through the Control Panel command in the File menu.

If you work with a PostScript printer, you should be using Windows' own printer driver or another viable Windows-compatible PostScript driver. Examples include the UltraScript PostScript interpreter from QMS and the PostScript driver provided with release 2.0 or later of Micrographix Designer.

Another adjustment you should make involves the use of the Windows print Spooler. You can make this adjustment by editing one line in the WIN.INI file. The short sections that follow will guide you through the process of reviewing and editing your printer setup.

Checking Printer Installation And Setup

If you did not specify the correct printer and port when you installed Microsoft Windows, you will not be able to print in Corel DRAW!. To check whether your printer is correctly installed to run under Microsoft Windows, follow these steps:

1. From the main screen of Corel DRAW!, select Control Panel from the File menu. The Control Panel window appears, as shown in Figure 18-1.

2. Your main concern is with the options in the pull-down Setup menu of the Control Panel window. Click on Setup, at the top of the Control Panel window, to pull down this menu. Then, select the Connections command in the Setup menu to access the Connections dialog box, an example of which appears in Figure 18-2. The Printer list box should contain the name of the printer you are going to use, and this name should be highlighted. If the name of your printer is in the list box but is not

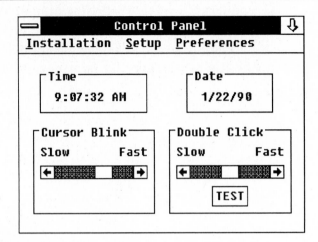

FIGURE 18-1   The Control Panel window

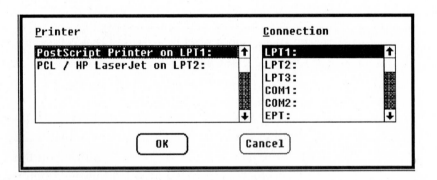

FIGURE 18-2   The Connections dialog box of the Control
Panel

highlighted, click on it with the mouse. If the name of your printer is missing in the Printer list box, select Cancel. Then, add the necessary printer driver using the Add New Printer command in the Installation menu of the Control Panel.

3. Return to the Connections dialog box, if necessary, and check the Connection list box. This box should contain the name of the parallel or serial port to which your printer is connected, and this name should be highlighted. If the port name is there but is not highlighted, click on it with the mouse. If the desired port name is missing, select Cancel, close the Control Panel, exit Corel DRAW!, and reinstall your printer using the Control Panel of the MS-DOS Executive.

4. When both the printer and the port names are highlighted in the list boxes of the Connections dialog box, click on the OK command button.

5. If your printer is connected to a serial port, click on the Communications Port command in the Setup menu of the Control Panel. When the Communications Settings dialog box shown in Figure 18-3 appears, make certain that the Baud Rate, Word Length, Parity, Stop Bits, Handshake, and Port settings are correct. Refer to your printer manual if you need assistance in defining these settings. When you are finished, click on OK to return to the Control Panel window. Leave the Control Panel on your screen.

If you need to alter your printer installation after performing this check, refer to your *Microsoft Windows User's Guide*. The chapter entitled "Using Control Panel" contains the necessary instructions; the Control Panel that you access from Microsoft Windows directory is identical to the one you access from within Corel DRAW!.

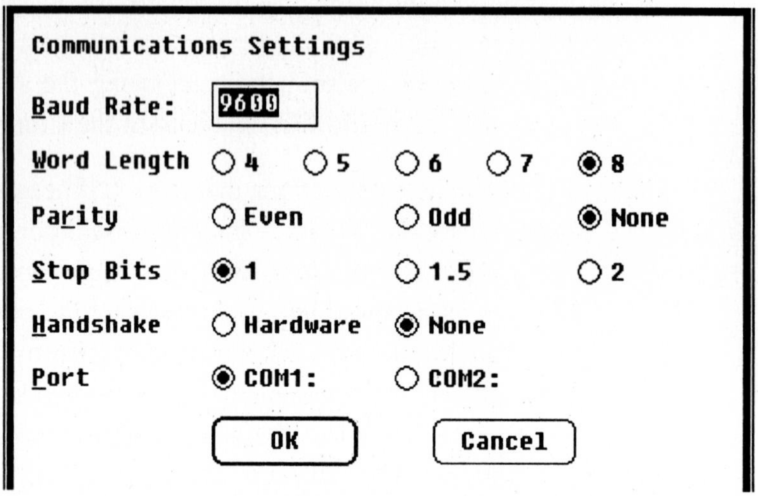

```
Communications Settings

Baud Rate:    9600

Word Length   ○ 4      ○ 5      ○ 6      ○ 7      ● 8

Parity        ○ Even        ○ Odd        ● None

Stop Bits     ● 1           ○ 1.5        ○ 2

Handshake     ○ Hardware    ● None

Port          ● COM1:       ○ COM2:

              [    OK    ]      [  Cancel  ]
```

FIGURE 18-3   The Communications Settings dialog box of the Control Panel

Checking and Adjusting Printer Timeouts

After checking for correct printer and port assignments, you should customize the Printer Timeouts settings, found under the Printer command in the Setup menu of the Control Panel. These settings define how long Windows waits before sending you messages about potential printer problems. The default Printer Timeouts settings installed with Microsoft Windows may be adequate for average Windows applications, but you should customize them to improve printing performance in Corel DRAW!. To edit Printer Timeouts,

1. From the Control Panel, click on the Printer option in the Setup menu. The Default Printer dialog box shown in Figure 18-4 appears. At the top of the dialog box is a list of the printers

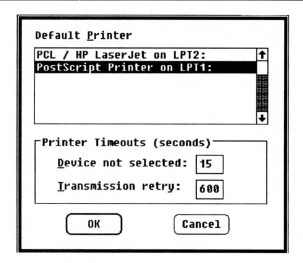

FIGURE 18-4   Adjusting Printer Timeouts

installed for use with Windows applications. If the printer you intend to use for the current printing operation is not highlighted, click on it now.

2. The Printer Timeouts section of the dialog box shows two settings: Device not selected and Transmission retry. The Device not selected setting determines how long Windows waits before informing you that the printer is not connected properly, not turned on, or otherwise not ready to print. Leave this setting at its default value of 15 seconds, because if the printer is not ready to perform, you want to find out as soon as possible.

3. Adjust Transmission retry from its default value of 45 seconds to 600 seconds (equal to 10 minutes), as is shown in Figure 18-4. The Transmission retry value determines how long Windows waits between transmission requests before a timeout error occurs. Although 45 seconds may be long enough for most software that runs under Windows, it is not always adequate for

graphics applications such as Corel DRAW!. The output file
that Corel DRAW! sends to your printer can contain complex
information, requiring more time to transmit.

4. Click on the OK command button to exit the dialog box. A third
   dialog box, specific to your printer, now pops up. Click on OK
   to exit this last dialog box and return to the main Control Panel
   window. Then, pull down the Installation menu and select Exit
   to leave the Control Panel and return to Corel DRAW!.

By checking your printer setup and Printer Timeouts settings
each time you run Corel DRAW!, you can prevent potential
printing and communications problems before you even attempt
to print. You can eliminate one more potential printing pitfall by
disabling the Windows Spooler, about which you will learn in the
next section.

Disabling the Windows Spooler

Microsoft Windows is installed to print all files through a Spooler.
The Spooler is a program that captures printing instructions and
sends them to the printer. The printer then runs in the background,
so that you can continue working in your application without
interruption. The Spooler doesn't always work efficiently with
graphics files, however. For this reason, you can avoid printing
problems if you disable the Windows Spooler. When the Spooler
is disabled, the printing operation runs in the foreground; you must
wait until printing is complete before you can continue with your
work. Printing takes place faster this way than when the Spooler
is enabled, however.

To disable the Windows Spooler, you edit a line in the WIN.INI
file, as the following exercise demonstrates:

1. Exit Corel DRAW! if it is currently running.

2. From the MS-DOS Executive, make sure you are in the Windows directory, and then double-click on NOTEPAD.EXE to open the Notepad text editor.

3. When the Notepad window appears, select the Open command from the File menu. A small file selection dialog box pops up.

4. The Open File Name text box shows a default file extension of .TXT. To change this to .INI so that you can access the WIN.INI file, backspace over the letters "TXT," type **ini** instead, and then click on the Open command button. The WIN.INI file now appears in the Files list box.

5. To open the WIN.INI file, double-click on its name. The [windows] section is at the head of the file. You will see a line that reads "spooler=yes."

 An alternative way to access the WIN.INI file is simply to double-click on the WIN.INI filename, without opening Notepad first. Using this method, you open Notepad and WIN.INI simultaneously.

6. Position the cursor after the "s" in "yes" and click once. Then backspace over the word "yes" to delete it and type **no** instead, as shown in Figure 18-5.

7. Select the Save command in the File menu to save the changes to WIN.INI, and then select the Exit command in the File menu to leave Notepad and return to the MS-DOS Executive.

8. To cause the changes you have made to take effect, exit and then restart Windows.

Now that you have customized Windows printer settings to improve printing performance in Corel DRAW!, you are ready to explore the options in the Printer Options dialog box. The next

FIGURE 18-5   Disabling the Windows Spooler in the WIN.INI file

series of sections lets you experiment with the choices available to you when printing.

WORKING WITH THE PRINT OPTIONS DIALOG BOX

To begin the process of printing in Corel DRAW!, you select the Print command in the File menu. An image must be on the screen before you select this command. The options Print Only Selected, Scale, Fit to Page, Tile, and Print to File are available for use with all printers.

If you use a PostScript printer, you can also include date and file information on the printout, prepare spot or process color separations, and print crop and registration marks with your graphic. You can also print the image in film negative format, change the default screen frequency for proofing images, or print using fonts resident in the host printer rather than the native Corel DRAW! fonts.

The following sections each explore one printing option or one aspect of the printing process. So that you can practice printing using the options in the Print Options dialog box, you will import a clipart image, save it in .CDR format, and then use it in the exercises that follow.

Preparing an Image for Printing

In Chapter 17, you imported a clipart image in bitmap format and traced it using Autotrace. Other sample clipart files provided with your software are in object-oriented format. In the following steps, you will import one such file, scale and regroup it, and save it in Corel DRAW! format. Then, you will print this file in each of the succeeding sections to practice using the options in the Print Options dialog box.

 The .CGM format file selected for printing throughout this chapter was chosen so that you could print the image on almost any printer that Corel DRAW! supports. If your version of Corel DRAW! is earlier than version 1.10, however, you will not be able to import a file in .CGM format. If you have an early version of Corel DRAW!, import one of the .CDR format files from the Artright Corporation as a substitute. The specific clipart samples provided by Artright vary from version to version of Corel DRAW!, so choose one that contains a variety of colors. You can then adapt the steps in the exercises to fit the graphic you have chosen.

1. Starting with a blank screen in Corel DRAW!, select the Import command in the File menu. When the Import dialog box appears, select Graphics Metafile (.CGM) format as shown in Figure 18-6, and then select OK. The Import Graphics dialog box displays. (If you have a version of Corel DRAW! that is earlier than 1.1, select .CDR format instead, and open one of the sample clipart files provided by the Artright Corporation.)

2. With the help of the Directories list box, change to the drive and directory where the Presentation Task Force sample clip-art

images from New Vision Technologies are located. If you did not install the sample clipart images when you installed Corel DRAW!, insert the appropriate diskette (#10 if your software is on 3 1/2-inch disks, #4 if it is on 5 1/4-inch disks) into drive A:. Then highlight the filename HUMAN23A.CGM and click on the Open command button. The image of a businessman using the telephone in front of his computer workstation displays at a size larger than the page. In addition, the image is in horizontal format; if you currently have a portrait-format page, you will need to change page orientation.

3. Change page orientation if necessary. Select the Page Setup command in the File menu. When the Page Setup dialog box appears, click on the Landscape option button, make certain that Letter is selected for Page Size, and then click on OK. (Later on in this chapter, you will have a chance to customize

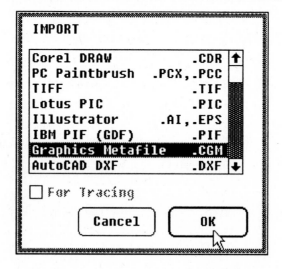

FIGURE 18-6   Importing a graphic in .CGM format

the page size for printing.) The image is still larger than the page, but the page is now in the correct format.

4. Reduce the size of the image so that it fits the page. Click on the Zoom-Out tool [Q] in the Magnification tool pop-out menu. The viewing window changes to allow you a view of the entire imported graphic superimposed on the much smaller page, as shown in Figure 18-7. (You may need to click on the Zoom-Out tool twice before you will see the boundary markers for the image.) Position the cursor at any one of the four corner boundary markers and drag the marker toward the center of the picture, scaling it until the value in the status line is approximately 35%. Then, move the reduced image into the page area and click on the Show Page icon in the Magnification tool pop-up menu. The entire page displays, as shown in Figure 18-8.

5. It is a good habit to save any imported graphic in Corel DRAW! format. Select the Save As command from the File menu. When the Save As dialog box appears, type **GETINFO** and click on the Save command button. Leave this image on the screen for the series of exercises that follow.

As you may recall from Chapter 17, images in .CGM format usually come into Corel DRAW! at a size that is much larger or much smaller than the page size. Scaling such an image down to fit a letter-sized page is only one way to print the entire image. For example, you could also define a custom page size to fit the picture, and then print the picture either on an imagesetter or using the Tile option in the Print Options dialog box. You will learn about these options in later sections of this chapter.

Now that you have an image ready for printing, you are ready to select the Print command and become acquainted with the Print Options dialog box.

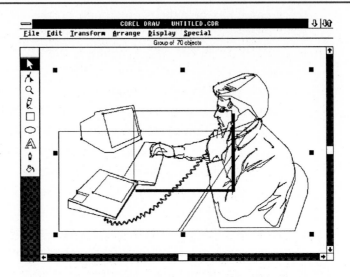

FIGURE 18-7   An imported graphic that is larger than the
Corel DRAW! page

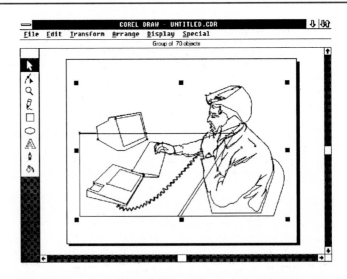

FIGURE 18-8   The same graphic scaled down to fit within the
page

Selecting the Print Command

Once you have an image on the screen, you are ready to begin the printing sequence. Select the Print command from the File menu. The Print Options dialog box appears, as shown in Figure 18-9.

The "POSTSCRIPT" designation that appears in parentheses in the title of the dialog box is misleading. Five of the options in this dialog box—Print Only Selected, Tile, Scale, Fit to Page, and Print to File—are available for any printer supported by Corel DRAW!. The other six options—Include File Info, Crop Marks & Crosshairs, Print As Separations, Film Negative, All Fonts Resident, and Default Screen Frequency—are available for PostScript printers only. In addition, you can select multiple options for any given print operation, as long as all of the ones you choose are available for your printer.

Before you experiment with the printing options, go on to the next section to learn how to check the printer setup.

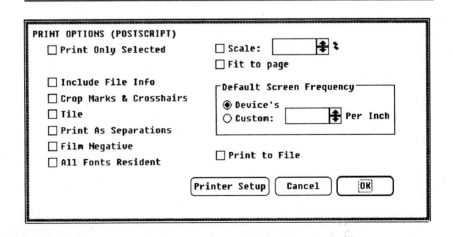

FIGURE 18-9   The Print Options dialog box

Checking Printer Setup

Whenever you print, it is advisable to develop the habit of checking the printer setup *before* you select any print options. The Printer Setup dialog box, which you access by clicking on the Printer Setup command button in the Print Options dialog box, contains controls that allow you to define the desired number of copies, paper size and orientation, printing resolution, and the brand name of your printer. The other items in the Printer Setup dialog box vary, depending on the printer you selected using the Connections command (Setup menu) of the Control Panel. For example, the Printer Setup dialog box shown in Figure 18-10 shows the controls available for a PostScript printer.

Some of the variable controls are important to know about, because they help you avoid possible pitfalls when you attempt to print complex images. Later on, in the series of sections following "Hardware-Specific Printing Tips," you will find hints on adjusting these settings to prevent or minimize printing problems. Take a moment to explore the contents of *your* Printer Setup dialog box and of any nested sub-dialog boxes that are accessible by clicking on special command buttons. When you are ready, click on the Cancel command button of the Printer Setup dialog box. Click again on the Cancel button of the Print Options dialog box to return to the image on your screen.

Each of the next series of sections presents a single option in the Print Options dialog box and allows you to test it using the GETINFO.CDR file you saved earlier in the chapter. The non-PostScript options are presented first, for the convenience of those who do not work with a PostScript printing device.

Printing Only Selected Objects

There are several reasons why you might choose to print only selected objects within a picture, rather than the entire graphic:

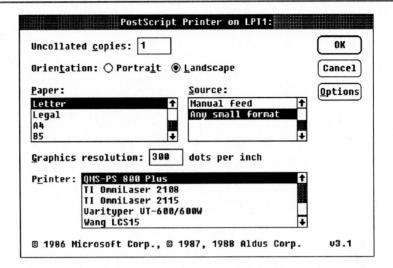

FIGURE 18-10.   Printer Setup options for a PostScript printer

- You want to save printing time and need to check only a portion of the image.

- Your picture contains a great deal of fine detail, such as in a technical illustration, and you want to examine certain areas for accuracy.

- Some of your picture elements contain complex or PostScript-only features that do not display in the preview window.

- You have experienced printing problems and want to locate the object or objects that are causing the trouble.

Whatever your reason, you can print just the selected objects within a picture by activating the Print Only Selected checkbox in the Print Options dialog box. You must select the desired objects before you select the Print command, however, or you will receive

an error message. Practice printing selected objects in the
GETINFO.CDR file now.

1. If the Print Options dialog box is still on your screen, click on
   Cancel to exit it and return to the GETINFO.CDR file. Turn on
   the preview window. The image contains several colors in
   addition to black. As you may recall from Chapter 16, files in
   .CGM format often transfer into Corel DRAW! with fill colors
   and outlines as two separate objects.

2. Select any object in the image; the status line shows you that
   all of the objects in the picture are grouped. Click on the
   Ungroup command in the Arrange menu to ungroup all of the
   objects, and then deselect all objects by clicking on any white
   space.

3. Magnify just the area of the image that contains the computer
   terminal, keyboard, and telephone base. Activate the Preview
   Selected Only command, and then draw a marquee around the
   objects that make up the terminal. As in Figure 18-11, you
   should be able to see the entire terminal, and the status line
   informs you that you have selected three objects.

4. Leave the objects selected and click on the Print command.
   When the Print Options dialog box appears, review your Printer
   Setup, and then click on the Print Only Selected checkbox. An
   "x" appears in the checkbox.

5. Select the OK command button to begin the printing process.
   After a short time, the image of the terminal should emerge from
   your printer. Leave the GETINFO.CDR image on your screen
   for the next exercise.

As you learn about the other options in this dialog box, you will
think of effective ways to combine one or more of them with Print
Only Selected. Assume, for example, that you are working with a

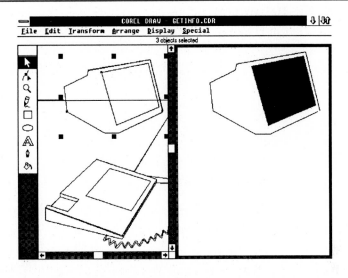

FIGURE 18-11   Selecting objects within the graphic for printing

complex technical illustration and need to proof just a small area. If you activate both the Print Only Selected and Fit to Page options, you can print the selected objects in magnified format in order to proof it more easily.

 When you print complex, memory-intensive images, it is a good practice to use the Select All command in the Edit menu to select all objects before you click on the Print command, and then print with the Print Only Selected option activated. Some objects in a memory-intensive image may be left out; by using the Select All command and the Print Only Selected option, you minimize this problem.

In the next section, you will learn about a way to print proofs of a graphic that is larger than the page area.

Tiling a Graphic

You can choose from several different methods of sizing a graphic in Corel DRAW!. The most obvious method is to use rulers when creating objects. Another method involves defining a custom page size with the Page Setup command and the Page Setup dialog box. You can also use the Select tool to scale an image to the desired size *after* you have created it.

Posters and other applications, however, require images that are larger than any paper size available for your printer. Even if you print final versions of these images on a Linotronic or other imagesetter that has fewer restrictions on paper size, how do you obtain accurate proofs? The answer is, through *tiling* the image. Tiling refers to the process of printing an oversize image in sections that fit together precisely to form the complete picture. If, for example, you create a poster that is 11 inches wide by 17 inches high and select Tiling as a printing option, the image will print on four 8 1/2- by-11-inch sheets (or on some multiple of whatever size paper you use for your printer).

In the following exercise, you will enlarge the page size for GETINFO.CDR, scale the image to fit the page, and print the entire image with the Tile option enabled.

1. With the GETINFO.CDR image still on your screen, deactivate the Preview Selected Only command in the Display menu, and turn off the preview window. Adjust the viewing magnification to ALL.

2. Click on the Select All command in the Edit menu to select all of the objects in the picture. Then select the Group command in the Arrange menu to keep all objects together.

3. Activate the Show Rulers command in the Display menu, and then select the Page Setup command in the File menu. When the Page Setup dialog box appears, click on the Tabloid option button to activate it. Selecting Tabloid will result in a page that

is 17 inches wide by 11 inches high in landscape format. Click on the OK command button to exit the dialog box. Your page is now approximately twice as large as the graphic. The rulers show you the change in page size, as shown in Figure 18-12.

4. With the Select tool 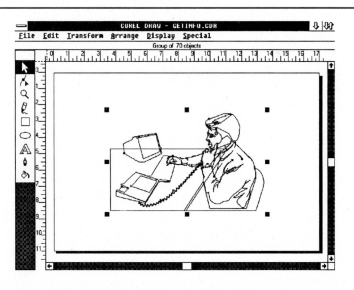 active, position the cursor at the upper-left corner boundary marker of the grouped image. When the cursor turns to a white cross, drag the mouse until you have scaled the image to fit the upper-left corner area of the page. Do the same for the lower-right corner boundary marker.

5. Move the scaled image so that it is centered on the enlarged page, and then select the Print command from the File menu.

6. When the Print Options dialog box appears, deselect any options that are currently active, and then click on the Tiling option to activate it. Select OK. After a few moments, the image

FIGURE 18-12 Changing page size through the Page Setup dialog box

begins to print. Depending on the algorithm your printer uses, the number of sheets used for tiling may vary.

7. When the file has finished printing, deactivate the Show Rulers command, and then select Open from the File menu. Do not save the changes you have made to the size of the page or the picture. When the Open File dialog box appears, double-click on GETINFO.CDR to re-open this file in its original state. Leave this image on the screen for the next exercise.

Since most printers do not print to the edge of the page, you may need to use scissors or a matt knife to cut and paste the tiled pieces together exactly. Still, this method gives you a fairly exact representation of your image as it will print on the imagesetter. If your cutting and pasting skills are also exact, you may be able to use the tiled version of the image as the master copy for commercial printing.

Scaling an Image

There is a difference in Corel DRAW! between scaling an image on the screen with the Select tool and defining a scaling value in the Printer Options dialog box. When you scale an image visually, you are altering its actual dimensions. When you adjust values for the Scale option of the Printer Options dialog box, however, you change only the way the file prints, not its actual size.

Perform the following exercise to print the GETINFO.CDR file at a reduced size, using the Scale option:

1. With the GETINFO.CDR file on the screen, click on any outline within the image. As the status line informs you, the entire image is grouped.

2. Select the Print command from the File menu. When the Print Options dialog box appears, deselect any options that are currently active, and then click on the Scale checkbox. The value 100% (actual size) appears in the associated numeric entry box as soon as you enable this option.

3. Using the bottom scroll arrow, scroll to the lowest value available. This should be 10%, as shown here:

If you have a PostScript printer and are running a version of Corel DRAW! previous to 1.02, the lowest value is 29%. Selecting this value causes the image to print at the specified percentage of its original size. (You may be able to print the graphic at a percentage smaller than 29%, but part of the graphic may be cut off as a result.)

4. Click on OK to begin the printing process. If you have a PostScript printer and version 1.02 or later of Corel DRAW!, the tiny scaled-down image will appear exactly centered on your page. If you are using a PostScript printer but have a version of the software earlier than 1.02, the image will print in the lower-left corner of the page. If you have another kind of printer, the image will probably print in the upper-left corner of the page.

5. Leave this image on the screen for further work.

You have seen how you can reduce the scale of an image to a lower limit of 10% of original size. You can also increase the scale of an image to an upper limit of 300% of original size. If you expand the scale of an image beyond the dimensions of the page, however, remember to activate the Tile option as well.

In the next section, you will experiment with another printing option that involves image size.

Fitting an Image to the Page

Like the Scale option, the Fit to Page option in the Printer Options dialog box does not affect the actual size of the graphic. When you select this option, Corel DRAW! automatically calculates how much it must increase the scale of the graphic or selected object(s) in order to make it fill the entire page. In the following exercise, you will combine the Fit to Page option with the Print Only Selected option you learned about previously.

1. Select any outline within the GETINFO.CDR image; since the entire image is grouped, you select all objects automatically.

2. Click on the Ungroup command in the Arrange menu, and then click on any white space to deselect all objects. As you did in the "Printing Only Selected Objects" section, select the three objects that make up the computer terminal.

3. With the computer terminal selected, click on the Print command in the File menu. When the Print Options dialog box appears, deselect any options that are currently active, and then activate the Print Only Selected Option.

4. Click on the Fit to Page option to activate it, and then select OK to begin printing. After a few moments, the computer terminal, which composes only a small fraction of the total image, appears on the paper, filling the entire sheet.

5. Leave the GETINFO.CDR image on the screen for the next exercise.

As mentioned earlier, the use of the Fit to Page option with Print Only Selected is useful when you want to blow up details within a complex graphic, such as a technical illustration. In the next section, you will experiment with printing an image to a file.

Printing to a File

There are two common reasons why you might choose to print an image to a file.

- You are creating files to send to a service bureau for output on a Linotronic or other imagesetter.

- Your printer is busy and you prefer to copy the print information directly to the printer at a later time.

To print to a file, you select the Print to File option in the Print Options dialog box and name the output file. Printer output files created in applications that run under Microsoft Windows bear the extension .PRN. Corel DRAW! then displays another screen, prompting you to set printing parameters specific to your printer.

The following exercise assumes that you are going to send an output file to a service bureau for use on a PostScript imagesetter. In order to do this, you do not need to have a PostScript printer, but you must have a PostScript printer driver installed in your Windows directory. If you do not have a PostScript driver installed, use the Add New Printer command in the Installation menu of the Control Panel, which you can access from the File menu of Corel DRAW!. Refer to your Microsoft Windows documentation for assistance. Once you have the PostScript driver set up, practice printing the GETINFO.CDR image to a file in the following exercise:

1. With the GETINFO.CDR file on the screen, deselect all objects in the image, and then click on the Control Panel command from the File menu. When the Control Panel window appears, use the Connections and Printer commands in the Setup menu to set up the printer to which you want to send an output file. When you have finished specifying printer parameters, select OK to return to your image.

2. Select Print from the File menu. When the Print Options dialog box displays, deselect any options that are currently active.

3. Click on the Print to File option. (Do not click on the Printer Setup option, because any changes you make at this point will be ignored. A dialog box similar to the Printer Setup dialog box but with a different name will pop up automatically after you finish specifying an output filename.) Select OK; a second dialog box appears with the title Print To File, as shown in Figure 18-13. This dialog box looks and operates similar to the Open File dialog box.

4. Type **GETINFO** in the File text box, and then select Print. Corel DRAW! adds the file extension .PRN automatically to designate this as a printer output file. A third dialog box appears; the contents vary depending on the type of printer that will receive the output file. Figure 18-14 shows a dialog box set up for a PostScript printer, which is the most common case if you are sending an output file to a service bureau. If you are printing a file for use by an HP LaserJet or other printer, the dialog box you see on your screen will be different.

5. Leave the Uncollated copies value at the default of 1, but change Orientation from Portrait to Landscape to match the orientation of the picture. Set Graphics resolution to 1270 dpi and select the Linotronic 100/300/500 option from the Printer list box, as shown in Figure 18-14.

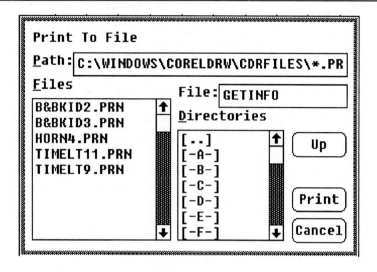

FIGURE 18-13   The Print To File dialog box for specifying an output filename

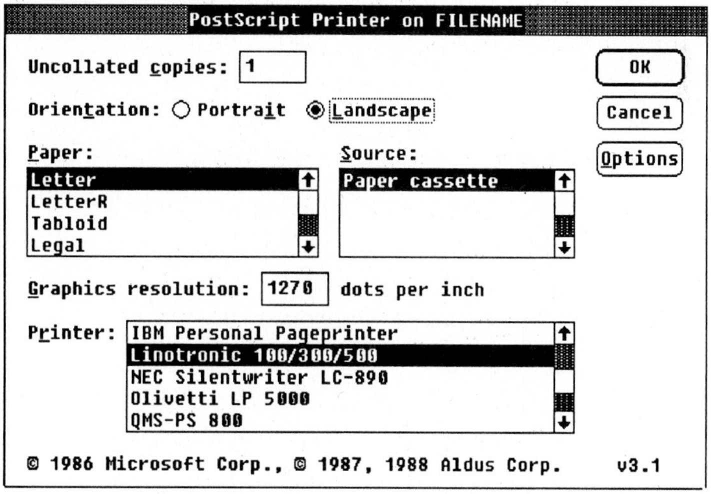

FIGURE 18-14   Printer Setup for a Linotronic imagesetter (Print To File)

6. Click on OK to begin the process of printing to a file.

7. When printing is complete, group all objects in the image and press (CTRL-S) to save your work. Then select New to clear the image from the screen.

There is one more optional step that you should know about if you plan to send an output file to a service bureau. Find out whether the imagesetter at the service bureau is driven by IBM-compatible or Macintosh equipment. If Macintosh equipment drives the imagesetter, you need to edit two characters out of your PostScript output file so that it will print smoothly. To edit the output file, use a word processor or text editor that accepts long files without converting them to another format. Remove the ^D character sequence that appears both at the beginning and at the very end of the file. This control code is specifically an IBM reset code; since the Macintosh equipment does not know how to interpret it, you can print your output file through Macintosh successfully only by deleting both occurrences of the code.

When printing an image to a file, you can combine several options. For example, if you are creating color separations for commercial printing, you might choose to activate the Crop Marks & Crosshairs, Print As Separations, Film Negative, and All Fonts Resident options at the same time.

The next group of sections introduces you to print options that apply specifically to PostScript printers. Since you may use some of these options in combination, the sections are ordered according to task, rather than according to their appearance in the Print Options dialog box.

Printing File Information with
A Graphic (PostScript)

If you are like most illustrators and designers, you probably revise a graphic several times, renaming it with each revision so that you can choose the best version later. You are therefore familiar with the bewilderment of viewing multiple printouts of the same graphic and not knowing which sheet represents which version.

Corel DRAW! provides a convenient solution to this common frustration, available to you if you print to a PostScript device. By activating the Include File Info option in the Printer Options dialog box, you can print the filename, date, and time of printing with your image. This information appears in 10-point Courier outside the left margin of your *page,* not of your graphic. If you activate this option, choose a page size in the Page Setup dialog box that is smaller than the nominal page size. For example, if your graphic fits on an 8 1/2-by-11-inch page, select a 10- by-14-inch or Tabloid page size before you print. This step is necessary because file information is visible *only* if you reduce Page Size below the size of the paper in your printer tray. If you are using 8 1/2-by-11-inch paper, for example, you must use the Page Setup dialog box to define a custom page size of smaller dimensions, and then fit the graphic within that page. You can practice defining a custom page size and printing file information in the following exercise:

1. Open the GETINFO.CDR file. When the file displays, select the Page Setup command in the File menu. Click on the Custom option button in the Page Setup dialog box, and define a page 4.0 inches wide (the Horizontal value) and 3.0 inches high (the Vertical value). Then select OK to exit the dialog box and return to your picture, which is now larger than the new page size.

2. Click on the Zoom-Out tool to be able to see the entire image. Then click on any object in the picture to select the entire grouped image. Scale the picture down to 34% of original size, using the status line for reference. Move the picture so that it fits entirely within the page.

3. Click on the Print command and activate the Include File Info option in the Printer Options dialog box. Check your printer setup and make sure that the Landscape orientation option is selected, and then click on OK to return to the Print Options dialog box. Click on OK again to begin printing. After a few moments, the image emerges from your printer. The filename, date, and time of printing appear in 10-point Courier just beyond the left boundary of the custom page, at a 90-degree angle to the image.

4. Select the Save As command in the File menu. When the Save As dialog box appears, type **GETINFO2**, and then click on the Save command button. Leave this image on the screen for subsequent exercises.

Since Corel DRAW! generates object-oriented art, you can scale your images without distortion. It is therefore convenient to change page size so that you can print file information for your own use. Another common use for the Include File Info option is in conjunction with the Print As Separations and Crop Marks & Crosshairs options, which you will learn about in the next section.

Printing Color Separations, Crop Marks, And Registration Marks (PostScript)

When you began to specify outline fill and object fill colors in Chapters 14 and 15, you learned about the differences between spot color and process color in the commercial printing process. If you have a PostScript printer or plan to send output files to a

PostScript imagesetter, you can reduce your commercial printing expenses by generating color separations on paper or in a file. This reduces the number of intermediary steps that commercial printers must perform to prepare your images for printing.

Put simply, *color separation* is the process of separating the colors that you specify for an entire image into the primary component colors. When you generate color separations using the process color system (CMYK), the output is four separate sheets, one each for the cyan, magenta, yellow, and black color components of the image. The commercial printer uses the four sheets to create separate overlays for each color, in preparation for making printing plates. When you generate color separations using the spot color system, the output is one sheet for each color specified in the image, and the commercial printer creates overlays for each color. This process becomes very expensive as the number of spot colors in an image increases, so it is a good idea to use the process color system if you plan to have more than six colors in a given image.

When you generate color separations using the Print As Separations option in the Print Options dialog box, it is also important to include *crop marks* and *registration marks* (called crosshairs by Corel DRAW!). You can see examples of these marks in Figure 18-15a through 18-15d. Crop marks are small horizontal and vertical lines printed at each corner of the image to show the exact boundaries of the image. A registration mark, two of which appear at the inside of each corner of an image, are crossed lines with a circle. Both crop marks and registration marks assist the commercial printer in aligning color separation overlays exactly; if misalignment were to occur, the final printed product would display a host of color distortions. When you activate the Crop Marks & Crosshairs option with Print As Separations, Corel DRAW! prints a color bar for correct color matching below the lower boundary of the image. The color for the page, together with the halftone screen angle and density, appear beyond the crop marks at the left side of the image.

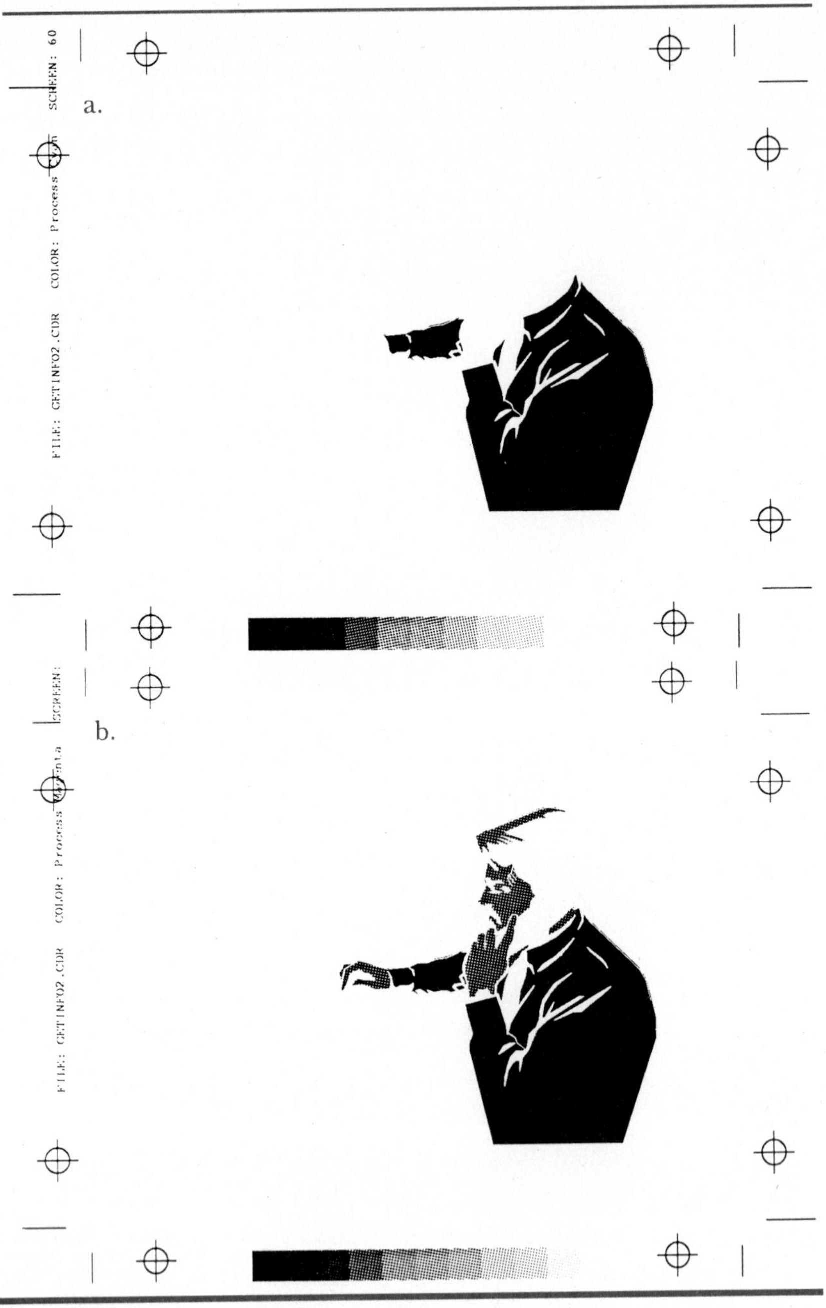

FIGURE 18-15 Process color separations for GETINFO.CDR: (a) cyan, (b) magenta, (c) yellow, (d) black

FIGURE 18-15 Process color separations for
GETINFO.CDR: (a) cyan, (b) magenta, (c)
yellow, (d) black (*continued*)

Just as with File Information, you can see crop marks and registration marks from your printer *only* if you define a custom page size that is smaller than the size of the paper you are using. This caution also applies if you are printing to Linotronic or other imagesetting equipment.

In the following exercise, you will generate PostScript color separations for selected objects in the GETINFO2.CDR file using the Print As Separations, Crop Marks & Crosshairs, and Print Only Selected options. If you send files to a PostScript imagesetter but do not have a PostScript printer for your draft copies, you may perform this exercise with the Print to File option activated as well.

1. With the GETINFO2.CDR image still on the screen, click on any object. Since all objects in the image are grouped, you select the entire picture. Click on the Ungroup command in the Arrange menu, and then deselect all objects by clicking on any white space.

2. Turn on the preview window and activate Preview Selected Only. Then, select various objects in turn, magnifying portions of the image if necessary for more accurate selection. When you select a color object (you will recall that imported .CGM images transfer into Corel DRAW! with outlines and colors as separate objects), access the Uniform Fill dialog box and check the process color values that have been specified.

3. After you have observed the fill colors of various objects, magnify just the right half of the image, which contains the male figure. With the Select tool active, draw a marquee around all of the objects that make up the upper body, hands, and head, as well as the telephone headset and part of the telephone cord. Your preview window should display only these objects, as shown in Figure 18-16. Since files in .CGM format transfer into Corel DRAW! with fill colors as separate objects, you may need

to experiment a little to make sure you have all necessary objects and fill colors selected. When you have the right combination, the status line will show 52 objects selected.

4. Click on the Group command in the Arrange menu to group all of the selected objects. These are the objects for which you will print color separations, so leave them selected.

5. Press (CTRL-S) to save your changes to the image, then select the Print command in the File menu. When the Print Options dialog box appears, deselect any options that are currently active. Then activate the Print Only Selected, Crop Marks &

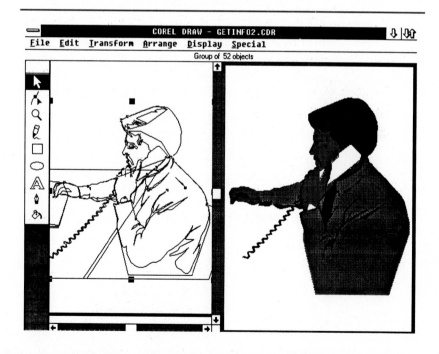

FIGURE 18-16   Selecting a portion of the image for printing
color separations

Crosshairs, and Print As Separations options. If your own draft printer is not a PostScript printer, you can select the Print to File option, too. (If you select Print to File, do not bother to check your printer setup yet. Changes you make in the Printer Setup dialog box will not take effect until that dialog box pops up automatically later in the process. You will specify printer setup automatically after you specify an output filename.)

6. Select OK. A second dialog box, the Color Separations dialog box, now appears, as shown in Figure 18-17. In the upper-left corner of the dialog box is a list box containing the names of the four process colors. (If you were preparing to print an image using the spot color method, you would see specific color names here instead.) Under Screen Angles are four screen angle values, one for each of the process colors. Do *not* alter these values unless you are very experienced in four-color printing

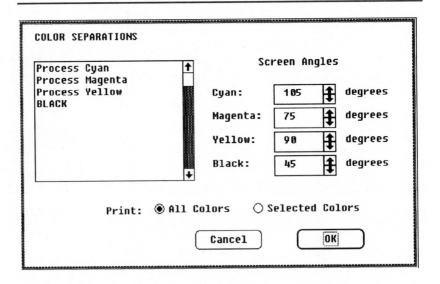

FIGURE 18-17   The Color Separations dialog box

and know exactly what you are doing. These angles are preset to ensure the best possible color alignment and registration. At the bottom of the dialog box is Print:, followed by two option buttons: All Colors and Selected Colors. For this exercise, leave All Colors selected, or click on this option if it is not selected already. For future reference, you can choose to print separations for either one color or a few colors at a time. To do so, just click on the Selected Colors option button and then on a desired color in the list box. To highlight more than one color, click on the name of the first color, press and hold (SHIFT), and click on each additional color.

7. Select OK to save these settings and exit the Color Separations dialog box. If you are printing directly to your own PostScript printer, Corel DRAW! now begins printing the separations. The printing of color separation sheets takes longer than simply printing the file normally. In a few moments, four sheets of paper appear. The first shows the color values for cyan, the second for magenta, the third for yellow, and the fourth for black. As shown in Figure 18-15a through 18-15d, each sheet also contains a color bar, crop marks, registration marks, file-name and date information, and color and screen information.

8. If you chose to print to a file, the Print to File dialog box appears when you exit the Color Separations dialog box, prompting you to name the output file. Type **COLORSEP** and select OK; Corel DRAW! adds the extension .PRN automatically. The Printer Setup dialog box now appears, bearing the title Post-Script Printer on Filename.

9. Make sure that the option button for Landscape orientation is highlighted, and (assuming that you are sending this output file to a Linotronic imagesetter) that you select the Linotronic 100/300/500 option in the Printer list box. Notice that the

Graphics resolution value changes from 300 to 1270 dpi as soon as you select this printer.

10. To check other important file printing parameters, click on the Options command button in the upper-right corner of the Post-Script Printer on Filename dialog box. Make sure that the Job timeout value is 0 seconds and that Download each job is specified for the header. Then, select OK to begin printing the file to the specified drive and directory. You can then send the file to a PostScript service bureau for output.

11. Leave the GETINFO2.CDR image on the screen for the next exercise.

If you fill objects with any PostScript halftone screen pattern other than the default pattern, your custom settings will have no effect when you print color separations for the objects, because Corel DRAW! uses the halftone screen function to calculate color separation angles. This limitation applies to every object in the file, not only to the objects for which you print color separations. If you assign non-default screens to objects for which you must print color separations, your screen assignments have no effect.

Keep in mind that you can combine any number of options when you specify color separations. For example, you can tile separations for an oversize image, include file information, make selected objects fit the custom page size exactly, or scale the selected image for printing. If you are sure that the current image is in a final version, you can also print it in film negative format, as you will do in the next section.

Printing in Film Negative Format (PostScript)

In commercial black-and-white or color printing, the transfer of the image or of color separations to film negative is one of the last steps to occur before the printing plates are made. Think of the difference between a snapshot and the negative from which it was produced: colors in the negative appear inverted and backward. The same thing happens when you activate the Film Negative option in the Print Options dialog box. White image backgrounds fill with printer toner, dark areas in the original image print as light, and the image is reversed horizontally. If you print in this format with Include File Info or Crop Marks & Crosshairs activated, even the file and color separation screen information is printed backward.

Use of the Film Negative option can save you money, but only if you are certain that the color separations in the image (if any) are in final form and will not need any further color correction or screen angle adjustments. If you intend to send a film negative file to a service bureau for output on a high-resolution imagesetter, ask the bureau management whether they can output your file in film negative format automatically. Many imagesetters can print your color separation file as a film negative just by flipping a switch. This might be preferable if your aim is to achieve a higher output resolution than that provided by your own 300 dpi laser printer.

In the following exercise, you will print one color separation screen for the GETINFO2.CDR file in film negative format. If you have your own PostScript laser printer, you can print this screen directly onto paper. If you use PostScript only to send files to a service bureau, steps are provided so that you can print the film negative format to a file.

1. With the GETINFO2.CDR file open, select the same grouped objects that you printed as color separations in the previous exercise. Then click on the Print command in the File menu.

2. Make sure that the print options that you used in the previous exercise—Print Only Selected, Crop Marks & Crosshairs, Print As Separations—are still active. (If you printed to a file in the previous exercise, make sure that the Print to File option is still active, too.) Then, click on the Film Negative option and select OK. The Color Separation dialog box appears, as before.

3. You do not need to print out all four color separation sheets to see how the Film Negative option works, so click on the Selected Colors option button at the bottom of the dialog box. Highlight the Process Magenta option in the process colors list

FIGURE 18-18   Color separation sheet for process magenta, printed in film negative format

box, and then click on the OK command button. If you are printing directly to your printer, the color separation now begins to print. In a few moments, the color separation sheet for process magenta appears in film negative format, as shown in Figure 18-18. The image in the figure shows only the graphic and its file information, but your output sheet is covered with toner all the way to the edges of the printable page area. If you elected to print to a file, the Print to File dialog box appears, prompting you to enter a filename.

4. If you are printing to a file, type **NEG-MAG** in the File text box, and then click on the Print command button. The Printer Setup screen (PostScript Printer on Filename) now appears, as in the previous exercise.

5. Repeat steps 9 and 10 of the previous exercise, and click on OK to generate your file. When you finish printing, leave the image on the screen, with the grouped objects selected.

You need not limit yourself to printing in film negative format when you are working with a spot or process color image. You can also use this printing option with black-and-white images.

In the next section, you will learn more about the Default Screen Frequency option and how it affects your printouts.

Setting Default Screen Frequency (PostScript)

The Default Screen Frequency option determines the value that appears in the PostScript Halftone Screen dialog box. As you may recall from Chapter 14, you can access this dialog box whenever you assign a spot color to an outline or object fill. The frequency of the default screen pattern determines how fine the halftone resolution will appear on the printed page. Each type of PostScript printer has a default screen frequency, with the most common being 60 lines per inch for 300 dpi printers and 90 or more for high-resolution imagesetters. The standard setting for Default Screen Frequency in the Print Options dialog box is Device's, because in most cases it is best to let the printer you are using determine the screen frequency.

You can override this standard value, however, by clicking on the Custom option button and entering the desired value in the associated numeric entry box. Thereafter, *all* of the objects in your image will have the custom screen frequency. The most common reasons for altering this value are

- You want to create special effects such as the text examples that appear on page 118 of the Corel DRAW! user's manual.

- You experience visible "banding" effects while printing objects with fountain fills and want the color transitions to occur more smoothly.

In the first case, you would increase the default screen value for the selected printer, while in the second, you would decrease it. If you have a 300 dpi PostScript printer, perform the following brief exercise to compare how reducing the default screen frequency alters the appearance of your output.

1. With the GETINFO2.CDR image open and the grouped objects selected, click on the Print command in the File menu. The Print Options dialog box appears.

2. Make sure that the Print Only Selected, Crop Marks & Crosshairs, and Print As Separations options are activated. Deselect any other options that show an "x" in their respective checkboxes. Then click on the Custom option button in the Default Screen Frequency section of the dialog box. If you have

a 300 dpi PostScript printer, the number 60 appears in the numeric entry box next to Custom. This is the default screen frequency for your printer.

3. Change the Custom value to 45 lines per inch, and then click on OK.

4. When the Color Separations dialog box appears, click on Selected Colors and highlight Process Magenta, as you did in the previous exercise. These settings will cause only the color separation for the color magenta to print.

5. Click on the Print command button of the Color Separations dialog box to begin printing. After a few moments, the color separation sheet appears. If you compare this output sheet with the one produced in the "Printing Color Separations, Crop Marks, and Registration Marks" section, you will not notice much difference in the appearance of the man's shirt. But if you look closely at the hair, hands, and face (all of which have a lower percentage of magenta), you will see that the dot pattern of the 45 lines per inch screen printout appears coarser.

6. Select New from the File menu to clear the screen of the GETINFO2.CDR file. Do not save any changes to the image.

If you alter the default screen frequency value in order to proof an image, be sure to change the frequency back to Device's before sending the final output file to a service bureau. Otherwise, your image will not appear to have a much higher resolution than what your printer could offer.

 If you assign a *custom* PostScript halftone screen pattern to an object while drawing, any changes you make to the *default* screen frequency at printing time will have no effect on the screen frequency of that object.

In the next section, you will become familiar with the uses of the All Fonts Resident printing option. Since the example image does not contain any text, you will not have an exercise, but the principle of the option is quite straightforward.

All Fonts Resident (PostScript)

The All Fonts Resident option in the Print Options dialog box is designed with the occasional user of Adobe PostScript fonts and laser service bureaus in mind. As you are aware, Corel DRAW! comes supplied with 102 different typeface and typestyle combinations. Although these are of very high quality, they do not contain the "hints" (program instructions) that allow genuine Adobe PostScript fonts to print at extremely small sizes with very little degradation. Therefore, if you use text with a small typesize in a drawing, you might choose to substitute equivalent Adobe PostScript fonts for the Corel DRAW fonts at printing time. You activate the All Fonts Resident option to instruct the PostScript printer to substitute the correct fonts.

The All Fonts Resident option is intended for temporary use. If you have purchased downloadable fonts from Adobe and *always* want your printer to automatically substitute Adobe fonts for Corel DRAW! typefaces, you should alter the [CorelDrwFonts] section of your WIN.INI file according to the instructions in Appendix D. If you use the All Fonts Resident option when you send output files to a laser service bureau, make sure that the service bureau has all of the necessary PostScript fonts downloaded. If you specify a PostScript font that is not in the host printer's memory, the font will print as Courier instead.

 The All Fonts Resident option does not apply to fonts from other manufacturers that you have designated as substitutes for Corel DRAW! fonts through the WFNBOSS utility. Windows considers any non-Adobe fonts that you substitute through WFNBOSS as non-resident fonts.

In the final sections of this chapter, you will find tips for smooth printing based on the type of printer you are using and the features of your artwork.

HARDWARE-SPECIFIC PRINTING TIPS

Even if you closely follow all recommended printing procedures, such as checking the Printer Setup options or setting Job timeout at 0 seconds and transmission retry at 600 seconds, you may encounter printing difficulties on occasion. Some difficulties involve settings for your specific printer type, while others may involve features of the artwork you are trying to print. This section deals with printing problems that could be dependent on hardware and makes suggestions for solving them. The final section, "Hints for Printing Complex Artwort on PostScript Printers," deals with printing problems that might be related to features of the artwork itself.

 Regardless of the type of printer you use, you may sometimes encounter one of several error messages indicating that you should cancel the printing process. In most cases, click on the Retry command button. Repeated attempts to print often force the data to and through your printer.

PostScript Printers and Controller Boards

Corel DRAW! is designed for the PostScript Plus type of printer, with its 11 resident typeface families and 2 or 3 MB of RAM. It also runs on older versions of PostScript printers that contain only

four typeface families, but you may experience slower performance or other limitations if the memory in your printer is not
sufficient. If this happens, check with your printer dealer to see
whether a memory upgrade is possible. If you run Corel DRAW!
with an older model of PostScript printer, you should edit your
Windows WIN.INI file to notify the printer that certain PostScript
fonts are not available. To do this, proceed through the following
exercise.

1. From the Windows directory of the MS-DOS Executive, double-click on the WIN.INI file name to begin editing this file.

2. Go to the [CorelDrwFonts] section of the WIN.INI file and look
   at the listings of fonts that are followed by the number 3 at the
   end of the line. These are PostScript Plus fonts, not available
   for the older models of PostScript printers.

3. Change each 3 to a 0. This tells Corel DRAW! always to
   substitute Corel DRAW! fonts for the PostScript fonts when
   you print the file to a PostScript printer.

4. Save these changes to the WIN.INI file and exit Notepad.

5. Exit and then restart Windows to cause your changes to take
   effect.

In today's market, a number of so-called PostScript compatible
controller boards are available for the HP LaserJet and compatibles. You should be aware that there is a distinction between
genuine PostScript-controller boards licensed by Adobe and Post-
Script-compatible controller boards that are only as compatible as
their interpreters. If your LaserJet printer is equipped with a
genuine PostScript controller board, you should be able to print
everything that would be possible on a genuine PostScript printer.

This is not necessarily true for a printer equipped with a Post-Script-*compatible* controller board, although some of these boards work extremely well.

If you have a genuine PostScript printer or if your printer has a genuine PostScript controller board, the following tips should help you prevent printing problems when running Corel DRAW!. Potential problems are organized according to whether your printer is connected to a parallel or a serial port.

PARALLEL PRINTERS   Many printing problems experienced with PostScript printers that are parallel-connected are printer or job timeout problems. To avoid such problems, check for the following:

- The Windows Spooler should be turned off (see the "Preparing to Print" section of this chapter).

- Make sure that your printer is set up for batch processing mode, not interactive mode. Interactive mode does not permit the printing of imported bitmaps.

- See whether you can change Wait timeout directly from the printer as well as from the Windows Control Panel. Many PostScript printers provide utilities that let you specify these times independent of any software application.

- Set Job timeout, Device not selected, and Transmission retry settings as recommended in the "Preparing to Print" section of this chapter.

You will find additional tips related to printing complex artwork with PostScript printers in the "Hints for Printing Complex Artwork on PostScript Printers" section at the end of this chapter.

SERIAL PRINTERS   Although most PostScript printers attach to IBM-compatible computers with a parallel cable (the faster and preferred printing method), some printers require the use of a serial cable. To ensure trouble-free printing with a serially connected printer, compare your printer setup with the following checklist:

- Check the Communications command in the Setup menu of the Control Panel and make certain that the Communications settings are correct. (Refer to your printer manual.) Make sure that hardware handshaking is active.

- Make sure that hardware handshaking is also activated from the Print Options dialog box. You will find this well-hidden control by clicking on the Printer Setup command button, then on the Options command button of the Printer Setup dialog box, and finally on the Handshaking command button within the Printer Options dialog box. Some older PostScript printer models do not permit hardware handshaking; if this is the case with your printer, you may want to contact Corel Systems technical support for assistance.

- Check your printer cable. Some serial cables seem not to transmit all available data with graphics applications.

- From DOS, check the COMM.DRV file on your Microsoft Windows disks. This is the serial driver for your printer. If the COM.DRV file is 4484 bytes long or shows a date of 9/07/88, you may have a faulty driver; contact Microsoft for an updated one.

HP LaserJet Printers and Compatibles

Since the HP LaserJet and compatible printers connect to your computer by means of a parallel rather than a serial cable, you should refer to the "Parallel Printers" section under "PostScript

Printers and Controller Boards." Printers that are guaranteed to be 100% LaserJet compatible perform equally well with the genuine HP LaserJet. Printers that are HP LaserJet clones and that do not guarantee 100% compatibility may present erratic problems, which vary with the printer driver and manufacturer.

If your LaserJet or compatible is an older model and you have only 512 K of memory, you may find that you are unable to print full-page graphics with complex features such as outlines and fountain fills. Many LaserJet-type printers split a graphic that is too large for memory into strips and print the strips over several sheets. If you plan to print large graphics regularly, see whether you can expand your printer's memory. If this is not possible, try reducing the size of the graphic on the page. Since object-oriented graphics can be scaled up or down without distortion, this should be a satisfactory solution. As a last resort, reduce the printing resolution of the graphic to 150 dpi, or even 75 dpi, in the Printer Setup dialog box.

HP DeskJet and PaintJet

The HP DeskJet is a black-and-white inkjet printer that is almost completely compatible with the HP LaserJet. There are different versions of the driver for this printer, however. Check to make sure that you have the latest model driver when printing graphics from Corel DRAW!. In addition, avoid designing large filled objects or layered objects; the ink for the DeskJet is water-based and could run or smear if you layer it too thickly.

The HP PaintJet manifests Corel DRAW! printing problems somewhat erratically, and there are no "cookbook" solutions. It is important to keep your ink jet nozzles for each color clean and unclogged, however, to avoid smearing colors. If you have checked your Printer Setup and cannot find a solution, try printing your problem image to a file and sending it to Corel DRAW! technical support.

Genuine HP and Other Plotters

The Windows driver for plotters seems to be written specifically for the HP Plotter line. If you have a clone from another manufacturer, the Windows driver may not work well for you when you print images from Corel DRAW!. Contact your plotter manufacturer to see if a driver for Corel DRAW! is available.

In addition, the driver for the HP Plotter supports only hairline outlines and no fills for objects that you create in Corel DRAW!.

Dot-Matrix Printers

The results of printing Corel DRAW! graphics on dot-matrix printers are very erratic, owing to the large number of printer types available and the many different drivers written for them. Some dot-matrix printers cannot print complex files at all, while others print part of a page and stop. Dot-matrix printers that have multi-color ribbons do not all lay colors down on the page in the same order. This can result in muddy colors that do not match what you see on your screen. Depending on the problem, you may wish to contact your printer manufacturer to see if a driver for Windows is available.

HINTS FOR PRINTING COMPLEX ARTWORK ON POSTSCRIPT PRINTERS

The term "complex" artwork, when applied to Corel DRAW!, can include a variety of features. Among them are curves with many nodes, multiple fountain fills in an image, PostScript halftone screens and textures, and text converted to curves. Many printing problems that are traceable to the complexity of features are encountered chiefly with PostScript printers. This happens because the PostScript language has certain internal limits. When these are exceeded, the affected object may not print at all or may print incorrectly. For example, objects that contain more than 200 to 400 nodes may cause your PostScript print job to crash.

You might not experience a problem with the same object if you are printing to an HP LaserJet printer, because the HP LaserJet does not recognize nodes; it interprets all graphic images simply as collections of pixels. Some PostScript printer manufacturers, such as QMS, allow you to run PostScript printers in LaserJet mode. If you have such a printer, try switching to LaserJet mode and printing your "problem" image again. If the file prints correctly, it is safe to guess that an internal PostScript limitation is causing printing problems in PostScript mode.

Using the Downloadable PostScript Error Handler

You may not be aware that Microsoft Windows provides an error handler that helps you diagnose PostScript printing problems. To understand how the error handler works, you need to know that PostScript prints the "bottom" or first-drawn object in the image first, followed by each succeeding layer. When you download the error handler and try to print a problem file, the printer begins with the first object and prints as far as it can. When the printer encounters an object that is problematic, it stops and prints out the objects completed so far, together with an error message. Although the messages are in PostScript code language, they are in many cases intelligible enough for you to decipher what the basic problem might be. The purchase of a relatively inexpensive PostScript manual, of which several are available, can help you even further.

To download the PostScript error handler to your printer and keep it resident there until you turn the printer off, follow these steps:

1. From the Print Options dialog box, click on the Printer Setup command button.

2. From the Printer Setup screen, click on the Options command button to access the PostScript Printer Options dialog box.

3. Click on the Errors command button. The Error handler options dialog box appears as shown here:

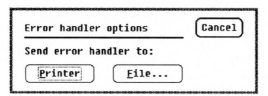

4. If you are printing to your own PostScript printer, click on the Printer option button to download the error handler directly to the printer. This setting has no effect if you sent a file to a service bureau, for most service bureaus use their own error handlers.

The Windows error handler should be helpful in fixing problems that already exist within a graphic. However, there are other measures you can take to design a graphic that will avoid printing problems entirely. The following sections explain a few of these measures briefly.

Printing PostScript Textures

The 42 PostScript textures described in greater detail in Chapter 15 and Appendix E were created with highly complex mathematical algorithms. Sometimes, you may not be able to make an object with a PostScript texture print correctly. If this happens, try adjusting the parameters to avoid extremely dense patterns. If the image does not print at all, try removing excess objects. PostScript textures can be so memory-intensive that they do not tolerate many other objects within the same graphic. In general, you should use these textures as fills in a limited number of objects within a given graphic. Short text strings used as headlines (but not converted to curves) are among the best applications for PostScript texture fills.

If you are a desktop publisher, you may sometimes find that a page containing a Corel DRAW! graphic with PostScript textures does not print. Try removing everything from the page except the PostScript texture graphic, and then attempt to print the page again. Sometimes a page becomes too complex for PostScript if it contains both PostScript textures and other elements.

Printing Complex Curve Objects

As previously mentioned, the current version of PostScript may give you difficulty when you try to print images that contain objects with more than 200 nodes. If you suspect that an object has too many nodes and could be causing problems, click on it with the Shaping tool. The number of nodes contained in the object appears on the status line. If the number of nodes seems too high or approaches the danger zone, reshape the object and eliminate any unnecessary nodes.

When you drag one or more control points of a curve object outward by a great distance, the boundary markers of the object may extend much further outward than you can see. If you print a file containing many curve objects and some objects just do not print, it may be that you have not selected them. One remedy is to click on the Select All command in the Edit menu before you begin to print, and then activate Print Only Selected in the Print Options dialog box. This procedure ensures that all objects in the graphic are selected, no matter how extensively you may have reshaped them.

Printing Fountain Fills

A common complaint when printing fountain-filled objects on PostScript printers is that "banding" effects can occur. In other words, the edges of each fountain stripe are clearly visible and do not blend into the next stripe smoothly. This occurs both with 300 dpi printers and with Linotronic or other imagesetters that have a higher resolution. With LaserJet and compatible printers, solving this problem is easy: you simply increase the Fountain Stripes value in the Preferences dialog box to create a smoother blend. When you alter this value with a PostScript printer, however, it affects your preview window only, not the way the image prints.

To reduce banding effects on Fountain Fills when you print to a 300 dpi PostScript printer, click on the Custom Default Screen Frequency option button in the Print Options dialog box, and reduce the frequency to a number between 30 and 45 lines per inch according to your taste. This procedure results in a somewhat coarser dot pattern, but definitely improves the smoothness of color transition in a Fountain Fill.

 If you alter the default screen frequency for a draft printout on a 300 dpi printer, remember to change the Default Screen Frequency setting back to Device's before you create an output file to be sent to a high-resolution imagesetter. When you alter the default screen frequency, your image can still contain objects that have a non-standard halftone screen pattern.

Printing on 300 dpi Printers Versus High-Resolution Imagesetters

It may sometimes happen that your graphic prints on your own 300 dpi PostScript printer, but causes a high-resolution imagesetter to crash. This occurs because at higher resolutions, the amount of information in a file multiplies. It is possible that your graphic exceeds certain internal PostScript limits at these higher resolutions, but didn't at the lower resolution. To avoid such problems, try reducing the resolution at which the imagesetter prints, using the Default Screen Frequency setting in Printer Setup dialog box. Alternatively, you can define a custom default screen frequency for the imagesetter before you create the output file. If you do so, make certain that your custom frequency is lower than that of the imagesetter. These measures help reduce the amount of data in fills and outlines.

SUMMARY

Although Microsoft Windows provides drivers for many different printers and plotters, not all of them work equally well with Corel DRAW!. PostScript printers and imagesetters, HP LaserJets and compatibles, and HP PaintJets and DeskJets are the printers that Corel DRAW! supports best. You may obtain satisfactory output with other printers and plotters, but your results will vary because of the multiplicity of standards. PostScript controller boards that are licensed by Adobe Systems may perform as well as genuine PostScript printers.

Before you print, check your printer setup in the Control Panel and adjust Printer Timeouts if necessary. The Device not selected setting should be at 15 seconds, while the Transmission retry value should stand at 600 seconds. This allows the computer sufficient time to send all of the data in a complex graphics file to the printer. You should also disable the Windows Spooler for improved graphics printing.

To print an image, you select options in the Print Options dialog box, which you access by clicking on the Print command in the File menu. The five print options—Print Only Selected, Tile, Scale, Fit to Page, and Print to File—are available for all printers. These options respectively let you print selected objects in lieu of an entire picture, print oversize images in pieces using several sheets, change the image size for printing purposes only, and send an output file to a laser service bureau.

With PostScript printers and imagesetters you have six other options available. The Include File Info option lets you print the filename and the date and time of printing on your printed page. The Print As Separations option lets you print color separation sheets for either spot or process colors for use by a commercial printer. Normally, you also activate the Crop

Marks & Crosshairs option when printing color separations, so that the commercial printer can align the separation masters exactly with a minimum of error. You can also choose to print your image in film negative format, in order to reduce the number of costly steps that go into the commercial printing of an image. For proofing purposes, you can alter the default screen frequency of all objects in a graphic through the two Default Screen Frequency options, Device's and Custom. Finally, you may activate the All Fonts Resident option to instruct a PostScript printer or imagesetter to substitute genuine Adobe fonts for the Corel DRAW! screen fonts at printing time.

The printing options offer you flexibility in determining what and how to print. You can combine multiple print options in accordance with your needs.

For PostScript printers, Windows provides a downloadable error handler. This error handler helps you understand why some images cause printing problems and how to fix them. You can avoid other PostScript printing problems by planning PostScript textures carefully, editing out extra nodes in complex curve objects, reducing banding effects in Fountain Fills, and monitoring the arrangement of objects before and after printing.

chapter 19

CREATING AND USING MACROS

Recording a Macro
Saving and Naming a Macro
Playing Back a Macro

I f you find that you are performing the same series of operations over and over, you will benefit by using a shortcut. With Corel DRAW!, you can design your own software shortcuts, called *macros,* at any time.

A macro is a custom command that lets you automate a sequence of repetitive steps. For example, you might define a macro that performs the following actions:

• Duplicates an object a specified number of times

• Groups all of the duplicated objects

- Moves the grouped objects to another location

- Skews all of the grouped objects at a specific angle

If you performed these operations manually, you would have to remember each step, strike a number of keys, and take several trips to the menus with your mouse. The macro saves you time and prevents omission errors in routine work.

The process of defining and using a macro in Corel DRAW! always involves these three steps:

- *Recording a macro*   The Record Macro command in the Special menu lets you record the series of steps that you want to automate. This command is available only when a single object, or a combined object is currently selected. In addition, the steps that you record must consist of operations that you perform on the selected object(s). Actions such as opening or importing a file, changing the magnification, or turning on the preview window cannot be recorded.

- *Finishing a macro*   When you are finished recording steps, you select the Finish Macro command from the Special menu to name and save the new macro.

- *Playing back the macro*   To apply an existing macro to single or multiple objects, you select the object(s), click on the Play Macro command in the Special menu, and then choose the name of the desired macro.

In this chapter, you will define, name and play back a sample macro, and perhaps develop ideas for macros that suit your own applications.

RECORDING A MACRO

Most word processors let you record any series of keystrokes or commands in a macro. In Corel DRAW!, however, you can record only those steps that consist of actions you can perform on an existing object or group of objects. Actions such as adjusting magnification, turning the preview window on or off, or opening a file cannot be recorded. In addition, the Record Macro command is available only when a single object, a grouped object, or a combined object is currently selected.

As soon as you select the Record Macro command, the word "Macro" appears at the left side of the status line as a reminder that you are in macro recording mode. Every action you perform directly on the selected object is recorded until you select the Finish Macro command. If you make a mistake, click on Undo in the Edit menu immediately to undo your last action; the macro will not "remember" a mistake that you have corrected.

While you are in macro recording mode, the availability of Corel DRAW! tools and menu commands is different than at other times. For example, other objects in the picture appear in your editing window with dotted outlines, as a reminder that you cannot select or edit them while recording. If the object you use to define the macro is a text object, you cannot use the Edit Text command or change text attributes while recording. If the steps in your macro involve creating duplicate objects from the selected object, however, you can use the commands in the Arrange menu to rearrange, align, or group those objects.

The toolbox behaves differently in macro recording mode, too. The Select, Outline, and Fill tools are all available, but you cannot activate the Shaping tool or any of the drawing tools.

File	Edit	Transform
Export	Clear	Rotate&Skew
Control Panel	Duplicate	Stretch&Mirror
	Copy Style From	Clear Transformations
	Select All	

Arrange	Display	Special
(varies)	Snap To Grid	Finish Macro
	Grid Size	
	Show Rulers	
	Show Status Line	
	Show Preview	
	Show Bitmaps	

TABLE 19-1   Menu Commands Available in Macro Recording Mode

Table 19-1 shows the menu commands that are available when you are in macro recording mode. A brief survey of these commands should give you ideas for potential macro applications. The commands most amply represented are in the Display menu—whatever your purpose, you should use the preview window and other display aids to see the results of your modifications.

In the following exercise, you will define a macro that designs a special type of shadow effect for any selected object or group of objects. You will define the macro using a text object, but later on you will apply it to another type of object.

1. To prepare the display for this exercise, activate the Show Rulers and Snap To Grid commands in the Display menu. Select Grid Size, set Grid Frequency to 8 per inch, and then select OK.

2. Select the Page Setup command in the File menu. When the Page Setup dialog box appears, click on the Portrait and Letter option buttons if they are not already selected, and then press (ENTER) or click on the OK command button. The Corel DRAW! page redisplays with a width of 8 1/2 inches and a height of 11 inches.

3. Select the Preferences command in the Special menu and set the Place Duplicate values to 0.25 and 0.25 inch. Select OK to save these new settings, and exit the Preferences dialog box.

4. Click on the Fill tool  and then on the fountain fill icon in the pop-up menu. The message box in Figure 19-1 appears. Because you have not selected an object, you are asked if you intend to set a new default fill color. Click on OK to access the 'New Object' Fountain Fill dialog box. When the Fountain Fill dialog box appears, adjust your settings to match the settings in Figure 19-2. Choose a linear fountain fill at an angle of 135 degrees, with a start color (From) of black (Color 0, Tint 100%) and an end color (To) of white (Color 0, Tint 0%). Select OK to save these settings.

'NEW OBJECT' UNIFORM FILL

(?) Nothing is currently selected. Change 'New Object' Setting -- used when new objects are created?

[OK]   [Cancel]

FIGURE 19-1   The 'New Object' Uniform Fill message box

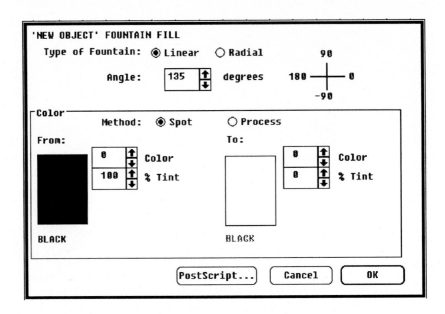

FIGURE 19-2   Linear fountain fill settings for the macro recording exercise

5. Click on the Outline tool ⬚ and the Custom Outline Pen icon. Again, the New Object message box appears. Click on OK to access the Outline Pen dialog box and set new outline pen default values. Your settings should match the ones in Figure 19-3: line Type solid, Behind Fill active, sharp corners, butt line cap styles, Width 0.08 inch, Angle 50 degrees, and Stretch 40%. Select OK to exit this dialog box with the new settings.

6. Click on the Outline tool again and then on the black fill icon in the second row of the pop-up menu. Once more, the 'New Object' Outline Fill message box appears, asking you if you mean to select a new default outline color. Select OK to save black as the new outline color.

7. Adjust your viewing magnification to 1:1. Now you are ready to draw.

8. Activate the Text tool 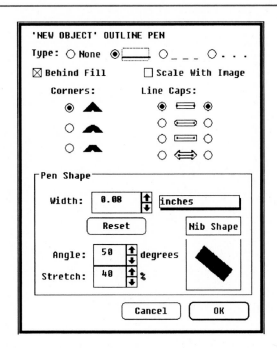 and select an insertion point at the 1-inch mark along the horizontal ruler and the 4 1/2-inch mark along the vertical ruler. When the Text dialog box appears, type **Shadow Cast** in the text entry box, and set text attributes as Homeward Bound Normal, Left Alignment, 60.0 points. Click on the Spacing command button and set inter-character spacing to 0.20 ems. Then click on OK. The text displays in your editing window.

9. Turn on the preview window, adjust it to a top-to-bottom format, and then magnify just the letters. The text displays as

FIGURE 19-3   Text string created with new default outline and fill settings

shown in Figure 19-4. The calligraphic angle and stretch of the outline gives the text a feeling of weight.

10. Activate the Select tool 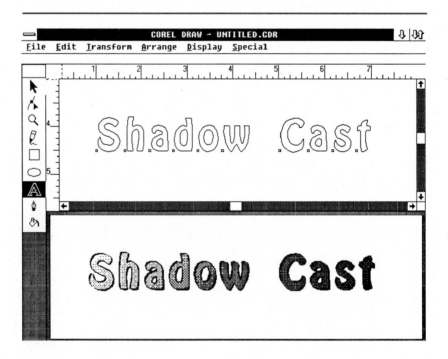 by pressing the spacebar. The text string is selected automatically.

11. Select the Record Macro command in the Special menu. This command is available only because you have selected an object on the screen. The screen redraws, and the word "Macro" appears at the left edge of the status line.

12. Create a vertical mirror image of the text string that is exactly the same size as the original. To do this, position the cursor over

FIGURE 19-4   Text string created with new default outline and fill settings

the top middle boundary marker of the highlighting box and begin to drag the boundary marker down. As soon as the dotted outline box appears, press and release + on the numeric keypad (the Leave Original key) to leave a copy of the original. Then, press and hold (CTRL) and continue to drag the boundary marker down. When the status line shows the value "y-scale:-100%," release the mouse button first, and then release (CTRL). Your results should look like Figure 19-5.

13. With the mirror image still selected, click on the Fill tool and then on the solid black icon ■. The vertical mirror image now contains the specified fill.

14. Click a second time on the outline of the selected mirror image

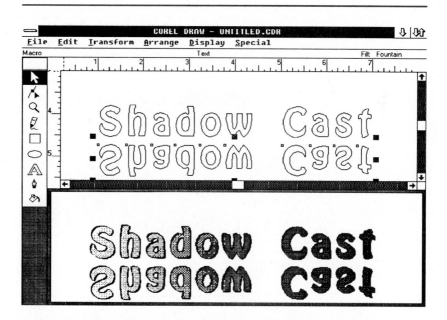

FIGURE 19-5   Text string with vertical mirror image

to enter rotate/skew mode. Then, position the cursor over the middle boundary marker along the bottom edge of the high-lighting box. Adjust the editing window if the boundary marker is not visible. Drag the marker toward the right until you have skewed the mirrored text string by an angle of 40 degrees, using the status line for assistance. Release the mouse button at this point, and adjust the preview window so that your work fills the entire screen. The mirror image text reappears as the shadow shown in Figure 19-6. The outline of the original text and the fill angle of its skewed mirror image lend the impression of a light source originating from behind and to the left of the subject.

15. Leave this image on the screen for now.

Since beginning to record a macro, you have created a mirror image of the selected object, assigned a fill to the mirror image, and skewed it. Now you are ready to complete the macro by saving and naming it.

FIGURE 19-6   Text string with skewed mirror image

SAVING AND NAMING A MACRO

When you have finished recording all of the desired steps of a macro, you select the Finish Macro command from the Special menu. A file selection box then pops up to let you save and name the macro. All Corel DRAW! macros have the default file extension .MAC. Continue where the previous exercise left off to name the macro you have recorded.

1. With the text string and its skewed shadow still on the screen, select the Finish Macro command from the Special menu. The Save Macro dialog box appears, similar in structure to the Open or Save As dialog box you have seen earlier.

2. Type **SHADOW** in the File text box, as shown in Figure 19-7, and then click on the Save command button. You exit back to your picture.

3. Save your picture at this point. Select the Save As command from the File menu and type **SHADE** when the Save As dialog box appears. Then press (ENTER) or click on the Save command button to save the picture under this name. Leave the picture on the screen for the next exercise.

If, during the recording process, you decide that you do not want to create a macro after all, simply select the Finish Macro command. Then, click on Cancel in the Save Macro dialog box. This is the only way to stop recording without saving the steps.

 If you find the macro feature convenient, you are likely to create a number of them. Always give each macro a name that will help you remember its function and the steps that it contains. You can

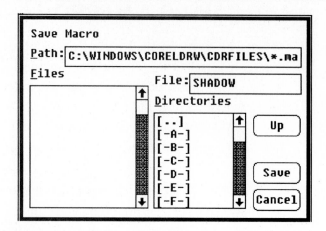

FIGURE 19-7   Naming the macro in the Finish Macro dialog box

also create a subdirectory of CORELDRW in which to store only macros, keeping them separate from your images.

In the next section, you will play back the macro you have just recorded, applying it to a different object.

PLAYING BACK A MACRO

The beauty of a Corel DRAW! macro is that you can replay it on any type of object, not only on objects that are similar to the one for which you created the macro. In other words, if you created the macro for a circle, you can play it back on a text string or a bitmap. You can also play back a macro on one object or multiple objects, as long as the multiple objects are selected, grouped, or combined. Macros are therefore ideal for stylizing key elements throughout an image.

In the following exercise, you will create several objects, combine them, and then apply the macro SHADOW.MAC to them.

1. Adjust the preview back to a top-to-bottom format. Press and hold down the scroll arrow in the vertical scrollbar, and scroll down the editing window until you can no longer see the text string.

2. Select the Rectangle tool ▢. Position the drawing cursor at a point at the 3-inch mark on the horizontal ruler and the 7-inch mark on the vertical ruler. Then, draw a rectangle from the left corner downward. Release the mouse button when the status line informs you that the rectangle is 1.25 inches wide and 0.75 inch high.

3. Press (CTRL-D) twice to create two duplicates of the rectangle, each offset above and to the right by 0.25 inch.

4. Press the spacebar to activate the Select tool, and then select all three rectangles using either (SHIFT) or the marquee method. Click on the Combine command in the Arrange menu to combine the rectangles into one object. As you may recall from exercises in previous chapters, combining objects causes transparent "holes" to appear where the objects overlap.

5. With the combined object selected, click on the Play Macro command in the Special menu. The Play Macro dialog box appears, as shown in Figure 19-8. Its structure is identical to that of the Save Macro dialog box.

6. Double-click on the filename SHADOW.MAC to exit the dialog box and apply the chosen macro to the selected object. In a few seconds, a mirror image of the combined rectangles appears at the identical angle and with the identical fill you defined for the text string earlier. You may not be able to see all of the skewed mirror image, but you will adjust the viewing window in the next step.

7. Adjust the preview window so that it fills the screen, and then click on the Show Preview Toolbox command in the Display

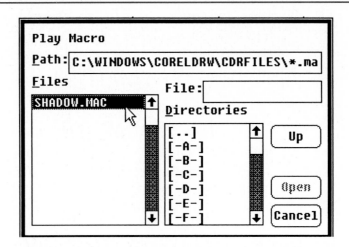

FIGURE 19-8   Selecting a macro in the Play Macro dialog box

window. Magnify just the abstract design that resulted from your macro. Your screen should look similar to Figure 19-9.

8. Adjust magnification of the preview window to ALL, and compare the original text design with the abstract rectangle design. When you are finished, press (CTRL-S) to save your changes to this file, and select New from the File menu to clear the screen.

The macro you have created is just one of many possible design effects that you can automate. You can combine any sequence of steps involving outline and fill attributes, transformation operations, object duplication, and arrangement of duplicated objects.

One way to automate a macro even further is to play it back on one object, select another object, and then press (CTRL-R) (the Repeat key combination) to repeat your most recent operation. Using the Repeat key combination in this way, you can play back the same macro many times within a picture, without ever selecting a menu command.

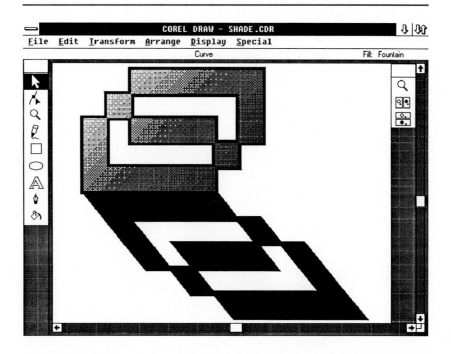

FIGURE 19-9   The result of playing back SHADOW.MAC on an abstract design

The next and final chapter, "Combining Corel DRAW! Features and Creating Special Effects," presents a number of creative design techniques that involve multiple steps. Some of these might provide inspiration for further macros, with which you can customize Corel DRAW! features to suit your talents and working habits.

SUMMARY

A macro is a user-defined command that lets you automate a series of steps that you perform repeatedly. In Corel DRAW!, a macro can consist of any sequence of steps that can be applied to a single object, a combined object, or multiple grouped objects.

To begin recording a macro, you select an object, and then click on the Record Macro command in the Special menu. You can duplicate objects, move, stretch, scale, rotate, and skew them, define outline and fill attributes, and rearrange them. You cannot reshape objects or activate any drawing tools while recording, however.

To save and name a macro, you select the Finish Macro command from the Special menu and enter the desired macro name in the Save Macro dialog box. Give each macro a name that suggests the task that it performs. All Corel DRAW! macros have the extension .MAC. If you plan to use macros often, you can create a special subdirectory of CORELDRW and store all of your macros there.

You can play back any existing macro on a selected single, combined, or grouped object. To play back a macro, you select the desired object, click on the Play Macro command in the Special menu, and then choose the name of the desired macro. The macro applies all of the stored steps to the selected object.

Macros are a convenient shortcut that you can use to automate special design effects. If you want to play back a macro repeatedly within a picture, you can automate the process even further by using the Repeat key combination, CTRL-R.

chapter **20**

COMBINING COREL DRAW! FEATURES AND CREATING SPECIAL EFFECTS

Poster: A Masked Ball
Chasing Rainbows
A Global Fax Transmission

The previous chapters in this tutorial concentrated on teaching you a specific set of skills. The key word is *concentrated,* for the exercises throughout the book built on skills you had already learned, even as you mastered new ones.

This final chapter, however, takes a different approach. It assumes that you have mastered all of the basic skills in Corel

DRAW! and are ready to explore applications that combine many different techniques. In this chapter you will find ideas, and perhaps some of these ideas may inspire you in your own work. However, you will not find a comprehensive catalog of every possible technique or special effect of which Corel DRAW! is capable. The three major exercises that make up this chapter feature text in the sample illustrations, because no other software for the PC allows you to turn text into word pictures as magnificently as Corel DRAW!.

This chapter is composed of three major sections, each containing one exercise in designing a graphic. The title of each section describes the graphic; the introduction to each exercise describes briefly the main Corel DRAW! techniques that help you create the graphic. If you need to review certain techniques, you can refer back to the chapter or chapters that first introduced these skills. Bon voyage!

POSTER: A MASKED BALL

In the following exercise, you will design a poster that integrates a bitmap image with line art; in this case, text. You can use this exercise to review text editing, stretch and scale, and outline and fill techniques (Chapters 5, 9, 11, 13, 14, and 15). Since the poster format is 11 inches by 17 inches, you also can brush up on the page setup, printing, and tiling skills you learned in Chapter 18. The end result of your exercise should look similar to Figure 20-7.

 The clipart file in .PCX format that you will import for this exercise is provided only with Corel DRAW! version 1.1 or later. If you have an earlier version of Corel DRAW!, you cannot perform the exercise exactly as written. However, you can import a .PCX image from another source and try your hand at merging it with appropriate text.

To create the poster:

1. Starting with a blank screen, activate the Show Rulers command in the Display menu. The Snap To Grid command should be inactive for this exercise.

2. Select the Page Setup command in the File menu. Click on the Portrait and Tabloid option buttons to design a page that is 11 inches wide and 17 inches high. Select the OK command button to return to your screen.

3. Select the Import command from the File menu. When the Import dialog box appears, click on the PC Paintbrush .PCX, .PCC option, making sure that For Tracing is *not* active. Click on the OK command button to exit to the Import Bitmap dialog box.

4. Using the Files and Directories list boxes, change to the drive and directory where the sample clipart file NEWSMAKR.PCX is located. You have sample clipart in .PCX format only if your version of Corel DRAW! is 1.1 or later. If you have an earlier version of Corel DRAW!, use a suitable .PCX file from a paint program or clipart package that you already own, or scan in a poster-like picture from a print source. If you have version 1.1 or later but did not install the clipart, insert the disk containing the METRO Image Base directory into drive A and import it from there. Double-click on the filename NEWSMAKR.PCX to import the bitmap. After a few seconds it appears, centered vertically on your screen and selected automatically.

5. Press (F3) to activate the preview window. Then, position the cursor at the bottom-middle boundary marker of the bitmap object. Stretch the bitmap vertically by dragging the marker downward until it reaches the 16-inch mark on the vertical ruler, and then release the mouse button.

6. Scale the bitmap from the boundary marker in the upper-left corner until the status line shows a value of approximately 114%. Scale the bitmap from the boundary marker in the lower-right corner until the status line shows a value of approximately 105%. The bitmap should now occupy an area of the screen similar to Figure 20-1.

7. Save and name the image at this point. Select Save As from the File menu, and type **MASKBALL** in the file text box. Then press (**ENTER**) or click on the Save command button to save the file and return to the Corel DRAW! screen.

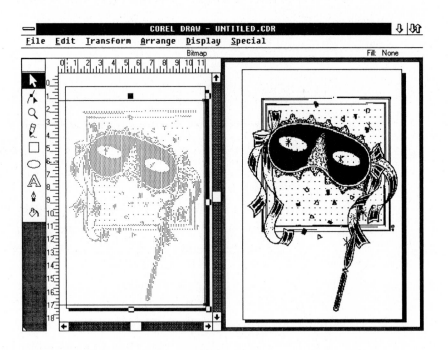

FIGURE 20-1   Incorporating a stretched and scaled bitmap into a poster format

8. Select the Zoom-In tool 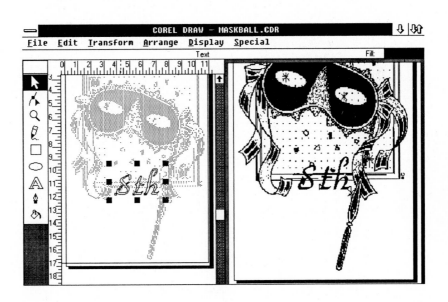 from the Magnification tool pop-up menu, and magnify just the lower half of the page, which contains a large white space and the wand of the mask

.9. Activate the Text tool and select an insertion point anywhere on the unoccupied white space. When the Text dialog box appears, type **8th** in the text entry window. Set text attributes to Left Alignment, Paradise Normal, 256.0 points. Click on the Spacing command button and set inter-character spacing to 0.10 em, and select OK. The text appears at the insertion point.

10. Activate the Select tool to select the text string automatically. Then, move it to the position shown in Figure 20-2. Press (CTRL-S) to save the changes you have made to the file.

FIGURE 20-2   Moving "8th" into position

11. With the text string still selected, click on the Outline tool
    [⬦] and then on the Custom Outline Pen icon [⬦] in the
    pop-up menu. The settings for this text string should be: solid
    line type, sharp corners, butt line caps, Width 0.01 inches,
    Angle 0 degrees, and Stretch 100%. Both the Behind Fill and
    Scale With Image options should be inactive. Click on the OK
    command button to save these settings for the text.

12. Select the Outline tool again, and then click on the black fill
    icon [■] in the pop-up menu to make the text outline black.

13. Click on the Fill tool [✎] and then on the 40% gray icon in the
    pop-up menu. This is the seventh icon from the left, or the fifth
    icon from the right. The preview window shows the change in
    the fill color of the text. Since the outline of the text is black,
    however, the word stands out against the backdrop behind the
    mask. Save your changes at this point by pressing (CTRL-S).

14. Activate the Text tool again and select another insertion point
    in the white space. When the Text dialog box appears, type
    Annual in the text entry window, and set text attributes to Left
    Alignment, Paradise Normal, 121.0 points. Click on the Spac-
    ing command button and set inter-character spacing to 0.10 em,
    then select OK. The text string appears at the insertion point.

15. Activate the Select tool and move "Annual" to the location
    shown in Figure 20-3.

16. With the "Annual" text string still selected, click on the Outline
    tool and again on the Custom Outline Pen icon. Make sure that
    the Outline Pen dialog box settings are the same as in step 11
    (solid line type, Behind Fill and Scale With Image deactivated,
    sharp corners, butt line caps, Width 0.01 inch, Angle 0 degrees,
    and Stretch 100%), and then select OK.

17. Click on the Outline tool icon again, and then click on the black
    fill icon in the second row of the pop-up menu.

18. Click on the Fill tool icon and again on the black fill icon in the pop-up menu. The text string in the preview window now has a black fill color and a thin black outline.

19. Activate the Text tool once more and select a third insertion point in the white space. When the Text dialog box appears, type **Masked Ball** in the text entry window. Set text attributes to Left Alignment, Paradise Normal, 121.0 points. Click on the Spacing command button and set inter-character spacing to 0.10 ems and inter-word spacing to 1.10 ems, and then select OK. The text string appears at the insertion point.

20. Activate the Select tool to select the text automatically. Move this text string to the position shown in Figure 20-4, making sure that the handle of the mask falls in the empty space between "Masked" and "Ball." The left edge of the three text strings should follow an imaginary diagonal line.

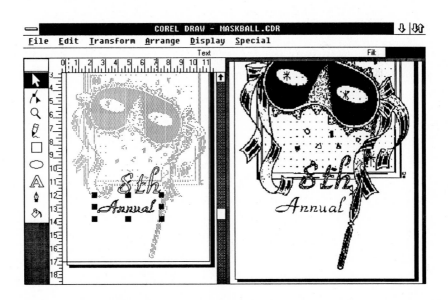

FIGURE 20-3   Moving "Annual" into position beneath "8th"

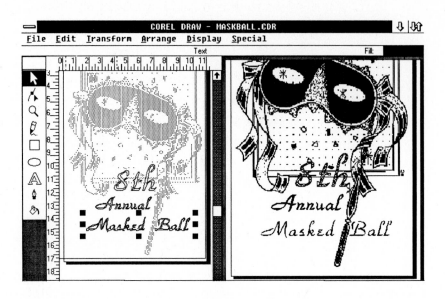

FIGURE 20-4   Aligning "Masked Ball" with the handle of the mask

21. With the "Masked Ball" text string still selected, click on the Copy Style From command in the Edit menu. Activate only the Outline Pen, Outline Color, and Fill checkboxes, and then select OK. When the From? cursor appears, click on the "Annual" text string to copy its outline and fill attributes to the currently selected text string. Make certain to click on the *outline* of the object from which you want to copy the style, or you will see an error message.

22. Activate the Text tool once more and select another insertion point in the white space. When the Text dialog box appears, type **Presented By:** in the text entry window. Set text attributes to an alignment of None, Timpani Normal, 42.0 points. Click on the Spacing command button and set inter-character spacing

to 0.10 em. Reset inter-word spacing to 1.00 em, and then select OK to display the text.

23. Activate the Select tool to select the new text string automatically. Move this text string to the position shown in Figure 20-5.

24. With "Presented By:" still selected, click on the Outline tool and again on the Custom Outline Pen icon in the pop-up menu. Set outline pen attributes as solid line type, Behind Fill and Scale With Image deactivated, sharp corners, butt line caps, Width 0.01 inch, Angle 0 degrees, and Stretch 100%. Click on the OK command button to save these settings for the text.

25. Click on the Outline tool again and then on the black icon in the second row of the pop-up menu.

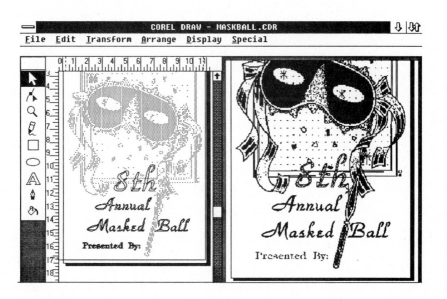

FIGURE 20-5   Moving "Presented By:" into position

26. Click on the Fill tool and again on the white fill icon (the third icon from the left). The preview window shows you a white fill for this text string.

27. Activate the Text tool once more, and select an insertion point in the lower-right area of the page, just to the right of the mask handle. When the Text dialog box displays, type **UPB** on the first line of the text entry window, then press (ENTER) and type **Symphony** on the second line. Set text attributes to Center Alignment, Timpani Normal, 39.5 points. Click on the Spacing command button. Set inter-character spacing to 0.10 em and inter-line spacing to 125% of point size, and then select OK.

28. Activate the Select tool to select the new text string automatically. Move this text string to the position shown in Figure 20-6, aligning it visually with the "Presented By:" text.

29. Click on the Copy Style From command in the Edit menu. When the Copy Style dialog box appears, make sure that only the Outline Pen and Outline Color options are activated, and then click on OK. Then, click on the "Presented By:" text string to copy its outline attributes to "UPB Symphony."

30. Click on the Fill tool and then on the black fill icon to fill the selected text with black.

31. Click on the Magnification Tool and again on the Show Page icon ▣ . Then, choose the Select All command in the Edit menu and apply the Group command in the Arrange menu.

32. Move the grouped objects upward to center them on the page more evenly, and then press (CTRL-S) to save your changes. Adjust the preview window to fill the screen. Your final picture should look like Figure 20-7.

33. Select New from the File menu to clear the screen.

You may choose to print this oversize poster on your own printer. If you do, be sure to activate the Tile option in the Print Options dialog box. This will result in your poster being printed on four separate sheets, each containing one quarter of the graphic. If your printer does not have enough memory to print this graphic at 11-by-17 inches, try scaling the image down. Then, change the page size to 8-by-11 inches, using the Page Setup command in the File menu.

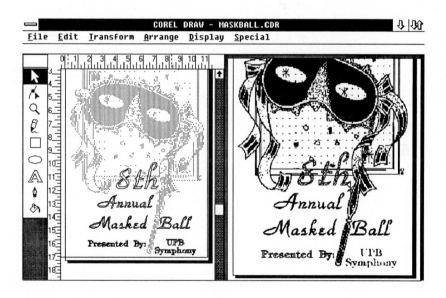

FIGURE 20-6   Aligning "UPB Symphony" with "Presented By:"

FIGURE 20-7   The completed poster illustration

To add to your Corel DRAW! applications gallery, continue with the next exercise. There, you will create a color design that takes advantage of the Corel DRAW! features that fit text to a path and mirror images.

CHASING RAINBOWS

If you have followed this book from the first chapter onward, you have learned nearly every available Corel DRAW! drawing technique. One important (and very creative) technique remains: fitting text to a path using the Fit Text To Path command in the Arrange menu. You can cause a text string to follow the outline of *any* object, be it a circle or an ellipse, a rectangle or a square, a line, a curve, a complex curved object, or even another letter that has been converted to curves.

Just how text aligns to a second object depends on the nature of the object. In most cases, the results are straightforward. When you fit text to a rectangle or ellipse, however, the text may appear upside down or along the bottom edge of the object. The placement of the text depends on how you drew the rectangle or ellipse. Figure 20-8a and b demonstrates how the "corner" from which you start a rectangular or elliptical shape determines where fitted text will appear. To summarize,

- If your starting point for a rectangle or ellipse is the *upper-left* corner or rim, fitted text appears right side up and outside the upper rim.

- If your starting point is the *upper-right* corner or rim, fitted text appears upside down and inside the upper rim.

- If your starting point for a rectangle or ellipse is the *lower-left* corner or rim, fitted text appears right side up and inside the bottom rim.

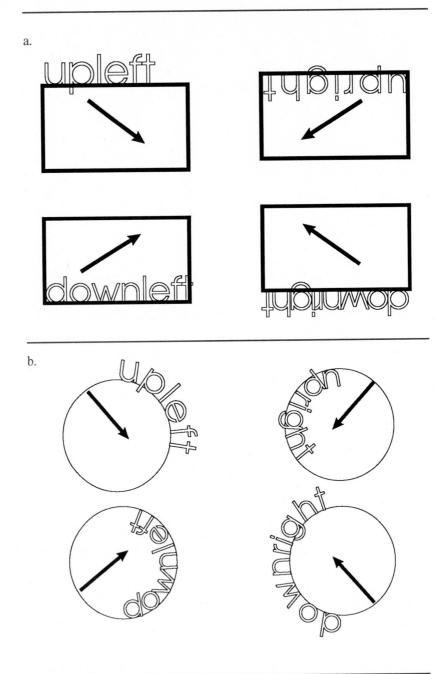

FIGURE 20-8   Start point determines how text wraps:
a) Rectangles; b) Ellipses

- If your starting point is the *lower-right* corner or rim, fitted text appears upside down and outside the bottom rim.

Once you have fitted text to an object, you can delete that object without causing the text to lose its newly acquired shape. If you edit text attributes later, however, the text may change its alignment. You can remedy this simply by fitting text to the same path again.

In the following exercise, you will design a stylized "rainbow" image that consists of a series of scaled and aligned wedges. You will then fit the word "Rainbow" to a curve, combine the text string with a background object to create a mask, and overlay the transparent letters on the rainbow colors. The result—after stretching and mirroring the mask and rainbow—is the illustration shown in Figure 20-19. If you have a color monitor, your results will appear more vivid than the one shown in the illustration. If you have a black and white display adapter and monitor, you can achieve a similar "rainbow" effect by filling the wedges with the gray shades indicated in parentheses in the following steps.

1. Starting with a blank screen, select Page Setup from the File menu. When the Page Setup dialog box appears, click on the Landscape and Letter option buttons, and then select OK. This results in a page that is 11 inches wide and 8 1/2 inches high.

2. To prepare the Corel DRAW! screen for the exercise, make sure that Snap To Grid is activated and that Grid Frequency is set to 8 per inch. Activate the Show Rulers command as well.

3. Set new outline and fill defaults so that all of the objects you draw will be standardized. First, click on the Outline tool and again on the None icon in the first row of the pop-up menu. The 'New Object' Outline Pen message shown in Figure 20-9 appears, asking whether you want to define outline pen settings

for objects you haven't drawn yet. Select OK to set no outline as the new default.

4. Click on the Fill tool and then on the black fill icon. The 'New Object' Uniform Fill message appears, asking whether you want to define fill colors for objects you haven't drawn yet. Select OK to define a default fill color of black for new objects.

5. Activate the Ellipse tool ⬭ , then position the cursor at the 3 1/4-inch mark on the horizontal ruler and the 6 1/2-inch mark on the vertical ruler. Press and hold (CTRL-SHIFT) and drag the mouse downward and to the right until the status line shows a width and height of 3 inches. As you may recall from Chapter 4, the use of (CTRL) and (SHIFT) together results in a circle drawn from the center outward. When you release the mouse button, the circle appears with the node at the top, as shown in Figure 20-10a.

6. Create a 90-degree wedge from this circle, as you learned to do in Chapter 10. Activate the Shaping tool 🖅 and position the Shaping cursor at the node of the circle. To turn the circle into

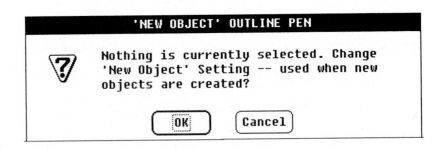

FIGURE 20-9   The 'New Object' message box

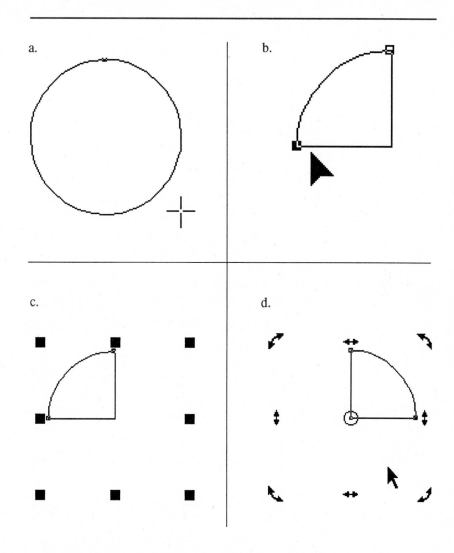

FIGURE 20-10 Creating a pie wedge from a circle and rotating it

a pie wedge, press and hold (CTRL) and drag the node in a clockwise direction until you reach the 9 o'clock position (90 degrees on the status line). Hold the tip of the Shaping cursor *inside* the rim of the circle as you drag, or you will see an open arc instead of a wedge. Release the mouse button when you reach the 9 o'clock position. The wedge appears, as in Figure 20-10b.

7. Activate the Select tool to select the wedge automatically. Notice that the highlighting box is much larger than the wedge, just as in Figure 20-10c. Corel DRAW! continues to treat the wedge as though it were a full circle.

8. Click again on the outline of the wedge to enter rotate/skew mode. Position the cursor at the arrow markers in the upper-right corner, press and hold (CTRL), and rotate the wedge in a clockwise direction until the status line indicates an angle of −90 degrees. Remember to release the mouse button before you release (CTRL); otherwise, the wedge may not snap to the exact −90-degree angle. The curve of the wedge now faces upward and to the right, as shown in Figure 20-10d.

9. Click again on the wedge outline to return to stretch/scale mode. You are ready to increase the scale of the wedge and leave a copy of the original. Position the cursor at the boundary marker in the upper-right corner and scale the wedge upward and to the right, until the status line value reaches approximately 116.7%. When you reach the desired point, continue to hold the mouse button, but press the + key on the numeric keypad to leave a copy of the original. Then, release the mouse button. The original wedge remains in position, and a scaled version overlays it, as in Figure 20-11.

10. Press (CTRL-R) (the Repeat key combination) five times to create five additional wedges, each larger than the previous one. Your screen should show a total of seven wedges, resembling Figure 20-12.

11. Your next step is to align the wedges so that they form one-half of a rainbow. Click on the Select All command in the Edit menu

to select all seven wedges, and then select the Align command in the Arrange menu. When the Align dialog box appears, click on both the Horizontal Center and Vertical Center option buttons, and then select OK. The wedges realign with a common corner point in the center of the page, as shown in Figure 20-13.

12. With the seven wedges still selected, click on the Reverse Order command in the Arrange menu. You will not see a visible change at this point, but you have positioned the larger wedges in the back and the smaller wedges in the front. When you turn on the preview window later in the exercise and begin to assign

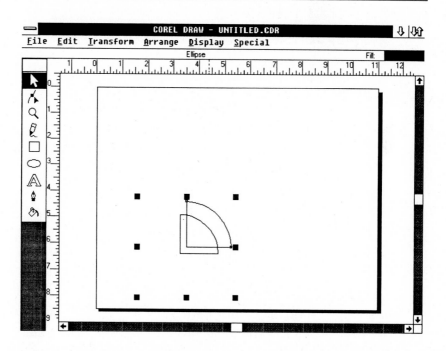

FIGURE 20-11 Scaling a wedge and leaving a copy of the original

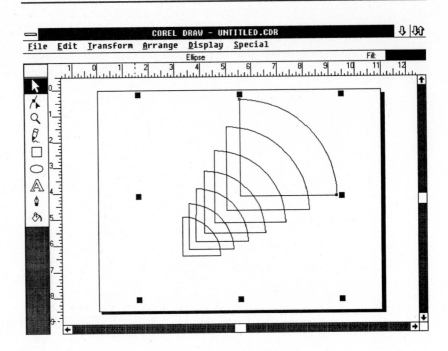

FIGURE 20-12   A series of scaled wedges created using the Repeat key combination

fill colors to the wedges, you will see each wedge as a ribbon-like band.

13. Select the Save As command from the File menu at this point. When the Save As dialog box appears, type **RAINBOW1**, and then press (ENTER) or click on Save.

14. To design the other half of the rainbow, you simply create a horizontal mirror image of the currently selected image. Click on the Stretch & Mirror command in the Transform menu to access the Stretch & Mirror dialog box. Then activate both the Horz Mirror command button and the Leave Original checkbox, and then select OK. The mirror image of the seven

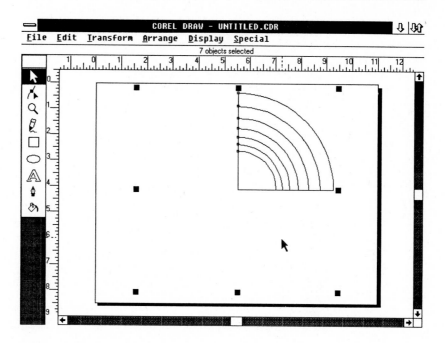

FIGURE 20-13   Wedges aligned using Horizontal Center and
Vertical Center options

wedges appears and fits tightly against the original group of
wedges, as shown in Figure 20-14.

15. You can now begin to assign fill colors to the wedges of the
"rainbow." Turn on the preview window and make sure that it
is in side-by-side format; for greater convenience, activate the
Preview Selected Only command in the Display menu. Adjust
magnification to ALL by clicking on the ALL icon in the
Magnification tool pop-up menu.

16. Deselect all of the wedges by clicking on any white space. Then,
select both the largest wedge on the left half of the "rainbow"
and the smallest wedge on the right half. To select them, click
on each of their curve outlines while holding (SHIFT). Just as in

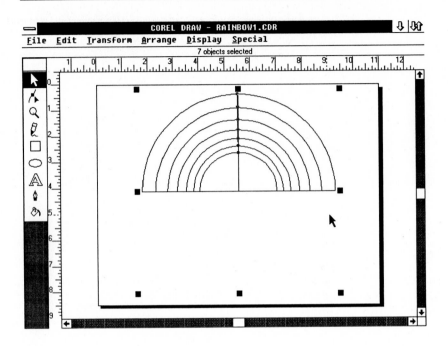

FIGURE 20-14   Original seven wedges with a horizontal mirror image

Figure 20-15, the editing window looks as though all of the wedges were selected, because the highlighting box of the largest wedge surrounds all of the objects. The preview window, however, shows you that only two wedges are selected.

17. With the two wedges selected, click on the Fill tool and again on the Uniform Fill icon. When the Uniform Fill dialog box displays, select Process color and set color values to 100% magenta, 75% yellow, and 10% black. Select OK; the two opposite wedges now redisplay with a red fill, the hue of which varies depending on whether you have an EGA or VGA display adapter. (If you have a black and white monitor, set black to 80% and leave all other colors at 0%.)

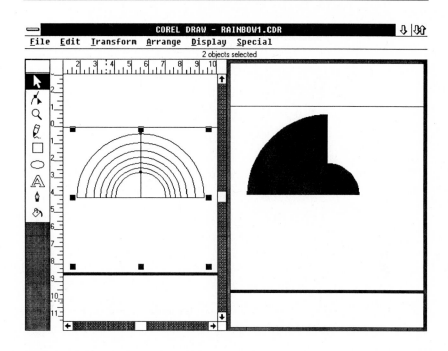

FIGURE 20-15   Selecting pairs of wedges with Preview
Selected Only in effect

18. Deselect the previous wedges. Then select the second largest
    wedge on the left half of the "rainbow" and the second smallest
    wedge on the right half, and then access the Uniform Fill dialog
    box once more. If you have a color monitor, set process color
    values to 100% magenta and 100% yellow, and then select OK.
    The two wedges now show a bright orange fill. (If you have a
    black and white monitor, set black to 40% and leave all other
    colors at 0%.)

19. Continue in the same way with the next five pairs of wedges. If you have a color monitor, assign colors as follows: third pair, 100% yellow; fourth pair, 40% cyan and 60% yellow; fifth pair, 100% cyan, 40% yellow, and 20% black; sixth pair, 100% cyan, 100% magenta, and 10% black; seventh pair, 100% magenta and 50% black. (If you have a black and white monitor, assign 15% black to the third pair, 40% black to the fourth, 30% black to the fifth, 75% black to the sixth, and 100% black to the seventh.) When you are finished, turn off the Preview Selected Only feature. The two halves of the rainbow show an opposite sequence of colors, as you can see by the black-and-white representation in Figure 20-16.

20. Click on the Select All command in the Edit menu to select all 14 wedges, and then apply the Group command from the Arrange menu. This prevents you from moving or editing an individual wedge accidentally, apart from the group.

21. Press (F3) to turn off the preview window for the next few steps of the exercise. Click on the Show Page icon in the Magnification tool pop-up menu to display the full page.

22. Now you are ready to prepare the text that will eventually overlay the rainbow as a transparent mask. First, activate the Ellipse tool and position the drawing cursor at the 2 1/2-inch mark on the horizontal ruler and the 1-inch mark on the vertical ruler. Drag the mouse downward and to the right and draw a circle 6 inches in diameter. Remember to use (CTRL) (but *not* (SHIFT)) to obtain a circle rather than an ellipse. The circle overlays most of the "rainbow" for now, but you will delete it when it has served its purpose.

23. Activate the Text tool and select an insertion point in any white space on the page. When the Text dialog box appears, type **Rainbow** in the text entry window. Set text attributes to Aardvark Bold, 105.0 points, and an alignment of None. Click on

the Spacing command button and set Inter-character spacing to 0.10 em, and then select OK to display the text on the page.

24. Activate the Select tool to select the text string automatically. Use (**SHIFT**) to also select the circle you have just drawn. Then, click on the Fit Text To Path command in the Arrange menu. After a few seconds, the text appears right side up but veering off the upper-right rim of the circle, as shown in Figure 20-17.

25. Deselect the text to leave only the circle selected, and then press (**DEL**) to delete the circle. The text retains its new shape.

26. Double-click on the outline of the text to enter rotate/skew mode. Position the cursor over the arrow marker at the bottom-

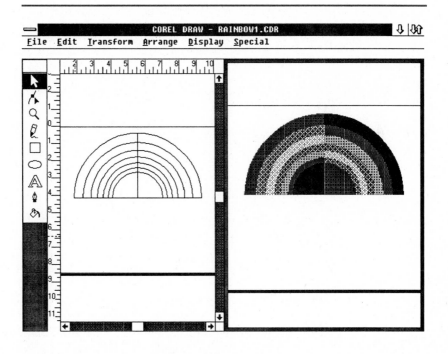

FIGURE 20-16 Opposite color sequences in each half of the rainbow

right corner, and then rotate the text counterclockwise by an angle of 67 degrees. When you release the mouse button, the text redisplays right side up and centered on the screen.

27. Click again on the outline of the text string to leave rotate/skew mode and return to normal select mode. Fill the text with white by clicking on the Fill tool and again on the white icon in the second row of the pop-up menu.

28. Create the rectangle that will become the background of the mask. Activate the Rectangle tool ▭ and position the drawing cursor at the zero point on both the horizontal and vertical

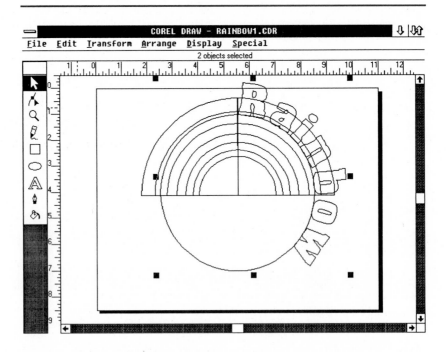

FIGURE 20-17   Fitting text to a circle

rulers. From this point, draw a rectangle 7 3/4 inches wide and 3 3/4 inches high, sweeping downward and to the right.

29. Press the spacebar to select the rectangle automatically. Give the rectangle a transparent fill by clicking on the Fill tool and then on the NONE icon in the pop-up menu. Make the edge of the rectangle also transparent by clicking on the Outline tool and again on the NONE icon on the first row of the pop-up menu.

30. Select the text string and move it on top of the rectangle. Position it so that the bottom of the text string is 1/4 inch above the lower edge of the rectangle.

31. To center the text horizontally on the rectangle, select both objects, click on the Align command in the Arrange menu, and choose the Horizontal Center option button. Select OK to leave the Alignment dialog box and redisplay the newly aligned objects.

32. With both the text and the rectangle still selected, move both objects into the empty space at the bottom of the page, out of the way of the rainbow wedges. Then, select the Reverse Order command from the Arrange menu to place the text behind the rectangle.

33. Turn on the preview window. You cannot see the rectangle because it is transparent, and you cannot see the text because it has a white fill and is behind the rectangle. With the text and rectangle both selected in the editing window, click on the Combine command in the Arrange menu. The two objects reverse colors when they combine, and the text becomes a transparent "hole" in the white rectangle.

34. Move the newly combined object back over the grouped rainbow wedges and align the bottom edge of the curve object with the bottom edge of the wedges.

The object that is in the background when you combine two objects determines the fill color of the combined object. If you see white letters over a transparent rectangle, you forgot to place the text behind the rectangle. Select Undo from the Edit menu, use the Reverse Order command in the Arrange menu to bring the rectangle to the foreground, and then combine the two objects again.

35. Drag the preview window so that it fills the screen. With the white rectangle invisible against the page, all you can see are

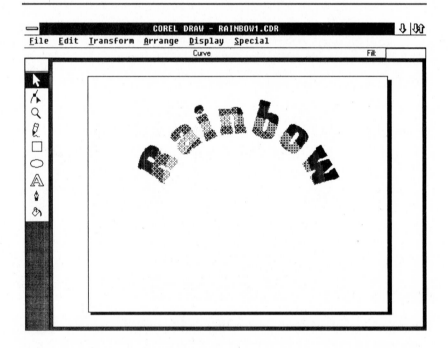

FIGURE 20-18   Rainbow colors appearing as fill through the mask object

the rainbow colors behind the transparent text string, as shown in Figure 20-18.

36. Readjust the preview window so that it fills only half the screen in a side-by-side format, and then adjust viewing magnification to ALL. Select both the combined object and the wedges and apply the Group command from the Arrange menu.

37. Create a mirror image of the grouped object. With the group still selected, click on the Stretch & Mirror command from the Transform menu. When the Stretch & Mirror dialog box appears, click on both the Horz Mirror and Vert mirror command buttons and make sure that a checkmark appears in the Leave Original checkbox. Select OK; an upside down and backwards

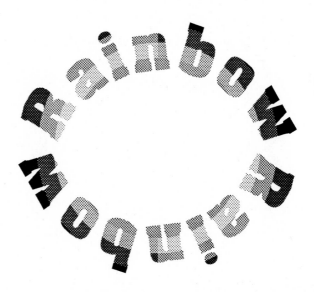

FIGURE 20-19   Rainbow with vertical flipped mirror image

version of the "Rainbow" text displays beneath the original, as shown in the full-screen preview in Figure 20-19. This object is selected automatically in the editing window.

38. Press (CTRL-S) to save the changes to your work, and then select New from the File menu to clear your screen.

The main emphases in this last exercise have been on fitting text to a path, working with color effects, creating a mask, aligning objects, repeating operations, and creating mirror images. In the next and last sample application, you can achieve 3-D effects using fountain and contrasting fills, outlines, and repeated scalings.

A GLOBAL FAX TRANSMISSION

The "FAX" image in Figure 20-27 has a vibrant, 3-D look; the graphic represents the power of facsimile to "broadcast" to the world quite literally. Several special effects techniques contribute to the dynamic quality of the image:

- Text fitted to a curve

- Text objects with drop shadows (shadows placed behind and offset from the original)

- A "globe" with an off-center radial fountain fill

- Repeated duplication and expansion of a text string

- Judicious use of contrasting fills

- Inclusion of a backdrop that makes the image seem to burst beyond its boundaries

You already have practiced the basic skills that make all of these special effects possible. In the exercise that follows, you will recreate this image, using the Leave Original and Repeat keys, fountain fill and node editing techniques, and the Duplicate, Fit Text To Path, Group, and Page Setup commands. For a review of shadow and fountain fill techniques, see Chapter 15.

1. Starting with a blank screen, select Page Setup from the File menu. When the Page Setup dialog box appears, click on the Landscape and Letter option buttons, and then select OK. This results in a page 11 inches wide and 8 1/2 inches high.

2. To prepare the Corel DRAW! screen for the exercise, activate the Snap To Grid command in the Display menu, select the Grid Size command, and set Grid Frequency to 8 per inch. Activate the Show Rulers command as well.

3. Change the default outline type to a hairline by clicking on the Outline tool and then on the HAIR icon in the first row of the pop-up menu. When the 'New Objects' dialog box appears to ask whether you want this outline type applied to future objects, click on OK.

4. Change the default outline color to black by clicking on the Outline tool and then on the black icon in the second row of the pop-up menu. The 'New Objects' dialog box appears once again; select OK as you did in the previous step.

5. Create a small circle to which you will fit text. To do this, activate the Ellipse tool and position the crosshair cursor in the approximate center of the page. Press and hold (CTRL) and draw a perfect circle 0.63 inch in diameter. Start with your cursor in the upper-left portion of the rim and drag downward and to the right. When you complete the circle, remember to release the mouse button before you release (CTRL) to ensure that you create a circle rather than an ellipse.

6. Now enter the text that you will fit to this circle. Activate the Text tool and select an insertion point about an inch above the circle. The exact location does not matter, because when you invoke the Fit Text To Path command later, the text will snap to the circle no matter where it is. When the Text dialog box displays, type **FAX** in all capital letters in the text entry window. Set text attributes to an alignment of None, Frankfurt Gothic Heavy, Normal, 30.0 points. Click on the OK command to display your text on the page.

7. Press the spacebar to activate the Select tool; the text string is selected automatically, since it was the last object you drew. While you press and hold (SHIFT), select the circle as well.

8. With both objects selected, click on the Fit Text To Path command in the Arrange menu. The text wraps around outside of the circle, centering itself around the upper-right segment of the rim, as shown in Figure 20-20. (The image on your screen is much smaller.)

9. Deselect the text string using (SHIFT), and then press (DEL) to delete the circle. The text remains curved, even though the circle is no longer there.

10. Double-click on the text string to enter rotate/skew mode, and rotate the text by 26 degrees in a counterclockwise direction.

11. Move the text to the lower-left corner of the page.

12. Now you are ready to begin creating a text pattern. With the Select tool still active, position the cursor at the upper-right corner boundary marker of the text object and begin to scale the object from this point. As soon as the dotted outline box appears, press and release + on the numeric keypad (to leave a copy of the original). Continue scaling the text until the status line indicates a value of approximately 127%. (The status line

will "snap" to this value because of the grid frequency you have selected.) Then, release the mouse button. A larger-scaled version of the text string appears on top of and offset from the original. You can see the proportions more clearly if you change magnification to ALL temporarily.

13. Select the Show Page icon from the Magnification tool pop-up menu to return to a full-page view. Then press (CTRL-R), the Repeat key, ten times, to repeat the scaling and duplication of the text. Ten scaled replicas of the text string overlay one another, each one larger than the last. The last text string exceeds the boundaries of the page, as shown in Figure 20-21.

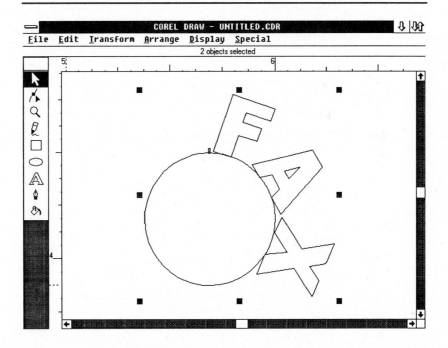

FIGURE 20-20   Magnified view of text fitted to a small circle

14. Leaving the most recently created text string selected, click on the Preference command in the Special menu. Make certain that the Place Duplicate values are at 0.25 and 0.25 inches, and then select OK. These values determine the placement of a duplicate object relative to the original.

15. Press (CTRL-D) to create an exact duplicate of the top text string, offset 1/4 inch above and to the right of the original. The duplicate is selected as soon as it appears.

16. Turn on the preview window. All of the text strings appear with black fills. Click on the Select All command in the Edit menu and then on the Group command in the Arrange menu to group

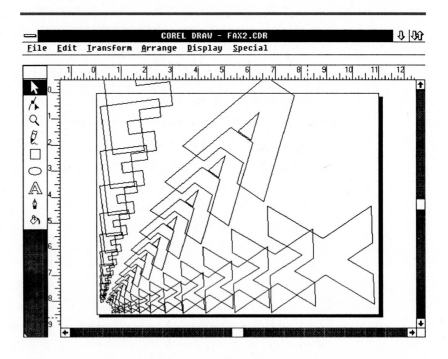

FIGURE 20-21   Scaled and repeated text strings exceeding to page boundaries

all of the text strings. Then, select the white fill icon in the Fill tool pop-up menu. The text strings redisplay in the preview window with a fill of white, making it easier to distinguish them from one another.

17. With all text strings still selected, click on the Outline tool and then on the Custom Outline Pen icon to access the Outline Pen dialog box. Change the settings to match the ones in Figure 20-22: Scale With Image active, Width 0.01 inch, Angle 0%, and Stretch 100%. Then select OK. The text strings redisplay with a fine outline of uniform width.

18. Ungroup and deselect all text strings, and then select only the last text string you created (the offset duplicate on top). Click on the Fill tool and again on the Fountain Fill icon ▨ to access the Fountain Fill dialog box. Make sure the Spot color option button is selected and assign a start color (From) of white (Color 0, Tint 0%) and an end color (To) of black (Color 0, Tint 100%). Choose a linear fountain fill and an angle of 45 degrees. Click on OK to make this fill color take effect.

19. Now create a drop shadow effect. Press (TAB) to select the text string in the layer just below the text string containing a fountain fill. Assign a fill of black to this object by clicking on the black icon ■ in the Fill tool pop-up menu. The preview window shows the result of your selection, as in Figure 20-23.

20. Continue pressing (TAB) to select each text string in the reverse order from which it was created. Fill the text strings in the following sequence, starting with the largest text string after the drop shadow: 80% black, 60% black, 40% black, 20% black, 10% black. Fill one more text string with 10% black and the remaining (smallest) text strings with white. You can use the icons in the Fill tool pop-up menu to select these shades quickly. The resulting gradation of fills and the drop shadow make the

repeated text strings seem to leap out of the screen, as shown in Figure 20-24.

21. To group all text strings so that you cannot separate them accidentally, click on Select All in the Edit menu, and then on the Group command in the Arrange menu. Then, move the group upward and away from the left side of the page. You will bring the group back later, but for now you need room to create more objects.

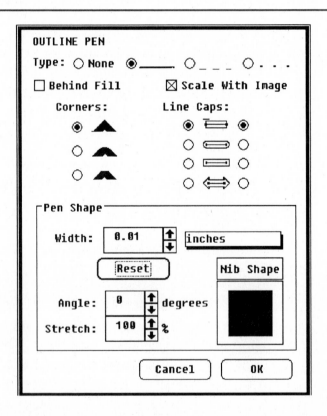

FIGURE 20-22   Outline pen settings for "FAX" text strings

22. Activate the Ellipse tool and position it 4 1/2 inches from the top of the page and 3/4 of an inch from the left margin. Press and hold (CTRL) and draw a circle 3 inches in diameter, starting from the upper-left area of the rim. Use the status line as a guide.

23. Turn the circle into a 3-D globe by giving it a radial fountain fill. To do this, activate the Select tool to select the circle automatically, and then click on the Fill tool and again on the Fountain Fill icon. When the Fountain Fill dialog box appears, change the start color (From) to black (Color 0, Tint 100%) and the end color (To) to white (Color 0, Tint 0%). Select a radial fountain fill, but leave the other settings unaltered. Select OK to make the fountain fill take effect. The globe reappears with

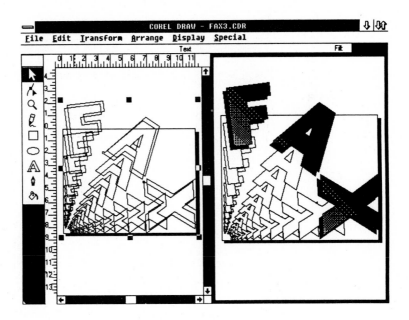

FIGURE 20-23   Drop shadow effect using duplicated text and black fill

a white highlight in the center and the fill gradually darkens toward the rim.

24. Prepare to create an off-center highlight so that the light source seems to be coming from above and to the right of the globe. Activate the Freehand tool 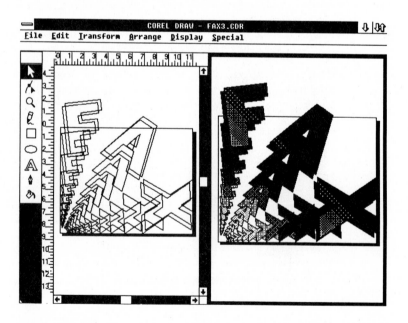, and draw a very short line segment above and to the right of the globe. Select both the line segment and the globe and click on the Combine command in the Arrange menu to combine these into one object. Whenever the preview window redraws from now on, Corel DRAW! extends the first stage of the fountain fill as far as the line segment, as shown in the magnified preview in Figure 20-25. This means that you can control the placement of the highlight

FIGURE 20-24   Gradation of fills, leading to a 3-D effect

on the globe by moving the nodes of the line segment with the Shaping tool.

25. If you wish to change the placement of the highlight on the globe, activate the Shaping tool and move the uppermost node of the line segment in a clockwise or counterclockwise direction. You can move either or both nodes; experiment until you find the placement you want.

26. Now, make the line segment invisible. Activate the Select tool to select the combined object automatically, and then click on the Outline tool and again on the white outline fill icon in the second row of the pop-up menu. The line segment seems to

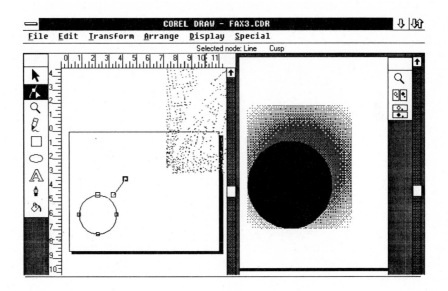

FIGURE 20-25   Changing the center of a radial fountain fill by combining line segment with globe

disappear from the preview screen, but you can still use it to manipulate the highlight on the globe.

27. Create a rectangle that will form a backdrop for the rest of the image. Activate the Rectangle tool and begin a rectangle at the 1-inch mark on the horizontal ruler and the 1 1/2-inch mark on the vertical ruler. Extend the rectangle downward and to the right until you reach the 7 1/2-inch mark on the horizontal ruler and the 7 1/4-inch mark on the vertical ruler, and then release the mouse button. The preview window shows that this object lies on top of all the other objects, obscuring them from your view.

28. Activate the Select tool to select the rectangle automatically, and then click on the To Back command in the Arrange menu. Now, the globe appears as the top layer.

29. Assign a black outline of 2.0 fractional points and a fill of 20% gray to the rectangle.

30. To make the globe stand out in 3-D from the background, select it and assign an outline 0.01-inch wide, using the Outline Pen dialog box.

31. Select the grouped text strings and move them on top of the globe so that they seem to be emerging directly from the highlight, as shown in Figure 20-26. To make certain that the text strings are the top layer object, click on the To Front command. This also hides the line segment that you used as a "handle" to change the center of the globe's fountain fill.

32. Adjust viewing magnification to ALL by clicking on the ALL icon in the Magnification tool pop-up menu. With the grouped object still selected, scale the text strings down until the status line displays a value of approximately 47%. Adjust the preview window to a full-screen view. Thanks to the insertion of the

background rectangle, the text strings still seem to thrust outward in 3-D, as shown in Figure 20-27.

33. Click on the Select All command in the Edit menu and then on the Group command in the Arrange menu to group all of the objects in the image.

32. Select Save As from the File menu. When the Save As dialog box appears, type **FAXTRANS**, and then press (ENTER) or click on Save.

33. Select New from the File menu to clear the screen.

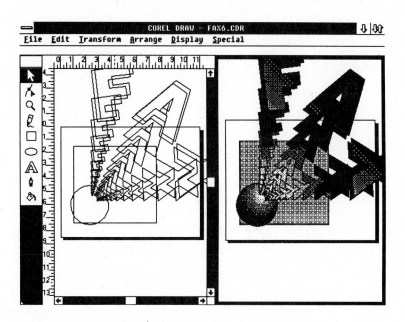

FIGURE 20-26 Grouped text strings overlaid on the globe highlight for 3-D effects

FIGURE 20-27   "FAX" illustration using fountain fill, drop
shadows, and background frame to enhance
3-D effects

If you have performed all three of the exercises in this chapter,
you are well on the way to understanding how to combine many
different Corel DRAW! features, tricks, and techniques. Perhaps
these exercises have stimulated you to create your own original
designs, or given you new ideas for embellishing on existing ones.
Whatever your field, your work in this tutorial has given you the
tools to create more effective illustrations, documents, presentations, and designs. Corel DRAW! makes it all possible!

INSTALLING COREL DRAW! AND ENHANCING PERFORMANCE

Installing Corel DRAW!
Enhancing Operating Speed and Performance

T he first half of this appendix guides you through the process
of installing Corel DRAW!. If you have installed your software already, you will find the second half of the appendix more
useful. It contains numerous tips on maximizing Corel DRAW!'s
operating speed that will benefit beginning, intermediate, and
advanced users equally.

INSTALLING COREL DRAW!

This section contains detailed instructions on installing Corel DRAW!. Before you install Corel DRAW!, you must install Microsoft Windows and ensure that it is working properly. Refer to the documentation that came with your Microsoft Windows software for full instructions on installing Windows correctly.

System Requirements

Before you begin the installation procedure, review the hardware and software requirements contained in this section. You can help ensure trouble-free operation of Corel DRAW! by checking to see that your system meets all requirements.

COMPUTERS AND HARD DRIVE SPACE   Your computer should be an IBM AT- or PS/2- compatible system (based on an 80286 or 80386 microprocessor) with a hard disk drive and at least one floppy disk drive. Your hard disk drive should have at least 8 to 10 megabytes (MB) of space available before you install Microsoft Windows and Corel DRAW!. Of this amount, at least 3 MB should remain free *after* you have installed the software. This memory is needed because Corel DRAW! generates large temporary files with the extension TMP each time you run the software. The size of these files can vary, depending on the complexity of your graphics and the number of bitmapped images you import (each bitmap generates a temporary file corresponding to the size of the image in Kb). However, you should ensure that the temporary files have plenty of room to work.

If you have less than 3 MB of hard drive space available after you install Corel DRAW!, remove any unneeded applications or files. Alternatively, you might choose not to install the sample Corel Systems or third-party clipart files that are provided with your software. You need a few of these files to perform some of the exercises in the book, but you can copy them to your hard drive individually as they are required.

DISPLAY ADAPTERS AND MONITORS Microsoft Windows, not Corel DRAW!, determines which display adapter and monitor choices are available to you. Not all graphics adapters work well with Corel DRAW!, however. For best operation, you should have an EGA, VGA, Hercules, or other display adapter that has a vertical resolution of 350 or greater. If you wish to preview your images in color, you need an EGA or VGA display adapter and compatible monitor.

A "bug" in the generic screen drivers supplied with Windows versions 2.1 and earlier causes problems when Corel DRAW! users preview fountain fills in color. The screen drivers supplied with Windows versions 2.11 and later, however, are problem free. Since Corel Systems cannot predict which version of Windows you will be using, Corel DRAW! is set to display fountain fill previews in black and white when you first install it. If you are using Windows 2.11 or later *and* you installed the Windows generic screen driver, you can edit your WIN.INI file to change this setting and preview fountain fills in color. See Chapter 15 for instructions on making the appropriate changes to your WIN.INI file.

Keep in mind that the "bug" in Windows version 2.1 and earlier is due to the screen drivers supplied with Windows, not to Windows itself. If you installed *any* version of Windows using a custom screen driver provided by your display adapter, this caution may or may not apply. Only the quality of that screen driver determines whether you can preview fountain fills in color successfully. To see if a custom Windows screen driver is adequate, edit your WIN.INI file as described in Chapter 15 and experiment with color fountain fills in the preview window.

DRAWING DEVICES   You must have a mouse or other drawing device, such as a graphics tablet, in order to run Corel DRAW!. The Setup program you run when you install Microsoft Windows lists the drawing devices that Windows supports. If you use a graphics tablet instead of a mouse, choose one that has the activation button on the side rather than on the top. This type of design gives you the best results because it minimizes unwanted movement on the screen.

This book assumes that most users work with a mouse instead of some other type of drawing device. References to a mouse therefore apply to any drawing device.

OUTPUT DEVICES   Using the Print and Export commands in the File menu, you can output your Corel DRAW! images to paper (standard printers) or to formats used by film recorders and slide generation equipment. Chapter 16 discusses output to 35mm slide generation or presentation equipment in greater detail. If you normally print your images to paper, however, you will achieve the best results with the following types of printers:

- PostScript printers, imagesetters, and PostScript controller boards licensed by Adobe Systems

- HP LaserJet series or 100% compatible

- HP PaintJet and DeskJet printers

Although Windows supports other printers as well, many of these cannot reproduce complex Corel DRAW! images exactly as expected. In addition, a few of the most complex Corel DRAW! features can be output on PostScript printers only. For more information on printer limitations, see Chapter 18.

MEMORY REQUIREMENTS   It may come as a surprise to you to learn that you can take advantage of all of Corel DRAW!'s advanced graphics and text handling abilities with only 640 Kilobytes (640K) of memory. Corel DRAW! itself does not support expanded or extended memory; if you have expanded or extended memory available, however, Windows can use it to speed file-handling functions in Corel DRAW!. The "Enhancing Operating Speed and Performance" section of this appendix covers this subject more fully.

OPERATING SYSTEM AND WINDOWS REQUIREMENTS You need DOS 2.0 or later and Microsoft Windows 2.0 or later to run Corel DRAW!. Please note, however, that if you create color fountain fills, the screen driver you installed with Windows determines whether or not you can preview them in color successfully. Refer back to the "Display Adapters and Monitors" section of this appendix for more information on screen driver limitations. Chapter 15 provides instructions for changing your WIN.INI file so that you can preview Corel DRAW! fountain fills in color.

Installing the Software

The INSTALL program for Corel DRAW! installs program files, fonts, and (at your option) sample files onto your hard disk. This requires anywhere from two to three disks, depending on the version of Corel DRAW! and whether you are using 5 1/4-inch or 3 1/2-inch disks. You also received several additional disks containing clipart images from a variety of clipart vendors. In most versions of Corel DRAW!, the INSTALL program does not install the clipart for you automatically. If you have sufficient space available on your hard drive, you can copy the clipart files onto separate directories, and then import the images while running Corel DRAW!. Chapter 16 discusses how to import these and other clip-art files.

The directions that the INSTALL program gives you vary slightly from version to version. The following step-by-step summary covers the essential information; if your procedure seems different, follow the on-screen instructions exactly. Before you begin, take note of the drive and directory where you have installed Microsoft Windows, and decide where you want to install Corel DRAW!.

1. Insert the Program Disk into the floppy drive from which you want to install Corel DRAW!. This book assumes that you are installing the software from drive A.

2. Type **a:install** and press (ENTER). (If you are installing Corel DRAW! from a different floppy drive, type that drive name instead of "a:".) INSTALL provides some preliminary information on the screen.

3. Read the preliminary information. When you are ready to proceed, press (ENTER) to continue or type **q** to quit without installing the program. Some versions of Corel DRAW! have an additional information screen. You can exit the additional screen using the same commands.

4. INSTALL now asks where you have installed Microsoft Windows and proposes C:\WINDOWS as the default path. To accept C:\WINDOWS, press (ENTER). If you have installed Windows in a different drive and/or directory, type the path name in full and then press (ENTER).

5. INSTALL asks you at this point for the name of the destination directory where you want to install Corel DRAW! and proposes a default path. To accept the pathname offered, press (ENTER). If you want to give your Corel DRAW! directory another name, type the path name in full and then press (ENTER).

6. INSTALL allows you to check to make sure you have specified the correct Windows and/or Corel DRAW! directory. In some versions of Corel DRAW!, you can type **d** if you make an error, and INSTALL will allow you to type an alternative path name. If the path name that appears on the screen is correct and you want to continue, press (ENTER).

7. Depending on your software version, INSTALL may ask you whether you are upgrading from an earlier version or installing Corel DRAW! for the first time. (Versions 1.11 and later allow you to choose whether to install the sample files only, without software.) Follow the on-screen instructions to respond properly so that INSTALL can edit your WIN.INI configuration file if necessary.

8. INSTALL now asks you to specify the drive you are using as the source drive for the installation and proposes drive A. If this is correct, press (ENTER) to begin installing the software. If drive A is not correct, type the drive name you are using and press (ENTER). INSTALL begins copying program files to the destination drive and directory you specified.

9. When INSTALL has installed the necessary program files, it prompts you to remove the program disk and insert a fonts disk. Insert the requested disk and then press (ENTER). INSTALL now uncompresses font files in alphabetical order and copies them to your hard drive. Depending on your software version and disk format, INSTALL may prompt you to insert a second fonts disk to continue the installation.

10. INSTALL asks whether you want to copy the sample drawing files from Corel Systems. If you are installing a version earlier than 1.11, these files occupy approximately 600K of hard disk space. If you are installing version 1.11 or later, the sample files require 1.1 MB of space. If you want to install these files and you have the required space available, type **y** and press (ENTER).

INSTALL then creates a directory on your hard disk, called CDRFILES, where you can store both the sample files and your own artwork conveniently. If you do not want to install the sample files, simply press (ENTER) to accept the default answer of No that INSTALL proposes. You can install them later by choosing the Install Sample Files Only option of the INSTALL program. Keep in mind, however, that if you do not install these files, INSTALL will *not* create a CDRFILES subdirectory of CORELDRW. If you wish to keep all your artwork in a single directory but have not installed the sample files, you can create this subdirectory later by manually using the MKDIR command in DOS (example: MKDIR CDRFILES).

11. In some versions of the software, INSTALL now displays a screen of information about third-party clipart images provided on separate disks and suggests how to copy them onto your hard disk manually.

This completes the automatic installation procedure. If you would like to install the sample clipart images on your hard drive, you can do so manually. Make directories for each clipart manufacturer, just as you see them on the disks provided with your software, and then copy the files into the appropriate directories.

You should also decide whether you want to make a backup copy of your drawings when you run Corel DRAW!. If you do, edit the [CDrawConfig] section of your WIN.INI file so that the last line in the section reads "MakeBackupWhenSave=1." If you do not want Corel DRAW! to make backup copies of your illustrations, edit this line so that it reads "MakeBackupWhenSave=0."

Before starting Corel DRAW!, read the following sections for hints on optimizing software performance. Then, turn to Chapter 1 to begin running Corel DRAW!.

ENHANCING OPERATING SPEED AND PERFORMANCE

Corel DRAW! boasts lightning speed in comparison with other graphics applications that run under Microsoft Windows. Nevertheless, you can increase software operating speed even further by taking one or more of the steps mentioned in this section. The suggestions under "Managing Memory" apply to all Corel DRAW! users. Review "Using SMARTDRV and RAMDRIVE" if you have expanded or extended memory available.

Managing Memory

Corel DRAW! uses only the 640K in your system's main memory. Whether or not you have expanded or extended memory, you will want to make available to Corel DRAW! as much of your system's main memory (640K) as possible. A good rule of thumb is to have at least 250K still available (300K or more is preferable) after you load both Windows and Corel DRAW!. Follow these steps to find out how much main memory is available when you are running Corel DRAW!:

1. Load Corel DRAW! with the Windows MS-DOS Executive running as an icon in the background. Review the "Starting Corel DRAW!" section in Chapter 1 if you need help on how to do this.

2. Click on the minimize arrow at the upper-right corner of the screen. The Corel DRAW! window becomes a small icon in the lower-left corner of the screen.

3. Maximize the MS-DOS Executive by clicking on the Windows icon and then on the Maximize command in the pop-up menu. The MS-DOS Executive again fills the screen and contains a listing of the files in the current directory.

4. Select the About MS-DOS Executive command in the File menu. The information box in Figure A-1 appears.

5. Check the "Conventional Memory Free" line. The figure listed here should be at least 250K.

6. Click on OK to remove the information box from the screen.

7. Click on the Windows control-menu icon 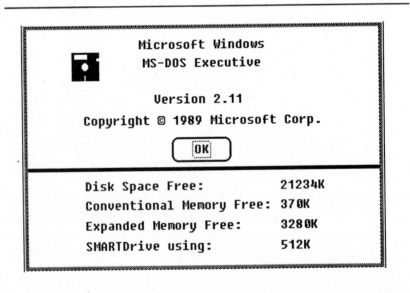 at the upper-left corner of the screen and select the Minimize command. Windows again becomes a small icon.

8. To return to Corel DRAW!, click on the Corel DRAW! icon and select Maximize from the pop-up menu.

```
                    Microsoft Windows
                    MS-DOS Executive

                       Version 2.11
          Copyright © 1989 Microsoft Corp.
                        ┌────────┐
                        │   OK   │
                        └────────┘

          Disk Space Free:           21234K
          Conventional Memory Free:  370K
          Expanded Memory Free:      3280K
          SMARTDrive using:          512K
```

FIGURE A-1   Checking available memory

If the figure in the "Conventional Memory Free" line on your screen was smaller than 250K, you may need to take further steps to free additional memory. The following sections describe some suggested steps in greater detail.

REMOVING TSR'S AND NONESSENTIAL DRIVERS FROM YOUR SYSTEM FILES   Remove any references to memory-resident programs (also known as TSR's, or terminate-and-stay-resident programs) from your AUTOEXEC.BAT file so that these programs do not load automatically when you start your computer. Memory-resident programs may include DOS shells and menuing systems, fax board or modem software, or anything else you normally store in main memory to run at the touch of a hot key.

After you have edited your AUTOEXEC.BAT file, check your CONFIG.SYS file as well. Remove all unnecessary drivers from your CONFIG.SYS file except for the hard drive manager, FILES and BUFFERS statements, and drivers needed to run Windows (may including HIMEM.SYS, RAMDRIVE.SYS, or SMART-DRV.SYS).

LOADING COREL DRAW! TO SAVE MEMORY   You can load Corel DRAW! in several different ways, and some consume more memory than others. For example, if you start Windows and then run Corel DRAW! without running the MS-DOS executive as an icon in the background (see Chapter 1), Windows takes up more system memory than it needs to. Always run Corel DRAW! with the MS-DOS Executive running as an icon in the background.

If this measure still does not free enough main memory, you can save a little more by loading Corel DRAW! a different way. Assuming that Corel DRAW! is installed in the path C:\WIN-DOWS\CORELDRW, start Corel DRAW! by typing the following command at the DOS prompt:

win :c:\windows\coreldrw\coreldrw

Be sure to leave a space after "win" and to type the colon (:) both before and after the drive name. The first "coreldrw" indicates the destination directory where Corel DRAW! is installed, while the second "coreldrw" invokes the CORELDRW.EXE command that starts the program. If Corel DRAW! is installed in a different location on your hard drive, customize the command to include the correct pathname.

The colon (:) in front of the drive name tells Windows to load Corel DRAW! without first loading the MS-DOS Executive. This method of running Corel DRAW! increases speed markedly and works well when you have no memory-resident programs running simultaneously, but it does have some limitations. For example, you cannot import or export images to another application through the Windows clipboard or run the WFNBOSS or Corel Trace! utilities automatically unless the MS-DOS Executive is running in the background. Start Corel DRAW! with the aforementioned special command when you do not need these features during a session.

CREATING MULTIPLE SYSTEM FILES TO RUN DIFFER-ENT APPLICATIONS   If you use many different software programs, you may need to retain most of the TSR's and drivers statements in your AUTOEXEC.BAT and CONFIG.SYS files. Removing many of these statements would be inconvenient because you might need these drivers in order to run applications other than Corel DRAW!. One solution to this problem is to create two different configuration files for your system: one to run Windows applications, and one to run all other programs. Follow these steps to run your system with two different CONFIG files:

1. Copy your CONFIG.SYS file twice using the DOS COPY command. Name the first copy CONFIG.WIN and the second

CONFIG.ALL. You will use CONFIG.WIN for your Windows applications and CONFIG.ALL with all other applications.

2. Copy your AUTOEXEC.BAT file twice in the same way. Name the first copy AUTOEXEC.WIN and the second AUTOEXEC.ALL. You will use AUTOEXEC.WIN for your Windows applications and CONFIG.ALL with all other applications.

3. Using DOS EDLIN or another convenient text editor, edit the CONFIG.WIN and AUTOEXEC.WIN files and eliminate all statements except the ones you need to run Windows applications. Save the files with these changes.

4. Edit the CONFIG.ALL and AUTOEXEC.ALL files so that they contain only the drivers you need to run non-Windows applications. Save the files with these changes.

5. Before running an application that requires the CONFIG.WIN and AUTOEXEC.WIN files, type **copy config.win config.sys** at the DOS prompt and press (ENTER). Then type **copy autoexec.win autoexec.bat** and press (ENTER) again.

6. Reboot your computer after copying these files. Your CONFIG.SYS and AUTOEXEC.BAT files now contain only the drivers needed by Microsoft Windows applications.

7. Before running an application that requires the drivers in the CONFIG.ALL and AUTOEXEC.ALL files, then type **copy config.all config.sys** at the DOS prompt and press (ENTER). Then type **copy autoexec.all autoexec.bat** and press (ENTER) again.

8. Reboot your computer after copying these files. Your CONFIG.SYS and AUTOEXEC.BAT files now contain only the drivers that other programs require.

Some users have difficulty remembering when to copy the correct configuration file, or they may prefer a shortcut command. To automate this file-switching process even further, you can create two simple batch files using DOS EDLIN or another text editor. Each batch file should contain commands for copying the appropriate configuration file to CONFIG.SYS and for rebooting the computer automatically. You might give each batch file convenient names such as BOOTWIN.BAT and BOOTALL.BAT to remind yourself of their purpose. Consult your DOS manual for assistance in creating batch files.

RUNNING MEMORY-RESIDENT PROGRAMS AND DRIVERS IN HIGH MEMORY   If you have extended or expanded memory, you can take advantage of popular utility programs that tell your computer to run memory-resident programs and drivers in the "high memory" between 640K and 1 MB. This method frees up most or all of your system memory (the first 640K) so that you can run Corel DRAW! as efficiently as possible. Example of such memory-management programs for 80386-based computers include Quarterdeck's QEMM and Qualitas Software's 386 to the Max, but other commercial and shareware utilities are available as well. Check with computer software dealers or shareware catalogs to find the utility that is right for you.

After trying one or more of the preceding suggestions, check the memory available to Corel DRAW! a second time. (If you choose to run Corel DRAW! without the MS-DOS executive, you cannot access the About MS-DOS Executive information screen.) You should now have sufficient main memory to use even the most advanced Corel DRAW! features without encountering speed limitations or other problems.

Using SMARTDRV and RAMDRIVE

If you have extended or expanded memory in your computer system, you can use the SMARTDRV and RAMDRIVE utilities that come with Microsoft Windows to improve the operating speed of Corel DRAW!. SMARTDRV.SYS is a *disk caching* utility that stores the most recently used software commands so that the software does not need to make many calls to the hard drive. Although Corel DRAW! program features do not directly support the use of extended or expanded memory, Windows can use it for SMARTDRV to speed up file-handling functions. Corel DRAW! performance benefits as a result.

A RAM drive, on the other hand, allows you to store the temporary files that Corel DRAW! generates when you are running the program. When you store these files at the speed of memory rather than at the speed of the hard drive, the operation speed of Corel DRAW! improves.

Follow these general guidelines to use SMARTDRV and RAM-DRIVE most efficiently with Corel DRAW!.

1 MB OR LESS OF EXPANDED OR EXTENDED MEM-ORY   If you have 1 MB or less of expanded or extended memory, reserve all of it for SMARTDRV. You will also need to alter your CONFIG.SYS file if you did not install SMARTDRV automatically when you installed Windows. Consult your Windows documentation for instructions on how to alter this file.

2 MB OR MORE OF EXPANDED OR EXTENDED MEM-ORY   If you have 2 MB or more of expanded or extended memory and are running DOS 3.2 or later, you can use both

SMARTDRV and RAMDRIVE. Reserve 1 MB of the expanded or extended memory for SMARTDRV, and then create a RAM drive with some of the remainder. Ideally, the RAM drive should contain enough memory to store all of the temporary files you generate. If you use multiple bitmap, for example, you may require several megabytes to store temporary files.

To create a RAM drive, edit your CONFIG.SYS file to include the following statement:

device=RAMDRIVE.SYS *size sector* /E /A

In this statement, *size* should indicate the amount of memory you want to set aside, expressed in kilobytes. This number should be a multiple of 16. The *sector* indicates the size in bytes of each sector in the RAM drive; you can specify 128, 256, 512, or 1024. If you do not enter a number, the value defaults to 512 for the file RAMDRIVE.SYS provided with Microsoft Windows. The /E in the statement tells DOS to put the RAM drive in extended memory, while the /A statement tells DOS to put it in expanded memory. You can use either /E or /A in your RAMDRIVE statement, but not both.

 Make sure that the directory where RAMDRIVE.SYS is located is in the path statement of your AUTOEXEC.BAT file if you want your computer to know where to find RAMDRIVE.SYS each time you reboot the system.

When you have finished editing your CONFIG.SYS file to include the RAMDRIVE statement, edit your AUTOEXEC.BAT file to include the following statement:

SET TEMP=*x*:

In this statement, x is the letter you have assigned to the RAMDRIVE. This letter should be one letter *beyond* the last letter of your hard drive. For example, if you have hard drives C through E, you should assign the letter F to your RAM drive.

caution When using a RAM drive to run Corel DRAW!, be sure that you are using the RAMDRIVE.SYS driver that comes with Windows. Some incompatibilities between Windows and the regular DOS RAMDRIVE.SYS driver may exist. Refer to the README.TXT file provided with your copy of Microsoft Windows.

MENU SUMMARIES

The File Menu
The Edit Menu
The Transform Menu
The Arrange Menu
The Display Menu
The Special Menu

This appendix provides a quick overview of the commands contained in the six Corel DRAW! menus and how they function. Since this book is a training guide rather than a reference manual, the chapters are organized according to the tasks that you perform, not according to the layout of the Corel DRAW! screen. You will find this appendix most useful when you need to refresh your memory about the function of a particular command.

THE FILE MENU

The File menu, shown in Figure B-1, contains commands that apply to file-handling functions rather than software features. A summary of each command in the File menu follows.

New   Select New when you want to clear the screen and begin creating a new picture. If you have made changes to the current picture, Corel DRAW! always gives you the option of saving your changes before erasing the picture from the screen.

Open   Choose this command to open an existing graphic that you have created previously. If you have another graphic on the screen, Corel DRAW! gives you the option of saving your current changes

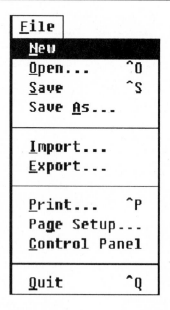

FIGURE B-1   The File menu

or simply clearing it from the screen without saving the changes. You use the controls in the Open Drawing dialog box to specify the name and location of the file you want to open.

Save   Select this command to save your work under the current filename, which appears at the top of the screen. If you have not saved the picture previously, you will be prompted to enter a name for it in the Save As dialog box.

Save As. . .   Choose this command to name a new picture, or to give an existing picture a different name so that you do not overwrite the previous version. You enter a name for the picture in the Save As dialog box.

Import. . .   Select this command when you want to import a graphics file from a paint program, object-oriented graphics program, or scanning software or clip-art. Corel DRAW! supports a wide variety of file formats.

Export. . .   Choose this command when you want to save your Corel DRAW! graphic in a format that can be exported to another application. Corel DRAW! supports export to a variety of desktop publishing and graphics programs, as well as to popular slide generation and presentation software and equipment.

Print. . .   Select this command to output some or all of the current graphic to a printer or to a file. You have many different printing options, which you specify in the Print Options dialog box. You cannot print a drawing that is not currently open.

Page Setup. . .   Choose this command to alter the size or format of the page that contains your graphic. You can specify a custom page size.

Control Panel   The Control Panel command is a convenient way for you to access Microsoft Windows functions without having to leave Corel DRAW! and return to the MS-DOS Executive. Select this command when you wish to add or delete printers, change printer configuration or defaults, add or delete fonts, or change screen colors and other Windows default settings.

Quit   Use this command to exit Corel DRAW!. If you have made any changes to the current graphic, Corel DRAW! gives you the option of saving them.

THE EDIT MENU

The Edit menu, shown in Figure B-2, contains a broad spectrum of commands that involve changes you make to selected objects. Other menus contain commands that let you edit objects, too, but their commands are specialized, whereas the commands in the Edit menu involve more general editing functions.

Undo   Select this command to undo the *last* change you made to a selected object or group of objects. This command is most handy when you need to reverse changes you have made accidentally. Undo is not available for operations such as changing magnification, selecting objects, and opening or exporting files.

Redo   This command becomes available only when you have just chosen to Undo an operation. It gives you the opportunity to change your mind again and restore the picture to the way it appeared before you applied Undo.

Repeat   Select Repeat to repeat the most recently performed operation on the currently selected object. This command is available only when an object is selected.

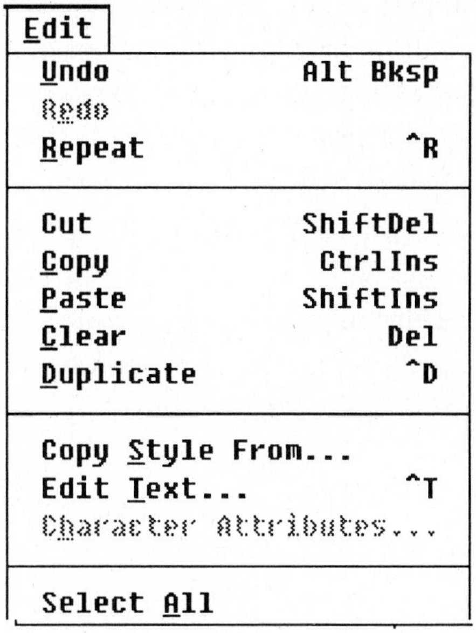

```
┌─────────────────────────────────┐
│ ┌─────┐                         │
│ │Edit │                         │
│ └─────┘                         │
│   Undo              Alt Bksp    │
│   Redo                          │
│   Repeat                  ^R    │
│ ─────────────────────────────── │
│   Cut               ShiftDel    │
│   Copy               CtrlIns    │
│   Paste             ShiftIns    │
│   Clear                  Del    │
│   Duplicate               ^D    │
│ ─────────────────────────────── │
│   Copy Style From...            │
│   Edit Text...            ^T    │
│   Character Attributes...       │
│ ─────────────────────────────── │
│   Select All                    │
└─────────────────────────────────┘
```

FIGURE B-2   The Edit menu

Cut   Choose Cut to delete the currently selected object from the page and send a copy of it to the clipboard. You can then paste the cut object to another picture or Windows application.

Copy   Select this command to send a copy of the currently selected object to the clipboard, while retaining the object on the page. You can then paste the copy to another picture or Windows application.

Paste   This command is available only when you have cut or copied an object to the clipboard. Choose this command to paste the cut or copied object to the current picture.

Clear   Select this command to delete the currently selected object from the page, without sending a copy to the clipboard. You cannot retrieve a cleared object again, unless you select Undo immediately.

Duplicate   Choose this command to make an exact duplicate of the currently selected object appear in the current picture. You use the Place Duplicate option in the Preferences dialog box to determine how far away the duplicate appears from the original.

Copy Style From. . .   Select this command to copy the text, outline, outline fill, and/or fill attributes of one object to the currently selected object. After making your selection in the Copy Style dialog box, you select the object from which you want to copy attributes.

Edit Text. . .   Choose this command to change the content, alignment, typeface, typestyle, point size, or spacing of a currently selected text string. The changes you make apply to all of the characters in the text string.

Character Attributes. . .   Select this command to change the typeface, typestyle, point size, horizontal shift, vertical shift, or angle of specified characters *within* a text string. This command is available only when you have selected characters with the Shaping tool.

Select All   Choose this command to select all of the objects in an image automatically.

THE TRANSFORM MENU

The commands in the Transform menu (see Figure B- 3) apply to a special group of editing operations that you can perform only when the Select tool is active: stretching, scaling, rotating, and skewing, and creating mirror images. Corel DRAW! refers to these operations collectively as transformations.

Rotate & Skew...   Choose this command when you want to rotate or skew the currently selected object or group of objects. Using the Rotate & Skew dialog box, you can specify the exact degree of rotation, as well as whether to leave a copy of the original object on the screen.

Stretch & Mirror...   Choose this command to stretch, scale, or create a mirror image of the currently selected object or group of objects. Using the Stretch & Mirror dialog box, you can specify the exact percentage of stretching, as well as whether to leave a copy of the original object on the screen.

```
┌─────────────┐
│ Transform   │
├─────────────┴──────────────┐
│  Rotate & Skew...          │
│  Stretch & Mirror...       │
├────────────────────────────┤
│  Clear Transformations     │
└────────────────────────────┘
```

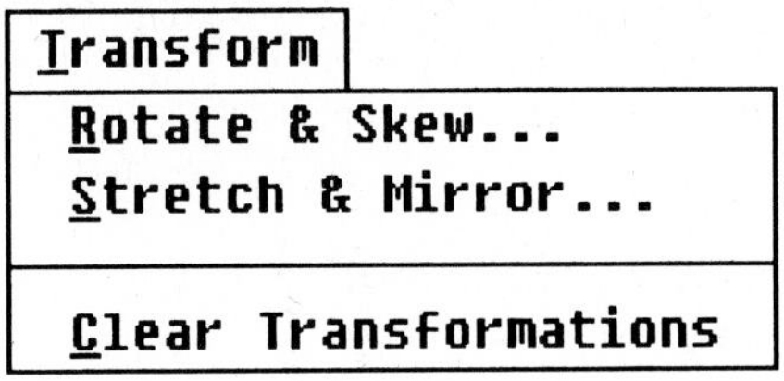

FIGURE B-3   The Transform menu

Clear Transformations   Choose this command to return a transformed (and currently selected) object to its original state, no matter how many times you have transformed it during the current session.

THE ARRANGE MENU

The Arrange menu, shown in Figure B-4, contains commands that alter the relative positions of objects within a picture.

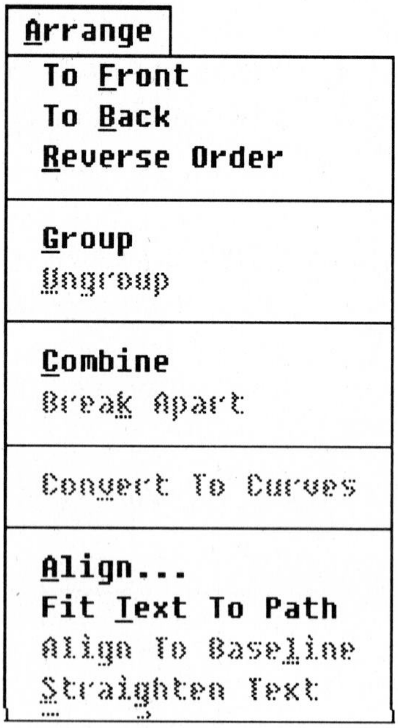

FIGURE B-4   The Arrange menu

To Front   Select this command to place the currently selected object in front of all the other objects in the picture (as the top layer in the picture).

To Back   Choose this command to place the currently selected object behind all the other objects in the picture (as the bottom layer in the picture).

Reverse Order   Choose this command to reverse the top-to-bottom arrangement of a group of selected objects.

Group   Select the Group command when you want Corel DRAW! to treat all of the currently selected objects as a unit. Changes that you make to a group apply to all the objects in the group.

Ungroup   Choose this command to separate the currently selected Group back into individual objects. You can then edit each object separately.

Combine   Select the Combine command to meld the currently selected objects into one object. Overlapping areas within the combined object display as transparent holes. This command is especially useful for creating masks and reducing file size.

Break Apart   Choose this command to break the currently selected combined object back into individual objects. When text is part of the combined object, selecting this command causes each closed path to become a separate curve object.

Convert To Curves   Choose this command to turn the currently selected object into a curve object so that you can alter its shape more freely.

Align. . .   Choose the Align command when you want to align two or more currently selected objects. You can align objects in one of fifteen different ways, using the six options in the Align dialog box.

Fit Text To Path   Use this command when at least one of two selected objects is a text string and you want the text (the first object) to follow the shape of the second object. You can fit text to any type of curve object in Corel DRAW!.

Align To Baseline   Select this command to align all the letters in a text string to their current baseline. Typically, you would perform this operation after changing the vertical shift or kerning individual letters with the Shaping tool, or after fitting text to a curve.

Straighten Text   Use this command when you have either fitted text to a path or edited individual characters with the Shaping tool and want to straighten the entire text string again.

THE DISPLAY MENU

The Display Menu, shown in Figure B-5, contains commands that affect the appearance of the Corel DRAW! screen or of objects on the screen.

Snap To Grid   Select the Snap To Grid command to turn the invisible grid on or off. When a checkmark appears in front of the command, the grid is turned on; when a checkmark does not appear, it is turned off. You specify the frequency of the grid using the Grid Size command, also in the Display menu. Work with the

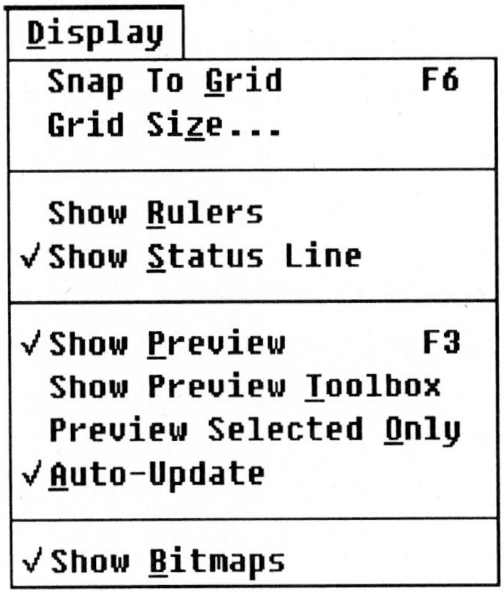

```
┌────────────────┐
│ Display │      │
├────────────────┤
│  Snap To Grid       F6 │
│  Grid Size...          │
├────────────────────────┤
│  Show Rulers           │
│ √Show Status Line      │
├────────────────────────┤
│ √Show Preview       F3 │
│  Show Preview Toolbox  │
│  Preview Selected Only │
│ √Auto-Update           │
├────────────────────────┤
│ √Show Bitmaps          │
└────────────────────────┘
```

FIGURE B-5   The Display menu

grid on when you want to align objects at precise increments on the page.

Grid Size...   Select this command to specify the frequency of the invisible grid. Using the controls in the Grid dialog box, you can change the unit of measurement in which the grid is measured, as well as the grid frequency value. Your changes have an effect only if the Snap To Grid command is turned on, however.

Show Rulers   Select the Show Rulers command to display or conceal the rulers. When a checkmark appears in front of the command, the ruler display is turned on; when a checkmark does not appear, it is turned off. The unit of measurement you specify using the Grid Size command determines the unit of measurement of the rulers.

Show Status Line   Choose this command to display or conceal the status line information. When a checkmark appears in front of the command, the status line is turned on; when a checkmark does not appear, it is turned off. Status line information varies, depending on the selected object or current operation, but is especially helpful for work that requires precision.

Show Preview   Select this command to display or conceal the preview window. When a checkmark appears in front of the command, the preview window is turned on; when a checkmark does not appear, it is turned off. The preview window allows you to see the fill colors, outline colors, and layering of objects in the current drawing.

Show Preview Toolbox   This command, available only when the preview window is currently displayed, allows you to turn the display of the preview toolbox on or off. When a checkmark appears in front of this command, the preview toolbox is turned on; when a checkmark does not appear, it is turned off. The preview toolbox allows you to adjust the display of the preview window independently of the editing window and to change the format of the preview window.

Preview Selected Only   This command is available only when the preview window is turned on. Select it to display only the currently selected object or objects in the preview window. This command is especially useful for determining the layers of objects within a graphic, or for viewing small details in a graphic containing many objects.

Auto-Update   This command is available only when the preview window is currently displayed. Choose it to determine whether Corel DRAW! updates the preview window display every time you make a change in the editing window, or only when you click on the preview window. When a checkmark appears in front of this command, the Auto-Update feature is turned on; when a checkmark does not appear, it is turned off. Turning this feature off is useful when you want to reduce screen redraw time.

Show Bitmaps   Select this command to turn the display of bitmapped objects in the editing window on or off. When a checkmark appears in front of the command, the bitmaps will display; when a checkmark does not appear, the command is turned off and bitmaps appear as a blank rectangle. Turn off the display of bitmaps if you want to lessen screen redraw time.

THE SPECIAL MENU

The Special menu, shown in Figure B-6, contains four commands. Three of them involve the Macro feature; the fourth allows you to set parameters for a variety of features in Corel DRAW!.

Record Macro   Choose this command to begin recording a macro, a series of steps that you want to automate. This command is available only when an object is currently selected, and you can record only operations that pertain to the editing of a selected object.

Finish Macro   Select this command when you have recorded all the steps in a macro and are ready to save and name the macro. This command is available only when you are in macro recording mode.

```
┌──────────────┐
│ Special      │
├──────────────┴──┐
│ Record Macro     │
│ Finish Macro...  │
│ Play Macro...    │
├──────────────────┤
│ Preferences...   │
└──────────────────┘
```

FIGURE B-6   The Special menu

Play Macro   Choose this command to replay an existing macro on the currently selected object. This command is available only when macros have already been created and one object or Grouped objects in the current picture are selected.

Preferences   The Preferences command accesses the Preferences dialog box, which contains a number of settings that you can alter to customize the way Corel DRAW! operates. Some of these settings affect the smoothness of curves when the Freehand tool is active. Others determine how fountain fills and outlines display on the screen, and how far duplicated objects are offset from the original object. Another setting lets you choose the character that appears in the preview display of the Text dialog box.

KEYBOARD AND
MOUSE SHORTCUTS

This appendix contains an alphabetical listing of the Corel
DRAW! operations that you can perform using keyboard
shortcuts, without having to select a menu option. A description
of the tasks you may wish to perform appears in the left column,
and their keyboard shortcuts appear in the right column.

This quick reference list does not include the Corel DRAW!
operations that you perform using the mouse only. However, if the
word "click" or "drag" appears in the right column as part of the
key combination, you must click or drag the mouse to complete
the specified action. If a particular tool must be active in order to
carry out the action, its icon appears within the description in the
left column.

Action	Key Combination
Action	**Key Combination**
Activate Select tool	Spacebar
Activate previous tool ([↖] active)	Spacebar
Align multiple selected objects ([↖] active)	(ALT-A)
Align selected text to baseline ([↖] active)	(ALT-A) + (L)
Arc, convert circle to, in 15-degree increments ([⌃] active)	(CTRL) + drag node
Auto-Update preview window (with preview window on)	(ALT-D) + (A)
Break apart selected combined object ([↖] active)	(ALT-A) + (K)
Clear Transformations to selected object ([↖] active)	(ALT-T) + (C)
Combine selected objects ([↖] active)	(ALT-A) + (C)
Control Panel, open	(ALT-F) + (C)
Convert selected object to Curves ([↖] active)	(ALT-A) + (V)
Copy selected object to clipboard ([↖] active)	(CTRL) + (INS), (ALT-E) + (C) + (ENTER)
Copy Style From one object to another	(ALT-E) + (S)
Cut selected object to clipboard ([↖] active)	(SHIFT) + (DEL)
Delete (clear) newly drawn or selected object	(DEL), (ALT-E) + (C) + (C) + (ENTER)
Dialog box, move to next field in	(TAB)
Dialog box, move to previous field in	(SHIFT-TAB)
Draw circle ([◯] active)	(CTRL) + drag
Draw circle from center outward ([◯] active)	(CTRL-SHIFT) + drag

Action	Key Combination
Draw ellipse from center outward (⬭ active)	(SHIFT) + drag
Draw line in increments of 15-degree angles (✎ active)	(CTRL) + click
Draw rectangle from center outward (▢ active)	(SHIFT) + drag
Draw square (▢ active)	(CTRL) + drag
Draw square from center outward (▢ active)	(CTRL-SHIFT) + drag
Duplicate selected object(s) (▲ active)	(CTRL-D), (ALT-E) + (D)
Edit attributes of selected characters (▢ active)	(ALT-E) + (H)
Edit text attributes, newly drawn or selected text	(CTRL-T), (ALT-E) + (T)
Erase portions of curve as you draw (✎ active)	(SHIFT) + drag
Export current picture	(ALT-F) + (E)
Finish Macro (save & name)	(ALT-S) + (F)
Fit Text to a path (▲ active)	(ALT-A) + (T)
Grid Size, specify	(ALT-D) + (Z)
Grid, turn on/off	(F6)
Group multiple selected objects (▲ active)	(ALT-A) + (G)
Import a file	(ALT-F) + (I)
Maximize Corel DRAW! window	(ALT-F10)
Minimize Corel DRAW! window	(ALT-F9)
Move Corel DRAW! window	(ALT-F7) + arrow keys + (ENTER)
Move selected objects at 90-degree angles (▲ active)	(CTRL) + drag outline
New (clear screen)	(ALT-F) + (N)
Open File	(CTRL-O), (ALT-F) + (O)
Page Setup	(ALT-F) + (G)

Action	Key Combination
Paste object from clipboard	(SHIFT) + (INS), (ALT-E) + (P)
Play existing Macro (object selected, [↖] active)	(ALT-S) + (P)
Preferences, edit	(ALT-S) + (E)
Preview Selected Only, turn off/on (with preview on)	(ALT-D) + (O)
Preview Window, activate/deactivate	(F3)
Print File	(CTRL-P), (ALT-F) + (P)
Quit Corel DRAW!	(CTRL-Q), (ALT-F4), (ALT-F) + (Q)
Record Macro (object selected, [↖] active)	(ALT-S) + (R)
Redo last undone operation	(ALT-E) + (E)
Repeat last operation on selected object ([↖] active)	(CTRL-R), (ALT-E) + (R)
Reverse Order of multiple selected objects ([↖] active)	(ALT-A) + (R)
Rotate & Skew selected object ([↖] active)	(ALT-T) + (R)
Rotate selected object in 15-degree increments ([↖] active)	(CTRL) + drag corner node
Save current picture	(CTRL-S), (ALT-F) + (S)
Save As, name current picture	(ALT-F) + (A)
Scale selected object in 100% increments ([↖] active)	(CTRL) + drag corner node
Scale selected object, leave original ([↖] active)	drag corner node, Plus key, drag
Select All objects	(ALT-E) + (A)
Select multiple objects ([↖] active)	(SHIFT) + click
Select next object in picture ([↖] active)	(TAB)
Select previous object in picture ([↖] active)	(SHIFT-TAB)
Show Bitmaps in editing window	(ALT-D) + (B)

Action	**Key Combination**
Show Rulers, turn on/off	(ALT-D) + (R)
Show Status Line, turn on/off	(ALT-D) + (S)
Show Preview Toolbox, turn on/off (with preview on)	(ALT-D) + (T)
Show Preview window, turn on/off	(F3), (ALT-D) + (P)
Size screen	(ALT-F8) + arrow keys + (ENTER)
Skew selected object in 15-degree increments (⬉ active)	(CTRL) + drag middle node
Snap To Grid, turn on/off	(F6), (ALT-D) + (G)
Straighten selected text (⬉ active)	(ALT-A) + (S)
Stretch & Mirror selected object (⬉ active)	(ALT-T) + (S)
Stretch selected object(s) in 100% increments (⬉ active)	(CTRL) + drag middle node
Stretch selected object(s), leave original (⬉ active)	(•) key, drag middle node
To Back, move selected object to (⬉ active)	(ALT-A) + (B)
To Front, move selected object (⬉ active)	(ALT-A) + (F)
Undo last operation	(ALT) + (BACKSPACE), (ALT-E) + (U)
Ungroup selected group (⬉ active)	(ALT-A) + (U)
Wedge, convert circle to, 15-degree increments (⬉ active)	(CTRL) + drag node

COREL CONNECTIVITY:
CLIP ART AND FONTS

Clip-Art Vendors with Supported Formats
Corel DRAW! Character Set Charts
Renaming Corel DRAW! Typefaces
Converting Third-Party Fonts with WFNBOSS

T he growing number of file formats now supported for import
by Corel DRAW! (11 different formats as of release 1.2) make
it possible for you to edit clip art from many manufacturers. In
addition, the WFNBOSS font conversion utility supplied with
versions 1.1 and later gives you access to more than 4000 popular
commercial fonts. This appendix provides supplementary information for Corel DRAW! users who wish to take advantage of clip
art and fonts produced by third-party manufacturers. It also contains tables of the character sets provided with the native Corel
DRAW! typefaces. If you own a PostScript printer, you will find
the instructions at the end of this appendix useful for renaming the

Vendor	Telephone Number	Format	Images Available
ArtRight Software	(613) 820-1000	.CDR	4000
Casady & Greene	(800) 331-4321	.EPS	130
Dream Maker	(800) 876-5665	.EPS	350+
Dynamic Graphics	(800) 255-8800	.EPS	1000+
3G Graphics	(800) 456-0234	.EPS	280+
Image Club Graphics	(800) 661-9410	.EPS	1800+
Marketing Graphics	(800) 368-3773	.CGM	700+
Metro Creative Graphics	(800) 525-1552	.PCX/.TIF	1400+
Micromaps Software	(800) 334-4291	.AI	65
Multi-Ad Services	(309) 692-1530	.EPS	350+
New Vision Technologies	(613) 727-8184	.CGM	800+
T/Maker Company	(415) 962-0195	.EPS	380+

TABLE D-1   Major Clip Art Vendors Providing Images in Importable Formats

Corel DRAW! typefaces to correspond with their PostScript counterparts.

CLIP-ART VENDORS WITH SUPPORTED FORMATS

As of version 1.2, Corel DRAW! can import clip-art in 13 different file formats: .CDR, .PCX, .TIF, Lotus .PIC, Adobe .AI or .EPS, IBM .PIF, .CGM, AutoCAD .DXF, .GEM, HPGL, and MAC PICT. Table D-1 provides a handy reference to the major vendors who have supplied clip-art samples with your software. You can, of course, use clip-art files from other vendors as well. Collectively, these vendors give you access to more than 11,000 images. When the Macintosh PICT import option becomes available, you

033	!	075	K	0117	u	0159		0201	É	0243	ó
034	"	076	L	0118	v	0160		0202	Ê	0244	ô
035	#	077	M	0119	w	0161	¡	0203	Ë	0245	õ
036	$	078	N	0120	x	0162	¢	0204	Ì	0246	ö
037	%	079	O	0121	y	0163	£	0205	Í	0247	œ
038	&	080	P	0122	z	0164	¤	0206	Î	0248	ø
039	'	081	Q	0123	{	0165	¥	0207	Ï	0249	ù
040	(	082	R	0124	|	0166	¦	0208		0250	ú
041	)	083	S	0125	}	0167	§	0209	Ñ	0251	û
042	*	084	T	0126	~	0168	¨	0210	Ò	0252	ü
043	+	085	U	0127		0169	©	0211	Ó	0253	
044	,	086	V	0128	`	0170	ª	0212	Ô	0254	
045	-	087	W	0129	^	0171	«	0213	Õ	0255	ÿ
046	.	088	X	0130	~	0172	¬	0214	Ö		
047	/	089	Y	0131	ı	0173	—	0215	Œ		
048	0	090	Z	0132	ƒ	0174	®	0216	Ø		
049	1	091	[	0133	"	0175		0217	Ù		
050	2	092	\	0134	"	0176	°	0218	Ú		
051	3	093	]	0135	‹	0177		0219	Û		
052	4	094	^	0136	›	0178		0220	Ü		
053	5	095	_	0137	fi	0179		0221			
054	6	096	`	0138	fl	0180	´	0222			
055	7	097	a	0139	†	0181		0223	ß		
056	8	098	b	0140	‡	0182	¶	0224	à		
057	9	099	c	0141	–	0183	•	0225	á		
058	:	0100	d	0142		0184	¸	0226	â		
059	;	0101	e	0143	ˇ	0185		0227	ã		
060	<	0102	f	0144	„	0186	º	0228	ä		
061	=	0103	g	0145	...	0187	»	0229	å		
062	>	0104	h	0146	‰	0188		0230	æ		
063	?	0105	i	0147		0189		0231	ç		
064	@	0106	j	0148		0190		0232	è		
065	A	0107	k	0149		0191	¿	0233	é		
066	B	0108	l	0150		0192	À	0234	ê		
067	C	0109	m	0151		0193	Á	0235	ë		
068	D	0110	n	0152		0194	Â	0236	ì		
069	E	0111	o	0153		0195	Ã	0237	í		
070	F	0112	p	0154		0196	Ä	0238	î		
071	G	0113	q	0155		0197	Å	0239	ï		
072	H	0114	r	0156		0198	Æ	0240			
073	I	0115	s	0157		0199	Ç	0241	ñ		
074	J	0116	t	0158		0200	È	0242	ò		

TABLE D-2   The Corel Character Set

will be able to browse through the advertisements in any Macintosh periodical and choose from thousands of additional clip-art images.

COREL DRAW!
CHARACTER SET CHARTS

As you may recall from Chapter 5, the 43 typefaces and 102 font combinations provided with Corel DRAW! include four typefaces with symbol character sets: Dixieland, Greek/Math Symbols, Geographic, and Musical. The other typefaces supplied with your software use the Corel character set.

If you are using one of the typefaces based on the Corel character set and wish to type a character not found on your keyboard, refer to Table D-2. Activate the Text tool and select an insertion point on your page. When the Text dialog box appears, select the desired typeface, press and hold (ALT), and type the three- or four-character numerical ASCII code that corresponds to the character you want. You *must* include the zero in front of the ASCII code in order for the character to be correct. Keep in mind that the Text dialog box can display only the Windows character set, which differs slightly from the Corel DRAW! character set. As a result, a few of the characters that you type in the Text dialog box look different from the characters that display after you exit the dialog box. All Corel characters display correctly in the editing and preview windows, however. Before typing a non-alphabetic Corel character in the Text dialog box, refer to the Character Chart that came with your software or to Table D-2. As long as the ASCII code that you type matches the character you want, the character will display correctly in the editing and preview windows of Corel DRAW!.

If you wish to use one of the symbol typefaces provided with Corel DRAW!, select the desired character using the appropriate character chart. Tables D-3 through D-6 show the ASCII code and corresponding characters for the Dixieland, Greek/Math Symbols,

033	079 ★	0125 "	0171 ♠	0218
034	080 ☆	0126 "	0172 ①	0219
035	081 ✳	0127	0173 ②	0220 ➜
036	082 ✺	0128	0174 ③	0221 →
037 ☎	083 ✳	0129	0175 ④	0222 →
038 ✆	084 ✳	0130	0176 ⑤	0223 →
039 ✳	085 ✳	0131	0177 ⑥	0224 ➡
040	086 ✳	0132	0178 ⑦	0225 ➡
041 ✉	087 ✳	0133	0179 ⑧	0226 ➢
042 ☛	088 ✳	0134	0180 ⑨	0227 ➢
043 ☞	089 ✳	0135	0181 ⑩	0228 ➢
044	090 ✴	0136	0182 ❶	0229 ➡
045	091 ✳	0137	0183 ❷	0230 ➡
046	092 ✳	0138	0184 ❸	0231
047	093 ✳	0139	0185 ❹	0232 ➡
048	094 ❀	0140	0186 ❺	0233 ⇨
049	095 ❁	0141	0187 ❻	0234 ⇨
050 ➡	096 ♣	0142	0188 ❼	0235
051 ✓	097	0143	0189 ❽	0236
052 ✔	098 ○	0144	0190 ❾	0237 ⇨
053 ✗	099 ✵	0145	0191 ❿	0238 ⇨
054 ✘	0100 ✾	0146	0192 ①	0239 ⇨
055 ✗	0101 ✺	0147	0193 ②	0240
056 ✘	0102 ✿	0148	0194 ③	0241 ⇨
057 ✚	0103 ✳	0149	0195 ④	0242 ⊃
058 ✚	0104 ✳	0150	0196 ⑤	0243
059 ✛	0105 ✳	0151	0197 ⑥	0244
060 ✜	0106 ✳	0152	0198 ⑦	0245
061 †	0107 ✳	0153	0199 ⑧	0246
062 ✞	0108 ●	0154	0200 ⑨	0247
063 ✝	0109 ○	0155	0201 ⑩	0248
064 ✠	0110 ■	0156	0202 ❶	0249
065 ✡	0111 □	0157	0203 ●	0250 →
066 ✢	0112 □	0158	0204 ●	0251
067 ✣	0113 □	0159	0205 ●	0252
068 ✤	0114 □	0160	0206 ●	0253
069 ✥	0115 ▲	0161	0207 ●	0254 →
070 ✦	0116 ▼	0162	0208 ●	0255
071 ✧	0117 ◆	0163	0209 ●	
072 ★	0118 ◆	0164 ♥	0210 ●	
073 ☆	0119 ◗	0165	0211 ❶	
074 ✪	0120	0166	0212 →	
075 ✫	0121 ▮	0167	0213 →	
076 ★	0122 ▰	0168 ♣	0214 ↔	
077 ★	0123 '	0169 ♦	0215 ↕	
078 ★	0124 '	0170 ♥	0216	
			0217 →	

TABLE D-3   The Dixieland Character Set

Geographic, and Musical character sets, respectively. To type any of these characters, activate the Text tool and select an insertion point. When the Text dialog box appears, select the desired symbol typeface. Then, press and hold (ALT) and type the three- or four-character numerical ASCII code that corresponds to the character you want. Be sure to include the zero at the beginning of the ASCII code. The Windows character set does not permit accurate representation of any of the symbol characters in the Text dialog box, but the Corel DRAW! screen displays them correctly, after you exit the dialog box. To find the character(s) you want to type, refer to the character chart that came with your software or to the appropriate table in this appendix.

 An interesting use for characters in the symbol typefaces is to create your own "instant" clip art. To do this, assign a very large point size to the desired character when you type its ASCII code in the dialog box. When the character appears on the Corel DRAW! page, activate the Select tool, select the character, and convert it to curves. You can then reshape the character as a curve object, using the Shaping tool.

RENAMING COREL DRAW! TYPEFACES

Corel DRAW! is shipped with 43 different typefaces; the combination of these typefaces with the typestyles available for each yields a total of 102 fonts. Corel Systems designed these typefaces and their names to resemble popular typefaces in common use by desktop publishers and graphic designers. In many cases, the names of the Corel DRAW! typefaces will remind you of their industry counterparts, as Table D-7 shows.

If you are more familiar with the industry standard, however, you may find it too inconvenient to memorize another set of typeface names. You have the option of renaming the Corel DRAW! typefaces so that the names you see in the dialog box

Code	Sym	Code	Sym	Code	Sym	Code	Sym	Code	Sym	Code	Sym
033	!	075	K	0117	υ	0159		0201	⊃	0243	
034	∀	076	Λ	0118	ϖ	0160		0202	⊇	0244	
035	#	077	M	0119	ω	0161	ϒ	0203	⊄	0245	
036	∃	078	N	0120	ξ	0162	′	0204	⊂	0246	
037	%	079	O	0121	ψ	0163	≤	0205	⊆	0247	
038	&	080	Π	0122	ζ	0164	/	0206	∈	0248	
039	∋	081	Θ	0123	{	0165	∞	0207	∉	0249	
040	(	082	P	0124	|	0166	ƒ	0208	∠	0250	
041	)	083	Σ	0125	}	0167	♣	0209	∇	0251	
042	∗	084	T	0126	~	0168	♦	0210	®	0252	
043	+	085	Y	0127		0169	♥	0211	©	0253	
044	,	086	ς	0128		0170	♠	0212	™	0254	
045	−	087	Ω	0129		0171	↔	0213	∏	0255	
046	.	088	Ξ	0130		0172	←	0214	√		
047	/	089	Ψ	0131		0173	↑	0215	·		
048	0	090	Z	0132		0174	→	0216	¬		
049	1	091	[	0133		0175	↓	0217	∧		
050	2	092	∴	0134		0176	°	0218	∨		
051	3	093	]	0135		0177	±	0219	⇔		
052	4	094	⊥	0136		0178	″	0220	⇐		
053	5	095	_	0137		0179	≥	0221	⇑		
054	6	096	—	0138		0180	×	0222	⇒		
055	7	097	α	0139		0181	∝	0223	⇓		
056	8	098	β	0140		0182	∂	0224	◊		
057	9	099	χ	0141		0183	•	0225	⟨		
058	:	0100	δ	0142		0184	+	0226	®		
059	;	0101	ε	0143		0185	≠	0227	©		
060	<	0102	φ	0144		0186	≡	0228	™		
061	=	0103	γ	0145		0187	≈	0229	Σ		
062	>	0104	η	0146		0188	…	0230			
063	?	0105	ι	0147		0189	|	0231			
064	≅	0106	φ	0148		0190	—	0232			
065	A	0107	κ	0149		0191	↵	0233			
066	B	0108	λ	0150		0192	ℵ	0234			
067	X	0109	μ	0151		0193	ℑ	0235			
068	Δ	0110	ν	0152		0194	ℜ	0236			
069	E	0111	o	0153		0195	℘	0237			
070	Φ	0112	π	0154		0196	⊗	0238			
071	Γ	0113	θ	0155		0197	⊕	0239			
072	H	0114	ρ	0156		0198	∅	0240			
073	I	0115	σ	0157		0199	∩	0241			
074	ϑ	0116	τ	0158		0200	∪	0242			

TABLE D-4   The Greek/Math Character Set

033	○	075	）	0117		0159		0201	△	0243	✖
034		076	□	0118		0160		0202	◆	0244	✚
035	△	077		0119		0161		0203	■	0245	†
036	◇	078		0120		0162	◆	0204	■	0246	
037	○	079	◯	0121		0163	▲	0205		0247	◆
038	✸	080	▽	0122		0164		0206	▥	0248	
039		081		0123	—	0165		0207		0249	
040		082		0124	↗	0166		0208	✖	0250	
041		083		0125	↖	0167		0209		0251	✕
042	✦	084	◎	0126		0168		0210		0252	
043	∴	085		0127		0169		0211	←	0253	▼
044		086		0128		0170	■	0212	↓	0254	▶
045		087	✦	0129		0171	★	0213	↑	0255	
046		088		0130		0172		0214			
047		089		0131		0173		0215			
048	◦	090		0132		0174	＋	0216	●		
049	₁	091		0133		0175	◯	0217			
050	₂	092		0134		0176	●	0218	●		
051	₃	093		0135		0177		0219			
052	₄	094	☆	0136		0178		0220	■		
053	₅	095		0137		0179	✕	0221	●		
054	₆	096		0138		0180	◯	0222	⬤		
055	₇	097		0139		0181		0223			
056	₈	098		0140		0182		0224	■		
057	₉	099	●	0141		0183	✳	0225			
058		0100	▲	0142		0184		0226			
059		0101	★	0143		0185	▷	0227	•		
060	○	0102		0144		0186		0228	★		
061		0103		0145		0187		0229	★		
062	✕	0104	⚓	0146		0188		0230	◦		
063		0105	◯	0147		0189	✉	0231			
064	□	0106		0148		0190	✕	0232	▽		
065		0107		0149		0191	◯	0233			
066		0108	□	0150		0192	✳	0234			
067		0109	▤	0151		0193	●	0235	⊏		
068	▲	0110	✳	0152		0194	□	0236			
069	☆	0111	◯	0153		0195		0237	∩		
070		0112	◇	0154		0196		0238	）（		
071		0113		0155		0197		0239			
072		0114	●	0156		0198	✈	0240	▲		
073	⬠	0115		0157		0199	↘	0241	✖		
074	✚	0116	◉	0158		0200	→	0242	◇		

TABLE D-5   The Geographic Character Set

Code		Code		Code		Code		Code		Code	
033		075		0117		0159		0201		0243	
034		076		0118		0160		0202		0244	
035		077		0119		0161		0203		0245	
036		078		0120		0162		0204		0246	
037		079		0121		0163		0205		0247	
038		080		0122		0164		0206		0248	
039		081		0123		0165		0207		0249	
040		082		0124		0166		0208		0250	
041		083		0125		0167		0209		0251	
042		084		0126		0168		0210		0252	
043		085		0127		0169		0211		0253	
044		086		0128		0170		0212		0254	
045		087		0129		0171		0213		0255	
046		088		0130		0172		0214			
047		089		0131		0173		0215			
048		090		0132		0174		0216			
049		091		0133		0175		0217			
050		092		0134		0176		0218			
051		093		0135		0177		0219			
052		094		0136		0178		0220			
053		095		0137		0179		0221			
054		096		0138		0180		0222			
055		097		0139		0181		0223			
056		098		0140		0182		0224			
057		099		0141		0183		0225			
058		0100		0142		0184		0226			
059		0101		0143		0185		0227			
060		0102		0144		0186		0228			
061		0103		0145		0187		0229			
062		0104		0146		0188		0230			
063		0105		0147		0189		0231			
064		0106		0148		0190		0232			
065		0107		0149		0191		0233			
066		0108		0150		0192		0234			
067		0109		0151		0193		0235			
068		0110		0152		0194		0236			
069		0111		0153		0195		0237			
070		0112		0154		0196		0238			
071		0113		0155		0197		0239			
072		0114		0156		0198		0240			
073		0115		0157		0199		0241			
074		0116		0158		0200		0242			

TABLE D-6   The Musical Character Set

Industry Name	Corel Equivalent
Aachen Bold	Aardvark Bold
American Typewriter	Memorandum
Avant Garde	Avalon
Benguiat	Bangkok
Bookman	Brooklyn
Bodoni Poster	Bodonoff
Brush Script	Banff
Carta	Geographic
Caslon	Casablanca
Century Old Style	Centurion Old
Cooper Black	Cupertino
New Century Schoolbook	New Brunswick
Franklin Gothic	Frankfurt Gothic
Franklin Gothic Heavy	Frankfurt Gothic Heavy
Freestyle Script	Freeport
Fritz Quadrata	France
Futura Condensed	Fujiyana Condensed
Futura Condensed Extra Bold	Fujiyama Condensed Extra Bold
Futura Condensed Light	Fujiyama Condensed Light
Garamond	Gatineau
Helvetica	Switzerland
Helvetica Black	Switzerland Black
Helvetica Light	Switzerland Light
Helvetica Narrow	Switzerland Narrow
Hobo	Homeward Bound
Machine	Motor
New Baskerville	Nebraska
Optima	Ottawa
Palatino	Palm Springs
Park Avenue	Paradise
Revue	Renfrew
Sonata	Musical
Souvenir	Southern
Stencil	Stamp

TABLE D-7   Commonly Used Typeface Names and Their Corel Counterparts

Industry Name	Corel Equivalent
Symbols	Greek/Math Symbols
Tiffany	Timpani
Tiffany Heavy	Timpani Heavy
Times	Toronto
Univers Black	USA Black
Univers Light	USA Light
University Roman	Unicorn
Zapf Chancery	Zurich Calligraphic
Zapf Dingbats	Dixieland

TABLE D-7   Commonly Used Typeface Names and Their Corel Counterparts (*continued*)

match the better-known industry typeface names. To do this, edit the typeface names in your WIN.INI file in the following way.

1. Load Windows and the MS-DOS Executive and change to the directory in which Windows is installed, if necessary.

2. Make a backup copy of your WIN.INI file using the Copy command in the Windows File menu. Give the copy either a different filename or a different extension to distinguish it from the original.

3. Double-click on the WIN.INI file to open it in the Notepad editing window.

4. Scroll through the file until you come to the [CorelDrwFonts] section. This part of the WIN.INI file contains the list of typefaces used in Corel DRAW!.

5. Go to the first typeface name you want to change. Position the cursor in front of the equal sign (=) character and click the mouse button, then backspace and erase the current typeface

name. Do *not* erase the characters that appear after the equal sign; these characters represent the DOS filename that Corel DRAW! refers to when identifying the typeface. Remember that you are changing the typeface name only, not the filename that contains the information about the typeface.

6. Type the name of the standard industry typeface, or an abbreviation of it. You must fit the name within 18 spaces in order to see all of it in the Text dialog box. Furthermore, you may not include any spaces in the new typeface name. If the standard industry name contains two or more words, type the spaces between the word as a hyphen (-) or underline (_) character. For example, to substitute the name Aachen Bold for the Corel name Aardvark Bold, you would type **Aachen_Bold**. To substitute the industry name New Century Schoolbook for its Corel equivalent New Brunswick, you might type **New_Century_Schbk**. Be sure not to leave any spaces between the new typeface and the equal sign (=) character.

7. Select the Save command in the Windows File menu to save your changes.

8. Continue editing in this way until you have changed all of the names. Save the WIN.INI file periodically so that you will not lose all of your changes if you make a mistake along the way.

9. If you would like to have the new typeface names in alphabetical order, reposition the lines by copying and then pasting them to the desired positions. Then you can delete the original lines that you copied. Figure D-1 shows part of a WIN.INI typeface list with industry typeface names substituted for Corel names. The industry typeface names in the figure have been rearranged in alphabetical order.

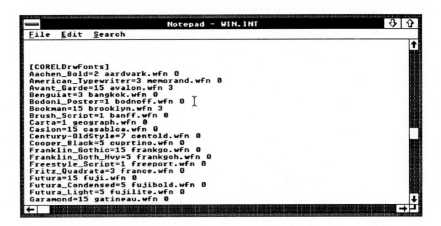

FIGURE D-1 Corel WIN.INI fonts list with common typeface names substituted in alphabetical order

10. When you have changed and repositioned the typeface names to your satisfaction, save the WIN.INI file once more and exit Notepad.

The procedure just described is handy if you want to call Corel DRAW! typefaces by the names of similar standard industry typefaces. If you regularly work with fonts from other vendors and want to use them in Corel DRAW!, however, you require a different solution. Using the WFNBOSS utility described in the next section of the appendix, you can convert fonts from other vendors into Corel DRAW! format.

CONVERTING THIRD-PARTY FONTS WITH WFNBOSS

Corel DRAW! typeface files have the extension .WFN, as you know if you have browsed through the file listings in the Corel DRAW! directory or the [CDrwFonts] section of your WIN.INI file. Corel DRAW! versions 1.1 and later include a utility called WFNBOSS, which allows you to convert other vendors' fonts into the .WFN format for use in Corel DRAW!. WFNBOSS effectively gives you access to more than 4000 commercial fonts by vendors such as Adobe Systems, Agfa Compugraphic, Bitstream, ZSoft, and others. Table D-8 lists the vendors whose typeface libraries are convertible to .WFN format using the WFNBOSS utility.

Converting Fonts to Corel Format: An Overview

WFNBOSS is installed automatically when you install Corel DRAW!. The process of converting a third-party vendor's fonts to Corel format (.WFN) always includes these steps in sequence:

1. Access the WFNBOSS Font Conversion Program.

2. Select the font type (Conversion Type) that you want to convert to Corel format.

3. Select the source directory where the vendor's fonts are located.

4. Choose the drive and directory where you want the Corel version of the font to reside on your hard disk.

5. Select the first font in the chosen source directory that you want to convert.

6. If desired, change the font name that WFNBOSS suggests. This is the name that will appear in the Corel DRAW! Text dialog

box after you convert the font from the original vendor's format.

7. Begin the conversion process.

The next section describes how to access the WFNBOSS utility and acquaints you with the contents of the WFNBOSS Font Conversion Program window.

Vendor	Product Name	Format	Number of Outlines	Telephone Number
Adobe	Type Library	Adobe Type 1	450	(415) 961-4000
				(800) 833-6687
Agfa Compugr.	Curvilinear Type Library	Type Director	1200	(508) 658-5600
				(800) 873-3668
Bitstream	Fontware	Bitstream	947	(617) 497-6222
				(800) 522-3668
Casady & Greene	Fluent Laser Fonts	Readable PostScript	83	(408) 624-8716
				(800) 331-4321
DigiFonts	Digi-Duit	DigiFont	272	(303) 526-2318
				(800) 242-5665
HP/Agfa Compugr.	Type Director	Type Director	53	(800) 538-8787 (HP)
				(800) 873-3668 (Agfa)
Image Club	PS Typeface Library	Readable PostScript	600	(403) 262-8008
				(800) 661-9410
The Font Company	URW Type Library	Readable PostScript	750	(602) 996-6606
				(800) 422-3668
Treacyfaces	Treacyfaces	Readable PostScript	8	(215) 896-0860

TABLE D-8 Typeface Vendors with Fonts in WFNBOSS-
Convertible Format

FIGURE D-2   Accessing WFNBOSS from the MS-DOS Executive

The WFNBOSS Font Conversion Program Window

You cannot access WFNBOSS directly from within Corel DRAW!; instead, you open it from the MS-DOS Executive as a separate program in the directory where Corel DRAW! is installed. To access WFNBOSS so that you can begin the process of converting fonts, follow these steps:

1. Start Windows and change to the CORELDRW directory (or the directory where Corel DRAW! is installed).

2. Double-click on the filename WFNBOSS.EXE, as shown in Figure D-2. The main window of the WFNBOSS Font Conversion Program appears, as shown in Figure D-3.

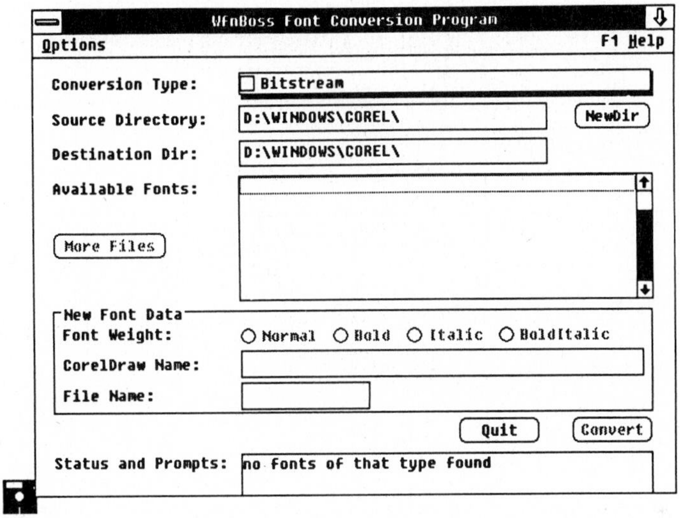

FIGURE D-3 The WFNBOSS Font Conversion Program window

The WFNBOSS window is similar to a standard Windows dialog box. Take a moment to become familiar with the components of this window. To move between options in the WFNBOSS window, you can either press (TAB) or (SHIFT-TAB), or click directly on the desired option.

Conversion Type When you open WFNBOSS, the Conversion Type is the first option you must define, as shown in Figure D-3. This option lets you determine which typeface format you are going to convert. The very first time you use WFNBOSS, the Bitstream typeface option is active. To select a different typeface family, click on the checkbox within the option line until you see the family you want, or press the spacebar repeatedly. Once you change the selected typeface, Windows remembers the last Conversion Type you selected.

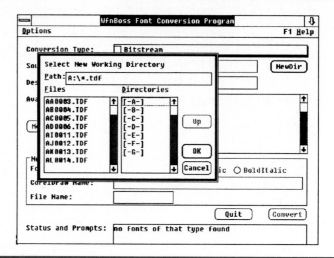

FIGURE D-4   Selecting a Source directory for fonts to be converted

Source Directory/NewDir   The Source Directory option shows you the drive and directory where WFNBOSS will search for fonts to convert. The very first time you start WFNBOSS, the directory where CORELDRW is installed is the default directory. To change the source drive and/or directory, you can either click on the NewDir command button, or press (TAB) until NewDir is selected and then press (ENTER). When you select NewDir, the Select New Working Directory dialog box pops up, prompting you to change the path. In Figure D-4, the drive A has been specified as the location of Bitstream file fonts in .TDF format. The available font filenames (not the popular names of the fonts) appear in the Files list box.

To accept the directory you have chosen, click on the OK command button or press (ENTER). The popular filenames of the fonts in the new source directory then appear in the Available Fonts box of the main WFNBOSS window, as shown in Figure D-5. The message appearing in the Status and Prompts box at the bottom of

```
 ┌──────────────────────────────────────────────────────────────┐
 │ ⊟                WFnBoss Font Conversion Program           ⇩  │
 │ Options                                           F1 Help     │
 │                                                               │
 │  Conversion Type:     ┌─────────────────────────────────────┐ │
 │                       │ ☐ Bitstream                         │ │
 │  Source Directory:    ┌──────────────────────────┐ ┌───────┐ │
 │                       │ A:\                      │ │ NewDir│ │
 │  Destination Dir:     ┌──────────────────────────┐           │
 │                       │ D:\WINDOWS\COREL\        │           │
 │  Available Fonts:     ┌──────────────────────────┐ ┌─┐       │
 │                       │ Swiss Roman              │ │↑│       │
 │                       │ Swiss Italic             │ │ │       │
 │                       │ Swiss Bold               │ │ │       │
 │  ┌──────────┐         │ Swiss Bold Italic        │ │ │       │
 │  │ More Files│        │ Dutch Roman              │ │ │       │
 │  └──────────┘         │ Dutch Italic             │ │ │       │
 │                       │ Dutch Bold               │ │↓│       │
 │ ┌─New Font Data──────────────────────────────────────────┐  │
 │ │ Font Weight:    ○ Normal ○ Bold ○ Italic ○ BoldItalic  │  │
 │ │                                                         │  │
 │ │ CorelDraw Name: ┌─────────────────────────────────────┐ │  │
 │ │                                                         │  │
 │ │ File Name:      ┌─────────────────────┐                │  │
 │ └─────────────────────────────────────────────────────────┘ │
 │                              ┌──────┐ ┌─────────┐            │
 │                              │ Quit │ │ Convert │            │
 │                              └──────┘ └─────────┘            │
 │  Status and Prompts:  ┌─────────────────────┐               │
 │                       │ 8 Fonts Found        │               │
 └──────────────────────────────────────────────────────────────┘
```

FIGURE D-5   A listing of available fonts in the specified
source directory

the window tells you how many fonts reside in the specified drive
and directory. If you have a version of Corel DRAW! earlier than
1.11, a single directory can contain only 32 fonts. If you have
version 1.11 or later, you can place any number of fonts in a
directory and, if there are more than 32, you can view additional
font names by clicking on the More command button.

Destination Dir   The Destination Dir option stands for Destination Directory, or the directory where you want the fonts to reside
once they are converted to Corel format. This is always the
directory where Corel DRAW! is installed, unless you deactivate
the Autoinstall command in the Options menu. (Refer to the
"Options Menu" section in this chapter.)

Available Fonts   The Available Fonts list box contains the names
of fonts in the currently selected source directory that match the
currently selected Conversion Type. The names that appear in this

this list box are the popular names of the fonts, not the filenames that contain those fonts. To select a font, simply click on it to highlight it, as shown in Figure D-6. As soon as you select a font for conversion, the New Font Data options and the Convert command button become available for selection.

In most cases, you should select and convert only one font at a time. However, if you are converting four different typestyles of the same bitstream font (weights—normal, italic, bold, and bold-italic), you can convert them all at once. The resulting *merged* fonts will be stored under a single filename in the destination directory. They will also appear in the Text dialog box under one name, with four typestyle options available.

New Font Data   The three options in the New Font Data box—Font Weight, CorelDraw Name, and File Name—become available only when you have selected a font to convert from the Available Fonts list box. The WFNBOSS program suggests settings for each of these options, based on the information in the file for the font(s) you have selected. You may change any or all of these settings, however. The setting you are most likely to alter is the CorelDraw Name, which determines the font name that appears in the Text dialog box when you enter new text. For example, the Bitstream Swiss Bold Italic font selected in Figure D-6 has been given the name Swiss_Bit for use in Corel DRAW!.

The File Name option determines the name that the converted font is stored under in the destination directory. You should leave the suggested File Name option unaltered, because this filename is stored on disk when you save your artwork. If you need to exchange your artwork files with other users who have converted the same fonts, the filenames of the converted fonts must be the same for both users. Otherwise, Corel DRAW! will not recognize the font in the other person's computer.

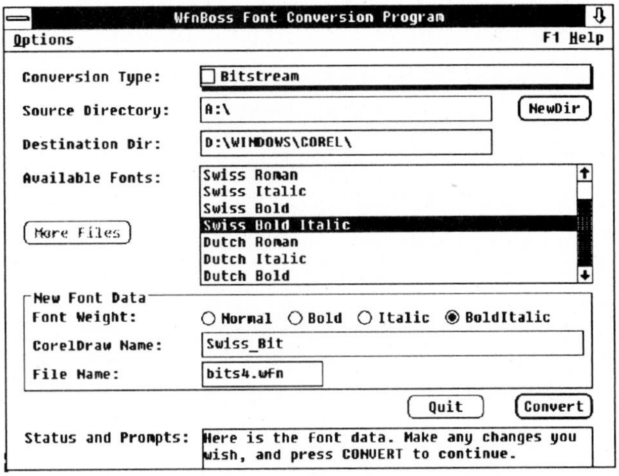

FIGURE D-6   Selecting a font for conversion and altering the Corel font name

The Convert Command Button   Clicking on the Convert command button begins the process of font conversion. This button becomes available as soon as you select one of the typefaces in the Available Fonts selection box. Make sure that all New Font Data information is correct before you click on Convert.

The time required to convert a particular font depends on the font manufacturer, but often ranges from three to five minutes. A single font can occupy between 10K and 25K of space on your hard drive, depending on how many ASCII characters are contained in the character set being converted. If you convert several typestyle weights of the same typestyle, merging them into one font file, the size of the font file can be much larger.

Status and Prompts   The message in the Status and Prompts box changes as you move through the font selection and conversion

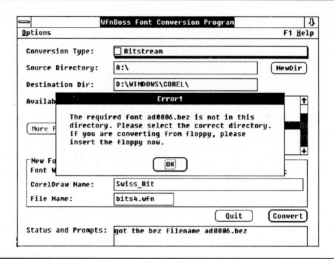

FIGURE D-7   Status and Prompts messages during the font conversion process

process. When you select a source directory, for example, Status and Prompts lists the number of fonts available in the specified format. When you select a specific font to convert, Status and Prompts reminds you to make changes to font data before beginning to convert the font to Corel format. Status and Prompts also keeps you informed about what is happening throughout the conversion process. Special message boxes also provide supplemental information. In Figure D-7, for example, a font is being converted from Bitstream to Corel format. Status and Prompts informs you that WFNBOSS is looking for a file with the extension .BEZ, and a supplemental error message box prompts you to insert a different floppy disk into the drive A to continue searching for the requested file.

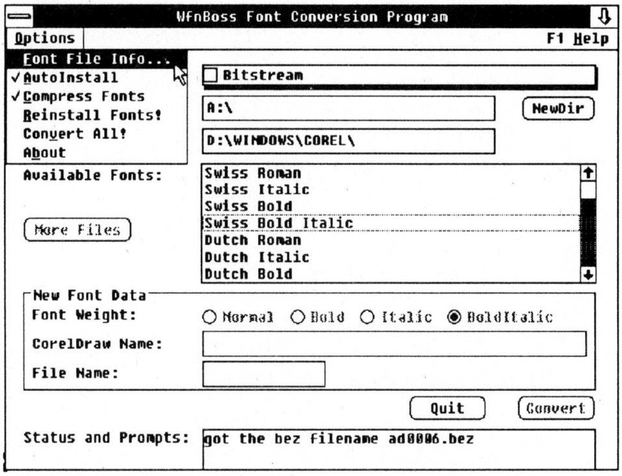

FIGURE D-8   The Options menu of WFNBOSS

The Options Menu

The Options menu is the only menu in the WFNBOSS program window. It contains several commands that can make the font conversion process more efficient or help you access information about fonts you have already converted. Figure D-8 shows the WFNBOSS program window with the Options menu displayed and the first command in the menu highlighted.

Font File Info   The Font File Info command allows you to change some features of font files that have already been converted to .WFN format. When you select this option, the Select Font File dialog box shown in Figure D-9 appears. This dialog box operates just like the other file selection dialog boxes within Corel DRAW!. Select the desired path and font filename; Figure D-9 shows the

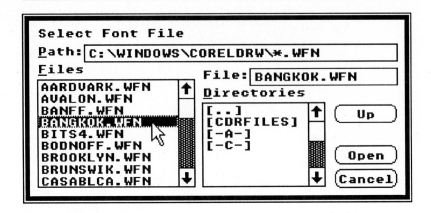

FIGURE D-9   Selecting a Corel .WFN font to edit font file
information

Corel font file BANGKOK.WFN selected. To confirm your selection, click on OK. The font file dialog box shown in Figure D-10

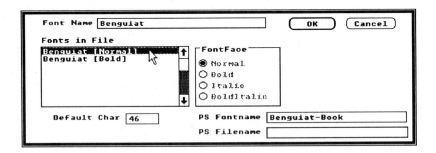

FIGURE D-10   Editing font information in the font file info
dialog box

then displays. Most of the data in this second dialog box is for your information only. The Font Name option, for example, displays the name of the currently selected font file. The Fonts in File list box displays the weights of the fonts included in the selected font file. However, you can change the Default Character (the character that appears in the preview display of the Text dialog box) and the PostScript Fontname information if you desire. Remember that the PostScript Fontname refers only to the commonly used name of the font, not to the name of the file that contains the font data.

AutoInstall   The AutoInstall command is activated when you first install Corel DRAW! and remains active until you deselect it. When this command is active, the directory where Corel DRAW! is installed is automatically the destination directory for all fonts converted through WFNBOSS. If you deselect AutoInstall, you can store the converted .WFN fonts in any directory you choose.

remember   Keep in mind that fonts stored in a directory other than the one where Corel DRAW! is installed will not appear in the WIN.INI file. However, the WFNBOSS.INI file, which is located in the same directory as the one where Corel DRAW! is installed, contains a listing of those fonts. To find out which fonts you have converted and where they are located, view the contents of WFNBOSS.INI.

Compress Fonts   You can use the Compress Fonts command only if the fonts you want to convert are in Readable PostScript format (Casady and Greene, Image Club, The Font Company, Treacyfaces). This command tells WFNBOSS to compress the data in the converted font so that it takes up less space on your hard drive.

Reinstall Fonts!   The Reinstall Fonts! command is useful when you have reinstalled Microsoft Windows, thereby losing Corel DRAW! configuration and font information in the WIN.INI file. WFNBOSS.INI "remembers" all of the fonts you have ever converted to Corel DRAW! format, so you can use this command to copy references to those fonts to the Windows WIN.INI file.

Convert All!   When you select Convert All!, WFNBOSS converts all of the fonts in the Available Fonts list box simultaneously. If you are converting different typestyles of the same typeface and the font manufacturer is Bitstream, WFNBOSS generates a single font file for all of the typestyles. When you convert fonts from vendors other than Bitstream, however, WFNBOSS generates a separate file and filename for each typestyle of each typeface. If this is not what you want, you should convert each font weight separately, with the Convert All command deactivated. When you convert individual weights of a single Bitstream typeface separately and in sequence, WFNBOSS merges and stores each weight in the same font file automatically.

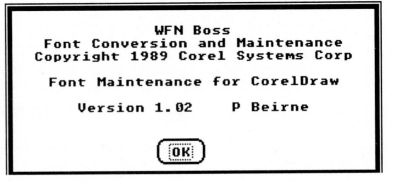

FIGURE D-11   The About WFNBOSS information box

About   Click on the About command to see the information
screen shown in Figure D-11. This screen contains information
about the current version of WFNBOSS and its release date.

Getting Help While Converting Fonts

WFNBOSS has its own help file, WFNBOSS.CHL, which gives
you step-by-step instructions as well as detailed information about
converting each type of font format. You can access this help file
in one of two different ways, depending on whether you are
currently running WFNBOSS.

If you are running WFNBOSS, simply click on the F1 Help area
of the menu line, or press (F1). The help screen that appears is keyed
to the option that is currently selected in the WFNBOSS program
window. The help screen about converting Bitstream fonts shown
in Figure D-12, for example, appears when the Conversion Type
option is selected and Bitstream is in the option line.

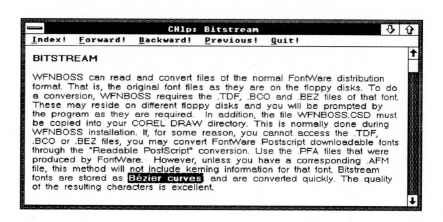

FIGURE D-12   Accessing the WFNBOSS help screens with
the (F1) key

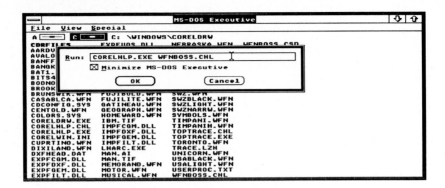

FIGURE D-13   Accessing the WFNBOSS help system from the MS-DOS Executive

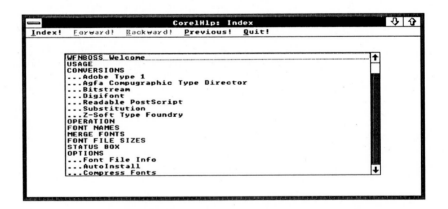

FIGURE D-14   The Index screen of the WFNBOSS help system

If you are not running WFNBOSS, you can access the WFNBOSS help screens from the MS-DOS Executive by following these steps:

1. Run the MS-DOS Executive and change to the directory where Corel DRAW! is installed.

2. Click once on the CORELHLP.EXE file and then select the Run command in the File menu of the MS-DOS Executive. The Run dialog box appears, with the filename CORELHLP.EXE in the text box next to the Run command, as shown in Figure D-13.

3. Click on the RUN: text box directly after the end of the CORELHLP.EXE filename. Press the spacebar and add the filename WFNBOSS.CHL, as shown in Figure D-13. In doing this, you are telling Windows to run the general Corel help system and enter the WFNBOSS help screen subsystem.

4. If no x appears in the Minimize MS-Dos Executive checkbox, activate this option by clicking once in the checkbox. Then select OK. The Index screen for the WFNBOSS help system displays, as in Figure D-14.

5. Select a WFNBOSS help topic from this index. Refer to the "Getting Help in Corel DRAW!" section of Chapter 1 to review moving between topics and using the help system menus.

POSTSCRIPT TEXTURES

Texture Parameters
PostScript Texture Examples

I f you have access to a PostScript printer or output device, you can take advantage of the PostScript fill textures that Corel DRAW! makes available through the Fill tool pop-up menu. As you may recall from Chapter 15, the preview window cannot provide a WYSIWYG display of PostScript textures, so objects that contain these as fills appear in the preview window filled with the letters PS. You must print the objects on a PostScript device in order to see the actual fill patterns.

Although the nominal number of available textures is 42, the actual number of possible fill patterns you can generate is almost infinite. The visual examples in this appendix represent only four possible results for each texture, yet they demonstrate that even a single texture can look like a multitude of different patterns. When you consider that you can edit up to five parameters for each texture, and that each parameter can be set to a wide range of values, you will see the creative possibilities in using the PostScript fill textures as a design tool.

TEXTURE PARAMETERS

Each of the 42 PostScript textures has its own set of four or five parameters that you can edit to alter the basic pattern. While the parameters vary for each texture type, many textures share common parameters. The following list explains the meaning of the most commonly used parameters.

Frequency   The Frequency parameter specifies how many times per inch the complete pattern is repeated.

Line Width   This parameter expresses the width of the lines in the pattern in terms of thousandths of an inch.

Foreground Gray, Background Gray   These parameters indicate the gray levels of the foreground and background areas of the pattern respectively. A value of 100% results in black, while a value of 0% results in white. Other values represent shades of gray.

Spacing   Spacing is expressed as a percentage of the spacing for the default values of that pattern. For example, motifs in a texture that has a spacing value of 50% seem more closely squeezed together than motifs with a spacing value of 100%.

Maximum and Minimum Values   Some PostScript textures have parameters that express maximum and minimum size, length, or gray values. These textures (the Bubbles texture is a good example) have a built-in mathematical random, or "chance," algorithm that chooses motifs of variable sizes or gray shades. The maximum and minimum values specify the allowable range in size or gray shade for that texture.

Random Seed   When a given texture has a "Random Seed" parameter, the pattern of the motif looks different every time you use the texture. This parameter gives the texture a "chance" or random look.

POSTSCRIPT TEXTURE EXAMPLES

Below each of the following sets of texture examples, you will find a brief table that lists the settings used to generate the fill patterns. The settings in the leftmost column represent the default settings for that texture. Notes following the examples describe any special features of the texture and whether it is transparent. If a particular texture is transparent, you can use it to fill objects that function as a mask in your picture.

PostScript textures generally take a long time to print. The exact amount of time depends on the settings you choose and the speed of your printer. If a picture containing one or more PostScript fills is very complex, or if the objects that contain PostScript texture fills also contain outline fills, you may experience difficulties in printing. Try selecting and printing only objects that contain PostScript textures if problems occur. If you import a picture containing PostScript textures into a desktop publishing program and the page will not print, empty the page of everthing except the picture and try again.

If you normally send output files to a Linotronic imagesetter but do not have your own PostScript printer, you will find the examples in this appendix especially helpful in choosing texture parameters. To review how to select and edit PostScript fill textures, see Chapter 15.

Archimedes

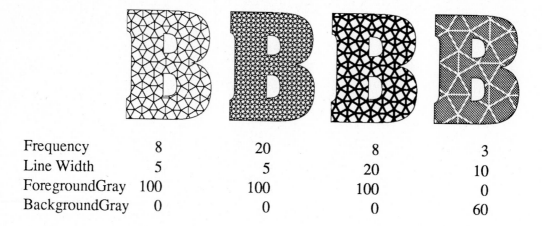

Frequency	8	20	8	3
Line Width	5	5	20	10
ForegroundGray	100	100	100	0
BackgroundGray	0	0	0	60

The Archimedes texture is transparent if you set Background-Gray to a negative number.

Bars

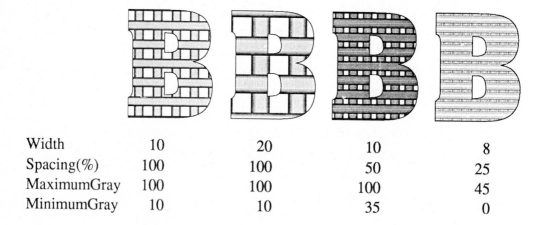

Width	10	20	10	8
Spacing(%)	100	100	50	25
MaximumGray	100	100	100	45
MinimumGray	10	10	35	0

The Bars texture is always transparent.

Basketweave

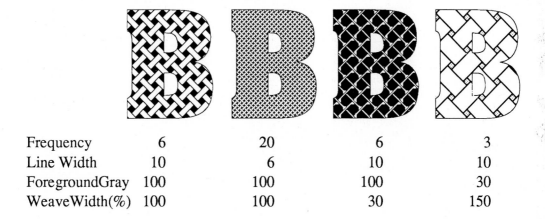

Frequency	6	20	6	3
Line Width	10	6	10	10
ForegroundGray	100	100	100	30
WeaveWidth(%)	100	100	30	150

The Basketweave texture is transparent.

Birds

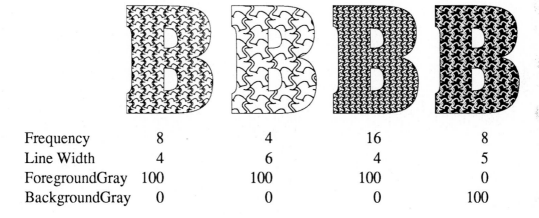

Frequency	8	4	16	8
Line Width	4	6	4	5
ForegroundGray	100	100	100	0
BackgroundGray	0	0	0	100

The Birds texture is transparent only if you set BackgroundGray to a negative number.

Bricks

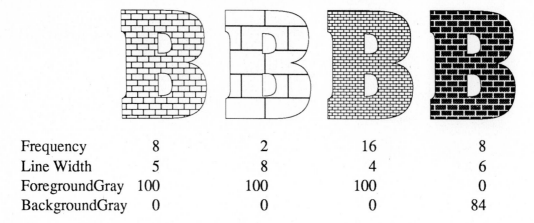

Frequency	8	2	16	8
Line Width	5	8	4	6
ForegroundGray	100	100	100	0
BackgroundGray	0	0	0	84

The Bricks texture is transparent only if you set Background-Gray to a negative number.

Bubbles

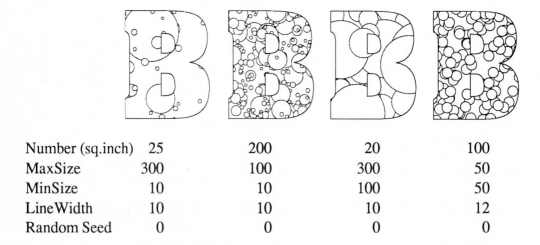

Number (sq.inch)	25	200	20	100
MaxSize	300	100	300	50
MinSize	10	10	100	50
LineWidth	10	10	10	12
Random Seed	0	0	0	0

The space between the white bubbles is transparent, but the bubbles are opaque.

Carpet

Frequency (dpi)	72	44	72	72
Gray	100	100	100	100
Gamma (box size)	50	50	25	50
ModFactor	3	3	3	2
Alpha	10	10	10	10

The Carpet pattern is transparent.

CircleGrid

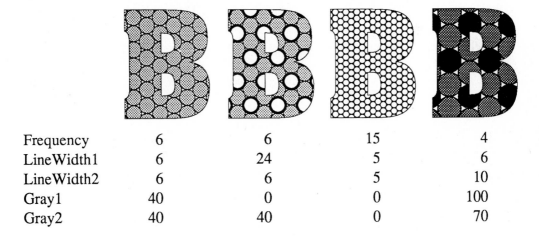

Frequency	6	6	15	4
LineWidth1	6	24	5	6
LineWidth2	6	6	5	10
Gray1	40	0	0	100
Gray2	40	40	0	70

Background areas between the circles are transparent. If you set Gray1 or Gray2 to a negative number, the circles to which they correspond are also transparent.

Construction

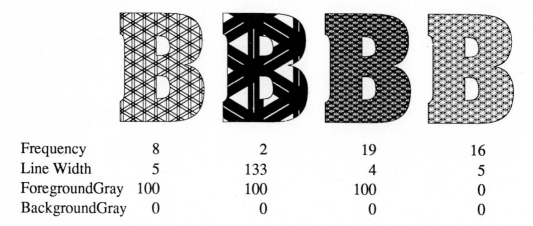

Frequency	8	2	19	16
Line Width	5	133	4	5
ForegroundGray	100	100	100	0
BackgroundGray	0	0	0	0

If you set BackgroundGray to a negative number, the pattern is transparent.

Cracks

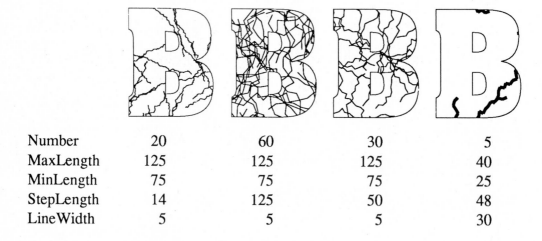

Number	20	60	30	5
MaxLength	125	125	125	40
MinLength	75	75	75	25
StepLength	14	125	50	48
LineWidth	5	5	5	30

The Cracks pattern is transparent.

Craters

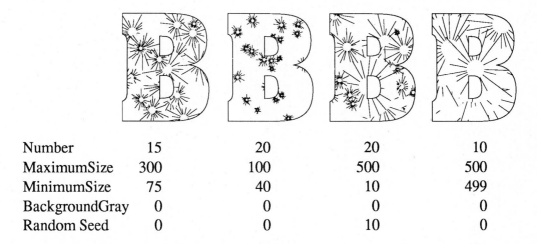

Number	15	20	20	10
MaximumSize	300	100	500	500
MinimumSize	75	40	10	499
BackgroundGray	0	0	0	0
Random Seed	0	0	10	0

The Craters texture is opaque.

Crosshatching

MaxDistance	75	30	50	150
MinDistance	0	0	0	50
LineWidth	5	4	6	13
Angle	45	45	8	60
Random Seed	0	5	0	0

The Crosshatching texture is transparent.

CrystalLattice

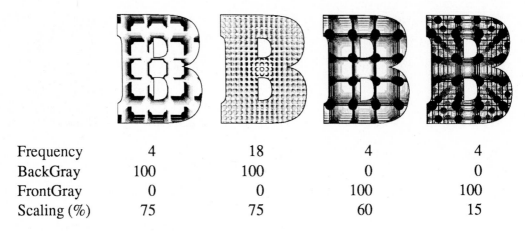

Frequency	4	18	4	4
BackGray	100	100	0	0
FrontGray	0	0	100	100
Scaling (%)	75	75	60	15

The CrystalLattice texture is transparent.

Denim

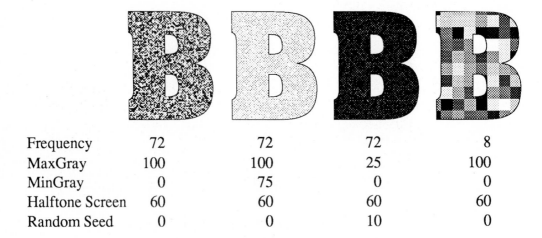

Frequency	72	72	72	8
MaxGray	100	100	25	100
MinGray	0	75	0	0
Halftone Screen	60	60	60	60
Random Seed	0	0	10	0

DNA

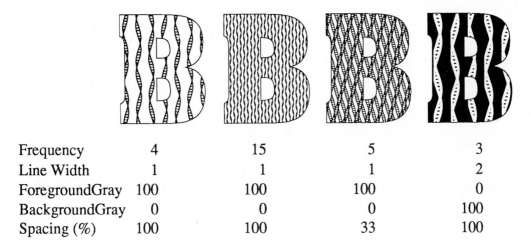

Frequency	4	15	5	3
Line Width	1	1	1	2
ForegroundGray	100	100	100	0
BackgroundGray	0	0	0	100
Spacing (%)	100	100	33	100

This pattern is transparent if you set BackgroundGray to a negative number. Spacing is measured relative to the default pattern; since DNA strands are .040 inch wide, a Spacing setting of 40% causes them to touch.

Fishscale

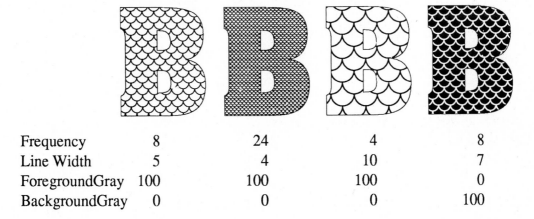

Frequency	8	24	4	8
Line Width	5	4	10	7
ForegroundGray	100	100	100	0
BackgroundGray	0	0	0	100

This pattern is transparent if you set BackgroundGray to a negative number.

Grass

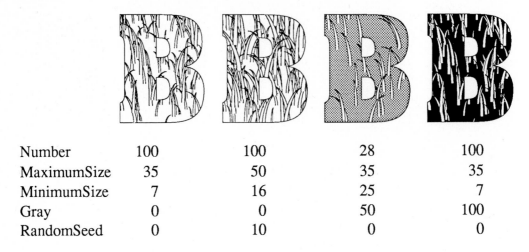

Number	100	100	28	100
MaximumSize	35	50	35	35
MinimumSize	7	16	25	7
Gray	0	0	50	100
RandomSeed	0	10	0	0

When you set Gray to a negative number, the Grass pattern is transparent.

Hatching

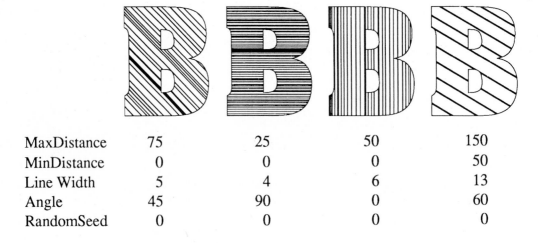

MaxDistance	75	25	50	150
MinDistance	0	0	0	50
Line Width	5	4	6	13
Angle	45	90	0	60
RandomSeed	0	0	0	0

The Hatching texture is transparent.

Hexagons

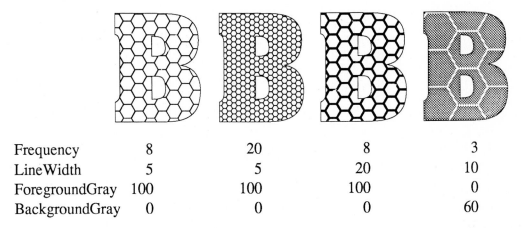

Frequency	8	20	8	3
LineWidth	5	5	20	10
ForegroundGray	100	100	100	0
BackgroundGray	0	0	0	60

This pattern is transparent when you set BackgroundGray to a negative number.

Honeycomb

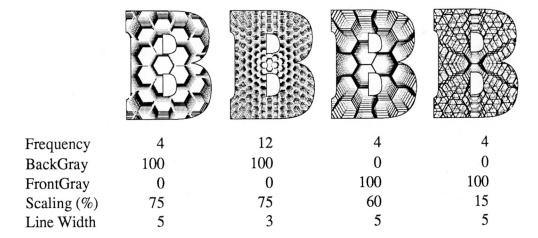

Frequency	4	12	4	4
BackGray	100	100	0	0
FrontGray	0	0	100	100
Scaling (%)	75	75	60	15
Line Width	5	3	5	5

The Honeycomb pattern is transparent.

Impact

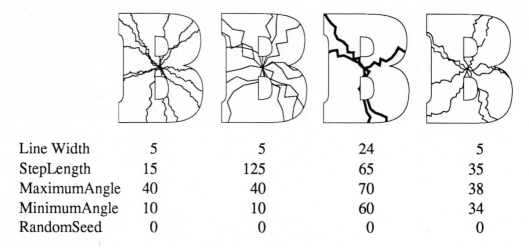

Line Width	5	5	24	5
StepLength	15	125	65	35
MaximumAngle	40	40	70	38
MinimumAngle	10	10	60	34
RandomSeed	0	0	0	0

The Impact texture is transparent.

Landscape

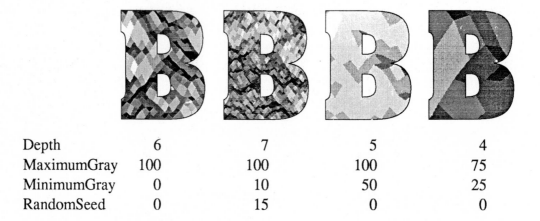

Depth	6	7	5	4
MaximumGray	100	100	100	75
MinimumGray	0	10	50	25
RandomSeed	0	15	0	0

The Landscape texture is opaque. Each time you increase the depth setting by one, the filled object takes four times as long to print. The fills that look the most shallow (low numbers) print fastest.

Leaves

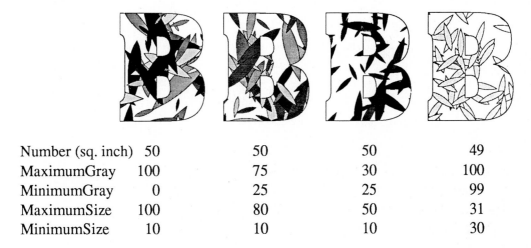

Number (sq. inch)	50	50	50	49
MaximumGray	100	75	30	100
MinimumGray	0	25	25	99
MaximumSize	100	80	50	31
MinimumSize	10	10	10	30

The Leaves texture is transparent.

Mesh

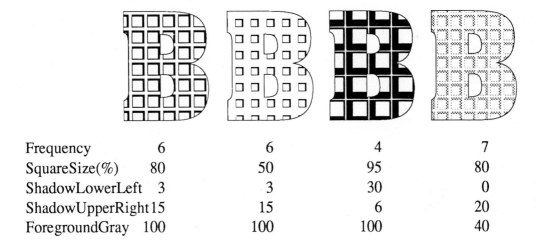

Frequency	6	6	4	7
SquareSize(%)	80	50	95	80
ShadowLowerLeft	3	3	30	0
ShadowUpperRight	15	15	6	20
ForegroundGray	100	100	100	40

The Mesh texture is transparent.

Motifs

Motif	1	2	3	4
Frequency	2	6	6	4
Spacing(%)	100	80	100	60
ForegroundGray	100	100	100	100

Motif	5	6	7	2
Frequency	4	6	6	4
Spacing(%)	75	75	100	50
ForegroundGray	100	100	75	100

Motifs is actually seven textures in one. Motif numbers 1 through 7 have already been defined by Corel Systems. You can select other motif numbers, but they will have no effect unless you program their content in PostScript language. All of the defined textures in Motifs are transparent.

Octagons

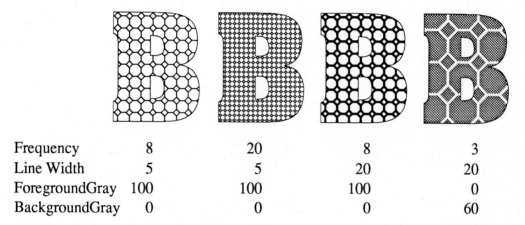

Frequency	8	20	8	3
Line Width	5	5	20	20
ForegroundGray	100	100	100	0
BackgroundGray	0	0	0	60

This texture is transparent only when you set BackgroundGray to a negative number.

Patio

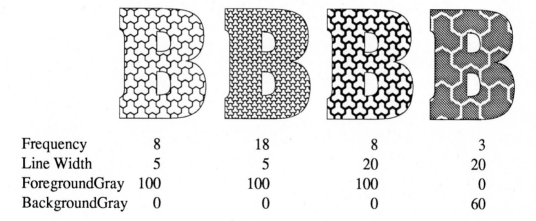

Frequency	8	18	8	3
Line Width	5	5	20	20
ForegroundGray	100	100	100	0
BackgroundGray	0	0	0	60

The Patio texture is transparent if you set BackgroundGray to a negative number.

Rectangles

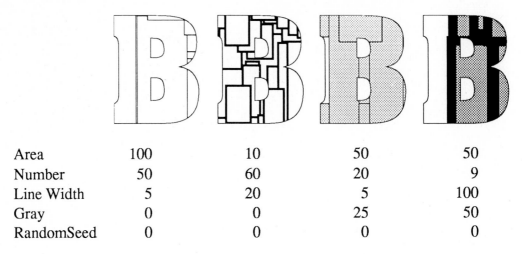

Area	100	10	50	50
Number	50	60	20	9
Line Width	5	20	5	100
Gray	0	0	25	50
RandomSeed	0	0	0	0

The spaces between the rectangles in this texture are transparent. The rectangles themselves are opaque.

Reptiles

Frequency	4	5	4	10
Gray1	60	0	100	100
Gray2	30	0	50	50
Gray3	0	0	20	0
Line Width	8	8	6	2

Gray3 is always opaque, regardless of the setting. Gray1 and Gray2 are transparent when you set them to a negative number.

SpiderWeb

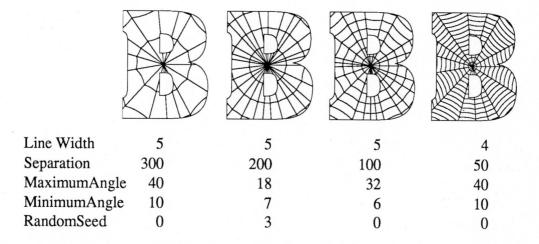

Line Width	5	5	5	4
Separation	300	200	100	50
MaximumAngle	40	18	32	40
MinimumAngle	10	7	6	10
RandomSeed	0	3	0	0

The SpiderWeb texture is transparent.

Spirals

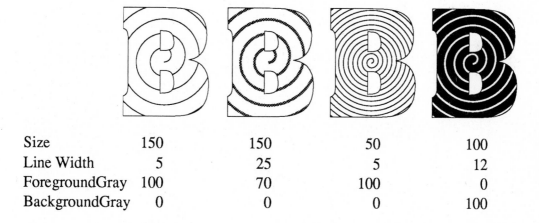

Size	150	150	50	100
Line Width	5	25	5	12
ForegroundGray	100	70	100	0
BackgroundGray	0	0	0	100

This pattern is transparent when you set BackgroundGray to a negative number.

Spokes

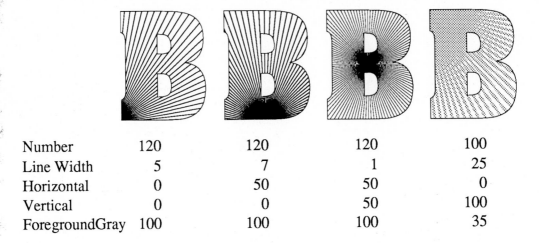

Number	120	120	120	100
Line Width	5	7	1	25
Horizontal	0	50	50	0
Vertical	0	0	50	100
ForegroundGray	100	100	100	35

The Spokes texture contains a number of interesting algorithms. The Number parameter refers to the number of spokes in an imaginary 360-degree circle. The Horizontal and Vertical parameters define the location of the center point of the object as a percentage of the highlighting box around the object. Spokes is a transparent texture.

Squares

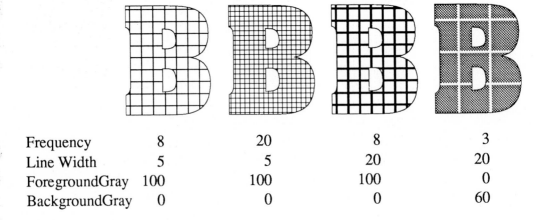

Frequency	8	20	8	3
Line Width	5	5	20	20
ForegroundGray	100	100	100	0
BackgroundGray	0	0	0	60

The Squares texture is transparent when you set Background-Gray to a negative number.

StarOfDavid

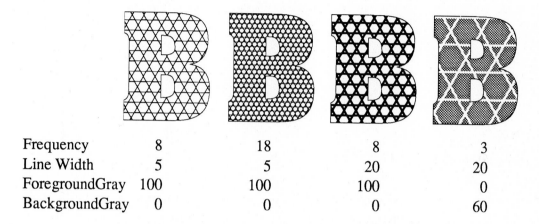

Frequency	8	18	8	3
Line Width	5	5	20	20
ForegroundGray	100	100	100	0
BackgroundGray	0	0	0	60

The StarOfDavid texture is transparent when you set Back-groundGray to a negative number.

Stars

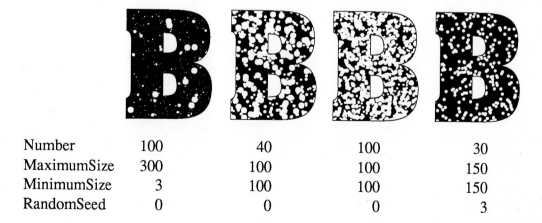

Number	100	40	100	30
MaximumSize	300	100	100	150
MinimumSize	3	100	100	150
RandomSeed	0	0	0	3

This pattern is always opaque. The Number parameter, unlike the Frequency parameter found in other PostScript textures, is measured in units per square inch.

StarShapes

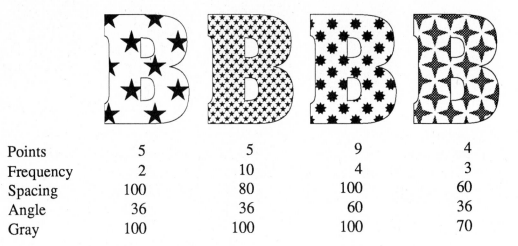

Points	5	5	9	4
Frequency	2	10	4	3
Spacing	100	80	100	60
Angle	36	36	60	36
Gray	100	100	100	70

You can use the Points parameter of this texture to define motifs with any number of points, not just five-pointed stars. The texture is transparent.

StoneWall

Frequency	15	20	5	12
MaximumGray	100	80	100	50
MinimumGray	0	30	0	5
Line Width	5	0	20	5

This texture is always opaque.

Text

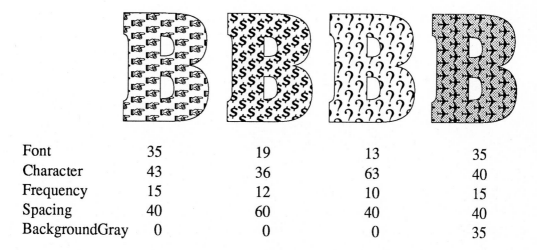

Font	35	19	13	35
Character	43	36	63	40
Frequency	15	12	10	15
Spacing	40	60	40	40
BackgroundGray	0	0	0	35

The Font parameter for the Text pattern must refer to one of the 35 fonts that come standard with a PostScript Plus type printer. Table E-1 lists the numbers that correspond to the valid fonts. The Text texture is transparent only when you set BackgroundGray to a negative number.

Font #	Font Name	Font #	Font Name
1	Times Roman	8	Helvetica-BoldOblique
2	Times-Italic	9	Courier
3	Times-Bold	10	Courier-Oblique
4	Times-BoldItalic	11	Courier-Bold
5	Helvetica	12	Courier-BoldOblique
6	Helvetica-Oblique	13	Symbol
7	Helvetica-Bold	14	AvanteGarde-Book Oblique

TABLE E-1   Valid Selections for the Font Parameter of the Text PostScript Texture

Font #	Font Name	Font #	Font Name
15	AvantGarde-BookOblique	26	NewCenturSchlbk-Roman
16	AvantGarde-Demi	27	NewCenturySchlbk-Bold
17	AvantGarde-DemiOblique	28	NewCenturySchlbk-Italic
18	Bookman-Demi	29	NewCenturySchlbk-BoldItalic
19	Bookman-DemiItalic	30	Palatino-Roman
20	Bookman-Light	31	Palatino-Bold
21	Bookman-LightItalic	32	Palatino-Italic
22	Helvetica-Narrow	33	Palatino-BoldItalic
23	Helvetica-Narrow-Bold	34	ZapfChancery-MediumItalic
24	Helvetica-Narrow-BoldOblique	35	ZapfDingbats
25	Helvetica-Narrow-Oblique		

TABLE E-1   Valid Selections for the Font Parameter of the Text PostScript Texture (*continued*)

Tiles

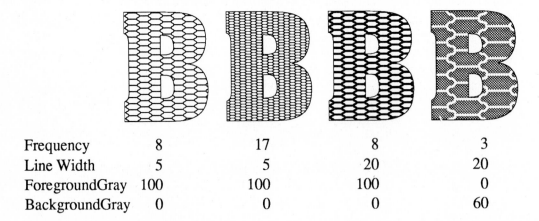

Frequency	8	17	8	3
Line Width	5	5	20	20
ForegroundGray	100	100	100	0
BackgroundGray	0	0	0	60

The Tiles texture is transparent when you set BackgroundGray to a negative number.

The Tiles texture is transparent when you set BackgroundGray to a negative number.

TreeRings

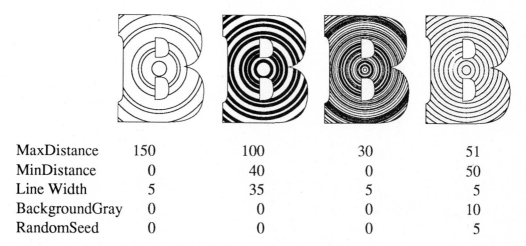

MaxDistance	150	100	30	51
MinDistance	0	40	0	50
Line Width	5	35	5	5
BackgroundGray	0	0	0	10
RandomSeed	0	0	0	5

The Distance parameters for this texture are measured in thousands of an inch, representing the space between adjacent rings. The texture is transparent when you set Background Gray to a negative number.

Triangle

Frequency	8	18	8	3
Line Width	5	5	20	20
ForegroundGray	100	100	100	0
BackgroundGray	0	0	0	60

The Triangle texture is transparent when you set Background-Gray to a negative number.

Waves

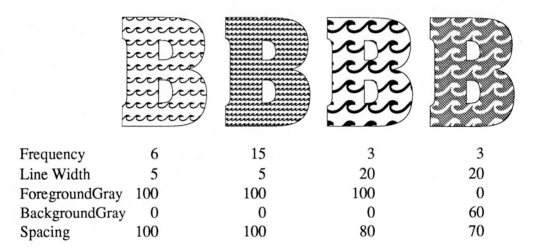

Frequency	6	15	3	3
Line Width	5	5	20	20
ForegroundGray	100	100	100	0
BackgroundGray	0	0	0	60
Spacing	100	100	80	70

The Waves texture is always transparent.

Index

PostScript printers, *continued*
 tips for printing complex
  artwork on, 710-715
 using Windows error handler
  with, 711-712
PostScript printing options, 689-705
 All Fonts Resident, 704
 color separations, 690-698
 default screen frequency
  setting, 701-704
 printing crop marks, 690-695
 printing file information,
  689-690
 printing in film negative format,
  699-701
PostScript textures
 and preview limitations, 157,
  532, 845
 and Windows clipboard limits,
  410
 defining, 532-534
 examples of, 847-870
 parameters for, 846-847
Preferences command, 808
 adjusting AutoJoin sensitivity
  with, 54-55, 92
 and Freehand Tracking, 80-81
 and Place Duplicate option, 413
 functions of, 14
Preferences dialog box
 and tracing bitmaps, 605
 changing sample display
  character in, 104-105
Preset gray shades
 filling objects with, 510-513
 outlining with, 482-485
Preset outline widths, 456-458
Preview boundary, 159
Preview Selected Only command,
 755-758, 806
 and preview operation speed,
  178, 180
Preview toolbox, 171-177
 displaying, 172
Preview window
 adjusting and sizing, 159-171
 adjusting format automatically,
  172-173
 and defining outline pen, 427
 and editing fill color, 491
 and imported bitmaps, 548-549,
  596
 and PostScript fill textures,
  532
 concealing, 157
 displaying, 154-157
 displaying fountain fills in, 779
 displaying PostScript textures in,
  845
 limitations of, 157-159, 464
 side-by-side format, 167-171
 top-to-bottom format, 160-167

Preview window, *continued*
 updating, 171
 with dashed or dotted lines, 431
Print command, 797
Print Options dialog box, 670-705
Print Spooler, disabling, 668-670
Printable page area, 7, 10
Printer installation, 663-665
Printer resolution, and halftone screen
 frequency, 477
Printer setup, checking before printing,
 676
Printer timeouts
 defined, 662
 setting, 666-668
Printers supported in Corel DRAW!,
 780
Printing, 659-715
 and adjusting image scale,
  682-684
 and disabling Windows spooler,
  668-670
 and fitting image to page size,
  604
 and Print Options dialog box,
  670-705
 checking printer setup before,
  676
 color separations, 690-698
 complex images, 679, 713
 crop marks and registration
  marks, 690-695
 fountain fills, 713-714
 hardware-specific tips for,
  705-710
 imported bitmaps, 549
 imported graphics, 671-705
 in film negative format,
  699-701
 oversize graphics, 680-682, 745
 PostScript-only options for,
  689-705
 PostScript textures, 712-713,
  847
 Selected Objects Only, 676-679
 setting default screen frequency
  for, 701-704
 to a file, 685-688
 using resident PostScript fonts,
  704
 with PostScript error handler
  installed, 711-712
Printing tips
 for PostScript printers,
  710-715
 hardware-related, 705-710
Process color
 advantages and disadvantages
  of, 506
 defined, 464
 defining b/w fountain fills with,
  525

Process color, *continued*
 defining linear fountain fills
  with, 523-526
 defining radial fountain fills
  with, 529-531
 filling objects with, 506-510
 outlining with, 478-482
 uses of, 464
Program operation speed, with
 imported bitmaps, 548

Q

QEMM memory manager, 790
QMS printers, 711
Quit command, 798
Quitting Corel DRAW!, 30

R

Radial fountain fills
 changing center of, 531,
  764-776
 creating 3-D effects with,
  764-776
 defined, 513
 defining with process color,
  529-531
 defining with spot color,
  527-529
 specifying, 526-531
Random algorithms, PostScript textures
 and, 533-534
RAM drive
 uses of, 792
 with expanded or extended
  memory, 791-793
Record Macro command, 807
Rectangle tool
 activating, 21, 68
 functions of, 21
Rectangles
 drawing from a corner,
  68-70
 drawing from the center
  outward, 71
 rounding corners of, 338-342
 shaping, 276, 338-345
 shaping stretched, rotated, or
  skewed, 342
Redo command, 798
Registration marks
 defined, 691
 printing, 90-698
Repeat command, 798
Repeat key combination, 269-271
Resolution
 when exporting to bitmapped
  file formats, 568
Retry command button, with printing
 error messages, 705